Levinas and Twentieth-Century Literature

Levinas and Twentieth-Century Literature

Ethics and the Reconstitution of Subjectivity

Donald R. Wehrs

UNIVERSITY OF DELAWARE PRESS
Newark

Published by University of Delaware Press
Co-published with The Rowman & Littlefield Publishing Group, Inc.
4501 Forbes Boulevard, Suite 200, Lanham, Maryland 20706
www.rowman.com

10 Thornbury Road, Plymouth PL6 7PP, United Kingdom

British Library Cataloguing in Publication Information Available

Library of Congress Cataloging-in-Publication Data
Library of Congress Cataloging-in-Publication Data Available
ISBN 978-1-61149-442-6 (cloth : alk. paper)
ISBN 978-1-6114-9650-5 (pbk : alk. paper)

To Frank Ward

Contents

Acknowledgments

The editor would like to thank all those who have helped make this volume possible. First of all, I would like to acknowledge the patience and good will of the contributors and the fine editors at the University of Delaware Press and Rowman & Littlefield Publishing Group, particularly the anonymous readers, Donald Mell, Julia Oestreich, Brooke Bures, and Christopher Basso. The example of Melvyn New's pioneering collection, *In Proximity: Emmanuel Levinas and the Eighteenth Century* (Texas Tech, 2001), as well as Professor New's encouragement and advice, have been a constant resource. Similarly, David P. Haney's editorial collaboration with me on our earlier collection, *Levinas and Nineteenth-Century Literature* (Delaware, 2009), contributed mightily to allowing this effort to come to fruition. The opportunity to teach Levinas in Auburn University's English Department's undergraduate and graduate literary theory classes over the years, as well as many conversations with colleagues and students, have deeply informed this project. Generous university and departmental funding for conference travel, and the institutional venues provided by the Modern Language Association, the International Association for Philosophy and Literature, the Society for Comparative Literature and the Arts, and the American Comparative Literature Association, have been indispensible both for honing ideas and for building productive interdisciplinary professional dialogue. I should particularly mention Robert Bernasconi, Patrick Colm Hogan, John Burt Foster, Ron Bogue, Dorothy Figueira, Elaine Martin, Hugh J. Silverman, Matthew Binney, Thomas Blake, and Benjamin Joshua Doty.

Appreciation is expressed here to the following publishers for permission to reprint cited material: Springer Science + Business Media B.V., for citations from Emmanuel Levinas, *Existence and Existents*, trans. Alphonso Lingis (Pittsburgh: Duquesne University Press, 1978) and Emmanuel Levinas,

Otherwise than Being, trans. Alphonso Lingis (Pittsburgh Duquesne University Press, 1981); Duquesne University Press, for citations from Emmanuel Levinas, *Time and the Other*, trans. Richard Cohen (Duquesne University Press, 1985) and Emmanuel Levinas, *Totality and Infinity*, trans. Alphonso Lingis (Pittsburgh: Duquesne University Press, 1969); Columbia University Press, for citations from Emmanuel Levinas, *Entre Nous: Essays on Thinking-of-the-Other*, trans. Michael B. Smith and Barbara Harshav (New York: Columbia University Press, 1998); Indiana Univeristy Press, for citations from Emmanuel Levinas, *Basic Philosophical Writings*, ed. by Adriaan T. Peperzak, Simon Critchley, and Robert Bernasconi (Bloomington and Indianapolis: Indiana University Press, 1996) and Emmanuel Levinas, *Nine Talmudic Readings*, trans. Annette Aronowicz (Bloomington and Indianapolis: Indiana University Press, 1990).

Material from Zahi Zallouia, *Reading Unruly: Interpretation and its Ethical Demands* (Lincoln: University of Nebraska Press, forthcoming) appears here by permission of the University of Nebraska. Citations from *As I Lay Dying* by William Faulkner, copyright 1930 and renewed 1958, are used by permission of Random House, Inc. Any third party use of this material, outside of this publication, is prohibited. Interested parties must apply directly to Random House, Inc. for permission. Citations from William Carlos Williams, *Paterson*, rev. ed. (New York: New Directions, 1992) and William Carlos Williams, *The Collected Poems: Volume 1. 1909-1939*, copyright 1938 by New Directions Publishing Group, are reprinted by permission of New Directions Publishing Corp. Citations from Tony Kushner, *Angels in America, Part One: Millennium Approaches* and *Angels in America: Perestroika* (New York: Theatre Communications, 1992) appear here by permission of Theatre Communications. Citations from *Gravity's Rainbow* by Thomas Pynchon, copyright 1973 by Thomas Pynchon, are used by permission of Viking Penguin, a division of Penguin Group (USA) Inc. Translations of excerpts from Gabriella Ghermandi, *Regina di fiori e di perle* (Milano: Donzelli, 2007) are used with kind permission of Donzelli. Citations from *Everything Is Illuminated* by Jonathan Safran Foer are reprinted by permission of Houghton Mifflin Publishing Company. All rights reserved. Citations from *Fugitive Pieces* by Anne Michaels (London and New York: Bloomsbury, 1998) are reprinted with permission of Bloomsbury and Random House. Assistance in paying publishers' permission fees has graciously been provided by Auburn University, Harper College, and the University of Witwaterstrand.

I must acknowledge the support of those dearest to my heart, my daughter Sylvia, whose commitment to excellence is always an inspiration, my son William, whose keen scholarly mind sets a standard to emulate, and my wife, Lorna Wood, whose acuity, rigor, intellectual breadth and passion, as well as her warmth and patience, sustain and refine all that I write. This project has led my thoughts frequently back to those I have known personally whose twentieth-century lives embodied Levinasian ethics. Of course, my parents and extended family came to mind, but also remarkable teachers at Holland Hall School in Tulsa, Oklahoma between 1962 and 1974, especially those whose work and sensibilities, I would to think, continue to shape my own— Father Ralph Taylor, Thomas Elmer, Rosemary Chase, Robert Krieckhaus, and Frank Ward. I would like to dedicate this volume to the last of these, but in recognition of all.

List of Abbreviations

WORKS BY EMMANUEL LEVINAS

AE   *Autrement qu' être, ou au-delà essence*. Dordrecht, Netherlands: Martinus Nijhoff, 1974.

BPW   *Basic Philosophical Writings*. Edited by Adriaan T. Peperzak, Simon Critchley, and Robert Bernasconi. Bloomington and Indianapolis: Indiana University Press, 1996.

BTV   *Beyond the Verse: Talmudic Readings and Lectures*. Trans. Gary D. Mole. Bloomington and Indianapolis: Indiana University Press, 1994.

CCP   *Collected Philosophical Papers*. Trans. Alphonso Lingis. The Hague: Martinus Nijhoff, 1987.

DF   *Difficult Freedom*. Trans. Seàn Hand. Baltimore: Johns Hopkins University Press, 1990.

EI   *Ethics and Infinity*. Trans. Richard Cohen. Pittsburgh: Duquesne University Press, 1985.

EE   *Existence and Existents*. Trans. Alphonso Lingis. Pittsburgh: Duquesne University Press, 1978.

Eel   *Ethique et infini*. Paris: Libraire Arthème Fayard, 1982.

En   *Entre nous*: Essais sur le penser-à-l'autre. Paris: Grasset, 1991.

EN   *Entre Nous: On Thinking-of-the-Other*. Trans. Michael B. Smith and Barbara Harshav. New York: Columbia University Press, 1998.

HOM   *Humanism of the Other*. Trans. Nidra Poller. Urbana and Chicago: University of Illinois Press, 2003.

ITR   *Is It Righteous to Be?: Interviews with Emmauel Levinas*. Ed. Jill Robbins. Stanford: Stanford University Press, 2001.

LR   *The Levinas Reader*. Ed. Seàn Hand. Oxford: Blackwell, 1989.

MS   "Meaning and Sense." In *Basic Philosophical Writings*, 33–64.

NeTR	*New Talmudic Readings*. Trans. Richard A. Cohen. Bloomington and Indianapolis: Indiana University Press, 1993.
NiTR	*Nine Talmudic Readings*. Trans. Annette Aronowicz. Bloomington and Indianapolis: Indiana University Press, 1990.
OB	*Otherwise than Being or Beyond Essence*. Trans, Alphonso Lingis. Pittsburgh: Duquesne University Press, 1981.
OS	*Outside the Subject*. Trans. Michael Smith. Stanford: Stanford University Press, 1993.
PN	*Proper Names*. Trans. Michael B. Smith. London: Athlone Press, 1996.
RS	"Reality and Its Shadow." In *The Levinas Reader* (*LR* 129–43).
S	"Substitution." In *Basic Philosophical Writings,* 79–95.
TI	*Totality and Infinity: An Essay on Exteriority*. Trans. Alphonso Lingis. Pittsburgh: Duquesne University Press, 1969.
TeI	*Totalité et infini: Essai sur l ' exteriorité*. The Hague: Martinus Nijhoff, 1961.
TO	*Time and the Other*. Trans. Richard Cohen. Pittsburgh: Duquesne University Press, 1985.
UH	*Unforseen History*. Trans. Nidra Poller. Urbana and Chicago: University of Illinois Press, 2004.
	Other abbreviations will be designated in individual essays.

I

Introductory Matters

Introduction

Levinas, the Twentieth Century, and Its Literature: From Ethical Trauma to the Reconstitution of Subjectivity

Donald R. Wehrs

Emmanuel Levinas (1906–1995), a Lithuanian-born French ethical philosopher whose challenging phenomenological and devotional texts were known only to a small circle before the 1980s, became by the end of that decade a revolutionizing force within philosophy and religious studies, and in the 1990s began exerting increasing influence upon literary theory and criticism.[1] Secondary literature on Levinas, now comprising thousands of volumes, addresses fields ranging from philosophy and religion to politics, psychology, social theory, and literary scholarship.[2] From 1930 to around 1990, Levinas produced a body of work combining phenomenological analysis as pioneered by Edmund Husserl and Martin Heidegger with traditions of Jewish philosophical piety exemplified by the eleventh-century commentaries of Rashi (Rabbi Shlomo ben Itzhak) and the proto-existentialist thinker Franz Rosenzweig (1886–1929).[3] From such heterogeneous sources, and in response to the philosophical challenge, moral horror, and personal devastation represented by Hitlerism and the Shoah, in which all his family, save wife and daughter, perished, Levinas fashioned a radically innovative account of how ethical significance underlay human subjectivity and how philosophy, culture, language, and reason were predicated upon and answerable to the ethical.

In a way new to Western philosophical writing, but implicit in both Jewish scriptural study and modern European literature, Levinas located the ethical not in contemplation of being or reality, as in the ontological tradition from Plato to Heidegger, nor in aspirations for self-consistent freedom, as in the deontological tradition inaugurated by Kant, nor in liberation of the self from social conformity or systematic, totalizing thinking, as in Rousseau, Kierkegaard, Nietzsche, early Derrida, middle Foucault, Deleuze, and Badiou. Instead, for Levinas the ethical inheres in encountering an Other whose presence puts in question, traumatically, the ego's claim to its own privilege and priority, a trauma from which human sociality and signification derive.

Levinas's ethics break starkly with previous paradigms. Plato originates an ontological tradition in which discerning the nature of being determines what is good. For Plato, Charles Taylor notes, "[r]ationality is tied to the perception of order; and so to realize our capacity for reason is to see the order as it is. . . . The surest basis for virtue is the perception of this order, which one cannot see without loving."[4] With variations, ontological thought governs Western ethical reflection from ancient through early modern times.[5] The nature of being is taken to provide *reasons* for being good, as in Cicero's demonstration that what is truly useful (*utile*) and what is upright (*honestas*) coincide, and in Augustine's insistence that, following the principle that "we must use this world, not enjoy it [*utendum est hoc mundo, non fruendum*]," we see that love of others (*caritas*) is useful for us: "[w]hen you enjoy a human being in God, you are enjoying God rather than that human being. For you enjoy the one by whom you are made happy."[6] Once the new science complicates demonstrating the self-interest of being good, philosophy's *justifying* of morality is thrown into crisis, as Alasdair MacIntyre observes.[7] Since knowing being/reality logically precedes knowing that morality is useful, philosophy's epistemological crisis prompted a vain search for "foundations" (recounted by Richard Rorty[8]) and threw moral thought into crisis, though the ontological tradition continued, as in the later Heidegger's insistence that humans should attend the unveiling of Being and adopt an attitude of letting be.[9]

A second tradition emerges in the late eighteenth century. Rather than deriving the good from the nature of being, Kant argues that the ethical emerges from human efforts to extract themselves, through willing compliance with what reason discloses to be moral, from heteronomies of natural necessity, chance, interest, and passion.[10] Kant thus breaks the connection forged in antiquity between the question of the good and pursuit of happiness,[11] a connection reinforced by Christianity's association of happiness with salvation, which helped make eudemonic ethics (thinking of the good in terms of how individuals may acquire happiness) central to moral and religious discourse from patristic times through the eighteenth century.[12] By insisting that moral reasoning not be influenced by concern for happiness, Kant turns against eudemonic-ontological ethics, but not against what Levinas calls the "egological" (*EN* 163) structure of Western reflection (taking an individual's concern with himself as thought's starting place). For Kant, disinterested moral reasoning procures consciousness of freedom or moral autonomy, and so consciousness of "the sublimity of one's own supersensuous existence"[13] and the inner satisfaction it breeds. Contemporary proceduralist moral and political philosophy takes Kantian deontological ethics as its starting point.[14]

A third current, what Taylor calls "the ethics of authenticity," originates with Rousseau's insistence that the self owes itself liberation from conformity, and that duty to self is co-equal to, or co-extensive with, duty to others, God, principles, or ideals.[15] Associating the good primarily with self-liberation leads, in a fairly straightforward manner, from Rousseau and currents of Romanticism to, first, the anti-Hegelianism of Kierkegaard, then to Nietzsche's valorization of increasing life or expanding power, and finally to the celebration of authenticity in Heidegger and championing of "being for oneself" in Sartre.[16] So early Derrida and middle Foucault present post-structuralist interpretation as iconoclastic epistemological exercises that liberate the self, in Nietzschean fashion, from linguistically instantiated totalizing violence.[17] In seeking to free the self from discursively induced conformity, their projects share common inspiration with Lacanian psychoanalysis and Althusserian ideology critique, enabling various combinations of these four thinkers to anchor much politicized 1980s academic literary criticism.[18]

While the axiom that "the personal is political" underlies such criticism, a certain tension between the personal and political, going back to Rousseau himself, runs through it. On the one hand, demonstrating patterns of coercive discursive and material subject construction is tacitly assumed to promote a personal freedom taken to be a self-justifying good. On the other, only by treating one's own liberation as a model for others to follow can it be reconciled with political commitment. This assumes that differences between and among people denote either trivial variations in aesthetic-consumerist taste or historical and ideological effects that historical revolution or political education may dissolve. Rousseauian duty of the self to itself can thus ground both revolt against convention (the tradition of Nietzsche) and identification of one's own will with a communal general will. This latter postulate underwrites utopian political thought from Rousseau's social contract theory, through Marx's notion of post-revolutionary freedom, to diverse hopes that solidarity must follow from escaping ideological interpellation: seeing the other as another me, identifying my (true) interests with the (objective) interests of the whole, will allow egocentrism to ground sociality.[19]

The breach between the Old and New Left that convulsed French intellectual life in 1968 had at its core advocates of the Nietzschean legacy of Rousseau challenging the Marxist legacy by valorizing difference as a *political* goal incommensurate with the totalizing collectivism of the Old Left. This quarrel, nonetheless, was posed within a Western egological framework: were the self's interests best served by recognition of its own and *so* others' radical alterity, or by mutual recognition of their solidarity-inducing sameness? Much subsequent thought seeks to revitalize the ethics of authenticity. Deleuze and Guattari attempt to reunite Nietzschean and Marxian legacies by arguing that liberation entails revolt against the (oedipal) subject formation that capitalism renders coercively normative, and Jean-Luc Nancy seeks to enunciate a social theory reconciling solidarity with singularity. By contrast, Alain Badiou and Giorgio Agamben re-assert Nietzscheanism by claiming that in embracing one's own creativity as the highest good, one escapes "unethical" complicity in self-betrayal.[20] Such efforts, however, confront the difficulties that Terry Eagleton finds in Marx's assumption that "emancipation of human powers" can be the measure of the good: Eagleton notes that "human powers are far from spontaneously positive," and so no possible social order could dispense with the need to "discriminate among human powers."[21] This puts in question the derivation of sociality from egocentrism that Western theorizing in general presupposes.

Levinas breaks with all this. The delay in his thought's reception reflects not only the barriers of a demanding writing style (in French mediated through Russian and Hebrew), but also disorientation: Levinas challenges the very place from which reflection upon the good should begin. He brings into the heart of philosophy, as he notes, "pre-philosophical experiences" anchored in "reading the Bible" and derived from "the reading of books," including "national literatures," wherein reading is experienced as a sequence of "initial shocks" which "become questions and problems, giving one to think" (*EI* 24, 21).[22] Engaging literature in ways marked by a certain approach to the Bible both prompts and contextualizes philosophical inquiry. Modern philosophy's quest for a "ground" anterior to presupposition or perspective must fail not simply because (as poststructuralism would have it) subjectivity and language are always already historically-culturally situated and/or metaphysically invested, but also because aspiration to truth presupposes concern for what *justly* may be claimed, and so for *justice* and responsibility to others woven into speech (*TI* 90–101).[23] This in turn presupposes that the ethical is already a matter of significance, indeed *grounds* significance, thus eliciting the "shocks" from which "questions and problems" emerge (see *OB* 61–81; *EN* 133–53). After disclosing to an interviewer that between his Biblical and philosophical studies, he encountered "the Russian classics . . . and the great writers of Western Europe," Levinas implies that encountering "[t]he philosophical problem understood as the famous 'meaning of life'—about which the characters of the Russian novelists ceaselessly wonder" was "good preparation" for academic study of philosophy (*EI* 22).

An interdisciplinary correction of philosophy's exclusivity stands behind Levinas's stress upon *lived experience* as the provocation of thought. One encounters in the presence of the Other a responsibility that is unsolicited and inescapable (*TI* 42–48, 197–209; *OB* 83–86), as constitutive of consciousness as it is determinative of corporeal sensation and signification (OB

135–40; *EN* 123–32, 159–177; *OG* 137–71). This issues in "traumatisms or gropings" (*EI* 21) and so informs experiences behind and within reading from which non-egological philosophy emerges. Non-egological thought's expression parts company with self-centered conceptuality by flowing from "the gravity of the love of one's fellowman—of love without concupiscence—on which the congenital meaning of that worn-out word is based, and which is presupposed by all literary culture, all libraries and the entire Bible, in which its sublimation and profanation are told" (*EN* 186). Phenomenological analysis and textual exegesis become distinct modalities within a common discerning of the ethical's weight upon experience and thought.

For Levinas, "Subjection to the order that orders man, the *I*, to answer for the other is, perhaps, the harsh name of love." (*EN* 174). Because "responsibility for the other" gives rise to concern for justice, and justice elicits rationality necessary for comparing "what is in principle incomparable, for every being is unique," ideas of "equity" and "objectivity" emerge, and with them the ethical orientation of "pondering": "in this sense philosophy would be the appearance of wisdom from the depths of that initial charity; it would be . . . the wisdom of love" (*EN* 104).[24]

Levinas's audacious predication of love of wisdom (philosophy) upon the wisdom of love motivates his relentless elaboration of the reordering of subjectivity that follows from the ethical structuring of both somatic and conscious signification.[25] Both the reordering and the premise that engenders it must be read in the context of tensions endemic to poststructuralism. Fundamentally, post-structuralism's twin achievements—completing philosophy's repudiation of any abstract, objective, or transcendental "foundation" grounding truth, value, and autonomous subjectivity, *and* asserting the *value* of difference, singularity, and liberating agency—stand in tension with one another. The first induces radical skeptical relativism, but also courts despair of agency's escaping co-option.[26] The second presupposes that valorization somehow escapes ubiquitous skepticism, even if valorization does not go beyond affirming abstract negativities (anti-totalization, anti-phallologocentrism, anti-imperialism, etc.).[27] Its impasses (however inadvertently) underscoring the indispensability, or inescapability, of ethics, post-structuralism helped prompt a resurgence of Anglophone moral philosophy beginning around 1980.[28] In putting at risk any notion of coherent agency, poststructuralism made urgent the need for an account of subjectivity tied neither to notions of autonomy nor to tropes of identity as merely a site prey to fluxes of heterogeneous forces or conflicted contexts, some of which might be vaguely emancipatory.[29] Anxiety that poststructuralism's epistemological skepticism could erode progressive political commitments underlay the 1987 "affair" triggered by revelation of Paul de Man's wartime collaborationist journalism.[30] Within these contexts, Levinas came to be read both as an ethical extension of poststructuralism and as an ethical critique of egological residues binding post-structuralism to normative Western thought from Plato to Sartre.[31] The fruit of such reading is not just the increasing presence of Levinas in literary criticism over past two decades, but also criticism increasingly attentive to how literary modes of signifying drive home the "prephilosophical" weight of the ethical upon subjectivity, a weight whose impress evokes criticism's responsibility *to* what it reads.[32]

The aspiration of this volume, like that of previous collections on Levinas and eighteenth-century studies, Levinas and medieval literature, and Levinas and nineteenth-century literature,[33] is at least threefold. It hopes, first, to explore the value of Levinas's thought for literary scholarship, both in prompting compelling readings and in opening new possibilities for generic, thematic, or historical–cultural research. Second, it seeks to trace how literary works develop via lines of thought that Levinas adumbrates, thereby allowing literary criticism to refine assessment of his work's strengths, limitations, untapped potential, or unexpected difficulties. Third, the collection endeavors to illuminate unsuspected proximities between Levinas's work and the preoccupations or climate of thought of a particular era and its literature.

Distinctive to this collection, however, is the enfolding of Levinas's life and work within the confines of the era whose literature is studied. Levinas's days spanned all but ten years of the twentieth century, and the forces shaping its literature motivate and structure his discourses. Moreover, Levinas's career itself constitutes a major event within twentieth-century studies. From his introduction of Husserl and Heidegger to a French readership in 1930, to the influence of his anti-totalizing phenomenology upon Derrida's early work, to the remarkable reception of his ethical thought in the century's last decades, Levinas's story and that of the twentieth century are intimately and extensively entwined.[34] While an overview is offered in the following essay, here it should be stressed that ethical trauma marks both the century and a life, as Levinas noted, "dominated by the presentiment and memory of the Nazi horror" (*DF* 291). In total war and totalitarianism, in racial extermination and ethnic cleansing, in ideological fanaticism and coldly theoretical extremism, the twentieth century went beyond naturalized exploitation and ideological obfuscation to experiment with self-conscious, programmatic "teleological suspensions of the ethical" far more bloody-minded than anything Kierkegaard, in originating the phrase, had in mind.[35]

Indeed, speculative innocence about the consequences of "suspension" helped foster impatience with the ethical as plodding impediment to leaps of faith, total victory, securing the revolution, reordering society along scientific lines, giving the master race sufficient living space, protecting the dictatorship of the proletariat, dealing with the natives, instituting cultural revolution, leading the free world, decolonizing the country, realizing the self's emancipating energies, or allowing the party of God to prevail. All such impatience intimates that the ethical is somehow extraneous or secondary—a luxury we cannot afford, a ruse of interests hoping to sap our will, or something (like cooking) for women to deal with, an afterthought to analysis, a corollary to self-emancipation, a benefit of peace at the end of history but thus something which only future objective conditions make possible or useful.[36] A certain diffidence, even disparagement, adheres to the ethical from the beginning of philosophy in the West, where it is a means to the end of self-sufficient happiness. By the turn of the twentieth century Christian reluctance to ascribe intrinsic value to ethics (intensified by many generations of preaching against "mere morality"), the consolidation of value-neutral scientific, economic, and social theory, and associations of morality with hypocritical moralistic cant all primed Europe to test the hypothesis that the ethical was an irksome anachronism impeding progress.[37] Auschwitz and the Gulag are the starkest consequences, but Western-exported suspensions of the ethical unleashed systemic violence from the European scramble for African colonies, to Mao's China to Pol Pot's Cambodia, to disappearances and death squads in South and Latin America. Of course (lamentably), ethnic hatred and massacres, injustice and exploitation, private cruelties and collective failures of conscience saturate every century. Distinctive to the twentieth, in addition to the mechanized, bureaucratized nature of the slaughter, and its breathtaking scope, was the thoroughness to which suspensions of the ethical were, as Razumikhin says of Raskolnikov's theories in *Crime and Punishment*, made a matter of conscience: "to condone the shedding of blood *on grounds of conscience* [*po sobesmi*] is . . . more terrible [*ctrashnee*] than if it were permitted officially, by law."[38]

Just as the twentieth century is defined, despite extraordinary transformations of the texture of daily life and expansion of human potencies, by a series of experiments in suspending the ethical, and by somatic-moral revulsion against what such exercises wrought,[39] so presentiments and memories of all that overriding the ethical in the name of principle or theory or privileged interests looses upon the world dominate twentieth-century literature from prescient psychological studies of political terror such as Dostoyevsky's *The Devils* (1871) and Conrad's *The Secret Agent* (1907) to gestures of witness and protest such as Huong thu Duong's *Paradise of the Blind* (1987) and Marjane Satrapi's *Persepolis* (2000–2003).

To recognize something as "terrible" in the sense implied by Razumikhin presupposes an ethical predication of significance whose inescapability Raskolnikov learns painfully in the course of *Crime and Punishment*. Levinas strives to make this inescapability explicit so as to render Western thought, after Auschwitz, radically incommensurate with what it had been before. The imperative of "Never again" radiates out of Levinas's texts, but on a more intimate level the incongruity of survival exacts an ultimate seriousness. In response to an interviewer's musing that the death of someone close brings us to "discover more intensely to what degree [death] is a part of the fabric of our lives," Levinas observes, "[M]y analysis does not begin in a relation to the death of those who 'are dear to us,' still less in the return to 'oneself,' which would bring us back to the priority of my own death. In starting from the Holocaust, I think about the death of the other man; I think of the other man for whom one may already feel—I don't know why—like a guilty survivor" (*ITR* 126). Levinas challenges the egocentric structuring of value deeply internalized in Western thought—exemplified by the same interviewer later arguing that the other's death may be for us "a deliverance; it saves us from living halfway," to which Levinas responds, "But that is not an ethical attitude" (129).

Such challenge should not be confused with advocating ascetic censoriousness or morbid self-denial, which Levinas explicitly rejects (*EI* 120–22).[40] Indeed, against Heidegger's disparagement of "everydayness," Levinas celebrates the simple material pleasures of shelter, warmth, food, sociability, family, and the possibility of actions of one's own (see esp *EE*, *TO*, *TI* 109–83), goods five years in a prisoner of war camp may help one appreciate. Such goods, however, take their place within non-egocentric predications of significance that for Levinas were exemplified by the convergence of a particular Jewish religious education with worlds of meaning and affectivity opened up by Russian literature.

As Derrida's 1995 eulogy "Adieu" notes, Levinas's long career involved getting readers to hear words such as *"droiture*—'straigthforwardness' or 'uprightness' . . . otherwise and to learn."[41] The effect of this adjustment of hearing, learning, and so reading, was that Levinas "slowly displaced, slowly bent according to an inflexible and simple exigency, the axis, trajectory, and even the order of phenomenology or ontology that he had introduced into France beginning in 1930," thereby "completely chang[ing] . . . the landscape of thought," and "in a dignified way, without polemic, at once from within, faithfully, and from very far away, from the attestation of a completely other place."[42] This collection seeks to delineate some of the implications of that changed landscape for literary criticism in general and for twentieth-century literary studies in particular. To attune one's hearing to what Levinas allows us to learn by reading otherwise need not imply unwillingness to criticize Levinas. His thought, like that of any major philosopher, contains internal tensions, and, given Levinas's treatment of language as tending to drift into rigid and flattening conceptual representation (the said) even though language starts from and returns to a signifying of pre-conceptual ethical concern or approach (the saying), it would be highly un-Levinasian to take any word, including his own, as totalizing or final. But a critique forgetful of saying would equally betray his work.

Whether or to what degree a specific politics emerges from Levinas's derivation of justice from ethics has been much addressed.[43] On the one hand, the Latin American political thinker Enrique Dussel has drawn upon Levinas for a Third World philosophy of liberation.[44] On the other, Dussel and others have viewed the reformist republicanism that Levinas associates with anti-totalizing thought as what Gad Horowitz calls Eurocentric "evasion of the appeal of the other. The other is not the poor who shall always be with us . . . , always urgently demanding that *we* do our duty to *them*. The urgent demand for justice is for *total* abolition, not simply recurrent significant remediation, of this particular material distinction between a prosperous 'we' and a relatively impoverished 'them.'"[45] Such reprises of Marxist revolution versus reform argumentation, however, may themselves be challenged as neglectful of Levinas's attentiveness to what he called the shocking actuality that "Marxism could have turned into Stalinism" (*ITR* 217), something his lifelong inhabiting of the Russian language kept strongly in view. Critiques of Levinasian reformism, especially when motivated by real concern for non-Western suffering and injustice, can seem inattentive to how pursuit of "total" solutions underwrote not only the Gulag, but also the Cultural Revolution and the killing fields of Cambodia.[46] Indeed, from Albania to Cuba to Vietnam, entrenched party elites administered bureaucratically codified inequality and repressed otherness (for example, Castro's campaigns against homosexuals and dissident writers converged in the persecution of the novelist José Lezama Lima, whose treatment of gay themes in his masterwork, *Paradiso*, angered the regime).[47]

Questions have also been raised about how much Levinas's thinking of gender and Europe are captive to patriarchal or ethnocentric assumptions, how closely his ecumenical enfolding of religion into ethics approximates atheism or universalizes particularism, and how much his stress upon radical alterity might be modified by alternative phenomenologies.[48] Such critical interrogations can illuminate, correct, supplement, and extend Levinasian reflection, but even in contestation they highlight why his work merits attention in the first place. Simon Critchley has identified five political "problems" in Levinas (fraternity, monotheism, androcentrism, filiality and the family, and Israel), but concludes that in making us aware of "an anarchic ethical injunction" and "experience of an infinite ethical demand" underlying any responsible politics, Levinas puts us in "infinite debt" to his work.[49] When critique assumes maximal vehemence, however, it risks lapsing into nostalgia for landscapes of thought innocent of Levinas's disruptive insistence upon a philosophy, politics, and criticism, as well as religion, "for adults" (*DF* 11–23), landscapes not yet marked by renunciation of egological privilege. One may suspect that such nostalgia permeates post-Levinas, post-French "new philosophy" reiterations of Nietzschean or Heideggerian themes in forms evoking the intellectual world of 1971.[50] A similar nostalgia seems to attend accounts of identity in which fixation upon one's own or a group's victimization diverts attention from how being for-the-other and pursuing justice for all the other others might make resistance more than "multiplicity of allergic egoisms which are at war with one another and are thus together" (*OB* 4).[51] And nostalgia certainly underlies vague invocations of "total" revolution incongruously yoked with an abstract lionizing of heterogeneity—as though twentieth-century experiments in totalized change had never taken place, as though the 1968 rupture between the Old Left and the New Left, or late-1970s French intellectual disenchantment with anti-humanism, or the dissolution of the Soviet empire, or the turn of China and Vietnam away from economic communism had never occurred.[52] Paradoxically, however, the danger that naturalizing egological habits of mind and feeling may become the West's most successful export underscores the global relevance and actual revolutionary radicalism of Levinas's work.

The essays collected here go beyond merely "applying" Levinas to their literary subjects, even as they keep in view how fundamentally Levinas's work reshapes what one hears and learns from literature. All explore how particular works challenge characteristic twentieth-century modes of identity, valorization, and uses of language opposed by Levinas. In the second section of this book, "Levinas and the Fugitive Other: Consciousness, Representation, Affectivity, and Memory," Rebecca Nicholson-Weir connects Virginia Woolf's desire to memorialize her deceased brother to her narrative experimentalism, thereby linking modernist anxiety about the ethics of representation to a Levinasian sense of responsibility: the obligation to conserve the Other's irreducibility motivates displacing perspective and judgment onto multiple characters whose heterogeneous partiality prevents knowledge of Jacob in *Jacob's Room* from dissipating the alterity that makes him, like Proust's Albertine, a subject the narrative cannot "consume." Lorna Wood argues that similar anti-imperializing currents of modernism inform A. A. Milne's Pooh books in ways that contest hegemonic categorizing and sentimental retreat within the narratives, thus problematizing not only the imperializing culture of Milne's time but also ideas about children's literature dominating criticism from Dorothy Parker to current academic theory. Showing how analogous concerns recur in feminism, Zahi Zalloua argues that Marguerite Duras's choice of a male narrator for her novel *The Ravishing of Lol Stein* (1964) both invites and subverts readings that would identify the narrator with an essentializing, logocentric, phallic "ravisher," for reading the narrator as *merely* so cannot but mirror the totalizing acts such readings would condemn.

In the third section, "Levinas and the Aesthetics of American Modernism," Benjamin Joshua Doty arrestingly connects Levinasian critique of totalizing thought with race theory and whiteness studies in a reading of American representations of "poor Southern whites" that culminates in an account of how William Faulkner, through the peculiar modes of narration he develops within *As I Lay Dying*, challenges not only hardened stereotypes but also the denigration of embodied, intuitive understanding and sociality that lies behind such stereotypes. N. S. Boone explores how a similar ethical unease with poetry's tendency to lapse into stylization and moralizing prompts William Carlos Williams in *Paterson* to strive for modernist verse composition in which dialogue and dance push back against, on the one hand, nineteenth-century American deployment of poetry for sentimental normalizing and, on the other hand, aestheticizing, elite cultural reaction to that American heritage in the modernist poetry of T. S. Eliot and Ezra Pound.

In the fourth section, "Levinas and the Embodied Voice: Listening and Performance," Todd Avery analyzes how the advent of radio raised the question of what kind of voice, what tone, what implied relation between speaker and audience should be valorized and cultivated on air. Contrasting Goebbels' mobilization of the medium for authoritarian propaganda with debates within the BBC regarding the degree of intimacy, dialogic sociality, and authoritative cultivation appropriate for speaking on the radio, Avery documents how the new medium's totalizing potentialities were consciously reflected upon, actively seized, conscientiously contested, and negotiated. Linking Levinas's ethics to Bakhtin's notion of dialogic communication in a study of twentieth-century drama from Luigi Pirandello's *Six Characters in Search of an Author* (1921) and Arthur Miller's *All My Sons* (1947) to Tony Kushner's *Angels in America* (1991-92), Richard Middleton-Kaplan argues that the embodied performative dimension of drama offers a particularly congenial generic space for the entwinement of Levinasian and Bakhtinian concerns.

In the fifth section, "Trauma and the Loss and Return of Character," I explore how Gabriel García Márquez's *One Hundred Years of Solitude* (1967) and Thomas Pynchon's *Gravity's Rainbow* (1973) depict psychological and social worlds in which the possibility of reconstituting subjectivity after and through ethical trauma, as Levinas articulates it, is precluded or forfeited. I consider how much the dissolution of character prominent within postmodern and postcolonial fiction follows from systemic impediments to ethical subject formation or reformation, and whether these works nevertheless allow possibilities of escape into ethical selfhood. In a related manner, in chapter 10 Mike Marais reads J. M. Coetzee's fictions and Michael Ondaatje's *The English Patient* as connecting ethical significance's origin in trauma to traumas of temporal and identity disruption so as to delineate subtle connections between identity confirmation and cognitive, colonizing violence. The unraveling of these connections in extraordinary, hospitable reception of an Other entails a radically disorienting eclipse of self and meta-critical self-consciousness, so that the texts themselves serve as subtle metonymies for the stakes in decolonization.

In the sixth section, "Levinas and Temporal Fracturing in New European and Postcolonial fiction," Nina L. Molinaro discusses the relationship between diachronic temporality, narrative disruption, and ethical dislocation in three post-Franco Spanish novels published in the mid-1990s, all of which contrast synchrony supporting the illusion of temporal mastery and narrative coherence with diachronic traumas through which temporal displacement and subversion of egoism are entwined. Molinaro demonstrates how welcoming the Other entails being remade and unmade by the Other's death in ways that, paradoxically, ground any relation to sociality and futurity that is not a living death. Norma Bouchard traces how the experience of being an African immigrant in Italy, depicted in Salah Methnani's *Immigrato* (1990), resonates with repressed dimensions of Italian historical identity even as the depiction of that experience calls to consciousness, along Levinasian lines, an ethical subjectivity rooted in memories of exile and wandering. Then, treating a novel structured like an oral storytelling session that depicts Ethiopia under Italian fascist colonization and its aftermath, Gabrielle Ghermandi's *Regina di fiori e di perle* (2007), Bouchard explores trauma's ambiguous consequences for both subjective and communal forms of identity and sociality, within Italy but also within Italy's former colonies in east Africa.

In the collection's final section, "Levinas, Apocalpse, and the Non-Imperializing Self," Merle Williams considers two contemporary novels, Anne Michaels' *Fugitive Pieces* (1996) and Jonathan Safran Foer's *Everything Is Illuminated* (2002), that address second-generation experience of the Shoah through protagonists who confront the murder of their relatives many years after the event. Horror that cannot be contextualized tears one away from a thinning out of selfhood amid postindustrial, welfare state securities, but at the risk of a level of psychic scarring that pushes one toward suicidal depression or self-enclosing acting out. Paradoxically, one can only have the heart for reparative work that does not betray or obscure the irreparable through engaging in displacements of self in concern for someone else. Only the divestment of egoism from futurity allows the present to become fecund; only then is enjoyment not obscene, affording one sufficient love of life to have something to give to others. In a deeply analogous manner, Daniel T. Kline reads Cormac McCarthy's *The Road* (2006) as revealing, through a father's unconditional love of his son in the wake of a worldwide apocalyptic disaster, a re-enactment and reversal of Abraham's intended sacrifice of Isaac that reiterates Levinas's critical reading of Kierkegaard's account of the Abraham story, from which the notion of a "teleological suspension of the ethical" emerges. The novel's premise allows a stripping away of material being to the essence of what separates human from inhuman persistence in being. Either life and understanding proceed from and attest to being-for-the-other, or they do not. The absolute reductions that McCarthy's novel develops find their correlative in the exorbitant rigor of Levinas's thought.

Taken together, the essays in this collection tell a story of the twentieth century and its literature different from grand narratives culminating in fragmentation, groundlessness, and pastiche. Instead, this collection affirms literature's abiding value and its interdependence with reconstitutions of ethical subjectivity upon foundations at once transcendent, pluralistic, and materialist.

NOTES

1. For Levinas's scholarly reception, see Salomon Malka, *Emmanuel Levinas: His Life and Legacy*, trans. Michael Kigel and Sonja M. Embree (Pittsburgh: Duquesne University Press, 2006), especially 205–211, 274–86. For his introduction to English readers, see especially Edith Wyschogrod, *Emmanuel Levinas: The Problem of Ethical Metaphysics* (The Hague: Nijoff, 1974); Richard A. Cohen, ed., *Face to Face with Levinas* (Albany: State University of New York Press, 1986); Robert Bernasconi and David Wood, eds., *The Provocation of Levinas: Rethinking the Other* (London: Routledge, 1988); Robert Bernasconi and Simon Critchley, eds., *Re-reading Levinas* (Bloomington: Indiana University Press, 1991); Simon Critchley, *The Ethics of Deconstruction: Derrida and Levinas* (Oxford: Blackwell, 1992); Adriaan T. Peperzak, *To the Other: An Introduction to the Philosophy of Emmanuel Levinas* (West Lafayette, IN: Purdue University Press, 1993); Adriaan T. Peperzak, ed., *Ethics as First Philosophy: The Significance of Emmanuel Levinas for Philosophy, Literature, and Religion* (New York: Routledge, 1995); Brian Schroeder, *Altared Ground: Levinas, History, and Violence* (New York: Routledge, 1996). For Levinas's emergence within literary theory, see especially Geoffrey Galt Harpham, *Getting It Right: Language, Literature, and Ethics* (Chicago: University of Chicago Press, 1992); David P. Haney, *William Wordsworth and the Hermeneutics of Incarnation* (University Park: Pennsylvania State University Press, 1993); Krzysztof Ziarek, *Inflected Language: Toward a Hermeneutics of Nearness: Heidegger, Levinas, Stevens, Celan* (Albany: State University of New York Press, 1994); Adam Zachary Newton, *Narrative Ethics* (Cambridge, MA: Harvard University Press, 1995); Robert Eaglestone, *Ethical Criticism: Reading After Levinas* (Edinburgh: Edinburgh University Press, 1997); Roland A. Champagne, *The Ethics of Reading According to Levinas* (Amsterdam: Rodopi, 1998); Donald R. Wehrs, "Sterne and Levinas: From the Ethics of the Face to the Aesthetics of Unrepresentability," in *Laurence Sterne: Critical Essays*, ed. Melvyn New (New York: G. K. Hall, 1998), 311–29; the essays in *The Eighteenth Century: Theory and Interpretation* (30, no. 3[1999]), special issue on "Levinas and the Eighteenth Century," guest editor Melvyn New; Jill Robbins, *Altered Reading: Levinas and Literature* (Chicago: University of Chicago Press, 1999); David P. Haney, "Aesthetics and Ethics in Gadamer, Levinas, and Romanticism: Problems in *Phronêsis* and *Technê*," *PMLA* (114, no. 1 [1999]), 32–45.

2. Representative examples include, in psychology, *Psychology for the Other: Levinas, Ethics and the Practice of Psychology*, ed. Edwin E. Gantt and Richard N. Williams (Pittsburgh: Duquesne Univeristy Press, 2002); in religion, Claire Elise Katz, *Levinas, Judaism, and the Feminine: The Silent Footsteps of Rebecca* (Bloomington: Indiana University Press, 2003); in political theory, *Difficult Justice: Commentaries on Levinas and Politics*, ed. Asher Horowitz and Gad Horowitz (Toronto: University of Toronto Press, 2006); in education, Sharon Todd, *Learning From the Other: Levinas, Psychoanalysis, and Ethical Possibilities in Education* (Albany: State University of New York Press, 2008); in literature, Steven Shankman, *Other Others: Levinas, Literature, Transcultural Studies* (Albany: State University of New York Press, 2010).

3. While Levinas's corpus divides between phenomenological philosophy (*EE*, *TO*, *TI*, *OB*, OG, *EN*) and devotional commentary (*DF*, *BTV*, *NiTR*, *NeTR*), the two contexts or inspirations are entwined. Levinas gave weekly commentaries on Rashi from the 1940s to the end of his life and pursued Talmudic studies in the early postwar years under the mysterious but brilliant scholar Mordechai Chouchani (see Malka, 107–39). For Levinas's discovery, around

1935, of Franz Rosenzweig's *The Star of Redemption* (1921), see Malka, 42–44, and Samuel Moyn, *Origins of the Other: Emmanuel Levinas Between Revelation and Ethics* (Ithaca: Cornell University Press, 2005), 129–63. Also see Robert Gibbs, *Correlations in Rosenzweig and Levinas* (Princeton: Princeton University Press, 1992); Richard A. Cohen, *Elevations: The Height of the Good in Rosenzweig and Levinas* (Chicago: University of Chicago Press, 1994); Michael Fagenblat, *A Covenant of Creatures: Levinas's Philosophy of Judaism* (Stanford: Stanford University Press, 2010).

4.   Charles Taylor, *Sources of the Self: The Making of the Modern Identity* (Cambridge, MA: Harvard University Press, 1989), 122–23.

5.   Ibid.; see especially 115–58.

6.   See Cicero, *De Officiis*, with trans. Walter Miller (New York: Loeb Classical Libray, 1913); Augustine, *De Doctrina Christiana*, with trans. R. P. H. Green (Oxford: Clarendon Press, 2001, rpt. 1995), 16–17, 46–47.

7.   See Alasdair MacIntyre, *After Virtue: A Study of Moral Theory*, 2nd ed. (Notre Dame: Notre Dame University Press, 1984 [1st ed. 1981]), especially 36–78.

8.   See Richard Rorty, *Philosophy and the Mirror of Nature* (Princeton: Princeton University Press, 1979).

9.   See especially the essays collected in Martin Heidegger, *Poetry, Language, Thought*, trans. Albert Hofstadter (New York: Harper and Row, 1971); also see "Letter on Humanism" and "The Question Concerning Technology," in Martin Heidegger, *Basic Writings*, ed. David Ferrell Krell (New York: Harper and Row, 1977), 193–242, 287–317.

10.   See Immanuel Kant, *Critique of Practical Reason*, trans. Lewis White Beck (Indianapolis: Bobbs-Merrill, 1956), especially "The Incentives of Pure Practical Reason," 74–92.

11.   See Plato's organizing *The Republic* around the claim that the just man is necessarily happier than the unjust (*Republic* 357b–358e) in Plato, *The Collected Dialogues*, ed. Edith Hamilton and Huntington Cairns (Princeton: Princeton University Press, 1961), 605–06, and Aristotle's deriving his account of the virtues from an inquiry into human happiness in *Nicomachean Ethics* 1095a 15-1098b 5, trans. Terence Irwin (Indianapolis: Hackett, 1985), 5–18. Also see Martha Nussbaum's account in *The Therapy of Desire: Theory and Practice in Hellenistic Philosophy* (Princeton: Princeton University Press, 1994) of how Hellenistic philosophy conceived argument about the (true) good as medicine counteracting susceptibility to unhappiness.

12.   See for example, Rebecca Konyndyk De Young, Colleen McClusky, Christina Van Dyke, *Aquinas's Ethics: Metaphysical Foundations, Moral Theory, and Theological Context* (Notre Dame: Notre Dame University, 2009; Thomas Hibbs, *Aquinas, Ethics, and the Philosophy of Religion* (Bloomington and Indianapolis: Indiana University Press, 2007); Richard Hooker, *Of the Laws of Ecclesiastical Polity*, in *Works of Richard Hooker*, gen. ed. W. Speed Hill, vol. 1., ed. Georges Edelen (Cambridge: Harvard University Press, 1977), Ch. 9, "Of the benefit of keeping that lawe which reason teacheth," 93–95; Joseph Butler, *The Analogy of Religion, Natural and Revealed* (London: George Bell and Sons, 1889 [1736]), especially 98–161, 275–327; "Sermon I-III.—Upon Human Nature," "Sermon V.—Upon Compassion," "Sermon XI-XII.—Upon the Love of Our Neighbour," in Butler, 385–414, 425–43, 484–511.

13.   Kant, *Critique of Practical Reason*, 91.

14.   See especially John Rawls, *A Theory of Justice* (Cambridge, MA: Harvard University Press, 1971); Thomas Nagel, *The View from Nowhere* (New York: Oxford University Press, 1986), *Equality and Partiality* (1991); Jürgen Habermas, *The Theory of Communicative Action*, trans. Thomas McCarthy, 2 vols. (Boston: Beacon Press, 1984, 1987).

15.   See Taylor, *Sources of the Self*, 355–70; *The Ethics of Authenticity* (Cambridge, MA: Harvard University Press, 1992), especially 25–29.

16.   See especially Rousseau's rejection, throughout the *Confessions* and *Reveries of a Solitary Walker*, of any judgment of his actions not rooted in appreciation of his distinctiveness and the sincerity of his intentions; see also the "Profession de foi du Vicaire Savoyard" (Jean-Jacques Rousseau, *Émile ou de l'éducation* [Paris: Garnier-Flammarion, 1966], 345–83). For the origins of anti-totalizing philosophy, see Søren Kierkegaard, *Concluding Unscientific Postscript*, trans. David F. Swenson and Walter Lowrie (Princeton: Princeton University Press, 1941), 115–224; Friedrich Nietzsche, *Beyond Good and Evil: Prelude to a Philosophy of the Future*, trans. Walter Kaufmann (New York: Vintage, 1966), "The Free Spirit," 35–56, "Our

Virtues," 145–70; *The Will to Power*, trans. Walter Kaufmann and R. J. Hollingdale (New York: Vintage, 1967), "Origin of Moral Valuations," 146–56, "The Will to Power as Life" 341–81. For authenticity (*Eigenheit*), see Martin Heidegger, *Being and Time*, trans. John Macquarrie and Edward Robinson (Oxford: Basil Blackwell, 1973), I. 4, "the 'they,'" 149–68, II, 2–3, "Dasein's authentic potential," 312–82. For being-for-itself, see Jean-Paul Sartre, *Being and Nothingness: A Phenomenology Essay on Ontology*, trans. Hazel E. Barnes (New York: Washington Square Press, 1956), "Being-for-itself," 119–58.

17. See especially Jacques Derrida, *Writing and Difference*, trans. Alan Bass (Chicago: University of Chicago Press, 1978), particularly the conclusion of "Force and Signification," 29–30 and "Structure, Sign, and Play in the Discourse of the Human Sciences," 292–93, and *Margins of Philosophy*, trans. Alan Bass (Chicago: University of Chicago Press, 1982), particularly "Différance," 3–27, and "The Ends of Man," 111–36; Michel Foucault, "Nietzsche, Genealogy, History," and "Revolutionary Action: 'Until Now,'" in *Language, Counter-Memory, Practice: Selected Essays and Interviews*, ed. Donald F. Bouchard (Ithaca: Cornell University Press, 1977), 139–64, 218–33.

18. See especially Jacques Lacan's argument that not giving up one's desire constitutes the ethical in *The Seminar of Jacques Lacan: Book VII, The Ethics of Psychoanalysis, 1959-60*, trans. Dennis Porter (New York: Norton, 1992), and Louis Althusser's relegation of the ethical to one of many modalities of manipulative ideological appellation in the writings collected in *Essays on Ideology*, trans. Ben Brewster (London: Verso, 1984). Broadly speaking, 1980s politicized literary criticism sought to integrate post-structuralist accounts of language and subjectivity with the social goals of 1960s activism: anti-racism, feminism, anti-colonialism, systemic critique of capitalism, and liberation from consumerist or corporate identity formations. For pioneering works, see especially Luce Irigaray, *Speculum of the Other Woman*, trans. Gillian G. Gill (Ithaca: Cornell University Press, 1985 [French original, 1974]; Edward W. Said, *Orientalism* (New York: Pantheon, 1978); Fredric Jameson, *The Political Unconscious: Narrative as a Socially Symbolic Act* (Ithaca: Cornell University Press, 1981).

19. For the French Revolution's deriving from Rousseau a monolithic notion of "the people" that discredits pluralism as a progressive value, and for the influence of such thinking upon Marx, see especially François Furet, *Marx and the French Revolution*, trans. Deborah Kan Furet (Chicago: University of Chicago Press, 1988). For philosophical impasses in seeking to derive a notion of the Other from the self, see Michael Theunisson, *The Other: Studies in the Social Ontology of Husserl, Heidegger, Sartre, and Buber*, trans. Christopher Macann (Cambridge, MA: MIT Press, 1984). For efforts within Marxism to articulate a theory of liberation in terms of the party-led articulations of general will (revealing difference to be a historical-ideological illusion), see Georg Lukàcs's notion of the vanguard in *History and Class Consciousness*, trans. Rodney Livingstone (Cambridge, MA: MIT Press, 1968 [1921]), Antonio Gramsci's formulation of the "organic intellectual" in *The Prison Notebooks* (New York: Columbia University Press, 1991), and the political writings of Maurice Merleau-Ponty, especially *Humanisme et terreur: Essai sur le problème communiste* (Paris: Gallimard, 1947) and *Adventures of the Dialectic*, trans. Joseph Bien (Evanston: Northwestern University Press, 1973), and of Jean-Paul Sartre, especially *Critique of Dialectical Reason*, trans. Alan Sheridan-Smith (London: Verso, 1990 [1961]), "Matérialisme et revolution," in *Situations III* (Paris: Gallimard, 1949), 135–225, "Les Communistes et la paix," in *Situations VI* (Paris: Gallimard, 1964), 80–384, and *Le Fantôme de Staline*, in *Situations VII* (Paris: Gallimard, 1964), 144–307.

20. See Gilles Deleuze and Félix Guattari, *Anti-Oepidius: Capitalism and Schizophrenia*, trans. Robert Hurley, Mark Seem, and Helen R. Lane (Minneapolis: University of Minnesota Press, 1983), *A Thousand Plateaus: Capitalism and Schizophrenia*, trans. Brian Massumi (London: Athlone, 1988); Jean-Luc Nancy, *The Inoperable Community* (Minneapolis: University of Minnesota Press, 1991); Alain Badiou, *Ethics: An Essay on the Understanding of Evil*, trans. Peter Havillward (London: Verso, 2001), *Being and Event*, trans. Oliver Feltham (New York: Continuum, 2005); Giorgio Agamben, "Absolute Immanence," in *Potentialities: Collected Essays in Philosophy*, ed. and trans. Daniel Heller-Roazen (Stanford: Stanford University Press, 1999).

21. Terry Eagleton, *The Ideology of the Aesthetic* (Oxford: Basil Blackwell, 1990), 222–23. The questions that Eagleton poses for Marx hold equally for any effort to make emancipation of

human powers the basis of the good. See Peter Atterton and Matthew Calarco's commentary on Judith Butler's career in "Editors' Introduction: The Third Wave of Levinas Scholarship," in *Radicalizing Levinas*, ed. Peter Atterton and Matthew Calarco (Albany: State University of New York Press, 2011), xi.

22. See Valerie Allen's astute "Difficult Reading," in *Levinas and Medieval Literature: The "Difficult Reading" of English and Rabbinic Texts*, ed. Ann W. Astell and J. A. Jackson (Pittsburgh: Duquesne University Press, 2009), 15–33. Also see Richard A. Cohen, *Ethics, Exegesis and Philosophy: Interpretation After Levinas* (Cambridge: Cambridge University Press, 2001) and Amit Pinchevski, *By Way of Interruption: Levinas and the Ethics of Communication* (Pittsburgh: Duquesne University Press, 2005).

23. Diane Perpich notes, "The subject is constituted in a manner that makes it unable to be totally deaf to the other's demands, whether those be demands for reasons, a cry for compassion, an expression of pain, or the pangs of hunger. . . . Subjectivity is ever too late to say that the other in no way concerns it" (*The Ethics of Emmanuel Levinas* [Stanford: Stanford University Press, 2008], 145; also see 124–46). In a related manner, Taylor argues that the self always finds itself situated in narrative movement toward or away from a complex of goods structuring both a sense of identity and moral deliberation. See especially Taylor, *Sources of the Self*, 3–52 and *The Ethics of Authenticity*, 31–41. MacIntyre articulates similar claims (*After Virtue*, 109–20, 204–25). Both advocate a return to Aristotle within contemporary moral philosophy. Significantly, affinities between Levinas and Aristotle have been subsequently pursued in Claudia Baracchi's *Aristotle's Ethics as First Philosophy* (Cambridge: Cambridge University Press, 2008) and Christopher P. Long's *The Ethics of Ontology: Rethinking an Aristotelian Legacy* (Albany: State University of New York Press, 2004). Deborah K. W. Modrak's *Aristotle's Theory of Language and Meaning* (Cambridge: Cambridge University Press, 2001) highlights bonds between language and ethical sociality also central to Levinas's thought (see especially *MS*, *OB* 45–59). Troels Engberg-Pedersen's *Aristotle's Theory of Moral Insight* (Oxford: Clarendon Press, 1983) emphasizes how for Aristotle desire for the good precedes moral deliberation. Also see Silvia Benso and Brian Schroeder, eds., *Levinas and the Ancients* (Bloomington: Indiana University Press, 2007).

24. See Corey Beals' discussion of the connection between deriving philosophy from wisdom's love and framing the ethical in terms of rendering the Other's singularity visible in *Levinas and the Wisdom of Love: The Question of Invisibility* (Waco, TX: Baylor University Press, 2007).

25. See especially Perpich, *The Ethics of Emmanuel Levinas*, 50–77; Sarah Allen, *The Philosophical Sense of Transcendence: Levinas and Plato on Loving Beyond Being* (Pittsburgh: Duquesne University Press, 2009), 176–218, 263–304); Fagenblatt, 84–96, 150–56.

26. For the problems that post-structuralist accounts of subjectivity present to theorizing political agency as genuinely progressive or liberating, see especially Peter Dews, *Logics of Disintegration* (London: Verso, 1987); Patrick Colm Hogan, *The Politics of Interpretation: Ideology, Professionalism, and the Study of Literature* (Oxford: Oxford University Press, 1990); John McGowan, *Postmodernism and Its Critics* (Ithaca; Cornell University Press, 1991); Richard J. Bernstein, *The New Constellation: The Ethico-Political Horizon of Modernity/Postmodernity* (Cambridge, MA: MIT Press, 1992).

27. See Taylor's delineation of these impasses in *Sources of the Self*, 53–90; *The Ethics of Authenticity*, 13–23, and MacIntyre's related argument in *After Virtue*, especially 1–22, 256–63.

28. See especially Stanley Cavell, *The Claim of Reason: Wittgenstein, Shakespeare, Morality, and Tragedy* (New York: Oxford University Press, 1979); Alasdair MacIntrye, *After Virtue* and *Whose Justice? Which Rationality?* (Notre Dame: Notre Dame University Press, 1988); Charles Taylor, *Collected Philosophical Papers*, 2 vols. (Cambridge: Cambridge University Press, 1985), *Sources of the Self*; Bernard Williams, *Ethics and the Limits of Philosophy* (Cambridge, MA: Harvard University Press, 1985); Martha Nussbaum, *The Fragility of Goodness: Luck and Ethics in Greek Tragedy and Philosophy* (Cambridge: Cambridge University Press, 1986), *Love's Knowledge: Essays on Philosophy and Literature* (New York: Oxford University Press, 1990), *Upheavals of Thought: The Intelligence of the Emotions* (Cambridge: Cambridge University Press, 2001); Richard Rorty, *Contingency, Irony, Solidarity* (Cam-

bridge: Cambridge University Press, 1991). Paul Ricoeur's *Oneself as Another*, trans. Kathleen Blaney (Chicago: University of Chicago Press, 1993) speaks to such Anglophone philosophical reflection.

29.   The most influential poststructuralist approach to subjectivity was probably Foucault's. A vexed recognition of the centrality of ethics to subjectivity marks Foucault's late, largely posthumously assembled work (see especially Michel Foucault, *Ethics: Subjectivity and Truth*, ed. Paul Rabinow, trans. Robert Hurley and others [New York: The New Press, 1997]). But the alternately co-opted and neo-Nietzschean subject of Foucault's middle period (see especially Michel Foucault, *Discipline and Punish: The Birth of the Prison*, trans. Alan Sheridan [New York: Pantheon, 1977], *The History of Sexuality, Volume One*, trans. Robert Hurley [New York: Pantheon, 1978], *Power/Knowledge: Selected Interviews and Other Writings, 1972-1977*, ed. Colin Gordon, trans. Colin Gordon et al. [New York: Pantheon, 1980]) lay behind efforts to think of repressive literary agency in terms of co-option, containment, and coercive subject-positioning. For early instances, see Stephen Greenblatt, *Renaissance Self-Fashioning: More to Shakespeare* (Chicago: University of Chicago Press, 1980); Frank Lentricchia, *Criticism and Social Change* (Chicago: University of Chicago Press, 1983); Richard Terdiman, *Discourse/Counter-Discourse: The Theory and Practice of Symbolic Resistance in Nineteenth-Century France* (Ithaca: Cornell University Press, 1985). Among recent reiterations are William H. Galperin, *The Historical Austen* (Philadelphia: University of Pennsylvania Press, 2003); Nancy Armstrong, *How Novels Think: The Limits of Individualism from 1719-1900* (New York: Columbia University Press, 2005); Perry Nodelman, *The Hidden Adult: Defining Children's Literature* (Balitmore: Johns Hopkins University Press, 2008).

30.   See Paul de Man, *Wartime Journalism, 1939-1943*, ed. Werner Hamacher and Thomas Keenan (Lincoln: University of Nebraska Press, 1988); Werner Hamacher and Thomas Keenan, eds., *Reponses: On Paul de Man's Wartime Journalism* (Lincoln: University of Nebraska Press, 1989); David Lehman, *Signs of the Times: Deconstruction and the Fall of Paul de Man* (New York: Poseidon Press, 1991); Marc Redfield, ed., *Legacies of Paul de Man* (New York: Fordham University Press, 2007).

31.   For examples of both, see Zygmunt Bauman's *Postmodern Ethics* (Cambridge: Blackwell, 1993) and *Postmodernity and Its Discontents* (Cambridge: Polity Press, 1997). For Levinas's affinities with and distinctiveness from post-structuralist thought, see especially Simon Critchley, *The Ethics of Deconstruction* and *Ethics, Politics, Subjectivity: Essays on Derrida, Levinas, and Contemporary French Thought* (London: Verso, 1999); Todd May, *Reconsidering Difference: Nancy, Derrida, Levinas, and Deleuze* (University Park, PA: Pennsylvania State University Press, 1997); Sarah Harasym, ed., *Levinas and Lacan: The Missed Encounter* (Albany: State University of New York Press, 1998); John Llewelyn, *Appositions of Jacques Derrida and Emmanuel Levinas* (Bloomington and Indianapolis: Indiana University Press, 2002); Michael L. Morgan, *Discovering Levinas* (Cambridge: Cambridge University Press, 2007).

32.   See especially Michael Eskin, *Ethics and Dialogue in the Works of Levinas, Bakhtin, Mandel'shtam, and Celan* (Oxford: Oxford University Press, 2000), Melvyn New, ed., with Richard A. Cohen and Robert Bernasconi, *In Proximity: Levinas and the Eighteenth Century* (Lubbock: Texas Tech University Press, 2001); Jil Larson, *Ethics and Narrative in the English Novel, 1880-1914* (Cambridge: Cambridge University Press, 2001); David P. Haney, *The Challenge of Coleridge: Ethics and Interpretation in Romanticism and Modern Philosophy* (University Park, PA: Pennsylvania State University Press, 2001); Donald R. Wehrs, *African Feminist Fiction and Indigenous Values* (Gainesville: University Press of Florida, 2001); Pamela Brown, "Levinas in 'Ithaca': Answering the Joycean Worldstage," *Partial Answers: Journal of Literature and the History of Ideas* 1, no. 2 (2003): 61–86; James A. Knapp, "Visual and Ethical Truth in *The Winter's Tale*," *Shakespeare Quarterly* 52, no. 3(2004): 253–78; Linda Bolton, *Facing the Other: Ethical Disruption and the American Mind* (Baton Rouge: Louisiana State University Press, 2004); Clark Davis, *Hawthorne's Shyness: Ethics, Politics, and the Question of Engagement* (Baltimore: Johns Hopkins University Press, 2005); Leslie Hill, "'Distrust of Poetry': Levinas, Blanchot, Celan," *MLN* 120, no. 5 (2005): 986–1008; Gabriel Riera, *Intrigues: From Being to the Other* (New York: Fordham University Press, 2006); Michael O'Sullivan, *The Incarnation of Language: Joyce, Proust, and a Philosophy of the Flesh* (Lon-

don and New York: Continuum, 2008); Donald R. Wehrs, *Pre-Colonial Africa in Colonial African Narratives: From* Ethiopa Unbound *to* Things Fall Apart, *1911-1958* (Aldershot UK: Ashgate, 2008), *Islam, Ethics, Revolt: Politics and Piety in Francophone West African and Maghreb Narrative* (Lanham, MD: Lexington, 2008); Joseph Ballan, "Divine Anonymities: On Transcendence and Transdescendence in the Works of Levinas, Celan, and Lispector," *Religions and the Arts* 12, no. 4 (2008): 540–558; Robert Eaglestone, *The Holocaust and the Postmodern* (Oxford: Oxford University Press, 2008); Ann W. Astell and J. A. Jackson, eds., *Levinas and Medieval Literature: The "Difficult Reading" of English and Rabbinic Texts* (Pittsburgh: Duquesne University Press, 2009); Donald R. Wehrs and David P. Haney, eds., *Levinas and Nineteenth-Century Literature: Ethics and Otherness from Romanticism through Realism* (Newark, DE: University of Delaware Press, 2009); Gerald Bruns, "Should Poetry Be Ethical or Otherwise?" *SubStance* 38, no. 3(2009): 72–91; Sara Crangle, *Prosaic Desires: Modernist Knowledge, Boredom, Laughter, and Anticipation* (Edinburgh: Edinburgh University Press, 2010); Steven Shankman, *Other Others: Levinas, Literature, Transcultural Studies* (Albany: State University of New York Press, 2010); Colin Davis, *Critical Excess: Overreading in Derrida, Deleuze, Levinas, Zizek, and Cavell* (Stanford: Stanford University Press, 2010); James A. Knapp, *Image Ethics in Shakespeare and Spenser* (New York: Palgrave Macmillan, 2011).

33. See New, ed., *In Proximity*; Astell and Jackson, eds., *Levinas and Medieval Literature*; Wehrs and Haney, eds., *Levinas and Nineteenth-Century Literature*.

34. For Levinas's early studies of Husserl and Heidegger, see his *Théorie de l'intuition dans la phenomenology de Husserl* (Paris: Alcan, 1930); *The Theory of Intuition in Husserl's Phenomenology*, trans. Andre Orianne (Chicago: Northwestern University Press, 1985) and *En découvrant l'existence avec Husserl et Heidegger* (Paris: Vrin, 1949); *Discovering Existence with Husserl*, trans. Richard A. Cohen and Michael B. Smith (Chicago: Northwestern University Press, 1998). For Derrida's and Levinas's relationship, see Malka, 172–85. Derrida's 1964 essay, "Violence and Metaphysics," reprinted in 1967 in his *Writing and Difference*, attests to his being impressed by Levinas's critique of totalizing thinking, while critical of Levinas's reliance upon ontological language (see *Writing and Difference*, 79–153). Levinas's effort in his later thought to separate signification from linguistic instantiation of ontological representation (*OB* 31–59; *BPW* 98–107; *OG* 152–71) is widely viewed as a response to Derrida's critique, though his engagement with Derrida's work is oblique ("Jacques Derrida: Wholly Otherwise," in *PN* 54–62). For Levinas's assessment of the "anti-humanism" of structuralism and post-structuralism, see especially "Humanism and An-archy" and "Without Identity," both written near the events of 1968, in *HOM* 45–57, 58–69. Derrida's post-De Man "affair" writings reveal abiding preoccupation with Levinas. See Jacques Derrida, "At This Moment in This Very Work Here I Am," trans. Rubin Bevezdovin, in *Re-Reading Levinas*, ed. Robert Bernasconi and Simon Critchley (Bloomington: Indiana University Press, 1991), 11–48; *Aporias: Dying—Awaiting (One Another at) the "Limits of Truth,"* trans. Thomas Dutoit (Stanford: Stanford University Press, 1993); *The Gift of Death*, trans. David Wills (Chicago: University of Chicago Press, 1995); *Politics of Friendship*, trans. George Collins (London: Verso, 1997); *Adieu to Emmanuel Levinas*, trans. Pascale-Anne Braut and Michael Naas (Stanford: Stanford University Press, 1999); *Of Hospitality*, trans. Rachel Bowlby (Stanford: Stanford University Press, 2000); *On Cosmopolitanism and Forgiveness*, trans. Michael Dooley and Michael Hughes (London: Routledge, 2001); *Psyche: Inventions of the Other*, ed. Peggy Kamuf and Elizabeth Rottenberg (Stanford: Stanford University Press, 2007).

35. See Søren Kierkegaard, *Fear and Trembling*, in *Fear and Trembling and The Sickness Unto Death*, trans. Walter Lowrie (Princeton: Princeton University Press, 1941), especially 64–77. For Levinas's response, see "Kierkegaard: Existence and Ethics" and "A Propos of 'Kierkegaard vivant,'" in *PN* 66–74, 75–79; also Merold Westphal, *Levinas and Kierkegaard in Dialogue* (Bloomington: Indiana University Press, 2008).

36. Sartre concludes *Being and Nothingness* with the promise of a sequel on ethics that he was unable to write. See *Being and Nothingness*, 795–98, and Sartre's *Notebooks for an Ethics*, trans. David Pellauer (Chicago: University of Chicago Press, 1992). Adorno similarly declines any concrete account of the ethical, suggesting it must await a revolutionary transformation of subjectivity, even though Adorno shares Levinas's anti-totalizing perspective and his critique

of "affirmative," triumphal culture's encouraging a complacent "good conscience." See especially *OG* 172–77; *EN* 191–92; Theodor W. Adorno, *Negative Dialectics*, trans. E. B. Ashton (New York: Continnum, 1973); *Minima moralia: Reflections from Damaged Life*, trans. E. F. N. Jephcott (London: Verso, 1979); *Against Epistemology: A Metacritique: Studies in Husserl and the Phenomenological Antinomies*, trans. Willis Domingo (Cambridge, MA: MIT Press, 1983).

37. Levinas often cited Gabriel Marcel's questioning of the Christian West's assimilation of "the eminent value of *autarkia*, or self-sufficiency" from classical antiquity (*OS* 22; Levinas's citation may be found in Gabriel Marcel, *Metaphysical Journal*, trans. B. Wall [London: Rockliff, 1952], 210–11; also see *EN* 61–63; *OG* 143); Levinas concludes, though, that in Marcel "dialogue is finally overwhelmed by ontology" (*EN* 119). While dissociations of intrinsic value from ethics within Christianity are evident in the theological conundrum of the virtuous pagan, they are intensified within Protestant attacks upon the spiritual usefulness of "works," as in George Whitefield, "The Nature and Necessity of Our Regeneration or New Birth in Christ Jesus," in *Whitefield & Wesley on the New Birth*, ed. Timothy L. Smith (Grand Rapids, MI: Francis Asbury Press, 1986), 75. The notion of value-neutral rationality derives from Hume's argument that *ought* cannot be deduced from *is*, which challenges ontological moral philosophy, but at the cost of making the ethical a matter of utility or feeling. See David Hume, *An Inquiry Concerning the Principles of Morals*, ed. Charles W. Hendel (Indianapolis: Bobbs-Merrill, 1957); also see MacIntyre, *After Virtue*, 48–56. In practice, philosophical moral neutrality intersected with the segregation of bureaucratic rationalization (in Weber's sense) from questions of value. See Max Weber, *The Protestant Ethic and the Spirit of Capitalism*, trans. Talcott Parsons (New York: Charles Scribner's Sons, 1958), 25. Suspicion that moral discourse must be contaminated by moralistic mystification, evident in much late-nineteenth century fiction (Samuel Butler and Thomas Hardy for example) as well as in Nietzsche's "genealogical" account of morals, was radically intensified by the horrors unleashed by World War I (as the poetry of Sassoon and Owens attests).

38. Fyodor Dostoyvesky, *Crime and Punishment*, trans. David McDuff (London: Penguin, 1991), 316; *Prestuplenie i Nakazhanie* (Moskva: Slavianka, 1993), 160.

39. See Beals, 99-105.

40. See Allen, 77–109; Beals, 65–92.

41. Derrida, *Adieu to Emmanuel Levinas*, 2.

42. Ibid., 11–12.

43. See especially Jeffrey Nealon, *Alterity Politics: Ethics and Performative Subjectivity* (Durham, NC: Duke University Press, 1998); Howard Caygill, *Levinas and the Political* (New York: Routledge, 2002); Horowitz and Horowitz, eds., *Difficult Justice*; Asher Horowitz, *Ethics at a Standstill: History and Subjectivity in Levinas and the Frankfurt School* (Pittsburgh: Duquesne University Press, 2008); the essays collected in Atterton and Calarco's collection, *Radicalizing Levinas*; John E. Drabinski, *Levinas and the Postcolonial: Race, Nation, Other* (Edinburgh, UK: Edinburgh University Press, 2011).

44. See Enrique Dussel, "'The Politics' by Levinas," in *Difficult Justice*, 78–96; *The Underside of Modernity* (Atlantic City, NJ: Humanities Press, 1996); *Philosophy as Liberation* (New York: Orbis Books, 1985); Michael Barber, *Ethical Hermeneutics: Rationality in Enrique Dussel's Philosophy of Liberation* (New York: Fordham University Press, 1998).

45. Gad Horowitz, "Aporia and Messiah in Derrida and Levinas," in *Difficult Justice*, 326. For similar calls for revolution rather than reform, recalling the Bolshevist/Menshevist-Social Democratic polemics of the early twentieth cetutry, see Paul Smith, *Primitive America: The Ideology of Captialist Democracy* (Minneapolis: University of Minnesota Press, 2007) and Slavoj Zizek, *Violence* (New York: Picador, 2008).

46. Asher Horowitz's *Ethics at a Standstill* is representative. In a 360-page argument that Levinasian political thought could dispense with liberalism because of affinities between Levinas's and Frankfurt School critique of totalizing conceptuality, Stalinism (98) is mentioned only once, to note that Levinas never argues that Stalinism *must* follow from Marxism. That is true, but his derivation of pluralism as the political correlative of ethics and his regard for republican institutions may be connected to an attentiveness to lived experience nowhere evident in Horowitz's book, despite the presence of "history" in its subtitle. Something in Marx-

ism, Levinas observes, did not prevent Stalinism (just as something in Western thought did not prevent the Holocaust): both facts should give thought pause. Despite trenchant criticism of liberalism's shortcomings, Levinas intimates that Marxism's disdain for liberal impediments to centralization of power may betray a *constitutive* vulnerability to Stalinism.

47. See José Lezama Lima, *Paradiso* (Buenos Aires: Ediciones de la flor, 1968); Eduardo González, *Cuba and the Fall: Christian Text and Queer Narrative in the Fiction of José Lezama Lima and Reinaldo Arenas* (Charlottesville: University of Virginia Press, 2010). Examples of twentieth-century literary works whose subject is radical left state violence include Anna Akmatova, *Requiem*, in *Poems of Akhmatova*, trans. Stanley Kunitz with Max Hayward (Boston and New York: Mariner, 1973), 98–117; Ahmadou Kourouma, *Les soleils des indépendances* (Paris: Seuil, 1970); Duong Thu Huong, *Memories of a Pure Spring*, trans. Nina McPherson and Phan Huy Duong (New York: Penguin, 2000).

48. On gender, see especially Sam B. Girgis, *Levinas and the Cinema of Redemption: Time, Ethics, and the Feminine Sex* (New York: Columbia University Press, 2010); Diane Perpich, "Levinas, Feminism, and Identity Politics," in *Radicalizing Levinas*, 21–39, *The Ethics of Emmanuel Levinas*, 177–98; Lisa Guenther, *The Gift of the Other: Levinas and the Politics of Reproduction* (Albany: State University of New York Press, 2006); Katz, *Levinas, Judaism, and the Feminine*; Tina Chanter, "Hands That Give and Hands That Take: The Politics of the Feminine in Levinas," in *Difficult Justice*, 48–62; *Time, Death, and the Feminine* (Stanford: Stanford University Press, 2001); Tina Chanter, ed., *Feminist Interpretations of Emmanuel Levinas* (University Park, PA: Pennsylvania State University Press, 2001); Stella Sandford, "Levinas, Feminism, and the Feminine," in *The Cambridge Companion to Levinas*, ed. Simon Critchley and Robert Bernasconi (Cambridge: Cambridge University Press, 2002), 139–60, *The Metaphysics of Love: Gender and Transcendence in Levinas* (London: Athlone Press, 2000). On Eurocentrism, see Drabinski, *Levinas and the Postcolonial*; Robert Eaglestone, "Postcolonial Thought and Levinas's Double Vision," in *Radicalizing Levinas*, 57–68; Gad Horowitz, "Aporia and Messiah in Derrida and Levinas," in *Difficult Justice*, 307–30; Dussel, *The Underside of Modernity*. On the ecumenical or atheistic currents within Levinas's religious thought, see especially Westphal, *Levinas and Kierkegaard in Dialogue*; Ethan Kleinberg, "The Myth of Emmanuel Levinas," in *After the Deluge: New Perspectives on the Intellectual and Cultural History of Postwar Europe*, ed. Julian Bourg (Lanham, MD: Lexington, 2004), 201–26; Hillary Putnam, "Levinas and Judaism," in *The Cambridge Companion to Levinas*, ed. Simon Critchley and Robert Bernasconi (Cambridge: Cambridge University Press, 2002), 33–62; Jeffrey L. Kosky, *Levinas and the Philosophy of Religion* (Bloomington and Indianapolis: Indiana University Press, 2001); Jeffrey Bloechl, *Liturgy of the Neighbor: Emmanuel Levinas and the Religion of Responsibility* (Pittsburgh: Duquesne University Press, 2000); Jeffrey Bloechl, ed., *The Face of the Other and the Trace of God: Essays on the Philosophy of Emmanuel Levinas* (New York: Fordham University Press, 2000). On Levinas's relation to alternative phenomenologies, see especially Judith Butler, "Precarious Life," in *Radicalizing Levinas*, 3–19, *Giving an Account of Oneself*; Jacques Rancière, *The Flesh of Words: The Politics of Writing* (Stanford: Stanford University Press, 2004); Jean-Luc Marion, *In Excess: Studies in Saturated Phenomena*, trans. Robyn Horner and Vincent Berraud (New York: Fordham University Press, 2002); Michael Henry, *Incarnation: Une philosophie de la chair* (Paris: Seuil, 2000); Giorgio Agamben, *Homo Sacer: Sovereign Power and Bare Life*, trans. D. Heller-Roazen (Stanford: Stanford University Press, 1998); Natalie Depraz, *Transcendance et incarnation: le statut de l'intersubjectivité comme alerité à soi chez Husserl* (Paris: J. Vrin, 1995).

49. See Simon Critchley, "Five Problems in Levinas's View of Politics and the Sketch of a Solution to Them," in *Radicalizing Levinas*, 41–53, 52 cited.

50. Perpich effectively identifies such nostalgia in Dominique Janicaud's criticizing Levinas for departing from orthodox Husserlianism and Giorgio Agamben's criticizing Levinas for departing from "celebrat[ing] the vertiginous groundlessness of Foucault's and Deleuze's theories of immanence" (*The Ethics of Emmanuel Levinas*, 22; also see 17–23, 44–49; Dominique Janicaud et al., *Phenomenology and the Theological Turn: The French Debate* [New York: Fordham University Press, 2001]; Agamben, *Potentialities*). For the complexities of Levinas's relationship with Nietzsche, see the essays collected in *Nietzsche and Levinas: "After the*

Death of a Certain God," ed. Jill Stauffer and Bettina Bergo (New York: Columbia University Press, 2009).

51. See Perpich's discussion of how Sonia Sikka's critique of Levinas relies upon incoherently conjoined discourses of equality and discourses of difference (*The Ethics of Emmanuel Levinas*, 176–98 and "Levinas, Feminism, and Identity Politics," in *Radicalizing Levinas*, 21–39; also Sonia Sikka, "The Delightful Other: Portraits of the Feminine in Kierkegaard, Nietzsche, and Levinas," in *Feminist Interpretations of Emmanuel Levinas*, ed. Tina Chanter [University Park: Pennslyvania State University Press, 2001], 96–118). Perpich delineates the extent to which radical critique of Levinas may involve a desire to prevent his work from challenging long-established academic discourses and modes of identity, a desire that naturalizes and totalizes conceptual matrices consolidated in the 1970s and 1980s.

52. Philip Goldstein's review, in *Symplokê* 18, nos. 1–2 (2011): 409–11, of Teresa L. Ebert's *The Task of Cultural Critique* (Urbana: University of Illinois Press, 2009) makes the same point about her advocacy of totalizing "transformative critique". "The history of Western communist parties, the collapse of the former USSR, the revisionist practices of China and now Cuba, or the very marginal, isolated position of the American left all pose serious issues for traditional Marxism, yet Ebert simply accepts Leon Trotsky's criticisms of Stalin as though it [*sic*] denies the left's need to rethink or reevaluate traditional Marxism" (409).

Chapter One

Emmanuel Levinas, 1906–1995

A Twentieth-Century Intellectual Life

Donald R. Wehrs

Levinas always stressed that the Judaism into which he was born in Kaunas (Kovno), Lithuania, shaped decisively by the Gaon (genius) of Vilna, Rabbi Elijah ben Solomon Zahman (1720–1797), eschewed the mystical and irrational (*ITR* 24): "The religious sentiment such as I received it consisted much more in respect for books—the Bible and its traditional commentaries . . .— than in determinate beliefs. . . . It is that extraordinary presence of [the Bible's] characters, that ethical plenitude and its mysterious possibilities of exegesis which originally signified transcendence for me" (*EI* 23). Rejecting "fervor and the cult of emotions" for "a Judaism more squarely rooted in study, rigor and sober observance,"[1] the Gaon opposed Hassidism, which embraced the Kabbalah, whose cornerstone was the Zohar (Radiance) (c. 1300), a vast text countering rationalism such as Moses Maimonides's with esoteric readings of the Torah arguably influenced by Christian Neoplatonism, Catholic Mariology, and *troubadour* poetry, though it presented itself as ancient,[2] a claim Hassidism accepted.[3]

Despite opposing Hassidism, the Goan was "also a Kabbalist" and some of his disciples "continued the study of Zohar,"[4] a point Levinas confirms while stressing that the Goan "always thought that the Zohar was in agreement with the Talmud" (*ITR* 93). Talmudic interpretation was in turn mediated by the great eleventh-century scholar from Troyes, Champagne, Rashi (Rabbi Shlomo Yitzhaki).[5] Rashi's scriptural readings stress the ethical, affective nuances of narratives; they strive to "stir up those human feelings which are the basic preconditions for the free-will acceptance of any system of law," and so "appeal to the heart rather than the intellect."[6] When encountering legal explanations that the "heart hesitates" to accept, he would fashion an interpretation more congruent with ethical rationality. [7] Levinas's post-war devotional teaching and writings are self-consciously rooted in these traditions. [8]

Though his childhood study of scripture reflected mediation by the Talmud as interpreted by Rashi, the Goan, and his followers, [9] Levinas's own encounter with Talmudic and Kabbalah writings came much later. His parents, who owned a Russian book and stationery shop, "saw the future of young people in the Russian language and culture" (*ITR* 24), and Levinas recounts imbibing from his parents deep love of Russian literature (*ITR* 24), observing, "The Russian novel was my preparation for philosophy" (*ITR* 89): "'We are each of us guilty with respect to all, and I more so than all the others,' says a character in Dostoyevsky's *The Brothers Karamazov*, thereby expressing this 'originary constitution' of the I or the unique, in a responsibility for the neighbor or the other, and the impossibility of escaping responsibility or of being replaced" (*ITR* 229). [10] The continuity of scriptural and novelistic reading by the young Levinas grounds his later insistence that "[t]here is a participation in Holy Scripture in the national literatures," for they signify "through the expression of the face of the other man" (*EI* 117).

In a 1990 study of Mikhail Bakhtin, Gary Saul Morson and Caryl Emerson delineate the distinctive Russian intellectual culture shaping the fiction of Tolstoy and Dostoyevsky in a commentary equally relevant to Levinas: "Bakhtin follows a tradition of Russian anti-ideological thinkers that includes Alexander Herzen, Leo Tolstoy, and Anton Chekhov. . . . In his essay, 'Why Do Men Stupefy Themselves?,' Tolstoy develops the idea that real ethical decisions are made, and one's true life is lived, at everyday moments we rarely if ever notice"; for both Tolstoy and Bakhtin, "moral wisdom derived from living rightly moment to moment and attending carefully to the irreducible particularities of each case." [11] The impress of the ethical upon language yields dialogue, a form of answerability to the other that goes beyond empathy, that by "'living into' another [*vzhivanie*]," yields understanding antithetical to "reducing everything to a single consciousness, dissolving in it the other's consciousness." [12]

While there are significant differences between Levinas and Bakhtin, both draw upon what "understanding" [*ponimanie*] and the verb "to understand" [*ponimat'*] signify within Tolstoy's and Dostoyevsky's novelistic discourse. In *Anna Karenina*, Levin's search for understanding from philosophy is baffled by its abstract terms, for as soon as he reflects upon "life [*ie zhieni*] itself," theorizing as a consolation for mortality collapses. [13] By chance Levin hears a peasant say that while "[o]ne man just lives for his own needs," another is "an upright [*pravibyj*] old man. He lives for the soul [*dushi zhivet*]. He remembers [*pomnit*] God" (794/419). Deeply struck, Levin realizes that to have "understood [*ponial*]" the peasant's words means to have been unable to doubt their "rightness [*spravedlivosti*]"; moreover, not only he "but everybody, the whole world, fully understands [*ponimaiut*] this one thing, and this one thing they do not doubt and always agree upon" (795/419–20). Levin discovers that ethics, the other before oneself, initiates the understanding that human living presupposes. When arguing that philosophy rests upon "a pre-philosophical experience, upon a ground that does not pertain solely to philosophy" (*ITR* 159), Levinas has in mind "life" in Tolstoy's sense, wherein the ethical gives words a communicative agency anterior to conceptuality or identity politics.[14]

Notably, what precedes "understanding" is feeling: Levin "felt [*chuvstvoval*] something new in his soul" (795/419) *before* he realized he understood.[15] The same word and its variants appear in *Crime and Punishment* almost exclusively in contexts when Raskholnikov experiences somatic revulsion at his own ideas or actions. But he remains locked in egocentrism until the novel's last pages, when discovering he loves Sonya "infinitely [*beskonechno*]" frees him from self-preoccupation, something she spontaneously "understood [*poniala*]."[16] Then sociality, and so redemption, becomes possible: "and he knew it, felt it [*enal eto, chuvstvoval*] completely in the whole of his renewed being" (629/331). Convergence of conscious knowledge (what he *knew—enal*) and somatically articulated moral sense (what he *felt—chuvstvoval*) make him a new man: "In place of dialectics life [*zhien'*] had arrived" (630/331). While stress upon feeling's intuitive uprightness suggests Rousseauian, Romantic influence, both Tolstoy and Dostoyevsky depict feeling leading us *away* from self-absorption, disrupting egoism.

The atmosphere of such religious and novel reading shaped Levinas's political and philosophical interests from youth to old age. When World War I erupted, his family, being Jewish, were obliged to relocate to Russia proper. Returning in 1920 to newly independent Lithuania, Levinas felt he was "leaving a messianic country," for, though not "a militant Marxist revolutionary," he believed "that in Russia history was reaching its ultimate goal, a bit like the ultimate flowering of justice. This, of course, was before Stalin" (*ITR* 189). Upon return to Lithuania, Levinas had his "first contact" with Europe through a Jewish German teacher at his *lycée*: "When he used to say, 'das ist goethisch (this is Goethean),' everyone shivered" (*ITR* 85). Levinas absorbed an idealizing love of Europe epitomized in its western Jewish form by the French scholar Léon Brunschvicg, who represents a "whole generation" who remembered of the Dreyfus Affair "less the fact that such an injustice had been possible in a civilized age than the triumph recorded by justice" (*DF* 43).

Just as Marxism and Europe were refracted through his early reading, so Levinas, as a philosophy student at the University of Strasbourg, was initially drawn to Bergson, whose focus upon human creative potentialities spoke to "fear of being in a world without novel possibilities, without a future of hope" (*EI* 28). He then discovered in Husserl's suspending theoretically con-

ditioned conventional perception in order to get to what consciousness immediately apprehends a philosophical method congruent with predicating
"understanding" upon "life."[17] Concurrently, his friendship with fellow student Maurice Blanchot introduced him to Valéry and Proust (*ITR* 30), and so
to a European modernism similarly challenging naturalized perceptions.[18]

In 1928 Levinas went to Freiburg to study with Husserl, and there discovered Heidegger, who, breaking with the contemplative *cogito*-oriented stance
that Husserl inherited from traditional Western philosophy, resituated philosophy in analysis of everyday, active, embodied immediacy. For Heidegger,
human being (*Dasein*, literally "there-being") entails being-toward a "world"
configuring and configured by intentionality, experiencing temporality as
moving toward a horizon, inhabiting modes of being-in-the-world colored by
moods and anxieties.[19] Heidegger's *Being and Time* (*Sein und Zeit*, 1927)
established for Levinas a way of doing philosophy that "aims at describing
man's being or existing—not his nature" (*EI* 40). In 1929 Levinas witnessed
a debate between Heidegger and Ernst Cassirer in which Heidegger's critique
of the metaphysical basis of traditional humanism (knowing *about* man implies essentialism, thinking in terms of timeless substances) seemed to liberate thought from reified abstractions: "I must admit that I did not even pity
Cassirer" (189). Writing in 1931 of his time in Freiburg, Levinas observed
that the "new philosophy" seemed not "a new theory," but rather "a new
ideal of life" (*UH* 63).

In 1930 he produced his pioneering study of Husserl and became a French
citizen, cementing lifelong allegiance to French culture and republican values, but Hitler's 1933 rise to power, accompanied by Heidegger's public
allegiance to Nazism, provoked a philosophical trauma of the first magni-
tude: "Naïve as I was then, I imagined that only vulgarity and hatred could
lead to Nazism" (*ITR* 189). In 1934, the same year he began working for the
Alliance Israélite Universelle, which provided religious and French academic
education to Jews from throughout the Mediterranean world, Levinas published an essay, "Reflections on the Philosophy of Hitlerism," that presents
Nazism as revolt against a liberalism perceived to be rootless, abstract, alienating.[20] Marxism begins to break with this abstract freedom by arguing that
the spirit has "an inevitable relation to a determined situation" (7), but in
National Socialism "[t]he biological . . . becomes more than an *object* of
spiritual life. It becomes its heart. . . . Man's essence no longer lies in
freedom, but in a kind of bondage [*enchaînement*]" and "society based on
consanguinity" concretizes "the spirit" (9). Levinas displays some sympathy
for critiques of a liberalism in which "[m]an revels in his freedom and does
not definitely compromise himself with any truth" (10), which echo similar
critiques in Tolstoy and Dostoyevsky.[21] But Nazism's embrace of blood and
force puts in question not just "a particular dogma concerning democracy,
parliamentary government, dictatorial regime, or religious politics," but "the

very humanity of man" (11). To counter Nazi racism what is needed is a way of reclaiming the "humanity of man" uncompromised by the essentialism that Heidegger so devastatingly dismantles.

Endeavoring to push ontology beyond Heideggerian limits, Levinas in 1935 published a short essay, "On Escape" (*De l'évasion*), in which, like Heidegger, he identifies "traditional philosophy" with "a revolt . . . against the idea of being," but links that revolt to seeking a "peace" or "rest" dissolving all that in "the brutal fact of being . . . assaults [human] freedom" (*OE* 48). But, Levinas claims, "modern sensibility" and "contemporary literature" suggest that simply acquiring more being (as in Hitler in seeking more living room) cannot quell an agitated desire to escape being itself. In a phenomenological analysis of *escape*, a term "borrow[ed] from the language of contemporary literary criticism" (52), Levinas distinguishes desire to escape from desire for a higher, better, or more creative plane of being. Escape seeks relief from "an acute feeling of being held fast [*rivé*]" (52), from "being itself or the 'one-self'" rather than from "being's limitation" (56). Consequently, Western thought's valorization of more or better being cannot bring this agitation peace or rest. But simply to accept being, "with the tragic despair it contains and the crimes it commits" (73) is to embrace "barbarian" thought (to follow Hitler or Heidegger in taking power or being as the measure of all things). Since romanticism, idealism, and barbarism offer delusive transcendence, one is left with the imperative "of getting out of being by a new path." (73).

The new path unites phenomenology with critique of totalizing thought. Levinas discovered a model for the latter by reading in 1935 Franz Rosenzweig's *Star of Redemption* (1921), which argues that philosophy, aspiring to "throw off the fear of things earthly," subsumes life into a totalizing "All" belied by the singularity of one's own death.[22] Anticipating Heidegger's similar claim, Rosenzweig argues that our impending death gives us "the singular life of the singular person" (11).[23] As in theist existentialism developed from Kierkegaard by Martin Buber, Rudolf Otto, Karl Barth, and others,[24] the self in Rosenzweig, finding its singularity effaced by totality, is driven to defiance and despair (106). Rearticulating human temporality in terms of creation (the past), revelation (the present), and redemption (the future), Rosenzweig depicts existence as the effect of primal divine love, responsiveness to which reorders communal and political life around the command, "Love thy neighbor."[25] Sociality so reformed repairs the damage done to the world by sin and redeems time by working toward bringing God's presence into the world.[26]

Rosenzweig's erotically charged language, "Thus love turns the world into a world animated with a soul" (240), highlights his transposition into existential-historicizing terms both imagery and narrative structure from the Zohar, wherein interaction among ten divine potencies generate the world and its order. These potencies are imaged as male or female, whose loving modifying interaction supports the world: so *Hokhmah* (wisdom) descends and penetrates *Binah* (understanding), which opens itself in fertile receptivity.[27] From this union emerge *Hesed* (loving-kindness) and *Din* (judgment), whose proper entwinement gives birth to "*Tif'eret* ('splendor'), *mishpat* ('balanced judgment'), and *emet* ('truth')," whence derives *Hod* (splendor, prophecy) and *Netsah* (endurance, prophecy), whose offspring is *Yesod* (foundation), the basis of the created and social world, "often called *tsaddiq* [righteous]. . . ."[28] All this may gravitate into theosophic mysticism, but may also metaphorically indicate the primacy of pluralism and dialogical conservation of alterity. Sexuality is put figuratively at the center of non-totalizing interaction, and presence (*Shekhinah*), at once dialogic, ethical, and erotic, "is depicted as the longing of God and cosmos alongside that of a suffering people. All of them long to be redeemed." Moreover, "Human efforts toward the restoration of the *Shekhinah* operate within the framework of certain rhythms, both historical and liturgical."[29]

Rosenzweig suggests that reordering of self through responsiveness to others' speech makes possible enacted ethical sociality and so invests time with redemptive hope. Concretely, "To learn the Torah and to keep the commandments is the omnipresent basis of Jewish life. Marriage brings with it the full realization of this life. . . . The household is the chamber of the Jewish heart. Revelation wakens something in creation [love] that is as strong as death. . . . The new creation of revelation is the soul." (326). Such life offers hope that individuals might be redeemed from anomic despair and that the West might learn that "walk[ing] humbly with thy God" opens "the gate" into "LIFE" (424), the last word of the text.

The appeal of Rosenzweig to Levinas appears evident. Making present the Good in everyday existence enfolds Enlightenment progressivism within Russian-Hebraic messianic ethical relations to time. Similar ethical translations of Kabbalah themes are pursued in Rabbi Hayim ben Issac of Volozhin's *The Soul of Life* (*Nefesh Hahayim*) (1824), though Levinas may have come to Rosenzweig first. According to Richard A. Cohen, "Rabbi Hayim invokes the entire Jewish mystical tradition" to invest human ethical actions with the power of bringing God's presence into the world, something Levinas later affirms, Cohen argues, in describing the ethical encounter as "nothing other than the movement 'to-God.'"[30]

Further, Claire Elise Katz notes that Levinas, like Rosenzweig, evokes "the Kabbalistic conception of *tikkun olam*, to repair the world."[31] Not only does repairing the world invest human time with meaning; it keeps the world, as in Kabbalistic teaching, from reverting to nothingness. In a 1964 Talmudic commentary, Levinas argues, "The world is here so that the ethical order has the possibility of being fulfilled. . . . To refuse the Torah is to bring being back to nothingness" (*NiTR* 41). Since Levinas's deployment of Kabbalistic tropes, like his reading of the Talmud and Scripture, is governed by ethical-rational hermeneutics, "Israel" denotes all for whom the ethical grounds understanding and life. But the metaphorical is in a sense literal. Refusing the ethical order not only can destroy the world, it has already done so—in the *Shoah*.

Mobilized as a translation officer in 1939, Levinas was captured and sent to a stalag in 1940. During this suspended time, when not just personal life, but the life of a world attesting the presence of God hung in the balance, Levinas's wife and young daughter were spared through the efforts of Maurice Blanchot and a cloister of Catholic nuns, but his mother-in-law, parents and two brothers, as well as his wife's family, all perished. He seldom spoke of those lost, even privately. The context for reflection, however, became irrevocably otherwise.

After becoming director of a Parisian secondary school, part of the Alliance Israélite Universelle, Levinas returned to philosophy in two short books, *Existence and Existents* (1947) and *Time and the Other* (1947), and three enigmatic essays on art. *Existence and Existents*, begun in captivity, picks up from "On Escape" to argue that "anxiety over Being" is just as "primal" as anxiety over death (Heidegger's theme), because pure Being, what Levinas calls the *il y a* (*there is*), is as horrific for humans as nothingness (*EE* 5). Levinas argues that intentional structuring of a world involves concrete material relations: "In desiring I am not concerned with being but am absorbed with the desirable, with an object that will slake my desire" (28). Embodied intentionality assumes imperialistic, fascistic resonances (30), but sociality lifts desire above this possessive-consumptive order: "Compare eating with loving, which occurs beyond economic activity and the world. For what characterizes love is an essential and insatiable hunger. To shake hands with a friend . . . is to convey . . . [that friendship is] something unfulfilled, a permanent desire . . ." (35). By contrast, possessing cognitively what shines in the light, and experiencing oneself as unavailable for a similar grasp, elicits a feeling of "power to withdraw infinitely" (43), akin to detached liberalism's abstract freedom. The opposite of free withdrawal involves putting oneself in a distinctive place, thereby "escap[ing] anonymity" (44), but at the price of forfeiting total freedom.

Art occupies an equivocal position, for perception is freed from possessiveness but withdrawal abides: "Instead of arriving at the object, the intention gets lost in the sensation itself. . . . In art, sensation . . . returns to the impersonality of *elements*" (47). Abstraction from both comprehension and sociality courts reversion to the *il y a*, impersonal "being in general" (52), whose "horror" literature well depicts (Levinas cites Rimbaud, Huysmans, Poe, Zola, Maupassant, Shakespeare, and Racine). The *il y a* as impersonalized being one cannot escape bears strong resemblance to the twilight existence of prisoners, or people de-composed as subjects by totalitarian force.

The central question becomes how to reconstitute subjectivity, or how reconstitution illuminates subjectivity's forgotten pre-history. Levinas concludes, "A subject does not exist before the event of its position. . . . Its action does not consist in willing, but in . . . a folding back upon itself," contrary to Heidegger's association of "being-toward" with standing out from oneself (ecstasy), and contrary to the association of foundation with entrapment in post-structuralist anti-humanism.[32] The subject Levinas would recover "is in a certain sense a substance" (81), for "taking position in the anonymous *there is*" involves "taking a position on solid ground, on a base, fulfilling the conditions, foundation" (82). An existent stands out from existence not simply by asserting its own freedom; it exerts being from a place, as though braced against something. Hypostasis, action generating existence, engenders sufficient freedom to enable withdrawal from the *il y a*, but by itself this merely delivers one to solitude, to "enchainment to oneself" (89), as in "On Escape."

For "being-toward" to cease being abstract and solipsistic, there needs to be "hope for the reparation of the irreparable" (93). Evoking *tikkun olam* and the idea of the future as redemption, Levinas links both to the question of what subjectivity after Auschwitz can be possible or bearable.[33] Having time, survival, is endurable only if "time is constituted by my relationship with the other" (96), a relationship irreducible to a "collectivity formed around something common" (98): "Intersubjectivity is . . . brought about by Eros, where in the proximity of another the distance is wholly maintained. . . . What is presented as the failure of communication in love in fact constitutes the positive character of the relationship: this absence of the other is precisely his presence qua other" (98–99).[34]

How "the very relationship of the subject with the Other" (*TO* 39) constitutes the subject's temporality is *Time and the Other*'s theme. Hypostasis begins with "freedom" experienced as the "existent . . . exert[ing] on its existence the virile power of the subject" (54), but while virile solitary freedom is a moment in subjectivity's constitution, it is hardly authenticity.[35] It is, rather, an immaturity.[36] Failure to see this yields naïve bourgeois individualism properly attacked by Marxist humanism (60–62), philosophical identification of transcendence with a *cogito*'s grasping objects caught by the light of reason (64–66), and romanticizing of aloof "resoluteness" (Heidegger's *Entschlossenheit*).[37] Given this immaturity, death can only scandalize thought, which Levinas illustrates by citing *Macbeth*, prompting the exclamation, "[I]t sometimes seems to me that the whole of philosophy is only a meditation of Shakespeare" (72).

Philosophy is literature's exegesis to the extent that literature, participating in Holy Scripture, speaks from and to a grown-up life in which "time itself refers to this situation of the face-to-face with the Other" (79). Because death is "the impossibility of having a project" (74), it reveals "that existence is pluralist" (75), for other existents have projects from which they too may be alienated by death. Moreover, others are real (not just representations or objects for us) by virtue of having existences that are "not unknown but unknowable, refractory to all light," so that "the relationship with the other is a relationship with a Mystery" (75). In *Time and the Other* this "very alterity" (83) is concretized in sexual difference (86). Linking gender to pluralism, as in the Kabbalah, Levinas argues that the erotic relation highlights how inexhaustible love of the Other proceeds from desiring the Other's abiding difference.[38] From desiring "the alterity of the feminine" (90), the male subject's relationship to the future is transformed by paternity, in which "a pluralist existing" (92) allows escape from enchainment to oneself without lapsing into the "collectivity of the side-by-side" (93). Whether or not this account opens to gender essentialism or to an ethics of sexual difference, it is later modified, for in *Totality and Infinity* eros does not anchor ethical subjectivity but lies to its side (*TI* 256–66), which raises a separate set of issues about gender and eros in relation to ethics.[39]

In *Time and the Other* Levinas may naturalize male subjectivity as normative, but there is also veiled homage from a man to the wife he nearly lost. This effort to think through without sentimentality the redemptive time women open for men is akin to Joyce's effort in *Ulysses*, set on the date of his first walk with his future wife, Nora. There is no evidence that Levinas knew Joyce, but his 1947 essay on Proust reveals how intimately the other towering high modernist novelist informed *Existence and Existents* and *Time and the Other*. Levinas separates Proust from a fashionable "literature of action, heroism and the soil" (*LR* 161) that naively celebrates virility. In the time regained (*retrouvé*) of Proustian narrative and memory, perception guided by intention to possess objects is displaced by "intention get[ting] lost in the sensation itself, and . . . wandering about in sensation, in *aisthesis* (*EE* 47), piercing through egoistic conceptuality to a life bound up with "the mystery of the other" (*LR* 163). Proust reveals that emotion aroused by places and things "exists through others (*les autres*), through Albertine, his grandmother, or his own past self" (163). Others captivate us because we cannot grasp them as objects, a point monumentalized by Albertine's inexhaustible elusiveness (163): "Marcel did not love Albertine, if love is a fusion with the Other" (164); rather, Marcel's love, like the entire novel, "situate[s] reality in a relation with . . . the Other as absence and mystery" (165), and so discloses that sociality and a possibly redemptive future lie in a "proximity that, far from meaning less than identification, precisely opens up the horizons of social existence, making the whole surplus of our experience of friendship and love burst forth" (164).

Given this literary correction of philosophy, Levinas's 1948 "Reality and its Shadow" may seem jarringly anomalous. The essay's prominent availability in English during Levinas's initial Anglophone reception helped foster a

notion that Levinas was hostile to art, despite his own evident literary culture.[40] Published in Sartre's journal, *Les Temps Modernes*, the essay was an
attack on Sartre's notion of "engaged" art, art taking the celebration of what
Levinas considered immature virility to be a form of ethical life, on the one
hand, and an attack on art for art's sake on the other.[41] In a context where
discussion revolved around these poles, Levinas sought to demonstrate the
inadequacy of both. While an image's "detachment from an object" puts us
in a realm of "sensation" that suspends intentional possessiveness (*RS* 134),
it also puts us at risk of losing the "position" or "base" keeping us from
reversion into the *il y a*. A simulacrum of time, its illusory abrogation, or its
freezing into fatality may be deeply seductive: "The fact that humanity could
have provided itself with art reveals in time the uncertainty of time's continuation and something like a death doubling the impulses of life" (141). Behind
such descriptions lies experience of time as unimaginable trauma and loss. It
may not be too fanciful to suggest that Levinas finds in art's magic a danger
equivalent to that which lurks, for Harry Potter, in the Mirror of Erised, and
for analogous reasons: art "brings the irresponsibility that charms as a light-
ness and grace. It frees. . . . We find an appeasement when . . . we throw
ourselves into the rhythm of a reality which solicits only its admission into a
book or a painting" (141–42).[42] Like Dumbledore warning against engross-
ment in the Mirror, Levinas warns that lingering in "artistic enjoyment"
partakes of something "wicked and egoist and cowardly." (142).[43] The way
to break the lure of such idolatry, however, is not to scorn literature, but to
engage in criticism, which "integrates the inhuman work of the artist into the
human world" (142) by building on "clear awareness" of the "insufficiency
of artistic idolatry" within "modern literature" itself (143).[44]

Indeed, "The Transcendence of Words" (1949) suggests that major art
challenges conventional perception via a "proliferation of erasures" (*LR*
147). Though in "creating beauty out of nature, art calms and quiets it," the
resulting "silence" prompts a "need to enter into a relation with someone,"
arousing "the necessity of critique" (147). We thus move into "social relations" with "the real presence of the other" when "[t]he use of words
wrenches experience out of its aesthetic self-sufficiency," which is why "criticism, which is the word of a living being speaking to a living being, brings
the image in which art revels back to the fully real being" (148). Literary
words that solicit criticism break free of idolatrous frozenness, return us to
the lived, face-to-face contexts of speech that in privileging the Other "ceases
to be incomprehensible once we admit that the first fact of existence is
neither being in-itself (*en soi*) nor being for-itself (*pour soi*) but being *for the
other* (*pour l'autre*)" (149).

In this "first fact" the ethical predication of significance comes into view.
During the late 1940s, early 1950s, Levinas engaged in intense Talmudic
study under Mordechai Chouchani, the fruit of which appeared in devotional

essays collected in *Difficult Freedom* (first edition 1963, second edition 1976) and Talmudic commentaries, published as *Quatre lectures talmudiques* (1968), *Du sacré au saint: cinq nouvelles lectures talmudiques* (1977), *L'Au-delà du verset: Lectures et discours talmudiques* (1982), and *Nouvelles lectures talmudiques* (1996). In his commentaries, Levinas celebrates polyphonic voices addressing texts as interlocutors forever surprisingly new in their alterity and forever rational in their ethicality. "The respect for the stranger and the sanctification of the name of the Eternal are strangely equivalent. And all the rest is a dead letter. All the rest is literature. The search for the spirit beyond the letter, that is Judaism itself" (*NiTR* 27–28). By evoking in this context the well-known conclusion of Paul Verlaine's "Art poétique," "All the rest is literature," Levinas associates Verlaine's call for a poetry responsible to real life against abstract, "artsy" poetry ("literature" in a degraded commercial sense) with the spirit of the letter. An ethical sense must anchor the letter, whether scriptural or literary, if it is to escape congealment into an idolized image by entering into a shared order of "understanding" in the Russian novelistic sense.

Similarly, in philosophical work of 1950s, preeminently "Is Ontology Fundamental?" (1951) and "The *I* and the Totality" (1954), work culminating in Levinas's first masterpiece, *Totality and Infinity* (1961), encountering the Other traumatically breaks apart worlds within which abstract dead letters support egological intentionality forgetful of real life. Relationship with the Other is actualized in speech, for this "tie to the other . . . does not reduce itself to the representation of the Other, but rather to his invocation" (*BPW* 7). Through its autonomous signifying, "[t]he face breaks the system. . . . The condition for propositional truth resides not in the revelation of a being or of the being of beings, but in the expression of the interlocutor" (*EN* 34).

It is not necessary here to repeat expositions of *Totality and Infinity* available elsewhere.[45] Suffice it to say, Levinas places virile intentional consciousness within a pre-history of the ethical in which "labor, habitation, the home, and economy" must stave off threats (including mortality) to an "enjoyment" where "I am absolutely for myself" (*TI* 134). Keeping us from collapsing into *il y a* is an originating and sustaining love, not attributed directly to God, as in Rosenzweig, but bound up with a maternal presence linking habitation and welcoming, giving us a "base" within an enfolding sociality: "And the other whose presence is discreetly an absence, with which is accomplished the primary hospitable welcome which describes the field of intimacy, is the Woman" (155). One may suspect veiled remembrance of his own murdered mother here, but Levinas's description accords with Proust's portrait of Marcel's mother and grandmother, just as his account of illusory egoistic independence recalls young Marcel's habitual inattention to their love's work. The advent of ethical maturity begins with the Other's presence disrupting our being "at home" (*chez soi*). Calling us out from ourselves, the

Other also confounds us with an absence in presence that "resists possession, resists my powers" (197). As Moyn notes, the divine Other of Kierkegaard and Buber is secularized,[46] but this is accomplished in part by transposing into phenomenological terms Marcel's experience of Albertine.

In Levinas's narrative, the Other's alterity pushes me into a world where "reason lives in language" (208), in the "first rationality" gleaming in "the opposition of the face to face" through which "[t]hings acquire a rational signification, and not only one of simple usage, because an other is associated with my relations with them" (209). Because "[t]he face opens the primordial discourse whose first word is obligation" (201), inability to totalize discloses totalizing's immorality, as when Marcel's efforts to objectify Albertine while she sleeps give him an illusory "impression de la posséder tout entière" [impression of possessing her completely] (III, 70). Unexpected, involuntary revulsion at oneself undoes imperializing cognition. So Marcel as a boy regrets his success in drawing his mother away from a dinner party, making her his (first) prisoner (I, 38–39). Discovering ethical violence at the heart of intentional consciousness, I encounter the ethical as what makes the spontaneous unfolding of my freedom answerable to something beyond itself (*TI* 302–04). Therein I *discover* my subjectivity by registering the simultaneity of the Other's vulnerability and height.[47] Responsibility for the Other leads to concern for justice to other others (212–16), and so enjoins pluralism (221–26) and ethical relation to time (226–40). This *temps retrouvé* culminates in a fecundity in which through children "the I is divested of its tragic egoity" (273), and a fraternity which is "the very relation with the face in which at the same time my election and equality, that is, the mastery exercised over me by the other, are accomplished" (279). Whereas Proust's Marcel spends many empty years at a sanatorium following a break-down (III, 854), in Levinas ethical maturity's entrance into determinate forms of sociality incarnates a transcendence "[s]ituated at the antipodes of . . . the isolated and heroic being that the State produces by its virile virtues" (306).[48]

Levinas provides a phenomenology of ethical subjectivity embracing childhood, eros, family, parenting, and sociality. While its adequacy or completeness may be debated, it presses upon philosophy the heterogeneous fullness of life that enables "understanding" in Tolstoy and Dostoyevsky. Moreover, as the older Derrida would note, Levinas makes receptivity, hospitality, and welcoming central to re-imagined subjectivity (*TI* 51).[49] This welcoming suggests the feminine receptivity attributed to *Binah* (understanding) in the Zohar, and so ascribes to ethical subjectivity a susceptibility to "fecund" modification. Levinas notes that *Rakhamin* (mercy) derives from *Rekhem* (uterus): "This maternal element in divine paternity is very remarkable, as is in Judaism the notion of a 'virility' to which limits must be set and whose partial renouncement may be symbolized by circumcision" (*NiTR* 183).

Bringing Hebraic ethical grounding of significance into Greek (philo-sophical) discourse, *Totality and Infinity*'s narrative functions as the counter-part of devotional texts and commentaries that transpose Hebraic discourse into (Greek) universalism. Derrida's 1964 essay, "Violence and Metaphys-ics" challenges Levinas's coupling of Jew and Greek by arguing that *Totality and Infinity*'s ethical critique of Heideggerian ontology is undercut by its own ontological language.[50] While Derrida's critique may be questioned,[51] Levinas, embarking on a professorial career in his mid-fifties, nevertheless did work to develop an account of language disengaged from virile, grasping representational conceptuality as he sought to bind ethical consciousness to pre-intentional affective susceptibilities in a series of essays culminating in his second great book, *Otherwise Than Being* (1974).

Partly inspired by Merleau-Ponty's phenomenology of bodily experience, partly responding to decolonization and the hopeful cultural relativism of the early 1960s, Levinas in "Meaning and Sense" (1964) distinguishes "sense" (*sens*) from "meaning" (*signification*).[52] Meaning, conveyed by cultural ob-jects produced by "incarnate minds" (*MS* 40), brings a way of life into being, uniting the body as "a feeling felt" with "a celebration of the world, a poetry" (41). Employing Heideggerian vocabulary, Levinas argues that meaning "shines forth in the works of poets and artists," and "shines forth in diverse ways in the diverse artists of the same cultures and is diversely expressed in the diverse cultures" (42).[53] Since meaning expresses particular ways of life, there is "no *meaning in itself*," for such a thought would have to jump "over the deforming or faithful but sensory reflections that lead to it" (42). Similar claims, precluding ethnocentric essentializing, were much embraced by 1980s–1990s postcolonial theory.[54]

Levinas argues, however, that if there is no intermediary between diverse cultural expressions, incommensurability rather than pluralism ensues (46). For there to be crosscultural translation and appreciation, there must be a sense (*sens*) anterior to meaning which orients it.[55] This sense comes from the ethical as disclosed by the face, whose "nudity . . . is without cultural ornament" (53), whose signifyingness is pre-cultural and so "confounds the intentionality that aims at it" (54). Sense orients meaning in *any* culture, and the measuring of meaning against sense *within* cultural works allows them to be mutually intelligible.[56] Dissociating diversity from relativism, Levinas argues that "before Culture and Aesthetics, meaning is situated in the Ethical, presupposed by all Culture and all meaning. Morality does not belong to Culture: it enables one to judge it" (57). The double "all" here counters Eurocentrism, including Levinas's own.[57]

The sense that calls meaning to responsibility, Levinas argues in "Enigma and Phenomena" (1965), is not an alternative "chain of significations," "an-other game" (*BPW* 66), for it "depends on the possibility of a signification that would signify in an irreducible disturbance" (66). Language should not be understood as one closed conceptual–representational system displaceable by others (as in Derrida), or as a synchronic, totalizing discourse formation discontinuous with others equally totalizing (as in Foucault).[58] Instead, "[a]cross the unbreakable chains of significations . . . a face facing and interpellating . . . cut[s] the threads of the contexts" (69), for "proximity and uprightness" break through every system's synchronizing horizons, coming as "expression, *saying*, in this universe of significations, *said*, of structures— Nature and History" (69). In the "destructuring" that "disturbance, a fissile present" (72) provokes, the saying signifies an ethical relation that transcends and measures all contexts, any said: "the significations *said* offer a hold to the *saying* which 'disturbs' them, like writing awaiting an interpretation. But herein is the—in principle—irreversible antecedence of the Word with respect to Being, the irretrievable delay of the Said after the Saying" (73). Moreover, in an essay paying homage to Maurice Blanchot, "The Servant and her Master" (1966), Levinas identifies "art and poetry" with "that exceptional event . . . which frees language from its servitude toward the structures in which the *said* prevails" (*LR* 153), for "No novel, no poem—from the *Iliad* to *Remembrance of Things Past*—has perhaps done anything else [than disrupt orders of the *said*]," without which "the world would know only the meanings which inspire official records or the minutes of the board meetings of Limited Companies" (156–57). This is not naïve traditionalism. Levinas stresses that "the poetic word . . . can . . . betray itself, become engulfed in order" (157), and so reading that is exegetical is alert to language's servant's (the *said*'s) inadequate account of her master (*saying*).

Criticism must then be to literature as Talmudic-rabbinic commentary is to scripture. As Levinas argues in a 1972 essay on Paul Celan, the poem bears "[a] language of proximity for proximity's sake, older that that of 'the truth of being' . . . the first of languages, response preceding the question, responsibility for the neighbor, by its *for the other*, the whole marvel of giving" (*PN* 41). In calling attention to "conscience—rectitude of responsibility before any appearance of forms, images, or things" (43), the saying of the poem unsays or ceases to be at home in its own said.[59] Poetry becomes "the spiritual act *par excellence*" by interrupting "the playful order of the beautiful and the play of concepts, and the *play of the world*" to give precedence to a "one-for-the-other" that is "the signifying of signification" (46).[60] Opposing poetic interruption not just to totalizing metaphysics but also to play (*jeu*), Levinas associates "play" as it circulates in Derrida's early texts with an alternative metaphysics. In a 1969 Talmudic commentary, Levinas notes that the text he is interpreting "opposes itself to . . . the metaphysical tendencies prevalent today, according to which being is play, according to which freedom is not free enough because it drags along responsibilities" (*NiTR* 107–08).[61] Levinas presents poetry in one text and scriptural commentary in the other as interrupting *both* totalizing and play, as both share egological structures that responsibility for the Other disrupts. Uniting literary and religious concerns, Levinas's 1973 essay on the Russian Jewish Holocaust novelist Agnon notes that as "[i]t is of the essence of art to signify only between the lines," only "exegesis" can distinguish between what poetry "*signifies*" and rehearsal of "its themes" (*PN* 7–8), for poetic saying is to said as ethical life is to cultural practice, exegetical spirit to letter.

Saying makes communicable subjectivity's ethical constitution and reconstitution. In "Substitution," a 1968 essay revised into the central chapter of *Otherwise Than Being*, "*touching* . . . as caress" and "*language* . . . as contact*" (*S* 80) become modalities of one another in a narrative of how consciousness as "total freedom" (82) is traumatically disrupted by responsibility to the Other experienced "an-archically" (80), before or behind all intentional worlds. Ethical trauma discovers a "oneself" living "alongside the movements of consciousness or intentionality" (84), whose "singularity" (85) is stumbled upon in responsibility's "irremissibility and . . . anguish" (86), in "recurrence" to an "*in itself*" (Levinas pointedly reverses the valence of Sartre's terms) where "an impossibility of slipping away" (87) discloses responsibility to be gnawing impossibility of withdrawal undergone somatically in an "original expiation . . . , prior to the initiative of the will" (91).[62] The oneself discovered in corporeally mediated singularity gives rise to a Self distinct from an Ego.

Ascension to such selfhood begins with "an unconditional *Yes* of submission" (93), a *Yes* evoking but contrasting with Derrida's "Nietzschean *affirmation*" [Derrida's emphasis] of a "play . . . try[ing] to pass beyond man and humanism" by eschewing all "presence" and "foundation."[63] Following Nietzsche in acknowledging as "true" a "[m]odern antihumanism" that "denies the primacy that the human person, a free end in itself, has for the signification of being" (*S* 94), Levinas nonetheless asks anti-humanism to make "a place for subjectivity positing itself in abnegation, in sacrifice, and in substitution" (94), for subjectivity finding "entrance into discourse" within "an absolute susceptibility" (95) peculiar to itself.

In his short *Humanisme de l'autre homme* (1972), Levinas notes that the "crisis of humanism in our times" begins with the "unburied dead of wars and death camps . . . making tragicomic the care for one's self and illusory the pretensions of the *rational animal* to a privileged place in the cosmos" (*HOM* 45), so that subjectivity appears "none other than the detour taken by the manifestation or intelligibility or truth of the order, in virtue of that order" (47)—whether the order is understood in Heidegger's, Derrida's, or Foucault's terms. Against dissolution of the subject in an order's effects, Levinas advocates finding subjectivity in "a responsibility, unimpugnable as a traumatism" (51), unable to "appear in the *said*" because anterior to "intentionality" (52). While the human sciences quite properly pry "the human" away from essentialist metaphysics, they, along with Heidegger, send "the subject . . . back into ideology, or else root[. . .] man in being, making him its messenger and poet" (61). Vulnerability, however, opens a third option: "From the moment of sensibility, the subject is *for the other*: substitution, responsibility, expiation" (64). Stressing that the West has a biblical heritage as well as the philosophical one, Levinas suggests that "the permanent *saying* of the Bible" (66) leads us neither to "metaphysics nor the end of metaphysics" (67), but to "subjectivity [as] a responsibility for others, extreme vulnerability."

All these threads come together in *Otherwise than Being* (1974).[64] Here Levinas identifies being's essence, underlying egocentric intentionality, as organic self-preservation denoted by Spinoza's term *conatus*—an "endeavor" toward survival and flourishing that situates the good in what enhances one's own being or that of one's in-group (*OB* 4-5). Extending Merleau-Ponty's corporeal phenomenology, Levinas contrasts "sensing" with "intentionality" (23). Intentionality's structuring of *conatus*-governed worlds is destabilized by sensing time and language to be traversed by "something irrecuperable, refractory to the simultaneity of the present, something unrepresentable" (38) that rivets subjectivity to saying as "responsibility for the neighbor" (47). A "corporeality" uniting "for the other, despite oneself" with a "tear[ing] me from myself" (55) reveals on "the hither side of consciousness . . . this pre-original hold of the Good over it" (57), which binds sensibility to proximity (61–97). Judgment, comparison, work, technical skills, and so intentions follow from and are answerable to being-for-the-other just as, in the Zohar, judgment (*Din*) is coupled with loving-kindness (*Hesed*) so as to engender foundational uprightness (*Tsaddiq*). Being-for-the-other also motivates pursuit of material, bodily well-being (*conatus*), for partaking of enjoyment precedes sharing and giving to others (74). Maternity as everyday practice, not abstract notion, incarnates goodness otherwise than being: "Signification signifies, consequently, in nourishing, clothing, lodging, in maternal relations." (77).[65]

Reiterating the argument of "Substitution," but now as exegesis of an epigraph from Celan, "Ich bin du, wenn / ich ich bin" [I am you, when / I am I] (99), Levinas argues that "uncancellable recurrence of the oneself in the subject" (104) discloses "responsibility for the freedom of the others" (109) constituting a self "abrogat[ing] the egoism of perseverance in being, which is the imperialism of the ego" (128). Through this disclosure, which determines being "on the basis of sense" (129), meaning is introduced "into being" (128). Therefore, "[s]ignification as proximity is . . . the latent birth of the subject" (139). There is a decentering here, but also a reconstitution of subjectivity in which freedom, creativity, initiative, flexibility follow from "[e]lection . . . extract[ing] me from the concept in which I continually take refuge, for I find in [election] the measure of an obligation which is not defined in the election" (145). This "anarchic being affected" (148) issues in saying calling for a said aspiring to and measured by rationality answerable to justice: "Synchronization is the act of consciousness which, through representation and the said, institutes 'with the help of God,' the original locus of justice, a terrain common to me and the others" (160). Saying and said entail one another. As with the Zohar's gendered pairings, what is bad is not one or the other term, but failed dialogic sociality between them. Concluding with commentary upon an epigraph from Goethe's *Faust* that solidifies poetry's relation to saying, Levinas expands upon Faust's claim that "Das Schaudern ist des Menschheit bester Teil" (175) [shuddering/trembling is humanity's better part] by insisting that "to tremble or shudder" (185) is a needed "weakness," since "relaxation of virility without cowardice," "fission of the ego," and "its consummation for the other" underlies subjectivity's self-realization in action (its existence preceding essence), long championed by the modern West and exemplified by Goethe's Faust.

The year before *Otherwise than Being*'s appearance saw the publication of Alexandr Solzhenitsyn's *The Gulag Archipelago*. This was followed in the late-1970s by an exodus of "Boat People" refugees from Communist Vietnam, the turn of China away from Maoism, and the revelation of genocide in Cambodia. In part as a consequence, both Sartre and the anti-humanism of circa 1966–1972 came under attack from "new philosophers" who, "[b]urying their own Maoist peccadillos of the sixties in a lava torrent of accusations directed at their teachers, . . . bundled Sartre and his generation . . . with Althusser, Heidegger, Marx, Hegel, Rousseau."[66] The new philosophical turn championed pluralism, republicanism, and moral–religious concerns along with anti-totalizing thought.[67] This shift, reflected in Foucault's rethinking his history of sexuality project and Kristeva's turn from semiotics to subject formation, both occurring around 1980,[68] helped acclimate readers to Levinasian texts, making them appear less incomprehensible or eccentric than before.

In 1982, and then in a second edition in 1986, Levinas published a collection of essays, *Of God Who Comes to Mind*, probing how awakening to modes of consciousness exceeding and challenging intentionality brings to mind an idea of God "in the concreteness of my relation to the other man, in the sociality which is my responsibility for the neighbor" (*OG* xiv). Levinas suggests that this "awakening" (31) opens up a "non-eudaimonic, non-hedonistic affectivity" (51) that pulls God "out of objectivity, out of presence and out of being" (69). Language begins in dialogic sociality (142), and an "ethical thought" is "a sociality that is proximity or fraternity, and not synthesis" (165), just as the "human" is "return to the interiority of the non-intentional consciousness, . . . return to the bad conscience, . . . dreading injustice more than death" (177).

As Levinas argues in "Transcendence and Intelligibility" (1984), "the proximity of the Infinite and the sociality that it founds and commands" makes "sociality . . . an irreducible excellence through its very plurality" (*BPW* 159). Despite his own Eurocentrism, Levinas insists in "Peace and Proximity" (1984) that Europe should overcome millennia-long assumptions that peace is the product of an eschatological or ideological achievement of sameness, wherein reconciliation of one with another presupposes a "revealed" identity of one with another (*BPW* 164–66). Instead, peace "as the *relation* with the unique and the other—a relation designated by the general term *love*" (166)—should be understood "as love of the neighbor, where it is not a matter of peace as pure rest that confirms one's identity but of always placing in question this very identity, its limitless freedom and its power" (167).[69] As an illustration of "the wisdom of love" (169), Levinas cites, as he did in multiple interviews throughout the 1980s, Vassili Grossman's *Life and Fate* (167), a novel published in 1980, which Levinas read in Russian, which depicts small acts of kindness during the Stalingrad siege that attest to the transcendence of the human under conditions of maximal inhumanity.[70]

Grossman's sounding of Levinasian motifs with no knowledge of Levinas (the manuscript having been written in the 1950s and confiscated by the KGB in 1961, three years before Grossman's death) discloses how much literary work that rises above Verlainean "literature" makes saying its foundation. Describing a prison camp whose uniformity reveals its "inhuman character," for "[e]verything that lives is unique" (19), Grossman notes that among prisoners separated by language, reduction of discourse to "ten or fifteen words" (32) signifying "solidarity, fellow-feeling," enabled understanding, whereas when common language permitted abstract talk, the more people "talked and argued, the less they understood each other" (33). Such hatred born of "lack of understanding" lay behind "much of the tragedy of the twentieth century."[71]

Levinas's final essay collection, *Entre nous*, published in 1991, strives to clarify whence such understanding proceeds and what it entails. "[N]onintentional identification" with the "the non-invested, the non-justified, . . . the stateless or homeless person" (*EN* 129) separates sense of oneself from one's situated contextualization (race, class, gender, etc.), but also separates response to the other from assuming a stance in relation to identity politics. The other's transcendence tears one away from "resting" upon contexts, so that "the self draws back," in "bad conscience," from "the eventual insistence that may be involved in identification's return to self" (129). Ethical affectivity issuing from "[p]rereflexive, nonintentional consciousness" (144) yields initiative, action, creative self-realization via "conversion of the for-self into for-the-other" (152), for "goodness pull[s] the self away from its irresistible return to self," so that we come to have an "intended future" going "beyond . . . [what] concerns me" (152–53).

Breaking with egologic thought uproots a synchronic representational perspective (*EN* 166). Instead, sociality entails such "re-presentation" (167) being capsized by an "objectivity . . . founded on justice" experienced as my *"nonintentional* participation in the history of humanity, in the past of others, who 'regard/look at me'" in ways that reveal "the dia-chrony of a past that cannot by gathered into re-presentation" (171). Sensing obligations imposed before any recollected, represented time makes a "bad conscience" (175) constitutive of human consciousness, but bad conscience, paradoxically, offers "a chance for holiness in a society of just men without good conscience, and, in the inextinguishable concern for justice, consent to the rigor of human justice" (175). Even as my singularity derives from responsibility to an Other unique in non-reducibility to others (194), so "love of one's fellowman . . . as unique and incomparable" tends, of its "own accord," to "make appeal to a Reason" striving for just comparisons, so that "objectivity, objectification, thematization, synthesis" (195) cease to be mere technologies of power. Original *hesed*, loving-kindness, mercy, calls for judgment, the state, and laws, but "justice itself cannot make us forget" that "justice is always a revision of justice and the expectation of a better justice" (196). Subjectivity's reconstitution through ethical trauma culminates in "a vocation of an existing-for-the-other stronger than the threat of death" (xii).

On Christmas, 1995 death took Levinas, but the responsiveness and dialogue his words have elicited bear witness to what Levinas called the "radical generosity" of the Work (*MS* 49) toward a future the Agent producing the Work will not share. This future continues slowly to unfold, attesting in intellectual life to something like love, stronger than death.

NOTES

1. Salomon Malka, *Emmanuel Levinas: His Life and Legacy*, trans. Michael Kigel and Sonja M. Embree (Pittsburgh: Duquesne University Press, 2006), 11.

2. See Arthur Green, *A Guide to the Zohar* (Stanford: Stanford University Press), especially 9–70. Maimonides's work grew out of Jewish responses to Islamic Mut'azlite thought (Green, 9), which seeks to reconcile Quranic teaching with ethical rationalism.

3. Green, 184.

4. Ibid., 185.

5. See Esra Shereshevsky, *Rashi: The Man and his World* (New York: Sephor–Mermon Press, 1982), 1–15.

6. Ibid., 134; also see 73–118, 133–37.

7. See Shereshevsky, 142–43.

8. See Malka, 107–24, 125–39; "A Religion for Adults" (*DF* 11–23), "Judaism" (*DF* 24–26), "Loving the Torah more than God" (*DF* 142–45), and *NiTR*, especially "Toward the Other" and "The Temptation of Temptation," 12–29, 30–50.

9. See Malka, 15–19.

10. See Alain Paul Toumayan, "'I More than the Other': Dostoyevsky and Levinas," *Yale French Studies* 104 (2004): 55–66.

11. Gary Saul Morson and Caryl Emerson, *Mikhail Bakhtin: Creation of a Prosaics* (Stanford: Stanford University Press, 1990), 23, 25.

12. Morson and Emerson, 54, 56, citing on p. 54 Mikhail Bakhtin, "K filopofi postupka," in *Filosofia i sotsiologiia nauki i tekhniki (1984-85)* (Moscow: Nauka, 1986), 93, and on p. 56 Mikhail Bakhtin, "From Notes Made in 1970-71," in *Speech Genres and Other Late Essays*, ed.

Caryl Emerson and Michael Holquist, trans. Vern W. McGee (Austin: University of Texas Press, 1986), 141.

13. Leo Tolstoy, *Anna Karenina*, trans. Richard Pevear and Larissa Volokhonsky (New York: Penguin, 2000), 788; *Anna Karenina* in *Sobranie Sochinenij*, vol. 10 (Moscow: Gosudarstvennoe Iedatel'stvo Khudozhestbennop Aiyeratury, 1963), 411. All further references are to this edition and will be cited parenthetically in the text.

14. The anti-theoretical thrust here intersects with that of Ordinary Language Philosophy descending from the later Wittgenstein. See Toril Moi, "'They practice their trades in different worlds': Concepts in Poststructuralism and Ordinary Language Philosophy," *New Literary History* 40, 4 (2009), 801–24. On identity politics and abstract conceptualization, see Judith Butler, "Precarious Life," and Diane Perpich, "Levinas, Feminism, and Identity Politics," in *Radicalizing Levinas*, ed. Peter Atterton and Matthew Calarco (Albany: State University of New York Press, 2010), 3–19, 21–39. The relation of Levinas's appeal to "life" to Nietzsche's is explored in *Nietzsche and Levinas: "After the Death of a Certain God,"* ed. Jill Stauffer and Bettina Bergo (New York: Columbia University Press, 2009): see especially John Drabinski, "Beginning's Abyss: On Solitude in Nietzsche and Levinas," 134–49; David Boothroyd, "Beyond Suffering I Have No Alibi," 150–64; Richard A. Cohen, "Levinas, Spinozism, Nietzsche, and the Body," 165–82.

15. See Sarah Allen's discussion of Levinasian affectivity in *The Philosophical Sense of Transcendence: Levinas and Plato on Loving Beyond Being* (Pittsburgh: Duquesne University Press, 2009), 263–304.

16. Fyodor Dostoyvesky, *Crime and Punishment*, trans. David McDuff (London: Penguin, 1991), 629; *Prestuplenie i Nakazhanie* (Moskva: Slavianka, 1993), 330. Further references will be to these editions and cited parenthetically in the text.

17. See Edmund Husserl, *Ideas: General Introduction to Pure Phenomenology*, trans. W. R. Boyce Gibson (New York: Collier, 1962), 91–167.

18. See the distinction between voluntary and involuntary memory in Marcel Proust, *A la recherche du temps perdu*, ed. Pierre Clarac et André Ferré (Paris: Bibliothèque de la Pléiade, 1954), vol. 1, 43–48. All further references are to this edition and will be cited parenthetically in the text.

19. See Heidegger, *Being and Time*, trans. John Macquerrie and Edward Robinson (Oxford: Blackwell, 1962), I. 2, 78–90; I. 3, 91–148; I. 6, 225–56. All further references are to this edition.

20. Emmanuel Levinas, "Reflections on the Philosophy of Hitlerism," in *Difficult Justice: Commentaries on Levinas and Politics*, ed. Asher Horowitz and Gad Horowitz (Toronto: University of Toronto Press, 2006), 6; originally published as *"Quelques réflexions sur la philosophie de l'hitlérisme,"* in *Esprit* 2, no. 26 (1934). Henceforth all references will be to this edition and cited parenthetically in the text.

21. On Levinas's reservations about liberalism, see Asher Horowitz and Gad Horowitz, "Is Liberalism All We Need? Prelude via Fascism," in *Difficult Justice*, 12–23; Jill Stauffer, "The Imperfect: Levinas, Nietzsche, and the Autonomous Subject," in *Nietzsche and Levinas*, 33–47.

22. Franz Rosenzweig, *The Star of Redemption*, trans. William W. Hallo (New York: Holt, Rinehart and Winston, 1970), 3, 5. All further references are to this edition and will be cited parenthetically in the text.

23. See Martin Heidegger, *Being and Time*, II. 1, 293–311; Robert Gibbs, *Correlations in Rosenzweig and Levinas* (Princeton: Princeton University Press, 1992), 36–40.

24. See Samuel Moyn, *Origins of the Other: Emmanuel Levinas between Revelation and Ethics* (Ithaca: Cornell University Press, 2005), 123–41. Like Buber, Rosenzweig had once been Hermann Cohen's student. See Gibbs, 17–23, 46–51, 176–91.

25. See Rosenzweig, 108–204; Gibbs, 40–60; Moyn, 146–55.

26. See Gibbs, 105–54; Richard A. Cohen, *Elevations: The Height of the Good in Rosenzweig and Levinas* (Chicago: University of Chicago Press, 1994), 40–66; Moyn, 155–63; Rosenzweig, 205–15, 217–25, 227–40.

27. Green, 40–41.

28. Ibid., 42–49, 46–47 and 49 cited.

29. Green, 152–53; also see 49–53, 109–15, 126–33.

30. Cohen, *Elevations*, 269–70.

31. Claire Elise Katz, *Levinas, Judaism, and the Feminine: The Silent Footsteps of Rebecca* (Bloomington and Indianapolis: Indiana University Press, 2003), 87.

32. See Heidegger, *Being and Time*, II. 3, 370–82; also Jean-Paul Sartre, *Being and Nothingness: A Phenomenological Essay on Ontology*, trans. Hazel E. Barnes (New York: Washington Square, 1956), 180–237. For entwinement of anti-foundationalism and anti-humanism, see especially Jacques Derrida, "The Ends of Man" and "White Mythology: Metaphor in the Text of Philosophy," in *Margins of Philosophy*, trans. Alan Bass (Chicago: University of Chicago Press, 1982), 111–36, 209–71. Michael Fagenblat links the *il y a* with the "without form void" of Gen. 1: 2, the *tohu wa'bohu* out of which YHWH creates. See his *A Covenant of Creatures: Levinas's Philosophy of Judaism* (Stanford: Stanford University Press, 2010), 33–66, 195–97.

33. See James Hatley, *Suffering Witness: The Quandary of Responsibility After the Irreparable* (Albany: State University of New York Press, 2000); also Fagenblat, 64–66.

34. Levinas's target here is Heidegger's notion of *Mitsein*, "being-with." See Heidegger, *Being and Time*, I. 4, 149–63; also Sartre, *Being and Nothingness*, 534–56.

35. See Heidegger, *Being and Time*, I. 4, 163–68; I. 4, 203–24; II. 3, 377–78; Sartre, *Being and Nothingness*, 619–707.

36. See Katz, 5, 96, 131, 150–55; Fagenblat, 73–79.

37. See Heidegger, *Being and Time*, II. 2, 343–46. For the Sartrean equivalent, the "for-itself" (*pour soi*) (see *Being and Nothingness*, 119–58).

38. See especially Drew M. Dalton, *Longing for the Other: Levinas and Metaphysical Desire* (Pittsburgh: Duquesne University Press, 2009); Allen, 151–75; *TI* 33–35, *OB* 153–62. In describing the feminine as "absolutely other" (*TO* 85), Levinas incurs the censure of Simone de Beauvoir, who in a footnote in *The Second Sex*, trans. H. M. Parshley (New York: Vintage, 1952), insists "that woman, too, is aware of her own consciousness, or ego" (xix). Arguably, Levinas does not so much deny woman her "ego" as view it as an uninteresting co-virility. Whether lack of attention to woman's similitude to man is anti-feminist or anticipates later valorizations of difference is debated in Catherine Chalier, *Figures du féminin* (Paris: La Nuit surveillée, 1982), the essays in Tina Chanter, ed., *Feminist Interpretations of Emmanuel Levinas*, Katz, and Diane Perpich, *The Ethics of Emmanuel Levinas* (Stanford: Stanford University Press, 2008), 177–98.

39. Such reflection finds its fountainhead in Jacques Derrida's "At This Moment in This Very Work Here I Am," trans. Ruben Berezdivin, in *Re-Reading Levinas*, ed. Robert Bernasconi and Simon Critchley (Bloomington: Indiana University Press, 1991), 11–48, and Luce Irigaray's "The Fecundity of the Caress," in *An Ethics of Sexual Difference*, trans. Carolyn Burke and Gillian Gill (Ithaca: Cornell University Press, 1993), 185–217. For summaries of critiques, see Diane Perpich, "Levinas, Feminism, and Identity Politics," in *Radicalizing Levinas*, 21–39.

40. See Robert Eaglestone, *Ethical Criticism: Reading After Levinas* (Edinburgh: Edinburgh University Press, 1997), Roland A. Champagne, *The Ethics of Reading According to Levinas* (Amsterdam: Rodopi, 1998), and Jill Robbins, *Altered Reading: Levinas and Literature* (Chicago: University of Chicago Press, 1999) for pioneering engagements with Levinas's seeming antipathy to art. For later elaborations, see Gerald L. Bruns, "The Concepts of Art and Poetry in Emmanuel Levinas's Writings," in *The Cambridge Companion to Levinas*, ed. Simon Critchley and Robert Bernasconi (Cambridge: Cambridge University Press, 2002), 206–33; Steve McCaffrey, "The Scandal of Sincerity: Towards a Levinasian Poetics," in *Prior to Meaning: Protosemantics and Poetics* (Evanston, IL: Northwestern University Press, 2001), 204–29. For Levinas's literary culture, see especially Alain Paul Toumayan, "Levinas and French Literature," in *Levinas and Nineteenth-Century Literature: Ethics and Otherness from Romanticism through Realism*, ed. Donald R. Wehrs and David P. Haney (Newark, DE: University of Delaware Press, 2009), 126–47.

41. See "Qu'est-ce que la literature?" in Jean-Paul Sartre, *Situations II* (Paris: Gallimard, 1948), 59–316.

42. In an enchanted mirror reflecting one's heart's deepest desires, Harry Potter sees his dead relatives, including the parents murdered while he was an infant, alive again, whole, and happy (J. K. Rowling, *Harry Potter and the Sorcerer's Stone* [New York: Scholastic, 1997],

209). Night after night he stares longingly at their images, until Dumbledore tells him to seek out the mirror no more, for "It does not do to dwell on dreams and to forget to live." (214).

43. See Gabriel Riera's discussion in *Intrigues: From Being to the Other* (New York: Fordham University Press, 2006), 85–195, of Judaic wariness of idolatry in this context.

44. For the critical criteria of such literary exegesis, see Lorna Wood, "Emmanuel Levinas and the American Renaissance Canon," in *Levinas and Nineteenth-Century Literature*, 166–206, especially 166–74, 197–98.

45. See Donald R. Wehrs and David P. Haney, "Introduction: Levinas, Twenty-First Century Ethical Criticism and Their Nineteenth-Century Contexts," in *Levinas and Nineteenth-Century Literature*, 19–21; Seán Hand, *Emmanuel Levinas* (New York: Routledge, 2009), 36–46; Michael B. Smith, *Toward the Outside: Concepts and Themes in Emmanuel Levinas* (Pittsburgh: Duquesne University Press, 2005); B. C. Hutchens, *Levinas, A Guide for the Perplexed* (New York: Continuum, 2004); Adriaan Peperzak, *To the Other: An Introduction to the Philosophy of Emmanuel Levinas* (West Layette, IN: Purdue University Press, 1993).

46. See Moyn, 164–94.

47. See especially Levinas, "Transcendence and Height," in *BPW* 11–31; also see Perpich's splendid discussion in *The Ethics of Emmanuel Levinas*, 50–77.

48. On incarnation in Levinas, see especially Michael O'Sullivan, *The Incarnation of Language: Joyce, Proust, and a Philosophy of the Flesh* (New York: Continuum, 2008), 41–54; in relation to Proust, see 111–36. Also see David P. Haney, *William Wordsworth and the Hermeneutics of Incarnation* (University Park, PA: Pennsylvania State University Press, 1993) and Fagenblat, 67–96.

49. See Jacques Derrida, *Adieu to Emmanuel Levinas*, trans. Pascale-Anne Brault and Michael Naas (Stanford: University Press University Press, 1999), 17–29; for Derrida's account of the centrality of welcoming in *Totality and Infinity*, see *Adieu*, 18n.

50. See Jacques Derrida, "Violence and Metaphysics: An Essay on the Thought of Emmanuel Levinas," in *Writing and Difference*, trans. Alan Bass (Chicago: University of Chicago Press, 1978), 79–153.503.

51. See Cohen's vigorous defense of Levinas in *Elevations*, 305–21.

52. See Maurice Merleau-Ponty, *Phenomenology of Perception*, trans. Colin Smith (London: Routledge & Kegan Paul, 1962); *The Visible and the Invisible*, trans. Alphonso Lingis (Evanston, IL: Northwestern University Press, 1968). For Levinas on Merleau-Ponty, see *OS* 96–103. In the early 1960s the militant anticolonialism of Sartre (see *Situations V: Colonialisme et néo-colonialisme* [Paris: Gallimard, 1964]) intermingled with cultural relativism such as Claude Lévi-Strauss's in *Tristes Tropiques*, trans. John and Doreen Weightman (New York: Washington Square, 1973 [Fr. ed. 1955]).

53. See Martin Heidegger, *Poetry, Language, Thought*, trans. Albert Hofstadter (New York: Harper and Row, 1971), 17–87, 91–142, 189–210.

54. See especially Bill Ashcroft, Gareth Griffiths, and Helen Tifflin, *The Empire Writes Back: Theory and Practice in Post-Colonial Literatures* (New York: Routledge, 1989).

55. On dangers of thinking of cultural difference as monolithic, see especially Abiola Irele, "In Praise of Alienation," in *The Surreptitious Speech: Présence Africaine and the Politics of Otherness, 1947-1987*, ed. V. Y. Mudimbe (Chicago: University of Chicago Press, 1993), 201–24.

56. Thus in different cultures the same "sense" can repudiate Stalinist dismissals of ethical concerns as "bourgeois" residues impeding revolutionary goals. See Nadezhda Mandelstam's *Hope Against Hope: A Memoir*, trans. Max Hayward (New York: Atheneum, 1970); Duong Thu Huong's *Paradise of the Blind*, trans. Phan Huy Huong and Nina McPherson (New York: Perennial, 1993).

57. For consideration of Levinas's Eurocentrism, see Robert Eaglestone, "Postcolonial Thought and Levinas's Double Vision," in *Radicalizing Levinas*, 57–68. For Levinasian comparative literature, see especially Steven Shankman, *Other Others: Levinas, Literature, Transcultural Studies* (Albany: State University of New York Press, 2010).

58. See especially Jacques Derrida, "Structure, Sign, and Play in the Discourses of the Human Sciences," in *Writing and Difference*, 278–93; Michel Foucault, "The Discourse on

Language," in *Critical Theory Since 1965*, ed. Hazard Adams and Leroy Searle (Tallahassee, FL: Florida State University Press, 1986), 148–62.

59. See especially Gabriel Riera, *Intrigues: From Being to the Other* (New York: Fordham University Press, 2006), 85–198; Alain P. Toumayan, *Encountering the Other: The Artwork and the Problem of Difference in Blanchot and Levinas* (Pittsburgh: Duquesne University Press, 2003); Wood, "Emmanuel Levinas and the American Renaissance Canon," in *Levinas and Nineteenth-Century Literature*, 166–206.

60. See Michael Eskin, *Ethics and Dialogue in the Works of Levinas, Bakhtin, Mandel'shtam, and Celan* (Oxford: Oxford University Press, 2000).

61. Derrida advocates "the joyous affirmation of the play of the world and of the innocence of becoming" in "Structure, Sign, and Play," in *Writing and Difference*, 292.

62. For the congruence of such analysis with recent cognitive and neuroscientific work, see especially Joel Krueger, "Levinasian Reflections on Somaticity and the Ethical Self," *Inquiry* 51, 6 (2008): 602–26; Donald R. Wehrs, "Touching Words: Embodying Ethics in Erasmus, Shakespearean Comedy, and Contemporary Theory," *Modern Philology* 104, no. 1 (2006): 1–33, "Placing Human Constants within Literary History: Generic Revision and Affective Sociality in Shakespeare's *The Winter's Tale* and *The Tempest*," *Poetics Today* 32, 3 (2011): 521–91.

63. Derrida, "Structure, Sign, and Play," in *Writing and Difference*, 292. For Levinas's complex relation to Nietzsche, see *Nietzsche and Levinas*.

64. For synopses of this work, see Wehrs and Haney, "Introduction," in *Levinas and Nineteenth-Century Literature*, 22–24; Hand, 48–62; Smith; Hutchins.

65. The role of the maternal as prototype of the ethical intersects with research on the origins of sociality in face-to-face caregiver-infant interaction (see Krueger, 616–20; Wood, this volume) and with Julia Kristeva's account of introjection (internalization) of the maternal. See especially her *Hatred and Forgiveness*, trans. Jeanine Herman (New York: Columbia University Press, 2010), 49–94, 177–94; *Melanie Klein*, trans. Ross Guberman (New York: Columbia University Press, 2001); *The Sense and Non-Sense of Revolt*, trans. Jeanine Herman (New York: Columbia University Press, 2000), 94–106. Also see Perpich's discussion of how "Subjectivity is ever too late to say the other in no way concerns it" (*The Ethics of Emmanuel Levinas*, 124–49, 145–46 cited), and Fagenblat's related argument, 140–70.

66. Tony Judt, *Past Imperfect: French Intellectuals, 1944-1956* (Berkeley: University of California Press, 1992), 304.

67. See especially Luc Ferry and Alain Renault, ed., *Why We Are Not Nietzscheans*, trans. Robert de Loaiza (Chicago: University of Chicago Press, 1997); Luc Ferry and Alain Renault, *French Philosophy of the Sixties: An Essay on Antihumanism*, trans. H. S. Cattani (Amherst: University of Massachusetts Press, 1990).

68. See Michel Foucault, *The Use of Pleasure: The History of Sexuality*, vol. 2, trans. Robert Hurley (New York: Vintage, 1985), *The Care of the Self: The History of Sexuality*, vol. 3, trans. Robert Hurley (New York: Vintage, 1986); Julia Kristeva, *Powers of Horror: An Essay on Abjection*, trans. Leon S. Roudiez (New York: Columbia University Press, 1982), *Tales of Love*, trans. Leon S. Roudiez (New York: Columbia University Press, 1987).

69. See Fagenblat's account of fraternity along these lines (171–94).

70. Vasily Grossmann, *Life and Fate*, trans. Robert Chandler (London: Collins Harvill, 1985). For Levinas's discussions of Grossman, see especially *ITR* 79, 80–81, 89–90, 191–92, 206–08, 216–18; *EN* 230–32.

71. Grossman's portrait recalls Raskolnikov's nightmare, near the end of *Crime and Punishment*, in which a strange disease makes everyone so convinced of his own truth that no agreement is possible: "All were in a state of anxiety and no one could understand anyone else . . ." ["*ne ponimali drug druga* . . ."] (626/329). Absence of understanding led people to kill one another "in a kind of senseless [*'bessmyslennoi'*] anger."

II

Levinas and the Fugitive Other: Consciousness, Representation, Affectivity, and Memory

Chapter Two

"There Are Things That Can't Be Said"

Levinas and the Ethics of Representation in Virginia Woolf's Jacob's Room

Rebecca Nicholson-Weir

In 1922, on the final page of the first draft of *Jacob's Room* (1922), Virginia Woolf wrote "Atque in perpetuum, frater, ave atque vale. Julian Thoby Stephen (1880–1906)."[1] Originally written by the ancient poet Catullus to his dead brother, the Latin translates as, "And forever, brother, hail and farewell." This is followed by the years of the birth and death of Woolf's brother Thoby, who died at twenty-six of the typhoid he contracted during a family trip to Greece. Although at the time Woolf's friends (and many commentators since) read Thoby into the character of Jacob, Woolf opted to leave this explicit tribute to her brother out of the published novel. The reference to Catullus's elegiac poem nonetheless demonstrates her conscious thoughts were of Thoby during the process of writing the text.

Sixteen years earlier, immediately following Thoby's death, Virginia Woolf maintained a correspondence with her friend Violet Dickerson, who had also contracted typhoid on the same journey.[2] In these almost daily letters, Woolf constructed fictional tales detailing Thoby's convalescence, recovery, and routines. In what Kathleen Wall terms "an early instance of Woolf's fictionalizing," the author kept up the deception for nearly a month after his death (305).[3] It was as if Woolf believed she could temporarily keep him alive in Violet's mind, or at any rate defer the knowledge of his death, through the act of writing. These two written responses to her brother's death, one ephemeral and epistolary, one a permanent and semi-public document, instead of being used to demonstrate a potentially reductive biographical justification for the themes in *Jacob's Room*, may rather be read as a way into Woolf's ongoing concerns with the form of the modern novel, with the potential of narration, and with the ethics of representation. Both the fictional letters Woolf wrote to keep Thoby alive in Violet's mind and her decision sixteen years later to include the honorific Latin postscript demonstrate her clear investment in doing more than just keeping the memory of her brother alive, both at the time of his death and years after. Her choice ultimately not to include the postscript in the published book, however, intimates her awareness of the potential ethical problems of representing others in narrative.[4]

This chapter reads *Jacob's Room* through the lens of Levinasian phenomenology to make visible the unique ways that Woolf exposes narrative representation as an ethically charged ground where both writers and everyday individuals make determinative choices that define others. Both the novel's form and its experimental narrator endeavor to model narrative practices that would allow for representation that is ethical. Lacking a central protagonist, the narration leaps around in time and utilizes 160 characters linked only in their acquaintance with the elusive Jacob. Jacob is never fleshed out or represented in a concrete way, and the sweeping narration continually raises the question of character and the impossibility of ever really knowing another person.[5] These formal stylistic frameworks allow Woolf to ask the larger aesthetic and ethical questions: if fiction is about representation, what are the ethical stakes? If representation isn't the only goal of fiction, how does one write beyond the limits of representation? The narrative, rather than glossing over problems inherent within acts of representation, enacts heuristic difficulties in order to point out the ethically fraught implications of representation and thematization. Throughout the novel, Woolf utilizes multiple narrative techniques that prevent readers from assuming access to the title character and thus forges beyond a formal modernist exercise in technique to engage with the philosophical interstices of perception, intersubjectivity, and proximity.

Woolf's on-going concerns with the ethics of textual representation appear in a diary entry she wrote when beginning *Jacob's Room*. On the day after her thirty-eighth birthday, January 26, 1920, Virginia Woolf wrote in her diary that she had

> some idea of a new form for a new novel. Suppose one thing should open out of another . . . not for 10 pages but 200 or so—doesn't that give the looseness and lightness I want: doesn't that get closer and yet keep form and speed, and enclose everything, everything? For I figure that the approach will be entirely different this time: no scaffolding; scarcely a brick to be seen; all crepuscular, but the heart, the passion, humour, everything as bright as fire in the mist. Then I'll find room for so much.[6]

From the beginning, Woolf wanted this novel to be different from her earlier work. Even when *Jacob's Room* was nothing more than an idea, she aimed for a conscious shift away from realist narrative toward a more radical mode of representational ethics.

Woolf never formally studied either ethics or philosophy, yet she was deeply invested in the ideas of her day, regularly attended lectures and actively read contemporary philosophy. From an early age, she was quite interested in the work of the analytic philosopher G. E. Moore, whose Cambridge lectures and text *Principia Ethica* (1903) profoundly influenced Bloomsbury. The crux of *Principia Ethica* rests on the idea that what is good defies concepts and cannot be assigned properties, but is fundamentally good and cannot, as such, be analyzed as a mere concept. That which is good is good in and of itself, and an object's being good or bad is in no way dependant on anything outside of itself. This definition of good is the foundation for Moore's ethics, and arguably, for Bloomsbury's affinity for Moore's ethics, in which the states with the highest degree of good are personal relationships and aesthetic enjoyment, and for Moore, "the ultimate and fundamental truth of Moral Philosophy" is "consciousness of beauty."[7] He asserts that "it is only for the sake of these things [personal relationships and aesthetic pleasure]—in order that as much of them as possible may at some time exist—that any one can be justified in performing any public or private duty; that they are the *raison d'être* of virtue; that it is they . . . that form the rational ultimate end of human action and the sole criterion of social progress."[8] This emphasis on personal connection and assertion of the intrinsic value of aesthetic experience worked as a liberating force for the Cambridge students who were to become the Bloomsbury group.

Cambridge at the time was exclusively a men's university, so, unlike her brother Thoby, friend Lytton Strachey and future husband Leonard, Virginia was never a formal student of Moore. Nonetheless, according to her husband Leonard, Woolf, like the rest, was influenced greatly by his philosophy. Leonard's memoirs reminisce about the beginnings of Bloomsbury in the Apostles group at Cambridge and the continuation of those friendships later in London. He notes in *Sowing*, his memoirs' first volume, that for the Bloomsbury group, "The tremendous influence of Moore and his book upon us came from the fact that they suddenly removed from our eyes an obscuring accumulation of scales, cobwebs, and curtains, revealing for the first time to us, so it seemed, the nature of truth and reality."[9] In *Beginning Again*, his memoirs' second volume, he notes that Virginia was

> deeply affected by the astringent influence of Moore and the purification of that divinely cathartic question which echoed through the Cambridge Courts of my youth as it had 2300 years before echoed through the streets of Socratic

Athens: 'What do you mean by that?' Artistically the purification can, I think,
be traced in the clarity, light absence of humbug in Virginia's literary style. [10]

As Tom Regan points out, "Virginia . . . swam in pools deeply affected by
the strong currents that flowed from Moore's character and teachings.
Though they were not directly touched by Moore, the Cambridge student and
Fellow, they were intimately linked to him by those who were. And that
linkage helped consolidate, even if by itself it did not create, the phenomenon
of Bloomsbury." [11]

At around the same time that Moore was developing his ethical philosophy at Cambridge, Edmund Husserl, teaching in Germany, was laying the
foundations for phenomenological inquiry into intersubjectivity, from which
emerged inquiries into ethics sharing Moore's interest in ordinary life and
suspicion of the conceptual. Emmanuel Levinas, who built upon the work of
both Husserl and Martin Heidegger to describe intersubjective responsibility,
asserts the primacy of an ethical obligation to the absolute other, another
person who is not defined by her relationship with me, but instead is encountered as someone radically other than myself, as unique in her difference.
This phenomenology calls into question the whole of Western philosophy
that since Descartes had sought to know the world through knowing the self.
Knowledge as an aim has limitations for Levinas because it "seizes hold of
its object. It possesses it. Possession denies the independence of being, without destroying that being—it denies and maintains" (*DF* 8). For Levinas, the
foundation of both ethics and subjectivity rests in the absolute alterity of the
other, which resists all our attempts at knowing, and at representation. Another major facet of Levinas's ethics is the fact that we are born into responsibility. In "Substitution," the central chapter in *Otherwise than Being,* he
asserts that before self-consciousness a prior subjectivity exists that is accessible only through proximity with another person. This prior subjectivity is
founded in responsibility and exists, unlike empirical knowledge, before the
self is aware. Levinas outlines the way he views subjectivity by first presenting how philosophy usually bases the construction of subjectivity within a
consciousness-based model. He then presents an alternative that functions
prior to the knowledge of one's existence or being: "the reduction of subjectivity to consciousness dominates philosophical thought, which since Hegel
has been trying to overcome the duality of being and thought, by identifying,
under different figures, substance and subject" (*OB* 93). For Levinas, subjectivity is larger, deeper, and prior to consciousness: thus a large part of the
Levinasian project can be read as an attempt to free ethics from the confines
of consciousness that are the foundation of most philosophical discussions of
responsibility. Epistemology, the branch of philosophy that investigates the
limits of human knowledge, constructs out of thematization and abstraction,
creating a knowledge system in which "we identify beings across the disper-

sion of silhouettes in which they appear" (99). As Levinas notes, "For the philosophical tradition of the West, all spirituality lies in consciousness, thematic exposition of being, knowing" (99). Levinas's project runs counter to this tradition in its desire to get at what is prior to and more foundational than this self-consciousness grounded in spirituality as one or another modality of knowing. By privileging individualized consciousness as superior to (as more real, essential, or authentic than) a consciousness grounded in relation, epistemology forecloses possibilities that can be found in other ways of learning that are more fundamental than ontology, and therefore marginalizes in ethical relationships all that is imperceptible to consciousness-based knowledge.

Levinas contends that any consciousness of another person is based in idealization. Ideality, as a capacity to idealize, is limiting because it is fixed and unchangeable. It is in working beyond this capacity to idealize that ethical consciousness of another being is possible. The way consciousness is usually presented, as the "adventure of consciousness" in which the self moves out from the known (self-knowledge) into the unknown (knowledge of other people), is really "no adventure" and "never dangerous" because it is self-contained (*OB* 99). It is impossible to create new knowledge of another person because "the detour of ideality leads to coinciding with oneself" and "certainty" (99). Because this concept of the self is founded on conscious knowledge, it cannot help but begin from the known, and that origin forecloses truly new information because "anything unknown that can occur to it is in advance disclosed, open, manifest, is cast in the mould of the known, and cannot be a complete surprise" (99). Within this framework, representations of reality are the only access the conscious mind has to reality. One has to imagine and abstract in order to comprehend the world. In this sense, any understanding or knowledge that hinges on abstraction and categorization is representation, and thus interpretation. In this way, subjectivity within an empiricist model, no less than within an idealist one, hinges on categorization and interpretation.

Levinas (and Woolf, as I argue in the next section) ask us to see not only the dangers of thematization and representation, but also the possibility of another way. Both the philosopher and the novelist see within the summative statements common in representational narrative the possibility of unethical thematizations that disallow the complexity, absolute otherness, and subjectivity of other people. The impetus to write in a way that takes account of these pitfalls is a motivating factor. Tammy Clewell argues that Woolf's "experience of losing a brother she loved, admired, and elegized in *Jacob's Room* may have motivated and informed Woolf's resolve to forge a new bereaved sincerity, a new language for loss capable of conveying genuine sympathy and profound solemnity."[12] This new language could not rely on the prior systemized elegiac rituals in place, but instead had to look to new narrative techniques to point out the dangers of summative approximations of loved ones lost. An epigraph or other traditional honorific is inadequate. Woolf's reluctance to include her brother Thoby's name in either *Jacob's Room* or *The Waves* corresponds to Levinas's suspicion of attempts to find meaning in death. In "Useless Suffering," Levinas argues that making meaning out of the death of another person in essence justifies their suffering, and "the justification of the neighbor's pain is certainly the source of all inhumanity" (*EN* 99). The suffering and death of another person is always "an excess" (91),[13] and "the least one can say about suffering is that, in its own phenomenality, intrinsically, it is useless" (93). To assign meaning to the death of another through turning that person into something symbolic is thus unethical because it in effect justifies his or her suffering and death.

The unethical implications become more clear when one considers the roles that narrative structure and chronology play in assigning meaning to events. In his classic analysis of *Jacob's Room* as parody, Alex Zwerdling notes, "Unlike the classic Bildungsroman, *Jacob's Room* lacks a teleology."[14] It is precisely by way of this lack of teleology that Woolf accomplishes her ethics of representation. The narrator in seemingly unconnected episodes relates Jacob's life. By not showing Jacob's existence as small steps inevitably building up to the moment of his death, Woolf denies that his death had monumental meaning, or that his life can be reduced into leading up to this moment of death. Woolf demonstrates through her textual gaps, narrative fragmentation, and limited perspectives how any meaning assigned to a life is only grounded in the perspective of those who would attempt to assign meaning, and therefore when anyone attempts to universalize her or his meaning as the one true meaning, what remains is both arbitrary and reductive. Both Woolf and Levinas question how identity occurs and the extent to which individuals use consciousness of the self to acknowledge the subjectivity of others. It is in interrogating the possibility of any knowledge of other individuals' subjectivity that Woolf engages with the ethical questions of Levinasian ethical phenomenology.

Subjectivity and the pitfalls representation engenders appear from the beginning of the novel. Jacob's mother, Betty Flanders, begins to cry while writing a letter on the beach when

> pale blue ink dissolved the full stop; for there her pen stuck; her eyes fixed, and tears slowly filled them. The entire bay quivered; the lighthouse wobbled; and she had the illusion that the mast of Mr. Connor's little yacht was bending like a wax candle in the sun. She winked slowly. Accidents were awful things. She winked again. The mast was straight; the waves were regular; the lighthouse was upright; but the blot had spread.[15]

Just as Betty Flanders's emotion caused her pen to linger and deposit more ink than she intended, forever marking the point in her letter where tears shook the horizon, the entirety of *Jacob's Room*, too, is marked with concern for how emotion and categories color our perception of the world and others as well as with how the inflection of this personal perspectivism limits our communication. For Betty Flanders, the world moves because her tears bend the light, altering her perception. The narrative at first records that the bay "quivered" and the lighthouse "wobbled," but grounds these in her perception when it records the "illusion" of the mast bending. The blinks that wipe away the pooled tears normalize her perspective, and had her pen not been touching paper, no record of the moment would exist. However, her pen *was* adding pale ink to the letter and it is this addition that begins Woolf's exploration of how the act of writing and representation has both ethical pitfalls and possibilities.

When the narrative turns from Betty Flanders to another party on the same beach, the text gives a foretaste of its larger ethical and phenomenological questions. Concern with the ethical dimension of recorded perception (and within it, a critique of aesthetics) is demonstrated early on in Charles Steele's painting of Betty on the beach. As Betty Flanders sits on the beach and adjusts her belongings, unaware that she is part of his composition, Charles Steele stops painting in frustration and thinks, "Here was that woman moving—actually going to get up—confound her! He struck the canvas a hasty violet-black dab. For the landscape needed it. It was too pale. . . . The critics would say it was too pale, for he was an unknown man exhibiting obscurely" (6). Steele's annoyance with his subject is quickly erased by concern for unity and consumer appeal for the painting as finished product. In his attempts to negotiate between rendering accurately what he sees and the demands of his imagined marketplace and consumers, Steele takes no account of the relationship between himself and that which he paints, in this case Betty Flanders. As the first of several attempts to render a person through aesthetic means, Steele's "hasty violet-black dab" can be read both as a failure by Steele to see how acknowledging the agency of the Other could potentially improve his art and as a problematizing of the ethics of artistic representation. When Steele observes that Betty Flanders would be easier to paint if she would only sit still, he is articulating the privileged position of an observer reducing her to an object status in his landscape. As Levinas points out, representation is a fraught territory: the artist—or indeed anyone conscious of and reflecting upon reality—runs a real risk of (and indeed almost cannot avoid) imposing their categorization and thematization on others, thus defining and limiting them.

The innovative narrative of *Jacob's Room* takes on another problem of representation—that of summary, exemplified by repeated references to the difficulty and futility of making an epitaph. As a phrase etched onto the tombstone along with the name and dates of a person's life, an epitaph functions as a public codification of the dead person's status and existence.

As such, it necessarily serves a summative function. Betty Flanders engages with the ethical quandary of representation when she composes her husband's epitaph. "'Merchant of this city,' the tombstone said; though why Betty Flanders had chosen so to call him when, as many still remembered, he had only sat behind an office window for three months, and before that had broken horses, ridden to hounds, farmed a few fields, and run a little wild—well, she had to call him something. An example for the boys"(12). Mrs. Flanders literally does "have to call him something," and the descriptor that he had 'run a little wild,' while perhaps more true than the one on the tombstone, would do nothing for her status in the community or that of her sons. She asks herself,

> Had he, then, been nothing? An unanswerable question, since even if it weren't the habit of the undertaker to close the eyes, the light so soon goes out of them. At first, part of herself; now one of a company, he had merged in the grass, the sloping hillside, the thousand white stones, some slanting, other upright, the decayed wreaths, the crosses of green tin, the narrow yellow paths, and the lilacs that drooped in April, with a scent like that of an invalid's bedroom, over the churchyard wall. Seabrook was now all that. (12)

It is not Seabrook's consciousness (or transcendental ego to use the phenomenological term) that has merged with the sights and smells of the cemetery landscape, but rather Betty Flanders's idea and memory of him, once singular and linked to her, now part of all the other people she knows who have died. Betty Flanders's cannot get far in her reflections on Seabrook's existential status after death, as the narration deems it an unanswerable question. He is to her now literally part of the landscape.

The reductive nature and futility of tombstones is reinforced later when the narrator recounts the scene in London near Waterloo Bridge of "a mason's van with newly lettered tombstones recording how someone loved someone who is buried at Putney" (88).These stones convey even less meaning than Seabrook's, as the narrator can only read the words "Putney" and guesses that like all other tombstones, those she sees tell how "someone loved someone." Freed from their meaningful location, these stones demonstrate how little information any tombstone yields. The narrator continues, telling how "the motor car in front jerks forward, and the tombstones pass too quick for you to read more" (88), as if more information, such as the names of who loved who, would somehow give the stone more meaning for the reader.

The attempts at summary are not only imposed on the dead, but also applied to the living by characters attempting to understand others through thematization. Many characters in addition to the narrator try to understand Jacob, or make summative judgments of him. One telling example occurs when Jacob first meets the Durrant family after his sailing trip. As the girls of the family scramble to assemble the costumes and sets for a private theatrical, Mrs. Durrant and Jacob talk, and she thinks to herself, "He is extraordinarily awkward . . . Yet so distinguished-looking" (48). This is to become a repeated theme that echoes through her mind anytime Jacob Flanders is mentioned within her hearing. Mrs. Durrant does not change her initial impression of Jacob, and the repetition of the phrase eventually strips it of any meaning. A bit later, when the girls come to get Jacob for their theatrical venture, Mrs. Durrant says quietly, "Poor Jacob. . . . They're going to make you act in their play" (48). While this line is often read to foreshadow Jacob's death in World War I, it also foregrounds the novel's possibility for ethical representation by undermining Mrs. Durrant's ambivalent position as one who would thematize Jacob. Even as she is repeatedly presented as one who, like others, thematizes and reduces Jacob, this thematization is filtered through language of performance, role-play, and costume.

Mrs. Durrant also contemplates Jacob later in the text when seeing him in a London opera house. In the repetition of her prior thoughts, she is further removed from any ethical connection with Jacob.

> "Extremely awkward," she said, "but so distinguished-looking." Seeing him for the first time that no doubt is the word for him. . . . [D]istinction was one of the words to use naturally, though, from looking at him, one would have found it difficult to say which seat in the opera house was his, stalls, gallery, or dress circle. A writer? He lacked self-consciousness. A painter? There was something in the shape of his hands . . . which indicated taste. Then his mouth—but surely, of all futile occupations this of cataloguing features is the worst. One word is sufficient. But if one cannot find it? (55)

Mrs. Durrant, perhaps more so than any other character in the novel, attempts to bring Jacob into her own categories of understanding so as to insert him into pre-existing cultural narratives for her own agenda. As the mother of Jacob's beloved Clara, Mrs. Durrant is also keenly invested in his future career.[16] Being a woman who can infer a man's economic and social station from where he sits in the opera house, Mrs. Durrant is attuned to the judgments inherent to the hierarchical classification of people. In thinking that Jacob looks as though he could sit anywhere in the opera house, however, she illuminates the innate impossibility of categorization in ways that ally Woolf's narrative with the Levinasian critique of knowledge as a seizure that would ignore the absolute alterity of the other. Durrant's speculation is superficial and fruitless—one cannot read taste and self-consciousness physiologically anymore than one can sum up a person with one sufficient word.

The failure of summary to represent adequately a life in *Jacob's Room* corresponds not only to Levinasian critiques of ontology, but also to Levinas's critiques of art. Levinas was both interested in, and highly sceptical of, the idea that artistic production could result in ethical engagement. [17] While implicit in much of his writing, Levinas's on-going concern for the ethical possibilities of art explicitly manifests itself in "Reality and Its Shadow" (1948), where he critiques what is often identified as modern literature's defining temptation, if not dictum, "art for art's sake" (*RS* 131). This formula fails as an ethos for Levinas because "it situates art *above* reality and recognizes no master for it," which "liberates the artist from his duties as a man and assures him of a pretentious and facile nobility" (131). It is for this reason that Levinas asserts "there is something wicked and egoist and cowardly in artistic enjoyment" (142). Beyond the concern that art for its own sake removes the artist from engagement with and responsibility for others, Levinas also suggests that novels attempting to represent reality fall short, due to the way they present events and characters as fated to the events in the text:

> The characters of a novel are beings that are shut up, prisoners. Their history is never finished, it still goes on, but makes no headway. A novel shuts beings up in a fate despite their freedom. Life solicits the novelist when it seems to him as if it were already something out of a book. Something somehow completed arises from it, as though a whole set of facts were immobilized and formed a series. . . . The events related form a *situation*—akin to a plastic ideal (139)

The fixed nature of events in a completed novel are fated, leading up to a conclusion; therefore, despite how much insight a writer may give a reader, "he spills half the water he brings us" (142–43).Yet, within this critique of literature, Levinas also articulates an ethical potential, for he concedes, "Modern literature . . . certainly manifests a more and more clear awareness of this fundamental insufficiency of artistic idolatry" (143). Art for its own sake is idolatry because it removes the artist from her responsibility, not only in the world of action, but also in the world of the novel.

These concerns are also present, and in some ways even more overtly articulated, in Levinas's 1947 essay "The Other in Proust," where he lays out some of the specific ways Proust's novel manifests the modern condition, and in so doing, presents the possibility of hope. Preoccupation with solitude and the inability to connect with another person in a meaningful and ethical way are the defining features of modernity: "The theme of solitude, of the basic incommunicability of the person, appears in modern thought and literature as the fundamental obstacle to universal brotherhood. The pathos of sociality crumbles against the eternal Bastille in which each of us remains his or her own captive" (*PN* 101). For Levinas, the idea that one cannot achieve intercommunion with another person is modernity itself, and this limit of communication is a limitation of how we conceive of knowledge. If, as in "Reality and its Shadow," the plastic ideal is false and lacks ethical potential, then the absence that some writers position at the heart of their narratives may open up the possibility of textual ethics:

> One does not see that the success of knowledge would in fact destroy the nearness, the proximity, of the other. A proximity that, far from meaning something less than identification, opens up the horizons of social existence, brings out all the surplus of our experience of friendship and love, and brings to the definitiveness of our identical existence all the virtuality of the non-definitive. (104)

Proximity, with its foundation of shared time and space, transcends mere understanding and offers the positive possibility of intersubjectivity. The other is never available to us through knowledge, we can never truly know the other, but we can experience a positive nearness to the other through proximity. The indeterminacy of textual absence, and the continued desire of Woolf's narrator for proximal understanding of Jacob, articulates hope for proximity. Writers, like Proust (and Woolf), who do not attempt to fill in all the gaps, articulate the hope for proximity. What Levinas finds in Proust is an awareness of solitude, and within the novel's "despair is an inexhaustible source of hope" (104).The possibility that modern literature can remind readers of the limits of their ego, and perhaps offer another way to conceive of subjectivity, constitutes its ethical potential. When Levinas reads Proust, and, as this chapter argues, when we read Woolf, what is communicated more than a reflection of reality is the absence at the heart of relation with the other. For Levinas, the capacity of literature to highlight this lacuna underlies its ethical potential.

The potential of this starting place for narrative ethics in *Jacob's Room* is most clear in the limited and subjective narrator, which, of all the inventive forms present in the novel, is perhaps its most discussed and critically analyzed aspect. Through the limitations of the female, embodied narrator, the text enacts an ethics of representation that does not totalize the object it is narrating, but rather opens up through its abiding absence the possibility for an ethics of representation.[18] Her continual, intrusive, and gendered presence links the otherwise unconnected perspectives on Jacob into a sustained, though fragmented, narrative. The point at which the narrator becomes most obvious and intrusive is in the descriptions of Jacob at college. By calling attention to the embodied and gendered nature of the narrator, the text enacts the possibility that a witness can provide a moment of proximal, ethical relation. The narrator, as a woman with "ten years seniority and a difference of sex" (*JR* 75) from Jacob, is not Jacob, but she is not entirely a free-floating omniscient narrator either, but one grounded in time and space. Hiroko Takai points out "the narrator's reluctant omniscience"[19] and Zwerdling notes that at times "the omniscient narrator suddenly and rather disturbingly pleads ignorance, becomes at best 'semiscient.'"[20] The intrusion of this eavesdropping and limited narrator, rather than operating undetected in the novel, serves to call into question the ethics of the other characters' desire to grasp and understand Jacob. By contrast, in highlighting the narrator's embodied perspective, Woolf opens up the potential that proximity holds for making nonrepresentational ethics possible within both life and literature.

This "semiscience" is a radical move demonstrated most distinctly when the narrator is privy to conversations on the boat when only Timmy Durrant and Jacob are physically present. On a sailing trip to visit Durrant's home, Jacob becomes pensive. The narrator attributes this malaise to a youthful existential crisis: "[W]e start transparent, and then the cloud thickens. All history backs our pane of glass. To escape is vain" (*JR* 39). Such an account articulates the very phenomenological problem the text enacts, that of knowing oneself or others. This interpretation is immediately undercut, however, because in the next paragraph the narrator asks herself "whether this is the right interpretation of Jacob's gloom," deciding "it is impossible to say; for he never spoke a word. . . . There are things that can't be said." This thought, ostensibly focalized through Timmy, who wonders "(only for a second) whether his people bothered him" (39), is actually the fusing by the narrator of Jacob and Timmy's thoughts—Jacob's musings on the weight of history determining individual life and Timmy's concern for his friend's family life. The narrator is able to connect the young men in intersubjective communion, but the *narrative* as a whole does not, because it allows space for acknowledging that "there are things that can't be said." Throughout the novel, the narrator continually attempts to access Jacob's consciousness, or to articulate what is particular and embodied about him. By staging these attempts that continually fail in their goal of understanding Jacob, the text gestures toward an ethics of representation that acknowledges this impossibility. Timmy has no access to Jacob's inner life or thoughts, and the narrator also agrees that such access is "impossible."

The failure of representation occurs back on the college campus when the female narrator, perhaps because of her gendered body, cannot go into the rooms of the young men at Cambridge. Her perspective is that of an outsider, left guessing what is going on within: "All the lights were coming out round the court, and falling on the cobbles, picking out dark patches of grass and single daisies. The young men were now back in their rooms. Heaven knows what they were doing. What was it could drop like *that*?" (33). The narrator is clearly invested in what is going on, wondering what they are doing and concerned about what was dropped to make the sound she heard. Looking up at the room from below and outside, this is the perspective of the narrator who can see precisely how the light hits daisies and grass, but not what the men are doing. For Zwerdling, "[T]he cumulative effect of such passages is to make it impossible for the reader to sympathize fully with the character. We are, in effect, told to keep our distance. . . . Woolf frequently pretends ignorance: she is pictured as so far away from the action that she literally can't hear the words of the characters."[21] This analysis, while astute in pointing out these potential alienating effects upon the reader, conflates Woolf with the narrator of *Jacob's Room*, blurring the difference between the author and narrator and thus discounting the ethical potential that the novel articulates. Woolf's narrator is not Woolf, but is a woman who, like Woolf, is ten years older than the character she describes, who literally cannot go into the rooms of Cambridge. Woolf, in creating such a limited narrator and by temporarily grounding this narrator in time and space, points out both the phenomenological reality of limited access to other minds and articulates the outsider status of women at Cambridge.

Later, the narrator's perspective becomes even more limited as only the voices inside are heard: "The low voice was Simeon's. The voice was even lower that answered him. The sharp tap of a pipe on the mantelpiece cancelled the words. And perhaps Jacob only said 'hum,' or said nothing at all. True, the words were inaudible. It was the intimacy, a sort of spiritual suppleness, when mind prints upon mind indelibly" (35). As the chapter ends, the reader's and the narrator's access fades out. But, seemingly inexplicably, the missing narration—which the preceding pages deny the reader—is suddenly supplied. Whereas before the narrator could not see Jacob and could only guess who was in the room with him, we are told that the "inaudible words" that Jacob said (the words the female narrator has no access to) are, "'Well, you seem to have studied the subject'" (35).These words the narrator so desires to hear, ultimately illuminate nothing. Here the experimental nature of the novel, by fragmenting the narrative and turning back time to supply the missing dialogue, foregrounds the naïveté of the narrator's belief that more facts and information could somehow grant her access to Jacob. The reader, acclimated to status of excluded outside observer, is in a position to question the value of this dialogue in indicating any larger insight into Jacob's character, something the narrator's hunger for its availability, only a few pages before, accepts as natural or self-evident.

This moment in the narrative requires that readers consider their own attitudes and reactions to an unseen narrating voice. By being so present and evident, the other narrator of *Jacob's Room*, separate from the ten-year older woman, also recalls the realistic narrators common in nineteenth-century fiction, who fade into the fabric of other novels. They too shape the reader's perspective on events and characters, even when they were unseen. By grounding her narrator in a gendered, limited physical body, Woolf opens up the possibility for the ethics of proximity even as she questions the interpretation and thematization of the world and other people that goes along with modes of narration that assume distance and otherness can be, or should be, overcome. As another phenomenologist, Levinas's contemporary Maurice Merleau-Ponty, writes in *Phenomenology of Perception* (1945), "[U]nless I have an exterior, others have no interior."[22] In other words, one must be grounded in the present and in the moment to moment of experienced life, one must be living life with the (exterior) body and analyzing it with one's (interior) consciousness, in order to know that, even though all we see are other people's exteriors, and so have no access to their interior lives, their interior consciousness nonetheless exists just as ours exists. Woolf's embodied narrator, with her repeated frustration, incomprehension, and lack of proximity to Jacob illustrates this point in a way that an omniscient third-person narrator could not.

Later in an even more artificially staged situation of access to Jacob, the narrative puts Jacob's thoughts in parenthesis, and he thinks such things as: "(I'm twenty-two. It's nearly the end of October')"; "('Bonamy is an amazing fellow')"; "('The truth is one ought to have been taught French')" (56). Here readers have access to Jacob's precise thoughts, banal and uninteresting as they are. The narrating voice points out how even this level of access, impossible except in a novel with an omniscient narrator, does not give readers the access to Jacob's interiority that they (and she) seek: "But though all this may well be true—so Jacob thought and spoke . . . there remains over something which can never be conveyed to a second person save by Jacob himself" (57). Despite this knowledge, the female narrator cannot help but continue "endowing Jacob Flanders with all sorts of qualities he had not at all—for though, certainly, he sat talking to Bonamy, half of what he said was too dull to repeat; much unintelligible (about unknown people and Parliament); what remains is mostly a matter of guess work. Yet over him we hang vibrating" (57). By foregrounding the lack at the center of understanding Jacob, this passage critiques both the narrator—and by extension, the reader—for examining Jacob so intently. The reader's partial access to Jacob's "dull" and "unintelligible" words is available only through the flawed narrator and her guesswork. The failure of representation here is an ethical gesture wherein both narrative and narrator posit the possibility for ethical proximity with others by making these failures and narrative gaps visible. Even as she is compelled to try to find the word or gesture that would reveal Jacob to us, the narrator is aware of the imperializing nature of her curiosity.

This passage is reminiscent in several ways of Levinas's reading of Marcel's love for Albertine. "Marcel did not love Albertine, if love is a fusion with the other. . . . The story of Marcel's love is laced with confessions apparently destined to put in question the very consistency of that love. But that non-love is in fact love; that struggle the ungraspable, possession; that absence of Albertine, her presence" (*PN* 104). Marcel's obsession with Albertine is not love, but Levinas reads in Proust's novel an ethical gesture: instead of foreclosing meaning, the novel in its "despair" at never attaining Albertine is "an inexhaustible source of hope" (104). Articulating this desire and its inevitable failure opens up what Levinas reads as "Proust's most profound teaching . . . , consist[ing] in situating the real in a relation with what for ever remains other" (104–05). Literature is capable of conveying an understanding of the ways that a totalizing desire for knowledge will inevitably fall short of ethical relation.

The narrator of *Jacob's Room* arrives at a similar conclusion when the many moments of failed or partial representation eventually lead her to assert that,

> it seems that a profound, impartial, and absolutely just opinion of our fellow-creatures is utterly unknown. . . . In any case life is but a progression of shadows, and God knows why it is that we embrace them so eagerly, and see them depart with such anguish, being shadows. And why, if this and much more than this is true, why are we yet surprised in the window corner that the young man in the chair is of all things in the world the most real, the most solid, the best known to us—why indeed? For the moment after we know nothing about him. Such is the manner of our seeing. Such the conditions of our love. (56)

This acknowledgment that "our seeing" and "our love" are limited is both the limit of narrative representation and the opening of a potential for ethical representation. Levinas goes further to articulate this potential in *Otherwise than Being* through the idea of witness: "a witness . . . does not thematize what it bears witness of, and [her] truth is not the truth of representation, is not evidence" (*OB* 146). In other words, the narrator, in bearing witness to Jacob, cannot succeed in thematizing him into a concept, or find the one summative word that would describe him. The truth of Jacob is beyond representation, which is frustrating to both the narrator and the readers seeking him. This frustration should be viewed as constructive, rather than destructive, however, because it opens the narrative up to the potential for an ethical engagement with the difficulties of representation. The reader is not given evidence by which to find meaning in Jacob, for the truth of representation is greater than any evidence the narrator could supply. As readers we can no more experience Jacob than his friends can. The narrator, as a witness, cannot thematize Jacob, and so the narrative technique itself enacts repeated failures of thematization, staging the ethics of witnessing as the way toward an ethics of representation. In acting as witness, the narrative presents a multiplicity of perspectives, privileging none for more than an instant, and thus positions the 160 characters who comprise *Jacob's Room* as multiple witnesses, a heteroglossic move, one containing multiple, varying discourses, that is less myopic that the traditional elegy with only one poetic voice.[23] This limited narrative position points out how dominating and oppressive the normally naturalized positions of both omniscient and first person limited narrators are in order to argue for a narrative that does not delimit the nature of another person.

The view that Woolf's novel presents of the possibility of intersubjectivity is not then altogether pessimistic. She does not rule out the possibility for ethical relationality and ethical representation, but she does argue strongly that the way people normally go about attempting to relate to others fails precisely because of thematization. The alienation this engenders is demonstrated in the solipsism of ordinary London commuters: "The proximity of the omnibuses gave the outside passengers an opportunity to stare into each other's faces. Yet few took advantage of it. Each had his own business to think of. Each had his own past shut up in him like the leaves of a book known to him by heart; and his friends could only read the title" (*JR* 50–51). This passage is reminiscent of Levinas's suggestion in *Otherwise than Being* that instead of a knowledge regarding the other person based in individualized perception, we move to "sensibility interpreted not as a knowing but as proximity"; thus "proximity appears as the relationship with the other" (*OB* 89). This new subjectivity based in relation "blocks all schematism" (89) and thus takes the other person as he or she is, rather than thematizing the other person or reducing him or her into a concept. Schematizing the other into a pre-existing set of characteristics limits both the possibility of new knowledge and relation with the other person. Both Woolf and Levinas locate the potential for ethical relation in the face to face that is proximity. That this Levinasian insight in Woolf occurs in an elegiac text stands as a call to take advantage of this opportunity and to engage in the potential for intersubjectivity that the face to face presents while there is still time. Once someone has died, the potential for the face to face is lost.

Before beginning *Jacob's Room*, Woolf questioned in her diary the possibility of authentic representation of human emotion: "My doubt is how far it will enclose the human heart—Am I sufficiently mistress of my dialogue to net it there?"[24] She echoed this fishing/net imagery when she wrote in the novel, "It is thus that we live, they say, driven by an unseizable force. They say that the novelists never catch it; that it goes hurtling through their nets and leaves them torn to ribbons. This, they say, is what we live by—this unseizable force" (*JR* 122). In the end, Woolf opted to assign herself the more difficult task and *not* attempt to net the human heart, but to use the finely crafted and torn ribbons of *Jacob's Room* to reveal the vitality and untotalizable nature of this "unseizable force." By calling attention to her narrator's machinations, Woolf asks her readers also to perform the ethics of her text, to attempt to construct Jacob from these fragments, and in failing to arrive at a totalizable entity, to see how the project of characterization is always already limited by representation. This limit is the ethical message of *Jacob's Room*.

NOTES

I would like to thank Maren Linett, Tony Russell, Paul Rutz, and Aaron DeRosa for their invaluable suggestions for improving earlier drafts of this chapter. Many thanks also go to Donald Wehrs for his helpful comments and enthusiasm during editing.

1. Hermione Lee, *Virginia Woolf* (New York: Knopf, 1997), 227.

2. The elaborate nature and depth of Woolf's construction mirrors in many ways the depth of her grief. Five days after Thoby died, Woolf wrote in a letter to Violet, "Thoby is going on splendidly. He is very cross with his nurses, because they won't give him mutton chops and beer" (quoted in Mark Hussey, *Virginia Woolf A to Z* [Oxford: Oxford University Press, 1995], 272–73).

3. Kathleen Wall, "Significant Form in *Jacob's Room*: Ekphrasis and the Elegy," *Texas Studies in Literature and Language* 44, no. 3 (2002): 302–323, 305.

4. The idea of dedicating a novel to Thoby, and her trepidation at this idea, stayed with Woolf. Years later, in 1931 when she finished *The Waves*, she wrote in her diary that she was "sitting these 15 minutes in a state of glory, & calm, & some tears, thinking of Thoby & if I could write Julian Thoby Stephen 1881-1906 on the first page. I suppose not," in Virginia Woolf, *The Diary of Virginia Woolf, Volume 4 1931-1935*, ed. Anne Oliver Bell (New York: Harcourt Brace, 1978), 10.

5. As Rachael Hollander points out, the central absence in *Jacob's Room* "highlights the necessity of reading such gaps as the very encounter with otherness that defines the ethics of modernism" ("Novel Ethics: Alterity and Form in *Jacob's Room*," *Twentieth Century Literature* 53 [Spring 2007], 41). In her analysis of form in *Jacob's Room*, Hollander notes that Woolf is "committed to a theory of literature that recognizes the capacity of the novel to engender an ethical response in its readers" (41). For Hollander, by "emphasizing the impossibility of full knowledge and the fleeting and unpredictable nature of intimacy between individuals," Woolf's novel "rethinks the politics of the relationship between reader and text" (62).

6. Virginia Woolf, *The Diary of Virginia Woolf: Volume 2 1920-1924*, ed. Anne Oliver Bell. (New York: Harcourt Brace, 1978), 13–14.

7. G.E. Moore *Principa Ethica* (New York: Barnes & Noble, 2005), 192.

8. Ibid., 192.

9. Leonard Woolf, *Sowing: An Autobiography of the Years 1880-1904* (London: Hogarth Press, 1960), 147.

10. Leonard Woolf, *Beginning Again: An Autobiography of the Years 1911-1918* (New York: Harcourt, Brace & World, 1964), 25.

11. Ibid., 22.

12. Tammy Clewell, "Consolation Refused: Virginia Woolf, The Great War, and Modernist Mourning," *Modern Fiction Studies* 50 (Winter 2004), 206.

13. By arguing that the death of another person is an "excess," Levinas makes the point that we cannot make sense of the death of another without doing violence. Another's death always exceeds us in both our experience of the event and in our understanding of it.

14. Alex Zwerdling, "*Jacob's Room*: Woolf's Satiric Elegy." *ELH* 48, no. 4 (1981): 894–913, 898 cited.

15. Virginia Woolf, *Jacob's Room* (Rockville, MD: Arc Manor, 2008), 5. All further references are to this edition and will be cited henceforth parenthetically in the text. The text will be referred as *JR*.

16. The futility of Mrs. Durrant's attempt to read indications of Jacob's future career in his hands and lips is magnified and colored by readers' knowledge that he will never have a career, that he will die in the war.

17. For more on the other moments in Levinas's work where he addresses art, see Alain P. Toumayan, *Encountering the Other: The Artwork and the Problem of Difference in Blanchot and Levinas* (Pittsburgh: Duquesne University Press, 2004) and Jill Robbins, *Altered Reading: Levinas and Literature* (Chicago: University of Chicago Press, 1999). Toumayan continues his exploration of Levinas's statements on art in "Levinas and French Literature," in *Levinas and Nineteenth-Century Literature: Ethics and Otherness from Romanticism through Realism*, ed. Donald R. Wehrs and David P. Haney (Newark: University of Delaware Press, 2009), 126–50.

18. Narrative fragmentation, of course, is not unique to *Jacob's Room*, and in fact most of Woolf's subsequent novels address the fragmentation of subjects in various ways. In outlining her reading of another Woolf novel *The Waves*, Lisa Marie Lucenti writes, "[T]he subject thus fractured is, for Virginia Woolf, the only *ethical* subject since it is actively and continually engaged in a process of interrogating both its own construction and its relationship to everything it cannot contain. This subject is ethical because it refuses to be content with the illusion that it is whole, autonomous, and therefore independent of all that eludes its grasp" ("Virginia Woolf's *The Waves*: To Defer that 'Appalling Moment,'" *Criticism* 40 no. 1 [1998]: 75–97, 92 cited).

19. Hiroko Takai, "On Not Speaking Out: *Jacob's Room* as a Conflation of Modernism and Feminism," *Virginia Woolf Bulletin* 4 (2000): 7–12.

20. Zwerdling, 902.

21. Ibid., 902.

22. Maurice Merleau-Ponty, *Phenomenology of Perception*. (New York: Routledge, 2002), 434.

23. In the *Ethics of Mourning*, R. Clifton Spargo argues, "Though anti-elegiac sentiment—wherein the emphasis falls to the anticonsilitory, nontranscendent perspective of modern grief—resists literary and social convention, it traces implicitly the survival of grief against a social totality that denies the dead" (R. Clifton Spargo, *The Ethics of Mourning:Grief and Responsibility in Elegiac Literature* [Baltimore: Johns Hopkins University Press, 2004],131). In the context of *Jacob's Room*, read through anti-elegiac poetics as articulated here by Spargo, one may see Woolf actually deferring the totalizing moment that would end grief through her refusal to elegize Jacob.

24. Virginia Woolf. *The Diary of Virginia Woolf: Volume 2 1920-1924*, ed. Anne Oliver Bell (New York: Harcourt Brace, 1980), 13.

Chapter Three

Milne and the Tonstant Weaders

A Levinasian Case for Winnie-the-Pooh and The House at Pooh Corner

Lorna Wood

Poststructural assessments of children's literature have not been kind to A. A. Milne. Taking their cues from Edward Said's influential *Orientalism*, some scholars have concluded that children's literature is a means of colonizing children, imperialistically asserting the power of adults to mold and define them.[1] Since the will to power is unquestioningly accepted by such criticism as a fundamental motivating force working to repress desire at every level of society, molding can never be benign, and the content of molding tools like literature perpetuates the repressive energies that generated it. Such criticism, again without question, implicitly takes empowerment, the liberation of desire, and recognition of the repressed other to be goods. Therefore a nostalgic children's fantasy penned by a representative of the British Empire that does not overtly repudiate, or even indicate awareness of, the many levels of repression in which it participates may be reduced to an idealization of narcissistic denial. As Daphne M. Kutzer puts it,

> in the fictive world of the Pooh books . . . , empire, its values, and its endurance, are rarely if ever questioned. Lofting's troubled view of empire is unusual in this period, and although his [Dr. Dolittle] books have been bowdlerized for their supposed insensitivity to racial issues, they are far more cognizant of the implications of empire. But for Milne, remaining in a mythical land of childhood and learning the values of a declining empire still seems more appealing than sailing off to Africa to confront troublesome issues of empire and imperialism. The Pooh books allow us to remain in a mythological world

of childhood, to retreat from adult responsibilities; Lofting's novels push us to confront these responsibilities.[2]

Kutzer's view may be understood as a rejection of the sentimental similar to Dorothy Parker's famous assessment of *The House at Pooh Corner*, "Tonstant Weader fwowed up."[3] Kutzer's call for engagement evokes the similar tastes of Parker and her friends. As a member of the liberal and politically active Algonquin Round Table,[4] Parker wrote socially engaged fiction herself, and, in a manner analogous to Kutzer's championing of Lofting, Parker and her friends praised such sentimentally stereotyping but purportedly anti-imperialist works as the novels of Edna Ferber. Though she does not ferret out Milne's political imperialism, Parker implicitly condemns Milne for imposing a sentimental twaddle on children that reflects his own narcissistic inability to leave the nursery.

Poststructuralist conceptions of children's literature add a theoretical underpinning to Parker's implicit accusation that threatens to nullify Milne's defense, that he wrote for children, not "Mrs. Parker."[5] According to Perry Nodelman, for example, all writing, especially a genre that arose out of imperialism and that addresses vulnerable children, constructs its target audience in ways that enhance the power of its purveyors:

> No matter how hard we try, we aren't ever going to escape the imperialist tendencies at the heart of human discourse. There will always be somebody out there finding a new way to think about children or write about childhood, and the new ways will always inevitably work to impose somebody's ideas of childhood on both other adults and children. ("The Other," 34)

> [Children's literature] offers children both what adults think children will like and what adults want them to need, but it does so always in order to satisfy adults' needs in regard to children. . . . It fulfills real adult needs and children's presumed needs by working to colonize children. (*Hidden Adult*, 242–43)

Kutzer agrees that Milne participates in this dynamic: "If we look at the Pooh books in the context of Nodelman's essay ["The Other"], we can see that Milne is colonizing both Christopher Robin and the reader" (97). After detailing the extent to which, in her view, the Pooh books colonize children after the manner of the West colonizing "the Oriental" in Said, Kutzer concludes that "if Said and Nodelman are accurate in their reading of the Orient and of childhood—Milne and his narrator are as guilty of colonizing and silencing children as the West was of colonizing and silencing the East" (97–98).

Yet concerns over such poststructuralist tenets have been expressed, from a variety of perspectives, for at least the past twenty years. Particularly troubling to Levinas and many others are the following assumptions: that the will to power is the motivating force in human existence, that this will is exercised by monolithic totalities, that resistance to power in the name of universal recognition and/or arbitrary freedom is always intrinsically good, and that human life is organized around such binary patterns as power and resistance, and they can never be escaped.[6] This array of dissenting or qualifying voices allows us to entertain the following Levinasian alternatives to poststructuralist ideas.

First, the ethical impulse is primary. Both the impulse to create work for children and the creation of specific techniques and devices designed to make works appeal to this audience are driven by care for the Other (see *MS*). As saids, such works retain only the trace of Levinas's "face," the ethical impulse. They may even reject the ethical for some self-serving end. But the assumption that *all* works for children inherently serve their authors' will to power is unwarranted.

Second, the audience are not necessarily powerless dupes. If the ethical is primary, children's literature cannot simply be foisted on its readers by totalizing hegemonic forces, but must arise from and enter into the saying of educators, parents, and children themselves. If we listen out of care and respect for Others, then their power is vastly increased, and it is no longer necessary to assume that texts manipulate their young readers into buying adult notions of what is good for them, though this may certainly occur.

The rejection of binary patterns of struggle as defining paradigms of human interaction has far-reaching implications. The reduction of every facet of a work to such patterns necessarily leads to glossing over details, particularly details troubling to the theoretical system one is deploying.[7] This moves criticism away from the respect for the Other entailed in Levinas's extrasensory listening, and therefore away from any assessment of an author's ethical saying—an ironic outcome for a criticism concerned with liberating the silenced.

The same ideas regarding ethical subjectivity that undermine poststructuralist conceptions of self and other allow us to "listen" to non-, even anti-, imperialist aspects of the Pooh books' exploration of childhood and nostalgia. Through a Levinasian lens, Milne's portrayal of Christopher Robin's character and relationships may be viewed not as a narcissistic retreat to childhood, but as an engagement with a subjectivity separating from a developmental stage analogous to what Levinas characterizes as "enjoyment" and beginning to confront mortality in ways that, Levinas argues, enable ethical relationships. Likewise, Levinas's views of paternity allow us to read the narrator's relationship to his son in the frame of *Winnie-the-Pooh* as an ethical exchange, rather than as evidence of repression. Finally, Levinasian listening reveals humorous slippages of language and power that attack imperialism—including, obliquely, Britain's actual empire—throughout the Pooh texts.

> But the egotism with which . . . a child is born, surely very quickly disappears as attachments are made and relationships established. When a child plays with his bear the bear comes alive and there is at once a child-bear relationship which tries to copy the Nanny-child relationship. Then the child gets inside his bear and looks at it the other way round: that's how *bear* feels about it. And at once sympathy is born and egotism has died. [8]

In line with such studies of subject formation and transitional objects as those of D. W. Winnicott, Melanie Klein, and Julia Kristeva, Christopher Milne (the inspiration for Christopher Robin in his father's Pooh books) here views the relationship of a young child with a favored toy as an essential step in moving from a dyadic infantilism to ethical selfhood. [9]

Similarly, Levinas views "Woman" and "the feminine" as providing an intimacy that is "simultaneously" a "presence" and an "absence" (*TI* 155) and that thereby conditions "representation," which "claims to substitute itself *after the event* for this life in reality, so as to constitute this very reality" (*TI* 169). [10] The terms of Levinas's discourse do not rest on developmental psychology's chronological framework of infantile growth; nevertheless,the subject's primordial experience of "living from" in "enjoyment" in Levinas bears significant similarities with infantile nursing, and the "insecurity" that opens "interiority" in the Levinasian subject is similar to the infantile negotiation of the "good breast" and "bad breast." In explanations of the development of language and ethical subjectivity through the transitional object, the infant learns to master the rage that arises when he internalizes the "bad" (absent) breast by internalizing, with the help of Winnicott's "good-enough" mother, the "good" breast and later representing it in the transitional object. In Levinas the subject masters the element that both nourishes and threatens by locating subjectivity in a "dwelling" conditioned by the intimacy of a gentle and welcoming feminine "presence"—which, however, is simultaneously an absence to be bridged (*TI* 155). Again, whereas the relationship with the transitional object and later language, play, and cultural creativity involves both control and a love that reflects and returns nurturing care, so representation in Levinas both comprehends the element in the "said" and is conditioned by intimacy, "the relation with the Other who welcomes me in the Home, the discreet presence of the Feminine" (*TI* 170). Finally, whereas the relationships to "transitional phenomena . . . become diffused, . . . spread out over the whole intermediate territory between 'inner psychic reality' and 'the external world as perceived by two persons in common,' that is to say, over the whole cultural field" (Winnicott, 5), for Levinas, analogously, "The cultural creation is not added on to receptivity but is its other side from the start. We are not the subject of the world and a part of the world from two different points of view; in expression we are subject and part at once. To perceive is both to receive and to express, by a sort of prolepsis" (*MS* 41). [11]

For Levinas mastery of representation is not only conditioned by vulnerability to the element, but, through language, continually recurs to that vulnerability. Even here one might pursue parallels between his views and psychology, but unique to Levinasian phenomenology is the view that the only means of transcending vulnerability is being "accused" by the Other.[12] While we may put off awareness of our own death through conscious mastery, language from the Other breaches any attempt at self-enclosure, not with hostility, but with the gift and accusation of the Other's face. Our perception of the Other's vulnerability returns us anew to the threat of the element, Levinas argues, but now with the awareness of the Other's exposure, an awareness that paradoxically deprives us of power and endows us with ethical humanity (see especially *TI* 110–20).

This stress on the sense of responsibility that comes with self-mastery opens a new perspective on works of childhood fantasy. As Christopher Milne's description suggests, play in such works represents not a retreat to the nursery, but a discovery of the ethical relation ("that's how *bear* feels about it") in the midst of mastery. The element in which this occurs is not a self-enclosed idyll of enjoyment and pretended mastery, but that idyll in the context of aging and the ungraspable horizon of death. The pathos of the moment when age forces the child to abandon the play world does not center on the child, as one might expect from a work promoting narcissistic identification. Rather, readers of the Pooh books, like auditors of "Puff, the Magic Dragon" or viewers of the *Toy Story* trilogy, are called to feel most concern for the toys left behind as the child continues. While Christopher Robin is apprehensive about the coming change at the end of *The House at Pooh Corner*, it is Pooh who is powerless to cope.

> Then [Pooh] began to think of all the things Christopher Robin would want to tell him when he came back from wherever he was going to, and how muddling it would be for a Bear of Very Little Brain to try and get them right in his mind. "So perhaps," he said sadly to himself, "Christopher Robin won't tell me any more," and he wondered if being a Faithful Knight meant that you just went on being faithful without being told things. (176)

Christopher Robin's promises to return sometimes "*really*," and his plea to Pooh to "understand" if he is "not quite—" and "*whatever* happens"—all only reinforce the knowledge that, while Christopher Robin will continue to develop mastery in coping with mortality, Pooh will henceforth be severed from the ethical engagement that gave him life.

The toys in such fantasies are Others in multiple senses. First, as explicitly represented in *The Velveteen Rabbit*, they have been made real by love.[13] The child's ethical concern for them transcends representation; she is not merely representing the transitional object to herself as an Other, but projecting and recurring to a sense of ethical concern for the caregiver that is becoming Levinasian accusation by and Substitution for individual Others. The representation of toys as real dramatizes a primal experience of "ethics as first philosophy," the dawning of concern for the Other. Further, as projections of the child's unique self, specially called to ethical responsibility, the toys, and by extension the consciousness that enlivened them, resist our identification and exceed our grasp. In grieving for the toys, therefore, we do not merely mourn and resist our own mortality; we also manifest our concern for the consciousness of the Other, the child whose life has gained meaning through his concern for his toys, and the toys whose abandonment reawakens our own ethical sense. [14]

It must be acknowledged that Levinas's well known suspicion of the effects of art (see, for example, *RS*) supports Tonstant Weaders' view of such fantasies as sentimental and dangerously disengaged, even complicit in oppression. While an actual child's relationship with her transitional object may be ethically moving and important, the representation of such relationships may remain distorting and manipulative. If, as Levinas contends in *Otherwise than Being*, works call for their own exegesis (41), perhaps stories about children and mortality cry out for Tonstant Weaders, and ethical readerly experience is corrupt until one's grief over Little Nell is disrupted by Oscar Wilde. [15]

Certainly, exegesis must examine whether A. A. Milne, as author and as the father character ostensibly narrating the Pooh tales, carries the enchanted reader away with a saccharine idyll that violates both his son and all children, while papering over the violence of British imperialism in which he and Christopher participate. Perhaps Tonstant Weaders can never be satisfied on such points, and perhaps it is ethical that their voices continue to ring in debate; nevertheless, Levinasian exegesis also demands attention to the ways in which Milne's Pooh books evince respect for children and suspicion of the said's inherent repression of the Other.

Levinas characterizes "Fecundity" (*TI* 267–69) as a renewal of being that in its recommencement (through the child) seems to signal the possibility of infinite being, but that in its alterity, its recapitulation of the "Desire" that is the orientation toward the Other, actually allows us to transcend being: "By a total transcendence, the transcendence of trans-substantiation, the I is, in the child, an other. Paternity remains a self-identification, but also a distinction within identification—a structure unforeseeable in formal logic" (267); and, "But the Other is not a term: he does not stop the movement of Desire. The other that Desire desires is again Desire; transcendence transcends toward him who transcends—this is the true adventure of paternity" (269). The not-quite confounding of self and Other inherent in fecundity frees us from the binary struggle habitually assumed by poststructuralist critics. For if we acknowledge the possibility that Christopher Robin, and especially Christopher Robin the literary character, is also in some sense A. A. Milne, it is absurd to argue that Milne's text is merely appropriatively distorting Christopher Robin's play world.

As critics have pointed out, the close relationships in the Pooh books, especially Pooh and Piglet's, seem to evoke A. A. Milne's fraternal bond with his brother Kenneth more than the play of a solitary only child whose closest relationship was with his nanny.[16] Pooh's role as author likewise relates more to the psyche of the father than the play of the son;[17] and the many instances of sophisticated verbal humor in the books could not be understood, let alone created, by most young children (see *Recovering Arcadia*, 47–50).

It is not necessary, however, to assert that A. A. Milne or his persona appropriates Christopher's play world for his own (nefarious) purposes. Milne's books must and should contain the trace of his own face if they are to constitute meaningful communication from the Other. The fantasy's ethical response to mortality probably derives not merely from the subjectivity of Christopher Milne, but also from that of A. A. Milne, survivor of World War I, and, indirectly, that of his brother Kenneth, who was diagnosed with tuberculosis in 1924 and died in 1929, the year after *The House at Pooh Corner* was published. Doubtless the subjectivity of Christopher's beloved nanny, and of Dorothy Milne, who played with her son and his animals more than his father did, as well as traces of illustrator E. H. Shepard, likewise haunt the tales.[18] The simultaneous continuation and disruption of the I in being that occurs through fecundity in paternity, filiality, and fraternity in Levinas provides grounds for sharing and blending, and permits us to interpret these in terms of sociability, rather than domination.

> TO HER
> HAND IN HAND WE COME
> CHRISTOPHER ROBIN AND I
> TO LAY THIS BOOK IN YOUR LAP.
> SAY YOU'RE SURPRISED?
> SAY YOU LIKE IT?
> SAY IT'S JUST WHAT YOU WANTED?
> BECAUSE IT'S YOURS—
> BECAUSE WE LOVE YOU. (*Winnie-the-Pooh*, dedication, v)

Sociability does not preclude domination; indeed, according to Levinas, the said, in investing saying with being, necessarily reduces the ethical self to a trace. From a Tonstant Weaderly perspective, the conventional sentimental dedication to Mother may be viewed as a deceitful minimizing of Dorothy Milne's contribution, through her play, to the Pooh tales, or a false glorification of a woman who appears to have been emotionally cold as both wife and mother. And Christopher Robin's involvement "hand in hand" with the author, may be viewed as swallowing him up in a "we" that makes him silent and powerless.

Ethical exegesis, however, must not remain willfully deaf to Milne's innovation of the convention. The sentimentality of the image of father and son "hand in hand" and the supplicatory laying the book "in your lap," along with the meter of the first three lines, are all disrupted by the questions of the next three. Superficially, these undermine what was threatening to become Victorian idealization of Mother with humorous anticipation of her possible conventional responses. In the form of repeated questions, each intimating a more intense acceptance by Mother, however, this dedication seems unconfident about the fundamental presumptive said of all dedications, that the Other will gratefully accept. The tone is hopeful but pleading, diffidently allowing for the unexpected in the Other. Together with these questions, the last two lines seem to offer a further Levinasian corrective to the pomposity of dedication. Whatever the answer to the questions, the dedicators can only continue to offer the book in hope, and they are compelled to do so by love, which makes the book always already given over to the Other and therefore not really theirs to dedicate.

Family sociability likewise pervades the relationship among Christopher Robin, his animals, and the narrator in the introductions to both Pooh volumes and the frame of *Winnie-the-Pooh*. To ignore it in exegesis is to enact against the text the same kind of violence that poststructuralist critics accuse Milne of perpetrating. Wherever he appears, the narrator constantly presents his work as responding to the call of (O)thers. For instance, in the Introduction to *Winnie-the-Pooh*, after a fantasy about Christopher Robin at the zoo that may be viewed as awkward or self-indulgent (see *Recovering Arcadia*, 45–46), the narrator says he heard Piglet say "What about Me?" at this point in the writing, "And now all the others are saying, 'What about *us*?' So perhaps the best thing to do is to stop writing and get on with the book" (viii). As in the Dedication, a typically Victorian gesture (here the dreamlike fantasy becoming "real") is disrupted by the call of the Other (here a toy animal enlivened by Christopher Robin's play). And, as in the dedication, this call is represented as leading the narrator to abandon control over "his" project.

Similarly, the narrator's supposed takeover of Christopher Robin's play world is instigated by the child character himself,

"What about a story?" said Christopher Robin.
"*What* about a story?" I said.
"Could you very sweetly tell Winnie-the-Pooh one?"
"I suppose I could," I said. "What sort of stories does he like?"
"About himself. Because he's *that* sort of Bear."
"Oh I see."
"So could you very sweetly?"

"I'll try," I said.

So I tried. (2)

The narrator enters into the imaginative world of his son not as an invader, but in response to an invitation, a request from the Other whose taste in stories, though it is linked to his father's, is also his own, inaccessible except through an imperfect sharing, face to face in a Levinasian sense. Here the need of the Other and his separateness are embodied in the Bear, the extension of the child's ethical self. In promising to "try" to answer the call of Bear and son, with the "sort of stories" Pooh likes, the father evinces a respectful understanding of both his separateness from his son as Other, and the responsibility to his son that designates him as father.

In this context, Christopher Robin's inquiry, repeated in the end of *Winnie-the-Pooh*, "Coming to see me have my bath?" and the narrator's flippant response, "I might" (19, 157) convey not so much the displays of anxiety and power critcs have alleged (see Hunt, 114, *Recovering Arcadia*, 44) as the intimacy of speech whose content is not as important as the routine of exchanging familiarities. Since Christopher Robin changes the subject immediately after, he is clearly not upset by his father's equivocation, and since the same exchange is repeated, it is clearly part of a nightly ritual. Insofar as meaning is considered at all between the two, it seems merely to play with the blurred and changing lines between father and son as the same, not needing or wanting boundaries like privacy, and as Others to one another, tenuously linked by the open-ended saying of speech.

Even Milne's least defensible practices may contain traces of saying along with the repressive said. Christopher Milne describes his girlish clothes and hair as old-fashioned, setting him apart (15, 38–39, 95, and see *Recovering Arcadia*, 99), and readers have found Ernest Shepard's faithful representations of them alienating or even orientalizing: "The figure of the oriental was often feminized, and Shepherd's [*sic*] illustrations for the Pooh books feminized the little boy as well, portraying an androgynous figure with a bowl haircut, shorts, and a blousey sort of tunic top" (Kutzer, 97); "To a modern child, Christopher Robin is not without his charm, but he is puzzling and even a little girlish" (Swann, 130, and see 80). Yet a desire to feminize Christopher Robin seems inconsistent with Milne's emphasis on Christopher Robin's manly, even imperialistic, Wellington boots.[19] A more satisfactory explanation for Christopher's garb is consonant with the intimate friendships represented in the stories despite their absence from Christopher's life: Milne's nostalgia for his boyhood and friendship with Kenneth Milne, together with his horror of World War I, may be expressed in this old-fashioned clothing choice (Carpenter, 190, suggests this is a possibility). While clearly a disrespectful imposition on Christopher, therefore, the clothes convey not only adult imperialism, but also adult vulnerability and loss.

As we have seen, poststructuralist Tonstant Weaders interpret displays of vulnerability in the Pooh texts as at once a disengaged retreat from "the real world" and its power struggles, and an imperialistic tactic in their own right. Milne is accused by such critics of at once feminizing Christopher Robin in an "orientalizing" move designed to disempower him, and of representing a sweetened, feminized idyll that hides the ugly socioeconomic power plays of the 1920s British Empire. Once again, however, a Levinasian reading of Milne's Pooh books shows that whatever violence may be perpetrated through Milne's said, the saying of his work is nevertheless consistently concerned with opposing the ethical to the grasping, and may therefore be read as rejecting, rather than hiding from, empire as power.

First, as Kutzer has shown (98–104), the books are full of imperialist projects (and see Lerer, 143–45, Connolly, 197). Some of these, such as Christopher Robin's expedition to discover the North Pole or Rabbit's attempts to rid the Forest of strangers (Kanga and Roo) and their strangeness (Tigger's bounciness) bear obvious reference to actual imperialism; others, like Pooh's attempt to rob bees of their honey, merely evince a greedy desire to dominate. It is wrong, however, to claim with Kutzer that "empire, its values, and its endurance, are rarely if ever questioned" in the text. In fact, imperialism in multiple forms is continually questioned.

On the most obvious level of allusions to empire and empire-building, imperialist projects in the books are invariably frustrated or significantly changed through ethical responses (Connolly's discussion of "Milne's Moral Vision" in *Recovering Arcadia*, 104–110, is consonant with this view). That this was Milne's intention is suggested by the fact that while Pooh, Piglet, Eeyore, Owl, and Rabbit, the original denizens of the Forest, were somewhat haphazardly assembled (Owl and Rabbit are not based on stuffed animals), Milne deliberately chose the newcomers, Kanga and Roo and Tigger, to see how they would fit into Christopher's play. Thus while Kutzer's analysis of these characters' outsider, colonial status (98–101) is acute, its neglect of Milne's stated purposefulness renders it incomplete in a manner that conveniently supports her view of Milne as at best passively complacent about empire.[20] In fact it seems likely that Milne, as father, author, and World War I veteran, was consciously interested in the ethical integration of colonial outsiders.

In light of this concern, Kanga's somewhat unpleasantly authoritarian maternal role may be viewed not merely as a relegation of female possibilities to the more threateningly conventional, but, as Kutzer suggests (100), a domestication of Australian femaleness, originally associated with thieving and prostitution. Kanga not only serves to reassure readers as to the ethical intention behind even the more chafing aspects of maternal solicitude, she also teaches a lesson against stereotyping and xenophobia.

Although he himself is unable even to remember how many family members he has, Rabbit objects to Kanga on the arbitrary grounds that she "carries her family about with her in her pocket!" (90) and conceives a nasty plan to force Kanga to leave the Forest by kidnapping Roo. Piglet joins in because he "was so excited by the idea of being Useful that he forgot to be frightened any more," and Pooh is similarly convinced by Rabbit that the "adventure would be impossible" (92) without him: "Pooh went into a corner of the room and said proudly to himself, 'Impossible without Me! *That* sort of Bear'" (93).

The imperialist adventure fails for Levinasian reasons. After running off with Roo, Rabbit forgets his scheme because he "was playing with Baby Roo in his own house, and feeling more fond of him every minute" (101–02). In accord with Levinas's discussion of fecundity, Rabbit's affection for "Baby Roo" appears based both on his vulnerability and his similarity to Rabbit (both are busy, self-important animals). Ironically, this leads to a lasting, uncle-like connection with Roo: "And every Tuesday Roo spent the day with his great friend Rabbit" (106).

Pooh, meanwhile, "had decided to be a Kanga" (102). He admires Kanga's jumping and, in Levinasian terms, represents it as an accomplishment he might master. The folly of such an attempt, emphasized by Shepard's illustrations (100, 102), disrupts the notion that Kanga can be contained by Pooh's or the other animals' representations of her. In the end, we learn that Pooh has moved beyond Being and its saids to the point where "every Tuesday Kanga spent the day with his [*sic*] great friend Pooh, teaching him to jump" (106).

Piglet undergoes the most severe disruption of Being. Having replaced the infant Roo in Kanga's pocket, Piglet is first jounced to her house and then, when Kanga realizes the trick the animals have played, deliberately deprived of his identity. First, he loses the ability to communicate: "'*Aha!*' said Piglet, as well as he could after his Terrifying Journey. But it wasn't a very good '*Aha!*' and Kanga didn't seem to understand what it meant" (101). When he tries to assert that he is Piglet, Kanga insists that he is only Roo representing Piglet: "'Yes dear, yes,' said Kanga soothingly. 'And imitating Piglet's voice too! So clever of him'" (102). Then Kanga refuses to acknowledge his face. When Piglet pleads, "Can't you *see*? . . . Haven't you got *eyes*? *Look* at me!" Kanga insists, "I *am* looking, Roo dear. . . . And you know what I told you about making faces. If you go on making faces like Piglet's you will grow up to *look* like Piglet—and *then* think how sorry you will be" (103). Finally she prevents him from talking altogether (by filling his mouth with a soapy "flannel" whenever he opens it) and alters his appearance by washing him.

Consequently Piglet does not get justice with the entry of Levinas' third party—in this case, Christopher Robin. By this time, Piglet almost doubts his own identity. "I'm *not* Roo, am I?" he asks. Christopher Robin agrees he is not Roo, but insists he is not Piglet because, "I know Piglet well, and he's *quite* a different colour" (105).

Thanks to Milne's forbearance, Piglet draws none of the many possible moral lessons from his experience. After escaping, he "rolled the rest of the way home, so as to get his own nice comfortable colour again" (106). Piglet returns as quickly as possible to the "disinterested joy of play," which in Levinas is characterized by its "carefreeness with regard to existence" (TI 134).

Yet the anti-imperialist implications of the tale are many and ironic. Having heard from Christopher Robin that "a Kanga was Generally Regarded as One of the Fiercer Animals" (91), Piglet finds that she is fierce indeed—like that cradle-rocker of imperialist respectability, the British nanny. Having carried out, as far as he could, a savage plan to evict savages, Piglet finds himself treated as an outsider, even by "his great friend Christopher Robin" because once cleansed to a paler color, he is unrecognizable as an insider. Only in flight from civilization can Piglet (like Huck Finn) rediscover the joys of dirt and freedom after enslaving himself to Rabbit's xenophobia. Only once all the creatures have been moved beyond projects of Being toward the horizons of the Other can the narrator conclude, "So they were all happy again" (106).

The importance of such ideas to Milne is clear from their repetition vis à vis Tigger in *The House at Pooh Corner*. In "In Which Tigger Is Unbounced" (108–26), Rabbit's project is to forcibly assimilate the bouncy Tigger, whose colonial resonance with India is discussed in Kutzer (99–100). Just as Kanga affronted Rabbit's conventional notions of propriety by carrying her family in her pocket, so Tigger violates Rabbit's (and Piglet's and Eeyore's) boundaries with his bounciness: "'There's too much of him,' said Rabbit, 'that's what it comes down to'" (110).

Interestingly, the idea that Tigger should be "taught a lesson" (108) conjures up in Pooh's brain an association with Christopher Robin's lessons, which, as critics have pointed out (see Kutzer, 98), are educating him to succeed from chief of the forest to representative, and possibly colonial officer, of the British Empire. "'There's a thing called Twy-stymes,' [Pooh] said. 'Christopher Robin tried to teach it to me once, but it didn't'" (110). In the conflated colonizing projects here, Rabbit's plan to subdue Tigger is mixed up with the British educational system's plan to subdue little boys, which is mixed up with their "duty" to subdue India, which brings us back to Tigger.

Indeed Piglet soon brings up the question of Christopher Robin's attitude toward the plan to reduce Tigger to a "a Humble Tigger. . . . a Sad Tigger, a Melancholy Tigger, a Small and Sorry Tigger, an Oh-Rabbit-I-*am*-glad-to-see-you Tigger" (111). Piglet, who often feels small and vulnerable himself, is jolted out of his previous apprehensiveness regarding Tigger into something approaching Levinasian proximity: "I should hate him to go *on* being Sad,' said Piglet doubtfully." Piglet requires Rabbit's assurance that Christopher Robin will approve before he can feel "very glad about" participating in the unbouncing (112). Piglet resigns the unicity that, according to Levinas, responsibility for the Other would impose on him, in deference to an authority corrupted by Rabbit's sophistry.

Pooh, whose enjoyment of life keeps him aloof from the adventure from the moment Rabbit begins talking, is persuaded to join by a different aspect of imperialism. After giving himself over to the Forest's "gentle sounds, which all seemed to be saying to Pooh, 'Don't listen to Rabbit, listen to me'" (108), Pooh learns that Rabbit plans to lose Tigger at the North Pole, which Pooh had discovered earlier. Once again the dream of being recognized for his achievements as "*That* sort of Bear" (113) seduces Pooh, but he retains an endearing befuddlement about the purpose of what they are doing.

The event literalizes Rabbit's misguidedness, and ironically transforms Pooh's fogginess into clarity and ethical purpose. Like Pooh with Kanga earlier, Rabbit has assumed a mastery he does not possess. He must humbly acknowledge his vulnerability in order to emerge from "the mist." As before, it is only when his existence in being is threatened and his imperial projects thwarted by their own ethical shortcomings that a "Small and Sorry Rabbit" can attain the ethical relation toward the Other that allows him to participate happily in the community. In Levinasian fashion, this occurs when the hopelessly lost Rabbit suddenly hears the "loud yapping noises" that Tigger is making to find him as ethical speech: "And the Small and Sorry Rabbit rushed through the mist at the noise, and it suddenly turned into Tigger: a Friendly Tigger, a Grand Tigger, a Large and Helpful Tigger, a Tigger who bounced, if he bounced at all, in just the beautiful way a Tigger ought to bounce" (125–26).

Pooh, meanwhile, has found that once Rabbit and his unreliable understanding are gone, his honey pots call him home (123–24). Never believing in the mission, Pooh abandons it for Levinasian enjoyment, thereby magically freeing himself from the literal and ethical miasma from which Rabbit must be rescued. In so doing, Pooh also assumes protection of Piglet. After beginning the adventure by reproaching Pooh for not "listening to what Rabbit was saying" (110), Piglet ends it by "taking Pooh's paw" (119) and trusting to his friend's unerring sense of the comforts of home: the Levinasian dwelling, whose "gentleness that spreads over the face of things" (*TI* 155) presupposes and opens upon ethical relations.

The imperialism of the North Pole "expotition" is likewise subordinated to ethical relationships. First, Christopher Robin's definition of an "Expedition"—"A long line of everybody" with "Provision" (*Winnie-the-Pooh*, 110)—essentially transforms it into a picnic.[21] Then the discovery of the pole occurs when Pooh uses it to rescue Roo from drowning. Christopher Robin immediately realizes that this helpful instrument must be what they were looking for and sticks it "in the ground" with a "message" commemorating Pooh's feat (125). The mission, complete with Christopher Robin in his "Big Boots" (108) and the possibility of ambushes (115–16), does imitate imperialist explorations. Yet such exploration is also satirized, for the value of discovering an arbitrary point on the globe is harder to understand than the value of the ethical solicitude Pooh unconsciously displays.

As references to "Twy-stymes" and the North Pole discovery suggest, A. A. Milne's attitude to learning as a means of grasping control is ambivalent at best. For poststructuralist critics, his representations of companionship and play are sentimentalizing retreats from imperialism that both mystify its horrors and replicate them in distorting and manipulative representations of children. Thus Christopher Robin's "Big Boots" are associated with masculine conquest though he is feminized by most of his clothing. He is also empowered as a sort of colonial governor of the Forest, yet frequently appears insecure or even helpless (Connolly, 193–96). Altogether, A. A. Milne perpetuates and romanticizes imperialism so as to retreat to the comforts it provides, suppressing all otherness that might threaten them, including the Otherness of Christopher. Yet a Levinasian examination of Milne's consistent opposition of ethics to the supposedly empowering aspects of education suggests that he is preoccupied with the disconnections between saying and said, and with disrupting the self-interestedness of Being on every level.

This is most noticeable in *The House at Pooh Corner*, where Christopher Robin's advancing learning is a central theme.[22] It is introduced in the "Contradiction" (ix–x) that begins the volume, where A. A. Milne's persona represents himself as thwarting Christopher Robin's request for a Pooh story with mathematical story problems. "We find these very exciting," he says ironically, "and when we have been excited quite enough, we curl up and go to sleep" (ix). He and Christopher Robin and Pooh all dream about adventures; "but now, when we wake up in the morning, they are gone before we can catch hold of them" (x).

Here the Milne persona as child-colonizing tyrant seems evident. He recalls the Doctor in *When We Were Very Young* who deprives the Dormouse of his favorite flowers as a "cure" for illness, forcing him to dream of them instead ("The Dormouse and the Doctor," 66–70). Unlike the Doctor, however, Milne's persona includes himself among those who dream, does not seem partial to the treatment (the Doctor approves the boring chrysanthemums he administers), and does not insist on its efficacy, except insofar as he clearly feels compelled to slip it in "very quickly" (ix), before he can get started on the story Christopher Robin has requested. He also seems to need to atone for his conduct, offering readers "some of the other [adventures], all that we can remember now" (x), in place of those lost to studies, and insisting, as he will again at the end of the book, that "the Forest will always be there. . . . and anybody who is Friendly with Bears can find it."

Although the father accepts his duty to educate his son, he represents himself as conflicted by a painful ethical dilemma. Teaching math is portrayed as inevitably violent. Arithmetic is devoid of ethical content, as the trivialities of story problems concerning "cows going through a gate" (xi) suggest. In substituting story problems for story, the father moves not only from a discourse of sharing, play, and exchange to one of imposing knowledge, but also from a discourse concerned with ethical subjectivity—friendship, paternity, intimacy—to one that merely helps one grasp the world by comprehending and acquiring.

The same dilemma is evident in regard to letters. As we have seen, Rabbit, the most literate character in the books, is also the most xenophobic and bossy. Although Pooh's greedy enjoyment leads him to invade the spaces of others (the bees in chapter 1 of *Winnie-the-Pooh*, 1–19; Rabbit's home in chapter 2, 20–31), these incidents, like Rabbit's unbouncing, hurt mainly their originator. When Pooh's ethical sensibility is juxtaposed with "learning," Pooh's attunement to physical well-being keeps his focus on his immediate environment and the well-being of others while the "learned" are distracted by self-importance and preconceived understanding.[25]

This is in keeping with Levinas: "To fill, to satisfy, is the sense of the savor, and it is precisely to leap over the images, aspects, reflections or silhouettes, phantoms, phantasms, the hides of things that are enough for the consciousness of " (*OB*, 72). And,

> The immediacy of the sensible is the immediacy of enjoyment and its frustration. . . . It is not a gift of the heart, but of the bread from one's mouth. . . . It is the opening . . . of the doors of one's home . . . , a "welcoming of the wretched into your house" (Isaiah 58). The immediacy of the sensibility is the for-the-other of one's own materiality. . . . The proximity of the other is the immediate opening up for the other of the immediacy of enjoyment, the immediacy of taste, materialization of matter, altered by the immediacy of contact. (*OB* 74)

This is also consonant with theories linking infantile nourishment and care to early development of ethical subjectivity. Although Pooh is often selfish, he is always the first to respond to those in need, the one who cares most deeply and goes to the greatest lengths to help, or helps others do so. As is clear from his honey pots helping him take Piglet home when Rabbit is unbounced, Pooh's sensitivity and effectiveness are directly related to his enjoyment. In the end he opens his home not only to Piglet, who has given his to the displaced Owl, but also to everyone, since Christopher Robin leaves him the Forest to keep, and Pooh promises to welcome Christopher Robin (and implicitly all Friends of Bears) back unconditionally at any time (see

Recovering Arcadia, 66–70 for the themes of home and aging in the Pooh books).

Against this heroism, the irrelevance of Christopher Robin's spelling and geography is an ongoing theme. Milne directly satirizes the ethical claims of imperialist education when Eeyore intimidates Piglet with three sticks arranged to form an "A." "It means Learning, it means Education, it means all the things that you and Pooh haven't got. That's what A means," Eeyore explains (*The House at Pooh Corner*, 87). Eeyore's worship of learning is linked to Christopher Robin's education in a manner reminiscent of racist colonialist humor depicting "native" attempts to ape educated English ways:

> What does Christopher Robin do in the mornings? He learns. He becomes Educated. He instigorates—I *think* that is the word he mentioned, but I may be referring to something else—he instigorates Knowledge. In my small way I also, if I have the word right, am—am doing what he does." (89)

Whether Eeyore is seen here as symbolizing a younger child or a character like Lofting's Prince Bumpo, his admiration of English education at once glorifies imperialist power and justifies his own disempowerment. Like the malapropisms that Bumpo acquires at Oxford, Eeyore's pretentious "instigorates" shows that he cannot understand the learning he honors and is therefore fit only to be subordinate to the (soon to be) truly educated English child. [24]

Unlike Lofting, however, Milne does not leave the subject there. When Eeyore learns that Rabbit already knows all about the letter "A," he abruptly dismisses education: "'What *is* Learning?' asked Eeyore as he kicked his twelve sticks into the air. 'A thing *Rabbit* knows! Ha!'" (89). Milne implies that *all* imperialist glorifications of "Learning" may be suspect power plays. Notably, the previously disempowered Piglet has the last word in the exchange: "'I think *Violets* are rather nice,' said Piglet. And he laid his bunch in front of Eeyore and scampered off" (89). And the well spelled note from Christopher Robin that ends the chapter is significant in indicating not only his progress along an imperialist path, but also his consideration toward the animals (who now know where he goes in the mornings), and the poignancy of his impending permanent departure:

> "GONE OUT
> BACK SOON
> C-R." (90)

Once again, Milne clearly thematizes the conflict between the said, with its empowerment of the speaker, and the ethical impulse toward saying, whether it issues in giving violets or writing a reassuring note.

Milne's implicit parody of his own career through the compositions of Pooh, especially in *The House at Pooh Corner*, similarly explores the possibilities of ethics and empowerment in literary writing. From the beginning of the second volume, the inherent contradiction of saying and said in authorship becomes apparent: "a hum came suddenly into Pooh's head, which seemed to him a Good Hum, such as is Hummed Hopefully to Others" (2). Despite his good intentions, however, Pooh's egotism is evident both in his confidence that Eeyore will be encouraged by the song, and in its lyrics. As Piglet points out, these are specific to Pooh's experience: "it isn't the *toes* so much as the *ears*," Piglet explains; and as Dorothy Parker's Tonstant Weader points out, Milne's mild irony may not save them from nauseating inanity.

The dual nature of the song, well-meaning yet thoughtlessly selfish, becomes the dual nature of the do-gooding it inspires. Warmed by singing it, and imbued with feelings of Levinasian proximity to Eeyore, Pooh and Piglet conceive the notion of building a warming house for him (7), but build it out of his old house (9). After some anxiety and inconvenience, however, Eeyore brags about the house as if he had built it, and Pooh's and Piglet's relief is bolstered by proud singing of the very song that inspired their mistake in the first place (18).

Literary writing's links to self-empowerment and imperialism are explicitly explored in "The Search for Small" (Ch. 3, pp. 36–53), when Pooh and Piglet fall into a pit that is possibly their own old trap for "Heffalumps," dug in *Winnie-the-Pooh* (Ch. 5, pp. 54–68). Kutzer argues (101–02) that the Heffalump may be a veiled allusion to British imperialism in Africa, though she acknowledges that India is also a possibility. Whatever the case, the project of trapping a Heffalump clearly represents an imperialist attempt to domesticate the exotic along the lines of Rabbit's projects to drive away Kanga and Roo or unbounce Tigger. Like those projects, the Heffalump trap backfires. Pooh is trapped through his own greed when he gets his head stuck in the bait (a honey jar), and Piglet's preconceptions about Heffalumps lead to his humiliation when he mistakes the trapped Pooh for a real Heffalump (67–68).

In the more sophisticated *House at Pooh Corner*, Pooh and Piglet imagine that the Heffalump is trapping *them*, and Pooh thinks up a scene in which, after finding them in his trap, the Heffalump is verbally intimidated into losing the upper hand. While Pooh's desire to save himself and Piglet is ethical, his scene perpetuates imperialism by bringing an imaginary foreign danger to life, satirizing and defeating it, and aggrandizing the author. When Piglet steals Pooh's idea and embellishes on it, making *himself* the hero (45–46), the imperial power of authorship only becomes more apparent.

As often happens, however, life exposes the shortcomings of art. The play goes horribly wrong when the character Piglet thinks is the Heffalump refuses to say his lines and turns out to be Christopher Robin (49–51). Piglet is only saved from utter humiliation by the accidental ethical act of finding Rabbit's relation, Small (51–52). A playwright himself, Milne leaves open the question of whether or not a better play might have avoided imperialism, but the pitfalls of authorship are clear.

Indeed, it is significant that Pooh's only critical success in the book is a commission from/gift to Piglet (146) celebrating Piglet's heroism (142–44) in saving Pooh and Owl from Owl's house when it blew over. Effacing Pooh's own role in coming up with the escape plan and magnifying Piglet's bravery in executing it (152), this poem (147–48) meets with communal praise (155), only slightly undercut by our understanding of its mock-epic character.

Finally, in what may be read as a painful adumbration of Milne's own career, Eeyore usurps Pooh's position: "hitherto, as I was saying, all the Poetry in the Forest has been written by Pooh, a Bear with a Pleasing Manner but a Positively Startling Lack of Brain" (163). Beginning with this parody of what critics were already saying about Milne's own work (see Wullschläger, 194), Eeyore proceeds to a poem whose comic ineptitude gives rise to a recognizably Modernist self-consciousness (164–65; for Milne's dislike of Modernism, see Swann, 126–27).

Although this work meets with only forced applause (165), in what may nevertheless be a grudging nod to Modernism, the poem's halting awkwardness effectively conveys not only Eeyore's inability, but also the general impossibility of capturing in any said the love between Christopher Robin and the animals that he is leaving. Lines like "I ought / To begin again, / But it is easier to Stop. / Christopher Robin, good-bye" (164) disrupt the rhythm of the poem, preventing it from carrying the reader away, emotionally, but in doing so they call attention to the gulfs between saying and said, and between literary and mortal time, that Levinas also points to. Christopher Robin's verdict, that "POEM" is "a comforting sort of thing to have" (170), emphasizes the subordination of said to saying that has characterized all the literary ventures in both Pooh books.

Levinas and the Tonstant Weaders are right to warn against the dangers of self-indulgence in aesthetic experience, and such dangers are especially apparent in stories like these. Works like *The Velveteen Rabbit*, or *Little Women*, where Beth cares for a damaged doll before her own illness and death, show that fantasies about toys brought to life by a child's imagination, then abandoned as the child grows up, are heirs to the Victorian *topos* of the death of the child.[25] In an era where such deaths can no longer be represented as commonplaces,[26] the "deaths" of toys can still conjure up pity, purportedly for the abandoned toys and the child now facing the "shades of the prison-house," but actually indistinguishable from a narcissistic regret over our lost youth. Like the deaths of children in earlier literature, these turnings toward death may romanticize childhood, blurring the identity of the Other into a concept that allows us to revisit and comprehend our own lost childhoods as similar "tragedies."

Nor are poststructuralists wrong to suspect that sentimentalizing in such works may extend to kindred, imperialistic conceptualizations. To idealize Western childhood requires at least ignoring the inequitably distributed wealth that makes it possible; when unethical aspects of that wealth are part of the childhood portrayed, they are often reduced to sentimental concepts. Thus from the slaves who devote themselves to the dying Little Eva to the dim-witted, mammy-like maid of *Raggedy Ann Stories*,[27] African Americans are often patronizingly infantilized in American romanticizations of childhood, and it is right to beware similar distortions of Others underpinning any privileged society and its representations.

If such views are themselves to avoid conceptual reductions of Others, however, exegesis must listen, in a Levinasian sense, to the traces of Face conveyed through the ethical interrelations among the child character, the toy characters with whom he is interdependent, the author who represents this material, and ourselves. When one listens for such traces in the Pooh books, it is clear that the dangers of reducing the Other to an extension of oneself, whether by telling the wrong kind of story or by changing otherness into sameness, is a central anxiety of the text. To counter such dangers, Milne offers Levinasian remedies. Repeatedly in his books, enjoyment, home, family, give rise to the responsiveness to ethical accusation that, in turn, designates the characters as uniquely necessary to the Other. Thus whatever the merit of the Tonstant Weaders' criticism, whatever sentimentalism or imperialism Milne's said may contain, *Winnie-the-Pooh* and *The House at Pooh Corner* also contain their own corrective to such faults. Conceptual grasping results in "unbouncing," a loss of self that can only be repaired by recurrence to the ethical grounding afforded by the Forest world. Fortunately, this world is always accessible to those who are "Friendly with Bears" and respectful of the ethical subjects who give them life.

NOTES

1. See Edward Said, *Orientalism* (New York: Pantheon, 1978). The seminal work applying Said's ideas to children's literature is Perry Nodelman's "The Other: Orientalism, Colonialism, and Children's Literature," *Children's Literature Association Quarterly* 17, no. 1 (1992): 29–35, henceforth cited as "The Other." Although not operative in all recent examinations of children's literature, these ideas continue to be central to Nodelman, *The Hidden Adult: Defining Children's Literature* (Baltimore, MD: Johns Hopkins University Press, 2008), cited hereafter as *Hidden Adult*, and to Daphne Kutzer, *Empire's Children: Empire and Imperialism in Classic British Children's Books* (New York and London: Garland, 2000), cited hereafter as Kutzer. Robert Hemmings links imperialism in children's books from the "golden age" of children's literature with nostalgia and sexual repression in "A Taste of Nostalgia: Children's Books from the Golden Age—Carroll, Grahame, and Milne," *Children's Literature* 35 (2007): 54–79. Peter Hunt, *An Introduction to Children's Literature* (Oxford: Oxford University Press,

1994), hereafter cited as Hunt, while viewing the relationship of children's literature to culture as highly complex, stresses the potential for adult control over children's literature to be limiting or manipulative (1–26). Seth Lerer's *Children's Literature: A Reader's History, from Aesop to Harry Potter* (Chicago and London: University of Chicago Press, 2008) asserts that children's literature "is . . . a kind of system, one whose social and aesthetic value is determined out of the relationships among those who make, market, and read books. No single work of literature is canonical; rather, works attain canonical status through their participation in a system of literary values" (7, and see n. 14, p. 338, for the implicit imperialism in the notion of "system"). One may infer from this that books with canonical status, such as the Pooh books, owe it to the system's imperialism. Interestingly, Lerer's work (cited hereafter as Lerer) proceeds to make cogent cultural and historical observations in which the notion of "system" virtually disappears. Finally, even critics less concerned with imperialism or other repressive systems may deprecate and oversimplify Milne's nostalgia: see Paula T. Connolly, "The Marketing of Romantic Childhood: Milne, Disney, and a Very Popular Stuffed Bear," in *Literature and the Child: Romantic Continuations, Postmodern Contestations*, ed. James Holt McGavran (Iowa City, IA: University of Iowa Press, 1999), 188–207, especially 201–02. (This will be cited hereafter as Connolly.) In her *Winnie-the-Pooh and The House at Pooh Corner: Recovering Arcadia*, Twayne's Masterwork Studies No. 156, Robert Lecker, gen. ed. (New York: Twayne, 1995), 4–5, 47–50, 96–100, Connolly complicates this view by suggesting Milne may be satirizing his audience and their expectations through his supposed sentimentalism, but she also points out that the comforts of Pooh's world reflect a sheltered, privileged life (100–03). Further, she reflects darkly on Milne's "control" of Christopher Robin's world, 44. (This work will be cited hereafter as *Recovering Arcadia*.) Though adopting a more traditional historical approach, Jackie Wullschläger, *Inventing Wonderland: The Lives and Fantasies of Lewis Carroll, Edward Lear, M. M. Barrie, Kenneth Grahame and A. A. Milne* (New York: Free, 1995), hereafter cited as Wullschläger, also views Milne as escapist and backward-looking (see 175–99).

2. Kutzer, 103–104. See A. A. Milne, *Winnie-the-Pooh*, illustrated by Ernest H. Shepard (New York: Dutton, 1945 [1926]) and *The House at Pooh Corner*, illustrated by Ernest H. Shepard (New York: Dutton, 1945 [1928]). These will hereafter be cited as *Winnie-the-Pooh* and *The House at Pooh Corner*, respectively. Despite Lofting's gifts as a writer and his antipathy toward greed, war, and cruelty, instances of racial and cultural "insensitivity" in his works are pervasive and too blatant for any informed reader to miss (see, for example, n. 24, below).

3. Dorothy Parker, "Far from Well," in Dorothy Parker, *Constant Reader* (New York: Viking 1970 [*The New Yorker*, Oct. 20, 1928]), 100–01; 101 cited.

4. For the Algonquin Round Table, see James R. Gaines, *Wit's End: Days and Nights of the Algonquin Round Table* (New York: Harcourt, Brace, Jovanovich, 1977) and Margaret Case Harriman, *The Vicious Circle: The Story of the Algonquin Round Table* (New York: Rinehart, 1951).

5. A. A. Milne, *Autobiography* (New York: Dutton, 1939) 281–82 (hereafter cited as *Autobiography*). This defense is cited in *Recovering Arcadia*, 15; and see Connolly's discussion of anti-sentimentalism in the critical reception of the Pooh books, 14–16. See also Thomas Burnett Swann, *A. A. Milne*, Twayne's English Authors Series, Sylvia E. Bowman, ed. (New York: Twayne, 1971), 133–34 (this work will hereafter be cited as Swann) and Wullschläger, 197–98.

6. For such concerns, see Richard J. Bernstein, *The New Constellation: The Ethico-Political Horizons of Modernity/Postmodernity* (Cambridge, MA: MIT Press, 1992), John McGowan, *Postmodernism and Its Critics* (Ithaca, NY: Cornell, University Press, 1991), and Charles Taylor, *The Ethics of Authenticity* (Cambridge, MA: Harvard University Press, 1992). For similar discussions of problematic assumptions in poststructural theory, see pp. 4–8 of Donald R. Wehrs's Introduction to this volume, and "Levinasian Criticism and Theories of Canon Formation," 172–74, in Lorna Wood, "Emmanuel Levinas and the American Renaissance Canon," in *Levinas and Nineteenth-Century Literature: Ethics and Otherness from Romanticism through Realism*, ed. Donald R. Wehrs and David P. Haney (Newark, DE: University of Delaware Press, 2009), 166–206. Uses of Levinas to modify poststructuralist assump-

tions include Peter Atterton and Matthew Calarco, eds., *Radicalizing Levinas*, SUNY series in Radical Social and Political Theory, Roger S. Gottlieb, ed. (Albany: State University of New York Press, 2010), especially Judith Butler, "Precarious Life," 3–19, and Diane Perpich, "Levinas, Feminism, and Identity Politics," 21–39 (hereafter cited as Perpich); in the same volume, Edith Wyschogrod, "Levinas' Other and the Culture of the Copy" (137–52) explores points of correspondence and dissonance between Levinas and developments in cognitive science.

Cognitive science and evolutionary biology offer evidence and explanations for ethical human subjectivity and behavior, non-totalizing impulses, communal organization, and altruistic goals that involve the imposition of limits on ourselves as well as others; these fields also suggest that reading and education influence ethical human development. See Marco Iacoboni, *Mirroring People* (New York: Farrar, Straus and Giroux, 2008), hereafter cited as Iacoboni; Giacomo Rizzolatti and Corrado Sinigaglia, *Mirrors In the Brain—How Our Minds Share Actions and Emotions*, trans. Frances Anderson (Oxford: Oxford University Press, 2008), hereafter cited as Rizzolatti and Sinigaglia; and Andrew N. Meltzoff and Wolfgang Prinz, eds., *The Imitative Mind: Development, Evolution, and Brain Bases*, (Cambridge: Cambridge University Press, 2002), hereafter cited as Meltzoff and Prinz. Iacoboni explains connections between phenomenological theories and the understanding of consciousness made possible by the discovery of neurons linking action and perception (16–17). Paul Bloom, *Descartes' Baby: How the Science of Child Development Explains What Makes Us Human* (New York: Basic, 2004), especially 131–32, 139–51, addresses the role of culture and reason in moral decision making (this will hereafter be cited as Bloom). Patrick Colm Hogan, *What Literature Teaches Us about Emotion*, Studies in Emotion and Social Interaction, 2nd Series, Keith Oatley and Antony S. R. Manstead, eds. (Cambridge: Cambridge University Press, 2011) stresses the roles of attachment and empathy in human emotions and ethics, and the ways in which literature and its reception support cognitive models of emotional responses.

7. An example is Kutzer's parenthetical allusion to "the black servant in Thackeray's *Vanity Fair*" as, like Lofting's Prince Bumpo, "one in a long string of native figures who aspire—comically—to be white" (84). While this Thackeray character is a racist stereotype, Kutzer's reading of colonialism in the simplified terms of victim/oppressor seems responsible for reducing a powerful mixed-race heiress to a mere "servant."

8. Christopher Milne, *The Enchanted Places* (New York: Dutton, 1975), 27. Hereafter this work is cited as C. Milne.

9. D. W. Winnicott, *Playing and Reality* (London: Tavistock, 1971) (hereafter cited as Winnicott) explicitly mentions "Winnie the Pooh" (*sic*), (xi, 40). There are, of course, many differences among the theories of these three thinkers, and many other thinkers who might be cited. Winnicott's naming and explorations of the "paradox" of the transitional object (it is both internal and external) are fundamental; Klein is the analyst to whom his thinking on this point seems most indebted; and Kristeva is the most prominent contemporary thinker who has elaborated the significance and mechanisms of pre-Oedipal development. See Melanie Klein, *Love, Guilt and Reparation and Other Works 1921-1945, The Writings of Melanie Klein*, ed. Roger Money Kyrle, in collaboration with Betty Joseph et al., Vol. 1 (London: Karnac, 1992); Julia Kristeva, *Melanie Klein*, trans. Ross Guberman, European Perspectives, Lawrence D. Kritzman, ed. (New York: Columbia University Press, 2001); *Tales of Love*, trans. Leon S. Roudiez (New York: Columbia University Press, 1987), especially "Freud and Love: Treatment and Its Discontents," 21–56; and *Powers of Horror: An Essay on Abjection*, trans. Leon S. Roudiez (New York: Columbia University Press, 1982), especially 1–72. Drawing on Winnicott, Jessica Benjamin has explored "intrasubjectivity" at length: see her *Like Subjects, Love Objects* (New Haven: Yale University Press, 1995), especially 44. Other explorations have distinguished between "primary" and "secondary" transitional objects: see Ryan Lamothe, "The Birth of Reality: Psychoanalytic Developmental Considerations," *American Journal of Psychotherapy*, 54, no. 3 (summer, 2000): 355–371. The real Pooh would have been secondary, appearing after separation from the nursing dyad and assisting social relationships. For other recent studies recognizing the importance of objects in psychic life, see Sherry Turkle, ed., *Evocative Objects: Things We Think With* (Cambridge, MA: MIT Press, 2007), hereafter cited as Turkle.

10. The concepts of "the feminine" in Levinas and psychoanalysis cannot be adequately addressed in the confines of this chapter. I merely reproduce Levinas's and Winnicott's uses of

them here. Perpich defends Levinas's contribution to the debate over identity politics by opposing Levinas's emphasis on singularity to his "cultural and religious biases" (24), including his
patriarchal representations of women. Claire Elise Katz, *Levinas, Judaism, and the Feminine:
The Silent Footsteps of Rebecca* (Bloomington and Indianapolis, IN: Indiana University Press,
2003), hereafter cited as Katz, treats the issue more fully.

11. This insight is similarly articulated by Caroline A. Jones in "The Painting In the Attic,"
in Turkle, 233–42, especially 242. Like Levinas in *MS*, Turkle juxtaposes the insight with an
introductory reference to Bergson (Turkle cites *Matter and Memory* on p. 232). The neurophysiological basis for such an intermediary realm between cultural productions and their
audience is currently being explored and confirmed by cognitive science (see Meltzoff and
Prinz, Rizzolatti and Sinigaglia, Iacoboni, and Bloom).

12. I do not intend to minimize the grounds of disagreement between Levinas and psychoanalysis, although psychoanalysis has significantly rethought much of what Levinas characterizes as its insistence on "fables" as "unequivocal" truth and continues to do so. For a
consideration of the relationship of Levinas to psychoanalysis in the context of the illumination
both ways of thinking bring to education, see Sharon Todd, *Learning from the Other: Levinas,
Psychoanalysis, and Ethical Possibilities in Education* (Albany: State University of New York
Press, 2003); n. 21, p. 149, cites *CCP* 40. Like my own, Todd's work links Levinas with
Kleinian psychoanalysis: see "Learning from Klein and Dick," 32–37. Edwin E. Gantt and
Richard N. Williams, eds., *Psychology for the Other* (Pittsburgh, PA: Duquesne University
Press, 2002), attempts to use Levinas to counteract "moral relativism" in psychology. See
especially Richard A. Cohen, "Maternal Psyche," 32–64; James E. Faulconer, "Levinas: The
Unconscious and the Reason of Obligation," 102–17; Suzanne Barnard, "Diachrony, *Tuché*,
and the Ethical Subject in Levinas and Lacan," 160–81. The title, "Maternal Psyche," derives
from *OB* (see Katz, 2–3, 126–55, for a consideration of its significance). In regard to the
maternal dimension of the psyche in Levinas, the discovery of cognitive science that perception
and imitation are neurologically linked, and therefore a "rhythmic interaction with another
would . . . resemble, in form, the infant's interaction with her own body" (Marcel Kinsbourne,
"The Role of Imitation in Body Ownership and Mental Growth," in Meltzoff and Prinz,
311–30; 324 cited) may possibly be a step toward providing a neurophysiological basis for the
Levinasian experience of Substitution.

13. Margery Williams, *The Velveteen Rabbit, or How Toys Become Real*, Illustrated by
William Nicholson (Garden City, NJ and New York: Doubleday, 1922), rpt. *A Celebration of
Women Writers*, http://digital.library.upenn.edu/women/williams/ rabbit/rabbit.html, accessed
July 10, 2011.

14. Tracy Gleason, "Murray: The Stuffed Bunny," in Turkle, 171–77 (hereafter cited as
Gleason), is an autobiographical account of the author's relationship to her younger sister's
stuffed bunny that describes these same emotional attachments to a loved child's special toy
occurring without the mediation of literary fantasy. She keeps a picture of Murray on her desk,
next to a picture of her husband: for her, Murray, too, has a face (176, and see photos, 171,
177). Perhaps intuitions of the selfhood attained by such objects underlie Winnicott's own
comparison of the classification of transitional objects to that of faces: the transitional object "is
universal and has infinite variety. It is rather similar to the description of the human face when
we describe one in terms of shape and eyes and nose and mouth and ears, but the fact remains
that no two faces are exactly alike and very few are even similar. Two faces may be similar
when at rest, but as soon as there is animation they become different" (xii).

15. Oscar Wilde is said to have remarked, "One must have a heart of stone to read the death
of Little Nell without laughing."

16. Connolly (189) cites p. 202 of A. A. Milne's "The End of a Chapter," from *By Way of
Introduction* (London: Methuen, 1929), to show that Milne associates the childhood he portrays
with his own. In *Recovering Arcadia*, 100–03, she contrasts Christopher Milne's and A. A.
Milne's childhoods at more length to illustrate this point. See also Humphrey Carpenter, *Secret
Gardens: A Study of the Golden Age of Children's* Literature (Boston: Houghton Mifflin,
1985), 192 (this will be cited hereafter as Carpenter). Implicit evidence for the link between A.
A. Milne, his brother Ken, and Piglet and Pooh, respectively, can be found in passages like the
following from *Autobiography*: "On another occasion . . . we found a big boy knocking about a

smaller friend. Ken thought that we could appeal to the big boy's better nature. I thought that we should be late for tea as it was" (22). Pooh's simple optimism and Piglet's cowardice are clearly reproduced in the tone and humor.

17.   For Milne's career, see Swann; also Wullschläger, 175–99.

18.   Hints of how such blending may occur ethically are provided in Gleason: "When [my sister] Shayna is upset, I watch as Murray dries her tears, and I am somewhat taken aback to discover that I, too, am comforted by his presence" (173); and "I could no more walk past Murray as he lies in an uncomfortable position than I could ignore my sister's pleas to play with her or the cat's meows for food" (175). Gleason also describes other family members projecting redemptive qualities of their own imaginative concoction onto Murray (perceiving him as "a kindred spirit," for example) without impinging on Shayna's play world. See also C. Milne, Ch. 12, "The Toys," 76–79, for his account of the role of the Pooh characters in his and his family's world, and Wullschläger, 180–81. It is possible that "the [Pooh] books were a way for [Christopher's] father to create the fantasy of a father-son relationship to compensate for reality" (*Recovering Arcadia*, 73 and 104, 104 cited), and to the extent that this false concept is present in the text, it may justly evoke criticism; such concepts should not be assumed to dominate Milne's aesthetic, however. For instance, Kutzer asserts that "the adult voice, not the child voice, has control of the fantasy stories, the reader, and Christopher Robin himself" [96]. For a kinder view of the relationship between A. A. Milne's inadequacies as a parent and his work for children, see Carpenter, 201. For Shepard's alterations to his models, see Swann, 90, and *Recovering Arcadia*, 129, n. 7.

19.   See *Winnie-the-Pooh*, 108–09, and Shepard's illustrations, 109, 113, 115 136, 141, 143. A. A. Milne also associates boots with aspirations to manliness in *When We Were Very Young* ([New York]: Dutton, 1943 [1924]), hereafter cited by its title: see "Happiness," 4, and "Bad Sir Brian Botany," 92–94.

20.   See C. Milne, 77, and *Recovering Arcadia*, 78, for Milne's choice of new Pooh characters. Yet Kutzer claims, "Although it may seem a stretch to consider Kanga and Tigger as figures of empire, I would argue that it is not a stretch. It certainly is not conscious on Milne's part—the stories were concocted based upon real toys the real Christopher Robin possessed, after all—but that is precisely the point. By the twenties empire is so interwoven into British life, social and private as well as political and public, that it makes an almost unavoidable appearance in children's nurseries and in children's stories" (99).

21.   Connolly, 188–200, sees the North Pole expedition as part of Christopher Robin's broader alienation from romantic affinity with nature, which, in turn, is part of Milne's "deconstruction of Romantic notions of childhood" (195). In *Recovering Arcadia* (97–98) she interprets it as a satire of pretensions to mastery. Kutzer, 102, notes that it was "usually" "native bearers" or "working-class underlings"—here the animals—who carried the provisions on such expeditions; however no provisions appear in the illustrations, and when Christopher Robin suggests "that we ought to eat all our Provisions now, so that we shan't have so much to carry" (117), each member of the expedition, including Christopher Robin (and excluding only Eeyore, as usual), unwraps his or her own supply.

22.   I therefore disagree with Connolly's argument in *Recovering Arcadia*, 45–47, that this disruption in the "Contradiction" at the beginning of *The House at Pooh Corner* (ix–x) is a flaw.

23.   Connolly, 194–200, notes the same contrast between characters of "brain" (including Christopher Robin) and Pooh in terms of Milne's "deconstruction" of Romantic ideals (see n. 19, above). See also her *Recovering Arcadia*, 78–83. Carpenter notes Pooh's visionary quality, humility, and selflessness (207), and see Swann, 130.

24.   See, for example the following from Hugh Lofting, *The Voyages of Doctor Dolittle* (Philadelphia and New York: Lippincott, 1950 [1922]). The African Prince Bumpo is addressing Doctor Dolittle in the presence of the English child, Tommy Stubbins:

"You are a man of great studiosity. To see the world in your company is an opportunity not to be sneezed upon. No, no, indeed."
"How did you like the life at Oxford?" asked the Doctor.

"Oh, passably, passably," said Bumpo. "I liked it all except the algebra and the shoes. The algebra hurt my head and the shoes hurt my feet. I threw the shoes over a wall as soon as I got out of the college quadrilateral this morning; and the algebra I am happily forgetting very fast—I liked Cicero—Yes, I think Cicero's fine—so simultaneous. By the way, they tell me his son is rowing for our college next year—charming fellow" (150).

Bumpo is a recurring, consistently stereotyped character throughout the Dolittle books.

25.   See Louisa May Alcott, *Little Women, or Meg, Jo, Beth and Amy*, Introduction by Anna Quindlen (Boston: Little, Brown, 1994 [1868]), 41, 379–85, 423–29.

26.   A. A. Milne's "Sneezles," in *Now We Are Six*, illustrated by Ernest H. Shepard (New York: Dutton, 1961 [1927]), 14–16, even reduces childhood illness to nonsense words.

27.   Harriet Beecher Stowe, *Uncle Tom's Cabin*, Afterword by John William Ward (New York: Signet, 1966), 314–21; Johnny Gruelle, *Raggedy Ann Stories* (Chicago: Volland, 1918), rpt. *Google Books*, accessed July 12, 2011.

Chapter Four

Fidelity to Sexual Difference

Feminism, Levinas, and Duras's The Ravishing of Lol Stein

Zahi Zalloua

If questions of exemplarity (the belief that literature teaches us through ex-amples and counter-examples) once dominated, if not exhausted, ethical crit-icism, a poststructuralist ethics of reading rethinks what it means to be faith-ful, linking fidelity less to the interpretation of a work's content or message than to the reader's receptivity and responsiveness to it. Attesting to the "singularity of literature," to borrow Derek Attridge's suggestive formula-tion, means vigilantly resisting literature's conflation with moral philosophy. And disentangling an ethical concern in a literary work from its universalist aspiration is perhaps the most distinctive feature of a poststructuralist literary ethics. An ethics of reading, articulated in the above terms, owes much to Levinas's philosophy of the Other. Analogously related to the self's exposure to the Other, characterized in Levinasian terms by asymmetry and excess, the reader's relation to the work takes the form of an interpellation. In the act of reading, the reader confronts a "double bind," a hermeneutic hesitation be-tween two conflicting injunctions. The first is to thematize or make sense of the work's aesthetic otherness, that is, to adhere to the rules of literary dis-course: to conform to the protocols of commentary in order to communicate the text's meaning to oneself and one's community of readers. The second, however, is to attend to the work's inventiveness—its seductive refractori-ness—to recognize that the attempt to give meaning and the appeal to con-textual markers (cultural, historical, or authorial) might very well elucidate aspects of a literary work but can never exhaust that meaning nor fully meet or answer its demands.[1]

In this chapter, I propose to explore how Marguerite Duras's 1964 novel *The Ravishing of Lol Stein* illustrates and enacts such a double bind within a feminist interpretive framework. In her novel, Duras frames the problem of interpretation around the issue of fidelity to sexual difference. Not surprisingly, her text has caught the attention of feminist readers, and has often produced tumultuous exchanges regarding, in particular, the validity of psychoanalytic readings.[2] The very subject matter of the novel is open to dispute: Is it the character of Lol Stein, who desires to perpetually relive the night of her abandonment or/as ravishment at the ball of T. Beach? Or is it Jacques Hold, the narrator/lover of Lol, who obsessively desires to know his beloved *object*? By choosing a *male* narrator talking about a "mad" woman, Duras seems to engage in a "feminist" critique of previous male narratives. Radically rewriting the male fantasy narrative about female madness—the paradigmatic example being the surrealist André Breton's 1929 autobiographic novel, *Nadja*—Duras, for many of her feminist readers, foregrounds the irreducibility of Lol's sexual difference to Jacques's scopic drive.[3] The narrator's own surname suggests the phallocentric wish *to hold*—that is, to contain, to pin down—the unruly feminine.[4] On this reading, Levinas's philosophy of the Other provides the reader with a useful grammar with which to read the ethical resistance of Duras's female protagonist. To recall, in *Totality and Infinity*, Levinas locates the ethical moment in the face-to-face encounter with the Other, which he describes as a primordial moment of cognitive frustration—since the other's face "exceed[s] *the idea of the other in me*"—that brings into question the autonomy, spontaneity, and self-sufficiency of the self (*TI* 50).

Extrapolating from Levinas, we could say that the ethical moment of reading unfolds in the recognition that Lol (as the feminine Other) exceeds *the idea of* Lol that Jacques reproduces but ultimately fails to master in his narrative of her ravishing. This skeletal reading of *The Ravishing of Lol Stein* would be typical of the early reception of Levinas in literary studies, which always risked instrumentalizing and reducing the disruptive Levinasian encounter with the Other to a series of predictable, familiar, and easily translatable pathetic scenes. I propose an alternative Levinasian reading of Lol/*The Ravishing of Lol Stein*, one that draws more heavily on Levinas's other philosophical masterpiece, *Otherwise than Being*. In this later work, Levinas, implicitly responding to the concerns Derrida expressed in "Violence and Metaphysics," moves away from the face-to-face encounter as the paradigmatic ethical scene to the question of language and the possibility of ethical figuring. Levinas comes to realize that the ethical can signify within the realm of representation, that the language of ontology does not preclude nor exhaust what he calls the "ethical Saying." Contrasting Saying (*le Dire*) with the Said (*le Dit*)—"the birth place of ontology" (*OB* 42)—Levinas argues that Saying "is not a modality of cognition" (*OB* 48) nor an "exchange of information" (*OB* 92). Reminiscent of the "phatic" function of language in its insistence on intersubjectivity—the contact between speaker and addressee without the transfer of information—Saying expresses nothing but the desire to communicate. Levinas is keenly aware, however, of the paradox that as soon as one utters something, once meaning happens, one enters into the domain of the Said. Yet, he does not stop there. Refusing the false choice between Saying and the Said, between pure alterity and comprehension, respect and violence, Levinas advocates a kind of skepticism, an "endless critique" (*OB* 44), or "an incessant unsaying of the said" (*OB* 181). From this Levinasian optic, then, the ethical question no longer lies in (the determination of) the author's gender politics but in the reader's attentiveness to Lol's Saying, a Saying that, as we shall see, invariably passes through the scene of language/Jacques's narrative.

This Levinasian approach to Duras's novel allows us as well to entertain the possibility of a different relation between Levinas and feminism. What Levinas actually said about women or the feminine—not unlike his reflections on literature[5] —often disappointed and disconcerted his most sympathetic of interpreters. Feminist theorists by no means agree in their assessment of Levinas's relevance for feminism.[6] While some find that Levinas's philosophy of the Other opens up the possibility for a radical ethics of sexual difference,[7] other critics view Levinas's ethical model as anathema to feminism.[8] It is primarily *Totality and Infinity* that is most frequently evoked and invoked in these debates: sexual difference and its claim to a *feminine* experience stand in an uneasy relation with, or simply in opposition to, the ostensibly un-gendered space of the face-to-face encounter. Reading Duras's feminist novel with the later Levinas of *Otherwise than Being* aims to reframe this debate, asking to what extent a feminist reading depends on the reader's ability to share Lol's "experience," and to what extent the complexity of the male narrator's writing of Lol, that is, his writing of her ravishing and the ravishing of his writing, undermines any straightforward identification with the female character, or with the "feminine," more generally.

THE SAYING OF DURAS/LOL OR THE SAID OF JACQUES

Duras's choice of a male narrator raises an immediate concern for the reader; no conflation between author and narrator will take place in this novel. The original French reveals the gender of the narrator in the second paragraph; in the English, the gender indeterminacy is prolonged for a few pages. Does this information authorize, or at the very least orient the reader towards, a feminist reading? Even if we assume that it does (appeals to extra-textual or biographical information about Duras's strong feminist leanings are typically deployed as justification for such an approach), just what a feminist reading of *The Ravishing of Lol Stein* would actually entail remains nonetheless unclear.

In *Gynesis: Configurations of Woman and Modernity*, Alice Jardine firmly asserts that the true subject of Duras's novel is Lol Stein. To give Jacques Hold Lol's place as the real matter of her story, that is, to claim that the novel is really about the teller of the tale—as does Jacques Lacan, for example, when he states in his "Homage to Marguerite Duras" that Jacques Hold is not "only displaying the machinery" of the novel but is "one of its mainsprings"[9] —amounts to violently silencing the feminine voice, turning a deaf ear to the Saying of Duras and Lol. Jardine takes issue in particular with Lacanian hermeneutics, which she considers non/anti-feminist, finding Lacan's comments and his identification with Jacques Hold highly problematic.[10] Critical of Jacques Hold/Lacan's reduction of Duras's otherness to Lacan's master discourse of the Same, of his arrogance and usurpation of Lol/Duras's story (Jacques Hold writes, "I shall relate my own story of Lol Stein" [4], while Lacan marvels, "Marguerite Duras knows, without me, what I teach" [18]), Jardine affirms that a feminist reader needs to identify with Lol (the woman) and not Jacques (the man): "for the feminist reader, this book written by a feminist has only one subject: Lol V. Stein" (175). Rather than reducing Lol, as Lacan does, to an object of psychoanalytical discourse, perceiving Lol *only* as a "perfect case of clinical delirium,"[11] Jardine sees in Duras's representation of Lol another kind of example, a call for a new kind of subjectivity: "For the feminist reader . . . the representation of Lol as a new kind of subject-in-the-world is *categorical*" (176, emphasis added).

It is at times unclear, however, whether Jardine's feminist reader is gender-specific, and whether her feminist reading presupposes its own version of the order of the Same.

> For to the extent that one always reads . . . through identification, the woman reader has most likely been identifying, not with either of the Jacques, but rather with two highly visible if improbable others: Lol and Marguerite Duras. . . . For the feminist reader, it is Lol V. Stein—the entire name—which forms the potential space of the text. (174–75)

Jardine's conflation here of the feminist reader and the woman reader (it seems that the feminist reader of *The Ravishing of Lol Stein* is the woman reader who "correctly" actualizes the text's potential by identifying with Lol) unfortunately ignores or sidesteps questions pertaining to the male reader of Duras's novel: Can a male reader genuinely identify with Lol's subjectivity? Or to put it in Levinasian parlance, can a male reader read *The Ravishing of Lol Stein otherwise than being* (where "being" here represents a male [phallo]-centric interpretive mode)? Can the male reader actually read not *as* a woman (which would arguably efface sexual difference) but *like* a feminist?[12] Although it is unquestionable that Duras writes "about" women,[13] it is doubtful that she writes *only* for women, or more importantly, that her textual practice or *écriture* does not also have a transformative effect on her male audience. The fact that she chooses a male narrator to tell the story of a woman might alert us to the hermeneutic complexities that await us as readers.

In sharp contrast to Jardine, Martha Noel Evans does not dismiss Jacques Hold as the narrator of the story. Quite the contrary, Evans posits Jacques's narration as Duras's true target: "Duras uses this male narrator as a kind of front: first to present and explore the characteristics of traditional male narrative and then to dramatize the undoing of that very narrative."[14] Likewise, Laurie Edson does not formulate her feminist reading around the imperative of sexual identification, but advocates a feminist reading which paradoxically removes Lol as the *subject* of Duras's novel. The matter of the novel is not "the story of the human subject that is Lol, but the story of the way any story of a human subject is mediated by cultural codes—language, desire, discourses of power, and epistemology itself."[15] What the reader confronts in the *Ravishing of Lol Stein*, then, is not a set of characters with whom one may or may not identify, but a hegemonic system of representation. Consequently Lol as an unmediated representation is unavailable to the reader; what emerges in Duras's novel is not a subject in its own right (Lol as speaking subject) but a feminine figure produced by Jacques's male desire. Rather than creating a space for the Saying of Lol to be heard (letting the female Other speak in her own voice), Jacques gives the reader the Said of Lol (*his meaning* of Lol).

Edson sees as futile any attempt to recuperate Lol's voice from a psychoanalytical male discourse, which, according to Jardine, has problematically divorced the sign from the referent, reducing Lol to a trope ("the figure of Lol . . . is the figure of femininity—not the representation of a woman" [173]). She is more interested in examining the ways in which Duras's novel *mimes* the traditional male narrative in order to disclose and deconstruct its patterns of "patriarchal thinking—in particular, assumptions of objectifiability and knowability."[16] For Edson, Duras exploits male logic only to undermine it from within. Thus, despite the fact that both Jardine and Edson approach *The Ravishing of Lol Stein* from a feminist perspective (both recognize that men speaking about and for women has become a suspicious activity), they differ radically in their assessment of Jacques Hold. Jardine wants to rescue Duras's novel from the appropriating impulses of Lacanian psychoanalysis and to refocus attention on what she sees as the true subject of the story, Lol V. Stein. Edson, on the other hand, denies the possibility of any direct access to Lol, turning her focus instead to the textual mediation at work in the novel. Yet it is unclear to what extent their critique of male narrators is generalizable and applicable to male readers. Jardine's feminism—which gives primacy to sexual identification[17] —seems to put into question all male readings of Lol's story: female experience and desire are inaccessible to "bodies-coded-as-male," to the male epistemological gaze. Indeed, two male perspectives are explicitly discredited by Jardine: Jacques Hold and Jacques Lacan (176). Although Edson intentionally avoids formulating an essentialist definition of feminism (an essentialism based on sexual difference, for instance), she does seem paradoxically to essentialize and totalize the male perspective. Situating Jacques Hold firmly within an allegedly monolithic literary male tradition, she proceeds to challenge his "male logic" systematically. Edson warns us that this all-powerful male logic governs even some ("contaminated") feminist readings of *The Ravishing of Lol Stein*. She argues, for example, that Evans's reading, though similar in devoting much attention to Jacques's role in the novel, accepts too readily his authority: "How can Evans know anything at all about what Lol wants or does, except through Jacques's mediation, which she herself has already called into question?"[18] In other words, Evans severely undermines her feminist argument once she diverts it from her oppositional reading and speaks as if Jacques Hold's words were truths, that is, unmediated representations of Lol's psychic state.

Like Jardine, Edson associates the problematic of male desire with psychoanalytical discourse, reinforcing in turn the difference between feminism and psychoanalysis. But according to Edson, the fundamental problem with a psychoanalytical reading of Duras's novel does not lie in a (mis)identification between the reader and the main subject of the novel (indeed, she even credits Lacan for having correctly recognized the primacy of Jacques Hold in the story of Lol: "It is not surprising that psychoanalyst Jacques Lacan... understood the central character to be Jacques Hold, not Lol"[19]). It lies instead in an uncritical analysis of Lol, one that does not take into consideration Hold's vested interest in his representation of Lol: "Any such psychoanalytical reading of Lol can only duplicate Jacques's (mis)reading of her."[20]

If Lacanian analysts indulged in abstraction with their accounts of Lol as a figure of the Real, Edson, for her part, transfigures Jacques Hold into a figure of phallocentric mediation, though she could have taken her type of feminist criticism to its logical conclusion: If the reader becomes suspicious of Jacques Hold's narrative, why should this suspicion be selective? Jacques is either fully credible or he is not credible at all (especially when it comes to deciphering the desire of the Other).

The feminist hermeneutics at work here models Paul Ricoeur's "hermeneutics of suspicion." For Ricoeur, a "hermeneutics of suspicion" stands in opposition to a "hermeneutics of faith"; it contests the legitimacy of consciousness and its production of meaning: "After the doubt about things, we have started to doubt consciousness," he writes.[21] Ricoeur warns however that a hermeneutics of suspicion should not be conflated with the less desirable form of nihilistic skepticism:

> These three masters of suspicion [Marx, Nietzsche, Freud] are not to be misunderstood, however, as three masters of skepticism. They are, assuredly, three great "destroyers." But that of itself should not mislead us; [. . .] All three clear the horizon for a more authentic word, for a new reign of Truth, not only by means of a "destructive" critique, but by the invention of an art of *interpreting*.[22]

Based on the above sample of readings, a feminist hermeneutics of suspicion takes the following form: the "Truth" of Duras's novel lies in the "'destructive critique" of Jacques's Said, his narrative appropriation of Lol's voice (his phallocentric determination of her meaning).[23]

Levinas's Said and Saying perhaps map too neatly onto this feminist landscape. Is the question of Saying only to be located on the side of Duras and Lol? Is the Said of Jacques condemned to stasis? Isn't Levinas's formulation of the relation between Saying and the Said also supplemented by the double imperative of "unsaying" and "resaying" the ontological Said? Doesn't Levinas further link this double imperative to the unruly practice of skepticism, philosophy's disavowed child? To take up these questions, we must first revisit Jacques Hold's representational economy, probing further his status as a dubious, phallocentric subject of representation. Then, we will be in a better position to evaluate Duras's staging of the ethical encounter in *The Ravishing of Lol Stein* as well as her staging of *The Ravishing of Lol Stein* as an ethical encounter with the reader.

As we have seen, what feminist readings of *The Ravishing of Lol Stein* seem to have in common is an essentializing propensity: Jardine's essentialist identification (biological and social women need to identify with Lol) and Evans's and Edson's gendering of ontology (Jacques's narrative is an unproblematic exemplar of male logic). This essentialist dimension of the critique ironically re-inscribes feminism within the tradition of ontology and its economy of the Same, decried by many of the same authors for its phallogocentric underpinnings. More specifically, it is to the notion of "experience" that much of the debate about feminism gravitates. If female experience and male experience are fundamentally incommensurable, then what chance does Jacques have of producing a faithful account of Lol? Is fidelity to Lol's difference always inevitably a betrayal of that difference? Is it possible to conceive of feminism as *otherwise than being*, a feminism that does not posit the meaning of (female or male) experience as unproblematic or pre-discursively given? Such a feminist reading of Duras's novel would subsequently depend less on the reader's ability to share Lol's "experience" than on the reader's alertness to the quality of Jacques Hold's writing of Lol. Rather than exclusively focusing on Jacques Hold's writing of Lol's *ravishing* (which for some feminists is synonymous with his ravishing of Lol, that is, his violent subordination of Lol to his narrative will-to-know), I suggest that we ask as well: Is Jacques—or, more importantly, is his narrative—at all transformed by his encounter with Lol? Is the novel not only about Jacques's writing of Lol's *ravishing* but also the *ravishing* of his writing? While Jacques's appropriation of Lol's story is to a certain degree undeniable ("je raconterai *mon* histoire de Lol V. Stein" (14) ["I shall relate *my own* story of Lol Stein" (4)], emphasis added), one must nevertheless resist the impulse to deny or negate the singularity and heterogeneity of Jacques's character and condemn his narrative *tout court*, as does Evans: "Jacques Hold's narrative embodies the principles and values of male literary tradition, a tradition that includes a territorial, if not proprietary, notion of language, an authoritarian concept of authorship."[24] One-sided readings of Jacques's male narrative (either by radically displacing the importance of his role [Jardine] or by treating him as a one-dimensional character/narrator [Evans-Edson]) run the risk of simply reversing the male totalizing reading of Lol (uncritical acceptance of the narrator's voice) to a feminist totalizing reading of Jacques (an irresponsible dismissal of Jacques's narratorial authority). Indeed, a critical reading of Duras's *The Ravishing of Lol Stein* must avoid what could be described as the blackmail of some feminist critics: a reader must be either *for* or *against* Jacques Hold.

Rather than separating the feminine and the masculine in any clear and distinct fashion, Duras's text mines the distinction intrinsic to sexual difference without, however, opting to collapse the categories. In the first pages of *The Ravishing of Lol Stein*, the text draws attention to Lol's indocility, to the way in which "une part d'elle-même eût été toujours en allée loin de vous" (13) ["part of her seemed always to be evading you" (3)], and later in the novel Jacques stresses the unidirectional relation between them. Lol is described as a fascinating and evasive individual: "L'approche de Lol n'existe pas. On ne peut pas se rapprocher ou s'éloigner d'elle. Il faut attendre qu'elle vienne vous chercher, qu'elle veuille" (105) ["There is no way of approaching Lol. One can neither get close to her or move away from her. You have to wait until she comes in search of you, until she wants to" (95)]. Analogously related to Jacques's exposure to Lol—where Lol figures as the object of radical alterity—the reader's relation to *The Ravishing of Lol Stein* takes the form of an interpellation. As we have seen, one way of understanding this interpellation is as an ethical response to Duras's invitation to dialogue. I would add that this interpellation—this call of/from the Other—emanates also from Duras's *male* narrator, that is, from Jacques's Saying. What makes part of *The Ravishing of Lol Stein* seem always to be evading the reader (to echo Duras's phrasing) is arguably the perplexing qualities of Jacques Hold as lover/knower/narrator of Lol.

THE SAYING OF JACQUES

Ironically, the cover blurb for the English translation significantly diminishes, if not altogether effaces, Jacques's presence in the novel:

> *The Ravishing of Lol Stein* is a haunting early novel by the author of *The Lover*. Lol Stein is a beautiful young woman, securely married, settled in a comfortable life—and a voyeur. Returning with her husband and children to the town where, years before, her fiancé had abandoned her for another woman, she is drawn inexorably to recreate that long-past tragedy. She arranges a rendezvous for her friend Tatiana and Tatiana's lover. She arranges to spy on them. And then, she goes one step further . . .

What the blurb does, however, is to turn the reader's focus to the "primal scene" of the novel, the event of Lol's abandonment (that is, her ravishing), and to her subsequent attempts to cope with her "long-past tragedy." For Jacques, this event marks simultaneously the beginning of Lol's madness and *his* story of Lol:

> Les dix-neuf ans qui ont précédé cette nuit, je ne veux pas les connaître plus que je ne le dis, ou à peine, ni autrement que dans leur chronologie même s'ils se recèlent une minute magique à laquelle je dois d'avoir connu Lol V. Stein. Je ne le veux pas parce que la présence de son adolescence dans cette histoire risquerait d'atténuer un peu aux yeux du lecteur l'écrasante actualité de cette femme dans ma vie. (14)

> As for the nineteen years preceding that night, I do not want to know any more about them than what I tell, or very little more, setting forth only the straight, unadulterated chronological facts, even if these years conceal some magic moment to which I am indebted for having enabled me to meet Lol Stein. I don't want to because the presence of her adolescence in this story might somehow tend to detract, in the eyes of the reader, from the overwhelming actuality of this woman in my life. (4)

The exclusion of Lol's adolescence from the realm of investigation might seem puzzling for someone who seeks to truly understand the Other. This repression of a significant part of Lol's facticity is all the more disturbing given the initial opposition of Lol's friend and Jacques' lover, Tatiana, to his reading of Lol: "Tatiana, elle, ne croit pas au rôle prépondérant de ce fameux bal de T. Beach dans la maladie de Lol V. Stein. Tatiana Karl, elle, fait remonter plus avant, plus avant même que leur amitié, *les origines de cette maladie*" (120) ["Tatiana does not believe that this fabled Town Beach ball was so overwhelmingly responsible for Lol Stein's illness. No, Tatiana Karl traces the *origins of that illness* back further, further even than the beginning of their friendship" (2, emphasis added)]. Tatiana had always perceived Lol as an unconventional subject, as always being not *there*. Unlike Jacques, and despite the importance of the ball scene at T. Beach, she does not believe that Lol had ever had a substantial and integral self that was subsequently traumatized by her *ravishment*. Lol's identity was always characterized by its fluidity and mobility. From Tatiana's perspective, then, Lol's absence *preceded* her trauma:

> Lol était drôle, moqueuse impénitente et très fine bien qu'une part d'elle-même eût été toujours en allée loin de vous et de l'instant. Où? Dans le rêve adolescent? Non, répond Tatiana, non, on aurait dit dans rien encore, justement rien. Était-ce le cœur qui n'était pas là? Tatiana aurait tendance à croire que c'était peut-être en effet le cœur de Lol V. Stein qui n'était pas—elle dit: là—il allait venir sans doute, mais elle, elle ne l'avait pas connu. (13)

> Lol was funny, an inveterate wit, and very bright, even though part of her seemed always to be evading you, and the present moment. Going where? Into some adolescent dream world? No, Tatiana answers, no, it seemed as though she were going nowhere, yes, that's it, nowhere. Was it her heart that wasn't there? Tatiana apparently inclines toward the opinion that it was perhaps, indeed, Lol Stein's heart which wasn't—as she says—there; it would doubtless come, but she, Tatiana, had never seen any sign of it. (3)

Although Tatiana suggests what seems to be a causal explanation of Lol's present condition, she is unable to locate the moment of Lol's breakdown. In contrast to Jacques's clear and distinct location of Lol's illness in her *ravishing* at the ball, the imprecision of Tatiana's analysis may well strike the reader as being less a causal explanation than an affirmation of the unknowability of Lol's identity.

Jacques, however, does not allow Tatiana to expand on her alternative reading and is quick to discredit any authority she may have had in virtue of both her friendship for/with Lol and her proximity to the so-called "originary" event:

> Je ne crois plus à rien de ce que dit Tatiana, je ne suis convaincu de rien. Voici, tout au long, mêlés, à la fois, ce faux semblant que raconte Tatiana Karl et ce que j'invente sur la nuit du Casino de T. Beach. A partir de quoi je raconterai mon histoire de Lol V. Stein. (14)

> I no longer believe a word Tatiana says. I'm convinced of absolutely nothing. Here then, in full, and all mixed together, both this false impression which Tatiana Karl tells about and what I have been able to imagine about that night at the Town Beach casino. Following which I shall relate my own story of Lol Stein. (4)

Tatiana will thus *only* supply Jacques Hold with the raw matter that the latter's imagination will fashion into his story of Lol Stein.

Jacques's abrupt decision to silence Tatiana is so drastic and forceful that it should raise concerns about a propensity to subdue or instrumentalize the feminine Other for his own narcissistic ends. Yet, at the same time, Jacques makes clear that he is not telling *the* story of Lol (as if such a story could be told, even by Tatiana) but *his* story of Lol; remaining faithful to "the overwhelming actuality of this woman in [his] life" seems to necessitate this interpretive decision to confine the parameters of his inquiry. The reader quickly discovers that Jacques means what he says; two pages later, when inquiring about the unfolding of the traumatic event, more specifically, about Anne-Marie Stretter, the *femme fatale*, he asks: "Avait-elle regardé Michael Richardson en passant? L'avait-elle balayé de ce non-regard qu'elle promenait sur le bal?" (16) ["Had she looked at Michael Richardson as she passed by? And this non-look of hers swept over him as it took in the ballroom?" (6)]. Uncertainty about what took place in this primal scene of seduction translates into doubts about the origins of his story: "C'était impossible de le savoir, c'est impossible de savoir quand, par consequent, commence mon histoire de Lol V. Stein" (16) ["It was impossible to tell, it is therefore impossible to know when my story of Lol Stein begins" (6)].

Jacques's assertion of wanting to tell the story of Lol's transformative impact on his life includes a seemingly unexpected but innocuous reference to the reader—"the presence of her adolescence in this story might somehow tend to detract, *in the eyes of the reader*, from the overwhelming actuality of this woman in my life"—the only reference of its kind in the novel. More than a literary convention through which the narrator establishes some intimacy with his reader, the reference might more fruitfully be seen as an intersubjective gesture, foregrounding Jacques's exposure to the reader, reflecting a deeply self-conscious narrator, that is, a narrator conscious that he is writing *about* Lol *for* a third party (Jacques does not reveal his identity until one third of the way into the story). This formulation, of course, reinscribes Jacques in the traditional position of the active subject (the knower) and Lol in that of the passive object (the as of yet not known).

Again, things are a bit more complicated than they initially appear. Jacques already possesses some knowledge of Lol, a knowledge that clearly precedes the narrating of his story. Jacques feels nevertheless compelled to write her story down, to inquire further into the being of Lol. Assuming something akin to a pre-ontological understanding of Lol, then, Jacques takes up the role of an archeologist, and engages in a poetics of unearthing. He proceeds to reconstruct the object of Lol's desire in order to better understand her state of mind and silence; in short, to bridge the temporal gap between the ball and the present:

> Aplanir le terrain, le défoncer, ouvrir des tombeaux où Lol fait la morte, me paraît plus juste, du moment qu'il faut inventer les chaînons qui me manquent

dans l'histoire de Lol V. Stein, que de fabriquer des montagnes, d'édifier des obstacles, des accidents. Et je crois, connaissant cette femme, qu'elle aurait préféré que je remédie dans ce sens à la pénurie des faits de sa vie. D'ailleurs c'est toujours à partir d'hypothèses non gratuites et qui ont déjà, à mon avis, reçu un début de confirmation, que je le fais. (37)

To level the terrain, to dig down into it, to open the tombs wherein Lol is feigning death, seems to me fairer—given the necessity to fill in the missing links of Lol Stein's story—than to fabricate mountains, create obstacles, rely on chance. And, knowing this woman, I believe she would prefer that I compensate in this way for the lack of cold, hard facts about her life. Moreover, in doing so I am always relying on hypotheses which are in no way gratuitous but which, in my opinion, have at least some slight foundation in fact. (27–28)

Jacques speculates about the being of Lol and claims to invent (to "fill in") the links of the chain in her story. Deborah N. Glassman suggestively connects Jacques's project to Freudian psychoanalysis:

Freud, in "Construction in Analysis," asks: "What sort of material does [the patient] put at our disposal which we can make use of to put him on the way to recovering the lost memories? All kinds of things . . . fragments of these memories in his dreams . . . ideas . . . repetitions of the affects belonging to the repressed. It is out of such raw material . . . that we have to put together what we are in search of . . . [the analyst's] task is to make out what has been forgotten from the traces which it has left behind, or more correctly, to construct it."[25]

Glassman's reading of Jacques as a crypto-psychoanalyst is all the more justified given the ambiguity concerning Jacques's medical profession. Having said this, however, we must pause and not assume a priori that a psychoanalytic framework produces a masterful body of knowledge, to see in Lol, *à la* Lacan, a "perfect case of clinical delirium." What Jacques fashions or invents about Lol at times produces insights that are peculiarly paradoxical in nature: "ne savoir rien de Lol était la connaître déjà. On pouvait, me parut-il, en savoir moins encore, de moins en moins sur Lol V. Stein" (81) ["To know nothing about Lol Stein was already to know her. One could, it seemed to me, know even less about her, less and less about Lol Stein" (72)], Jacques observes. Here *knowing Lol* does not correspond to the traditional subject/object epistemological relation: a self-detached, autonomous, and authoritative knower in relation to his known object.[26] In this light, Jacques Hold's "psychoanalytic" approach to Lol would resemble more that of Jean Laplanche for whom psychoanalysis is better understood as anti-hermeneutics, as a skeptical practice that foregrounds the enigmaticity of the signifier, the untranslatability of the analysand's message into the analyst's pre-established hermeneutic code, that is, the classic Freudian language of typicality or symbols.[27] In Levinasian parlance, the Laplanchian analyst maintains a "relation without relation" (*TI* 80) with the analysand. Paradoxically entailing both a relation and a non-relation to the Other, this relationless relation joins *and* disjoins; it answers the aporetic demands made upon the analyst by the analysand: to be heard without being reduced to an object of comprehension (made into a case and thus reduced to the economy of the Same), to never dissolve the "without" of the "relation without relation" that interrupts any traditional, static subject-object relation and respects (by sustaining through discourse) the enigmaticity of the Other's message.

Jacques's observation that "to know nothing about Lol Stein was already to know her" makes it clear that Lol's identity is incomprehensible from within an egological universe; indeed, Lol's enigmaticity is not only uncontainable but often contagious, affecting not only Jacques's representation of Lol but also the foundations of his own identity. After his erotic encounter with Lol, Jacques no longer feels that his ego coincides with itself; her alterity obscures his self-transparency: "Mais qu'est-ce que j'ignore de moi-même à ce point et qu'elle me met en demeure de connaître? qui sera là dans cet instant auprès d'elle?" (105) ["But what is there about me I am so completely unaware of and which she summons me to know? Who will be there, at that moment, beside her?" (96)]. Jacques experiences a similar kind of defamiliarization later in the novel when Lol disturbs his very process of nomination. After she pronounces his name, he finds himself utterly bewildered, *ravi* (captivated and enchanted): "Fulgrante trouvaille. . . . Pour la première fois mon nom prononcé ne nomme pas" (112-13) ["A dazzling discovery. . . . For the first time my name, pronounced, names nothing" (103)]. Here we might say that ravishment functions as an ethical category akin to Levinas's notion of persecution from his 1968 essay "Substitution": "Persecution reduces the ego to the self, to the absolute accusative whereby the Ego is accused of a fault which it neither willed nor committed, and which disturbs its freedom. Persecution is a traumatism, violence par excellence, without warning, without a priori, without the possibility of apology, without logos" (*BPW* 183, n.44). Thrown into a profoundly heteronomous state, Jacques experiences Lol's ravishment as a traumatism, as an uprooting and disappropriation of the self; Lol's sexual difference fractures Jacques's masculinist self and disrupts his patriarchal reason (compelling him to see himself as an enigmatic signifier of his own). As Susan Rubin Suleiman puts it, Lol "feminizes" Jacques's masculine narrative,[28] introducing a ravishing unruliness within his phallocentric discourse. Enmeshed in transference, deeply affected by Lol's story (evidenced by his obsessive identification with Michael Richardson, for instance), Jacques resembles a compromised analyst, a less than masterful *subject supposed to know*.[29]

Seeing Jacques as completely transformed by his encounter(s) with Lol, though, would be to grossly overstate the situation. Suleiman, for example, likens Jacques's "hesitant" mode of narration to Duras's notion of *écriture feminine*,[30] whereas other critics have problematized the *effect* of Jacques's self-critical assertions, his uncertainties about his writing of Lol: "ce que j'invente" (14) ["what I have been able to imagine" (4)]; "Ce que je crois" (45) ["Here is my opinion" (35)]; "Je vois ceci" (55) ["I see this" (45)]. Rather than limiting or undermining his narratorial authority, "they increase our confidence in the narrator's reliability";[31] "When Jacques Hold the analyst . . . systematically engages in a reification of his own ignorance, he is striving to secure his own . . . authority."[32] A critical evaluation of Jacques's textual strategies, however, must keep in mind that Jacques's character is not one-dimensional, that the complexity of his narrative eludes both types of totalization: *écriture féminine* and male domination. While Duras's text invariably, and infuriatingly, solicits both of these mutually exclusive readings of Jacques, it also blocks the clear dominance of either one.

Jacques's desire to know Lol is never far from his desire to control her. Well after his "epiphanic" epistemological moment, where he states that "to know nothing about Lol Stein was already to know her," Jacques reiterates his irresistible thirst for Lol's speech/story: "Je désire comme un assoiffé boire le lait brumeux et insipide de la parole qui sort de Lol V. Stein" (106) ["Like one parched, I desperately want to drink of the hazy, insipid milk of the word which emerges from the lips of Lol Stein" (97, translation modified)]. He quickly follows this statement with a paradoxical yearning to be both possessed by Lol: "qu'elle me broie avec le reste, je serai servile." (106) ["let her consume and crush me with the rest, I shall bend to her will." (97)] and to possess her: "Mes mains deviennent le piège dans lequel l'immobiliser, la retenir de toujours aller et venir d'un bout à l'autre du temps" (107) ["My hands are becoming the trap wherewith to ensnare her, immobilize her, keep her from constantly moving to and fro from one end of time to the other" (97)]. Jacques's bizarre mixture of phantasmatic passivity with physical/hermeneutic violence (containing Lol physically and interpretively) makes evident that the ethical encounter does not unfold in any linear fashion: first, there is Jacques's desire for comprehension (the reduction of Lol to the realm of egology), then resistance resulting from his "ethical" recognition of Lol's otherness (Lol as an enigmatic signifier). Narrating the ethical encounter complicates a teleological understanding of the Levinasian encounter. It might also reveal why Levinas was deeply suspicious of the literary as such, as he says in "Reality and its Shadow": "The characters of a novel are beings that are shut up, prisoners. Their history is never finished, it still goes on, but makes no headway" (*RS* 139). It is precisely a lack of progression that Duras's novel displays time and time again. Narration and the ethical encounter as such are not necessarily locked in a negative dialectic. Rather, Duras's novel persistently resists the "pathos of understanding," as Lacan puts it,[33] fostering interpretive irresolution through its constant framing and reframing of the ethical encounter. Even the most idyllic image of ethical coexistence, such as Jacques's affectionate claim of being utterly *riveted* to Lol, "Nous voici chevillés ensemble" (113) ["here we are, bound together inextricably" (103)], is not immune to ironic recontextualization, to its reinscription within the many twists and turns of the narrative. In an exchange with Lol toward the end of the novel, for instance, Jacques (as well as the reader) is reminded of Lol's enigmaticity:

> —Je ne vous aime pas cependant je vous aime, vous me comprenez?
> Je demande:
> —Pourquoi ne pas vous tuer? Pourquoi ne vous êtes-vous pas encore tuée?
> —Non, vous vous trompez, ce n'est pas ça. (169)

> "I don't love you and yet I do. You know what I mean."
> I ask:
> "Why don't you kill yourself? Why haven't you already killed yourself?"
> "No, you're wrong, that's not it at all." (159)

Lol's statement that she does not love Jacques and does love him at the same time violates, or ravishes, the principle of non-contradiction, a principle of great utility for the analytic mind. Lol's subversion of Jacques's logic is followed by her thwarting of his hermeneutical astuteness: "No, you're wrong, that's not it at all." Here a feminist reading would not hesitate to privilege Lol's alterity and irreducibility, and interpret Lol's unruliness as Duras's call for a heroic new female subjectivity. Yet the novel asks us to do more. *The Ravishing of Lol Stein* dramatizes Levinas's statement that "to require that a communication be sure of being heard is to confuse communication and knowledge" (*OB* 167).[34] What the novel narrates or communicates is *not* knowledge of sexual difference, of a new female subjectivity, or the like. Rather, the Saying of the novel lies in its invitation to the reader to take up the ethical imperative of "unsaying" and "resaying"—not only the Said of Jacques's discourse, but also, or, better yet, especially, the Said produced by any reading of *The Ravishing of Lol Stein*, including one's own. Doing justice to Duras's novel, then, involves a constant alertness to one's interpretive maneuverings, creatively hesitating between competing injunctions: to interpret but not to translate Lol/Jacques/*The Ravishing of Lol Stein* into a pre-established hermeneutic code—feminist or otherwise.

NOTES

This chapter includes material from my book, *Reading Unruly: Interpretation and its Ethical Demands*. Reproduced by permission of the University of Nebraska Press. Forthcoming.

1. Zahi Zalloua, "Preface: Fidelity to the Unruly," SubStance 38, 3 (2009): 3-17, especially 4-5.

2. Leslie Hill attests to the dominance of the psychoanalytic framework in the reception of Duras's novel: "To this day, *Le Ravissement de Lol V. Stein* is the text of Duras's which has given rise to the greatest amount of critical commentary. Much of this, largely in the wake of Lacan, has been framed by issues derived either from psychoanalytic theory or from feminism, if not from both, and questions of desire, sexual difference, and gender identity loom large in discussions of the novel" (Hill, "Lacan with Duras," *Writing and Psychoanalysis: A Reader,* ed. John Lechte [New York: Arnold, 1996], 147). Levinas's presence in these debates has been largely negligible. Critics of the novel inclined to develop an ethical reading of *The Ravishing of Lol Stein* have pursued the feminist and/or psychoanalyst route. Martin Crowley makes brief but insightful observations about the affinities between Duras and Levinas in relation to the ethical. See his *Duras, Writing, and the Ethical: Making the Broken Whole* (Oxford: Clarendon Press, 2000).

3. Zahi Zalloua, "Reading Duras's *Le Ravissement de Lol V. Stein* like a Feminist," *Women in French Studies* 10 (2002): 228-42.

4. Michael Sheringham, "Knowledge and Repetition in *Le Ravissement de Lol V. Stein,*" *Romance Studies* 2 (1983): 124-40.

5. As Colin Davis puts it, "Levinas attacks art because it is irresponsible and inhuman, it is a form of idolatry which puts the mind to sleep and shrouds it in darkness" (Davis, *Critical Excess: Overreading in Derrida, Deleuze, Levinas, Žižek and Cavell* [Stanford: Stanford University Press, 2010], 97).

6. For a lucid overview of Levinas's reception among feminist critics, see Tina Chanter's edited volume *Feminist Interpretations of Emmanuel Levinas* (University Park: The Pennsylvania State University Press, 2001). See also Chanter's *Time, Death, and the Feminine: Levinas with Heidegger* (Stanford: Stanford University Press, 2001).

7. Luce Irigaray, for example, makes ample use of Levinasian rhetoric in her critique of Western phallocentric thought: "Now this domination of the philosophic logos stems in large part from its power to *reduce all others to the economy of the Same.* The teleologically constructive project it takes on is always also a project of diversion, deflection, reduction of the other in the Same. And, in its greatest generality perhaps, from its power to *eradicate the difference between the sexes* in systems that are self-representative of a 'masculine subject'" (Irigaray, *This Sex Which is Not One,* trans. Catherine Porter [Ithaca: Cornell University Press, 1985], 74). See, also, Ewa Plonowska Ziarek's article, "The Ethical Passion of Emmanuel Levinas," in *Feminist Interpretations of Emmanuel Levinas.*

8. For example, Sonia Sikka "question[s] the notion of alterity, or at least *radical* alterity, as a model for either ethics in general or feminism in particular" (Sikka, "The Delightful Other: Portraits of the Feminine in Kierkegaard, Nietzsche, and Levinas," in *Feminist Interpretations of Emmanuel Levinas,* 97). See, also, Stella Sandford's "Levinas, Feminism and the Feminine," in *The Cambridge Companion to Levinas,* eds. Simon Critchley and Robert Bernasconi (Cambridge: Cambridge University Press, 2002), 139–60.

9. Alice Jardine, *Gynesis: Configurations of Woman and Modernity* (Ithaca: Cornell University Press, 1985), 17. Further references will be cited parenthetically in the text.

10. This affinity between the two Jacques (which extends beyond their shared name to their shared medical training) results from a dubious affective economy. It is suggested that Hold is a psychiatrist: "Trente-six ans, je fais partie du corps médical. Il n'y a qu'un an que je suis arrivé à S. Tahla. Je suis dans le service de Pierre Beugner à l'Hôpital départemental" (Marguerite Duras, *Le ravissement de Lol V. Stein* [Paris: Gallimard, 1964], 75) ["I'm thirty-six years old, a member of the medical profession. I've been living in South Tahla only for a year. I'm in Peter Beugner's section at the State Hospital" (Duras, *The Ravishing of Lol Stein* [New York: Pantheon, 1986], 66)].

11. Lacan's interview with Duras, quoted in Karen Kaivola, "Marguerite Duras and the Subversion of Power," in *Critical Essays on Marguerite Duras,* ed. Bettina L. Knapp (New York: G. K. Hall & Co., 1998), 125.

12. See Diana Fuss's *Essentially Speaking: Feminism, Nature & Difference* (New York: Routledge, 1989). For a more explicit engagement with Fuss's argument, see Zalloua (2002).

13. Alice Jardine highlights the gender-oriented matter of Duras's works: "[Duras] never fails to emphasize that her texts and films are, above all, *about* women" (175).

14. Martha Noel Evans, *Masks of Tradition* (Ithaca: Cornell University Press, 1987), 125.

15. Laurie Edson, "Knowing Lol: Duras, Epistemology and Gendered Mediation," *SubStance* 68 (1992): 17–31, 30 cited.

16. Ibid., 19.

17. It should be noted that sexual identification is a necessary but not sufficient condition of Jardine's version of feminism, since she distinguishes between feminist (non-analyst) readings and psychoanalytical readings produced by women readers who "valorize Lol as character in one way or another" (176).

18. Edson, 20.

19. Ibid., 16.

20. Ibid., 20.

21. Paul Ricoeur, *Freud and Philosophy: An Essay on Interpretation*, trans. Denis Savage (New Haven: Yale University Press, 1970), 33.

22. Ibid., 33.

23. To be sure, Jardine's hermeneutic feminist model still relies a bit on a "hermeneutics of faith" to the extent that a restoration of Lol's voice through identification (responding to Duras's Saying, that is, to her invitation to dialogue) remains possible. Such a faith is not shared by the other feminist camps, who take the point of the novel to be not to identify with Lol but to criticize Jacques.

24. Evans, 140.

25. Deborah N. Glassman, *Marguerite Duras: Fascinating Vision and Narrative Cure* (London: Associated University Press, 1991), 128, n.18.

26. One is reminded of Levinas's essay, "The Other in Proust," in which Levinas associates mystery with the question of the other ("The mystery in Proust is the mystery of the other" [*PN* 102]). Here, as in the case of Lol, Albertine embodies a "deep strangeness" that remains unknowable or ungraspable to Marcel (Jacques's male counterpart); it "laughs in the face of knowledge," producing in him "an insatiable curiosity about the alterity of the other, at once empty and inexhaustible" (*PN* 103).

27. See Jean Laplanche's "Psychoanalysis as Anti-Hermeneutics," *Radical Philosophy* 79 (1996), 8. While Levinas was usually hostile to the discourse of psychoanalysis, Laplanche's practice strikes me as fruitful for a potential *rapprochement* between Levinas and psychoanalysis. This is evidently beyond the scope of this essay.

28. Susan Rubin Suleiman, *Subversive Intent: Gender, Politics, and the Avant-Garde* (Cambridge: Harvard University Press, 1990), 231.

29. Lynsey Russell-Watt, "The Terrors and Pleasures of Analysis: *Le Ravissement de Loi V. Stein*," *Nottingham French Studies* 43, 3 (2007): 121-133, especially 126.

30. Ibid., 116.

31. Evans, 131.

32. Karen McPherson, *Incriminations: Guilty Women/Telling Stories* (Princeton: Princeton University Press, 1994), 71.

33. Jacques Lacan, "Homage to Marguerite Duras, on *Le ravissement de Lol V. Stein*," in *Critical Essays on Marguerite Duras*, ed. Bettina L. Knapp (New York: G.K. Hall & Co., 1998), 20. On the narrative level, the last paragraph of the novel registers Jacques's ambivalent hermeneutics. Waiting for Tatiana in L'Hôtel des Bois, Jacques perceives Lol in the rye field, and comments: "Lol nous avait précédés. Elle dormait dans le champ de seigle, fatiguée, fatiguée par notre voyage" (191) ["Lol had arrived there ahead of us. She was asleep in the field of rye, worn out, worn out by our trip" (181)]. Lacking unequivocal closure—the narrative could go on indefinitely—Jacques Hold's narration sustains and prolongs Lol's enigmaticity, suspending, as it were, his desire to contain or normalize Lol, or to "save" her from her ravishment (Lacan, "Homage to Marguerite Duras," 20). This resistance to a recuperative logic, to a lack of "cathartic potential," as Kristeva describes it, characterizes Duras's art, reflecting the ways her aesthetics sabotages any readerly desire for appropriable meaning (*Black Sun: Depression and Melancholia*, trans. Leon S. Roudiez [New York: Columbia University Press, 1989], 228).

34. Likewise, Duras can be seen as dramatizing the anti-narrative ethos of her fellow *nouveaux romanciers* ("new novelists"), an ethos eloquently captured by Alain Robbe-Grillet in his

manifesto *For a New Novel*: "tell[ing] a story has become strictly impossible [*raconter est devenu proprement impossible*]" (*For a New Novel*, trans. Richard Howard [New York: Grove Press 1966], 33).

III

Levinas and the Aesthetics of American Modernism

Chapter Five

William Faulkner's Embodied Subjectivities

Benjamin Joshua Doty

John Duvall has written insightfully about how William Faulkner's works show "that not all Caucasians are fully white in a South that wishes to absolutize all racial difference," especially "poor whites."[1] This chapter examines the ethical dimensions of this limited whiteness first as it is conceived in American literature from the colonial period to the twentieth century and then as it is manifested and revised in Faulkner's novel *As I Lay Dying.* I structure my discussion as follows: I first examine American literary representations of poor whites in light of Emmanuel Levinas's ethical phenomenology and argue that the history of the poor white in American literature is one in which she is habitually dehumanized. I further argue that Levinas's work provides a framework for usefully relating current findings in neuroscience to narrative fiction in ways that open new lines of discussion for studies of race and literature. I seek to demonstrate such claims through my reading of *As I Lay Dying* in which I argue that the novel's dramatized modes of subjectivity may be given philosophical and analytical articulation within terms that Levinas and current neuroscience make available. Both Levinasian phenomenology and the new cognitive sciences envision a dynamic relationship between the mind and body in which bodily processes modify and are modified by conscious thought. In Faulkner's novel, the permeability of the boundaries between mind and body reflects a similar permeability between interiority and exteriority and between self and Other. I argue that the novel's troubling of these boundaries constitutes a check against the dehumanizing effects of racial and class signification, a check that creates the possibility of recognizing poor white Others as fully human. Understanding both how white poverty came to be associated with dehumanization and how Faulkner's novelistic depiction of subjectivity works actively to humanize poor white Others may suggest ways of rethinking intersections of race and class prevalent within American literature generally.

ALMOST WHITE: POOR WHITES IN AMERICA

The last two decades have seen much scholarly work in whiteness studies, an interdisciplinary field in which much of this chapter is rooted.[2] This field commonly examines the roots and effects of white privilege and power and the historical roots of whiteness as such. Theodore Allen posits that "the white race" was invented by the eighteenth-century slaveholding class as a "social control formation," one reliant upon the participation of both slave-holding and non-slaveholding classes to maintain a racist social order.[3] Noel Ignatiev defines white people as "those who partake of the privileges of the white skin in society."[4] While these analyses offer powerful revelations about the history of race in America, they tend to think of "whiteness" as being necessarily homogenous. Typically, in whiteness studies, immigrant groups such as the Irish historically became "white" once they attained white privilege, joining a homogenously white collective. I agree with David Hardigan when he writes that "treating whiteness in generic terms" as a "historically determined ideology of dominance" can lead to neglecting lines of stratification within whiteness.[5]

Much current work in whiteness studies comes from history, sociology, and anthropology. While these disciplines excel at offering comprehensive analyses of race and class, studying whiteness from the perspective of literature may allow for more finely nuanced cultural analyses than the social sciences typically perform. In the following section of my chapter I will make three arguments: (a) that the concept of "white trash" has inhabited American literature since colonial times; (b) that "white trash" are often "white" in name only and constitute a racial exception to homogenous whiteness as ideologically constructed by the white bourgeoisie; and (c) that American literary representations of "white trash" largely, in Levinas's words, typically engage in ethically dubious"[t]hematization and conceptualization" (*TI* 46).

I will first offer a brief overview of poor whites' presence in American culture since the early eighteenth century.[6] The depictions of poor whites discussed below all, to some extent, cast poor whites in a light that is distinctly racialized: their skins are tallow-colored, cadaverous, or, time and again, "sallow." Matt Wray, taking note of the off-white skin tones ascribed to poor whites in eighteenth-century literature, asks, "Under present-day regimes of perception, wouldn't this [attention paid to one's complexion] qualify as a racial observation? Perhaps, but in a historical context such as this . . . what exactly constitutes a racial observation can be a matter of guesswork."[7] However, as Allen writes, a 1705 "act declaring the Negro, Mulatto, and Indian slaves within this dominion [the Colony of Virginia] to be real estate" demonstrates a "desire not only to impose lifetime hereditary bond-servitude on African Americans, but to implement it by a system of *racial oppression*" based on skin color.[8] Clearly, a white supremacist racial system was in place before one of the earliest accounts of poor whites in the New World, William Byrd's report on the 1728 survey of the boundary between Virginia and North Carolina, was written. In his report, Byrd describes "indolent" poor whites, whose aversion to labor makes them suitable inhabitants for North Carolina, "where plenty and a warm sun confirm them in their disposition to laziness for their whole lives."[9] Byrd gives a few asides comparing the poor whites he encounters to Native Americans to differentiate them from more respectable whites such as himself. Their methods of animal husbandry are "just like the lazy Indians," and the poor white men, "just like the Indians," put their work upon the women.[10] Further, mosquitoes and disease "give them a cadaverous complexion."[11]

In the nineteenth century, poor whites were put at a further distance from the white bourgeoisie with the literary advent of the "clay-eater," particularly in Augustus Baldwin Longstreet's 1835 *Georgia Scenes.* Longstreet's stories feature a character named "Ransy Sniffle," whose diet of dirt and clay gives him "a complexion that a corpse would have disdained to own," among various physical deformities.[12] Richard Hildreth, in his 1852 *White Slave: Another Picture of Slave Life in America*, blames poor white ignorance and degeneracy on slavery, which, he claims, robs whites who are not landowners of jobs. This interpretation emphasizes cultural and economic realities as the progenitor of poor whiteness rather than "bad blood" or miscegenation. However, Hildreth also writes, "[I]t is freedom which makes the chief difference between the slaves and those poor whites," and that they are not intellectually "superior to the generality of the plantation slaves."[13]

Robinson Hundley, in his 1860 *Social Relations in Our Southern States,* presents a decisively genealogical view of poor whiteness in which poverty and blood are twined together: by Hundley's account, the ancestors of the poor whites arrived in the New World as mere chattel much like African slaves—"indentured servants or paupers."[14] Having arrived in the New World in such a socioeconomic state, Hundley asks, is there "any thing in the nature of our soil and climate which would soon transmogrify such untutored, uncultivated, and servile creatures into freemen and gentlemen?"[15] His answer is negative: they, "as a class, as a Community, remain in *statu quo.*"[16] Those poor whites who do manage to muster any ambition are able to do so because they "are not usually of the pure, unadulterated pauper blood. Their origin is somewhat mixed."[17] Upper-class whites, the "Southern Gentlemen," in contrast, come from "good stock."[18] Poor whites, Hundley says, also have "sallow complexion[s]."[19] Subsequent accounts of poor whites offer further focus on physiognomy as racial/class markers. Mark Twain created perhaps the most enduring poor white literary character in Pap Finn, whose skin is "not like another man's white, but a white to make a body sick, a white to make a body's flesh crawl."[20] W. J. Cash, in his 1941 *The Mind of the South*, describes poor whites as having misshapen heads and "a peculiar sallow swartness, or alternatively a not less peculiar and not less sallow faded-out colorlessness of skin and hair."[21]

Further emphasis given by these descriptions on "sallow" or "cadaverous" complexions and on lackadaisical behavior point to an emergent racial logic that ensures white privilege and nonwhite abjection by holding the full label of "white" in reservation. The "off-whiteness" of poor whites continues today. Allan Bérubé, describing his childhood growing up in a trailer park, writes that "other whites who looked down on us because of where we lived could call my whiteness into question. Ashamed, I kept these and other social injuries to myself, channeling them into desires to learn about how to act and look more white, and to find other ways to move up and out of this life that more and more felt like a trap I had to escape."[22] Likewise, Annalee Newitz observes, "When middle-class whites encounter lower-class whites, we find that often their class differences are represented as the difference between civilized folks and primitive ones. Lower class whites get racialized, and demeaned, because they fit into the primitive/civilized binary as primitives."[23]

LEVINASIAN ETHICS AND WHITENESS

The stuff from which whiteness is made—class exploitation and boundary-making—can be aptly analyzed with a methodology informed by Emmanuel Levinas's ethics. Levinasian approaches to literature are a key outgrowth of postmodernism's "ethical turn," or the reorientation of Western philosophy towards non-dominating relations with the Other.[24] Levinas's arguments for the place of ethics as first philosophy enable discussions of literature that illuminate texts' ethical dimensions, often by locating textual elements that establish relationships between text and reader analogous to those between self and Other. For Levinas, one's world and one's complacent existence within it become shattered by the encounter with the Other who "cannot be comprehended, that is, encompassed"; one encounters the Other's face, which is itself the Other's discernible presence or "trace," but cannot totalize it into comprehension (*TI* 194).This inability to assimilate completely into one's own terms or otherwise totalize the Other founds an ethical relation between self and Other that is the basis for all sociality. This ethical relation, variously defined by Levinas as "height," "vulnerability," and "passivity more passive than all patience," places the self in an automatic, non-elective relationship defined by infinite responsibility to do no harm to the Other (*TI* 75, *OB* 15, 54). This responsibility manifests itself in conscious but habitual gestures such as allowing someone else to go through a door before oneself. In a 1991 French documentary, *Penser Aujourd'hui: Emmanuel Levinas*, he says, "'*Après vous*': *cette formule de politesse devrait être la plus belle définition de notre civilization*"[25] ['After you': this salutation should be the most beautiful definition of our civilization]. The privileging of another before myself, enacted in such elementary gestures and woven into everyday sociality, founds and presupposes truth, justice, and reason.

The counterpoint to the ethical relationship in Levinas's thought is being-for-oneself. For Levinas, to be-for-oneself is to give in to the selfish demands of *conatus*, the putatively natural tendency of organic entities to secure well-being through the accumulation of power and resources. This self-interested striving in spite of the Other is facilitated by making a habit of encountering the Other as an "object-cognition," which can only reinforce belief that "the world [is] possessed by me" (*TI* 75). Levinas describes this state of illusory world-possession as "enjoyment" or "jouissance" (*TI* 75). Much like Sartre's voyeur peering through the keyhole, the subject enveloped in enjoyment experiences a feeling of self-sufficiency—we are what is necessary within our own worlds; we are, quite literally, the measure of things, the reference-point that gives objects cognized, including people, significance.

The logic of white supremacy is centered on such an illusory conception of the world. Once preserving white power becomes integral to maintaining the world in which the white subject is privileged, then "white trash" and other racial categories may usefully reinforce a sense of "world-possession," allowing bourgeois whites to abide in indulgent illusions of their own self-sufficiency. The enjoyment this illusion fosters, as Donald Wehrs notes, "an aesthetic relation to exteriority,"[26] as the aestheticizing of white (and non-white) destitution and deprivation for elite white consumption attests. Once the white bourgeoisie can aestheticize, caricature, totalize, or otherwise distance itself from racial and economic Others as a normative part of socialization, it can make adaptation of condescending attitudes integral to its own identity formation and so consolidate certainty of its own superiority and moral rightness. Enjoyment so articulated, so ritualized in social practice and reinforced in aesthetic recreation, comes to naturalize avoidance of real ethical engagement with the very Others whose putative lack of full humanity becomes both part of the Southern regional landscape and an object of bemused contemplation and popular disdain.

White bourgeois enjoyment or uncritical aesthetic consumption is aided by the remarkable homogeneity ascribed to "poor whiteness." From the colonial period to the present day, "poor whites" have shared in the popular imagination the same durable features: "sallow" complexions, morally repugnant behavior, and stultifying ignorance. These features serve as racial markers and give the white bourgeoisie "a pretext—humanity reduced to physicality—for defacing or misrecognizing" Others.[27] This sameness also adds an element of durable timelessness that petrifies poor whites into conceptual stasis. The suspension of time in such a conceptual framing resembles the suspension of time that art, according to Levinas, tends to effect. Art differs from life in lacking the element of temporal progression. Levinas cites the Mona Lisa. Her smile, "about to broaden," will never broaden. She is frozen in time; no matter what, she will always smile just as da Vinci painted her. She is "the paradox of an instant that endures without a future" (*RS* 138). The static, durable portraits of poor whites throughout American history are similar—not being possessed of temporal change, they are "never finished, still enduring—something inhuman and monstrous" (141).

EMBODIED SUBJECTIVITY

Levinas opposes conceptual and ethical violence, such as that evinced by the logics totalizing the concept of the "poor white," by providing an account of subjectivity rooted in embodiment. This subjectivity is founded in a pre-rational, somatic connection between individuals that Levinas terms "sensibility," which denotes an "exposedness to the other. It is a having been offered without any holding back and not the generosity of offering oneself, which would be an act, and already presupposes the unlimited undergoing of the sensibility" (*OB* 75). Further, sensibility "does not belong to the order of thought but to that of sentiment, that is, the affectivity wherein the egoism of the I pulsates. One does not know, one lives sensible qualities" (*TI* 135).This account of subjectivity is parallel to but not the same as that offered by Maurice Merleau-Ponty, who writes, "[E]very human use of the body is already *primordial expression*."(67)[28]. Where Levinas differs from Merleau-Ponty is that the subjectivity he discovers within embodiment is an *ethical* subjectivity, one animated by the commanding presence of an Other who "cannot be comprehended, that is, encompassed" (*TI* 194). The Levinasian subject finds herself given grounding by her relation to the radical and incomprehensible alterity of the Other, a relation she enters, through sensibility, "on the surface of the skin, at the edge of the nerves" (*OB* 14).

Interestingly, recent findings from cognitive science paint a picture of subjectivity largely congruent with Levinas's analysis. Just as Levinas situates subjectivity within the natural body rather than within a metaphysical Cartesian *res cogitans*, so cognitive scientists from a variety of subfields argue that subjectivity is "inextricably tied to our bodies and the peculiarities of our brains."[29] In recent years, this argument has migrated from scientific fields into philosophical and literary studies. In pioneering accounts linking interpretation of empirical neural research to the concerns of the social sciences and humanities, the neuroscientist Antonio Damasio in *Descartes' Error: Emotion, Reason and the Human Brain* (1994) and *Looking for Spinoza: Joy, Sorrow, and the Feeling Brain* (2003) explores the neural-physiological grounding of human reason upon emotion, which in turn is grounded upon cognitive processing of sensory data.[30] In *Philosophy in the Flesh: the Embodied Mind and Its Challenge to Western Thought* (1999), George Lakoff and Mark Johnson, coming respectively from the fields of linguistics and philosophy, examine the philosophical implications of Damasio's and others' findings, based in part upon tracing neural interactions through magnetic imaging, in part upon investigating the localized effects of neural or cognitive damage on the relationship on the mind and body. They note that Western philosophy has long largely assumed the "autonomous capacity of reason" removed from the body, but argue instead for an "empirically responsible philosophy informed by an appropriately self-critical cognitive science."[31]

Scholars have recently been examining the implications of embodied theories of subjectivity for humanist inquiry. Evan Thompson, a philosopher, further develops the philosophical implications of such work by suggesting in *Mind in Life: Biology, Phenomenology, and the Sciences of Mind* (2007) that Husserl's phenomenology offers a useful way of describing how developments in neuroscience bear upon the subjective experience of consciousness: pre-reflective bodily consciousness and its influence on conscious thought enacts "a dynamic linkage of outward perception and inward feeling" that shows the body to be "a material thing, but one animated from within by sensation and motility."[32] Recent literary studies have drawn upon cognitive science to examine the connections between the body, mind, emotions, and reasoning in literature. In *Why Do We Care About Literary Characters?* (2009), the literature scholar Blakey Vermeule draws on evolutionary psychology and cognitive science to explain our emotional attachments to literary characters. She argues that we evolved to care about fictional characters because "we need to know what other people are like, not in the aggregate, but the particular"; further, "the reasons we care about literary characters are finally not much different from the question of why we care about other people, especially people we have never met nor are likely to ever meet."[33] Jane Thrailkill's *Affecting Fictions* (2007), "a sustained argument in defense of the Affective Fallacy," draws upon American Pragmatism and cognitive science to argue for emotion's role as a predominant element of American Realist fiction.[34] Thrailkill observes that an interdisciplinary approach to literary criticism that combines mind science and traditional modes of humanistic study frees critics to "attend more rigorously, and with less embarrassment, to the emotional and aesthetic entailments of literary works."[35]

Cognitive science and Levinasian ethics illuminate each other. The primordial, somatic, pre-reflective state that Levinas identifies with giving rise to ethical consciousness strikingly correlates with much of cognitive science's "deep sense that our conceptual systems and our capacity for thought are shaped by the nature of our brains, our bodies, and our bodily interactions."[36] Such a correlation includes, for example, pursuing the implications for social theory of revolutionary new understandings of affectivity arising from the discovery of mirror neurons. Recent research suggests that when one sees someone else perform bodily actions such as lifting an arm, certain pre-motor neurons activate in a pattern corresponding to the pattern activated if one had actually raised one's own arm.[37] There is a degree of spontaneous neural imitation that applies not just to actions, but also to emotional states. One cannot see another's distress without feeling, through neural activation, as though one were undergoing the same emotional state (albeit to a lesser degree). What is particularly interesting about the connections between mirror neurons and Levinasian ethics is the automatic, non-elective nature of each: sociality, then, is not a conscious and rational process but rather a systematic interplay between the body and the mind. Marco Iacoboni writes that when we see another in pain, "mirror neurons help us to read his or her facial expression and actually make us feel the suffering or the pain of the other person."[38] Further, he asserts that such "mirroring" "is the foundation of empathy and possibly of morality."[39] Joel Krueger, discussing the Levinasian elements of mirror neurons, notes that they support Levinas's conception of our fundamental, pre-rational awareness of Others: "others' actions affectively resonate within the somatic space of my own motor possibilities."[40] As we will see, these pre-rational connections have many implications for literary studies of race, ethnicity, gender, and class. In the final portion of this chapter, I will read *As I Lay Dying*, William Faulkner's 1930 novel on poor, rural Mississippians, in the light of Levinasian ethics and congruent developments in cognitive science in an endeavor to provide a fresh analysis of intersections of race and class in literature.

FAULKNER AND POOR WHITE IDENTITY

Staging the kinds of dynamic mind–body relationship suggestive of those described by Levinasian philosophy and supported by recent neuroscientific findings, Faulkner's novel undoes Cartesian separations between mind and nature, interiority and exteriority, by positing a natural body that exists prior to culture. Indeed, modernist narrative experimentation in *As I Lay Dying* allows exteriority (objective form, "reality") and interiority (subjective experience) to permeate one another so as to yield a sensory–experiential portrayal of subjectivity that not only resists what Adam Newton calls "the culture of definition," but also makes such resistance explicable—pushing it beyond the sphere of the stubborn, the sentimental, the ineffable, and the exotic[41]. Significantly, the dialogic narrative form of Faulkner's novel mirrors Levinasian and scientific accounts of cognition in its stress upon how primordial social relations structure signification. This is to say that this portion of the chapter offers a reading of *As I Lay Dying* that shows how the novel works to portray its poor white characters in terms beyond those long recruited for conceptualizing race and class. Breaking with the categories of received conceptuality, Faulkner's novel humanizes what was previously Other, but in ways that do not simply apply to poor whites the valorized notions and motifs of an old-fashioned literary humanism, one which posits a monolithic, metaphysical "Human" that stifles difference and non-Western identity, to which "good" characters of heterogeneous backgrounds are assimilated. On the contrary, the argument here is that *As I Lay Dying* explores its characters' pre-rational sociality and ethical feeling in a way that gives witness to their humanity without reducing that humanity to, betraying it to, a unified concept.

Much recent scholarship on *As I Lay Dying* already focuses on the role of bodies in the novel. Jolene Hubbs writes that the passage of time in the novel is most notably marked by Addie's "corporeal putrefaction."[42] Later, she convincingly argues that a "sweat economy" in the novel measures "the labor that is masked within the dominant economic order."[43] Erin Edwards discusses the novel's "necropoetics," which she defines as an "experimental and vertiginously uncertain tropology through which the body is composed and decomposed."[44] These necropoetics, she argues, are "the defining mode of corporeal existence in the novel."[45] Christopher White argues that the use of animal metaphors in *As I Lay Dying* unmasks the limits of logic: animals in the novel, partly because of their bodily language, "expose the limitations of *logos,* and the insufficiency of a philosophical tradition, going back to Aristotle, that aims to secure the purity and privilege of the (human) subject."[46] I think White's assertions are especially perceptive, but animal metaphors and bodies are not the only elements in the novel that challenge *logos;* so, I will argue, do human bodies. White's claim that the novel renders Western philosophical tradition's privileging of the subject insufficient echoes, as we will see, Levinasian arguments defining the Good as one's infinite and unavoidable responsibility to the other rather than personal freedom.

Scholarship has long situated the Bundren family of *As I Lay Dying* specifically as poor whites. In *From Tobacco Road to Route 66*, Sylvia Jenkins Cook notes that "[t]he southern poor white is one of America's oldest and most enduring folk figures. His image is an elusive one, compounded of popular prejudice . . . but most typically it derives from the alliance of extreme material deprivation with slyness, sloth, absurd folly, and random violence."[47] Her discussion of *As I Lay Dying* includes a description of Anse that firmly ties him with the slyness and sloth she says defines poor whites: Anse "is a man of unbounded laziness."[48] The Bundren family's journey to bury their matriarch is, according to Cook, "the grim antics of the poor whites."[49] Nicolas Tredell calls *As I Lay Dying* Faulkner's "book most fully about the poor white."[50] Within the novel itself even other rural characters treat the Bundrens as something apart. The country doctor Peabody associates Anse with a dearth of movement. Noting that Anse had not been off his own property for twelve years, he laments, "[t]oo bad the Lord made the mistake of giving trees roots and the Anse Bundrens He makes feet and legs."[51] The plural he gives to Anse's name reflects the doctor's belief in a social type exemplified by Anse Bundren. A local farmer named Quick says that God has "took care of Anse a long time, now," because of Anse's sloth, and his friend Billy agrees: "'I reckon He's like everybody else around here.' . . . 'He's done it so long now he cant quit'" (58). Thus, the social boundaries between the Bundren family and the other characters in the novel are not totally drawn, as some might expect, along the rural/urban dichotomy. Even among other rural characters, they are something apart—social pariahs, white trash.

Both the novel's form and content play a role in asserting an embodied cognitive mode of subjectivity; I will first address form. *As I Lay Dying* is told entirely through the first-person narrations of its characters. Unlike *The Sound and the Fury*, in which the final section is told from the point of view of a disembodied narrator rather than one of the three Compson brothers, in *As I Lay Dying* there is no section where one might hope for an objective portrayal of the novel's world. Even characters that a reader might trust to offer an objective narrative add their own desires and beliefs to their narrations. One might be led, for instance, to think that Peabody's narration will be objective—he is a doctor, after all, and obviously a respected member of the community. However, Peabody's narration, far from being a standard by which to judge the novel's events, carries within it cultural assumptions that prejudice his perception. When he narrates a conversation with Anse, he reports Anse's speech in dialect (e.g., "That ere corn me and the boys was aimin to git up with, and Dewey Dell a-takin good keer of her, and folks comin in, a-offerin to help and sich, till I jest thought . . .") (30). Peabody narrates his own speech in standard English. However, when Darl narrates Anse's speech, there are no such dialectal markers; for example, Darl reports Anse saying, "She'll rest easier for knowing it's a good one, and private. She was ever a private woman. You know it well" (13). Peabody's urge to show the linguistic distance between him and Anse underscores the presence of his personality when he narrates. If one relies on him to report the novel's events objectively, one probably does so simply because his narration is easier to understand than that of most of the others. However, clarity does not guarantee objectivity. Because the form of *As I Lay Dying* refuses to allow the events of the novel to be narrated outside of the particular viewpoints of its characters, it makes an argument for the role of lived bodily experience in our perceptions of reality.

The novel's typographical elements also contribute to an embodied cognitive model of subjectivity by emphasizing the body's role in grounding signification. In the novel's first section, Darl, narrating Cash's working on their mother's coffin, notes the "Chuck. Chuck. Chuck. of the adze" (4). White space breaks up the onomatopoeic "chucks" into intervals, conveying the steadiness and temporality of Cash's work. This method of narration privileges sensory data—the sense of time passing and auditory information—over mere verbal description (e.g., "Cash worked steadily"). The novel's typography demonstrates that bodily experience is not simply a (separate) supplement to mental experience: both twine and have footing in the narrative.

Another important typographical innovation in Darl's sections is found in how switching between roman and italic type is handled. In *The Sound and the Fury*, Benjy's and Quentin's sections often move from roman to italic type to signify the narration of associative memories. These italic sections are typically in a traditional stream of consciousness style: they convey the narrator's thoughts but do not venture out of his head. By contrast, in *As I Lay Dying,* switching from roman to italic type, particularly in Darl's sections, signals the ability to read minds and communicate without words. In the scene in which Darl narrates Addie's death, Dewey Dell leaves the room, but Darl continues to narrate her actions:

> Then without looking at pa she goes around the bed and leaves the room.
> *She will go out where Peabody is, where she can stand in the twilight and look at his back with such an expression that, feeling her eyes and turning, he will say: I would not let it grieve me, now.* (35)

Later in the same section, Darl speaks to Jewel, who is not present: "*Jewel, I say, she is dead, Jewel. Addie Bundren is dead*" (35).

This scene is important to note because it illustrates both the infinite responsibility that Levinas ties to the face and the neuroscientific account of the role of social relations in structuring cognition. Dewey Dell faces Peabody's back in such a way that, eschewing sight's traditional role in recognizing another's face, he senses her attention and responds with what comfort he can. Peabody is, in Levinasian terms, called by and obligated to Dewey Dell's face, opening lines of ethical discourse that manifest themselves in his attempt to comfort her. In neuroscientific parlance, Darl dramatizes, by narrating Peabody's interactions with Dewey Dell, "affective resonance," in which two or more individuals affect each other's emotional states.[52] Here we see the emphasis the novel puts on binding sociality and emotion to produce signification. Darl's communicative abilities argue against the notion that we are each an unadulterated and lone subject, "each against all, in the multiplicity of allergic egoisms which are at war with one another" (*OB* 4). We may see how Faulkner's experiments with form make powerful arguments against generalizing poor whites into homogeneity: by emphasizing the influence of embodiment on consciousness, the novel portrays subjectivities resistant to reductive discursive construction and containment.

The novel's form further argues against traditional Western accounts of subjectivity by frustrating attempts to read any one character's section meaningfully outside of its context. For example, anyone who has taught *As I Lay Dying* will be familiar with the class being fixated on the shortest section of the novel, Vardaman's "My mother is a fish" (54). Taken alone, Vardaman's statement makes little sense; someone familiar with *The Sound and the Fury* might even wonder if Vardaman, like Benjy, is mentally disabled. Understanding Vardaman's comment requires contextualizing it with Anse's earlier assertion that, after catching and attempting to clean a fish, Vardaman is "bloody as a hog to his knees, and that ere fish chopped up with the axe like as not" (26). The reader then understands that Vardaman makes sense of his mother Addie's recent death by equating her dead body with the dead body of the fish. More generally, each character's sections are titled merely with his or her name, lending them a sense of characteristic *particularity.* The novel's form implies, then, that signification is structured and formed by social relations and dramatizes these relations within a "discursive community" of sorts, creating a horizon distinctive to each character. This runs counter to thinking of signification and meaning as stemming from culture as an enveloping, synchronic semiotic system or thinking of discourse in terms of textuality alone. Yet, in ethical and somatic responsiveness to others, as in Darl's preternatural intuition of Peabody's sensing the import of Dewey Dell's gaze and in Vardaman's association of his mother's bodily vulnerability with the abject bloodiness of the fish, characters breach the boundaries of their own horizons and are pushed away from reposing upon their own modes of "being-in-the-world."

The novel's content, like its form, stages Levinasian and neuroscientific modes of subjectivity. As in so many of Faulkner's novels, the beating heart of *As I Lay Dying* lives in its first paragraph, narrated by Darl: "Jewel and I come up from the field, following the path in single file. Although I am fifteen feet ahead of him, anyone watching us from the cottonhouse can see Jewel's frayed and broken straw hat a full head above my own" (3). What a reader might notice first is that Darl narrates in the present tense, a stylistic choice that places the act of Darl's narration in contemporaneity with the action he narrates. This gives a sense of partial omniscience and exteriority to Darl's narration, which is only underscored by his observation that someone standing near the cottonhouse could see Jewel's head above his own: the peculiarity of this observation lies in Darl's ability to situate Jewel's head in relation to his own despite his walking in front of Jewel and so, presumably, being unable to see him. The aforementioned heart of the novel thus is, as Erin Edwards writes, the erosion and permeability of the boundaries between "external, visible form and subjective inwardness."[53] This permeability is suggestive of a subjectivity that is not hermetically sealed from bodily and material existence but is rather constituted from such existence.

The sections of the novel narrated by Darl's seventeen-year-old sister, Dewey Dell, similarly assert her embodiment and removal from culturally constructed modes of subjectivity, but they do so in a less straightforward way than his. Dewey Dell, being unmarried, secretly pregnant, and deeply impoverished, represents the stereotypical portrayal of the poor white woman as "barefoot and pregnant." Her embodiment at first seems to be a problem: it is the fetus growing within her body that violates her desire to be "all right alone" with herself (39). However, as we will see, her embodiment and the narrative strategies stemming from that embodiment ground and structure her eligibility for moral consideration, consideration typically denied "white trash."

A section that Dewey Dell narrates is more often a monologue or self-declamatory space than a site of reportage: one such section begins with "The signboard comes in sight. It is looking out at the road now, because it can wait. New Hope. 3 mi. it will say. New Hope. 3 mi. New Hope. 3 mi. And then the road will begin, curving away into the trees, empty with waiting, saying New Hope three miles" (78). We may see that the novel eschews fact-oriented reportage in a way that obligates the reader to encounter and interpret Dewey Dell; her language relies on narrative excesses to demonstrate her radical alterity and, in the Levinasian "anarchy of passivity" that follows, humanity (*OB* 113). Her thoughts swirl around the approaching sign and the road near it, now in the present tense as the sign takes on personification and "look[s] out at the road now, because it can wait," and now in the future tense when "the road will begin, curving away into the trees." She mourns that "[i]t is because in the wild and outraged earth too soon too soon too soon. It's not that I wouldn't and will not it's that it is too soon too soon too soon" (78). Dewey Dell's narration, in its desperate excesses, demands an interactive rather than a legislative order of understanding. The structure of this section, with its narrative cracks that obligate the reader towards interaction, allows the reader to move towards an understanding of Dewey Dell not as "poor white Dewey Dell" and a target for ridicule or bourgeois sympathy, but towards an understanding of her embodied singularity as a young woman whose desire and reasons not to have a child in her present circumstances make themselves powerfully understood. Dewey Dell's language combines relatively simple words with sublime structural cadences that show a subtlety and fineness of feeling that her words alone cannot express.

TOWN FOLKS

Thus far I've discussed how *As I Lay Dying* humanizes poor white Others, but, as Vermeule notes, while humans are inclined towards recognizing each others' humanity, "we can just as easily deanimate other people, excluding them from the circle of personhood."[54] Citing developmental psychologist Paul Bloom's argument that disgust for others is a reaction to their bodies, Vermeule observes that it would follow that, to the extent that we see others only as bodies removed from individual identities, we would tend to remove them, subconsciously, from any consideration of moral behavior.[55] The reduction of identity and humanity to bodily markers (such as skin tone), an all too familiar culturally encoded trope, would seem to constitute a social-political correlative of the psychological patterns that Bloom's research documents.[56] White bourgeois writers' habitual deployment of terms such as "sallow" to denote poor whites' skins, then, may be understood as efforts to patrol economic and social boundaries, to regulate to whom a full range of human motives and feelings may be attributed. Consistent with Bloom's account, then, elite discourse's identification of poor whites with their bodies—here, the obsession shown by writers over skin tone—legitimates their dehumanization. Matt Wray calls attention to "the heightened sense of moral repugnance and disgust that energizes and animates the descriptions [of poor whites]. Talk of *poor white trash* consistently provoked strong emotions of loathing and contempt."[57] This disgust, he continues, "enabled those who used the term to unite in a shared experience of moral superiority and moral outrage and simultaneously to absolve themselves of responsibility for what was a deplorable state of affairs."[58] The phrase "to absolve themselves of responsibility" recalls Levinas's account of the ethical as something woven into subjectivity, as something one would like to outrun or mystify but never entirely can. Wray's insightful perception of what Levinas makes the subject of ethical phenomenology attests to the acuity of Levinas's analysis, and to its applicability to contexts (the American South) about which Levinas appears to have known and thought little. If Levinasian sensibility and neural sense-awareness of other humans ultimately ground rationality and ethical behavior, then to refuse to acknowledge one's obligation to the Other is to refuse rational deliberation on moral behavior towards that Other. We may see this self-absolution at work in two sections of *As I Lay Dying* narrated by town-dwelling members of the white bourgeoisie. Mosley, a Mottson store worker, narrates the first of these.

Mosley's section begins with his looking at Dewey Dell's face and seeing her "not looking at anything in particular; just standing there with her head turned this way and her eyes full on me and kind of blank too like she was waiting for a sign" (133). Here, the possession of a face attached to a recognizably poor person "already provides the culture of definition with a pre-text—humanity reduced to physicality—for defacing or misrecognizing it; being culturally 'marked,' in other words, legitimates a more violent marking of the face."[59] Mosley, by defining Dewey Dell as poor, as "culturally 'marked,'" transfers his cultural attitudes towards the poor onto her. The blankness Mosley sees in Dewey Dell's eyes exists in a background of indeterminacy. Her face, rather than offering him recognition or inviting speech and so a sharing of minds, instead merely mystifies. Mosley operates within "the culture of definition"; for him, Dewey Dell is an object of socioeconomic and racial categorization instead of a person. Further, he thinks that "she had a quarter or a dollar at the most, and that after she stood around a while she would maybe buy a cheap comb or a bottle of nigger toilet water," thus simultaneously sizing up Dewey Dell's capital value and assigning her to a racialized family of products ("nigger toilet water") based on what he sees. At one point, Mosley thinks that he perceives some signification in her eyes: "She stopped and looked at me. It was like she had taken some kind of a lid off her face, her eyes. It was her eyes: kind of dumb and hopeful and sullenly willing to be disappointed all at the same time. But she was in trouble of some sort; I could see that" (134). He then asks, "What's your trouble?" Despite Mosley's racially tinged assumptions about Dewey Dell, the trace of recognition remains: facing her feels as if she's taken a lid off her face. Further, he recognizes she is "in trouble" and offers to help. Such a lifting of lids off faces mirrors the novelistic depictions of embodied subjectivities at work in *As I Lay Dying*.

However, when Mosley learns that Dewey Dell is seeking an abortion, he takes a position of moral superiority. This scene dramatizes the complex interplay between morality as the involuntary Good that "has chosen me before I have chosen it" and moralizing as culturally received mores (*OB* 11). He tells her, "A thousand dollars wouldn't be enough in my store and ten cents wouldn't be enough" (135). He insists upon his moral righteousness by informing her he is "a respectable druggist, that's kept store and raised a family and been a church-member for fifty-six years in this town" (ibid.). At this point, he is seemingly pushed to the limits of indignation and the limits of his willingness to interact with in a way uninformed by received class and gender roles, for her eyes and face appear to him as "kind of blank again like when I first saw her through the window" (ibid). The more he is unwilling to accommodate the "interruption of the irreversible identity of [his] essence," the less able he is to understand and empathize with her thoughts and feelings, instead retreating into his comfortable role as town druggist and churchgoer (*OB* 13).We see here the effacement of Mosley's earlier recognition of Dewey Dell's humanity, its subsumption into his desire (perhaps well-intentioned but certainly self-important) to help her into moral orthodoxy. This subsumption is challenged, however: he says to the reader, "But it's a hard life they have; sometimes a man. . . . . . .if there can ever be any excuse for sin, which it cant be. And then, life wasn't made to be easy on folks: they wouldn't ever have any reason to be good and die" (136). He verges on an empathy rooted in a genuine, non-conceptually processed desire to help Dewey Dell, but goes on instead to rely upon his idea of Christian doctrine as his ethical guide, eventually telling her to leave his store (ibid). Mosley, encountering Dewey Dell, must reckon with the break of pre-ethical enjoyment that she represents, and he responds by thematizing her into abstract ethnicity and womanhood to avoid that very break; rather than considering her humanity, he categorizes her. One might argue that Dewey Dell's blank stare is a defense mechanism designed to disarm others by assuming a received role as a dumb country woman. However, Dewey Dell blankly staring at the druggist could hardly be disarming, and her singular focus on obtaining an abortion suggests she would attempt to be accommodating towards someone she thinks could help her, as she is, tragically, later with Macgowan.

Macgowan, a drug store clerk in Jefferson like Mosley, carries condescending and stereotypical attitudes towards all "country people" (165). When his coworker Jody tells him a woman (Dewey Dell) has come into the store, he replies, "What kind of a woman is it?" (164). He explains of rural people that "[h]alf the time they dont know what they want, and the balance of the time they cant tell it to you" and that "like as not, they aint heard yet out there that they use rings [to signify marriage]" (165). He tricks Dewey Dell into believing that he is a druggist and can provide her with an abortion, giving her a dose from an unlabeled "bottle that looked all right" and telling her to return that night for an "operation" (168). When she returns to the store, he gives her six capsules of talcum powder and directs her to go in the cellar for the "procedure," where he rapes her.[60] This event, curiously underreported by both Dewey Dell and literary critics, demonstrates the collapse of ethical behavior within the context of class signification. Mosley and Macgowan are unable or unwilling to see Dewey Dell as an individual, but instead see her as part of a collective—the dull-witted poor white. This is because they insist upon racial, economic, and sexual categories and boundaries as the parameters of their interactions with her. These very same boundaries also limn their identities: similarly to how Mosley and Macgowan see Dewey Dell within the rigid confines of class and race, they assert their identities as a "churchgoing druggist" and "cosmopolitan townsman," respectively. Such identification allows them to comfortably locate themselves "in terms of in-group/out-group divisions."[61]

By refusing to allow their enjoyment to be interrupted by Dewey Dell, Mosley and Macgowan situate her as something less than human, or at least less than self. This refusal to devote individuated consideration to the ethical challenge that Dewey Dell presents, in order to conserve *a priori* categorizations, highlights a key distinction between the flexible, provisional practical wisdom (*phronesis*) with which one, according to Aristotle, should judge particulars so as not to reduce them to mere instances of universals, on the one hand, and the ethically violent universalism with which Mosley and Macgowan judge Dewey Dell, on the other.[62] My argument for the failure of the ethical systems with which Mosley and Macgowan approach Dewey Dell faults these systems for their inability to reckon with particular ethical dilemmas, not the action of judgment itself, which is a valuable function of practically deliberated ethical decisions. With Mosley and Macgowan, *As I Lay Dying* stages, if by negative examples, modes of embodied subjectivity in which the potential to liberate individuals, both as subjects and objects, from categorization remains stubbornly alive. Within that resistance abide challenges to the totalization and indifference towards the Other. Such challenges, the novel intimates, are the vocation of responsible literature: to be disruptive of stereotypical aestheticized consumption.

EMBODIED SUBJECTIVITY, RACE, AND POOR WHITES

Discussion of the body's role in constructing subjectivity, it should be noted, may be interpreted as carrying connotations that poor whites, especially women, are somehow limned and limited by their bodies. Such an interpretation is developed by Diane Roberts in *Faulkner and Southern Womanhood* when she writes that Dewey Dell "is all body as Darl is all language," and that "[h]er consciousness, *such as it is*, looks inward toward the life growing in her" (emphasis mine).[63] This kind of interpretation is ultimately grounded (however paradoxically) in patriarchal Western philosophical traditions that invariably press toward denigrating the body. Recourse to such traditions, often unreflectively, reveals contemporary criticism's continuing prioritization of semiotic systems over natural bodies in identity construction, a legacy of poststructuralist theorizing oddly congruent with the philosophical inheritance it sought to transcend. Thinking from within the deeply rooted conceptual-evaluative contexts of dominant Western traditions, whatever one's conscious ideas may be, is apt to lead one to view claims about the body's role in subjectivity as necessarily giving putatively rational justification to movements towards suppression, particularly in light of traditional associations of women and people of color with the body. Such thinking is transcended by the novelistic depiction of subjectivity *As I Lay Dying* presents for its characters.[64] However, Levinasian ethics and contemporary cognitive science, in challenging Western philosophy's degradation of the body, open lines of discussion that attend to valorizing the body's role in ethical subjectivity by providing terms that make a non-reductive account of such subjectivity possible. Dewey Dell's body, then, rather than merely marking her according to economic, social, and racial boundaries, founds her identity as someone worthy of ethical behavior and capable of nuanced moral reasoning, as evidenced by ruminations such as *"That's what they mean by the womb of time: the agony and the despair of spreading bones, the hard girdle in which lie the outraged entrails of events"* and "[I]f I were not alone, everybody would know it. And he could do so much for me, and then I would not be alone. Then I could be all right alone" (78, 39). Such passages mark a complexity of thought and feeling that exceeds conceptual boundaries.

Further, Levinasian ethics, by suggesting and founding aesthetic value in infinite alterity, carries powerful implications for studies of race in literature. Lorna Wood, in a discussion of *The Narrative of the Life of Frederick Douglass* that "focuses on alterity in the work, rather than insisting on some (unstated) ideal of 'unity,'" notes that Levinas praises Proust for his "revelation that what is loved in the beloved is her unknowable Otherness."[65] Readings of literature informed by Levinas and cognitive science, then, can help reorient discussions of race towards the recognition and obligation grounded in the infinite alterity and singularity of the Other by moving such discussions away from reliance upon self–Other subjective paradigms that, however well-intentioned, naturalize *conatus* as the essence of the human and so gravitate toward locating both the Self and the Other within the "irresistible imperialism of the same and the I"(CCP 55). It is in such an understanding of race and literature that the power of *As I Lay Dying* to illustrate humanity emerges.

NOTES

1. John Duval, "'A Strange Nigger': Faulkner and the Minstrel Performance of Whiteness," *Faulkner Journal* 22, no. 1/2 (2006): 106–119, 106 and 108 quoted.

2. I am thinking in particular of Eric Lott, *Love and Theft: Blackface Minstrelsy and the American Working Class* (Oxford: Oxford University Press, 1993); Theodore Allen, *The Invention of the White Race: Volume One; Racial Oppression and Social Control* (New York: Verso, 1994), and its subsequent volume, *The Invention of the White Race: Volume Two: The Origin of Racial Oppression in Anglo-America* (New York: Verso, 1997); Alexander Saxton, *The Rise and Fall of the White Republic* (London: Verso 1990); David Roediger, *Working Toward Whiteness* (New York: Basic Books, 2005); Noel Ignatiev, *How the Irish Became White* (New York: Routledge, 1995), among others.

3. Allen, 251.

4. Ignatiev, 1.

5. David Hardigan, *Odd Tribes: Toward a Cultural Analysis of White People.* (Durham: Duke University Press, 2005), 26.

6. My discussion of the history of "white trash" in American culture owes much to Matt Wray's treatment of the subject in *Not Quite White: White Trash and the Boundaries of Whiteness* (Durham: Duke University Press, 2006).

7. Wray, 40.

8. Allen, 250. The legal action to which Allen is referring is an act of the Colony of Virginia titled "An act declaring the Negro, Mulatto, and Indian slaves within this dominion, to be real estate." The text of the act is viewable at the University of Virginia's *The Geography of Slavery in Virginia* website at http://www2.vcdh.virginia.edu/gos/laws1700-1750.html. Earlier acts of the Colony of Virginia that arguably demonstrate racial hierarchies based on skin color include "An Act to Discourage English Running Away with Negroes" (1660) and "An act for the apprehension and suppression of runawayes, negroes and slaves" (1672).

9. William Bryd, *History of the Dividing Line Betwixt Virginia and North Carolina* (New York: Dover Publications, 1967 [1728]), 54, 92.

10. Ibid., 54.

11. Ibid., 74.

12. Augustus B. Longstreet, *Georgia Scenes, Characters, Incidents, &c., in the First Half Century of the Republic. By a Native Georgian. UNC Library of Southern Literature* (New York: Harper & Brothers, 1850), 54.

13. Richard Hildreth, *The White Slave: Another Picture of Slave Life in America.UNC Library of Southern Literature* (George Routledge and Co., 1852), 156.

14. Daniel R. Hundley, *Social Relations in Our Southern States.UNC Library of Southern Literature* (New York: Henry B. Price, 1860), 255.

15. Ibid., 256.

16. Ibid., 256.

17. Ibid., 274.

18. Ibid., 274.

19. Ibid., 264.

20. Mark Twain, *The Annotated Huckleberry Finn*, ed. Michael P. Hearn (New York: Norton, 2001[1885]), 53. This whiteness that is so white as to be sickening has interesting connections with the final chapter of Edgar Allan Poe's *The Narrative of Arthur Gordon Pym*, but I do not have room for that discussion in this essay.

21. W. J. Cash, *The Mind of the South* (New York: Vintage Books, 1941), 24.

22. Allan Bérubé and Florence Bérubé, "Sunset Trailer Park," in *White Trash: Race and Class in America*, ed. Matt Wray and Annalee Newitz (New York: Routledge, 1997), 33.

23. Annalee Newitz, "White Savagery and Humiliation, or a New Racial Consciousness in the Media," in *White Trash: Race and Class in America*, ed. Matt Wray and Annalee Newitz (New York: Routledge, 1997), 134.

24. See especially Mikhael Bakhtin, *Art and Answerability*, eds. Michael Holquist and Vadim Liapunov, trans. Vadim Liapunov and Kenneth Brostrom (Austin: University of Texas Press, 1990[1974-79]), Jacques Derrida, *The Gift of Death*, trans. David Wills (Chicago: University of Chicago Press, 1995), and Jean-François Lyotard, *The Differend*, trans. Georges Van Den Abbeele (Minneapolis: University of Minnesota Press, 1989) for examples of the "ethical turn" in philosophy. See especially Clark Davis, *Hawthorne's Shyness: Ethics, Politics, and the Question of Engagement* (Baltimore: Johns Hopkins University Press, 2005); *Levinas and Nineteenth Century Literature*, ed. Donald R. Wehrs and David P. Haney (Newark: University of Delaware Press, 2009), Jill Robbins, *Altered Reading: Levinas and Literature* (Chicago: University of Chicago Press, 1991), and Adam Newton, *Narrative Ethics* (Cambridge, MA: Harvard University Press, 1995) for examples of Levinasian approaches to literature.

25. Nat Lilenstein, *Penser Aujourd'hui: Emmanuel Levinas. Une 2 Plus.* 1991.

26. Donald R. Wehrs, "Levinas and Sterne: From the Ethics of the Face to the Aesthetics of Unrepresentability," in *In Proximity: Emmanuel Levinas and the Eighteenth Century*, ed. Melvyn New with Rober Bernasconi and Richard A. Cohen (Lubbock, TX: Texas Tech University Press, 2001), 144.

27. Newton, 183.

28. Maurice Merleau-Ponty, *Signs*, trans. Richard McCleary (Northwestern University Press, 1964 [1960]), 67.

29. George Lakoff and Mark Johnson, *Philosophy in the Flesh: The Embodied Mind and Its Challenge to Western Thought* (New York: Basic Books, 1999), 17.

30. See especially Antonio Damasio. *Descartes' Error: Emotion, Reason and the Human Brain* (New York: Harper Perennial, 1994), 127–201, 223–52; *Looking for Spinoza: Joy, Sorrow and the Feeling Brain* (Orlando: Harcourt, 2003).

31. Lakoff and Johnson, 17, 342

32. Evan Thompson, *Mind in Life: Biology, Phenomenology and the Sciences of Mind* (Cambridge: Harvard University Press, 2007), 250.

33. Blakey Vermeule, *Why Do We Care about Literary Characters?* (Baltimore: Johns Hopkins University Press, 2009), xii-xiii.

34. Jane Thrailkill, *Affecting Fictions: Mind, Body, and Emotion in American Literary Realism.* (Cambridge: Harvard University Press, 2007), 1.

35. Ibid., 17.

36. Lakoff and Johnson, 265–66.

37. Thompson, 394.

38. Marco Iacoboni, *Mirroring People: The New Science of How We Connect to Others* (New York: Farrar, Straus and Giroux, 2008), 5.

39. Ibid., 5.

40. See Joel Krueger, "Levinasian Reflections on Somaticity and the Ethical Self," *Inquiry* 51, no. 6 (2008): 603–26, 620 cited.

41. Newton, 183.

42. Jolene Hubbs, "William Faulkner's Rural Modernism," *Mississippi Quarterly* 61, no. 3 (2008): 461–75, 462 cited.

43. Ibid., 468.

44. Erin E. Edwards, "Extremities of the Body: The Anoptic Corporeality of *As I Lay Dying*," *MFS: Modern Fiction Studies* 55, no. 4 (2009): 739–64, 739-40 cited.

45. Ibid., 740.

46. Christopher White, "The Modern Magnetic Animal: *As I Lay Dying* and the Uncanny Zoology of Modernism," *Journal of Modern Literature* 31, no. 3 (2003): 81–101, 82 cited.

47. Sylvia Jenkins Cook, *From Tobacco Road to Route 66: The Southern Poor White in Fiction* (Chapel Hill: University of North Carolina Press, 1976), ix.

48. Ibid., 41.

49. Ibid., 43.

50. Nicolas Tredell, *William Faulkner: The Sound and the Fury and As I Lay Dying* (New York: Columbia University Press, 1999), 55.

51. William Faulkner, *As I Lay Dying* (New York: Library of America, 1985 [1930]), 42. All further references are to this edition and will be cited parenthetically in the text.

52. Thompson, 395.

53. Edwards, 745.

54. Vermeule, 25.

55. Ibid., 26.

56. Bloom writes in *Descartes' Baby: How the Science of Child Development Explains What Makes Us Human* (New York: Basic Books, 2004) that "by stating that certain people are disgusting, you inspire negative thoughts toward them . . . Disgust is a response to people's bodies, not their souls. If you see people as souls, they have moral worth: You can hate them and hold them responsible; you can view them as evil; you can love them and forgive them, and see them as blessed. They fall within the moral circle. But if you see them solely as bodies, they lose any moral weight. Empathy does not extend to them" (177).

57. Wray. 60.

58. Ibid., 60.

59. Newton, 183.

60. The fact of Dewey Dell's rape is oddly unmentioned in either *As I Lay Dying* or in criticism of the novel. A notable exception is Caroline Garnier's "Temple Drake's Rape and the Myth of the Willing Victim," in *Faulkner's Sexualities,* eds. Annette Trefzer and Ann J. Abadie, (Oxford, MS: University of Mississippi Press, 2010). Garnier writes, "Dewey Dell's

rape is surprisingly a nonevent: She never says a word about it, and McGowan [sic] only alludes to preparing for it" (176).

61. Hogan, Patrick Colm. *Understanding Nationalism: On Narrative, Cognitive Science, and Identity* (Columbus: The Ohio State University Press, 2009), 8. Hogan distinguishes between "practical identity" or "someone's entire set of representational and procedural structures" and "categorical identity" or "any group membership that I take to be definitive of who I am" (27, 29). See also Paul Bloom, "The Moral Life of Babies," *The New York Times*, May 5, 2010, Sunday Magazine, MM44+. Bloom notes that "studies with young children have found that once they are segregated into different groups—even under the most arbitrary of schemes, like wearing different colored T-shirts—they eagerly favor their own groups in their attitudes and their actions." Of further interest is Julia Kristeva's treatment of abjection in *Powers of Horror: An Essay on Abjection,* trans. Leon S. Roudiez (New York: Columbia University Press, 1982). Kristeva observes that "abjection is elaborated through a failure to recognize its kin; nothing is familiar, not even the shadow of a memory" (5). Thus we see from a variety of perspectives (cognitive science, developmental psychology, and philosophy, respectively) the ways in which self-selection into a group not only sets us against out-groups, but also paralyzes us within our in-groups and their mores, much as we see with Mosley and Macgowan.

62. See Aristotle, *Nicomachean Ethics*, trans. Terence Irwin, 2nd ed. (Indianapolis: Hackett, 1999), 1142 a. On the flexibility of Aristotelian *phronesis* and its attentiveness to singularizing particularity, see Martha C. Nussbaum, *The Fragility of Goodness: Luck and Ethics in Greek Tragedy and Philosophy* (Cambridge: Cambridge University Press, 1986). On connections between Aristotle's stress upon responsibility to the singularity of the particular in ontology and epistemology and his ethical thought's relation to Levinas's, see Christopher P. Long, *The Ethics of Ontology: Rethinking an Aristotelian Legacy* (Albany: State University of New York Press, 2004) and Claudia Baracchi, *Aristotle's Ethics as First Philosophy* (Cambridge: Cambridge University Press, 2008).

63. Diane Roberts, *Faulkner and Southern Womanhood* (Athens: University of Georgia Press, 1995), 202.

64. It would be naïve at best to argue that Faulkner's novels offer such movements towards humanization that I've described in this essay to all female characters and characters of color. Notable African American characters such as Charles Bon and Joe Brown are indeed given complex treatment, but this might be partially due to Faulkner's fascination with mixed-race bloodlines. Analyses of Faulkner's African American characters within the context of humanization and embodied subjectivity deserve further work, but I have no room to do such work here.

65. Lorna Wood, "Emmanuel Levinas and the American Renaissance Canon," in *Emmanuel Levinas and Nineteenth-Century Literature*, ed. Donald Wehrs and David Haney (Newark: University of Delaware Press, 2009), 166–206, 175, 174 cited.

Chapter Six

Paterson as a Satyrical Work

Epistemology of the Dance

N. S. Boone

William Carlos Williams's *Paterson* (published in five books between 1946 and 1958, and as a single volume in 1963) is a strange and improbable poem. Primarily rooted in the tradition of modernist collage, it also opens into the postmodern in its unceasing interruptions of its own discourse, its undercutting of its own narrative authority, and perhaps most importantly, its self-reflexive grounding in what I call "the epistemology of the dance"—a way of understanding that refuses systematic thought and abstract categories. In the following pages, I make two basic suggestions. First, using Mikhail Bakhtin's genre criticism in *The Dialogic Imagination*, I argue that *Paterson* claims for itself the genre of "satyrical literature," which is a type of satire with a particular bodily or carnal emphasis. Second, using Levinas's contrast between the saying and the said, I suggest that *Paterson* embodies an aesthetics of the saying whose claim for knowledge is strikingly similar to Levinas's in *Otherwise than Being*, namely that knowledge can be figured outside of subject/object, presence/absence binaries. Considering some salient features of *Otherwise than Being* may inform a reading of *Paterson*.

LEVINAS'S *OTHERWISE THAN BEING*

Levinas is typically thought of in terms of ethics, but his late work, *Otherwise than Being, or Beyond Essence*, carries enormous implications for ontology and epistemology as well. Its opening pages present the project of viewing human existence outside of the dialectic of being and non-being as contesting Western philosophy's construing of ontology via binaries of being/nothingness, presence/absence, essence/emptiness, in which being, presence, and essence are invariably privileged. Levinas insists, however, that since "Essence is interest" (4), presence is contest, and being is war. Western philosophy, in its privileging of being, promotes contest, war, through its discourse. Levinas would find a way to talk about existence without resorting to being/nothingness, presence/absence binaries, making possible a discourse in which human existence can be understood as "otherwise than being."

To accomplish this, Levinas separates the human subject from the dominating perspective of the abstractly rational subject, or the ego, founding human existence, instead, on the subject's, that is on my, proximity to, and thereby my relationship with, alterity. Alterity, the otherwise-than-me, is always already before me. It is before my beginning, an-archic, and I am always late in coming to its call. The an-archic is a past that is more than past, an irrecoverable past, of which I can only find a trace. The other is the locus of the trace of this an-archic alterity whom I encounter face-to-face. The other, before whom I am always already late in coming, calls me into responsibility for itself, and so holds me hostage. In sum, my existence is founded on a proximity to alterity which is an-archic and irrecoverable, but of which a trace is seen in the other who calls me into responsibility for itself.

In *Totality and Infinity*, Levinas focuses on the face-to-face encounter as the foundational moment of philosophy and ethics. The face of the other "cannot be comprehended, that is, encompassed" (194), for totalizing the other, reducing the other to a set of ideas, would evade the face's infinity, its inability to be comprehended, which calls me, as a subject, into question.[1] This ethical moment, in *Otherwise than Being*, does more than just call me into question; it founds my own subjectivity. No one else can take this burden; I must do it. But this singling me out seems to suggest that I am a being with an identity, one that can be held accountable as an individual. Levinas, however, explains how being singled out in responsibility does not presume one's essence or one's individual identity. Levinas's views on time can help clarify this claim.

While treatment of time in *Otherwise than Being* is too complex for a full account here, one key point bears upon responsibility's calling forth subjectivity. For Levinas, the structure of diachrony is built into the present, as the present is never fully present, but is always slipping away from itself.[2] The present is never at home with itself. Indeed, only a trace of the present is ever actually present, so presence's essence is never manifest, and the present has no "being," as "being" is typically understood. Recognizing the structure of diachrony built into the present allows Levinas to discuss how a subject (me) can be singularly called to take responsibility for the other without "being" an identity, an essence. To do this, Levinas uses linguistic terms (the saying and the said), which are tied to time terminology—the saying to diachrony, the said, synchrony.

Responsibility is a relationship with alterity by which my subjectivity is always already determined. But my subjectivity takes the form(s) of expression, signification, the saying (which is produced out of my proximity to alterity), and the said (which the saying inevitably becomes). The said is language; it assembles into a system; it is a field where the past and the future can be (re)presented; and it establishes togetherness through exchange and interpretation in synchronous time.[3] The saying, though, precedes and sustains the said (*OB* 6). The said is identification, but the saying "signifies prior to essence, prior to identification" (*OB* 46). The said takes comfort in identity and can be protected in dissimulation; it can hide behind interpretation. But the saying is full exposure, disclosure to the other "which uncovers beyond nudity . . ." (*OB* 49), exiling one from oneself: "The subject in saying approaches a neighbor in expressing itself, in being expelled, in the literal sense of the term, out of any locus, no longer *dwelling*" (*OB* 48–49). The saying in expressing itself is always moving ahead of itself or slipping away from itself, never experiencing presence. The subject, in saying, is never at home, dwelling in an identity.

However, my saying is not an active, willful exposure, but a supremely passive one. Levinas writes, "The passivity of exposure responds to an assignation that identifies me as the unique one, not by reducing me to myself, but by stripping me of every identical quiddity" (*OB* 49). My relationship with alterity, which is saying, is determined by a responsibility I always already have, before I choose to say, to be exposed to the other. At one point, Levinas describes this passivity as *creation ex nihilo*, in which creation obeys the call of the creator to come into existence before ever being able to hear the call and/or decide to obey the call.[4] Similarly, I am "incarnated" through my responsibility to the other.[5] The call of the other requires exposure, my denuding in the saying. It is, as Levinas calls it, an assignation by the other, for the other, which one never actively chooses, but always already is called by. My subjectivity, then, a saying structured as diachrony, dislocates me from myself. But paradoxically, in this dislocation lies my uniqueness, for my subjectivity is tied to my responsibility to bear the burdens of the other, or my accountability to the other in such a way that no other can take my place. I have been singled out in what Levinas calls "an election in persecution" (*OB* 56), and he provides the image of being held hostage to describe it.[6]

The saying, exposure to the other, expiation, expelling oneself, taking responsibility for the other—all of this is integral to Levinas's concept of substitution. At one point, Levinas writes, "Substitution is signification" (*OB* 13). Substitution is the structure of existence as being-for-the-other, "taking charge of the other" (*OB* 14), which is my very uniqueness. My subjectivity is my exposure to the other (saying), which is my being-for-the-other (responsibility), which is substitution. I take the other's place in the face of accusation. But, once again, I do not find an identity or a dwelling place in substitution. Substitution is a signifying, a saying, an exposure, an expelling/expiation of self—a diachrony never at home in itself.

A LEVINASIAN READING OF *PATERSON*: THE AESTHETICS OF THE SAYING AND THE EPISTEMOLOGY OF THE DANCE

As Williams himself describes it, "Paterson is a long poem in four parts,"[7] and he added a fifth, seven years after the fourth part was published. Williams began with a basic outline for the poem, which he describes in different ways. Essentially, the poem began as an attempt to reconcile man and his cities—to explore the modern American city as a kind of objective definition of man, himself. The first part (1946) digs into the "elemental character" of Paterson, New Jersey, through a pastiche of poetry, historical documents, and brief narratives about early inhabitants. Part II (1948) "comprises the modern replicas"—that is, it presents the city in its contemporary guises. Williams's poetry variously describes scenes from the park above the Passaic River Falls, and the scenes tend to focus on lust of one sort or another (especially for money or for sex). He intersperses prose texts about the economics of the early U.S., newspaper stories about present-day Paterson, and many letters he received over the years from Marcia Nardi, who is identified as "Cress"—many of which call into question Williams's character. The third book (1949) focuses on "a language" through which the city can live. The setting begins at the library, where the stale deadness of the past cannot be the source of new language that the city must discover to live now. Williams burns down the library and moves to the scene of the Falls, where the tumbling water reveals that needed language. Williams titles the first part of Book IV (1951) "an idyll." It is comprised of the conversations a young lady, confused, trying to succeed on her own in the city, has with her two employers—both of whom express their sexual desire for her. After some scattered depictions of Madame Curie (tied in with Pound's economic theories), and a final poetic sequence that repeats the refrain, "the sea is not our home," Book IV ends with a figure (Williams calls him Odysseus in his comment on the poem) who washes ashore on the beach to walk inland with his dog. Book V (1958) has no central setting, but it focuses on a couple of classic works of art, the most important of which are "The Hunt of the Unicorn" tapestry and Brueghel's "The Adoration of the Kings." Williams's most conspicuous concern in this book is aesthetics.

As the above summary demonstrates, *Paterson* is held together neither by a strong narrative string nor by any easily definable theme.[8] Its most memorable characteristic is its use of collage or pastiche, a motley assemblage of Williams's poetry, newspaper articles, various historical writings, personal letters, and other miscellanea. Key to Williams's aesthetic is his notion that the otherness of experience, the alterity of the exterior world, must be kept alive in the writing. Gabriel Riera's recent book on Levinas and aesthetics demonstrates the same concern. He asks, "If the other is both unnaratable and indescribable, how to write the other and to conceive of this writing as its welcoming?"[9] Otherness totalized, thematized, results in the dead language that Williams, especially in Book III, explicitly seeks to escape. His task is to make art that keeps otherness alive, allowing it, in fact, to be created by that otherness, and to do its bidding. This attitude is, I think, perfectly in line with Levinas.[10] I believe that Levinas's ideas, particularly regarding the saying and the said, open the door for an appreciation of satyrical literature, especially in the self-effacing way that Williams pieces together the pastiche of his epic. According to Leslie Hill, what Levinas prizes most in a poet such as Celan is disjunction—how the poet is interrupted consistently by otherness, and how the poem is thereby not a perfect artifact of high culture, but a living openness to the vagaries of experience—alterity, otherness.[11] Disjunction and the effacing of the poet's own voice through the piecemeal gathering of others' materials are what most characterize the "saying" of *Paterson*.

Throughout *Paterson*, Williams is keenly aware of his own writing. Thomas LeClair has suggested that, in many ways, it "is a long poem about writing a long poem."[12] Paul Bové suggests that Williams, as a postmodern poet, no longer separates aesthetics and ethics, and that in *Paterson*, "the perceiving subject loses its authority" and "the subject is not a privileged point of origin of the work." In losing the privileged position of the subject, "the tyranny of the ego's perspective in projection and perception is displaced."[13] Similarly, Jill Robbins argues that Levinas privileges the philosopher's language, which stands in an expressive relationship to its object, over poetic language which is more totalizing as it creates its object.[14] Perhaps, though, by dropping the privileged position of the subject-perceiver-ego-poet, *Paterson* stands in a more expressive relationship to that which he includes in the poem.

Kinereth Meyer believes that Williams explicitly deals with problems of representation in *Paterson*, arguing that Williams perceives "the inevitable belatedness of word to thing."[15] In a Levinasian vein, as a poet Williams, then, sees himself as always coming late to the alterity he is called to write for. Meyer writes, "The language of the poem performs, rather than merely thematizes, the interaction in American literature between aesthetics as an ideology of power."[16] For Meyer, aesthetic representation, especially in American literature, is about appropriating and/or possessing the other, but *Paterson*, by presenting otherness (rather than just conceptualizing it), "forces the reader to question those assumptions which posit the power of language to 'own' reality."[17] When Williams writes, "How strange you are, you idiot! / So you think because the rose / is red that you shall have the mastery?" (29),[18] he indicts the poetic tradition (the oft-repeated trope of the rose as love), which reminds the reader of the limitations, "the partial victory," of the poem they are reading. Meyer insists that though the American poet tries "to set himself up as the sole owner" of the other, in *Paterson* "the specific and incontrovertible *out there*" is always disrupting that totalizing impulse, ending her essay by claiming that in performing the act of representation, *Paterson* opens up the possibility of the poet being possessed by that which he represents.[19] Going further, I see in *Paterson* the poet's subjectivity being determined by the other, held hostage, called into responsibility for the other. But this can really only be understood within a broader view of *Paterson* as a satyrical work, as a work that embodies the epistemology of the dance—a dance that, within a Levinasian framework, is a saying which "resists the final crystallization" (*OB* 109) that is the said.

Williams ends Book V with a stunning epistemological claim: "We know nothing and can know nothing / but the dance, to dance to a measure / contrapuntally, / Satyrically, the tragic foot" (*P* 236). Tied directly to this epistemological claim is the image of the satyr—an image that plays an important role throughout *Paterson*, and especially in Book V. The image appears explicitly twice in both Books II and IV.[20] In Book II Williams describes "the peon in the lost Eisenstein film" (57) as a satyr—actually, as one of the mythical leaders of the satyrs, Priapus (58). Imbibing his wine, he is described as a "Heavenly man!" (58). Soon after that image, Williams shows us a young girl lounging beside her sleeping boyfriend, both of them drunk and "flagrantly bored" (59). Williams says she is "lean as a goat" as she "leans / her lean belly to the man's backside" (59). Mentioning the goat implies that she, like the old peon, is also a kind of modern-day satyr.

In Book IV, during a dialogue between the lesbian poet, Corydon, and her young, naive friend, Phyllis, Corydon describes herself as "more horse / than woman" (157); satyrs were at one time represented as having attributes of horses. Then, Corydon asks Phyllis to switch roles in their interpersonal drama: "Let's change names. You be Corydon! And I'll play / Phyllis. Young! Innocent! One can fairly hear the pelting / of apples and the stomp and clatter of Pan's hoofbeats. Tantamount / to nothing" (157). Of course, the sylvan god Pan is often linked to satyrs, but also of interest is the implication that the two women's play will be a tragedy—"Tantamount / to nothing." This foreshadows Book V when tragedy and the satyr dance are juxtaposed and in some way united. Also, near the end of Book IV, the satyr image appears again, this time as "the great theatre of Dionysus" (200). The satyric plays were all devoted to Dionysus, the god of ancient theater.[21] Here Williams laments the loss of the satyric, and wishes that "it could be aroused by some modern magic / to release / what is bound in it" (200). The satyr imagery is increased in Book V, but it builds upon the images provided in Books II and IV. For instance, the concupiscence demonstrated in the satyr references in Book II will be important in Book V, and so will the juxtaposition of tragedy and the satyr, as well as the nostalgia for a literature of the satyric that can be seen in the image of the theater of Dionysus at the end of Book IV.

"Satyr" and related words ("satyrical" and "satyrically") show up in three strategically important places in each of Book V's three sections. In the first section, the word characterizes a young man who has more than the average young man's concupiscent tendencies. The use of the term in the second and third sections is more extensive and important. It is placed almost exactly in the center of Book V the second time it is used, and the last time it shows up is in the poem's last line. In the middle of the second section , the speaker, who is the poet, Dr. Paterson, obsesses over a woman whom he will, ostensibly, never meet. He impulsively dedicates everything he has ever written to her: "have you read anything that I have written? / It is all for you // or the birds . / or Mezz Mezzrow // who wrote . // [enter a long prose section about a white man's experience with "Negro music"] // . . or the Satyrs, a / pre-tragic play, / a satyric play! / All plays / were satyric when they were most devout. / Ribald as a Satyr! // Satyrs dance! / all the deformities take wing" (218–19). Williams has obviously provided a double meaning for satyr. Not only does he recall the mythical goat-man followers of Dionysus, but he also conjures up the literary genre of satire. Both meanings are relevant here. First, the speaker describes his poems as literally existing for satyrs—those libido-driven creatures. He suggests that his writing is full of carnal desires, and also in some way driven or manufactured by libidinous elements. Second, use of "satyrical" is obviously intended to bring to mind the literary genre of satire. But "satyrical," I contend, isn't exactly satire, but satire infused with the carnal, perhaps even debauched urges of the satyrs. I would suggest that Williams is creating his own genre, "satyric literature," while he simultaneously elevates it beyond what is arguably the most revered literary genre, tragedy. But specifying the nature and purpose of Williams's satyric mode requires some preliminary clarifying of issues regarding tragedy and satire and satyr plays.

First, the satyr plays Williams refers to are not related to the later literary genre of satire. (Though through a twisted Anglophone etymology, they are linguistically related; this is due to similar pronunciation, not similar meanings from the Greek originals.[22]) Emily Wallace suggests that Williams "carefully" avoids the scholarly debate concerning the development of tragedy (i.e., whether or not it developed directly out of the satyr plays) by referring to the satyr plays as "pre-tragic," since no one claims they postdate tragedies.[23] While I doubt Williams would seek "carefully" to avoid any scholarly debate, he certainly is distinguishing satyr plays from tragedy, in fact elevating them above tragedy by nostalgically appealing to their more "devout" nature. Williams implies that tragedy is a later, less devout (at least in a Dionysian sense), and inferior invention that unfortunately holds a place of honor today. This is why he looks back with nostalgia to the theater of Dionysus at the end of Book IV.

Williams likely draws upon Nietzsche's *The Birth of Tragedy*, which argues that tragedy's original impulse stems from Dionysian rites, the choral sections of the tragedies being not simply ancillary to the action, but its original root as plot grew out of the need to present a visual image or objectify the chthonic impulse of the Dionysian chorus. Nietzsche writes, "[T]he Dionysian reveler sees himself as a satyr, *and as a satyr, in turn, he sees the god* which means that in his metamorphosis he beholds another vision outside himself as the Apollonian complement of his own state."[24] The satyr-reveler experiences ecstatic devotion to the god—unpredictable, uncontrollable. Apollonian objectification of this devotion is the plot or narrative, the truly ancillary aspect of the tragedy. However, because of Socratic logocentrism, Nietzsche claims, the Apollonian became the celebrated aspect of the genre as reason, and its resultant formalism, pushed out the more primal, dissonant original of tragedy.

Nietzsche's view was roundly criticized by classical scholars of his day, who were trained to see tragedy as primarily rational, symmetrical, balanced, and healthy, a notion that persists into twentieth-century genre criticism with Northrop Frye's *Anatomy of Criticism*. For Frye, true tragedy must "make a tragic *point*" morally or philosophically.[25] Forcing one to think on the "seriousness of life,"[26] tragedy takes itself seriously and insists its audience take themselves seriously. Against such academic perspectives on tragedy, Williams presents his Nietzsche-inspired satyrical genre, which will not strive towards making moral and philosophical points, but will be concrete, corporeal—given to the nature of the dancing, singing, love-making satyrs— rather than abstractly moral or philosophical.

Williams's idea of the satyrical is more than just plain satire, but includes satirical elements. Frye's genre analysis suggests why satire would appeal to Williams; whereas philosophy, of which tragedy partakes in heavy doses, is dogmatic, satire is pragmatic, anti-philosophic literature.[27] It is also more corporeal, *satyr*-ic: Fyre notes that "practically every great satirist" becomes "obscene" at some point, and speaks of "a bodily democracy,"[28] which I take to mean that everyone, kings and peasants alike, is presented corporeally, with the crudeness of the body emphasized. Williams cites on the final page of Book I, a long passage from John Addington Symonds's chapter on satirists in *Studies of the Greek Poets*, where Symonds argues that, unlike later satirists, such as Swift, who used satire as a serious moral indictment of society, the Greek satirists "knew nothing" of "serious invective" or "moral preaching."[29] Following Symonds's lead, Williams makes satire his own by making it "satyrical."

One more genre critic can help shed light on *Paterson* as a satyrical work. Several scholars have noticed in Williams' poetry the kind of heteroglossia (interwoven heterogeneous discourses or voices) that Mikhail Bakhtin sees as key in the development of the novel.[30] Certainly, heteroglossia can be found in *Paterson*, but I want to focus on a genre that Bakhtin mentions as crucial to Western literature's movement toward the novel form: the parodic-travestying genre. Bakhtin mentions four accomplishments of the parodic-travestying genre, which I believe *Paterson*, as satyrical literature, accomplishes as well. First, it "liberated the object from the power of language [as almighty interpreter] in which it had become entangled"; second, it "destroyed the homogenizing power of myth over language"—meaning now becomes contingent rather than eternal, or fixed; third, it "freed consciousness from the power of the direct word, destroyed the thick walls that had imprisoned consciousness within its own discourse." This leads to the fourth point, the creation of a distance between language and reality—the word becomes its own concrete reality, and consciousness is freed from the logos, opening it up to the concrete, corporeal, and the carnal.[31]

Bakhtin argues that the parodic-travestying genre paved the way for the novel, but he doesn't mention its implications for epistemology. If this genre accomplished a divorce of consciousness from its own discourse and of language from reality, then people would have to question the authority of their knowledge. The speaker at the end of *Paterson* addresses problems of epistemology, intimating that the only literary form that is epistemologically valid is satyrical literature: "We know nothing and can know nothing / but / the dance, to dance to a measure / contrapuntally, / Satyrically, the tragic foot."

In another late poem, Williams writes, "[O]nly the dance is sure."[32] Insisting that embodied knowledge is superior to abstractions, Williams, in his theoretical essay, *The Embodiment of Knowledge*, consistently criticizes those who would use "Science and Philosophy" to order human existence. People should see the distortions that can occur when abstractions "stand beyond us to order us,"[33] and we should value instead a real knowledge "anterior to all systems of thought."[34] *Paterson*, as satyrical literature, exhibits this embodied knowledge, this epistemology of the dance, which leads to a language that is concrete (no ideas but in things) and carnal. At moments, Williams explicitly denies the ability of language/reason to order reality: "How strange you are, you idiot! / So you think because the rose / is red that you shall have the mastery? / The rose is green and will bloom, / overtopping you, green, livid / green when you shall no more speak, or / taste, or even be" (*P* 29).

The concrete and carnal are essential pieces of the "satyr" aspect of satyrical literature, and elements can be seen all over *Paterson* (wine drinking, sex, and the hilarious picture of the giant urinating, among others). But another important part of "satyrical" literature is more involved in the "satire" aspect, and that is the ability of satyrical literature to incorporate earlier texts, playing upon their meaning through reordering and recontextualization. By positing that the satyrical is the only literature that can achieve real knowledge, Williams is essentially arguing that language, and literature as language, cannot produce fixed, stable meanings, cannot lead humankind toward eternal ideals. The satyrical does not interpret, but rather plays upon already existing texts. We can only know satyrically. Knowledge then becomes play, contingent; it is not serious, fixed, or eternal, but concrete, corporeal, local, rooted in experience, and application. *Paterson* embodies this aesthetic, stemming from the epistemology of the dance. *Paterson*'s "beautiful thing" is vulgar, which "surpasses all perfections" (120) of philosophy, all abstract ordering of reality by language and reason. [35]

Of course, one of *Paterson*'s striking features is the amount of material from other sources that it incorporates within itself. Satire and parody, in the broadest definition of those terms, basically achieve their humor, or other purposes, through playing off of earlier texts by recontextualizing them, thereby creating irony. *Paterson* exhibits satire and parody in many ways. First, there is the inclusion of other texts from histories of the city and letters Williams had received over the years. But other texts and forms of texts show up that are less easily identifiable. Most of the prose in *Paterson* obviously seems taken from other sources; some, however, is Williams's own invention. To complicate matters further, some of the prose is from Williams's typist, who researched and summarized material for him. Even more problematic is his transformation of a prose text into poetry, which takes up a substantial portion of Book IV. A reader (even an astute one) is rendered incapable of separating what is original to Williams from what he is incorporating. Williams even parodies himself, by using portions of a poem ("The Wanderer"), which he had already published separately. [36] Such play with earlier texts radically questions the authority of language, as well as the authority of the author to produce meaning. But Williams's play with the language of other texts, according to Joseph N. Riddel, has a more positive aesthetic value than simple questioning of the authority of meaning; recontextualization of the historical piece on Sarah Cummings (and by implication all the historical prose pieces in *Paterson*) works to give the writing "a sense of presentness to itself." [37] In its original environment, the details of the Sarah Cummings piece were put in service of another motive, namely an interpretation of a strange historical event. Riddel argues that by recontextualizing certain parts of the narrative, Williams brings the writing alive to itself, alone. Like the epistemology of the dance, which doesn't rely on abstraction to order reality, but orders reality itself through its contact with it, this writing now exists knowingly in itself.

Perhaps most interesting of all is the poem's satirizing of itself. Kathleen D. Matthews describes what she calls "the satiric bedrock" of *Paterson* in Book I. Concentrating upon Williams's critique of Eliot, Cummings, Hart Crane, and Pound, she states briefly at one point that Williams saw "the need for the satirist to place himself in the same position as those he satirized." With this formulation, Matthews argues that Williams creates *Paterson* as "an anthropomorphic myth which competes with Eliot's myths and a mock-heroic giant who competes with other literary giants."[38] Williams, I think, believes he beats his "competition" not because he satirizes them, but because he is able to satirize himself even as he satirizes them. His hero is only a mock hero. Matthews doesn't mention the inclusion of the Nardi letters in *Paterson*, but this is perhaps the most powerful example of Williams satirizing himself. In Book II, Williams includes long letters from Marcia Nardi (who, in the poem, is identified as "Cress"), a young, female writer who called, many times desperately, upon him for literary and financial assistance. As Robert Coles suggests, "Cress" calls the poet out from behind his desk in front of the world for inspection, and she finds him wanting: Williams may write against intellectualism, but really he's a snob; he doesn't live what he writes.[39] By including these accusations, *Paterson* performs a self-satire that is as vicious, or even more vicious, than any invective it conducts against Eliot.

Williams's inclusion of other texts is a demonstration of satyric play upon previous texts, but it also is an act of self-effacement as the other texts take over and challenge the authority of the poet-ego. The Nardi letters have multiple implications along these lines in *Paterson*, because, as "other" texts, their inclusion already disrupts the tyranny of the singular poet/subject/ perception. However, the text of the letters plunges even more deeply into the problem of subjectivity.[40] The first appearance of a Nardi letter in Book II speaks of "exiling one's self from one's self": "That kind of blockage, exiling one's self from one's self—have you ever experienced it? I dare say you have, at moments; and if so, you can well understand what a serious psychological injury it amounts to when turned into a permanent day-to-day condition" (45). This letter obviously implicates the poet in the problem of self-exile. The next letter continues in the same vein, but the sense of exile relates to Williams as a satyric poet by questioning the validity of any poet's writing and the alienation between the poet and his or her writing. In speaking of the exchange of letters between Williams and Nardi (which Williams has, at this point, put a stop to on his part), the letter states that the result of the exchange has been "to destroy the validity of myself to myself," and that "the whole side of life connected with those letters should in consequence take on for my own self that same kind of unreality and inaccessibility which the inner lives of other people often have for us" (48). Williams may here be intimating that in the writing of this poem, which is the saying, there is a losing of self in the self-expression.

Later in Book II, another Nardi letter speaks of the loss of personal identity which is needed to write (76), and in the last astonishingly long letter at the end of Book II, something similar is stated: "*Only* my writing (when I write) is myself: only that is the real me in any essential way" (87). In the inclusion of these parts of Nardi's letters, Williams displays an anxiety over the relationship between writing and personal identity. However, Nardi's voice may also serve as a counterpoint on which Williams works his satire; for though Nardi claims that a writer needs a personal identity to write, Williams shows that he can produce poetry through effacing his identity— partially accomplished by including her letter in his poem. Ironically (satyrically), he uses her own expression of desire for an identity as a writer to demonstrate the effacement of his own identity as a writer. [41]

These examples of the poet's self-effacement in *Paterson* demonstrate what occurs, according to Levinas, in the saying—a full expression, a vulnerability, and a nudity that is an expulsion of the self, which takes responsibility for the other as substitution for the other. The self is never identical with itself, but is self-effacing in its taking responsibility for the other—which is its fullest expression of itself. But this saying is not a chosen response; rather, it is the result of an extreme passivity towards the other. Thus the saying, which I am arguing is the dance that is *Paterson* as a satyrical work, has a problematic origin. From whence does this saying come? How does it come about?

First of all, it does not come from anything like a categorical ethical imperative willed by the subject. The saying is called out of the subject's extreme passivity in regard to alterity. At times, *Paterson* hints at such a passivity: "— that love, / that is not, is not in those terms / to which I'm still the positive / in spite of all; / the ground dry,—passive-possessive" (44). Here we see an expression, love that cannot be formulated in normal terms "to which I'm still the positive"—that is, in which one is still posited as an identity, as possessing being and a presence. The love is a saying that is from a subject who does not possess being or presence, but that *is* a passive expression, an existence that slips from itself in its expression.

Terri A. Mester, drawing on Riddel, sees the dance in Williams's work as a pre-reflective state anterior to language and/or consciousness. [42] In *The Embodiment of Knowledge*, Williams states that knowledge is anterior to mind, or any branch of human thought, and that science, philosophy, ethics, and religion (those branches) are preceded by the illogical, "a region unsusceptible to argument." Williams asserts that the basis of all knowledge is "the unknown," and this unknown is figured not as any abstraction, but as a place (i.e., "the region unsusceptible to argument.") [43] Passages such as these underlie what critics often see as Williams's pre-occupation with a sense of origins. Some critics, such as Nancy K. Barry, believe that "Williams persistently valorized the moment of origin as antecedent to language, undefiled by words and the 'trick of history,'" and that he thought he could recover a sense of this primordial origin through the new measure he often speaks of, or the dance, the playful language of *Paterson*.[44]

Another approach towards Williams's concern over origins is that of Riddel, whose project, as Hugh T. Crawford sees it, is to view *Paterson* as a postmodern text that 1) takes itself as its own subject, and 2) denies origins.[45] According to Riddel, the poet refuses to believe he can recover lost origins.[46] The best the poet can achieve is "writing in search of the origin of writing."[47] The origin of writing is unnameable, "primordial." It is "a dissonance," a "violent and inaugural beginning of the word which the word can never name."[48] The dance that is Williams's poetry seeks to return to that moment of original violence so as to provide an imaginative freedom of the play of words no longer subjected to the "Word."[49] Riddel's reading has some similarities with a Levinasian one in that he recognizes the poem's relationship to a past that is anterior to language and which is irrecoverable. In Levinas, the subject recognizes the trace of the an-archic in alterity (the other), which is an infinite, irrecoverable past. The response to this recognition is the saying, a non-totalizing expression/expulsion of the self. So, while Riddel sees Williams's *Paterson* as seeking to enact an originary violence, I see *Paterson* as a response that, if it does any violence, does violence to the self in its radical disclosure of the selfhood which takes oneself out of oneself in response-ability for the other in whom was recognized this primordial trace of the an-archic.

Thomas Bertonneau, who sees *Paterson* as presenting a doggedly humanist ethics, is most in line with a Levinasian reading of *Paterson*'s concern with origins. Using the anthropological theories of Eric Lawrence Gans and René Girard, Bertonneau states that, for Williams, "representation emerges from the victimary scene."[50] The "victimary scene" is actually a cadaver of a human propitiatory sacrifice. This cadaver is the origin from which all future fate of the culture springs; yet, it is an empty signifier: "Self-presence [of the culture, and individuals within the culture] . . . depends originarily on the presence of an Other, a radical Other who has been expelled or eliminated and who is present, therefore, in the form of a conspicuous absence."[51] Though I disagree with Bertoneau's too-easy alignment of Williams and humanism (more on this later), his idea that the poem finds its beginning in the presence of an absence (what Levinas calls "the trace") is very much how I read *Paterson*'s concern over origins. This is why, when Williams is describing a Dionysian moment with wine drinking and dancing in Book II, he writes, "This is the old, the very old, old upon old, / the undying: even to the minutest gestures, / the hand holding the cup, the wine / spilling, the arm stained by it" (57). The "minutest gestures" partake in this past, an an-archic past that is irrecoverable (why else repeat "old" four times?), old upon old. Also, this can be seen in Book III when Williams is questioning how one writes poetry that is a saying, a dance. He writes, "How to begin to find a shape—to begin to begin again" (140). Williams could have written, "to begin again" if he did not want to emphasize the primordial, essentially irrecoverable nature of this an-archic trace that is found in alterity. "To begin to begin again" is to move beyond beginnings.

As I've previously described it, Levinasian signification takes on a dualistic formulation as the saying and the said. Unlike the saying, which is a diachronic expression that never rests within itself, the said is a synchronic gathering up of things into a language, a system—it begets the dissimulation of interpretation. Riera suggests that "Levinas locates the possibility of a saying that exceeds the grasp of the said . . . in the amphibology of language," and that this possibility of an aesthetics of the saying could open a way towards ethical writing.[52] I believe that for Williams the dance figures as a kind of saying that resists "the final crystallization" of the said. But before the dance appears in all its glory in Book V, Williams presents the struggle of the poet to write a "dance," a saying, rather than to reduce the other to a totalizing system of language, the said. This struggle is especially apparent in Book III, where Williams writes,

> It is dangerous to leave written that which is badly written. A chance word, upon paper, may destroy the world. Watch carefully and erase, while the power is still yours, I say to myself, for all that is put down, once it escapes, may rot its way into a thousand minds, . . . // Only one answer: write carelessly so that nothing that is not green will survive. (129)

This passage is difficult because the carelessness Williams ends up suggesting seems at odds with the exertion of power over the text he seems to promote earlier in the passage. Eventually, Williams suggests carelessness, I believe, as a protection against ego control. By "carelessly" I believe Williams means without regard for one's own cares or concerns. "Carelessly" means a willingness to become vulnerable to the strangeness of alterity. Williams is presenting the struggle between the saying and the said, between an expression that denudes, makes one vulnerable (which we see in Book III when the beautiful thing is taken advantage of), and an expression that can be reduced to categorization, and so interpretation or a meaning. Williams wants a fresh, "green" writing which doesn't allow that radiant gist to crystallize into a "shelly rime" hard "baked by endless dessications" (143).

But how can a poet resist the said? The saying stops, eventually, and can be interpreted as a synchrony. The end of Book III seems to suggest that the poet, to maintain the "green" of the saying, must continue in the present, continue diachronically, not look at the past or into the future. The poet speaks in the present that, like the falls, is always slipping by itself, never at home, "unrelenting": "The past above, the future below / and the present pouring down: the roar, / the roar of the present, a speech— / is, of necessity, my sole concern" (144–45). The said can be interpreted; it is at home within itself, in the protective shell of its own meaning, not exposed or vulnerable. But the saying resists interpretation. Williams ends Book III on this note:

> No meaning. And yet, unless I find a place
> apart from it, I am its slave,
> its sleeper, bewildered—dazzled
> by distance . I cannot stay here
> to spend my life looking into the past:
> the future's no answer. I must
> find my meaning and lay it, white,
> beside the sliding water: myself—
> comb out the language—or succumb
> —whatever the complexion. Let
> me out! (Well, go!) this rhetoric
> is real!
> (145)

The only meaning the poet can find is that which he can lay "beside the sliding water"; he can only remain saying in a present that, like the falls, is continually sliding past itself. Williams uses the term "rhetoric" because it is that kind of expression that has been thought, throughout history, to be empty of meaning. But rhetoric, then, is the only kind of speech for the poet since, without a protective shell of meaning, its exposure of itself, it doesn't totalize the other it represents.

Williams recognizes the totalizing danger of the said (it "may destroy the world" that it seeks to represent), but he also sees it as inevitable. Even as the poet seeks to maintain the saying by being "the voice" rather than becoming the interpreter of the voice, "Who am I?—the voice!" (108), Williams has to face the reality of the said, which tells him,

> Give it up. Quit it. Stop writing.
> "Saintlike" you will never
> separate that stain of sense,
> an offense
> to love, the mind's worm eating
> out the core, unappeased
> —never separate that stain
> of sense from the inert mass. Never.
> Never that radiance
> quartered apart,
> unapproached by symbols.
> (108–9)

But Williams continues to strive after the radiant gist that resists symbolic meaning. And he continues to write, to say, to dance, beyond his original concept of four books into five, even six, as he tries to counter the said that would have him "give it up." Williams continues to "Go where all / the mouths are rinsed: to the river for / an answer / for relief from 'meaning'" (111–12). Only in that saying of the river and the falls, which is a presence never at home in itself, sliding by itself always resisting what we typically think of as knowledge, can Williams find what he is looking for, which is how to speak of, to represent Paterson—the other who faces him.

A temptation might arise to see in Williams a bond with Heideggerian aesthetics of being. As a poet who was refined in the crucible of modernism, and who was consistently re-inventing his poetics throughout the thirties and forties, Williams may have encountered Heideggerian and existential ideas among his friends and associates. And the repetition of "the beautiful thing" through Books II and III and of "the radiance" in Book III and IV could possibly suggest a complicity with a Heideggerian aesthetics of the poem as a lighting of the clearing, opening a space of clarity out of the darkness of earth in which being can dwell.[53] Williams's biographer, Paul Mariani suggests that "the radiant gist" is a central metaphor of the aesthetics of *Paterson*. Out of muck, grime, waste, or out of "unstable elements," "pitchblende," shines forth a radiance that is useful.[54] In a way, Heidegger plays upon Nietzsche's notion of tragedy as a synthesis of Dionysian (earthy, chthonic) and Appolonian (rational, clarifying) impulses. Mariani, while not explicitly invoking Heidegger, sees Williams in *Paterson* as working through the Dionysian darkness of earth to perhaps finally reveal the radium, allowing the clarity to shine forth through the darkness.

However, Williams and Heidegger differ on the position or posture being takes in light of the poem or artwork. With Heidegger, the posture is an uprightness of standing forth that is the freedom of letting be. With Williams, however, one never sees this letting be. One sees only "exasperation," which, as Riera points out, is Levinas's word for the task of writing.[55] The posture of being in Levinas is not standing forth in the uprightness of the freedom of letting be, but it is a prostrate obedience before the other who calls one to being for it. Williams's posture is much more prostrate than upright throughout *Paterson*, as he is consistently undermining his own authority, piecing together multitudes of voices, along with his own, hearing their call, not for the clarity of being, but for the urgent necessity of the call itself. "Rigor of beauty is the quest" (3), Williams writes at the outset of the poem, and such engagement with the dark and dissonant earth, such prostrating oneself before it, to it, requires a rigorous openness. A Levinasian reading of *Paterson* can demonstrate that the poem enacts a kind of aesthetics of the saying where beauty is shown not as a fixed concept, but rather as a saying maintained outside of stable presence/absence dyads. Beauty is a virgin/whore—it maintains itself (virgin) in giving itself (whore) in full expression.

Paterson begins with beauty locked in the mind—it is a concept, reduced to the said of the rational: "'Rigor of beauty is the quest. But how will you find beauty when it is locked in the mind past all remonstrance'" (3). But Williams struggles against beauty as a self-contained concept throughout *Paterson*. In Book II he says, "Unless it is beauty // to be, anywhere, / so flagrant in desire" (71). To be flagrant is to, in a sense, be outside oneself, or at least outside fixed concepts of propriety. This aesthetics of the saying begins to find fuller expression in the beautiful thing of Book III, which is "counter to all staleness" of the said (100). The beautiful thing is exposed ("TAKE OFF YOUR CLOTHES! [105]), and is beaten ("scarred . . . by the whip" [126], and "socked across the nose" [127]), probably even raped (128), and yet in its vulgarity, this saying, this vulnerability, surpasses all fixed, "perfect," concepts of beauty: "Beautiful thing, your / vulgarity of beauty surpasses all their / perfections" (120).

Williams begins to figure beauty as a whore (and possibly a virgin, too[56]) at the end of section two of Book II, and the virgin/whore figuration of beauty becomes a dominant theme in Book V: "The whore and the virgin, an identity" (208). Beauty's identity here is not really an identity because of its constant slippage between two antithetical poles. Just as Levinas posits an otherwise than being that is neither presence nor absence, Williams posits a beauty that is otherwise—whore/virgin rather than virgin or whore. Beauty is virginal in its newness, its "green"-ness as Williams said of writing in Book III—"nothing that is not green will survive" (129). However, beauty as saying is a whore in its "beautiful thing"–like exposure and vulnerability and vulgarity—its continual openness to the other. Williams figures this same thought a bit differently when he says, "no woman is virtuous [virgin] / who does not give herself to her lover [whore] / forthwith" (226, brackets are mine). Beauty is most uniquely itself (whole, virginal), in its losing of itself (whoredom) in full expression. Though *Paterson* begins with beauty as a concept "locked in the mind," it ends with a beauty disrupting fixed binary concepts like virgin or whore. *Paterson* itself becomes this beauty—the vulgarity of the openness and exposure of the satyr dance that diachronically slips by itself in its own expression of itself.

In *Paterson* Williams challenges the notion of a rational subject-poet in control of the poem and presents a self that is other to itself, one that, constantly slipping away from itself, is a passive response to an infinite, anarchic past. And it makes a claim for knowledge that seems particularly Levinasian. All that can be known is the dance, which never completes itself, but instead loses itself in its diachronic expression.[57] Only a literature that is satyrical (along the lines of Bakhtin's parodic-travestying literature) can achieve this knowledge. Anything else is a reduction, a dissimulation hiding in its meaning or interpretation. As Williams says in Book VI, which is symbolically significant in its very attempt towards existence, "Dance, dance! loosen your limbs rom that art which holds you / faster than the drugs which hold you fater" (238).[58]

CONCLUSION: WILLIAMS AND HUMANISM

Literati sympathetic to the doctrines or aims of humanism, as distinct academic scholars, have consistently read Williams's work as advocating a humanist *ethos*. In fact, Denis Donoghue declared, "*Paterson* is a humanist manifesto enacted in five Books, a grammar to help us live."[59] It is my sense that many of those who tag Williams with the label "humanist" wish to provide him with a badge of honor in the face of what they see as a postmodern takeover of literature in the academy. The tendency is to see Williams as a concerned social worker-poet whose goal is to lift up the common man through earthy, tough, politically inflected poems that register the difficulty of urban life.[60] Thomas Bertoneau provides the most convincing reading of *Paterson*'s sense of origins, and his reading (which uses René Girard and E. L. Gans) is parallel to my own in many ways. However, Bertoneau goes too far when, at the end of his article, he claims that Williams's "moral obligation" was "to speak for the universality of the human."[61] It is important to understand that Williams had a problem with humanism, as he did with most "isms." Paul Mariani describes an exchange between the editor of the magazine *The Humanist* and Williams. The editor had asked Williams if he considered himself a humanist and, if so, was he a secular or theistic humanist? Williams, it seems, disliked the question as it too easily pigeonholed the uncertainty of lived, contingent existence. He never felt the need to take a position on God. But, he does say, "[A] humanistic naturalism is all that is left to me lit by the lightnings which play about the minds of saints and sinners."[62] Mariani characterizes the rest of Williams's letter as declaring, in effect, unconcern with taking such positions, and unconcern over whether or not he may contradict himself from time to time on the nature of the transcendent or the human. Of this time in Williams's life, Mariani notes, "[H]is senses kept coming up on a dead end with the large questions . . . so [he] had immersed himself instead into the random flow of experience, to let whatever patterns there were in his life gather as they would."[63]

The above is a familiar characterization of Williams—skeptical, perhaps agnostic, in regards to any sort of theoretical knowledge. This skepticism is sometimes seen as being in league with the postmodern decentering of logocentrism. However, Williams's work does not end in endless aporia. Especially in *Paterson*, we see how Williams is much closer to Levinas's concept of a "humanism of the other man" than to Derridean deconstruction.[64]

In many ways, Heidegger's fears over humanism are relevant for Williams (as they are also, I believe, for Levinas). The tendency of the ism to dominate lived existence, and to codify being, rendering it inauthentic, seems right in line with much of what Williams fears in philosophy and science. Williams's most famous sentence, "No ideas but in things," is stated multiple times at the outset of *Paterson*. Ideas are rooted in the things and people of the world, and they can't become, so to speak, the tail that wags the dog. This is where Bertoneau's statement on the "universality" of Williams's humanism is troubling. According to Heidegger, the universalizing tendency in humanism is its metaphysical stance, which allows for the domination of the perception of the subject over the object, the technological gaze of philosophy as a science that manipulates being.[65] In this sense, Williams is in league with Heidegger. However, Heidegger's resistance to a conceptual dominance of human being leads to an ethics of "letting be" that tends to valorize freedom of individual being as well as the essential alienation of beings.[66] His aesthetics valorizes art that presents an opening for being to dwell authentically in its freedom, and perhaps, aloneness.

Certainly Williams tends to valorize the individual who stands forth authentically, and "the beautiful thing" could possibly be read as a Heideggerian artwork "shining forth" and lighting a place in which being can dwell authentically. However, as I hope I've shown, Williams conceives of himself, as the poet, as passive, self-exiled, called into his saying by the other who confronts him. Williams's work ends in neither Derrida's infinite deferral of meaning nor Heidegger's dwelling in authentic freedom, but instead in self-giving at the behest of alterity. His writing, especially of *Paterson*, was a compulsion, an exasperation that literally took hold of his life. So Levinas can help us see that Williams should not be classified as a humanist (because of his fears of thematization), nor as a posthumanist in the poststructuralist vein of a Derrida; neither is his anti-humanism properly Heideggerian. Instead, he exhibits a "humanism of the other man" that revels in openness to alterity, and attempts to stand in that responsible position to which that otherness calls him, non-conceptually, but sensually.

The last lines of the poem wonderfully realize the Williams epistemology of the dance as it has been worked out in *Paterson*: "We know nothing and can know nothing / but / the dance, to dance to a measure / contrapuntally, / Satyrically, the tragic foot" (236). Knowledge comes out of sensuous experience of alterity. Epistemology does not begin in the mind, but in "contrapuntal" response-ability to otherness. Whenever knowledge, or theories of knowledge, lose contact with the sensual alterity of the world, the music stops. There's nothing to dance to.

NOTES

1. In *Totality and Infinity*, Levinas writes, "The strangeness of the Other, his irreducibility to the I, to my thoughts and my possessions, is precisely accomplished as a calling into question of my spontaneity as ethics" (43).

2. Alphonso Lingis, in his introduction to *Otherwise than Being*, states, "The present is already passing, bypassing itself" (xix). Lingis's excellent introduction will often be used in these notes to explain certain aspects of Levinas's philosophy.

3. See Lingis, *OB* xxix.

4. Levinas writes, "But in creation, what is called to being answers to a call that could not have reached it since, brought out of nothingness, it obeyed before hearing the order. . . . The self as a creature is conceived in a passivity more passive still than the passivity of matter, that is, prior to the virtual coinciding of a term with itself. The oneself has to be conceived outside all substantial coinciding of self with self" (*OB* 113–14).

5. Lingis writes, "It is as responsible that one is incarnated" (xiii). Levinas also uses the term "incarnation" (see page 109, for example).

6. Levinas writes that proximity to alterity "provokes this responsibility against my will, that is, by substituting me for the other as a hostage" (*OB* 11).

7. The quoted statements on *Paterson* in this paragraph come from William Carlos Williams's "Author's Note" (xiv) that Christopher MacGowan includes in his Preface to the scholarly edition of *Paterson*: William Carlos Williams, *Paterson*, rev. ed. (New York: New Directions, 1992).

8. Marjorie Perloff reads *Paterson* as more of a closed poem, especially when compared to Williams's early work. See her *The Poetics of Indeterminacy: Rimbaud to Cage* (Evanston, IL: Northwestern University Press, 1999), 151. Perloff's reading is fair; however, she emphasizes certain image clusters, and tends to read them uni-dimensionally, relying heavily on Robert Lowell's review of *Paterson*, Book II, to confirm her own suspicions of Williams's more conservative, almost New Critical approach. I suggest that Perloff's reading has been too influenced, perhaps, by Lowell's and others, so much so that the amazing centrifugal, projective power of the poem has been lost on her. Perloff admits that her reading is the minority and that Williams's best critics read *Paterson* as an open rather than closed poem (151). Also see 148–54.

9. Gabriel Riera, *Intrigues: From Being to the Other* (New York: Fordham University Press, 2006), 87.

10. Lorna Wood makes a similar claim in "Emmanuel Levinas and the American Renaissance Canon," in *Levinas and Nineteenth Century Literature: Ethics and Otherness from Romanticism through Realism*, ed. Donald R. Wehrs and David P. Haney (Newark: University of Delaware Press, 2009), 166–206, when she quotes Levinas approving of literature that stretches its forms in an attempt to keep "awake everywhere the verbs that are on the verge of lapsing into substantives" (*OB* 40, quoted in Wood, 168).

11. Leslie Hill, "'Distrust of Poetry': Levinas, Blanchot, Celan." *MLN* 120 (2005): 986–1008, 990 cited.

12. Thomas LeClair, "The Poet as Dog in *Paterson*," *Twentieth Century Literature* 16 (1970): 97–108, 97 cited.

13. Paul Bové, "The World and Earth of William Carlos Williams: Paterson as a 'Long Poem,'" *Genre* XI (1978): 575–96, 596 cited.

14. Jill Robbins, *Altered Readings: Levinas and Literature* (Chicago: University of Chicago Press, 1999), 79–80.

15. Meyer, 159.

16. Ibid., 155.

17. Ibid., 155.

18. William Carlos Williams, *Paterson*, rev. ed. (New York: New Directions, 1992), 29. All further references are to this edition and will be cited parenthetically in the text. This text will be indicated as *P*.

19. Meyer, 164.

20. Actually the image appears two more times, albeit less explicitly, in Book I, if one counts Sam Patch's jump off of *Goat* Island (16) and the mention of the etymologically related "satire" (40).

21. Emily Wallace, "The Satyr's Abstract and Brief Chronicle of Our Time," *William Carlos Williams Review* 9, nos. 1–2 (1983): 136–55, 139 cited.

22. See the *Oxford English Dictionary Online*, "satyr,' definition 1.c.

23. Wallace, 139.

24. Friedrich Nietzsche, *The Birth of Tragedy*, in *Basic Writings of Nietzsche*, trans. and ed. Walter Kaufmann (New York: Modern Library, 2000), 64.

25. Northrop Frye, *Anatomy of Criticism: Four Essays* (Princeton: Princeton University Press, 1957), 282.

26. Ibid., 95.

27. Ibid., 229.

28. Ibid., 235.

29. John Aldington Symonds, *Studies of the Greek Poets* (n.p.: n.d.), 236.

30. See Kinereth Meyer, "Possessing America: William Carlos Williams's *Paterson* and the Poetics of Appropriation," in *Mapping American Culture*, ed. Wayne Franklin and Michael Steiner (Iowa City: University of Iowa Press, 1992), 152–67; Sergio Rizzo in "Can 'Beautiful Thing' Speak?: Race and Gender in *Paterson*," in *Critical Essays on William Carlos Williams*, eds. Steven Gould Axelrod and Helen Deese (New York: G. K. Hall, 1995), 199–212; and Gerald L. Bruns (though somewhat indirectly) in his *Tragic Thoughts at the End of Philosophy: Language, Literature, and Ethical Theory* (Evanston: Northwestern University Press, 1999), especially 170–75. In this section (pp. 170–75), Bruns also briefly discusses Levinas, taking a view of the saying that is similar to mine.

31. M. M. Bakhtin, *The Dialogic Imagination: Four Essays*, trans. Caryl Emerson and Michael Holquist (Austin: University of Texas Press, 1981), 60.

32. William Carlos Williams, "The Dance," in *The Collected Poems of William Carlos Williams Volume II: 1939-1962*, ed. Christopher MacGowan (New York: New Directions, 2001), 407–8, 408 cited.

33. William Carlos Williams, *The Embodiment of Knowledge* (New York: New Directions, 1974), 63.

34. Ibid., 132.

35. Unexpected interconnections between the corporeal philosophies of Nietzsche and Levinas are explored in Rosayln Diprose's "Nietzsche, Levinas, and the Meaning of Responsibility," in *Nietzsche and Levinas: "After the Death of a Certain God"*, ed. Jill Stauffer and Bettina Bergo (New York: Columbia University Press, 2009), 116–33.

36. Fortunately, if the "typical reader" picks up the version of *Paterson* edited by Christopher MacGowan, she can distinguish the original authorship of all the passages. The prose of Williams's typist occurs on page 132, the prose that Williams turns into poetry occurs on pages 192–97, and a portion of "The Wanderer" appears on page 229. Brian A. Bremen discusses the prose that Williams converts into poetry in his article, "'The Radiant Gist': 'The Poetry Hidden in the Prose' of Williams' *Paterson*," *Twentieth Century Literature* 32, no. 2 (1986): 221–41.

37. Joseph N. Riddel, *The Inverted Bell: Modernism and the Counterpoetics of William Carlos Williams* (Baton Rouge: Louisiana State University Press, 1974), 14.

38. Kathleen D. Matthews, "Competitive Giants: The Satiric Bedrock in Book One of William Carlos Williams' *Paterson*," *Journal of Modern Literature* 12 no. 2 (1985): 237–60, 241–42 cited.

39. Robert Coles, "Instances of Modern Anti-Intellectualism," in *Modernism Reconsidered*, ed. John Kiely, assisted by John Hildebidle (Cambridge: Harvard University Press, 1983), 215–28, 224 cited.

40. For explorations of connections between Nietzschean and Levinasian modes of disruptive, non-self-enclosed subjectivity, see Jill Stauffer, "The Imperfect: Levinas, Nietzsche, and the Autonomous Subject," in *Nietzsche and Levinas*, 33–47.

41. Sandra Gilbert, in her article on the Nardi letters, quotes from a letter Williams wrote regarding the use of the letters: "In the first place it was a reply from the female side to many of my male pretensions. It was a strong reply, a reply which sought to destroy me. If it could

destroy me I should be destroyed. It was just that it should have its opportunity to destroy. If I hid the reply it would be a confession of weakness on my part" (quoted. in Gilbert 7—"Purloined Letters: William Carlos Williams and 'Cress,'" *William Carlos Williams Review* 11.2 (1985): 5–15). Gilbert goes on to focus on the letters within the context of other "uses" of female figures in the poem, and suggests that the letters (and the entire poem) are an expression of anxiety over being dominated by the female. Thus he has to include the letters as a foil for his strength; he knows he'll overcome them. By contrast, I read the letters as part of Williams's attempt at writing vulnerably; they are an act of writing by not writing—a brilliant escape from the dominating ego tendency. They are a gesture towards otherness that exiles the author from himself in the poem—in a way, a destruction.

42. Terri A. Mester, *Movement and Modernism: Yeats, Eliot, Lawrence, Williams and Early Twentieth-Century Dance* (Fayetteville, University of Arkansas Press, 1997): 123, 157.

43. Williams, *The Embodiment of Knowledge*, 130–32.

44. Nancy K. Barry. "The Fading Beautiful Thing of *Paterson*," *Twentieth Century Literature* 35 no. 3 (1989): 343–63, 344 cited. See also William Sharpe, That Complex Atom': City and Form in William Carlos Williams' *Paterson*," *Poesis* 6 no. 2 (1985): 65–93.

45. Hugh T. Crawford, *Modernism, Medicine, and William Carlos Williams* (Norman: University of Oklahoma Press, 1993): 138.

46. Riddel, *The Inverted Bell*, 99.

47. Ibid., 35.

48. Ibid., 40.

49. Ibid., 298.

50. Thomas F. Bertonneau, "The Sign of Knowledge in Our Time: Violence, Man, and Language in *Paterson* Book I (An Anthropoetics)," *William Carlos Williams Review* 21 no. 1 (1995): 33–51, 41 cited.

51. Ibid., 41.

52. Riera, 144.

53. See "The Origin of the Work of Art," and in the other essays collected in the volume Martin Heidegger, *Poetry, Language, Thought* (New York: Perennial Classics, 2001).

54. Mariani writes in *William Carlos Williams: A New World Naked* (McGraw-Hill, 1981), "The image of extracting a residue of radium out of a mass of seemingly inert pitchblende was very much on Williams' mind in the spring of '44. It would serve as one of the most widespread and profound metaphors throughout *Paterson*" (492).

55. Riera quotes Levinas's statement that "exasperation" was his "philosophical method" (88), and explains that Levinas's exasperation is registered in the hyperbolic, more poetic language of *Otherwise than Being* (139).

56. In the same passage that speaks of "beautiful thing" being roughed up and possibly raped, "beautiful thing" wears a "white lace dress," which connotes virginity (127).

57. Speaking of "dance" as a verb, Mester writes, "The beauty of this verb is that it never quite manages to complete its action" (126).

58. Williams worked on Book VI of *Paterson* in the last years of his life, after a round of debilitating strokes. The typos ("rom" for "from" and "fater" for "faster") demonstrate the difficulty Williams faced in attempting write anything in the final years of his life.

59. Denis Donoghue, "The Long Poem," *The New York Review of Books* (14 April 1966), 18.

60. Not many academic critics have explored Williams's relationship with humanism. Bertoneau is nearly alone in relatively recent treatments of this topic. However, the fact that many readers do associate Williams with humanism may be easily ascertained by scanning the Internet. See Richard Carter, "William Carlos Williams: Physician Writer and 'Godfather of Avant-Garde Poetry,'" *The Annals of Thoracic Surgery*, 67 (1999) 1512–17, ats.ctsnetjournals.org/cgi/content/full/67/5/ 1512; Jan Henderson, "The Physician as Humanist," *The Health Culture: Yesterday, Today, Tomorrow*, (July 4, 2010), www.thehealthculture.com; Arthur Dobrin, "Humanist Literature in Perspective," *Humanism Today* 2 (1986): 59–62,www.humanismtoday.org.; Cliff Notes, American Poets of the Twentieth Century: The Poets, William Carlos Williams, www.cliffnotes.com.

61. Bertonneau, 49.

62. Quoted. in Mariani, 723.

63. Mariani, 723–24.

64. This phrase is a translation of Levinas's 1972 title, *Humanisme de l'autre homme*. The essays that comprise that volume ("Meaning and Sense," "Humanism and An-archy," and "No Identity") are most easily accessed in CP. In these essays Levinas consistently upholds the basic Heideggerian critique of Humanism as a system of values (see "Humanism and An-archy," 132–the "inanity of man as principle"—and the resistance to rendering man as a value in "a bi-polar field of values," 134). However, his critique of Heidegger is poignant in "No Identity" as he upholds his "humanism of the other man" when he says, "[M]an also has to be conceived on the basis of the responsibility more ancient than the *conatus* of a substance or inward identification, a responsibility which, always summoning from the outside, disturbs just this inwardness" (150). This conception of man becomes what Levinas calls his "defense of man understood as a defense of the man other than me" (151).

65. Throughout his "Letter on Humanism" (*Basic Writings*, ed. David Farrell Krell [San Francisco: Harper, 1993]), Heidegger links the forms of humanism that he has witnessed with metaphysics: "Every humanism is either grounded in a metaphysics or is itself the ground of one" (225). The tyrannical (manipulative, technological) gaze engendered by the metaphysical stance of humanism is well described in the following passage, and it opens the way for Heidegger to begin to think of possibility for humanism outside of metaphysics: "Of course the essential worth of man does not consist in his being the substance of beings, as the 'Subject' among them, so that as the tyrant of Being he may deign to release the beingness of beings into an all too loudly bruited 'objectivity'" (234).

66. Numerous citations could be given of Heidegger's notions of "letting be" and of freedom. One way that he characterizes the "realm of the truth of Being," which art reveals, is in his "Letter on Humanism," in which he calls it "the free space in which freedom conserves its essence" (247). In terms of the alienation central to aesthetics, Heidegger writes, "The more solitarily the work, fixed in the figure, stands on its own and the more cleanly it seems to cut all ties to human beings, the more simply does the thrust come into the Open that such a work *is*, and the more essentially is the extraordinary thrust to the surface and the long-familiar thrust down" ("The Origin of the Work of Art," 64).

IV

Levinas and the Embodied Voice: Listening and Performance

Chapter Seven

The Trumpets of Autocracies and the Still, Small Voices of Civilization

Levinas and Radio in a Time of Crisis

Todd Avery

THE NEW MODERNIST STUDIES, RADIO, AND ETHICS

The keynote of the New Modernist Studies is fascination with the ordinary. Its driving assumption is that, far from embodying an elitist, aestheticized hostility to the popular, cultural modernism actively engages with everyday life in the early twentieth century. Practitioners of this multifaceted and continually evolving congeries of critical approaches to modernism have expanded conventional notions of who and what counts as modernist, partly by shattering the conventional critical assumption of high modernism's contempt for mass cultural forms and, by extension, for that nebulous modern collectivity known as the "masses." In a succinct summary of major trajectories in the New Modernist Studies, Douglas Mao and Rebecca L. Walkowitz include "the concentration of work around mass media rhetorics." Such work contributes to the ongoing "vertical reconfiguration" of modernist studies, a reconfiguration that blurs "boundaries between high art and popular forms of culture."[1] As Mao and Walkowitz see it, the growth of this critical interest in relations between modernism and mass media marks, at the very least, a "momentary convergence . . . of individual scholarly projects," and may represent "the leading edge of a major trend."[2]

Regardless of the precise degree of pressure that interest in mass media ultimately exerts on the on-going reconfiguration of modernist studies, and to put aside whether it signifies the emergence of a "major trend," it is unlikely that this interest will fade soon: within the New Modernist Studies and elsewhere, scholars from a wide variety of fields continue vigorously to dig into long-languishing archives, and to recuperate, explore, and interpret many aspects of the early history of electronic mass telecommunications as it emerged and flourished during the modernist period. The birth and early development of radio as a technology and a cultural form coincided with the emergence and growth of modernism in literature and the arts, from its early stirrings and vibrations in the last decades of the nineteenth century to its maturation over the course of the following thirty or forty years. This coincidence also represented a convergence, as radio became an ineluctable feature of the social and cultural landscape within which writers and artists generated their experiments and, in Peter Gay's sense of the term, their heresies.[3] Radio technology, sending sound waves through the mysterious "ether," demanded engaged reflection and generated a great deal of excitement; when it was institutionalized as the cultural form of broadcasting in the United States and across Europe over the course of the 1920s, it offered modernists a new venue for artistic experimentation as well as a new forum for (and often an object of) social and cultural critique, and a new type of communications technology within which to promote their ethical beliefs. In short, radio wove its way during the early twentieth century into the fabric of everyday life and, therefore, constituted an inextricable thread in the cloth of modernism itself.

In a parallel recent coincidence, the emergence of the New Modernist Studies and the growth of radio studies as a loose interdisciplinary affiliation have occurred simultaneously with the so-called "ethical turn" in literary studies. Lawrence Buell lists "four interlocking influences" that help to explain "why ethics now." Among these influences he counts "the emergence of Emmanuel Levinas as a post-poststructuralist model for literary-ethical inquiry," and, in a footnote to this comment, cites foundational works in this regard published over the course of the 1990s by Robert Bernasconi, Simon Critchley, and Robert Eaglestone.[4] A year earlier than Buell, in a *Modern Fiction Studies* review of Jill Robbins's *Altered Reading: Levinas and Literature* (1999), Sandor Goodhart noticed, "Levinas's work is hot right now."[5] Thus, the period that has been marked by the "turn to ethics" and the rise of the New Modernist Studies, with its own partial turn toward the mass media, has also been characterized by a widespread critical embrace of the work of Emmanuel Levinas.

Levinas has become a presiding spirit in ethically concerned literary criticism across historical periods and national boundaries and a significant presence in the world of the New Modernist Studies. It would be going too far to assert either a causal relation between the turn to Levinas and the growth of the New Modernist Studies or that his influence on the New Modernist Studies has been a game changer. But this influence has been significant, and will no doubt continue to influence the New Modernist Studies' explorations of the everyday and the ethical. In the, in many ways, most satisfying application of Levinasian ideas to the interpretation of modernist literature to date, Sara Crangle's *Prosaic Desires: Modernist Knowledge, Boredom, Laughter, and Anticipation* (2010) makes a strong case that a great deal of modernist writing (specifically, fiction by Joyce, Woolf, Stein, and Beckett) explores the Levinasian idea that the self "comes into being through the facial expression of the other and can provide a lived experience of the infinite."[6] Crangle adopts Levinas's "reject[ion of] the suggestion that a being can . . . exist alone authentically"; she embraces Levinasian epiphany as "a very literal, quotidian transcendence of the self, as it involves a recognition of, and complete acquiescence to, something beyond subjectivity"[7]—what Levinas terms "radical alterity"[8]—and she shows how modernist writers discovered new types of authenticity and redemption in face-to-face relations between individuals, not only in the absence of traditional religious and philosophical certainties, but also outside the tyranny of the autonomous self. In these ways, *Prosaic Desires* shows how four major modernist writers "abandon" the effort to create "characters struggling for autonomy" in favor of characters who discover a sense of self through their encounters with others.[9]

More generally, Crangle is interested in reciprocal relations between literary modernism and Levinasian philosophy. For as fruitfully as modernist fiction may be read through a Levinasian lens, for Crangle bold traces of modernism's relentless engagement with problems of otherness and sure evidence of its persistent exploration of how the self is constituted through encounters with others may be read in Levinas's location of transcendence in the epiphanic encounter with the other in the work he produced from the post-War years onward. For this reason, Crangle explains, "Levinas is clearly influenced by the ideologies of modernism, a period in which subjectivity is continually under fire. Modernists such as Woolf, Joyce, and Stein break the ground that Levinas cultivates, and do so by abandoning grand narratives of desire and the subject in favour of prosaic longings and a centralization of otherness." In modernist literature, that is to say, and in anticipation of Levinas's philosophical treatment of the issue, "an ideological shift toward other-driven everydayness . . . occurs" which is marked by the "transcendence" to be found in "the everyday social exchange."[10]

This chapter is motivated by the desire to understand the usefulness of Levinas to the elucidation of the ethical elements of a constitutive but still relatively underexplored aspect of literary and cultural modernism—namely, radio broadcasting, a technological and cultural phenomenon grounded in the arena of "everyday social exchange" of which Crangle writes. To refine this topic further, my purpose is to explore some of the ethical complexities of broadcasting philosophy and practice as it developed as a technocultural mode of "everyday social exchange" in different ways in different national contexts in the late 1920s and the early 1930s, during a time of grave political and human crisis in Europe. More particularly, even, I examine through a

Levinasian lens the sharp contrast in broadcasting philosophy and practice at that time between British and German radio, with a broad focus on the ethics of broadcasting and a narrower focus on the theoretical, administrative, and editorial work of Hilda Matheson, an early Talks Department producer at the British Broadcasting Corporation. Matheson formatively influenced the sound of the BBC through her development of the "intimate" mode of address beginning in 1927. After leaving the BBC in 1931, she continued to comment, on British broadcasting and, later, with the rise of the Nazis, on German broadcasting under Joseph Goebbels and the Programming Director Eugen Hadamovsky, in a column for the *Week-End Review* that she wrote weekly in 1932–1934. Ethical concerns played a central part in Matheson's vision for radio as a vehicle of cultural uplift and moral progress. "War," Levinas writes in *Otherwise than Being or Beyond Essence* (1974), "is the chronicle or the drama of the essence's interestedness" (*BPW* 111). The contrast between, on the one hand, the ethical underpinnings of German broadcasting in the early 1930s, and, on the other, Matheson's vision for British broadcasting and broadcasting as such during the years leading up to the Second World War, represents the drama of a contest between the interested assertion, promotion, and reinforcement of (racial) essence, and a liberal affirmation, promotion, and endorsement of a type of "everyday social exchange" devoted to the sustained, though typically implicit, critique of such an essence—or, to use one of Levinas's own terms, to its "interruption." In other words, the difference between German broadcasting in the early 1930s and the broadcasting philosophy that Matheson embraced, and partly implemented at the BBC, represents a conflict between what Matheson called the trumpets of autocracies and the "still, small voices" of civilization. Moreover, Matheson's allusion here to a Biblical passage (1 Kings 19) in which the solitary prophet Elijah hears the voice of the Lord not in a spectacularly dramatic wind, earthquake, or fire, but as a "still small voice" connects her ethical thinking on radio in an interesting way with "Levinas's effort to bring Hebraic ethics into contemporary discourse." Regardless of her specific intentions, she certainly intended this phrase to be heard as a call to conscience in the face of blaring trumpets.[11]

Matheson argued, "The basic fact of broadcasting is that the microphone transmits an intimate voice *to* the individual; it is not a microphone shouting *at* a crowd."[12] What, as Matheson understood the situation, were the ethical investments of radio broadcasting in the 1920s and 1930s? How did broadcast styles signify specific ethical purposes? How does the desire to speak to and not at listeners resonate with a Levinasian injunction to attend to the face of the Other? How does the intimate mode of address embody an ethics of responsibility, a call to conscience, that challenges the "philosophy of Hitlerism" in German radio, with its exhortatory style designed to "awaken . . . elementary feelings" of identity and with the Nazi regime's mass organizational means—mandatory community listening—for recruiting the listening population into a fundamental order of the Same?[13] To address such questions is to illuminate a fundamental yet still obscure aspect of early radio broadcasting theory and practice in Britain and in Germany during the modernist period, at a time when these carried immense political and, indeed, moral weight—a time when "the very humanity of man," as Levinas puts it, was "in question."[14]

If, as Levinas says in one of his interviews, alluding to a favorite phrase from Pascal, "the war of 1939 . . . broke out because Nazi Germany demanded a vital space, its 'place in the sun,' the order where being strove to persevere in being" (*ITR* 99), then German radio broadcasting, as a propaganda vehicle for the Nazi party, performed a vital role in this demanding. This was, of course, in the nature of the case: Joseph Goebbels spoke of radio as, with the airplane, one of the two technologies that had enabled the Nazi political triumph; he also celebrated its capacity to perpetuate the being of Nazi Germany's being, through its power to disseminate to a mass audience composed of tens of millions of listeners the message of the Party as the material embodiment of the spiritual essence of the nation. "The radio," Goebbels said in an August 1933 speech at the opening of a radio exhibition, "is the most influential and important intermediary between a spiritual movement and the nation, between the idea and the people."[15] In this speech, Goebbels's reflections on radio's "responsibility to the future of the nation" concisely articulate the political and ethical motivations for broadcasting in the Third Reich. Radio would be a showcase for "the best spiritual elements of the nation . . . the most multifaceted, flexible means of expressing the wishes, needs, longings, and hopes of our age."[16] Goebbels's speech amounts to an affirmation of radio's role in the Nazi claiming of a "place in the sun"; radio under Goebbels was relentlessly to affirm the rightness of a specific spiritual order—the transcendent greatness of the German spirit, embodied in the Nazi Party and in the German people—in its work of "national construction." While (disingenuously) disavowing the "partisan" character of Nazi radio—because there should be "room for entertainment, popular arts, games, jokes, and music"—Goebbels subsumes all radio programming to a unified political agenda: "everything should have a relationship to our day. Everything should include the theme of our great reconstructive work, or at least not stand in its way. Above all it is necessary to clearly centralize all radio activities, to place spiritual tasks ahead of technical ones, to introduce the leadership principle, to provide a clear worldview, and to present this worldview in flexible ways."[17]

By definition, German radio under the leadership of Goebbels and the National Programming Director Eugen Hadamovsky was "Hitlerist," and therefore available to the elucidation and critique of Hitlerism developed by Levinas in the mid-1930s, at the very time when the Nazi regime was quickly developing a theory of broadcasting and consolidating its control over all broadcasting activities in Germany, and when Hitler himself was beginning to hold, as Hadamovsky writes, "enormous mass meetings that radio brought to the whole nation." The result of the Nazi "radio revolution that rebuilt it [broadcasting] according to National Socialist principles," Hadamovsky continues, was that radio came to "follow . . . absolutely clear lines in the . . . racial area . . . knowing no compromise."[18] That Hadamovsky is speaking approvingly of this development is a gross understatement. There is a more significant philosophical point here, though, given the Nazi regime's recognition of the power of broadcasting in the promotion of National Socialist ideals, and in light of Hadamovsky's remark on Nazi broadcasting's uncompromising racial essentialism. Arnold Davidson observes that in Levinas's "Reflections on the Philosophy of Hitlerism," "Levinas insists on comprehending Hitlerism not simply as some mad aberration, but as harbouring a philosophy and so requiring philosophical analysis."[19] So too should Nazi radio be seen as a historical, cultural, and political phenomenon that harbored a coherent philosophy—and specifically an ethical philosophy that demands analysis. For inasmuch as Hadamovsky and, in Hans Fritzsche's phrase, "the creative artist Joseph Goebbels"[20] thought of radio as a technocultural opportunity to promote the National Socialist worldview, they also understood it as a medium of electronic mass telecommunications that was bound by a moral responsibility to express—to "introduce," "provide," and "present"—what Levinas calls "the Germanic ideal of man [which] seems to promise sincerity and authenticity."[21] For the administrators of Nazi radio no less than for Hitler himself—as indeed for radio listeners in Germany after 1933—"Man no longer finds himself confronted by a world of ideas in which he can choose his own truth on the basis of a sovereign decision made by his free reason. He is already linked to a certain number of these ideas, just as he is linked by birth to all who are of his blood."[22] In Goebbels's and Hadamovsky's paeans to radio, what one hears, in Levinasian terms, are two broadcasting theorists giving voice to "[t]he mysterious urgings of the blood, the appeals of heredity and the past."[23] Seán Hand explains that in his "Reflections" Levinas "directly links a drama of destiny with racialist essentializations" and maintains that this "acceptance of racial purity sees man 'himself refusing the power to escape from himself' through the contemplation of truth."[24] In other words, the ideal of racial purity as it found expression in German radio beginning in 1933 demanded the abdication of responsibility to truth in favor of the embrace of that "elementary Evil" which, Levinas claims, "is inscribed within the ontology of a being concerned with being."[25]

HILDA MATHESON AND THE POLITICS AND ETHICS OF STYLE

In mid-1932, shortly after she began writing a regular column for the *Week-End Review*, Hilda Matheson began to hear over the airwaves, not the fruits of Nazi broadcasting policy—she, along with everyone else in possession of a radio receiver and within range of transmission, would begin to hear those the following year—but the first hints of the radio revolution that Hadamovsky would speak of in 1934. In June, for example, Germany's presidential election spurred her thoughts on "[t]he significance of broadcasting in public affairs."[26] In columns over the following few months, she encourages her readers to pay close attention to developments in German broadcasting: "The most interesting country at the moment from the broadcasting point of view is Germany," she writes in December 1932: "No student of German politics can afford to ignore the immense use which is being made of the microphone in the conscious development of a new nationalism."[27] The following April, she repeats, "The most interesting laboratory for experiments in broadcasting policy and technique is to be found at the present moment in Germany."[28]

Matheson was better positioned than almost anyone in Britain to understand the administrative and practical, as well as the theoretical, aspects of the German radio laboratory, just as she was to understand those aspects of British broadcasting: she had been instrumental in defining them, and especially in developing and refining the technique of broadcast speech and in articulating the moral and social aims of the early BBC. To be sure, Matheson's *Week-End Review* columns do not compose a coherent ethical critique of the German radio laboratory; nor did Matheson bring to her weekly reflections on radio a refined philosophical sophistication in the subtleties of ethical discourse. Be that as it may, these columns, together with her 1933 Home University Library monograph, *Broadcasting*, one of the best early surveys of radio as a cultural form (as opposed to a technological phenomenon), emerged from years of experience with broadcasting policy and production during which she advanced an agenda for British broadcasting that was motivated by a considered engagement with questions regarding the social and moral value and potential of radio.

Matheson was the BBC's first Director of Talks; in this role she oversaw the BBC's news, educational, and cultural programming. This was a position she held from the beginning of 1927, when BBC Director-General John Reith invited her to join the organization, until late 1931, when she angrily resigned in the middle of a protracted censorship dispute with Reith about a series of talks by the writer, diplomat, and Bloomsbury Group associate Harold Nicolson on modern fiction. In one of a series of talks on "The New Spirit in Literature," Nicolson wanted to praise two controversial novels, James Joyce's *Ulysses* and D. H. Lawrence's *Lady Chatterley's Lover*, which epitomized, in Desmond MacCarthy's phrase, "the [literary] sensibility and thought of the moment."[29] Reith forbade Nicolson from praising these novels, or indeed from even mentioning them by name. In doing this, Reith was following a 1925 internal memo that he had distributed to all BBC station managers, "*NOTICE TO ENTERTAINERS*," which had categorically proscribed "vulgar" and morally "doubtful" matter and, in general, compelled an exacting moral rectitude in the nation's broadcasting booths.[30] Nicolson grudgingly submitted to Reith's orders but shortly thereafter, in a *Spectator* article titled "Are the BBC too Cautious?" publicized his frustrations with a Corporation that was, he thought, "afraid" of "the strange power of the human voice" to "irritate but more often attract."[31] This was in November 1931; Matheson resigned in December when it had become clear that her vision for Talks in particular and for British broadcasting in general diverged sharply and in important ways from that of Reith.[32]

Matheson and the autocratic Reith—some employees dubbed him "Mussolini"—disagreed strategically and on a fundamental philosophical level about how, as a public service utility in the national interest, the BBC should pursue its mission to enlighten, inform, and elevate. They agreed that the BBC should maintain high standards as a way of elevating cultural discourse. But they disagreed about the ethos that the BBC should cultivate in a complex technological, cultural, social, and political context. However, notwithstanding their divergent opinions on the threshold of decency in the content of individual radio talks, as well as on other matters, Matheson and Reith shared a common conviction that broadcasting ought to be deployed in the service of "democracy"—a conviction that implied a shared sense of moral purpose for broadcasting, however differently they defined this moral purpose.[33]

Reith considered radio broadcasting—and more particularly, public service broadcasting—a "democratic" medium. He was suspicious of the American commercial model, though he also appears to have sympathized in the mid-1930s with Nazi methods of social control.[34] Under his leadership, British radio as Reith imagined it was to be a help to "democracy" by functioning—it is not too strong to say—as a hypostasis of the divine. According to the royal charter that established the British Broadcasting Corporation as of 1 January 1927, the BBC was bound by a specific set of obligations. As Andrew Crisell writes: "It was, and is, obliged to inform, to educate and to entertain; to report the proceedings of Parliament; to provide a political balance; and in a national emergency to broadcast government messages. It may neither editorialize nor carry advertising. Its income is guaranteed from broadcast receiving licences and it strives to maintain a position of editorial independence."[35]

Operating within these general guidelines, Reith forged an agenda for radio that constituted a sort of third way between two broadly accepted notions of democracy. Crisell explains:

One notion, to which the BBC broadly subscribed, was that democracy consists of giving all the people what they want. But this is undemocratic in the sense that within a limited resource such as broadcasting then was, and because people have differing tastes, nobody gets *enough* of what they want. The second notion, to which many of the corporation's critics subscribed, was that democracy consists of giving the *majority* of the people what it wants—which is also undemocratic, positively despotic, in the sense that the minority gets nothing at all. The complaint against the BBC, then, was that the majority did not get enough of what it wanted—and a great deal of what it did *not* want.[36]

As a believer in the fundamentally "democratic" nature and responsibility of the medium of radio itself and of the BBC as its guardian, Reith attempted a way out of this critical impasse by

posit[ing] . . . a third notion of democracy which was concerned neither with majority nor universal preferences but with what [he] perceived as universal needs: for the aim was to open up to all those who had been denied by a limited education, low social status and small income the great treasures of our culture. . . . Reith's policy offered a chance of spiritual if not material enrichment [and] was always ready to discriminate on the listeners' behalf between "the good" and "the inferior" in popular culture—often on moral rather than aesthetic or intellectual grounds.[37]

In the Reithian view of democracy, radio broadcasting functions as a public resource that respects no traditional demarcation of social or economic class in its ability to unite an entire population. It is able to do so, for example, through the sonic dissemination of imperial standards—by bringing "rural areas . . . into direct contact with . . . Empire institutions," for "the clock which beats the time over the Houses of Parliament, in the centre of the Empire, is heard echoing in the lowliest cottage in the land." It exerts its "consolidating influence" also by making quickly and universally available such phenomena as "the momentous utterance of a statesman, the exposition of a scientist, the eloquence of a preacher, or a great ceremony of widespread interest."[38]

Ultimately, the Reithian view of democracy, based on the idea of universal needs, relies on a centripetal belief in the moral supremacy of his Arnoldian notion of "the best." Furthermore, broadcasting, for Reith, was to be neither a mere communications utility nor a simple conveyor of culture, but rather, a moral and religious benefit, to the nation first, and then to humanity in general. As a cultural form, broadcasting, because it "offered a chance of spiritual . . . enrichment," represented a way of mitigating the promiscuity of radio technology. "As we conceive it," Reith writes, apparently speaking for the BBC as a whole in one of his most famous pronouncements on the social obligation of broadcasting,

Our responsibility is to carry into the greatest possible number of homes everything that is best in every department of human knowledge, endeavour and achievement, and to avoid the things which are, or may be, hurtful. It is occasionally indicated to us that we are apparently setting out to give the public what we think they need—and not what they want, but few know what they want, and very few what they need.[39]

Notwithstanding its capacity for diffusing cultural touchstones to the largest audience in history, broadcasting, as Reith understood its potential, subsumed these concerns to a higher, nobler one. "Best of all," he writes in *Broadcast over Britain*, "the message of peace on earth, proclaimed in the first Christmas to a few shepherds, can reach the hearts of all men of goodwill. And [this benefit is] neither merely national nor international, but supranational."[40] In the final sentence of his book, Reith drives home the religious basis for this sense of mission, imploring British radio listeners to "turn to the contemplation of the Omnipotence holding all things together by the word of power, in Whom, as in the ether, we live and move and have our being."[41]

Reith, a strident moralist, wanted to tell listeners what was the best that has been thought and said in the world; as a moral idealist, he believed that individual and social health were both necessary preconditions and likely results of adherence to eternally valid ethical truths. In brief, Reith valued the preservation of conventional moral norms such as the intrinsic rightness of a patriarchal social order more highly than he prized ethical uncertainty or relativism as a theoretical principle, or intimacy between individuals as an irreducible locus and goal of ethical practice. This moral belief informed Reith's understanding of "democracy" and led to his reluctance to air culturally, socially, politically, or morally controversial material. Hilda Matheson, for her part, wanted to help listeners to make up their own minds by presenting a, to Reith, too-great variety of often conflicting opinions on cultural, social, and political topics. "In the end," as Matheson's biographer, Michael Carney, puts it, "Reith was essentially middlebrow, content that broadcasting should reflect a conventional, lower-middle-class view of what was best," while Matheson "was the genuine creative spirit, an administrator and programme-maker of genius who had a particular gift for presenting serious programmes in an entertaining way."[42] Matheson's most significant contribution to broadcasting was a stylistic one: she imagined, crafted, and institutionalized the "intimate" mode of address, a conversational, though in fact highly practiced, manner of speaking *to* a listener as opposed to a declamatory manner of talking *at* a listener. The distinction is a subtle one, but it was an important one in the BBC's early years, when, as Reith wrote in his manifesto *Broadcast over Britain* in 1924, under the heading "Uncharted Seas," "Very few knew what broadcasting meant; none knew what it might become."[43]

The intimate mode of address that Matheson developed was the aesthetic expression of a specific philosophy of broadcasting, which also possessed political and ethical elements. Matheson saw radio broadcasting not as an opportunity for the mass projection of voice or for the distribution of information and entertainment to an undifferentiated mass audience, but rather, as a chance for intimate connection between individuals. She understood broadcasting as a communicative act, not between a broadcaster and a listening public—one man or woman talking at the masses—but between a broadcaster and individual listeners: one man or woman speaking to another man or woman in a transaction repeated thousands or even millions of times simultaneously. In *Broadcasting*, Matheson puts it more succinctly: "[T]he basic fact of broadcasting," she writes, is "that the microphone transmits an intimate voice *to* the individual; it is not a microphone shouting *at* a crowd."[44] She elaborates: "Early experiments with broadcast talks showed that it was useless to address the microphone as if it were a public meeting, or even to read it essays or leading articles. The person sitting at the other end expected the speaker to address him personally, simply, almost familiarly, as man to man."[45]

Matheson is writing of British broadcasting, and with the understanding that other experiments were being tried, elsewhere—in the United States, for example, where commercial popular entertainment trumped public service. She is also thinking of the ways that totalitarian states such as Germany, Italy, and Russia were developing broadcasting on what she saw as the "tub-thumping" propagandistic model of "a megaphone shouting at a crowd." Geoffrey Wheatcroft discusses the three main models of broadcasting that developed in Europe and the United States in the first two decades of radio. "Appropriately enough," he writes, "in the age when the business of America was business, American radio became wholeheartedly commercial. Appropriately enough in the age of totalitarianism, [state-owned] European radio became a prime vehicle for party propaganda and indoctrination. As usual," he concludes, "the British way fell somewhere in between."[46]

In addition to being an aesthetic choice, then, Matheson's theorization and implementation of the intimate mode of address also implied an ethical purpose and a political agenda. In light of the different ways that the technology of wireless communication was institutionalized in the United States and in totalitarian European countries, Matheson's assertion of "the basic fact of broadcasting"—that "the microphone transmits an intimate voice to the individual; it is not a megaphone shouting at a crowd"—should be read as an ideologically motivated, historically grounded prescription and not as an objective, historically decontextualized description of the way that radio works in some supposed essence. Outside the facts of wireless technology—which are themselves an unstable, continually evolving complex of scientific, social, and cultural elements—there is no essence of radio once it becomes a cultural form. Moreover, in the context of the growth of totalitarian, megaphonic, propaganda radio during the early 1930s, Matheson's understanding of broadcasting as an intimate medium should also be read as an expression of hope for what D. L. LeMahieu calls "a culture for democracy," in a way that recalls the romantic, revolutionary, bliss-was-it-in-that-dawn-to-be-alive-but-to-be-young-was-very-heaven moment when a mild corresponding breeze and not sound waves through the ether had carried the metrically enhanced language of a man speaking—"personally, simply, almost familiarly"—to men.[47]

Matheson wanted, as David Cardiff puts it, to "domesticate . . . the public utterance, as an attempt to soften and naturalize the intrusion of national figures into the fireside world of the family," and thereby "to reach people whose lack of literary education barred them from access to 'complicated, difficult and novel ideas.'"[48] Ethically speaking, Matheson's creation of the intimate mode of address circumvented the often rigidly moralistic vision for broadcasting championed by Reith and many of the BBC's early administrators. They wanted to give the best that has been thought and said to listeners who would discover their own best selves through a process of cultural orthopedics. For Matheson the conversational, personal, intimate art of the radio talk, especially when applied to culturally or politically provocative subjects, should encourage listeners to cultivate their own selves as they tuned in privately. In Matheson's promotion of the intimate mode of address, aesthetics, ethics, and politics merge. In fact, her embrace of the intimate mode was one expression of her broader vision for broadcasting as a techno-cultural means for promoting a vigorous democracy of sensibility and liberality of opinion. Her clash with Reith was at root the expression of a conflict in broadcasting as well as political philosophies: his paternalism, her liberalism. This clash was also the expression of an ethical conflict—one between a Director-General who saw radio as an opportunity for enlisting the listening population into a moral order of the same, and a producer who understood it as a potential model of and catalyst for messier and less easily controlled interpersonal connections.

To understand the ethical significance of Matheson's vision for broadcasting as a familiar art, it is necessary to locate it in the domestic context of intramural ideological struggles at the BBC. But Matheson focused her vision in a broader political context, too—one marked by the development of authoritarian broadcasting in Germany after Hitler became Reich Chancellor and Joseph Goebbels took control of German radio. Beginning in May 1932, in her *Week-End Review* column, Matheson commented regularly on German broadcasting, which she calls more than once "a menace to peace."[49] Michael Carney probably overstates the case in portraying his subject as a modern Cassandra. "At a time," he writes, "when most commentators ignored it, she regularly drew attention to the threat posed to democratic values by Nazi Germany."[50] Carney is right, though, to recognize Matheson's keen awareness of the place of radio in this threat; she repeatedly called attention to it, and her many references to German broadcasting under the Nazis show her a keen observer of how modes of address tended at that time to correspond both to specific political and ethical agendas and to the degree of state control over broadcasting.

Some of the early columns in which Matheson reflects on presentation methods also express concern with whether the BBC itself was beginning to "sound . . . the note of a new and militant nationalism;" these columns ask, for example, "[D]oes our *national* habit need special encouragement at the moment?"[51] This is in June 1932. A few months later, she defines that "moment," introducing the question of the relation between German politics and German radio. She writes, "The most interesting country at the moment from the broadcasting point of view is Germany"—a claim she repeats several times over the next year. "No student of German politics," she continues:

> can afford to ignore the immense use which is being made of the microphone in the conscious development of a new nationalism. . . . It has now become the principal channel for announcing policy, national and international to the German people. It is interesting to speculate whether the extreme impersonality of ordinary German politics has something to do with this enthusiasm for a peculiarly personal and human medium. . . . Whether deliberately or not, broadcasting in Germany is emphasizing the personality element in politics. This, together with the recent reorganization and centralization of the service, may well make the microphone one of the determining factors in forming that national opinion with which the rest of the world will have to deal during the next few years.[52]

Over the course of the following, momentous year, 1933, Matheson would frequently link stylistic issues with political ones. On 11 March 1933, for example,[53] Matheson contrasted German radio "oratory" with both American and English "intimacy," beginning with a reference to Franklin D. Roosevelt's famous fireside chats. "In these days of crisis," she writes,

> Broadcasting provides some interesting side-lights on the personalities of political figures. We have heard President Roosevelt, and gained an impression of a pleasant and friendly nature facing immense problems seriously and quietly. We have also heard Herr Hitler; it was indeed difficult not to hear him. I tuned in to listen the other evening, and, when I had had enough, his hoarse and strident tones pursued me as I turned my dial. I found myself wondering how far German psychology differs from English in the matter of listening to oratory. In this country it seems to have been proved beyond doubt that an intimate studio talk carries greater weight than the relay of platform appeals. Tub-thumping through the loud-speaker, in other words, does not go down well over here; what effect did it produce on those German families listening all over Germany? Its effect on the polls was probably negligible, since the

result was presumably a foregone conclusion; but can we safely assume that
the frenzied manner is unsuccessful in all places and at all times? I should like
to think it so.[54]

Because she had been so intimately involved in shaping British broadcasting,
and especially the liberal presentation of often controversial political, social,
and cultural subject matter, Matheson understood from the outset the subtle
relations among form, content, and political intention in German radio under
the leadership of Goebbels and Eugen Hadamovsky, who also well understood the differences between the spoken and written word, and between the
spoken word as broadcast and the spoken word as delivered in a lecture,
theatrical performance, or speech. "The spoken word over radio," Hadamovsky writes in 1934, "is in an entirely different context than a speech in a
meeting or a theater." And so, for radio to be effective, "a real human connection between receiver and sender must be established."[55] But where
Matheson accepted broadcasting as "an intimate contact between individuals,
between the listener and the speaker" designed to encourage independent
thought in private, and based her entire philosophy of broadcasting on that
belief, Hadamovsky assumed axiomatically that the purpose of broadcasting
was to "realize a common will." This was an intention that required the
practical step of the physical mobilization of the masses—what he calls with
bureaucratic banality, "human organizational means. One of the most important ways of doing this," he says, "is to bring many radio listeners together
for community listening, which National Socialism has developed to a major
degree."[56] In a formulation that uncannily recalls the Community Sings of
the Fordist state in Aldous Huxley's recently published *Brave New World*
(1932), this "organizational form," Hadamovsky goes on to say, will help to
ensure "the fact of connection" between the National Socialist state and "the
people . . . the river of strength flowing from popular life . . . the broad
masses."[57]

In his August 1933 radio exhibition speech, Goebbels speculated not only
that "the radio will be for the twentieth century what the press was for the
nineteenth century," but also, and more grandly, that radio would end up
having "as great an intellectual and spiritual impact on the masses as the
printing press before the beginning of the Reformation."[58] Radio, as Goebbels saw it, was both the most important "modern method of influencing the
masses" and "the most influential and important intermediary between [the
Nazi] spiritual movement and the nation, between the idea and the people."[59]
The "subordination" of the collective will to the National Socialist state was
the prime and patent aim of German broadcasting under his control, as Goebbels makes clear in his concluding salute to "One People, one Reich, one will
and a glorious German future!"[60] Four months earlier, Matheson had argued
that "the most interesting laboratory for experiments in broadcasting policy

and techniques is to be found at the present moment in Germany," where "the old conception of broadcasting as an instrument of non-political entertainment and education, reflecting all points of view, has been replaced . . . by a new conception of broadcasting as a means of influencing the masses in favor of a political and social ideal."[61] In the face of this threat, she calls the next week for "a world-wide campaign to insist that the loud-speaker is, psychologically, not a trumpet but a still, small voice. . . . The sooner this is generalized," she concludes, "the better it will be for broadcasting as well as for our general comfort."[62] In one of her final columns on this issue, and indeed one of her final columns, in late October 1933, she admits that "To dictatorships broadcasting offers a weapon readily available for war"; but she insists on a counterbalancing potential in the medium: "To a free people it offers an instrument equally apt for peace, provided that there is [a] fortunate divorce from Government . . . and provided that broadcasters are encouraged to keep alive . . . that human and informal contact with the widest public which is the essence of good broadcasting." And she hopes against hope that "the still, small," intimate voice "may be a more powerful agency for peace than the harsh tones of the German Chancellor may be for war."[63]

LEVINAS AND THE ETHICS OF RADIO

Matheson's development of the intimate mode of address during her five-year tenure at the BBC, and her continuing promotion of it while at the *Week-End Review*, was simultaneously an aesthetic, an ethical, and a political activity. It was an aesthetic one as an experiment in style, and it represented a contribution to cultural politics when Matheson appealed to it to critique both the militancy of German radio under Hitler and Goebbels and what she feared was becoming over the course of the 1930s, under Reith, a dangerously militaristic ethos at the BBC itself. Matheson's celebration of radio's fundamental intimacy as a communications medium also possessed an ethical resonance, in part as it critiqued the homogenizing moral agenda for British broadcasting that was promoted by John Reith. But Matheson was driven in her *Week-End Review* columns, and therefore presumably in general, both as a theorist and an administrator, by a moral anxiety which transcends the Arnoldian cultural politics of the BBC and lends itself to a more pointed ethical analysis. For, although she did not use these precise terms, and though for obvious reasons she did not think in explicitly Levinasian terms, she nevertheless listened to German radio with a keen awareness that Nazi broadcasting represented the eruption of what Emmanuel Levinas calls the "barbarism of being" (*EN* 187), and she repeatedly insisted on radio's intimacy as a way of encouraging individual listeners' as well as individual broadcasters' responsible attentiveness to the voices (or ears) of others as a way of interrupting this barbarism. Moreover, Matheson developed the intimate voice in broadcasting as a way of counteracting the strong tendency toward impersonality in modern telecommunications. The question remains, though, of how Matheson's vision for broadcasting as the transmission of an intimate voice between individual speaker and individual listener, given the particular institutional, political, and historical contexts in which she developed this vision, expresses a belief in the "transcendence" possible in the "everyday social exchange" that Sara Crangle speaks of and that occupied Levinas. How much does such a voice embody, articulate, or harmonize with a specifically Levinasian ethics? How can Levinas help us better to understand the ethical complexities of early broadcasting?

Levinas appeared numerous times on radio—he used the medium as a vehicle for the explanation and transmission of his ethical ideas. But he has very little to say about radio as such. However, the comments he does make on radio as a technology, and the references he makes to radio in his published interviews, happen rather serendipitously to speak to some of Hilda Matheson's central concerns, and thereby help to illuminate the ethical commitments and stakes of broadcasting in England and Germany in the late 1920s and early 1930s. Levinas demonstrates a passing interest, but an interest nevertheless, in radio's place as one among many types of communications and other technologies that play a large role in defining the place of the individual and in shaping the forms and felt experiences of human relationships in the modern world. In the introductory paragraphs to his 1982 Talmudic reading "The Pact," Levinas speaks of

> the unease felt by man today within a society whose boundaries have become, in a sense, planetary: a society in which, due to the ease of modern communications . . . each person feels simultaneously that he is related to humanity as a whole, and equally that he is alone and lost. With each radio broadcast . . . one may well feel caught up in the most distant events, and connected to mankind everywhere; but one also understands that one's personal destiny, freedom or happiness is subject to causes which operate with inhuman force. One understands that the very progress of technology . . . which relates everyone in the world to everyone else, is inseparable from a necessity which leaves all men anonymous. Impersonal forms of relation come to replace the more direct forms . . . in an excessively programmed world. (*LR* 212)

Levinas's thoughts reverberate with those of the many cultural theorists who have explored the ways that modern telecommunications technologies impose a sense of time–space compression on the individual's experience of the world. Levinas also goes on to raise an important question about the relation between the highly interconnected world of technological modernity, on the one hand, and, on the other, the realm of the ethical. He does this in a comment that opens up interesting possibilities not only for a Levinasian ethics of communication in general—as, for example, Amit Pinchevski uses that phrase in a book that explores, among other aspects of Levinas's thoughts on communication, the inverse relation between knowledge and responsibility, "the paradoxical realization that the more informed one is of the Other, the less one is responsible for the Other"[64] —but also for a Levinasian ethics of electronic mass telecommunications during the years leading up to the Second World War. "The cohesive nature of the modern world," Levinas writes, "planned by means of law and regulation, and all the 'remote connections' it sets up are constitutive of today's reality, even if these relationships make us march forward together rather than turn our faces toward each other" (*LR* 213). Levinas's characterization of modernity echoes his definition of the totalitarian state as one "in which the interpersonal relation is impossible, in which it is directed in advance by the determinism proper to the State" (*ITR* 167). This echo contains another one, of Levinas's often-cited question on relations between politics and ethics:

> It is extremely important to know if society in the current sense of the term is the result of a limitation of the principle that men are predators of one another, or if to the contrary it results from the limitation of the principle that men are for one another. Does the social, with its institutions, universal forms and laws, result from limiting the consequences of the war between men, or from limiting the infinity which opens in the ethical relationship of man to man? (*EI* 80)

Levinas is perhaps overstating the case in his characterization of modern life as "excessively programmed" by communications technologies as the facile tools of a unified and unifying State. Nevertheless, his comment on the pervasive constitutiveness of "remote connections" enabled by modern communications technologies speaks directly to ethical challenges faced by early broadcasting administrators. Even more importantly, his insight into how twentieth-century communications technologies "make us march forward together rather than turn our faces toward each other" constitutes an apt commentary on the tub-thumping, community-organizing, mass-listening, propaganda radio broadcasting of the Third Reich—as well as on the American (though now, of course, much more widespread) model of commercial broadcasting whose purpose is to encourage individuals to submerge themselves in the forward march of consumerism.

Elsewhere, Levinas makes an even closer connection among radio, totalitarianism, and the philosophical tradition from which he strove to distance himself even while vigorously grappling with it from the mid-1930s onwards. In two interviews, Levinas mentions radio in discussing Martin Heidegger, in whose very voice Levinas heard the harsh tones, the tub-thumping totalitarianism of the "Hitlerist" radio that provoked such keen anxiety in Hilda Matheson. In reply to the question, "How do you explain Heidegger's relation to National Socialism?" Levinas recalls that Heidegger's "firm and categorical voice came back to me when I used to hear Hitler on the radio." In another interview, in response to the observation that "Hitler could be directly derived from [Heidegger's] thinking," Levinas says, "I heard Hitler on the radio, and Hitler did always sound a bit like Heidegger to me. I mean in the way in which someone approves of something and proceeds to holler about it" (*ITR* 36, 141).

This conjunction of National Socialism, the voice of Martin Heidegger, and radio is interesting in itself; but it gains a special significance in the present context from what Robert Bernasconi calls Levinas's tendency to "associate" the "*conatus essendi*" with National Socialism.[65] The Spinozan concept of the *conatus essendi*—being persevering in being, the tendency of a being to persist in its being—occurs repeatedly in Levinas's work; it also constitutes "the focus of his polemic against . . . Heidegger."[66] With respect to the question of the ethics of radio broadcasting in the Third Reich, and the question of the relation between broadcasting style or voice, and politics, in the early 1930s in both Germany and Britain, it is significant that the voice of Hitler, in which Levinas heard a strong echo of the "firm and categorical voice" of Heidegger, was, as such Nazi radio theorists and administrators as Goebbels and Hadamovsky saw it, the very embodiment of the spirit of the Third Reich—the broadcast materialization of "Nazi Germany demand[ing] a vital space, its 'place in the sun,' the order where being strove to persevere in being" (*ITR* 99). When Hilda Matheson, tuning in to German radio during the historic month of March 1933, heard "the hoarse and strident tones" of Hitler which "pursued me as I turned my dial," and went on to link this hoarse stridency with a quickly developing "spirit of persecution" in Germany, she also worried about Nazi Germany's embrace of radio as a means of "mass persuasion." For her, radio was an opportunity to enhance connection between individuals and to encourage independent thought in the service of democracy. This can be put in a more specifically Levinasian ethical register. For Matheson the ultimate purpose of radio broadcasting as "a peculiarly personal and intimate medium" was to foster a state of social affairs in which people would move through the world with their faces turned toward each other, rather than one in which individuals, enlisted through the strange power of the broadcast voice into an "imperialism of the same" (*TI* 87), would "march forward together," bound by what Levinas calls in his "Reflections on the Philosophy of Hitlerism" "[t]he mysterious urgings of the blood, the appeals of heredity and the past" which impose "a kind of bondage"—a bondage to, in Goebbels's stock phrase, "One People, one Reich, one will and a glorious German future!"

Levinas speaks of ethics in one of his interviews as a type of "comportment," a manner of encountering the world, an attitude toward the world and to others "in which the other, who is strange and indifferent to you, who belongs neither to the order of your interest nor to your affections, at the same time matters to you. His alterity concerns you." This is an attitude in which one "encounters the face as face, where the obligation with respect to the other is imposed before all obligation: to respect the other, to take the other into account." This type of comportment constitutes a direct challenge and indeed a reproach to a possessive, knowledge-driven type of comportment towards others that expresses the urge "to embrace," to "hold in my thought," to make them "become mine." For it is the face of the other, the other in his or her radical alterity, that "rupture[s] . . . the immanent order," and offers the hope of liberation from a kind of spiritual bondage (*ITR* 48–49).

Hilda Matheson shared with Levinas a conviction as to the social desirability of such a comportment, such a non-possessive openness not only toward difference of opinion but also toward otherness as such. For her, the intimate mode of address, in contrast to oratory or pronouncement, respected independence, autonomy, and the ability as well as the desirability of individual listeners to make up their own minds. She was dubious toward the Reithian BBC's project of moral uplift. Her attitude toward that project, as well as toward the Nazi broadcasting laboratory with its determination to hail listeners into a National Socialist order of the same, may be read as embodying a generalized countercultural tendency or a commonly felt anxiety, without any deep ethical import. After all, it required no special fluency in ethical philosophy in the years 1927–1932 to bristle at Reithian paternalism. Still less did it require such fluency in the early 1930s to object to or feel threatened by the "hoarse and strident" voice of Hitler or by the rapid and successful growth of totalitarian broadcasting in Germany under Goebbels and Hadamovsky, both of whom insisted on what Levinas calls the "primacy of the same" (*TI* 45). Hilda Matheson shuddered before her radio receiver when Hitler's hoarse and strident voice trumpeted the autocracy and categorical possessiveness of Nazi Germany. What she heard was the beating of a sanguine economy that threatened precisely through its pursuing bellicosity and its bloody insistence on the "primacy of the same" to demolish the infinite possibilities for human relationships represented by the still, small voices of civilization.

NOTES

1. Douglas Mao and Rebecca L. Walkowitz, "The New Modernist Studies," *PMLA* 123, no. 3 (2008): 737–38.
2. Ibid., 738.
3. See Peter Gay, *Modernism: The Lure of Heresy: From Baudelaire to Beckett and Beyond* (New York: Norton, 2008).
4. Lawrence Buell, "What We Talk About When We Talk About Ethics," in *The Turn to Ethics*, ed. Marjorie Garber, Beatrice Hanssen, and Rebecca L. Walkowitz (New York: Routledge, 2000), 2, 10–11.

5. Sandor Goodhart, review of Jill Robbins, *Altered Reading: Levinas and Literature*, *MFS: Modern Fiction Studies* 45, no. 4 (1999), 1098.

6. Sara Crangle, *Prosaic Desires: Modernist Knowledge, Boredom, Laughter, and Anticipation* (Edinburgh: Edinburgh University Press, 2010), 184.

7. Ibid., 63.

8. Ibid., 14.

9. Ibid., 19.

10. Ibid., 10, 14.

11. I am indebted to Donald Wehrs for calling my attention to Matheson's allusion to 1 Kings 19 and for explaining the significance of this allusion in the present context. The quotations here are taken from private e-mail communication.

12. Hilda Matheson, *Broadcasting* (London: Home University Library, 1933), 127–28, italics added.

13. Emmanuel Levinas,"Reflections on the Philosophy of Hitlerism," *Critical Inquiry* 17, no. 1 (Autumn 1990), 64.

14. Ibid., 71.

15. Joseph Goebbels, "Radio as the Eighth Great Power" (1933), German Propaganda Archive, online: www.calvin.edu/academic/cas/gpa/goeb56.htm, 2.

16. Ibid., 4.

17. Ibid., 4.

18. Eugen Hadamovsky, "The Living Bridge: On the Nature of Radio Warden Activity" (1934), German Propaganda Archive, online: www.calvin.edu/academic/cas/gpa/hada3.htm, 1–2.

19. Arnold Davidson, "1933-1934: Thoughts on National Socialism: Introduction to Musil and Levinas," *Critical Inquiry* 17, no. 1 (Autumn 1990), 36.

20. Hans Fritzsche, "Dr. Goebbels and His Ministry" (1934), German Propaganda Archive, online: http://www.calvin.edu/academic/cas/gpa/goeb62.htm, 8.

21. Levinas, "Reflections," 70.

22. Ibid., 70.

23. Ibid., 69.

24. Seán Hand, *Emmanuel Levinas* (London: Routledge, 2009), 29.

25. Levinas, "Reflections," 63.

26. Matheson, "Broadcasting," *The Week-End Review* (11 June 1932), 735.

27. Matheson, "Broadcasting," *The Week-End Review* (17 December 1932), 747.

28. Matheson, "Broadcasting," *The Week-End Review* (22 April 1933), 454.

29. Desmond MacCarthy, "The Magnifying Glass on Modern Literature," *The Listener* (23 September 1931), 479.

30. John Reith, British Broadcasting Company memo, BBC Written Archives Centre file R 34/292/1.

31. Harold Nicolson, "Are the BBC too Cautious?" *Spectator* (21 November 1931), 670.

32. Her resignation was an event that at least one newspaper, the *News Chronicle*, reported as the unfortunate result of an explicitly gendered, Manichean conflict between Matheson, a politically and culturally liberal, female administrator, and Reith, the BBC's dictatorial, politically conservative (or, to put it more favorably, politically pragmatic), staunchly masculine Director-General. H. G. Wells, who owed his popular broadcasting career to Matheson, later recalled that the episode represented a fight between a "courageous and indefatigable" woman who was devoted to "that liberal thought and free expression which is the essence of democratic freedom," and a man who was inspired by loyalty to "duller influences from above." See Wells's contribution to the "little memorial volume" published after Matheson's death, *Hilda Matheson, Born June 7th, 1888, Died October 30th, 1940* (Letchworth, Hertfordshire: Hogarth Press, 1941), 56.

33. Max Horkheimer and Theodor Adorno, in their analysis of the culture industry in the mid-1940s, write of the "democratic" character of radio. Focusing on two of the three major modes of broadcasting administration then in existence—or, to borrow Raymond Williams's phrase, two of the three existing "cultural formations" of broadcasting: namely, commercial broadcasting (as pioneered in the United States) and totalitarian mass communications (as in

their native Germany under the Nazi regime)—Horkheimer and Adorno overlook the third model, that of public service broadcasting in the national interest, a model peculiar at that time to Britain. Radio, they nevertheless write in their radically skeptical analysis of the uniform broadcasting practices of the former two models (that is to say, the practice of broadcasting uniformity that they embody), "democratically makes everyone into listeners, in order to expose them in authoritarian fashion to the same programs put out by different stations. No mechanism of reply has been developed. . . . Any trace of spontaneity in the audience of the official radio is steered and absorbed into . . . a selection of specializations . . . and sponsored events of every kind." See Horkheimer and Adorno, "The Culture Industry as Mass Deception," in *Media and Cultural Studies: Keyworks*, rev. ed., ed. Meenakshi Gigi Durham and Douglas Kellner (Oxford: Blackwell, 2006), 42.

34. John Reith, *The Reith Diaries*, ed. Charles Stuart (London: Collins, 1975), 56–57.

35. Andrew Crisell, *An Introductory History of British Broadcasting* (London: Routledge, 2002), 28.

36. Ibid., 33, italics in text.

37. Ibid., 35.

38. John Reith, *Broadcast over Britain* (London: Hodder and Stoughton, 1924), 219–20.

39. Ibid., 34.

40. Ibid., 222.

41. Ibid., 224.

42. Michael Carney, *Stoker: The Life of Hilda Matheson OBE, 1888-1940* (Published by the Author, 1999), 81.

43. Reith, *Broadcast*, 23. The passage continues: "A broadcasting service was expected, and had to be initiated and developed. . . . All that could definitely be gathered was that this new organisation had agreed to establish a certain number of broadcasting stations and transmit therefrom at certain times, programmes composed of whatever a programme can be composed. . . . There it was" (23).

44. Matheson, *Broadcasting*, 127–28.

45. Ibid., 75–76.

46. Geoffrey Wheatcroft, "Who Needs the BBC?"*The Atlantic* 287, no. 3 (March 2001), 53.

47. D. L. LeMahieu, *A Culture for Democracy: Mass Communication and the Cultivated Mind in Britain between the Wars* (Oxford: Clarendon Press, 1988).

48. David Cardiff, "The Serious and the Popular: Aspects of the Evolution of Style in the Radio Talk, 1928-1939," *Media, Culture and Society* 2, no. 1 (1980), 30–31.

49. Matheson, "Broadcasting" (6 May 1933), 508; (20 May 1933), 608–9.

50. Carney, 89.

51. Matheson, "Broadcasting" (4 June 1932), 704, italics added.

52. Matheson, "Broadcasting" (17 December 1932), 747.

53. This was a month after the first German radio broadcast of one of Hitler's speeches and within two weeks following the Reichstag fire, the Reichstag Fire Decree (which explicitly restricted "freedom of opinion" and of the press), and the subsequent election of March 5 which made possible the Enabling Act giving Hitler dictatorial powers.

54. Matheson, "Broadcasting" (11 March 1933), 230. Of course, "the frenzied manner" was indeed successful in Germany in 1933, and would remain so for "the next few years." The next month she writes of "recent ominous developments in German broadcasting" (1 April 1933, 300), and of how "the spirit of persecution" in Germany at that time seemed inexorably to be "putting the clock back in broadcasting as in other things" (15 April 1933, 430). She made this latter comment in a column in which she also lamented the tragic and untimely death of Walter Schaffer, "the creator . . . of the German broadcasting system on its technical side, who, with his wife, committed suicide the other day in face, presumably, of the anti-Jewish campaign" (430). Two weeks later, deriding "the growing use of . . . loud-speaking in public places, the compulsory open windows for those with wireless sets," Matheson upholds the "real broadcasting" of the intimate, liberal type that she had developed, and worries about "the habitual diffusion of programmes in public places" for the purpose of "mass persuasion" (29 April 1933, 480).

55. Hadamovsky, 3.

56. Ibid., 3.
57. Ibid., 4.
58. Goebbels, 1.
59. Ibid., 1–2.
60. Ibid., 5.
61. Matheson, "Broadcasting" (22 April 1933), 454.
62. Matheson, "Broadcasting" (29 April 1933), 480.
63. Matheson, "Broadcasting" (21 October 1933), 402.
64. Amit Pinchevski, *By Way of Interruption: Levinas and the Ethics of Communication* (Pittsburgh: Duquesne University Press, 2005), 79.
65. Robert Bernasconi, "Globalization and World Hunger: Kant and Levinas", in *Radicalizing Levinas*, ed. Peter Atterton and Matthew Calarco (Albany: State University of New York Press, 2010), 78.
66. Ibid., 78.

Chapter Eight

Dialogic Ethics through Levinas and Bakhtin

Dialogism and Infinite Obligation to the Other in Three Twentieth-Century Dramas

Richard Middleton-Kaplan

This chapter seeks the common ground underlying Levinas's concept of infinite obligation to the Other and Mikhail Bakhtin's concepts of dialogism and polyphony. Fulfilling the Levinasian obligation depends upon an infinite openness to the voice or cry of the Other, an openness in some ways equivalent to the open play of voices that characterizes Bakhtinian polyphony. Remaining open to those voices, and resisting the urge to impose any totalizing monologic authority, constitutes not only the essence of Bakhtinian dialogism but also an ethical imperative.

When they turned to literary texts as exemplars of this ethical imperative, Levinas and Bakhtin focused on novels—Dostoevsky's novels in particular—and rarely on drama. I will argue, however, that drama is the genre *par excellence* that illustrates, or dramatizes, the dialogic principle and the ethical command to remain infinitely open to the voices of Others. I use three dramas that span the twentieth century to demonstrate the dovetailing theories of Levinas and Bakhtin: Luigi Pirandello's *Six Characters in Search of an Author* (1921), Arthur Miller's *All My Sons* (1947), and Tony Kushner's *Angels in America* (1991–1992).

To the ongoing dialogue about Levinas's importance for literary studies, I hope to contribute two seldom-discussed points of connection, first in the unification of Bakhtin and Levinas as ethicists, and second in the application of Levinas to dramatic literature.

COMMON GROUND BETWEEN LEVINAS AND BAKHTIN

While literary scholars might think of Bakhtin chiefly as a literary theorist associated with Formalism and narratology, the ground for viewing him as a philosopher has been thoroughly cultivated. Michael Eskin notes that "Bakhtin began his career as a philosopher."[1] Ken Hirschkop reminds us that Bakhtin "warned the young postgraduate literary scholars who 'rediscovered' him in the 1960s that he was 'a philosopher, not a literary scholar' who had turned to ostensibly literary studies as a way of prosecuting philosophical questions in peace."[2] In present-day Russia and Ukraine, many scholars regard Bakhtin primarily as a philosopher.[3]

The common soil beneath the feet of Levinas and Bakhtin has been tilled in Eskin's *Ethics and Dialogue in the Works of Levinas, Bakhtin, Mandel'shtam, and Celan.* Eskin locates crucial similarities between Bakhtin and Levinas: "abounding thematic resemblances" (66), "methodological affinity" (67), a view of "human sociality" as "fundamentally dialogic" (7), and an ethical framework in which "the unique ethical subject . . . is dialogically constituted" (19).

Without burying the differences which Eskin unearths, we can see an equivalence between Levinas's principle of infinite obligation and Bakhtin's conceptualization of the polyphonic novel militating against the closing off of dialogue. Imposition of a monologic truth terminates dialogue. Since a dialogic narrative refuses monologic closure, a reader must remain poised to entertain the characters' voices in an ongoing polyphonic dialogue . . . even if the novel itself must end. Viewed through the prism of Levinasian ethics, Bakhtin's determination to preserve open-ended dialogism emerges as a moral imperative to remain always open to the voice of the Other. At this point, Bakhtinian dialogism and Levinasian ethics converge.

We customarily connect Levinasian ethics to the encounter with the face of the Other rather than with dialogic exchange—and for good reason. "The irreducible and ultimate experience of relationship appears to me in fact to be . . . in the face to face of humans, in sociality, in its moral signification," Levinas writes (*EI* 77). The face summons us to ethical relationships: "The first word of the face is 'Thou shalt not kill.' It is an order" (89). Moreover, this obligation is infinite: "one is never quits with regard to the Other. . . . At no time can one say: I have done all my duty" (105).[4]

However, we can also be summoned by the voice or cry of the Other. Levinas asks us,

> Is not the evil of suffering—extreme passivity, helplessness, abandonment and solitude—also the unassumable, when the possibility of a half opening . . . that a moan, a cry, a groan or a sigh slips through—the original call for aid, for

curative help, help from the other me whose alterity, whose exteriority promises salvation? (*EN* 93)

Openness to the voice, cry, and groan of the Other forms the essence of dialogism, for dialogism resists silencing the Other by keeping at bay a totalizing, authoritative (or authoritarian) voice.

Dialogue, or the dialogic principle, should thus be seen as foundational and fundamental for Levinas. It forms the basis for his view of Talmud as an exchange of unmerged voices whose conflicting, spiky opinions are not flattened into monologic syntheses; his own Talmudic commentaries contribute to a living tradition of ongoing dialogue. Theodore De Boer says "that 'Levinas integrates phenomenological ontology into dialogical thought.'"[5] In the conversational and the transcendental realm, the dialogic principle is intertwined with ethical exchange.[6]

This passage from Bakhtin illustrates where he and Levinas converge: "The being of the human being . . . is, fundamentally, interaction. To be— means to *interact*. . . . To be means to be for the other and through the other—for oneself."[7] Here they agree that interaction leads us to be and to act for the Other. That call can only be heard through openness to the Other's voice.

BEYOND NARRATIVE: DIALOGISM AND DRAMA

In Dostoevsky's novels, both Bakhtin and Levinas found support for their theories of polyphony and infinite obligation. Dostoevsky's centrality for Bakhtin requires no elaboration. Levinas often quoted from *The Brothers Karamazov*: "each of us is guilty in everything before everyone, and I most of all."[8] The *Levinas Concordance* lists forty references to "Dostoïevski,"[9] most involving that passage. Noting the frequency with which he invokes the quote, Alain Toumayan comments that "Levinas's biographer, Marie-Anne Lescourret, goes so far as to characterize [this quote] as his mantra or talismanic quotation, *'sa citation fétiche.'*"[10]

Given the frequency of Levinas's invocation of Dostoevsky, it is not surprising that literary applications of Levinasian ethics have focused on novels. The same holds true for literary studies that extend Bakhtin's dialogism. A search of the *MLA International Bibliography* produced 944 results for "Bakhtin + Novel," but just 149 for "Bakhtin + Drama." When I entered "Levinas + Novel," the search generated 106 results; the search for "Levinas + Drama" produced a mere 24 results.[11] Studies of Bakhtin and the novel thus outnumber studies of Bakhtin and drama by more than 6 to 1; in the case of Levinas, the ratio in favor of novel studies stands at more than 4 to 1.

In seeking to understand this disparity, it is worth noting that Eskin and Hirschkop both insist on the importance of genre. Hirschkop says that critics who embrace Bakhtin's dialogism "ignore the other great emphasis of Bakhtin's work—an insistent and ceaseless interest in the 'generic,' as the textual form in which the dialogical is embodied" (10). That form must be the novel, Hirschkop reports, for Bakhtin does not want mere dramas but rather

> "novels," and what distinguishes novels are their heroes, which are not persons but socio-ideological languages. But the novelist who strives to represent these socio-ideological languages must nevertheless shape them as actors in a narrative.
> . . . To represent heteroglossia, one must therefore have narrative. (228)

This seems to me an untenable distinction. What is Joe Keller from *All My Sons* if not a socio-ideological language in dialogue with the position of his son Chris? They are indeed "actors"—the term drawn from drama is noteworthy here—in a plot if not in a narrative. In *Angels in America*, virtually every character represents a socio-ideological position in dialogue with others. The absence of narrative does not eliminate the characters' function as "actors" nor rein in heteroglossia; rather, it positions them unmistakably as "actors," and not having a narrator removes the last trace of monologism that might restrict unencumbered heteroglossia.

Eskin's study expands beyond fiction to poetry, but still omits drama: For Levinas and Bakhtin, he says, ethics and "the poetics of dialogue" unite in poetry, which is "the dialogically most significant speech genre" (113). One wonders why drama, which consists entirely of dialogue (except for stage directions), is not "the dialogically most significant speech genre."

Since a play by definition consists of dialogue and has no monologic narrator, drama is actually the genre that best exemplifies Bakhtinian dialogism and the comparable Levinasian call to heed the face and cry of the Other. It is on stage, in drama, that we witness the full, unfettered enactment of those voices in free play, with each of those voices calling upon each other, and most significantly calling upon us as audience members implicated in the drama, to respond ethically in recognition of our infinite obligation to all whose faces and voices we encounter.

PIRANDELLO'S *SIX CHARACTERS IN SEARCH OF AN AUTHOR*: "I WANT TO ACT MY PART, *MY PART!*"

Pirandello's play, as its title suggests, audaciously overthrows the authority of the author as well as the narrator. The play opens with an acting company cast and crew rehearsing another Pirandello play. To their consternation, their rehearsal is interrupted by six lost characters who report that they were conceived by an author but then abandoned before he completed the play for which he imagined them. They have come in search of an author to give voice to their stories, to give them life, and to give their lives meaning. The six characters persuade the company manager to turn their aborted story into a play. Chaos results, with frequent arguments erupting between the six characters, the company actors vying to play them, and the stage crew.

The six characters constitute a family. They are The Father, The Mother, The Son, The Boy, The Step-Daughter, and The Child. These generic names suggest that we should view them as types, quite possibly as socio-ideological categories, rather than as unique individuals. (For example, The Manager explains to the actor who plays The Father, "You stand for reason, your wife is instinct."[12]) As their story of torment and anguish unfolds in fits and starts, tragic events come to light: The Father encouraged The Mother to pursue an affair with his male secretary, and eventually turned her out; The Mother, driven to desperation, obtained work as a seamstress in a brothel but was incompetent at it; the brothel Madame pressed The Step-Daughter into prostitution to compensate for The Mother's inept work; The Father went to the brothel, where he was presented as a client to his Step-Daughter; The Child, a four-year-old girl, is witnessed drowning by The Boy, or perhaps is drowned by him; and The Boy goes mad and shoots himself.

Free from a narrator, unencumbered dialogue flows between actors, between actors and characters, and between our real and artificial selves. Dialogue rises to the level of dialogic ethics as Pirandello lifts his characters' "naked masks" and exposes illusions to reveal the naked human suffering underneath. The play forces us to recognize that we are all subject to being misunderstood and to enduring psychic anguish. With no monologic authority to privilege any one character's suffering, we must remain open to the voices of all . . . even to the silence of the non-speaking characters, the little Boy who goes mad and The Child who drowns. In Levinasian terms, that openness to the Other's voice is the prerequisite for acting on the ethical call of the Other.

Or at least that is how it should go. From a Bakhtinian perspective, the dialogic opposition of "one point of view opposed to another, one evaluation opposed to another, one accent opposed to another"[13] should result, as he argues it does in the world of Dostoevsky's novels, in "*coexistence* and *interaction*."[14] From a Levinasian perspective, the uncircumscribed polyphony should open us to hear and respond to the anguish of the Other. In fact, it has the opposite effect in Pirandello's play. The characters are consumed with telling the tale of their suffering, but they do not heed the voices and cries of their family members. In the end, we are left with a kind of hell—or rather, with three kinds of hell: a Sartrean hell of other people; a Bakhtinian abyss of warring monologisms; and a Levinasian nightmare of unanswered suffering and isolation. The characters' failure to engage in dialogism results in a failure to respond ethically to one another.

Pirandello does topple monologic authority. He "abandon[s] . . . the authorial position and allow[s] his characters to engage in autonomous confrontation on the stage (relegating his own voice to the stage directions)."[15] Dialogue, an irrepressible force, erupts everywhere, including where it does not belong (as in rehearsals). The Manager leading the rehearsal might be seen as a surrogate authority figure. But his authority is overthrown by the six characters who interrupt the rehearsal and who continually correct, contradict, and challenge him. At the same time, they plead with him to take on the role of author in order to give their stories meaning. He declines. With no author/authority/authoritarian figure, stage and script are free for unconstrained dialogic exchange. Instead, we witness a tragic breakdown of communication and ethical responsibility.

An ethic founded on dialogism requires listening to the Other. If we want Pirandello's characters to model dialogic ethics for us, they fail. The dialogue here is really just covert monologue; rather than engaging in true dialogism, they enact a series of monologues, verbally stumbling over each other as they fight to be heard, but not listening. Thus The Father attacks The Mother's "mental deafness" (Pirandello 224), but remains deaf to her pleas. The Mother sees The Step-Daughter's agony but only feels and wants recognition of her own, and does not respond with action or compassion: "she . . . has run away, she has left me, and is lost. If I now see her here before me, it is only to renew for me the tortures I have suffered for her too" (260); The Step-Daughter hears her mother's cries, but rather than comforting her, she exclaims, "It's driven me mad, that cry!" (260). The Step-Daughter also complains that The Father "wants to get at his complicated 'cerebral drama,' to have his famous remorses and torments acted; but I want to act my part, *my part!*" (258). These words epitomize the selfishness that each character exhibits.

Why does dialogism fail? First, in Felicity Firth's words, "Conflict and confusion ensue as each tries to hold the stage and impose his or her version of events on the others" (487). In this struggle to impose their own monologic versions, the characters repeatedly cut each other off; a revealing exercise would be to count the number of ellipses in the dialogue. They also repeatedly try to silence each other. The two potential authoritarian masters, The Father and The Manager, try to clamp down on the proliferating polyphony: The Father orders his family members to "Shut up!" several times, while The Manager often cries for "Silence!"

These responses illustrate a failure to heed the Other's cry; they also might be seen as illustrating the desire for recognition described by Hegel in his account of the master/slave dialectic and developed by Alexandre Kojève, Lacan, Lyotard, and others. The characters' desire for recognition of their own suffering could be interpreted in Hegelian terms as desire to enslave the others, or as a collective desire to enslave themselves to the director or an author.

Hegel's claims about lordship and bondage can be applied to the play. We see in several characters that "self-consciousness is . . . certain of itself only by superseding this other that presents itself to self-consciousness as an independent life"[16]; that each character "does not see the other as an essential being, but in the other sees its own self" (Hegel 111, par. 180); that "the outcome is a recognition that is one-sided and unequal" (116, par. 191); and that any satisfaction derived from negating the other is "only a fleeting one" (118, par. 195). Pirandello's characters stake their lives—that is, their existences as characters, which are already tenuous because they have been denied recognition by their originating author—in their cries for recognition from each other and from the director. The conflicting calls for recognition lead to war between them.

Psychological experiments conducted by R. D. Laing that developed Hegel's ideas, in which a person's self-perceptions were repeatedly contradicted and invalidated, found that within "a closed institution such as the family this persistent denial of recognition may, quite literally, lead to the disintegration of a person's sense of identity and to a condition of schizophrenia."[17] The identities of Pirandello's characters do tremble on the verge of disintegration through the entire spectacle. Once the production disbands, their existence disintegrates entirely.

Kojève also emphasized the role of family dynamics in conferring or withholding recognition. Through his influential seminars in Paris in the 1930s, Kojève introduced Hegel to many French intellectuals who would become important thinkers in their own right; Althusser, Bataille, Breton, Lacan, Merleau-Ponty, Queneau, and Sartre all attended in the city they shared with Levinas. Conferring recognition constitutes an act of love, Kojève says, and so "we can also say that Love is what is realized in and by the ancient Family."[18] But Pirandello's characters are denied recognition, as symbolized in their lack of individualized names. With that denial, they are denied love. Perhaps Kojève is right that love was realized in and by the ancient family; Pirandello depicts its absence in the modern family.

Individuals clamoring for recognition only for their own existences, stories, and sufferings will not produce a harmonious whole—nor even a group of harmonious, well-integrated individual personalities; rather, clashes between individual desires for recognition militate against self-realization, against love, against dialogism, against pluralism, and against ethical conduct toward the other. All of these failures are embodied in the dramatized failure of dialogism to bridge the chasm separating individuals. The Father says, "For the drama lies in all this—in the consciousness that I have, that each one of us—look—it seems to be single but it's not: it's many, sir, many, in accordance with all the ways of being that are within us."[19]

The Father blames lost faith and an atmosphere of moral desolation as the causes of this division. Within his lament, one finds Modernist acceptance of the death of God and of a shattered, fragmented world with no monolithic truth or metanarrative to help make sense of that world. Whereas an unconventional narrative would still be trapped inside the narrative genre in trying to depict the limitations of narrative, the genre of drama is ideally suited to dramatizing the absence of such a narrative. Firth elaborates: "The central thesis of Pirandello's 'new theatre' is that since no . . . verifiable world exists, each individual has to create a truth of his own to live with. Sometimes these 'truths' conflict, a situation made for theatre" (485). Pirandello allows the truths, and the characters who embody them, to remain in this state of unresolved conflict.

Finally, dialogism fails because not all the characters wish to reveal their private anguish. The Son wants his voice removed. The Boy and The Child, the chief victims, do not speak. In the cacaphonic cackle of self-centered cries for compassion, they are rendered voiceless, their suffering unheeded. In their silence, they stand for all voiceless victims. As Eric Bentley reminds us, Pirandello's plays "speak for all the tormented and, potentially, *to* all the tormented."[20]

Six Characters contains a sad sequence of failures to respond to the ethical command to respond to the Other. Only The Child, innocent and voiceless and drowned, does not violate that obligation, though she does nothing to fulfill it either.[21] The refusal to hear the Other's cry manifests itself at a political level in the fascism that arose in Italy at the same historical moment when Pirandello wrote *Six Characters* and then rose in Germany with a strong emphasis on despising weakness and rooting out sympathy for others; in fact, the play debuted the year before Mussolini's march on Rome. In terms of Hegel's notion of the family prefiguring the state, we can see in this play a pre-history or allegory of how fascism silences and dominates the weak. The characters' failure to embrace dialogism leads directly to failure to fulfill their obligations to the Other—a failure we can interpret on the individual, family, social, and political levels.

On discrete occasions, a deeper human connection almost materializes between divided consciousnesses. After a moving speech by The Step-Daughter, the stage directions tell us this:

> [The MOTHER at this is overcome with emotion, and breaks out into a fit of crying. ALL are touched. A long pause.] (259)

Here is an opportunity for all who are touched—family, actors, and crew—to fulfill their ethical obligation. The Mother's plea comes through the universal language of a cry, as if speech could neither contain nor express her agony. Levinasian ethics requires a response here, and not merely compassion, but an action to relieve the suffering of the Other "for whom I can do all and to whom I owe all" (*EI* 89). As Levinas writes, "the Other hails me and signifies to me, by its nakedness, by its destitution, an order. Its presence is this summons to respond" (*HOM* 33).[22] But after the long pause, no one responds. The potential of the moment evaporates.

Another failure occurs at the end, after The Child's drowning and The Boy's suicide. The stunned characters, actors, and crew grapple to come to terms with what they have witnessed. The last words before the final curtain belong to The Manager: "Pretence? Reality? To hell with it all! Never in my life has such a thing happened to me. I've lost a whole day over these people, a whole day!" (276). Here, as he turns his back on the family and inward to his own lost time, he squanders an opportunity to act for the Other. Insofar as he has been our surrogate in the play (in trying to make sense of the spectacle) and represents authority, his response reflects the defeat of dialogism and our own failure to heed the cry of the Other. This leaves us with only "loneliness, isolation, alienation. . . . For, if the great human gift is that of words, by what diabolic plan does it happen that words multiply misunderstanding? . . . Pirandellian man is isolated not only from his fellows but also from himself at other times. Further than this, isolation cannot go."[23]

Pirandello dramatically captures the post-World War I era's psychic devastation, and in his portrayal of isolation he anticipates themes of existential solitude that would become prominent by mid-century in works by Sartre, Camus, Ionesco, and Beckett. Indeed, depicting the shattered, lost, and lonely self of modern consciousness could be seen as his great subject.

But if Pirandello's major concern is the drama of consciousness, the depiction of the "primal moments when the Self uncomfortably confronts the Other within itself,"[24] how do we get from there to an artistic statement consistent with Levinasian ethics? Jonathan Druker provides a salutary caution not to transmute Pirandello into a proto-Bakhtinian or proto-Levinasian. "The true Pirandellian drama is interior," he reminds us, and "the external Other is only secondary."[25] Even though Pirandello says that comedic art should produce compassion and sympathy for the Other, in actuality, "Pirandello's art seldom emphasizes a moralizing sympathy for the tribulations of others, and seldom turns on the ability of Pirandello's characters to identify profoundly with the Other."[26] Are we, then, left with a play best described as a depiction of the split self, and not as a critique of the failure to establish dialogue with the Other?

I would argue that we can extend Pirandello's drama of consciousness to the social arena by observing the same splits between people that he dramatized inside the psyche. His genius exceeds his intentions . . . or, put differently, through his brilliance what was only secondary for him may emerge as primary for us. Thus he was able to bring to life "loneliness, isolation, alienation"[27] between as well as inside individuals—and the failure of dialogue to overcome that isolation. He accomplishes this through what Bentley calls "the great human gift . . . of words," staging the drama of consciousness enfleshed in characters, constructing a script that allows its audience to visualize the chasm between *dialogue* as words spoken in a play and *dialogue* in the deeper sense of an exchange of meanings, intentions, sympathies, and souls.

Ethical obligation and polyphonic dialogism are complementary and interdependent; if the first is not heeded, the second cannot occur. Monologue by definition silences others. When we replace dialogism with monologues designed to gain self-recognition, and when we lack a vision that respects the integrity of others and a readiness to respond to their cries, language drives us apart, and we end with a Levinasian nightmare of ethical failure that multiplies private agonies.

Whereas Pirandello's characters fail completely in fulfilling their ethical obligations to the Other, we shall see next that Miller's characters in *All My Sons* do somewhat better, aiming to succeed within the sphere of the family, but dramatically failing beyond that sphere.

MILLER'S *ALL MY SONS*: "DON'T YOU LIVE IN THE WORLD?"

All My Sons gives free voice to conflicting views of where Joe Keller's chief obligation resides: with his own family or with the family of man. The drama centers on the Keller family. During World War II, Joe Keller owned an aircraft manufacturing business that supplied parts for Army Air Force fighter planes. Joe allowed a series of cracked cylinder heads to be shipped out, fearing that if he shut down production for repairs, he would lose his military contract . . . and ultimately his business. Joe hoped to pass that business on to his sons Chris and Larry, both of whom were serving in the military. When the faulty parts result in twenty-one fatal crashes, Joe is brought to trial. He shifts blame to his innocent business partner, Steve Deever, who is sentenced to jail. Three years after the end of the war, Chris has returned home but Larry, an Army Air Force fighter pilot, remains missing and is presumed dead. The mother, Kate, clings to the hope that Larry is missing in action, and the other family members encourage or tolerate her delusion, complicit in a family drama of denial.[28] Crisis is set in motion when Chris plans to marry Ann Deever, Larry's erstwhile fiancée and the daughter of the business partner whom Joe let go to prison in his place. Kate fully understands what is at stake if Ann marries Chris, telling him, "Your brother's alive, darling, because if he's dead, your father killed him. . . . God does not let a son be killed by his father."[29]

The climax reveals that Larry read news of his father's trial. Unable to live with the shame of knowing his father was profiting while three or four of his fellow pilots crashed to their deaths each day, he then disappeared on a mission certain to take his life, essentially committing suicide in the line of duty. Confronted with the revelation of how Larry died, Joe Keller reaches an epiphany: "Sure, he was my son. But I think to him they were all my sons. And I guess they were, I guess they were" (83). Pressed by his other son, the idealistic Chris, to turn himself in to the police and serve the sentence that should have been his and not his partner Steve's, Joe kills himself.

Whereas Pirandello's characters enacted their desires for recognition of their own stories, Miller's characters battle over desire for recognition of a different sort. Kate insists that everyone recognize that Larry is alive. In contrast, Chris and Ann want recognition of Larry's death, for only with that will they gain recognition of their love. As Larry Krasnoff explains in amplifying Hegel, "without recognition by other human beings, without a sense that one is valued by others, no real happiness is possible."[30] This is one reason that Chris and Ann do not elope: family recognition is essential for their happiness; denial of that recognition would paralyze Chris (and has done so). "The fundamental unit of social recognition is, of course, the family,"[31] and in Miller as much as in Pirandello we witness the devastating consequences of a family refusing to recognize one of its own. This happens not just with the Kellers, but also the Deevers.

Because personhood can only come through recognition by a group, the group possesses "tremendous power over individuals."[32] As John McGowan says in discussing the importance of the master/slave dialectic for social relations, "The great threat that [social] power holds is not suppression but nonacknowledgment."[33] It was nonacknowledgment that Joe Keller faced when he returned from trial and found himself shunned by his neighbors; he did everything he could to reintegrate himself into the community and regain recognition. Steve Deever truly suffers the consequences of nonacknowledgment. Believing him guilty, Ann and her brother George withdraw acknowledgment from their father to the point that they do not visit him in prison and do not even send him Christmas cards. Denied recognition by community and family, Steve has become invisible, a non-entity, and is about to lapse into non-existence; after George visits him, he reports that his father "got smaller" and adds, "It's good I went to him in time—another year there'd be nothing left but his smell" (53). Perhaps this is why Steve never appears in the play . . . and does not even appear in the dramatis personæ. In going to the prison George has acknowledged his father, and now seeks recognition of the truth—the truth of his father's innocence and Joe Keller's guilt.

In contrast to Pirandello's six characters who fail in their responsibility to each other as family members, Joe Keller recognizes his responsibility to protect his family but fails to see that his moral obligations extend beyond that sphere. At first glance, that certainly seems to be the moral, and it is easy to conclude that Miller unequivocally condemns Joe for his blinkered vision of responsibility. The sound of Keller echoes "killer," inviting us to construe Joe as a murderer. Yet Miller's carefully constructed dialogism presents a more complicated view than such a monologic moral would allow. As Christopher Bigsby observes, the text "avoids . . . polarization."[34]

A reading that lapses into the polarization that Miller skillfully avoids might parse the play into tempting dichotomies: pursuit of profit versus pursuit of higher values; obligation to family versus obligation to a wider social sphere; Joe as a kind of inverted Antigone who wants to psychically bury Larry (as do Chris and Anne) in opposition to Kate who refuses to accept her son's death.

It is tempting to propose dialectical readings of *All My Sons* because of its resonances with *Antigone*:[35] a major conflict revolves around whether to bury Larry (that is, to accept his death and bury him in memory), and Joe's choices seem to pit obligation to family against a wider obligation. But we must not be fooled into thinking that Miller's drama is so schematic or dualistic. For example, at least four entities vie for loyalty—self, family, state, and the larger human community. In Miller's dialogic drama, characters can be seen as "socio-ideological languages," yet there are more than two languages, and they do not square off in direct, dialectical opposition. Joe represents ideologies of self-preservation, pragmatism, and capitalism; Chris represents Christian purity; George embodies what Miller himself called "return of the truth, the notion of the repressed";[36] he is a kind of St. George self-appointed to slay the dragons of falsehood.

Joe's position rejects the ethic of infinite obligation to the Other. He believed that his moral duty extended no further than his family, and he acted to protect their economic interests. The responsibility for the Other that forms the basis of Levinasian ethics is sacrificed to family, to pragmatism, and to profit. Bigsby puts the issue in perspective, asserting that "this is not primarily a play about a crime. It is about a man's failure to understand the terms of the social contract."[37]

It is this failure that Joe's son Chris indicts him with. When Chris learns that Joe knowingly allowed defective parts to be shipped out hoping that the defect would be caught later down the line, by which time he would have corrected the manufacturing error, Joe pleads that he did it for Chris, so that he could one day turn the business over to him. Furious, Chris lacerates his father:

> For me! Where do you live, where have you come from? For me!—I was dying every day and you were killing my boys and you did it for me? What the hell do you think I was thinking of, the Goddam business? Is that as far as your mind can see, the business? What is that, the world—the business? What the hell do you mean, you did it for me? Don't you have a country? Don't you live in the world? What the hell are you? You're not even an animal, no animal

kills his own, what are you? What must I do to you? I ought to tear the tongue out of your mouth, what must I do? (70–71)

In the end, Joe realizes that the Army Air Force pilots who plunged to their deaths because of his negligence were "all my sons." But this recognition does not satisfy Chris. Prepared to take his father to the police station so that Joe can surrender and be sent to prison, Chris chastises his father, "Once and for all you can know there's a universe of people outside and you're responsible to it, and you know that you threw away your son because that's why he died" (84). This articulation of obligation seems to seal Joe's ethical guilt and to justify a wider responsibility.

Tragically, these words drive Joe to suicide. Thus, they call into question Chris's severe application of idealism, as does his name, which suggests his self-perception as a holy figure. "There is a self-righteousness to him . . . a neighbour complains about the difficulty of living next door to the Holy Family. His standards are too absolute."[38] His sanctimony dramatizes the claim that "consciousness' quest for recognition reveals itself as a narcissistic longing and self-fulfilling aggrandizement"[39]; as in Pirandello, desire for recognition undermines pluralism that respects the Other—and undermines justice. Explaining the circumstances that led him to let the cracked cylinders be shipped, Joe pleaded with Chris to "see it human, see it human" (32). Perhaps his plea is compromised by self-interest,[40] yet the grim ending cautions about the dangers of self-righteousness, sanctimony, and unduly severe judgment.

A similar caution can be found in Levinas's writings about justice. Once the conditions for justice have been established, the person being judged has a right to *hesed* (charity or mercy) (*ITR* 68–69). Having judged Joe guilty, Chris then denies to his own father the *hesed* that any judge must grant to the accused. "To soften this justice, to listen to this personal appeal, is each person's role" (*ITR* 68); Chris fails in this role as he rejects his father's appeal to "see it human." If Joe has failed to recognize his ethical obligation to a wider human community, Chris has rejected the legitimate demands of family and of justice upon his mercy.

Thus, both Levinasian ethics and the play's dialogism mitigate against an outright condemnation of Joe Keller. As Bigsby rightly points out, "They all act in their own interests, serve their own psychic needs," and the accusations "levelled at [Joe] . . . are directed by those themselves guilty of offences, if not against the criminal code."[41] If human beings are to be judged wanting for serving their own interests, then we are all guilty. Encouraging citizens to extend their spheres of obligation and put their own interests at risk requires going beyond the hypocritically self-serving condemnation that Chris and others aim at Joe; rather, it requires the kind of ethical foundation that Levinas laid in developing his ideas around the interests of Being.

Crucial for this discussion is the fact that Miller began writing this as a novel. Unable to complete it satisfactorily, he ultimately transformed the subject matter into a play. In so doing, he avoided the trap of imposing monologic judgment on his well-rounded characters. They themselves try to silence the polyphony—as when Chris wants to tear out his father's tongue or when Kate smashes Joe across the face and exclaims, "Nothing. You have nothing to say. Now I say" (68)—but Miller never does. The polyphony leaves viewers with troubling questions: How harshly do we judge? Can we render severe judgment, as Chris does, without falling prey to sanctimony and self-righteousness? Must we always "see it human"? When, if ever, should we not? How do we balance duty to family, to country, and to our fellow beings beyond our borders? At what cost to our families do we extend our obligations to the entire human community?

For an audience in January 1947 when the play debuted, these questions were neither remote nor abstract. Miller does not reduce the complex dilemmas that people faced into an occasion for simplistic moral pronouncements; the sanctimony spurts from Chris Keller, not from Arthur Miller. Steven R. Centola confirms Miller's resistance to a monologic moral or message:

> The play conveys the complexity in life that transcends and belies a plot's tight lines and overt philosophical or social positions. *All My Sons* is indeed a tightly constructed play with ideas of importance, but the drama's success derives more from Miller's ability to capture the spirit and rhythm of a life not easily reducible to terse summary in a single assertion. In fact . . . despite its traditional form and adherence to the conventions of the realistic theatre, *All My Sons* resonates with ambiguity from the opening curtain to its powerful climactic close. [42]

In other words, some dramatic conventions pull toward monologic, totalizing final statements and tidy resolution; Miller resists the tug of this generic undertow and does not let the dialogic principle wash out to sea like ideological driftwood in the last act. Thus his choice of drama over the novel should be viewed as serving an artistic purpose rather than merely being the by-product of artistic frustration. Drama best served his dialogic exploration of multiple voices and truths.

Miller laid out a theory of drama supportive of this purpose in his 1949 essay "Tragedy and the Common Man." There he asserted that tragedy centers on a character "who is ready to lay down his life, if need be, to secure one thing—his sense of personal dignity" in response to "the fateful wound . . . of indignity. . . . Tragedy, then, is the consequence of a man's total compulsion to evaluate himself justly."[43] A character feels impelled to search for a just understanding of his conduct and how the universe has treated him, and in that quest discovers a moral law.

Levinas might have seen this way of construing the universe as characteristic of Western philosophy's egocentric obsession with Being, but he would have sympathized with the quest for just evaluation and a moral law. A playwright must be fearless in this quest, Miller says: "No tragedy can therefore come about when its author fears to question absolutely everything, when he regards any institution, habit or custom as being either everlasting, immutable or inevitable."[44] Such fearless questioning is what Bakhtin and Levinas would have seen in Dostoevsky, a fervent Christian who with each novel brought his own beliefs more into question, culminating in Ivan Karamazov rejecting heaven if the price of his entrance ticket is the suffering of children. Miller's equally fearless ideal would produce a stage for a democracy of ideas in which no position has privileged status—not family, not capitalism, not the state—and in which all are vigorously questioned, all allowed a voice. Consistent with his essay, Miller deploys polyphony in the service of democracy, with the play as a microcosm of an ideal democratic state in which all voices are heard. Because Miller does not silence any of the voices, Levinas's ethic of infinite obligation meets strong challenges within the play—as does every other ideological position.

The exact contours and limits of extended obligation lead us to the problem of the Third in Levinas. As William Paul Simmons observes, "With the appearance of the Third, the ego must respond to more than one Other. The ego must decide whom to respond to first. This decision is the foundation of all politics."[45] Joe's actions thus have an inescapable political dimension.

Miller's polyphony is consistent with Levinas's pluralism as described by Simmons, Oona Eisenstadt, Michael L. Morgan, and others.[46] Concisely stated, Levinas's pluralism "places the Other person, not the State or impersonal history, as the ultimate value."[47] In this sense, Chris's indictment of Joe puts forward an ethic of obligation similar to Levinas's. In its critique of both capitalism and its detractors (as enfleshed in Chris), Miller's dialogic drama also advocates a pluralism consistent with Levinasian pluralism . . . and with Bakhtinian dialogics.

Where are the limits of dialogism? Hirschkop says, "Dialogism, a sense of history, and heteroglossia in themselves could not deliver the novelistic historical world Bakhtin hoped for, but they articulated the terrain on which a democratic culture would have to be fought for and won in any reasonably modern society" (294). This is the fight going on in *Angels in America*, where dialogism and infinite obligation to the Other take center stage in a drama about repairing our broken democracy. Perhaps drama can deliver the hoped-for world that the novel could not.

KUSHNER'S *ANGELS IN AMERICA*: "IT'S NOT POLITE TO CALL OTHER PEOPLE'S BELIEFS PREPOSTEROUS"

The full title of Kushner's play is *Angels in America: A Gay Fantasia on National Themes*. It consists of two parts, *Part One: Millennium Approaches* and *Part Two: Perestroika*.

The play shares Miller's concern with the state of our democracy. It depicts a nation governed by ideologues, certain of their monologic truths, who have fostered a lifeboat society which throws the dying overboard and fails in its ethical obligation to those with AIDS. This ideology is embodied in Roy Cohn, a kind of anti-Levinas, who teaches his protégé Joe that there are limits to obligations to the Other, that service to self is primary, that moral responsibility is a trap. And yet even Cohn's voice is admitted into the polyphony. Much of the play concerns the possibility of dialogue with radically different Others. Ultimately, its dialogism leads to an assertion that unifies both the dialogic principle and the ethic of infinite obligation: One must always remain open to the cry of the Other and must respond to it despite ideological differences.

The play centers on two couples, one homosexual and one heterosexual, whose lives gradually intersect. The homosexual couple consists of Louis Ironson and Prior Walter. When the signs of Prior's fast-advancing AIDS become too obvious to ignore, Louis leaves his lover, abandoning him to isolation and certain death. The heterosexual couple is comprised of Joe Pitt, a devout Mormon and a Republican, and his wife Harper Pitt. When Joe can no longer resist his homosexual longings, he leaves Harper; when he hints at his homosexuality and seeks solace from his mother, Hannah Pitt, she cuts him off and shuts down the dialogue. Joe later accepts an offer to go to work for Roy Cohn, a New York lawyer and powerful political broker with ties in Washington, D.C. Roy is a self-hating Jew and a closeted homosexual dying from AIDS.[48]

As if transported from a Pirandellian universe, many characters reject dialogism. They renounce any obligation to the Other—infinite, finite, or infinitesimal. At the start, Louis has abandoned his grandmother. At her funeral, even as he performs the ritual act of putting dirt on her coffin and explains that "It's a Jewish custom to express love," he undercuts the loving act by adding, "Here, Grandma, have a shovelful."[49] In fact, he abandoned his grandmother before her death: "She was up there in that home for ten years, talking to herself. I never visited. She looked too much like my mother" (19). Forsaking his grandmother can thus be seen as a rejection of his mother . . . and of his Jewish heritage, for he recalls that his grandmother "actually saw Emma Goldman speak. In Yiddish" (19). Louis is truly a Pirandellian after Pirandello's time.

When Prior reluctantly confesses that he has AIDS, his worst fears are fulfilled as Louis, in panic, leaves him. The diagnosis walls off dialogue, or as Prior puts it, "No wall like the wall of hard scientific fact" (20). Once again, abandonment of one's ethical obligation coincides with abandonment of dialogue. Recognizing his moral failure, Louis asks the rabbi officiating at his grandmother's funeral, "Rabbi, what does the Holy Writ say about someone who abandons someone he loves at a time of great need?" (25). The rabbi asks, "Why would a person do such a thing?" Louis replies, "Because he has to," and then stammers through self-justifying claptrap about being a "neo-Hegelian positivist" before approaching the truth about himself: "maybe that person can't, um, incorporate sickness into his sense of how things are supposed to go. Maybe vomit . . . and sore and disease . . . really frighten him, maybe . . . he isn't so good with death" (25). Cutting off dialogue, the rabbi says, "The Holy Scriptures have nothing to say about such a person" (25), and tells him that if he wants to confess his failures, he should see a priest instead.

Hannah Pitt too fails at dialogism and at family obligations. When Joe calls her in despair to confess his homosexuality, she refuses to engage in dialogue. To his simple, desperate appeal "Mom," she responds, "We will just forget this phone call . . . No more talk" (76). Resorting then to monologic religious authority, she erupts in anger, assuming that he is drunk: "Drinking is a sin! A sin!" (76). With that, she closes off dialogue . . . and her openness to her son's suffering.

Hannah also rejects dialogue and response to suffering when she encounters a psychotic homeless woman in the South Bronx. Having gotten off the train at the wrong stop, lost in a dangerous area, frightened and wet and cold, Hannah asks the woman to direct her to the right station. As the woman talks to herself, Hannah snaps. "Shut up. Please. Now I want you to stop jabbering and pull your wits together and tell me how to get to Brooklyn" (105), she says, ignoring the woman's psychic anguish. Although the woman does help Hannah and even offers some of her soup, Hannah does nothing to reciprocate. The Biblical Hannah put community needs and social responsibility before her own desires, relinquishing her beloved son Samuel to the priests in order to fulfill a promise and so that Samuel could serve the people; in contrast, Kushner's Hannah closes herself off to community. She fails to respond to the suffering Other, and in her failure we see reflected the societal failure that results in homelessness.

Other such failures abound. When Harper encounters Prior in one of her pill-induced hallucinations, she reacts by exclaiming, "Oh! In my church we don't believe in homosexuals." He replies, "In my church we don't believe in Mormons" (32). Neither exists for the other; they may be having a dialogue, but they are denying the possibility of dialogism. With her husband, Harper feels so alone that she says, "God won't talk to me. I have to make up people to talk to me" (40). Much of the play concerns itself with the possibility of dialogue, and all too often the characters deny or refuse that possibility. They are isolated, adrift, suffering not silently but solo.

Harper's words to Joe beautifully encapsulate the tension between the pull to dialogism and the push away from it: "We are talking. Aren't we. Now please shut up. OK?" (77).

When ethical obligation to the Other fails, so does dialogism; they are interdependent. Roy epitomizes the rejection of both. A serpent counselor of selfishness, he plants in Joe's mind the idea that marital obligation has limits. When Joe says, "I am responsible for her," Roy counters, "Whatever. She's your wife. And so there are obligations. To her. But also to yourself" (54). Roy advises, "You do what you need to do, Joe. What *you* need. *You*. Let her life go where it wants to go. You'll both be better for that. *Somebody* should get what they want" (54). He teaches Joe that responsibility is a trap and replaces Levinasian ethics with an ethic of putting self first.

In the same year that Kushner staged Part One of *Angels in America*, 1991, philosopher Charles Taylor published *The Ethics of Authenticity*.[50] Taylor argues that we develop and define our identity "in dialogue with, sometimes in struggle against, the identities our significant others want to recognize in us" and he emphasizes the "fundamentally *dialogical* character" of human life.[51] At its best, an identity negotiated dialogically "allows a richer mode of existence" (74). Here the desire for recognition—which led to war in Hegel and had disastrous consequences in Pirandello and Miller—can positively effect identity development and relationships.

At its worst, though, the pursuit of self-determining freedom disavows dialogism and treats others as means. "Justifying in the name of authenticity a concept of relationships as instrumental to individual self-fulfillment should . . . be seen as a self-stultifying travesty" (22)—yet Roy perpetrates this travesty upon himself and Joe. Regarding others as instruments for our ends goes against the Levinasian pluralism that views the Other as unique and recognizes "that I cannot wholly conjoin or subsume the other to myself" (*TI* 221). Such a stance results in the "fading of moral horizons" (Taylor 10) characteristic of Roy's world view and conduct.

Roy's advocacy of an ethic of self does not stop with advice to others or with a hypocritical personal life in which he cuts himself off from his fellow homosexuals and Jews; that ethic also forms the basis of his political ideology. Kushner associates Cohn with Reagan Republicanism, and to the extent that the play has a villain, it is Cohn as an individual and Reaganism as a social force. Enshrining selfishness as national policy, Reaganites create a society that abandons its ethical obligations and throws the sick, the dying, and the homeless overboard without a life raft. Their absolute confidence in their views turns them into monsters of monologism. By treating others as means, Roy and Reagan Republicans forsake dialogism—and with it they forsake ethics, pluralism, and democracy. And for Kushner, democracy depends on dialogism.

The relationship between "democracy" and "dialogism" demands clarification here. For Levinas, dialogism cannot be separated from ethics; the ethical relation between self and Other is "primordially enacted as conversation" (*TI* 39) and is "accomplished in goodness proceeding from me to the other" (309). That ethical relation, based on the recognition that I cannot subsume the Other to myself, constitutes "the foundation of pluralism" (221). While pluralism is more than a matter of "numerical multiplicity" (121), like the relation to a single Other it recognizes "the radical alterity of the other, whom I do not simply *conceive* by relation to myself, but *confront* out of my egoism" (121). In contrast to Western metaphysics that he views as hostile to pluralism, Levinas regards pluralism as a bulwark against the dystopia sure to follow from totalizing authoritarian systems that impose a single monologic truth on their people. [52]

Levinas does not dictate how pluralism should manifest itself politically. [53] He writes in "Reflections on the Philosophy of Hitlerism," "It is not a particular dogma concerning democracy, parliamentary government, dictatorial regime, or religious politics that is in question. It is the very humanity of man." [54] What matters to Levinas is that the system upholds pluralistic ideals by protecting humanity and treating the Other as the ultimate value ahead of even the state. For Bakhtin too, democracy is less important than protecting the individual against totalizing authority. Contextualizing what democracy meant for Bakhtin, Hirschkop says that Bakhtin "writes about . . . a vernacular language, in which all have a right to speak, in which no speaker holds absolute authority" (viii). Bakhtin's dialogism and Levinas's pluralism describe Kushner's ideal of democracy: all have a right to speak and no monologic voice holds absolute authority. But how can we achieve, or even imagine, such a dialogic democracy?

If we only had Roy's and Joe's monologism, if we only had the denials of dialogism and responsibility detailed above, we would be trapped inside the world of Prior Walter, abandoned by his lover, by his government, by his society. We would be back inside Pirandello's world. But rather than reproduce Pirandello's world of isolation and unrelieved suffering, Kushner uses dialogism to rescue us from it. The play features dialogue among those who are supposed not capable of it—angels and humans, leftists and anti-Communists, homosexuals and homophobes, and so on. We have modeled on stage the national conversation which we need to have but which we run from, just as Louis ran from conversations he needed to have. Dialogue takes place not just across ideological divisions but across time, across continents, across genres, across dream states and waking, across the barriers dividing living from dead and illusion from reality. All voices, all positions—even the monologic ones—are absorbed into the democratic dialogue. Kushner resists the convention of excluding the anti-social Other as an exiled or marginalized character. The monologic Cohn's voice is not silenced; rather, it contributes to the polyphony.[55]

In thinking of Bakhtin's term "polyphonic" novel, we should recall its meaning in music; "Music that simultaneously combines several musical lines of individual design, each of which retains its identity as a line to some degree, in contrast to monophonic music, which consists of a single melody, or homophonic music, which combines several lines of similar, rhythmically identical design."[56] Thus, even a Roy Cohn—described by Louis as "the polestar of human evil, he's like the worst human being who ever lived, he isn't *human* even"[57]—retains his identity and individuality. Difference is not drowned out because each voice sounds roundly in humanized tones; for example, we hear Roy as a political power broker but also as a self-hating homosexual frightened of dying from AIDS. At the same time that no section of identical voices is allowed to dominate, neither is any single voice excluded; each player contributes to the harmonious whole.

This is not to say that Kushner presents all views as equally valid, but that he gives them all an equal opportunity to speak. Even if some part of Kushner might wish to silence the Roy Cohns and Ronald Reagans of the world, his commitment to a democracy of all voices trumps his political leanings. As for Louis, his abandonment of Prior may seem cowardly, but Kushner gives him a voice deserving to be heard, for no one would deny that it is frightening to watch a loved one be ravaged with disease and then die. Before judging Louis too harshly, or Cohn, we must learn to "see it human," as Joe Keller would say.

Polyphonic harmony can only emerge if each orchestra member is permitted to play. Kushner composes this so deftly that Frank Rich wrote, "this play, by turns searing and comic and elegiac, is no earthbound ideological harangue."[58] Rich asked, "When was the last time a play embraced intellectual poles as seemingly antithetical as Judy Garland and Walter Benjamin, Joseph Smith and Mikhail Gorbachev, Emma Goldman and Nancy Reagan?"[59]

By allowing each voice to sound itself in the dialogistic harmony, Kushner enables the characters to learn from, and to learn to listen to, each other. At the end of Part One, a dent appears in the metal surface of Joe's monologic certainty. Harper comes to see the possibility of *tikkun*, or repairing the world: "We'll mend together. That's what we'll do; we'll mend" (103).

The most striking transformations appear in the character arcs of Louis and Hannah, who illustrate our ability to develop a dialogic ethic and fulfill the obligation to the Other. Even at the end of Part One, Louis defended abandoning Prior, saying, "I have to find some way to save myself" (79). He still had a lifeboat mentality. In Part Two, he recognizes his part in a universal nexus and understands suffering in a Levinasian way: "To suffer for others is to serve them: to provide for their concrete material needs for nourishment, clothing, health, shelter, and employment; to assuage their pains, anxieties, and fears; to respect their freedom and dignity; to care for the other's requirements before protecting or catering to one's own various social identities."[60] In the end, he accepts the need to assuage Prior's pains and anxieties. The dying man's name is apt: Louis realizes he must put Prior's needs prior to his own. He fulfills his obligation to the Other and returns to Prior. Although Prior tells him he cannot come back, the two men reach an accord and state their mutual love.

Similarly, Hannah, who had rejected her obligation to heed the cry of the homeless woman and even of her own son, ultimately acts upon her obligation to the Other when she transcends monologic religious dogma to care for Prior. While this might seem an abandonment of polyphony and a privileging of Kushner's own ethic, Hannah reminds us that we must always remain open to the Other's voice. "It's not polite to call other people's beliefs preposterous," she rebukes Prior when he scoffs at her Mormonism. "You don't make assumptions about me, mister; I won't make them about you" (Part Two, 103). Ethical action entails overcoming the impulse to recoil from the Other's difference and instead heeding the impulse to respond to the Other's vulnerability and destitution. Here is the dialogic ethic at work: Hannah's openness to Prior's story generates a Levinasian response that causes her to act to relieve his agony.

Creating a space for the ethical in turn creates a space for the dialogical. Kushner creates a space where Ethel Rosenberg can engage with Roy Cohn without trying to deny or assimilate him. When Hannah and Prior allow themselves to be surprised by each other, and allow themselves and their most deeply held beliefs to be called into question, they find themselves surprised not just by each other but also by their own responses. It is at this moment that through dialogue they have arrived at the fulfillment of the Levinasian ethical.

The play's final words remind us, as Levinas would, that the process of *tikkun*, of mending the broken world, goes on: "The Great Work begins" (Part Two, 148). The play propels us outside the domain of theatrical illusion and back into the world; the work of perfecting our democracy now lies with us. From Kushner's continually unfolding series of Sayings that resist petrifying into a monologic Said—from Harper learning that mending is an ongoing process to Hannah and Prior shedding their totalizing beliefs about each other—we discover that listening to the Other's cry is inextricably intertwined with acting on our infinite obligation to respond.

CODA

The three plays discussed here form an arc of development. We began with Pirandello's *Six Characters in Search of an Author*, where the characters' failure to communicate dialogically led directly to their failure to fulfill their ethical obligations even within the limited sphere of the family. From there we moved to Miller's *All My Sons*, in which Joe Keller believed his obligations ended with his immediate family; however, challenges to that view arose within the polyphony. *All My Sons* allowed a multiplicity of ethically valid voices to argue over a morally complex situation. If the strongest argument is that Joe was wrong to not see all the pilots as his sons, then perhaps that constitutes both an acceptance of a Levinasian ethic and a limitation of the play's dialogism. After all, that acceptance stops short of extending to the entire human family. Joe Keller concedes that all the Army Air Force pilots were his sons; he does not go so far as to say that pilots from the Luftwaffe and Imperial Japanese Navy Air Service were also his sons. No doubt such an all-embracing statement would have been inconceivable so soon after the war. With *Angels in America*, the arc of development culminates in the fullest expression of both the dialogic principle and the ethic of infinite obligation to the Other. Dialogic ethics, successfully integrating Bakhtinian and Levinasian elements, blossoms in Kushner's drama.

Levinas aspired to let the "'dialogical' proximity in [his] discourse . . . embrace or collect in an 'ensemble'" that "is irreducible to syntheses" (*ITR* 211). We see the enactment of that aspiration in these plays, where the dialogue among an ensemble of characters embraces complex problems of family relations, justice, ethical obligation, and democracy, but refuses to reduce them to simplified syntheses. In all three plays, there are characters who try to silence others and impose their own totalizing, monologic voices; in contrast to their efforts, willingness to engage in dialogue, to allow polyphony, constitutes an ethical act. In all three plays, dialogue with the Other leads directly to an embrace of one's infinite obligation to the Other.

NOTES

1. Michael Eskin, *Ethics and Dialogue in the Works of Levinas, Bakhtin, Mandel'shtam, and Celan* (Oxford: Oxford University Press, 2000), 68. Further references will be cited parenthetically in the text.

2. Ken Hirschkop, *Mikhail Bakhtin: An Aesthetic for Democracy* (Oxford: Oxford University Press, 1999), 15. Further references will be cited parenthetically in the text.

3. According to Mykhaylo Kalinichenko, a literary scholar in the Department of English at Rivne State University of Humanities in Rivne, Ukraine, "The question of professional identification (or professional affiliation) of Bakhtin (whether he was a philosopher, or a philologist and linguist) remains open to this day, and gives no rest to many scholars (in Russia and Ukraine as well as other countries). As far back as 1995, during the 7th international conference dedicated to studies of his life and work (at MSPU—Moscow State Pedagogical University),

one could feel that there was a concealed and evident conflict between those scholars who treated Bakhtin as a philosopher, and those who preferred to see him in the ranks of Russian philologists. Such a contradictory reception of Bakhtin was influenced by a whole series of historical, biographical and even personal reasons." E-mail from Mykhaylo Kalinichenko to author, 12 June 2010.

4. Also, this responsibility cannot be shifted to another person. "My responsibility is untransferable, no one could replace me" (100). See also his statement, "The uniqueness of the Ego is the fact that no one can answer in my stead. . . . The Ego is infinitely responsible in face of the Other" (*HOM* 33).

5. Michael L. Morgan, *Discovering Levinas* (Cambridge: Cambridge University Press, 2007), 50. Morgan's attribution of the quote he cites on his page 50 is to Theodore De Boer, *The Rationality of Transcendence: Studies in the Philosophy of Emmanuel Levinas* (Amsterdam: J. C. Giehen, 1997), 2.

6. For an account of how discourse and the ethical content of the face-to-face encounter are intertwined, see Morgan, 71–75.

7. From *Problems of Dostoevsky's Poetics*, quoted in Eskin 72.

8. Fyodor Dostoevsky, *The Brothers Karamazov*, trans. Richard Pevear and Larissa Volokhonsky (New York: North Point, 1990 [1880]), Part II, Book Six, Chapter 2, 289.

9. Cristian Ciocan and Georges Hansel, *Levinas Concordance* (Dordrecht, The Netherlands: Springer, 2005), 879–80.

10. Alain Toumayan, "'I more than the others': Dostoevsky and Levinas," *Yale French Studies* 104 (2004): 55.

11. Searches performed on 6 July 2012 through EBSCO, Harper College, Palatine, IL.

12. Luigi Pirandello, *Six Characters in Search of an Author*, English version by Edward Storer, in *Naked Masks: Five Plays by Luigi Pirandello*, ed. Eric Bentley (New York: Dutton, 1952), 213.

13. M. M. Bakhtin, *The Dialogic Imagination: Four Essays*, trans. Caryl Emerson and Michael Holquist, ed. Michael Holquist (Austin: University of Texas Press, 1981), 314.

14. Mikhail Bakhtin, *Problems of Dostoevsky's Poetics*, ed. and trans. Caryl Emerson. Theory and History of Literature, Vol. 8 (Minneapolis: University of Minnesota Press, 1984), 28.

15. Felicity Firth, "Pirandello," in *The Cambridge History of Italian Literature*, ed. Peter Brand and Lino Pertile, Revised edition (Cambridge: Cambridge University Press, 1999), 485. All further references will be cited parenthetically in the text.

16. G. W. F. Hegel, *Phenomenology of Spirit*, trans. A. V. Miller (Oxford: Oxford University Press, 1977), 109, par. 174. All further references are to this edition and will be cited parenthetically in the text.

17. Richard Norman, *Hegel's Phenomenology: A Philosophical Introduction* (London: Sussex University Press, 1976), 48. Norman cites R. D. Laing, *The Divided Self* (London: Harmondsworth, 1965) and *Self and Others* (London: Harmondsworth, 1971), and R. D. Laing and A. Esterton, *Sanity, Madness and the Family* (London: Harmondsworth, 1970). Norman recommends "Part II of *Self and Others*, in particular...as a valuable elaboration of Hegel's concept of 'recognition'" (Norman 66, endnote 2).

18. Alexandre Kojève, *Introduction to the Reading of Hegel: Lectures on* The Phenomenology of Spirit *Assembled by Raymond Queneau*, trans. James H. Nichols, Jr., ed. Allan Bloom (New York: Basic, 1969), 61.

19. Throughout this section, I use the translation in Bentley's edition cited in note 12 above...except here. The Bentley edition uses "consciences" here and can be found on p. 231. I have instead used Jonathan Druker's translation. As Druker explains, "Anglophone readers have missed the psychological dimensions of this passage, and of the play as a whole, because the most widely available translation, Eric Bentley's, translates 'conscienza' as 'conscience' leaving the reader to surmise that mere moral weakness is at the center of Pirandello's drama (231)." The change is important because, Druker argues, the drama of consciousness is Pirandello's primary concern, and particularly the "interior torments" of consciousness in the modern age (66). See the Druker article cited below in note 24, passage translation on 61 and explanation on 70, endnote 17.

20. Eric Bentley, "Introduction," in *Naked Masks: Five Plays by Luigi Pirandello*, ed. Eric Bentley (New York: Dutton, 1952), xxvii.

21. In a play in which illusion and reality become hopelessly confused, we too are called upon to respond as audience members. Are the sufferings we witness, the cries we hear, real? In a rather Levinasian vein, John McGowan writes, "On the basis of the other's 'pain behavior' I cannot know for certain whether he is really in pain. But this skeptical question about my ground for knowledge misses the point that pain behavior is about the other's call for my help, my response, my sympathy, not about the other's trying to give me certain information," *Postmodernism and Its Critics* (Ithaca: Cornell University Press, 1991), 218 footnote 3.

22. In terms of what action we are summoned to take, B. C. Hutchens observes that nowhere does Levinas "emphasize what someone must do," but does insist *"that one must do something."* See B. C. Hutchens, *Levinas: A Guide for the Perplexed* (New York: Continuum, 2004), 51.

23. Bentley, xxvi–xxvii.

24. Jonathan Druker, "Self-Estrangement and the Poetics of Self-Representation in Pirandello's *L'umorismo*," *South Atlantic Review* 63.1 (Winter 1998): 57.

25. Ibid., 67.

26. Ibid., 67.

27. Bentley, xxvi.

28. For a discussion of each character's denials and evasions, see Steven R. Centola, *"All My Sons,"* in *The Cambridge Companion to Arthur Miller*, 2nd ed., ed. Christopher Bigsby (Cambridge: Cambridge University Press, 2010), 51–62.

29. Arthur Miller, *All My Sons* (New York: Penguin, 2000 [1947]), 68. All further references are to this edition and will be cited parenthetically in the text.

30. Larry Krasnoff, *Hegel's* Phenomenology of Spirit: *An Introduction*. Cambridge Introductions to Key Philosophical Texts (Cambridge: Cambridge University Press, 2008), 98.

31. McGowan, 219.

32. Ibid., 219.

33. Ibid., 219.

34. Christopher Bigsby, *Arthur Miller 1915-1962* (Cambridge: Harvard University Press, 2009), 269.

35. Hegel and Lacan both interpreted *Antigone* in dialectical terms. See Hegel 284, par. 470. Also see Hegel's *Aesthetics: Lectures on Fine Art*, Vol. II, trans. T. M. Knox (Oxford: Clarendon Press/Oxford University Press, 1998), 1217–18. For Lacan's dialectical reading, see "The Essence of Tragedy: A Commentary on Sophocles's *Antigone*," in *The Seminar of Jacques Lacan, Book VII: The Ethics of Psychoanalysis 1959-1960*, trans. Dennis Porter, ed. Jacques-Alain Miller (New York: Norton, 1997), 243–87, especially the section "Antigone between two deaths" beginning on page 270. See also Lacan's continuing discussion of two types of death in *Antigone* in *The Seminar of Jacques Lacan, Book VIII: Transference 1960-61*, trans. Cormac Gallagher, Seminar 19 of 3 May 1961, 264–66. Web. 8 Apr. 2011.

36. Quoted in Bigsby, 267.

37. Christopher Bigsby, "Introduction," in *All My Sons*, by Arthur Miller (New York: Penguin, 2000 [1947]), x.

38. Bigsby, *Arthur*, 266–67.

39. Brian Schroeder, *Altared Ground: Levinas, History, and Violence* (New York: Routledge, 1996), 70, quoted in Simmons 88. William Paul Simmons, *An-Archy and Justice: An Introduction to Emmanuel Levinas's Political Thought* (Lanham, MD: Lexington, 2003).

40. See Bigsby's reading in *Arthur*, 269.

41. Bigsby, *Arthur*, 268, 269.

42. Centola, 53.

43. Arthur Miller, "Tragedy and the Common Man," in *Death of a Salesman: Text and Criticism*, ed. Gerald Weales. Viking Critical Library (New York: Penguin, 1996), 144.

44. Ibid., 146.

45. Simmons, ix. See also 68–72.

46. It should be noted that for some commentators such as Charles Scott, C. Fred Alford, and Philip J. Harold, one cannot derive even a generalized pluralism from Levinas's work; for

these thinkers, Levinasian ethics remain too abstract to have any practical application in the mundane realm of politics. See Harold, *Prophetic Politics: Emmanuel Levinas and the Sanctification of Suffering* (Athens, OH: Ohio University Press, 2009), xv–xvii.

47. Simmons, 90. Clarifying Levinas's stance as distinct from Hegel's. Simmons writes, "Levinas claims that the Hegelian solution, the modern nation-state, totalizes the irreducible alterity of the Other. Against the totalizing politics of Hegel, Levinas posits a radical pluralism based on the Other" (79). Levinas's profound differences from, and with, Hegel are outlined in Levinas's essay "Hegel and the Jews," in *DF*, 235–38.

48. Kushner based Cohn on the historical Roy M. Cohn, as he explains in "Playwright's Notes," in *Angels in America: Part Two: Perestroika* (New York: Theatre Communications, 1992), 7. The historical Cohn served as Sen. Joseph McCarthy's chief counsel during the McCarthy hearings and was instrumental in prosecuting and seeking the death penalty for Julius and Ethel Rosenberg.

49. Tony Kushner, *Angels in America, Part One: Millennium Approaches* (New York: Theatre Communications, 1992), 19. All further references are to this edition and will be cited parenthetically in the text.

50. The book was based on Taylor's Massey Lectures delivered under the title *The Malaise of Modernity*. The title was changed to *The Ethics of Authenticity* for U.S. publication.

51. Charles Taylor, *The Ethics of Authenticity* (Cambridge, MA: Harvard University Press, 1991), 33.

52. The same uniqueness and multiplicity that Levinas wants to defend for individuals he also wants to defend for political structures. Asher Horowitz notes that in "Peace and Proximity," Levinas asserts "the extreme importance in human multiplicity of the political structures of society (PP, 168) [*BPW* 168]". "Beyond Rational Peace: On the Possibility/Necessity of a Levinasian Hyperpolitics," in *Difficult Justice: Commentaries on Levinas and Politics*, ed. Asher Horowitz and Gad Horowitz (Toronto: University of Toronto Press, 2006), 28.

53. Morgan, 263. See also Morgan's *Cambridge Introduction to Emmanuel Levinas* (Cambridge: Cambridge University Press, 2011), 7–8, and Oona Eisenstadt, "Levinas in the Key of the Political," in *Difficult Justice: Commentaries on Levinas and Politics*, ed. Asher Horowitz and Gad Horowitz (Toronto: University of Toronto Press, 2006). Kushner appears willing to take the same risk and, as a Jewish writer himself, he seems to share Levinas's stake in "the Jewish doctrine [of] pluralism" (74) that Eisenstadt discusses.

54. Emmanuel Levinas, "Reflections on the Philosophy of Hitlerism," trans. Seán Hand, rpt. in *Difficult Justice: Commentaries on Levinas and Politics*, ed. Asher Horowitz and Gad Horowitz (Toronto: University of Toronto Press, 2006), 11.

55. Excluding and exiling Cohn's voice would run the risk delineated by Asher and Gad Horowitz: "A simple reassertion or strengthening of liberalism as determination to expunge fascist-type Reaction and impose universal freedom could only facilitate fascist revivals by turning once again the wheel of the vicious circle of the dialectic of enlightenment" ("Is Liberalism All We Need? Prelude via Fascism," in *Difficult Justice: Commentaries on Levinas and Politics*, ed. Asher Horowitz and Gad Horowitz [Toronto: University of Toronto Press, 2006], 22). Kushner avoids this trap, not trying to expunge the Roy Cohn character but giving his voice and his suffering a place within the plurality.

56. Don Michael Randel, *Harvard Concise Dictionary of Music* (Cambridge: Belknap Press of Harvard University Press, 1978), 397.

57. Tony Kushner, *Angels in America, Part Two: Perestroika* (New York: Theatre Communications, 1992), 95. All further references are to this edition and will be cited parenthetically in the text.

58. Frank Rich, "Review/Theater: Marching Out of the Closet, Into History," *New York Times*, 30 Nov. 1992. Web. 20 Nov. 2010.

59. Ibid.

60. Richard A. Cohen, "Introduction: Humanism and Anti-humanism—Levinas, Cassirer, and Heidegger," in *HOM*, xxxiv.

V

Trauma and the Loss and Return of Character

Chapter Nine

Levinasian Subjectivity and Diminution of Character in *Cien años de soledad* and *Gravity's Rainbow*

Donald R. Wehrs

PROXIMITY AND THE CRISIS OF NOVELISTIC CHARACTER

During the same years that Emmanuel Levinas elaborated phenomenological pre-histories of ethical selfhood, Gabriel García Márquez in *Cien años de soledad* (*One Hundred Years of Solitude*) (1967) and Thomas Pynchon in *Gravity's Rainbow* (1973) depicted cultural and social life as ceasing to foster the psychic-affective resources that Levinas identifies as crucial to ethical selfhood.[1] Further, their works question whether such resources, once lost, may be retrieved.

To counterbalance egocentric intentionality, Levinas argues, the subject must have recourse to non-intentional dimensions of identity: "In starting with *touching*, interpreted not as palpation but as caress, and *language*, interpreted not as the traffic of information but as contact, we have tried to describe *proximity* as irreducible to consciousness and thematization" (*S* 80). Proximity gives rise to a Self non-coincident with Ego (*OB* 61–97), something to fall back upon when the Other's presence challenges naïve egoism (99–129). If identity is equated with intentional consciousness, the Other's difference will be experienced as danger, even murderous refutation.[2] Then, as in Hitlerian psychology, self-interest identified as the essence of being (*OB* 4–5, 131–36) will demand guilt be thrown off, others sacrificed, to secure one's own "Lebensraum."[3]

While fascism may be concordant with both the essence of being and the deep structure of Western metaphysics, Levinas insists that the phenomenological anteriority of proximity to *for itself* egoism gives subjectivity some-

209

thing to recur *to*. Subjectivity discovers "the Self [to be] . . . a traumatism of responsibility and not causality" (93–94). Such "awakening" allows "my uniqueness as myself, instead of being alienated, [to be] intensified" (*PN* 6), enabling genuine self-realization. Since what is recovered in recurrence is richer than what is broken, the Other Man need not (as in anti-Semitism) induce hatred,[4] for ethical selfhood denotes neither "hyperbolic" self-laceration nor masochistic self-effacement.[5] By the same token, pluralism becomes a substantive value.[6] What one is thrown back upon, proximity, has a solidity, significance, even glory (*OB* 140–52) that "gives meaning to my relations with all the others" (159). Individuated character follows from proximity's predication of signification.

García Márquez and Pynchon depict proximity's foreclosure within particular cultural-historical horizons. *Cien años de soledad* correlates the Buendía family's drive toward extinction with Spanish American cultural-political history, and in *Gravity's Rainbow* the descent of V-2 rockets upon wartime London prefigures not just nuclear warfare but also the fall of characters toward alternating despair and death drives.[7] In both novels, cultural meanings become systemically estranged from the ethical sense that, for Levinas, is "presupposed by all Culture and all meaning" (*MS* 57). Yet the ethical abides somatically. Characters find themselves pushed toward recurrence even though proximity has been dislodged from daily experience and estranged from memory. Hope for redemptive subjectivity migrates from the novels' narrative worlds to transactions between texts and readers. This is the case with many modernist texts, but in García Márquez and Pynchon it is unclear whether literature's simulation of proximity denotes regenerative possibilities or reveals literature's archaic inconsequentiality.

PROXIMITY UNDER SIEGE: FROM EARLY MODERN ESTRANGEMENT TO POSTMODERN DISASSEMBLY

Discussing *Cien años de soledad* in 1971, Mario Vargas Llosa notes that "previous fictions are assimilated for the fictive reality" of the novel.[8] While Vargas Llosa has in mind *Cien años de soledad*'s author's earlier fiction, García Márquez's recapitalization of Spanish-Hispanic subgenres—the family saga, the *hacienda* novel, the civil war novel, the neocolonialist novel— has as its mainspring an inverted *Don Quijote*. The madness (*locura*) of José Arcadio, like that of the knight-errant, monumentalizes an egoistic intentionality that Levinas associates with the West (*TI* 37–38). Quijote, in coming upon a burial procession, believes the deceased must be "algún mal ferido o muerto caballero, cuya venganza a él solo estaba reservada"["some knight either dead or badly wounded, and it was for him, Don Quixote, and him alone, to exact vengeance"].[9] Buendía's descent into solitude (*soledad*) is similarly marked by egoistic single-mindedness: "Habiendo abandonado por completo las obligaciones domésticas, permaneció noches enteras en el patio vigilando el curso de las astros. . . . Fue ésa la época en que adquirió el hábito a hablar a solas, paseándose por la casa sin hacer caso de nadie" ["Having completely abandoned his domestic obligations, he spent entire nights in the courtyard watching the course of the stars . . . . That was the period in which he acquired the habit of talking to himself, of walking through the house without paying attention to anyone"]."[10]

Yet Cervantes' hero derives his identity from a notion (to be sure, degraded and class-coded) of ethical service: "se instituyó la orden de los caballeros andantes, para defender los doncellas, amparar las viudas y socorrer a los huérfanos y a los menesterosos. Desta orden soy yo" ["the order of knights-errant was instituted, for the protection of damsels, the aid of widows and orphans, and the succoring of the needy. It is to this order that I belong"] (106/82). Quijote's insane belief that Sancho will govern an island is counterbalanced by conviction that virtue is a better qualification for rule than birth, "porque la sangre se hereda, y la virtud se aquista. . ." ["for blood is inherited but virtue is acquired. . ."] (841/781). If ethical sense opens speech to sociality and justice,[11] reformative possibilities abide, sustained partly by cultural meanings' continued intercourse with ethical sense, as Quijote's proverbial formula here indicates.

By contrast, in *Cien años de soledad* cultural modes of identity and ideality seem divested of all but the thinnest residue of proximity. Rather than engaging like Quijote and Sancho in "discretos coloquios" ["shrewd conversations"] (491/435), the extravagantly imaginative José Arcadio Buendía and his practical wife Úrsula move into silence and isolation, as when she thwarts his scheme of removing from Macondo by "[e]n una secreta e implacable labor de hormiguia" [with the secret and implacable labor of a small ant"] (70/21) disposing all the women of the village against it. When speech is employed, it becomes the instrument of single-minded, inhuman (ant-like) self-exertion, as in José Arcadio's lyrical evocation of "la promesa de un mundo prodigioso donde bastada con echar unos liquidos mágicos en la tierra para que las plantas dieran frutos a voluntad del hombre, y donde se vendían a precio de baratillo toda clase de aparatos para el dolor" ["the promise of a prodigious world where all one had to do was sprinkle some magic liquid on the ground and the plants would bear fruit whenever a man wished, and where all manner of instruments against pain were sold at bargain prices"] (71/22). He gravitates toward the infantile regressions of golden age motifs often applied to the New World,[12] from which Quijote, by associating knight-errantry with the *end* of the Golden Age, strikingly dissents. However delusionally, Quijote associates self-realization with being *for another*, whereas José Arcadio associates heroic achievement with making being *for another* dispensable or painless.

Úrsula's opposition usually denotes an equally monomaniacal fixation upon family. Though devotion to the lineage keeps her from her husband's total self-absorption, her single-mindedness (never singing, always working) matches his (66/18). Her mania for the clean and proper anticipates the suffocating, imperializing domestic administration of Fernanda del Carpio; her ability to seem everywhere at once anticipates the magical self-effacing omnipresence of Santa Sofía de la Piedad. Úrsula mirrors in material, familial spheres José Arcadio's projecting of worlds for imagination to order and dominate (as her repeated, ultimately disastrous postponements of Rebeca's wedding for propriety's sake attest). Both resemble New World colonizers, and their will to reduce exteriority to their respective images of ideality denotes an intolerance of difference and pluralism akin to Counter-Reformation militancy. José Arcadio can see his own children entering existence only at the moment that Úrsula calls attention to them as potential subjects for educational endeavors: they seem to be "concebidos por el conjuro de Úrsula" ["conceived by Úrsula's spell"] (71/23). Far from reconnecting him to a world outside himself, as she intends, the sons' education becomes an excuse to incorporate them into his solitary universe (72/24).

Nothing could be further from Levinasian ethical subjectivity. As Joel Krueger notes, "The world in which the bodily self is rooted is, according to Levinas, from the start a thoroughly *human* world saturated with intersubjective significance and affective valence," which is the pre-condition for a "body-based conception of ethical relatedness" and its possible actualization.[13] From the intimacy of the home presided over by welcoming, one comes into community as one whose "center of gravitation" (*TI* 183) lies outside oneself. The breakdown of proximity nurturing "love of life" (145) constitutes much of what García Márquez means by *soledad* (solitude). Without proximity's sustaining ethical relatedness, concern for justice, and so investiture of community, politics, and time with significance, can only seem a phantasmagorical daydream.[14]

SOLITUDE, NOSTALGIA, AND LABYRINTHS OF NON-RECURRENCE IN *CIEN AÑOS DE SOLEDAD*

Like Genesis, *Cien años de soledad* recounts two creation stories. In the first chapter, José Arcadio's "espiritú de iniciativa social" ["spirit of social initiative"] is "arrastrado por la fiebre de los imanes, los cálculos astronómicos, los sueños de transmutaciones y las ansias de conocer las maravillas del mundo" ["pulled away by the fever of the magnets, the astronomical calculations, the dreams of transmutation, and the urge to discover the wonders of the world"] (67/18). Original sin and Quixotic madness coincide with instrumental rationalism's alienating, reifying nature[15] to lose a paradise in which "ninguna casa recibía más sol que otra a la hora del calor" ["no house got more sun than another during the hot time of day"] (66/18). [16] Early Macondo exemplifies modes of "embodiment and embeddedness" that "knit us into living communities alongside other bodily subjects," where "otherness" is "built into the very structure of subjectivity." [17] José Arcadio's quasi-biblical fall entails retreat into his alchemist's laboratory, separating exteriority and interiority so that the only outsiders able to arouse desire or interest are those promising power or pleasure, as when touching ice makes José Arcadio forget both his projects and his friend Melquíades's apparent death, "abandonado al apetito de los calamares" ["abandoned to the appetite of the squids"] (75/26).

This fall, we learn in the second chapter, repeats an earlier one. Francis Drake's raiding of Riohacha had so terrified Úrsula's great-great-grandmother that, sitting upon a lighted stove, she became "una esposa inútil para toda la vida" ["a useless wife for the rest of her days"] (76/27). Pathological fear of exteriority forces the woman's husband, an Aragonese merchant, to remove far inland to a village of Indians and to build a windowless bedroom so that the pirates of her dreams cannot get in (76/27). García Márquez thus presents the Buendías as genetic consequences of defensive, self-enclosed cultural meanings woven into Catholic-Hispanic history. Early medieval Iberian ethnic, cultural pluralism gave way to ever more rigid insistence upon sameness of thought and blood—from the 1492 expulsion of the Jews to embrace of fascism in the twentieth century. [18] Social-cultural imperatives to maintain pure blood and psycho-pathological imperatives to remain guardedly isolated push the Buendías into a centuries' long drift toward incest, [19] the sexual analogue of the return of the same to itself, which, for Levinas, is Western thought's characteristic error (*MS* 51).

Úrsula and her relatives, however, are afraid only of "la vergüenza" ["the shame"] of engendering literal monsters, people with tails (77/28). Thus she refuses to consummate her marriage, making José Arcadio vulnerable to Prudencio Aguilar's aspersions upon his manhood. The need to remain inviolable, outside shames's reach, compels him to kill his friend, though residual ethical sense impels him to force Úrsula to yield so he will not kill again. Shielding oneself from another's reductive gaze induces murder, but indifference to an other's (Úrsula's) demands through rape, like indifference to futurity through incest, estranges sex from proximity.

Ethical significance, however, cannot simply be pushed aside, as worldwide stories of ghosts haunting murderers suggest. [20] Lois Parkinson Zamora notes that ghosts' "presence in magical realist fiction . . . dissent[s] . . . from modernity's (and the novel's) psychological assumptions about autonomous consciousness and self-constituted identity," but we may add that their doing so goes beyond what Zamora calls "postmodern . . . rejection of binarisms, rationalisms, and reductive materialisms": ghosts affirm the inescapability of the ethical.[21] Jean-Pierre Durix distinguishes European fantastic fiction's contesting scientism from magical realism's "incorporat[ing] the old [non-European] values and beliefs into the modern man's perception."[22] Rather than simply championing non-Western meanings, magical realism may reiterate an underlying ethical sense "orienting" all cultural meanings (see *MS* 46–47, *EN* 109).[23] José Arcadio's dismissal of Prudencio's ghost (79/30) is belied by his inability to make the ghost "be reasonable" and go away.

Like Cain, José Arcadio tries to outrun the Other's persecution, but in doing so he leads his young friends to "la tierra que nadie les había prometido" (80/31), land that no one had promised them. Such language recalls Exodus, but also the *conquistadors*. It stresses, in a Faulknerian manner, how endeavoring to possess "la tierra" constitutes, in the words of Pascal that Levinas uses as an epigraph for *Otherwise than Being*, a "usurpation" born of claiming one's "place in the sun."[24] Months of wandering culminate in José Arcadio's dreaming of "una ciudad ruidosa con casas de paredes de espejos" ["a noisy city with houses having mirror walls"] (81/31–32). There Macondo is founded, though years later, when José Arcadio discovers ice, he associates mirror walls with coldness, imagining Macondo "una ciudad invernal" ["a wintry city"] (81/32).

Mirroring and coldness are entwined, not as José Arcadio imagines, but in solitude's displacement of proximity. Just as his interest in educating his sons never escapes self-adulation, so the second José Arcadio's growing indifference to the laboratory, while correlated to awakening sexuality, moves him not outward toward others, but rather inward and backward. Wanting to be with Pilar Ternera "en todo momento" ["all the time"] merges with wanting her "fuera su madre" ["to be his mother"] and wanting them "nunca salir del granero" ["never to leave the granary"] (82/33). Erotic desire remains "need" in Levinas's sense, "return itself," "nostalgia" (*MS* 51), and so isomorphic with post-1492 Hispanic Counter-Reformation culture.

That Pilar Ternera evokes earth-goddess vitality and generosity, in contrast to such prim and iron-willed female characters as Úrsula, Amaranta, Rebeca, and Fernanda del Carpio, has often been noted.[25] Although José Arcadio's and Pilar's liaison produces a son, Arcadio, nothing of her really touches him.[26] Her ways of being "alegre, indiferente, dicharachera" ["merry, indifferent, chatty"] only irritate him (85/35). With the prospect of fatherhood weighing upon him, young José Arcadio, "[a]nsioso de soledad" ["anxious for solitude"] (88/39), wanders among visiting gypsies, where he encounters "una gitana muy joven, casi una niña" ["a very young gipsy girl, almost a child"], whose beauty so entrances him that he follows the gypsies when they leave Macondo. Instead of integrating "simultaneity of need and desire, of concupiscence and transcendence" (*TI* 255), erotic life binds need to anxiety for solitude.

Soledad evokes the poet Octavio Paz's iconic *El laberinto de la soledad* (*The Labyrinth of Solitude*) (1951, second edition 1959). Consistent with Sartrean existentialism, Paz's essay posits a primal aloneness that Levinas, emphasizing proximity, sharply contests.[27] On Paz's account, Mexicans embrace their solitude, rather than seek to mystify or evade it, as North Americans do. Having masks where others have faces,the Mexican "se encierra y se preserva" ["shuts himself away to protect himself"], making everythng serve him "para defenderse" ["as defense"] (26/29).

The closeness of this to the Buendías, and to the general xenophobic tenor of post-1492 Hispanic culture, is evident, but while Paz treats absence of proximity as normative, if radicalized by Latin America's history of defeat and humiliation, García Márquez presents it as pathological. Paz, like Husserl and Sartre, recuperates the Cartesian *cogito*, though it is experienced (like self-consciousness in Hegel) as a breach with totality so painful as to motivate elegy and nostalgia. Longing for primal oneness, projected toward an idealized future, Paz argues, lies behind religious eschatology and secular utopianisms (186/206). He wavers between intimating that accepting *soledad* is grown up, sobered up behavior and hoping that "la sociedad vuelva a su libertad original y los hombres a su primitiva pureza" ["society will return to its original freedom, and man to his primitive purity"] (191/211), so that, as in the Christian paradise, ontological transfiguration may make ethical exertion dispensable.[28] For Levinas, by contrast, "proximity with the Other" should be progressive politics' goal (*S* 80–82, *OB* 99–102).

In García Márquez's novel, *soledad* becomes an imperious, cancerous force. Úrsula agrees to take in the infant Arcadio "de mala gana" [grudgingly] (93/44) on condition he never know his identity. Prudery tied to Hispanic cultural naturalizations of self-enclosure pushes the boy toward a solitude that general inattention reinforces: "el cuidado de los niños quedó relegado a un nivel secundario" ["the care of the children was relegated to a secondary level" (93/44). In translation "quedó" (remained) becomes "was," but "quedó" stresses continuous neglect. Unsurprisingly, Arcadio becomes a petty, pompous tyrant when his uncle makes him revolutionary governor of Macondo. The narrator notes that Arcadio is not "lost," as Úrsula thinks, at the moment he puts on his absurd uniform, but has been so "desde siempre" ["from the beginning"] (162/110), for he grew up "un niño solitario y asustado" ["a solitary and frightened child"] (162/111). Reasons for lack of proximity are multiple: the harshness of settler community life; the monomaniac industry of Úrsula; José Arcadio's mad theoretical obsessions; Aureliano's self-protective, self-loathing withdrawal; Amaranta's and Rebeca's anchoring of meaning and self-worth in securing the same man.

If Melquíades's Sanskrit manuscripts are to be identified with the novel, his foreseeing the destruction of the Buendías and Macondo is less magical than morally prescient.[29] Financing and building a grand house draws Úrsula's time and attention away from others as Others. The new prosperity follows the insomnia plague, which has been read as emblematic of both "the destruction of Indian culture at the hands of the Hispanic and Creole populations" and "the loss of oral culture's ways of thinking that are symptomatic of leaving early childhood,"[30] both alienations from proximity. Pietro Crispi, the Italian pianola engineer who becomes the object of Amaranta's and Rebeca's adolescent competition, is desired not for himself, but as a marker of social ascension (for Úrsula), a means of self-validation (for Amaranta), or a way to ease insatiable inner hunger (for Rebeca). Rebeca's yearning to consume dirt merges drives toward primal unity with reversion to oral assimilative aggressiveness. This drive compels her ecstatic but infertile, quasi-incestuous sex with fantastically virile José Arcadio. It assumes political form in both allergy to pluralism (insistence that all houses be painted blue for Conservative), and the use of public life to pursue personal enrichment (José Arcadio), salve wounded egoism (Arcadio), or sanction regressive desires (Aureliano José).

The novel suggests possibilities for reversing this lethal dynamic, but all healing forces come to nought. After a brief reprieve of civic-mindedness following the insomnia plague, José Arcadio Buendía appears to sink back into a world of his own imagining, as announced by Prudencio's ghost finally catching up with him, and immediately followed by his "discovering" that every day is Monday (131/80). The conjunction of Prudencio's re-appearance and Buendía's account of time evokes Faulkner's celebrated observation that ethical consequences render illusory any such word as "was." José Arcadio Buendía learns from Prudencio that "eran tan intense la añoranza de los vivos, tan apremiante la necessidad de compañía" ["the yearning for the living was so intense, the need for company so pressing"] that he (Prudencio) "había terminado de querer al peor de sus enemigos" ["had ended up loving his worst enemy"] (131/80). Even the dead discover solitude to be unbearable, so great is the need for companionship and speech.

José Arcadio Buendía and Prudencio "conversó" ["conversed"] all night long, after which the former is found "llorando con el llantito sin gracia de los viejos, llorando por Prudencio Aguilar, por Melquíades, por los padres de Rebeca, por su papá y su mamá, por todos los que podía recordar y que entonces estaban solos en la muerte" ["weeping for Prudencio Aguilar, for Melquíades, for Rebecca's parents, for his mother and father, for all of those he could remember and who were now alone in death"]. As Levinas argues, the death of the Other (not our death) calls us away from forgetfulness of proximity.[31] Tragically, such recurrence comes too late, though he smashes his laboratory and instruments, recalling Don Quijote's dying renunciation of knight-errantry. As he speaks a new language, his descendants cannot understand; but a few glimpse possible remedies (remedios) for the sickness they share. Facing the firing squad (170/118), Arcadio wants his unborn child named either José Arcadio, not for his monstrously virile, asocial father, but for his grandfather, or Remedios, for Aureliano's deceased child-wife, who alone could learn to converse with his grandfather.

The preternaturally withdrawn Aureliano gravitates toward Remedios because for him, unlike his brother, the erotic pushes toward recurrence. Encountering a child prostitute maniacally exploited by a fantastically heartless grandmother, Aureliano moves from feeling "indiferente y terriblemente solo" ["indifferent and terribly alone"] (107/58) to being obsessed by the tactile immediacy of the girl's destitution, "el pellejo pegado a las costillas y la respiración alterada por un agotamiento insondable" ["skin stuck to her ribs and her breathing . . . forced because of an immeasurable exhaustion"] (107/58). Persecuted as his father was by Prudencio's ghost, Aureliano is filled with "una mezcla de deseo y conmiseración" ["a mixture of desire and pity"] (108/58), from which "una necesidad irresistible de amarla y protegarla" ["an irresistible need to love her and protect her"] resolves him to marry her. But, as with his father, it is too late. Finding she has left town, he retreats into his workshop "ocultar la vergüenza de su inutilidad" ["to hide the shame of his uselessness"] (108/58).

This is the context for Aureliano's headlong plunges into love and politics. He gravitates to Remedios, a girl the child prostitute's age, for, despite her extreme youth, in Aureliano's uncontainable love ethical obsession issues in an eros promising fecundity. "Remedios había llevado a la casa un soplo de alegría. . . . Cantaba desde el amanecer. Fue ella la única persona que se atrevió a mediar en las disputas de Rebeca y Amaranta" ["Remedios had brought a breath of merriment to the house. . . . She would start singing at dawn. She was the only person who dared intervene in the arguments between Rebecca and Amaranta"] (139–140/89). She begins learning Latin to communicate with José Arcadio Buendía, and when the infant son of Aureliano and Pilar (Aureliano José) enters the house, she welcomes him as her eldest child. Remedios offers remedies: Pilar's vitality without her vulgarity, singing to moderate Úrsula's unrelieved non-singing, fellow-feeling with both Rebeca and Amaranta, care and understanding for José Arcadio Buendía, and a welcoming feminine presence magically uncontaminated by centuries of Hispanic-Catholic self-enclosure, prudery, and gender warfare.

Remedios' devastating death is ostensibly cruel chance, but Amaranta's fear that her homicidal jealousy of Rebeca may be implicated suggests that, like a deranged organism, the Buendía household treats all healing otherness as invasive threats, sending out equivalents of antibodies to destroy all that might restore health. The same pathology marks the political-cultural sphere. Another defenseless female's victimization, the killing of a woman by Conservative soldiers, pushes Aureliano into political warfare as a way to expiate, or rewrite, a past whose shamefulness tears at him until resignation and despair drive him to a willful deadening of affect. Ethical consciousness proves as useless and tormenting as a toothache.

Colonel Aureliano Buendía's thirty-two rebellions, a composite of the late nineteenth-century Thousand Days' War and the police and street terrorism that convulsed Columbia between the late 1940s and early 1960s, recapitulates a progress from naïve idealism to cynical opportunism iconically expressed in such Mexican civil war novels as Mariano Azuela's *Los de abajo* (1915) and Carlos Fuentes' *La muerte de Artemio Cruz* (1962).[32] Distinctive to these themes in García Márquez is the Colonel's enduring disgust at himself—both for imagining that politics could remake the world so as to alleviate his shame and for allowing politics to serve, badly, personal therapeutic needs. In the diminished world that follows the war's failure, the inability of remedies to take root makes the ethical even unreal, as when José Arcadio Segundo's labor union activity against the banana company resolves into nothing or when Aureliano Segundo's paternal affection for Meme cannot protect her against her mother's, Fernanda del Carpio's, manipulations. Absent rational faith in an ameliorative future, ethical sensibility can only induce despair, as it does for José Arcadio Segundo. So one calls upon spectacle, apathy, and mystification to keep recurrence from disturbing solitude.[33]

Totalizing the self-enclosing tendencies of the first three generations of Buendías, Fernanda del Carpio, a variant of the phallic, passive-aggressive, sterile and sterilizing ultra-Conservative mother figure monumentalized in Galdos' Doña Perfecta and Lorca's Bernarda Alba, dominates the second half of the novel. The third Remedios (Meme), in loving the lower-class chauffeur Mauricio Babilonia, enacts receptivity to alterity, but, in a close restaging of the climax of Galdos' novel, Fernanda arranges to destroy Meme's lover in body and reputation, driving the daughter into madness.[34]

After this extirpation of proximity from private life—correlated with the massacre of the striking banana workers, a similar extirpation in public life— nature revolts against a humanity without ethical sociality. This great rain, unlike its biblical precedent, brings no renewal. Both Macondo and the Buendías are beyond amendment. Fernanda's son, in whom the narcissism of his ancestors becomes undiluted, is murdered by boys he picks up, and the last of the Buendías, Amaranta Úrsula and Aureliano Babilonia, sink into an autarkic, solipsistic, incestuous idyll, giving over exteriority to ravenous ants and the whirlwind of the novel's final page. Without proximity sustaining ethical subjectivity, the human world is left to being's interest in its own continuance, which paradoxically breeds solitudes that ensure genetic-cultural suicide. Macondo is founded in delusory effort to outrun the Other's pull upon conscience; the same may be said for the Hispanic colonial adventure, the ideology of purity in post-1492 Spain, the dream that instrumental rationality might yield sufficient material abundance to liberate self-indulgence from disruption and reproach. Forfeiture of proximity punishes all such sin. To the extent that the novel itself is exterior to the social and psychic terrain it depicts (as the supposed authorship of Melquíades and use of Sanskrit imply), it may be viewed as offering readers initiation into simulated relations of proximity. Translating these from imagination to life offers the only hope of preventing other centuries of solitude from equivalent self-protective eradication.

ELEGIAC RECURRENCE: PYNCHON, RILKE, AND ORPHIC LAMENT

While García Márquez implies that Catholic-Hispanic modernity's blockage of recurrence induces ethnocide, Pynchon suggests that Protestant-northern European estrangements threaten human survival altogether despite recurring proximity. From its opening evocation of a V-2 rocket's soundless approach to its concluding sketch of a missile's fall, *Gravity's Rainbow* addresses *you*, enacting a somatic-incantatory sociality, but one antithetical to identification of the triumphant being of a race, group, or interest with the Good that, for Levinas, characterizes fertility-cult paganism and Western ontological thought (*OB* 3–20, *BPW* 129–48, *LR* 76–87). Pynchon's narrative precludes the ecstatic immersion Levinas associates with a folk-cultural Sacred (*TI* 77–79) and with modernity's totalizing identity politics (*LR* 164, *BPW* 162–69).[35] Art, originating in cultic ritual, seems particularly to host neopagan and/or fascistic propensities (*RS* 132–34, *DF* 14–19, *TI* 53–60, *MS* 38–42),[36] and Pynchon's incantatory prose, evoking Dionysian excess, may seem to celebrate rapturous scattering of identity.[37] The narrative, however, obsessively makes "a despite-me, for-another . . . signification par excellence," enacting in recurrence "the very fact of finding oneself while losing oneself" (*OB* 11).

Implication of the reader evokes Rainer Maria Rilke's proto-Heideggerian modernist poetry from the novel's first sentence, "A screaming comes across the sky," to the last, "the Rocket, falling nearly a mile per second . . . reaches its last unmeasurable gap above the roof of this old theatre, the last delta-t."[38] Rilke identifies separation, as Paz does *soledad*, with existential homelessnes, and likewise longing for transcendence with nostalgia for original oneness.[39] The "screaming" that "comes across the sky" recalls the first lines of the *Duino Elegies* (1922), "Wer, wenn ich schriee, hörte mich denn aus der Engel / Ordnung?" ["Who, if I cried (screamed), would hear me among the angelic orders?"], but by conflating human "screaming" with the rocket's descent, Pynchon establishes a troubled link between "angelic" transcendence of alienated human cognition in Rilke and a rocket's transcendence of gravitational limits. Each form of "stärkeren Dasein" ["stronger existence"] coerces recognition, lauded by Rilke but rendered disturbing by Pynchon, that "das Schöne ist nichts / als des Schrecklichen Anfang, den wir noch grade ertragen" ["Beauty's nothing / but beginning of Terror we're still just able to bear"].[40] Similarly, the rocket's fall on the novel's final page suggests cryptic parody of Rilke's final verses (X. 110–114, pp. 84–85) celebrating happiness's "fall."

Pynchon, like Rilke, draws on the Orphic myth. In *Sonnets to Orpheus*, Orpheus's animation of a world become inanimate (Ovid, *Metamorphoses*, XI. 1–4) evokes poetry's awakening within us nature and things from the death-like reification imposed by instrumental rationality and consumerist values.[41] The kingdom of death (i.e., separation from nature and things) has made us "nicht sehr verläßlich zu Haus . . . / in der gedeuteten Welt" [not "very securely at home / within our interpreted world"] (*Duino Elegies* I.13–14, pp. 20–21). Art helps us become more securely (verläßlich) at home (zu Haus). This trajectory, anticipating Heidegger's, runs opposite to that of Levinasian recurrence, which "break[s] up . . . in me" all "rest in itself characteristic of definition" (*OB* 114).[42] Pynchon draws upon the larger Orpheus story (*Metamorphoses* X. 1–XI. 67), loosely correlating his protagonist Slothrop's misadventures with Orpheus's quest for Eurydice, her loss, the grief that follows, and dismemberment amid bacchant frenzies. Within the novel identity is "scattered," not body parts.[43]

Central to Slothrop's connection to Orpheus is his reversing Orpheus's iconic action, but to identical effect—not looking back consigns another to death's kingdom.[44] The scene inverts Aureliano's encounter with the child prostitute, as Bianca is, in Slothrop's imagination at least, an abused child/ Lolita fantasy girl. In "allowing the days' targets more reality than anything that might come up" (471), Slothrop, following the hardening of intentionality that military jargon conveys, refuses the Other's disruption of his being "at home." His failure to look back, his absorption in his own ascent, constitutes a refusal of the "recurrence of the self in responsibility for others" (*OB* 111). Such disruptions, Pynchon implies, are where "salvation could be" (471). The half-conscious nature of Slothrop's action reflects, partly, corporate-cultural forces denaturalizing receptivity to proximity, thereby precluding separation, as Levinas defines it: "the radical impossibility of seeing oneself from the outside and of speaking in the same sense of oneself and of the others, and consequently the impossibility of totalization—the impossibility of *forgetting* the intersubjective experience that leads to that social experience and endows it with meaning" (*TI* 53). Pynchon's novel, like much Cold War fiction, describes a world where social engineering facilitates totalization.[45] For all its non-linearity, the novel's first half is largely about how Slothrop's *not* looking back becomes possible.

The victim of plots to preempt agency, Slothrop is nonetheless, like others, half in love with loss of separation, and so easeful death. This is not simply because death drives intersect with entropy.[46] Rather, "tension" in organic matter, which Freud sees motivating "the instinct to return to the inanimate state,[47] *in humans* includes not only burdens of "judgment and decision" that "they" (*das Man*) promise to alleviate by making "[e]veryone . . . the other, and no one . . . himself,"[48] but also the annoying weightiness of finding oneself "the one" answerable for the Other. Gravitational tropes compete with the entropic motifs of Pynchon's earlier fiction.[49] Revolt, associating freedom with unconstrained will, motivates hostility toward the "they" (*das Man*), whose "stubborn dominion" coerces "each '*who*'" into "the '*nobody*,'"[50] but the same revolt elicits hostility toward all that encumbers ascent. This in turn pushes us toward an indifference to the Other that both the powers-that-be and our own susceptibility to power desire.

Criticism has long pondered "whether [Pynchon] takes in his work a radical postmodern position that verges on nihilism (through its totalizing representations of a paranoid and entropic social order) or affirms the possibilities of care, love, responsibility, and community."[51] The question may be reframed in terms of how much saying, signifying "the proximity of one to the other" (*OB* 5), works against the entropic pull of the said toward totalizing ontology. Within contexts both horrific and ludic, Slothrop's not looking back, in its very ethical failure, discloses saying's transcendence of the said and so the centripetal force of "fissioned" selfhood (*OB* 125). Paradoxically, saying fastens us to the Other in ways that both fission the self and impede its dispersal.

As with Aureliano encountering the child prostitute, Slothrop meets Bianca by chance, but only after many events estrange affectivity from proximity. An American lieutenant in wartime London, Slothrop becomes the subject of first experiments, then vendettas by scientists and "para-normal" experts assigned to a psychological warfare unit (PISCES) who imagine that correlations between where Slothrop is sexually aroused and where V-2 rockets *later* fall can be of military or academic use (and so capitalized upon for personal and institutional gain). Slothrop discovers that he was subjected to erotic conditioning experiments as an infant (payment for which covered his Harvard expenses) by a visiting European scientist connected with early rocket research, plastics, and, through I. G. Farben, the first articulation of a military-industrial complex. Stripped of his identity (literally, his uniform and military ID) by the plotting of the psychological warfare group, Slothrop enters newly occupied Germany, taking on a series of assumed identities, to chase down in V-2 rocket facilities links between science, business, and the military that he imagines will explain what *they* have endeavored to make him. Ending up in Berlin, he discovers in an abandoned movie studio Margherita Erdmann, a faded, mentally disturbed star of 1920s semi-pornographic German cinema, at whose instigation he re-enacts a sadomasochistic scene from the film *Alpdrücken* (*Nightmare*). This scene once so stimulated future V-2 rocket engineer Franz Pökler that he went home from the theater and fathered a daughter, Ilse (397–98). The filming of this scene culminated with stagehands gang-raping Margherita, who consequently conceived Bianca. Slothrop's quest for the V-2 testing site of Peenemünde leads him and Margherita to the cruise ship *Anubis*, where they discover Bianca, who performs a vamp-erotic Shirley Temple routine that inspires an outlandish orgy among the ship's decadent, elite fascist "guests."

Slothrop's hyperbolic, zany story precariously balances elegiac recurrence and elegy for recurrence, whose embattled possibility is measured by Slothrop's and others' wavering susceptibility to ethical significance. The novel's opening evacuation scene directs readers' attention, before anything else, to exposed and destitute anonymous others, "all the others pressed in around, feeble ones, second sheep, all out of luck and time" (3), linking organized passivity—"the crowd moves without murmurs" (4)—with hierarchical exploitation within an Orphic underworld ("No one was ever going to take the trouble to save *you*, old fellow"). Then it addresses the reader in the imperative, placing the other "in me and in the very midst of my identification" (*OB* 125): "There is no way out. Lie and wait, lie still and be quiet." (4).

Steven G. Weisenburger notes that in Calvinist theology, "second sheep are *preterite*, those predestined for abandonment" as opposed to "the *elect* who are predestined for redemption."[52] Pynchon links Protestant thought to colonization, the European "settlement" of the Americas, ecological extirpations, capitalist-corporate rationalization of science and the military, Soviet statism, and Nazi racial theory.[53] Like García Márquez, he depicts blocked recurrence. Slothrop is introduced as one whose "rocket-hunting routine" is getting "a little old," though "[o]nce upon a time, [he] cared. No kidding. He thinks he did, anyway" (21). Dissociation from oneself aligns with dissociations from the past and from modes of proximity uprooted in total war: "Individuals are reduced to being bearers of forces that command them unbeknown to themselves. . . . The unicity of each present is incessantly sacrificed to a future appealed to to bring forth its objective meaning" (*TI* 21–22). Slothrop's not caring is entwined with the passage from buzzbombs, whose shut-off of sound provides the illusion of warning, to V-2 rockets, whose soundlessness leaves Slothrop "really scared," inducing narcissistic retreat ("drinking heavier, sleeping less, chain-smoking") and a suspicion of victimization ("feeling in some way he'd been taken for a sucker") rooted in conviction that *he* should be untouchable, elect: "Christ, it wasn't supposed to keep on like *this*" (21).

Stefan Mattessich notes that Pynchon's novel's peculiar "discontinuous temporality" displaces "America in the late 1960s and early 1970s" into "Europe in 1945."[54] Slothrop's, "Christ, it wasn't supposed to keep on like *this*," evokes attitudes of white male suburban college students confronted with the Vietnam draft. Patrick McHugh argues that *Gravity's Rainbow's* most "surprisingly intense affect" is that "particular to white male postmodernism. . . . In one way, the white guys are victims like everyone else of the forces of capitalism, patriarchy, and colonialism. Yet . . . [these very forces] grant privilege to white guys. Moreover, the patriarchal ritual of succession happens precisely through (oedipal) resistance."[55]

Slothrop copes by marking the location of encounters with "a multitude of girls he seldom saw again" (23) on a map "celebrat[ing] a flow, a passing from which . . . he can save a moment here or there . . . , the feeling of Jennifer's breasts inside cold sweater's wool held to warm a bit in a coal-smoke hallway he'll never know the daytime despondency of . . ." (23). From such callow ordinariness, in which "flow" assimilates other people into images one can hoard, Slothrop elaborates a chart of his imperializing ego's meanderings. Its coincidence with V-2 landfalls will particularize his victimization.

But Slothrop is not entirely at "at home" adrift in flow.[56] Time has ethical significance. He reflects, "Yesterday happened to be a good day. They found a child, alive, a little girl, half-suffocated under a Morrison shelter" (24). When she asked for gum, Slothrop "felt like a fool" as "all he had for her was a Thayer's Slippery Elm [cough drop]." This rupture in egoism reseals as Slothrop slides into cinematic romanticizing: "he knew that's what he'd been waiting for, wow, a Shirley Temple smile, as if this exactly canceled all they'd found her down in the middle of" (24). Translating a "very faint" smile into a Shirley Temple one, Slothrop would insulate himself from trauma by recoding the encounter in more comfortable terms, but he ends by experiencing the ethical upend, the aesthetic-erotic just when he would "cover over" with cultural representation the nudity of the face signifying itself absolutely (*BPW* 53).[57]

Slothrop's subjection to the PISCES group's plotting both undermines and deepens him. It places Slothrop in the postmodern double bind of "mov[ing] between the pleasures of a hippie-like resistance to 'The Man' and the paranoia that such 'resistance' is yet another manifestation of the power of 'The Man.'"[58] It deepens, however, when proximity is glimpsed on the hither side of both pleasure and paranoia. "[H]ospitalized" by the Pavlovian Dr. Pointsman to discover the mechanism of his erotic affinity for V-2 landing sites, Slothrop experiences a sodium amytal induced delirium, akin to a 1960s drug trip, that connects guarding one's bounded autonomy to both fascistic nightmare and wild west romance. A garbled memory of losing his harmonica in a Roseland Ballroom toilet mutates into a paranoiac scenario of being sodomized by Negro shoeshine boys led by the future Malcolm X (64–65), a hyperbolic elaboration of his anxiety in being probed and confined by Pointsman and his associates. An inverted, compensatory counter-fantasy ensues, conflating Old West genre conventions and sado-masochist pederasty: "Crutchfield's little pard" (68) Whappo "bait[ed] his master in hopes of getting a leather-keen stripe or two across those dusky Afro-Scandinavian buttocks" (69).

Fear of being "taken for a sucker," focalized by PISCES, is traced via drugs to its most elemental psychic levels. As in Úrsula's ancestor's fantasies of violation, anxiety about the permeability of one's boundaries precipitates colonializing reactions—for the Buendía ancestors, insularity and withdrawal, for Slothrop compensatory libidinal-political identification with European conquest and homoerotic mastery. Slothrop's psyche thus intersects with that of his apparent opposite, Major Weissmann/Blicero. The Major's German Southwest African colonial background and S.S. V-2-unit command, correlated with black (Enzian) and white (Gottfried) boy lovers, pushes into actuality what remains virtual within Slothrop. Both, however, are erotically drawn to missiles as each aspires to evade embodiments linked to vulnerability and thus proximity.

Slothrop's hallucinatory "trip" suggests that he and Weissmann both articulate white male "elect" privilege in revolt against intimations that they too may only be preterites, the "abandoned" of Calvinist theology. Each feels the seductiveness of "leaving . . . human touch forever" and "climbing all alone" (98), gaining the solitary transcendence of Orphic ascent. Moreover, in finding similitude to Weissmann (white man) at the most uninhibited reaches of himself, Slothrop discovers that seeking to undo the centered, repressed, oedipal self—as in being drugged, "getting in touch with oneself," or Orphic-bacchante rhapsodies—leads one back to bodily exposure and so (without proximity's conversion of materiality into sociality) to an archaic, primal fear of invasion, penetration, absorption monumentalized in the Nazi psyche. Whether directed against "*das Man*" or "The Man," assertions of one's inviolability or transcendence encourage seeing the Other as monster— hence Weissmann's obsessive-compulsive sado-masochistic re-enactments of Hansel and Gretel, where maternal nurturer turns cannibalistic devourer and innocent ingenue pushes "the one" guilty into an oven's suffocating, entrapping solitude. Within fantasy worlds of dualistic psychic economies and dialectical-Gnostic metaphysics, proximity has no place; it is u-topia.

But the narrative contests this binary logic. When PISCES arranges for Slothrop, ostensibly on R&R on the French Riviera, to meet Katje, formerly undercover in Holland as Weissmann's mistress, it contrives to have him "rescue" her from Octopus Grigori, the "biggest" he "has ever seen outside the movies" (186). The outlandish scene compounds espionage and monster movie conventions, but Slothrop actually risks his life for another: "in the presence of certain death, [he] can't quit staring at her [Katje's] hand," partly because, already suspicious, he wants to read the name on her ID bracelet, partly because the "poor hand," "a soft-knuckled child's hand," is about to be "separate[ed] from Earth——." Slothrop's friend Teddy Bloat conveniently has a crab to divert the octopus, allowing Slothrop to complete a rescue whose staginess he intuits (188). Still, the orders of signification denoted by conspiratorial pastiche and by the poignancy of "a soft-knuckled child's hand" remain for Slothrop and the reader incommensurate. The same holds for others. Slothrop's officemate, Tantivy, confronted with Slothrop's anguished questioning, hesitatingly acknowledges that Bloat is "receiving messages in code," and declares, "face reddening a bit" (194), that if Slothrop needs help, "well, I'll help you."

As his fox hunting name indicates, Tantivy is pursued both by ethical responsibility and by *their* efforts to co-opt him. Other characters seem similarly hunted animals. Katje (whose name is Dutch for "kitty"), her sexuality having been recruited into the war effort, may sleep with Slothrop, but "will not surrender her face" despite his urgent "needing to see" it (197), either to retain part of herself apart or to avoid the direct look of one she will betray. His ID and clothes stolen, Tantivy suddenly missing, Slothrop finds himself rendered preterite, and can only think to return to Katje, though he knows she has set him up. "It's the only place I knew to come" (205), he tells her, words that echo the last sentence of Part One of Nabokov's *Lolita*, "You see, she had absolutely nowhere else to go," itself an echo of Marmeladov's explanation in *Crime and Punishment* of why his wife married him: "Do you understand, young man, do you understand what it means to have nowhere left to turn to?"[59] Slothrop, too, seeks to find a place to go, to recover agency, in knowledge, but the more he learns about the infantile conditioning that binds him erotically to a plastics used in V-2 rockets, the more coherence becomes paranoiac, labyrinths solitary, and a sense of personal grievance (however justified) narcissistically self-isolating.

Increasing knowledge is no substitute for lost human contact. Reflecting upon how the shape of the Mittelwerke missile tunnels resembles two sleeping lovers, Slothrop "wishes he were . . . all the way back with Katje, even lost as he might feel again, even more vulnerable than now—even (because he still honestly misses her). . . . He wants to preserve what he can of her from Their several entropies, from Their softsoaping and Their money: maybe he thinks that if he can do it for her he can also do it for himself" (302). Katje's alterity, to which *his* vulnerability is tied, is precisely what he misses and wants to conserve. The erotic transcends concupiscence in longing to "save" the Other's otherness. Slothrop here may go beyond Aureliano, for whom the child prostitute and Remedios are ultimately valorized in terms of their meaning for him. By contrast, Katje's separateness provokes Slothrop to knight-errantry, moving vestigial ethical sense toward nascent politics: "that's awfully close to nobility for Slothrop" (302). But it is only close. Saving her slides toward preoccupation with saving himself.

Perched (again like Aureliano) between self-absorption and ethical revolt, Slothrop encounters variants of his own internal dissonance in the occupied Zone, where, in competition with American, British, and Russian teams, he seeks out V-2 sites and equipment. The Zone-Herero community, exiles from former German Southwest Africa, divide between those who, responding to the trauma of genocide, seek purity in racial suicide, and those who, led by Enzian (Weissmann's former lover), seek to make the rocket retrieve agency and significance. The latter, like Slothrop, search out missile parts in hopes of piecing together sustainable identity. But self-preoccupation drifts toward Buendía-like solitude. Slothrop shields himself from attachment to others by aestheticizing exteriority and assuming increasingly stylized, outlandish identities: "Slothrop regards bombed-out Berlin, another Orphic underworld, as he would the preparation and expense of a movie scene," and habitually "characters and people make little or no distinction between film and traditional reality."[60] While Slothrop achieves heady freedom retrieving hashish from President Truman's Potsdam villa in the guise of a comic-book hero, Rocketman, his frenetic self-assertions serve (as in this case) other people's projects (see 359–83). This becomes particularly problematic when, in the abandoned movie studio, he encounters Margherita Erdmann and blandly agrees to re-enact a whipping scene (396). Feeling uncannily "at home" in his (interwar German) role, Slothrop loses Levinasian separation as the unicity integral to ethical identity unravels: "No—he still says 'their,' but he knows better. His meadows now, his sky . . . his own cruelty" (396).

The scene initiates a flashback to the life of German rocket engineer Franz Pökler, whose abiding but flawed love for his Leftist wife Leni resembles Slothrop's for Katje, and whose searing relationship with the daughter conceived under Margherita's spell, Ilse, anticipates Slothrop's with Bianca. Desire to sink into and to master the earth (Erdmann, earth man) connects Pökler's erotic life with the rocket's promise of transcendence: "Pökler was an extension of the Rocket, long before it was ever built. [Leni]'d seen to that. When she left him, he fell apart. . . . Then he moved to Kummersdorf, outside Berlin, to help his friend Mondaugen at the rocket field" (402). The lure of escaping the vulnerability inherent in proximity exposes him to Major Weissmann's co-option and tyranny. Weissmann keeps him in line by reminding him that wife and daughter, in a concentration camp, are at his (Weissmann's) disposal. Each year he is allowed a "vacation" visit from his daughter, but, in a dark parody of Marcel's discovering a new Albertine each time he encounters her, Pökler wonders if the girl is the same, or his. Poignant uncertainty is juxtaposed with the absurdity of a Nazi Disneyland, for in "a Corporate state, a place must be made for innocence, and its many uses" (419). Suspicious of being "played" by a fraudulent daughter, attracted to and repulsed by her abjectness, hungry for human contact and primed for masochistic fury, he lapses, upon her making an equivocal remark, into a hypnotic daydream in which she initiates "hours of amazing incest" after which they escape by ship to a free Denmark (420–21).

Instead of actually acting/lashing out, however, he chooses "to believe she wanted comfort that night, wanted not to be alone. Despite Their game, Their palpable evil, though he had no more reason to trust 'Ilse' than he trusted Them, by an act not of faith, not of courage but of conservation, he chose to believe that" (421). In Pökler's fantasy even egregious appropriation of the Other is lined with desire for her rescue, freedom, well-being. His ability, like Slothrop's, to hold himself apart from Their plots involves determination to act as though the Other were not totalized and cannot properly be at one's, anyone's, disposal. Collapse of identity into either brutal self-interest or despair may be evaded only by stubbornly, gratuitously, conceiving the world as not foreclosing all proximity, by acting in the present "for remote things, of which the present is an irrecusable denial" (*MS* 51).

But non-co-option demands extending non-disposability from loved ones to all others. After the Reich's collapse, in a vain, Orpheus-like search for wife and daughter through the camp adjacent the missile plant, Pökler confronts all the other singular ones, "each face so perfect, so individual, the lips stretched back into death-grins" (432). Just as the said, in aesthetic elaboration, profanes but also witnesses saying, so Pökler, suddenly aware of what he always knew, cries tears that cannot dissolve "prison walls" in finding "on every pallet, in every cell, that the faces are ones he knows after all, and holds dear as himself" (433). He cannot but cry, in part for his own relief, and is too tainted by egoism ever to cry and rage enough. The same may be said of the reader in encountering the novel's one direct Holocaust scene. No act or feeling is adequate, or offers hope of exculpation. If there is redemption in Pökler's inverted Orpheus journey, it lies in giving up associating transcendence with any "home" outside the gravity binding oneself to the other.

Slothrop, however, is diverted in the opposite direction, entering with Magherita the cruise ship, *Anubis*, where he encounters Bianca, perceived by him (fitting into his Shirley Temple/Lolitaesque preferred way of seeing) as "a knockout, all right, 11 or 12" (463), though she would have to be sixteen or seventeen.[61] When they meet the day after her performance has stimulated an orgy, she, acting like the briefly fantasized "Ilse," invites him into a carefree sexual romp that he insouciantly accepts. Whereas García Márquez stresses the child prostitute's bodily vulnerability, Pynchon presents a figure all cartoon-pornographic surface, in sharp distinction to "Ilse," to Katje, and to Nabokov's Lolita. Bianca is without otherness because Slothrop, in whose imagination she is seen, would elude separation. John Hamill claims that Slothrop seeks to evade "guilt and entrapment" by "evad[ing] responsibility" through "dissolv[ing] into a reverie reminiscent of the gritty style of the beat poets," for, fearing "anything that threatens mastery," he would avoid the

trap "of Orpheus, in which the looking back results . . . in loss."[62] To fear
loss, however, is to experience the other's significance in denying it.

After their coupling, Slothrop comes to a belatedly Humbert-like intuition
of there being more to Bianca than his pleasure in her: "Somewhere in their
lying-still are her heart, buffeting, a chickadee in the snow, her hair, draping
and sheltering both their faces" (470). He would "disentangle" himself from
all that through "a bureaucracy of departure, inoculations against forgetting,
exit visas stamped with love-bites," tropes affiliating him with "they-systems," even though "Her look now—this deepening arrest—has already
broken Slothrop's seeing heart" (471). To look away he must lose what
recurrence brings home by dissolving himself into a pastiche of "on the road"
self-elegizing lyricism: "that same look swung as he drove by, . . . looked for
how many Last Times up in the rearview mirror" (471). Just as Orpheus
retreats into cynical despair, and the Buendías retreat into labyrinths of solitude, so Slothrop dissolves not into heterogeneous individualities but into a
totality, refusing any distinction between himself and a "they," an American
inflection of "*das Man*": "Of course, Slothrop lost her and kept losing her—it
was an American requirement—out the windows of the Greyhound . . . ," and
anyway, "she has moved on, untroubled, too much Theirs" (472). In refusing
Pökler's act of conservation, Slothrop loses the knight-errantry that Levinasian separation enjoins. Totalizing American variants of being *for itself*, he
seems to confirm the transfer to America of an ethos of disposing of others to
facilitate one's own transcendence that Weissmann offers as a self-serving
philosophy of history: "In Africa, Asia, Amerindia, Oceania, Europe came
and established its order of Analysis and Death. What it could not use, it
killed or altered. . . . American Death has . . . learned empire from its old
metropolis" (722).

Were the novel to end here, it would be bleak indeed, and *Gravity's
Rainbow's* artistry would be "aesthetic" in Levinas's negative sense, imposing a fixity in which the "present, impotent to force the future, [is]. . . fate
itself" (*RS* 138). But Slothrop cannot be at home in abandoning Bianca. He
wanders the *Anubis* "feeling none too keen" (490), searching for her amid
orgiastic distractions. Imagining he sees her, he makes a "lunge after her
without thinking much" (491), falls overboard, and so parts company with
this ship of the morally dead. Rescued by a gruff maternal black marketeer,
he resumes his quest for Peenemünde accompanied by a German engineer,
Närrisch, and the former movie director/black marketeer. Once they reach
Peenemünde and are attacked by Russians, Närrisch (whose name means
"foolish") sacrifices himself to save the others, which Slothrop perceives
through a filter of associations with the killing of John Dillinger and the last
pages of *For Whom the Bell Tolls*. Out at sea, Slothrop again encounters the
Anubis, where on a surreptitious boarding he encounters or imagines he
encounters Bianca's dangling corpse: "Icy little thighs in wet silk swing

against his face. They smell of the sea. He turns away, only to be lashed across the cheek by long wet hair. No matter which way he tries to move now" (531). Nightmarishly, the Other's presence, rather like Prudencio's ghost, pursues one. Slothrop becomes part of the summer of 1945's great migrations of Displaced Persons, affectively waterlogged by the destitution surrounding him: "Tattersall dresses, thick-knitted shawls with babies inside, women in army trousers split at the knees, . . . the detritus of an order, a European and bourgeois order they don't yet know is destroyed forever" (550–51).

Elemental community emerges: "When Slothrop has cigarettes he's an easy mark, when somebody has food they shared it" (551); he befriends a wandering German boy, Ludwig, who, Orpheus-like, is searching for his lost lemming Ursula; he is connected by analepsis to his seventeenth-century ancestor William, who wrote a book arguing "holiness for these 'second Sheep,' without whom there'd be no elect" (555). From such roots, disruption of corporate-military totalization becomes possible. Slothrop warns Enzian of an impending ambush (562), and so preserves the Rocket-Hereros as an anarchic-pluralistic force. He assumes the costume of a pig used to celebrate a pig-hero's tenth-century deliverance of a village from Viking invaders, thereby aligning identity with being *for another*. Slothrop encounters Pökler, and the similitude of their ambiguous erotic/ethical quests for Ilse/Bianca, denoting Orphic selfhood prior to intentionality, is brought home: "She's still with you, though harder to see these days, . . . still she is there, cool and acid and sweet, waiting . . . to work among your saddest dreams" (577). If objectification of Ilse/Bianca underscores the appropriativeness shadowing human consciousness, insistence that "still she is there" suggests both the Other's irreducibility to consumption and desire's hunger for a relationship "whose positivity comes from remoteness, from separation" (*TI* 34). Attachment to particular others fosters broader, properly political ethics. Slothrop, preternaturally sensing the advent of the atomic age on August 6, 1945, "became a crossroad . . . [H]is chest fills and he stands crying, not a thing in his head, just feeling natural" (626).

Stubborn holding onto others extends from Slothrop not to all, but to enough to create what Pynchon calls "the Counterforce." The PISCES statistician, Roger Mexico, is as haunted by Slothrop's destitution as Slothrop is by Bianca's. He reflects, "I can't just leave the poor twit out there, can I? They're trying to destroy him—" (627). Much to his surprise, Roger discovers that he is not alone. His friend Pirate tells him, "For every They there ought to be a We. In our case there is" (638), but We-systems committed to pluralism can never "interlock" as They-systems do. Among the "we" is Katje, who enters the Zone and encounters Enzian while seeking Slothrop for reasons she cannot explain: "I don't just want to—I don't know, pay him back for the octopus, or something. Don't I have to know *why* he's out here, what I did to him, for Them?" (662).

Roger's temporary partnership with the anarchic, obscene, drug-dealing Seaman Bodine in serving Roger's wartme girl friend, Jessica, and her corporate They-man fiancé, Jeremy, a septic feast (713–17) underscores the ambivalence of Pynchon's depiction of the Counterforce. On the one hand, there is an ethical core arising from being haunted by what is done to others; on the other, there is a self-indulgent, paranoiac romancing of victimhood and/or cynical coolness prefiguring the sixties' counterculture: "The Man has a branch office in each of our brains, his corporate emblem is a white albatross, each local rep has a cover known as the Ego" (713). The implication is that egocentric intentionality always threatens to make "we" an inverted image of "they," especially when "we" insists upon "our" purity; yet the "fission" of the ethical offers hope for a "kinder" universe, where love challenges creation's ordering by dark, agonistic forces.[63]

Gravity Rainbow's lack of closure, like that of *Ulysses*, suggests unease with traditional narrative's tendency to import a fatality into art that obscures lived subjectivity's freedom. One strand of the novel drives toward Weissmann's launching the missile bearing Gottfried, but another describes how Tchitcherine, a Russian analogue of Slothrop, who has an Ahab-like obsession with killing his half-brother Enzian, under the influence of the nubile German witch Geli Tripping, encounters Enzian, fails to recognize him, and allows him to go in peace. Geli's magic is correlated with sex and nature, but also with what Levinas calls "dwelling" and "welcoming."[64] The last we hear of Tchitcherne is, "Then he goes back to his young girl beside the stream. They will have to locate some firewood before all the light is gone" (735). Entwining the girl and stream with the ethical sociality of locating firewood suggests precisely the choices that iconically American characters, such as Melville's, do not make.[65] Such choices break with *soledad* and undo the isolating reifications that concern Rilke. They make Orpheus-like "go[ing] back to his young girl" an orienting of oneself toward the Other.

This remains one possibility among many, as the novel fractures into discontinuous episodes and heterogeneous voices. Counterbalancing the gravitational pull of proximity is the desire, epitomized by Weissmann, to throw off the limits of the merely human, crystallized in the "wine rush" of "defying gravity, finding yourself on the elevator ceiling as it rockets *upward*" (743), and the despair that comes from conviction that all revolt must fail, just as all V-rockets must fall: "[W]e are condemned in our weakness to impersonate men of power our own infant children must hate, and wish to usurp the place of, and fail" (747). Slothrop's ambiguous scattering could be fertile if his inner dissonance embeds in nature and human nature a turning back toward the Other. Even at the novel's last moment, when humanity and the reader appear fixed, objectified, by the missile about to strike the old theater, itself a Hades-like refuge for solitary consumption of aestheticized, commercialized pleasures, "if you need the comfort," you might "touch the person next to you, or . . . reach between your own cold legs" (760). The choice of turning to another or retreating into oneself abides. If physical gravity's "rainbow" is the parabola of a missile's arc, announcing not a happiness that falls, but the death that ascent sealed off from recurrence brings, moral gravity's arc pushes us back toward the Other, toward the ground of ourselves prior to egoisms. In that trajectory alone the promise signified by the rainbow in Genesis may yet hold.

NOTES

1. Levinas elaborates an implicit narrative in which subjectivity, ideally, moves from self-preoccupation to "devoting-of-oneself-to-the-other" (*EN* xii; also see *EN* 13–38, 123–53, 159–77).

2. Thus the "look" of the Other in Sartre must be objectifying, invasive. See Jean-Paul Sartre, *Being and Nothingness: A Phenomenological Essay on Ontology*, trans. Hazel E. Barnes (New York: Washington Square Press, 1956), 340–400.

3. Robert G. L. Waite notes Hitler's recurrent fears of suffocation (see *The Psychopathetic God: Adolf Hitler* [New York: New American Library, 1977], 86, 488) and his stated need to eradicate feelings of guilt (17).

4. See the dedication of *Otherwise than Being* to the memory of "all victims of the same hatred of the other man, the same anti-semitism."

5. For charges of self-laceration, see Paul Ricoeur, *Oneself as Another*, trans. Kathleen Blamey (Chicago: University of Chicago Press, 1992), 335–55; for self-effacement, see Alain Badiou, *Ethics: An Essay on the Understanding of Evil*, trans. Peter Hallward (London: Verso, 2001).

6. For the problem of valorizing at once particular differences and difference as a category, see David. P. Haney, "Coleridge's 'Historic Race': Ethical and Political Otherness," in *Levinas and Nineteenth-Century Literature: Ethics and Otherness from Romanticism through Realism*, ed. Donald R. Wehrs and David P. Haney (Newark, DE: University of Delaware Press, 2009), 61–88.

7. See especially Lois Parkinson Zamora, *Writing the Apocalypse: Historical Vision in Contemporary U.S. and Latin American Fiction* (Cambridge: Cambridge University Press, 1988), 25–75.

8. Mario Vargas Llosa, *García Márquez: Historia de un deicidio* (Barcelona-Caracas: Monte Ávila Editores, 1971), 479. The translation is mine.

9. Miguel de Cervantes, *Don Quijote de la Mancha*, ed. Martín de Riquer (Barcelona: Éditorial Juventud, 1955), 172; *Don Quixote*, trans. Samuel Putnam (New York: Modern Library, 1949), 140. Further references will be to these editions and cited parenthetically in the text.

10. Gabriel García Márquez, *Cien años de soledad* (Madrid: Espasa-Calpe, S. A., 1982), 62; *One Hundred Years of Solitude*, trans. Gregory Rabassa (New York: Avon, 1970), 13, 14. Further references will be to these editions and cited parenthetically in the text.

11. This contrasts with the total asociality of similarly "mad" protagonists in "El licenciado Vidriera" and "El coloquio de los perros" in Miguel de Cervantes, *Novelas ejemplares II*, ed. Harry Sieber (Madrid: Ediciones Cátedra, 1982), 43–74, 299–359.

12. See Iris M. Zavala, "*One Hundred Years of Solitude* as Chronicle of the Indies," in *Gabriel García Márquez's* One Hundred Years of Solitude: *A Casebook*, ed. Gene H. Bell-Villada (Oxford: Oxford University Press, 2002), 109–25.

13. Joel W. Krueger, "Levinasian Reflections on Somaticity and the Ethical Self," *Inquiry* 51, 6 (2008): 603–26, 607 cited.

14. Lorna Wood elaborates these themes in relation to *Moby-Dick* in "Emmaneul Levinas and the American Renaissance Canon" in *Levinas and Nineteenth-Century Literature*, 189–97. Also see Claire Elise Katz, *Levinas, Judaism, and the Feminine: The Silent Footsteps of Rebecca* (Bloomington: Indiana University Press, 2003), esp. 55–65.

15. See Brian Conniff, "The Dark Side of Magical Realism: Science, Oppression, and Apocalypse in *One Hundred Years of Solitude*," in *Gabriel García Márquez's* One Hundred Years of Solitude: *A Casebook*, 139–52; Joyce Wexler, "The German Detour from *Ulysses* to Magic Realism," *Modern Language Quarterly* 79, 2 (2009): 245–68.

16. For García Márquez's loosely Marxist politics, see Gene H. Bell-Villado, *García Márquez: The Man and His Work*, 2nd ed. (Chapel Hill: University of North Carolina Press, 2010), 64–69.

17. Krueger, "Levinasian Reflections on Somaticity and the Ethical Self," 613, 615–16.

18. These themes, later monumentalized by Carlos Fuentes in *Terra Nostra*, trans. Margaret Sayers Peden (New York: Farrar, Straus, Giroux, 1976), *Terra Nostra* (Barcelona: Seix Barral, 1975), appear in Benito Perez Galdos's *Doña Perfecta* (Mexico: Editorial Orion, 1972 [1876]); Federico García Lorca, *La casa de Bernarda Alba*, in *Teatro selecto de Federico García Lorca*, ed. Antonio Callego Morell (Madrid: Escelicer, 1969); Julio Cortázar, "Casa tomada," in *Bestiario* (Buenos Aires: Editorial Sudamericana, 1951), 9–18.

19. This is thematically central to Cortázar's "Casa tomada," and equally prominent in Faulkner, whose influence upon García Márquez has been much remarked. See especially Bell-Villada, *García Márquez*, 81–85; Zamora, *Writing the Apocalypse*, 34–45.

20. See Pascal Boyer's *Religion Explained: The Evolutionary Origins of Religious Thought* (New York: Basic Books, 2001).

21. Lois Parkinson Zamora, *The Usable Past: The Imagination of History in Recent Fiction of the Americas* (Cambridge: Cambridge University Press, 1997), 77. For García Márquez's receptivity to Columbia's Indian and African cultural resources, see Bell-Villada, *García Márquez*, 15–24. Wexler points out that discussions of magical realism divide between "internationalists" and "Americanists" (249). See especially *Magical Realism: Theory, History, Community*, ed. Lois Parkinson Zamora and Wendy B. Faris (Durham, NC: Duke University Press, 1995); Jean-Pierre Durix, *Mimesis, Genres, and Post-colonial Discourse* (New York: St. Martin's Press, 1998); Wendy B. Faris, *Ordinary Enchantments: Magical Realism and the Remystification of Narrative* (Nashville, TN: Vanderbilt University Press, 2004).

22. Durix, 81.

23. See Bell-Villada's discussion (*García Márquez*, 103–13) of magical realism as articulating what Macondo or the Buendías experience collectively, communally, in memory, rather than as what actually happened.

24. See especially conjunctions of land ownership with crimes of incest and slavery in William Faulkner, *Go Down, Moses* (New York: Vintage, 1942), especially 254–315, 350–52.

25. See especially Lorraine Elena Roses, "The Sacred Harlots of *One Hundred Years of Solitude*," in *Gabriel García Márquez's* One Hundred Years of Solitude: *A* Casebook, ed. Gene H. Bell-Villada (Oxford: Oxford University Press, 2002), 67–78; Molly Monet-Viera, "Brujas, putas y madres: el poder de los márgenes en *La Celestina* y *Cien años de soledad*," *Bulletin of Hispanic Studies* 67 (2000): 127–46.

26. By contrast, the "charm" that Proust's Marcel discovers in various women, and in travel and art, follows from their evocations of alterity, as Levinas notes (*LR* 162–63).

27. Octavio Paz, *El laberinto de la soledad* (Mexico: Fondo de Cultura Económica, 1959), 9–17; *The Labyrinth of Solitude: Life and Thought in Mexico*, trans. Lysander Kemp (New York: Grove; London: Evergreen, 1961), 9–19. Further references will be to these editions and cited parenthetically in the text. For Levinas on solitude, see *TO* 42–57.

28. See Christian Moev's treatment of this theme in *The Metaphysics of Dante's* Comedy (Oxford: Oxford University Press, 2005), 77.

29. On Melquíades as supra-temporal narrator, see especially Michael Bell, "Nietzsche, Borges, García Márquez on the Art of Memory and Forgetting," *The Romantic Review* 98, nos. 2–3 (2007): 123–34.

30. See Lorna Robinson, "Latin America and Magical Realism: The Insomnia Plague in *Cien años de soledad*," *Neophilogus* 90 (2006): 249–69, 263 cited.

31. Emmanuel Levinas and Richard Kearney, "Dialogue with Emmanuel Levinas," in *Face to Face with Levinas*, ed. Richard A. Cohen (Albany: State University of New York Press, 1986), 26–27; *LR* 38–58; *EN* 207–17.

32. On Columbian political contexts, see Bell-Villada, *García Márquez*, 24–29, 103–05; Miguel Cabañas, "El sicario en su alegoría: la ficcionalización de la violencia en la novela columbiana de finales del siglo XX," *Taller de letras* 31, no, 2 (2002): 7–20; Roberto González Echevarría, "Archival Fictions: García Márquez's Bolívar File," in *Critical Theory, Cultural Politics, and Latin American Narratives*, ed. Steven M. Bell, Albert H. Le May, and Leonard Orr (Notre Dame: Notre Dame University Press, 1993), 183–207. On Mexican contexts, see Mariano Azuela, *Los de abajo: novella de la Revolutión Mexicana*, ed. John E. Englekirk and Lawrence B. Kiddle (New York: Mederith Corporation, 1971 [1915]); Carlos Fuentes, *La muerte de Artemio Cruz* (Mexico: Fondo de Cultura Económica, 1962).

33. Aureliano Segundo's extravagant celebrations much resemble Paz's account of the Mexican fiesta as a modality of solitude (see *El laberinto de la soledad*, 42–58, *The Labrinth of Solitude*, 47–64). On Macondo citizens' indifference to their own futures, see John Krapp, "Apathy and the Politics of Identity: García Márquez's *One Hundred Years of Solitude* and Contemporary Criticism," *LIT* 11, no. 4 (2001): 403–25.

34. See García Márquez, *Cien años de soledad*, 322–30, *One Hundred Years of Solitude*, 264–71; Galdos, *Doña Perfecta*, 133–87, *Doña Perfecto*, trans. Mary J. Serrano (New York and London: Harper and Brothers, 1895), 225–319.

35. On Pynchon's "collapse of the line separating the person reading the novel from the persons being read about," see Joel Bettridge, "Prurient Ethics: Representing Multiple Subjectivity in *Gravity's Rainbow*," *Pynchon Notes* 44–45 (Spring–Fall 2003): 53–72, 54 cited; Paul A. Bové, "History and Fiction: The Narrative Voice of Pynchon's *Gravity's Rainbow*," *MFS: Modern Fiction Studies* 50, no. 3 (2004): 657–680; John Hamill, "Looking Back on Sodom: Sixties Sadomasochism in *Gravity's Rainbow*," *Critique: Studies in Contemporary Fiction* 41, no. 1 (1999): 53–70. For Levinas's distinction between religion (stressing separation, responsibility) and cultic-ecstatic participation in the sacred, see especially Jeffrey Bloechl, *Liturgy of the Neighbor: Emmanuel Levinas and the Religion of Responsibility* (Pittsburgh: Duquesne University Press, 2000); Jeffrey Bloechl, ed., *The Face of the Other and the Trace of God: Essays on the Philosophy of Emmanuel Levinas* (New York: Fordham University Press, 2000); Jeffrey L. Kosky, *Levinas and the Philosophy of Religion* (Bloomington: Indiana University Press, 2001). On this distinction and advocacy of pluralism, see especially *NiTR* 136–60, *OS* 116–25, *EN* 155–58, *LR* 236–48; Howard Caygill, *Levinas and the Political* (London: Routledge, 2002).

36. For ways that art for Levinas may resist such appropriation, see Alain Paul Toumayan, "Levinas and French Literature," and Lorna Wood, "Emmanuel Levinas and the American Renaissance Canon," in *Levinas and Nineteenth-Century Literature: Ethics and Otherness from Romanticism through Realism*, ed. Donald R. Wehrs and David P. Haney (Newark, DE: University of Delaware Press), 126–47, 166–206.

37. Stefan Mattessich reads *Gravity's Rainbow* in terms of Deleuze and Guattari's *Anti-Oedipus* in *Lines of Flight: Discursive Time and Countercultural Desire in the Work of Thomas Pynchon* (Durham and London: Duke University Press, 2002), 70–206.

38. Thomas Pynchon, *Gravity's Rainbow* (New York: Viking, 1973), 3, 760. All further references are to this edition and cited parenthetically in the text.

39. Much discourse in *Gravity's Rainbow* links human suffering to consciousness's alienation from a primal unity. See Joseph W. Slade, "Religion, Psychology, Sex, and Love in *Gravity's Rainbow*," in *Approaches to Gravity's Rainbow*, ed. Clarles Clerc (Columbus: Ohio State University Press, 1983), 153–198; also James W. Earl, "Freedom and Knowledge in the Zone," and Charles Russell, "Pynchon's Language: Signs, Systems, and Subversions," in *Approaches to Gravity's Rainbow*, 229–50, 251–72; Lawrence Wolfley, "'Repression's Rainbow': The Presence of Norman O. Brown in Pynchon's Big Novel," *PMLA* 92 (1977): 873–89. For Heidegger's engagement with Rilke, see his "What are Poets For?" in *Martin Heidegger, Poetry, Language, Thought*, trans. Albert Hofstadter (New York: Harper and Row, 1971), 91–142.

40. Rainer Maria Rilke, *Duino Elegies*, trans. J. B. Leishman and Stephen Spender (New York: Norton, 1939), I. 1–2, 4–5, pp. 20, 21. References will be to this edition and henceforth cited parenthetically by line and page number. Except where amended, the translation is Leishman and Spender's. They comment that in the Angel "the limitations and contradictions of present human nature have been transcended," so that "the actual and the ideal, are one" (87–88). Also see Charles Hohmann, *Thomas Pynchon's* Gravity's Rainbow: *A Study of Its Conceptual Structure and of Rilke's Influence* (New York: Peter Lang, 1986), 283–324; Raymond M. Olderman, "The New Consciousness and the Old System," in *Approaches to* Gravity's Rainbow, ed. Clarles Clerc (Columbus: Ohio State University Press, 1983), 199–228; Mark Richard Siegel, *Pynchon: Creative Paranoia in* Gravity's Rainbow (Port Washington, NY: Kennikat Press, 1987), 89; Richard Locke, "*Gravity's Rainbow*," *The New York Times Book Review* (March 11, 1973): 2.

41. See Rainer Maria Rilke, *Sonnets to Orpheus*, trans. M. D. Herter Norton (New York: Norton, 1962), especially I, 23, pp. 60–61; also Heidegger, "What Are Poets For?," 97–98; Hohmann, *Thomas Pynchon's* Gravity's Rainbow, 325–33.

42. See Heidegger's "The Worldhood of the World" in *Being and Tme*, trans. John Macquarrie and Edward Robinson (Oxford: Basil Blackwell, 1973), I.3, 91–122, and Levinas's critique in *BPW* 5–8, *TI* 42–48, *OG* 172–77.

43. See Victoria de Zwaan, "*Gravity's Rainbow* as Metaphoric Narrative: Film, Fairy Tale and Fantasy in Pynchon's Germany," *Pynchon Notes* 54–55 (Spring–Fall 2008): 154–68; also Mattessich, *Lines of Flight*, 181–96; Hohmann, *Thomas Pynchon's* Gravity's Rainbow, 339–49; John O. Stark, *Pynchon's Fictions: Thomas Pynchon and the Literature of Information* (Athens: Ohio University Press, 1980), 152; Joseph W. Slade, *Thomas Pynchon* (New York: Warner, 1974), 237; Lance W. Ozier, "The Calculus of Transformation: More Mathematical Imagery in *Gravity's Rainbow*," *Twentieth Century Literature* 21, 2 (1975): 193–210.

44. Hohmann notes, "Slothrop/Orpheus is guilty of losing his Eurydices" (341), citing *Gravity's Rainbow* 471–72.

45. This theme is elaborated in George Orwell's *1984*, Joseph Heller's *Catch-22*, the works of Kurt Vonnegut. It is featured in critiques of corporate culture from Nathaniel West's *Miss Lonelyhearts* to the parody of insurance jargon in the film *The Incredibles*. Stencil, the protagonist of Pynchon's first novel, attempts to efface the singularity of responsibility by thinking and speaking of himself in the third person. See Thomas Pynchon, *V.* (New York: Modern Library, 1963), 62. The control *they* exercise over language and conceptuality in *Gravity's Rainbow* recalls Heidegger's treatment of how lapsing into the vocabulary of "the they" (*das Man*) immerses us in an "idle talk" (*Gerede*) "forgetful" of authentic being (*Being and Time*, I.4, 163–68; I.5, 203–24).

46. See Zamora, *Writing the Apocalypse*, 69–70; Hohmann, *Thomas Pynchon's* Gravity's Rainbow, 305–16.

47. Sigmund Freud, *Beyond the Pleasure Principle*, trans. James Strachey (New York: Liveright, 1950), 50.

48. Heidegger, *Being and Time*, I.4, 165.

49. See Thomas Pynchon, "Entropy" (1960), in Thomas Pynchon, *Slow Learner* (New York: Bantam, 1984), 65–86; *The Crying of Lot 49* (New York: Bantam, 1966), 61–62.

50. Heidegger, *Being and Time*, I.4, 165–66.

51. Mattessich, *Lines of Flight*, 83. For variations of humanism amid postmodern knowingness, see Thomas Schaub, *Pynchon: The Voice of Ambiguity* (Chicago: University of Chicago Press, 1981); Peter L. Cooper, *Signs and Symptoms: Thomas Pynchon and the Contemporary World* (Berkeley: University of California Press, 1983); Molly Hite, *Idea of Order in the Novels of Thomas Pynchon* (Columbus: Ohio State University Press, 1983); Louis Mackey, "Paranoia, Pynchon, and Preterition," and Craig Hansen Werner, "Recognizing Reality/Realizing Responsibility," in *Thomas Pynchon's "Gravity's Rainbow,"* ed. Harold Bloom (New York: Chelsea House, 1986), 53–68, 85–96. For a sharply nihilistic reading, see Zamora, *Writing the Apocalypse*, 66–71.

52. Steven G. Weisenburger, *A* Gravity's Rainbow *Companion: Sources and Contexts for Pynchon's Novel*, 2nd ed. (Athens and London: University of Georgia Press, 2006), 17.

53. See especially Slade, "Religion, Psychology, Sex, and Love in *Gravity's Rainbow*" and Charles Russell, "Freedom and Knowledge in the Zone," in *Approaches to* Gravity's Rainow, 153–68, 255–64.

54. Mattessich, *Lines of Flight*, 79.

55. Patrick McHugh, "Cultural Politics, Postmodernism, and White Guys: Affect in *Gravity's Rainbow*," *College Literature* 28, no. 2 (2001): 1–28, 2 cited.

56. If something like nomadic, deterritorialized anti-oedipal subjectivity is at play here, it seems to denote less transcendence through resistance, as Mattessich argues, than an alluring but ruinous temptation.

57. Levinas presents erotic objectification as paradoxically self-undermining: "It is necessary that the face have been apperceived for nudity to be able to acquire the non-signifyingness of the lustful. . . . The in appearance asocial relation of eros will have a reference—be it negative—to the social" (*TI* 262).

58. McHugh, "Cultural Politics, Postmodernism, and White Guys," 2.

59. Vladimir Nabokov, *Lolita* (New York: Berkeley Medallion, 1955), 130; Fyodor Dostoevsky, *Crime and Punishment*, trans. Jessie Coulson, ed. George Gibian, rev. ed. (New York: Norton, 1975), 13.

60. Charles Clerc, "Film in *Gravity's Rainbow*," in *Approaches to* Gravity's Rainbow, 103–51, 108 cited.

61. See Weisenburger, *A Gravity's Rainbow's Companion*, 258–59; also Bernard Duyhuizen, "'A Suspension Forever at the Hinge of Doubt': The Reader-Trap of Bianca in *Gravity's Rainbow*," *Postmodern Culture* 2, no. 1 (1991): 1–23.

62. John Hamill, "Looking Back on Sodom," *Critique: Studies in Contemporary Fiction* 41, no. 1 (1999): 53, 66.

63. On Pynchon's intimations of a "kinder" universe contesting dualistic metaphysics, see Hohmann, 144–56. Hohmann notes that Pynchon draws on Jewish mystical traditions, both Zohar and pre-Zohar sources (150–52). Levinas does likewise. See *EN* 228–31.

64. For Geli's association with the Zohar's *Shekhinah*, divine presence as a woman (bride of God or Israel), and so with time's redemption through creation's reparation [*tikkun*], see Hohmann, 151.

65. See Wood, "Emmanuel Levinas and the American Renaissance Canon," in *Levinas and Nineteenth-Century Literature*, 192–93.

Chapter Ten

The *Augenblick* of Reading in the Writing of J. M. Coetzee and Michael Ondaatje

Mike Marais

We yield to a stranger's embrace or give ourselves to the waves; for the blink of an eyelid our vigilance relaxes; we are asleep; and when we awake, we have lost the direction of our lives. What are these blinks of an eyelid, against which the only defence is an eternal and inhuman wakefulness? Might they not be the cracks and chinks through which another voice, other voices, speak in our lives? By what right do we close our ears to them?[1]

Emmanuel Levinas describes the self's "face-to-face" encounter with the otherness of the Other as an "unrelating relation" between "separated beings" (*TI* 295): while the self finds itself in a relationship, it is not with anything identifiable. What is at stake here is the pre-reflective, pre-cognitive, and non-intentional nature of the encounter. In terms of the trope of hospitality, which Levinas repeatedly enlists in his descriptions of this encounter, the Other, when he arrives, slips through the "outstretched nets" of consciousness like "a thief in the night." He arrives "unbeknownst to myself, 'slipping into me like a thief,'" that is, without "knocking," and hence "assigns me before I designate" him (*OB* 150). While the Other is a "visitor," in this idiom, he is one that exceeds the bounds of conventional hospitality: being uninvited, his arrival is wholly unexpected. Not having any advance knowledge of him, the host is unable to identify and thus place and locate this visitor. Accordingly, his visit is also a visitation in which he visits himself upon the host.

Jacques Derrida, in his description of unconditional hospitality, explains and elaborates on precisely this point. Unconditional hospitality, he argues,

237

denotes a receiving of difference "before any determination, before any anticipation, before any *identification*."[2] Given that the arrival of the stranger or Other is unannounced and wholly unexpected, she cannot be known in advance from within a priorly formed system of linguistic conceptuality. It follows that the host, in not being able to name, to grasp in language, the stranger, loses her sovereignty over and distance from this visitor. This is exactly what Levinas means when he says that the Other "assigns me before I designate" him. While I am in a relationship, it is not one of correlation.

Importantly, the time of this visit or visitation is beyond historical time. In Husserlian phenomenology, the consciousness of time, like all conscious experience, is intentional, that is, directed toward something. It follows that the self's inability, in the face-to-face encounter, to reduce the otherness of the Other to an object for intentional consciousness interrupts temporal experience: since this otherness is not an object, it is not present, presentable or representable. The *Augenblick* (which may be translated as "moment," "instant" or, literally, the "blink of an eyelid") of this encounter is thus a "lapse of time" (*OB* 38) or discontinuity, that cannot form part of a retentional past or a present from which the future may be anticipated. What is more, it cannot be remembered because a memory, in Husserlian phenomenology at least, must be intentional, that is, it must be of a specific experience that an intending subject has engaged in and thus undergone. For this reason, Levinas describes the *Augenblick* as "something irrecuperable, refractory to the simultaneity of the present, something unrepresentable, immemorial, prehistorical" (*OB* 50). The time of the Other is always immemorially past. In fact, the *Augenblick* can interrupt temporal experience precisely because it cannot be recuperated into history.

It is because of its immemorial nature that Levinas describes the effect on the self of the *Augenblick* of its encounter with the Other's otherness as a "trauma"(*OB* 148, 197). As I have already indicated, the self does not experience excessive alterity as a subject in control. Indeed, the event of the face-to-face encounter is marked by a loss of controlling consciousness. What characterizes the encounter with the Other, then, is exactly the subject's absence. In this regard, what Maurice Blanchot says about ecstasy has an obvious relevance for the face-to-face encounter:

> Ecstasy is without object, just as it is without a why, just as it challenges any certainty. One can write that word (ecstasy) only by putting it carefully between quotation marks, because nobody can know what it is about, and, above all, whether it ever took place: going beyond knowledge, implying un-knowledge, it refuses to be stated other than through random words that cannot guarantee it. Its decisive aspect is that the one who experiences it is no longer there when he experiences it, is thus no longer there to experience it. The same person (but he is no longer the same) may believe that he recaptures it in the past as one does a memory: I remember, I recall to mind, I talk or I write in a

rapture that overflows and unsettles the very possibility of remembering. All mystics, the most rigorous, the most sober (and first of all Saint John of the Cross), have known that that remembrance, considered as personal, could only be doubtful, and, belonging to memory, took rank among that which demanded escape from it: extratemporal memory or remembrance of a past which has never been lived in the present (and thus a stranger to all *Erlebnis*).[3]

To the extent that it is ecstatic, that it occurs when the self is beside itself, the event of the encounter with the Other's otherness is traumatic: it is an immemorial memory of a past that was never lived as a present; a past that cannot be forgotten because it cannot be remembered, and which therefore insists on being recalled. Through its refusal to be either remembered or forgotten, this memory traumatizes, even persecutes, the self.

My purpose in this chapter is to examine the seemingly intractable problems posed for novelistic representation by the *Augenblick* of the face-to-face encounter. How does one represent in fiction an encounter with that which is beyond presentation? In Blanchot's formulation, this question reads as follows: "How can I recover it, how can I turn around and look at what exists *before*, if all my power consists of making it into what exists *after*?"[4] Due to the extratemporal nature of the encounter with the Other, the fact that it was never "lived in the present," the writer is always belated and his representation is itself the loss of that which it seeks to present. In considering this question—a literary version of the ethical conundrum of how to receive the stranger without compromising his strangeness—I focus on Michael Ondaatje's and J. M. Coetzee's catachrestic depictions of unconditional hospitality in *The English Patient* (1992) and *Age of Iron* (1990), respectively. My ultimate argument is that these novels seek not so much to thematize such hospitality as to secure its enactment in their reception by the reader.

Ondaatje's *The English Patient* is about names and how the essences they assign overdetermine the ways in which we experience both others and ourselves. Throughout this novel, this preoccupation is evident in the manner in which characters identify themselves through identifying others. Kirpal Singh, for instance, is named Kip by the English, but later reasserts his Indian name and cultural identity as a determinate negation of Englishness. Even the European explorers' expeditions into the Libyan desert are portrayed as attempts at naming and claiming a space that is resistant to such procedures: "The desert could not be claimed or owned—it was a piece of cloth carried by winds, never held down by stones, and given a hundred shifting names long before Canterbury existed, long before battles and treaties quilted Europe and the East."[5] Importantly, too, this novel never allows the reader to forget that, since it was waged on the grounds of national identity, World War II was, in fact, enabled by the compulsion to identify, to construct forms of difference that inscribe indifference. In one of the novel's many reflections on how generic and generalizing discourses reduce singular entities to instances of the universal, the English patient, after asserting that "We are deformed by nation-states," describes how he, in the desert, wished "to remove the clothing" of his country, to "erase" his "name and the place" he had "come from," and eventually "came to hate nations" (147–48).

This, then, is the context in which Ondaatje introduces the novel's principal setting, the Villa San Girolamo. Albeit briefly, and quite incongruously, the Villa becomes the locus of a fragile ethical community in a world at war. As David Roxborough points out, this setting is "an Eden-like sanctuary, isolated from the horrors of the war that has mutilated the neighbouring countryside and continues to propagate destruction outside of Italy."[6] Or, in Ondaatje's own description, it is a "little cul-de-sac during the war."[7] What is particularly noteworthy about the Villa is its openness to the outside world. In this regard, it should be borne in mind that the boundaries of a house delimit not only an interior, but also an exterior. "[I]n order to constitute the space of a habitable house and a home," Derrida reminds us, "you also need an opening, a door and windows. There is no house or interior without a door or windows, you have to give up a passage to the outside world."[8] Since the very circumscription of the space of home opens it to the outside, against which it defines itself, against the intrusion of which it fortifies itself, it is telling that the Villa has been shelled and that now not just its windows and doors, but some of its walls open out to the external world, "accepting the habits of weather, evening stars, the sound of birds" (12). Quite self-consciously, then, this setting is figured as a site of unconditional hospitality in which visitors may arrive without knocking, without being invited or welcomed and therefore named. It is entirely apposite that the narrator should describe the Villa as a "palace of strangers" (312).

First and foremost among these strangers is Almásy who, in this makeshift hospital, receives the generous hospitality and unstinting care of the nurse Hana. Early in the novel, this character is described as "A man with no face. . . . All identification consumed in a fire . . . [with] nothing to recognize in him" (48), and is thereafter consistently depicted in terms of his anonymity and refractoriness to names. Strangeness is not peculiar to Almásy, though. The novel makes it clear that the respect for difference that distinguishes this community is even evinced by characters like Caravaggio and Hana who knew each other before the war. Rather than presuming any familiarity, Caravaggio responds to Hana as a stranger, loves her because of her strangeness:

> She had grown older. And he loved her more now than he loved her when he had understood her better, when she was the product of her parents. What she was now was what she herself had decided to become. . . . He could hardly believe his pleasure at her translation. Years before, he had tried to imagine

her as an adult but had invented someone with qualities moulded out of her community. Not this wonderful stranger he could love more deeply because she was made up of nothing he had provided. (234–35)

In that they do not exhibit the warring world's compulsion to identify, the "international bastards" (188) who populate this house form a community that is premised on an openness to strangeness. This is why the narrator, late in the narrative, describes the Villa and its residents as a tableau "flung ironically against this war" (296).

In Coetzee's *Age of Iron*, Mrs. Curren's house is also a site of hospitality in a society riven with conflict. Or, at least, it becomes such a site. Initially, it is described in terms of the absence of love: built "without love," it is "cold, inert," and "even the African sun has never succeeded in warming" it.[9] In this novel, house and host are clearly homologous structures. Like Mrs. Curren, the building is in a state of decay: "This house is . . . tired of holding itself together. The floorboards have lost their spring. The insulation of the wiring is dry, friable, the pipes clogged with grit. The gutters sag where screws have rusted away or pulled loose from the rotten wood. The rooftiles are heavy with moss" (13).[10] Significantly, too, the novel contains a description of the installation of burglar bars on the windows of the house (24–25). What is connoted here is the self's fear of exposure to difference, the integument or uncrossable boundary formed by intentional consciousness between the linguistically and culturally embedded subject and otherness. In fact, the very same idea emerges earlier in the text when Mrs. Curren, on pondering the paradox of the ugliness of a "not unattractive" woman she sees, ascribes the person's appearance to "A thickening of the membrane between the world and the self inside," an integument, that has been erected out of fear "that light, air, life itself were going to gather and strike her" (116).

By extension, Coetzee, through the image of the bars, suggests that the house is a jail , that the self is entrapped in itself, and that it is precisely "the thief in the night" who can save it from its incarceration in itself. Tellingly, in this regard, the house is referred to as a "cage" in which Mrs. Curren is "locked up" (25), and she later describes herself as "a woman in a burning house running from window to window, calling through the bars for help" (170). This description resonates with Levinas's ethic of hospitality, in which the self, through becoming a home for the other, is liberated from its imprisonment in itself. In substituting itself for the other person, the self "frees" itself "from ennui, that is, from the enchainment to itself, where the ego suffocates in itself" (*OB* 124). To open oneself to the Other is, for Levinas, "to free oneself . . . from closure in oneself" (*OB* 180). In this philosopher's imbricated stock of metaphors, the Other is a visitor, a breath of air that animates the host, releases him from suffocating or stagnating in the prison of monadic selfhood.

It is the arrival of Vercueil that precipitates the change that Mrs. Curren undergoes in the course of *Age of Iron*. On the very first page of the novel, the former, whose name is later associated with the Afrikaans word "Verskuil" (34), which means "concealed" or "hidden," is described as homeless, a stranger, and "A visitor, visiting himself on me [that is, Mrs. Curren]" (3)— this is to say in language similar to that which Levinas and, more latterly, Derrida use in talking of the advent of the Other. When Mrs. Curren returns from a visit to the hospital, Vercueil follows her into her home, "Uninvited" (74), a description that later recurs in her reference to him as "A man who came without being invited" (165). In the ethic of hospitality, Vercueil's uninvited entry into Mrs. Curren's house connotes the opening up of the self to the otherness of the other person, its infiltration of the self's consciousness. This is further suggested by Mrs. Curren's following thought on watching Vercueil eat the bread she has given him: "My mind like a pool, which his finger enters and stirs. Without that finger stillness, stagnation. . . . His dirty fingernail entering me" (74). The sexual innuendo in the passage implies that Vercueil, in entering Mrs. Curren's house, enters her very being. What is figured, here, is the self's penetration and possession by the Other.

Not surprisingly, the loveless, "cold" and "inert" house hereafter transforms into a place of love and care. In the closing pages of the novel, we learn that Vercueil, who has earlier moved into the house to minister to the dying Mrs. Curren's needs, now also occupies her bed: "We share a bed, folded one upon the other like a page folded in two, like two wings folded" (173). Although the transformation it has undergone is understated, and it cannot be described as ringing with "angelic chanting" (13) like the generous shoemaker's house in Leo Tolstoy's "What Men Live By," the house on Schoonder Street has nevertheless strangely and almost imperceptibly become a locus of selfless hospitality in a society in the throes of a civil war.

In both Ondaatje's *The English Patient* and Coetzee's *Age of Iron*, then, we find highly metaphorical descriptions of the effect on the self of the visit of the Other. What we do not find, however, is an attempt constatively to describe the *Augenblick* of the visit itself. In this respect, *Age of Iron* appears to differ markedly from *In the Heart of the Country*, a novel in which Coetzee does seem to attempt to present the protagonist Magda's possession by the voices of sky-gods. Paragraph 238 of this earlier novel describes a visit that Magda is paid by a boy, and ends with the following sentence: "That was the one visit" (125).[11] Paragraph 239 then commences with the words "I also hear voices" (125). The implication is that these voices *visit* Magda. At night, when she is asleep and thus no longer has the power, the self-possession, to invite, name, and therefore select, her guests, she receives these voices. They arrive uninvited "from another world" (127), we are told. Magda's following description of the visitation of the voices emphasizes the absence of intentionality in her hospitality: "The words I hear . . . sift down as they grow colder, just as the dew does . . . and to reach my ears by night, or more often in the early morning just before dawn, and to seep into my understanding, like water" (126–27). She becomes host to invisible and therefore uninvited visitors.

Even in this novel, though, we find that the description of the *Augenblick* of the Other's arrival undermines itself. Clearly, Magda describes what she cannot know and what is therefore beyond description: as much is implicit in the novel's concluding depiction of her hospitality, of her non-intentional waiting for visitors of whom she has no advance knowledge: "I do not dream at all nowadays, but sleep a blissful passiveness waiting for the words to come to me, like a maiden waiting for the holy ghost" (127). She waits without waiting for anything that may be defined as an object constituted by an intentional act of consciousness. That is, she waits without inviting, without awaiting, without expecting anything. It follows that her representation of the voices as "sky-gods" is a catachresis that announces its infinite distance from that which it only ostensibly seeks to denote, which it, in fact, self-consciously fails to denote. Accordingly, this novel indicates that its portrayal of the *Augenblick* of arrival destroys what it purports to present.

In *Age of Iron*, Coetzee does not appear overly concerned with representing the *Augenblick* of exposure to the otherness of the Other. Like Ondaatje, he seems satisfied simply to represent an effect of an absent cause. Nonetheless, the mere fact that much of what we read gestures towards this cause means that it is actually never entirely absent from the novel. For instance, the passage describing Vercueil's entry into Mrs. Curren's house is finally about its inability to describe the *Augenblick* of arrival. Through this passage, the text gestures elsewhere and, in the process, places the reader in relation to what exceeds its economy. My argument is that, in reading a novel like *Age of Iron*, the reader runs the risk of being exposed to and so acted upon, even traumatized, by this excession, this immemorial memory that the text cannot forget because it cannot be remembered. Differently put, the reader may come to share the trauma borne by the text. In the next section of this chapter, I show that both *The English Patient* and *Age of Iron* are self-reflexively aware of this possibility. They are aware, that is, that the reader, in the moment of reading them, could be visited by that which they have failed to thematize.

Earlier, I argued that Ondaatje's ethical community in the Villa San Girolamo is distanced from the violence of the warring world. I must now qualify this assertion: despite the fact that the patient, like the Libyan desert, is shorn of all identity, the other characters, initially at least, attempt to name him. What is important is not simply the failure of these attempts and the patient's resistance to names, which, incidentally, aligns him with the desert, but the effect of this failure on those who seek to name him. In the case of Hana, who first poses the question "Who are you?" to which he replies with the words "I don't know. You keep asking me" (5), we find that the compulsion to identify is inexplicably replaced with an urge to protect him from further such attempts. So, for instance, it is Hana who eventually tries to dissuade Caravaggio from *his* endeavor to divine the patient's identity: "I think we should leave him be. It doesn't matter what side he was on, does it? . . . You're too obsessed. It doesn't matter who he is" (176).

What precipitates Hana's change? While this question is not directly addressed in the novel, an answer of sorts does emerge in its description of Caravaggio's attempt to name and position the patient, to establish that he *is* Almásy and therefore a Nazi collaborator. Curiously, and very importantly, this interrogation proceeds along markedly literary lines: in listening to the patient's "errant" and "apocryphal" story, and "reorder[ing] the events" in its elliptical, non-linear sequence (263), Caravaggio behaves like a reader. This is further suggested by the patient's following question: "Or am I just a book? Something to be read" (269).[12] Significantly, too, Caravaggio abandons his attempt "to discover, to divine [information] out of this body on the bed" (262) because he is affected by what he hears:

> Caravaggio wants to rise and walk away from this villa, the country, the detritus of a war. . . . [H]e must get out of this desert, its architecture of morphine. He needs to pull away from the invisible road to El Taj. . . . It no longer matters which side he [that is, the patient] was on during the war. (267)

Despite his conscious, rational intentions, the horizon of expectations from within which he approaches it, the advance knowledge he possesses of it, Caravaggio is affected by the patient's story of ineffable pain and suffering, of unspeakable and therefore unforgettable loss. In the process, he loses the power, separation and distance inscribed by the subject position he has adopted in relation to it, and this enables the tale to invade his very being. What happens to him is thus very similar to the novel's description of what happens to Hana when she reads a novel: "She entered the story knowing she would emerge from it feeling she had been immersed in the lives of others, in plots that stretched back twenty years, her body full of sentences and moments, as if awaking from sleep with a heaviness caused by unremembered dreams" (13). Like Hana, Caravaggio does not simply enter the story he hears: it enters him. Through its affects, the trauma of pain and loss that its reduction to silence enables it to convey, this story penetrates his very being and, when he emerges from it, it is with "his body full of sentences and moments." The patient's story visits itself upon him.

It is for this reason that Caravaggio, in his turn, protects the patient from Kip's attempt to identify him as an "Englishman." The point of Caravaggio's words, "You don't know who this man is" (303), is palpably not that the patient is Hungarian rather than English but that he is more than these names.

Having been affected by the patient's story, Caravaggio is aware of the distance between the sign "Englishman" and that which it purports to designate. His intervention, which testifies to a restless dissatisfaction with the name's betrayal of what it names, constitutes an act of responsibility for the patient's otherness, difference, and strangeness.

Through the technique of irony, Ondaatje strives to align the response of the actual reader of the novel with that of its internal reader in the scene in which Kip names and comes close to killing the patient. Unlike Kip, the reader has been privy to the patient's story of ineffable suffering: she reads what Caravaggio hears. Consequently, in this scene, she, along with Caravaggio, knows that Kip is wrong, that he does not know who the patient is. The point, once again, is not just a case of mistaken identity but that the patient exceeds all markers of identity. In other words, the irony in this scene is not simply predicated on a disparity in knowledge between Kip, on the one hand, and the external and internal readers, together with the narrator, on the other hand. Instead, it is grounded in Caravaggio's and the reader's sense of the patient's singularity and therefore of his excession of generic and generalizing discourses. The reader's knowledge of the patient's singularity establishes an ironic disjunction between him and the identity that Kip imposes upon him. Because of her sense of his singularity, the reader is aware that the word "English" makes rather than represents an essence, and that the significatory field into which it incorporates the patient is extraneous to him.

Should the reader respond to the novel in the way I have described, he will have been affected despite himself, that is, notwithstanding the expectations about literature and assumptions about life in general that he has brought to the textual encounter. More to the point, he will have been affected by the otherness that the novel has failed to present but toward which its failure nonetheless gestures. In a manner prefigured by Hana's and Caravaggio's experience of reading, he will leave the text with it now in him, with his "body full of sentences and moments, as if awaking from sleep with a heaviness caused by unremembered dreams." Since they cannot be named, these sensations, catachrestically referred to as a "heaviness," cannot be fully remembered in the present. It follows, too, that, being "unremembered," they cannot be forgotten and so relegated to the past. They will thus live on in the reader and traumatize him because they cannot be conceptualized. The reader's inability to name and so control the "heaviness" of these sensations will enable them, like "unremembered dreams," to suffuse his waking life, to act on his actions through interrupting his uncontrollable compulsion to identify.

In *Age of Iron*, Coetzee also strives to expose the reader to an otherness that cannot be included in the text. If anything, this novel's self-reflexive exposition of how this may be achieved is even more detailed than it is in *The English Patient*. At one point in Coetzee's epistolary novel, his protagonist,

Mrs. Curren, addresses the reader of her letter, that is, her daughter, the actual reader's counterpart, as follows:

> I tell you the story of this morning mindful that the storyteller, from her office, claims the place of right. It is through my eyes that you see; the voice that speaks in your head is mine. Through me alone do you find yourself here on these desolate flats, smell the smoke in the air, see the bodies of the dead, hear the weeping, shiver in the rain. It is my thoughts that you think, my despair that you feel. . . . To me your sympathies flow; your heart beats with mine.
>
> Now, my child, flesh of my flesh, my best self, I ask you to draw back. I tell you this story not so that you will feel for me but so that you will learn how things are. It would be easier for you, I know, if the story came from someone else, if it were a stranger's voice sounding in your ear. But the fact is, there is no one else. I am the only one. I am the one writing: I, I. So I ask you: attend to the writing, not to me. If lies and pleas and excuses weave among the words, listen for them. Do not pass them over, do not forgive them easily. Read all, even this adjuration, with a cold eye. (95–96)

Here, Mrs. Curren confronts her reader with the unreliability concomitant on her location in language and culture. Because of her fallibility and the "worldliness" of her text,[13] her reader must read her account with a "cold eye" and thereby attempt to encounter those characters, like Vercueil, whom she has misunderstood, misrepresented, and therefore silenced. The reader, this is to say, must venture beyond the economy of Mrs. Curren's text through reducing the reductions of her representation. Should she do so, the "stranger's voice" may sound in her ear, that is, she may encounter Vercueil, whose strangeness has been familiarized by Mrs. Curren's generalizing discourse.

By implication, the reader must not follow the text, or must follow it through not following it. The paradox, here, is very similar to one that Derrida outlines in response to a question from Nicholas Royle in Michael Payne and John Schad's collection of interviews:

> [T]here is no simple opposition between the acolyte, or the "acoluthon" and the "*an*acoluthon." That is a problem, because to accompany, or to follow in the most demanding and authentic way, implies the "*an*acol," the "not-following," the break in the following, in the company so to speak. So, if we agree on this, a number of consequences will follow: you cannot simply oppose the acolyte and the anacoluthon—logically they are opposed; but in fact, what appears as a necessity is that, in order to follow in a consistent way, to be true to what you follow, you have to interrupt the following.[14]

Not to follow is part of the process of following. It may even enable following. This is the purport of what Coetzee seems to be saying in *Age of Iron*. The reader must follow the novel through interrupting the process of following. Instead of complying with its expectations of him, he must disobey the text, even its injunction to disobey it, and thereby refuse its address, its interpellation, its invitation, and its welcome. In order to be faithful to it, he must reject its appeal for love, loyalty, and friendship. Like Mrs. Curren's daughter, whom she describes as "someone grown strange, estranged" (127), he must estrange himself from the text and so become a stranger to it. If he succeeds in doing so, he will have entered the novel like a "thief in the night": that is, he will have invaded and penetrated it. In other words, he will have done what the police, Mrs. Curren's other unintended, and therefore unexpected, letter-readers, do. During their raid, these visitors not only invade Mrs. Curren's house, but also the text of her letter. When she reflects on this "visit" (154), she imagines "Soiled fingers turning the pages, eyes without love going over the naked words" (154). In fact, the uninvited visit these strangers pay the text is likened to rape: "The true purpose the touching, the fingering. The spirit malevolent. Like rape: a way of filthying a woman" (154). Only by violating the text, can the reader encounter the limits of not Mrs. Curren's but Coetzee's, and indeed his own, discourse, and thus the otherness of Vercueil. For the *Augenblick* of reading to become a possibility, the reader must read with a hostile eye.

In reading it with a "cold eye," and thereby perturbing and affecting it, the reader will have reduced the novel's reductions and thereby have altered it, made it different to, other than, the text she had initially expected. In short, the novel will have become a stranger to her and so have gained the ability to affect her, to place her in unrelating relation to the otherness to which it has failed to guide and lead her.[15] Precisely this possibility is suggested by the conjunction between Mrs. Curren's description of the "Soiled fingers" of her uninvited readers and her aforementioned reflection on Vercueil's uninvited entry into her house: "My mind like a pool, which his finger enters and stirs. Without that finger stillness, stagnation. . . . His dirty fingernail entering me" (74). In entering the text anonymously, the unwelcomed and unwelcome reader enables the text to enter her, uninvited. In terms of the imbricated metaphor of the self's entrapment, suffocating enclosure, and stagnation within itself, each liberates, animates, and "stirs" the other.

Coetzee's novel thus self-reflexively indicates that, should the reader follow it by parting company with it, he may experience the *Augenblick* of the encounter with the Other that is absent from its description of Mrs. Curren's relationship with Vercueil but nevertheless suggested by her reflection on the latter's penetration of her mind. The reader's reading will thus have performed what the text has been unable to thematize. What would have transpired is exactly what is, quite impossibly, represented in *Foe*. This earlier novel concludes with two companion passages describing two visits by an anonymous first-person narrator to Foe's house. In the first of these passages, an unnamed visitor, on arriving at Foe's house, enters a still and close space ("matches," we are told, "will not strike" in the "air of this room"[16]) where she or he encounters various of the novel's characters in postures of sleep. Like Magda at the end of *In the Heart of the Country*, they "sleep a blissful passiveness." Unlike her, though, they wait not for the words of sky-gods, but for the animating arrival of the uninvited, and therefore unexpected, reader, the estranged reader, or reader who has grown strange. They wait without awaiting, and expect the unexpected.[17] Figured here, through catachresis, is the *Augenblick* in which the novel unconditionally receives the reader who has refused its interpellation, its invitation and welcome.

In the second passage, the anonymous reader-figure again arrives uninvited, enters Foe's house, finds a manuscript, and begins to read, which is to say follow, the opening sentences of the novel. While this reader-figure may set out by following the text, she or he, it must be added, soon breaks company with it by proceeding to a space where it cannot take him or her: that is, to a wreck off Cruso's island, a watery underworld that is "not a place of words" (157). There, she or he finds the mute Friday (who, like Vercueil, is one of Coetzee's many "figures of alterity"[18]), and is reduced to a state of passivity on trying to question him and to open his mouth:

> From inside him comes a slow stream, without breath, without interruption. It flows up through his body and out upon me; it passes through the cabin, through the wreck; washing the cliffs and shores of the island, it runs northward and southward to the ends of the earth. Soft and cold, dark and unending, it beats against my eyelids, against the skin of my face. (157)

The point of this catachrestic passage is clear: through interrupting her following of it, the reader may enable the text to expose her to an otherness that exceeds its limits and which could therefore shut her eyes.

To moot the *Augenblick* of reading as a *possibility* open to the reader is, of course, quite simply outrageous. How can a reader read in order to *attain* a loss of control over himself, to *accomplish* a dispossession of himself? Although what is here at stake may begin as a possibility, it surely becomes a process that is not open to a subject acting in an arena of action, and is therefore, strictly speaking, an impossibility. Coetzee overcomes this particular objection not through the paradox of the impossible possibility but with the argument that the reader, in investing the text with agency, enables it to act on him. As I have argued, the reader, in reducing the text's reductions, furnishes it with the *ability* to affect him. It is in this way, then, that the *Augenblick* of reading becomes a possibility. The text inspires the reader to put in place the conditions that will enable it to affect him in a way that makes of reading an impossibility. By extension, the ending of *Foe* indicates that, as one reads its opening sentences, one reads of the possibility of forgoing all possibility, of invading and taking over the text so that it can invade and dispossess one of oneself.

If the reader's eyes were to be shut in the moment of reading, how would she respond? What would happen to her? Although I have argued throughout this chapter that one, in opening oneself to the Other, is freed from one's self-entrapment, that such exposure, in Levinas's lexicon, is "animation itself, breath, the breathing of outside air, where inwardness frees itself from itself, and is exposed to all the winds" (*OB* 180), I must now add that this freedom is a liberation into persecution and tyranny. To be liberated from one's onto-logical solitude is to be taken hostage by an otherness, to become responsible for it and, in the process, to be persecuted and traumatized by it. This, at least, is how Levinas describes self-substituting responsibility:

> It is being torn up from oneself, being less than nothing, a rejection into the negative, behind nothingness; it is maternity, gestation of the other in the same. Is not the restlessness of someone persecuted but a modification of maternity, the groaning of the wounded entrails by those it will bear or has borne? In maternity what signifies is a responsibility for others, to the point of substitution for others and suffering both from the effect of persecution and from the persecuting itself in which the persecutor sinks. Maternity, which is bearing par excellence, bears even responsibility for the persecuting by the persecutor. (*OB* 75)

For Coetzee, too, one's obligation to the Other is akin to maternal respon-sibility. Indeed, Friday, in his encounter with the reader-figure at the end of *Foe*, occupies the fetal position (157), a description that echoes Susan Bar-ton's depiction of him as "the child of his silence, a child unborn, a child waiting to be born that cannot be born" (122).

At issue in both Barton's description of Friday and Levinas's understand-ing of self-substituting responsibility as a "gestation of the other in the same" is the absolute nature of alterity, the irreconcilable, non-dialectical difference between the domains of the Same and the Other. Although it cannot enter the Same, the Other, through its infiltration of the self, demands to be born. This is why Barton evinces a restless dissatisfaction with the forms through which she, and indeed Foe, attempt to make sense of Friday and his silence. Be-cause she feels that these forms reduce and so betray Friday's otherness, she must not only betray them and so reduce their reductions, but also produce yet more. Whatever is "born," in terms of the metaphor of maternity, will therefore always be "stillborn or perhaps stifled," like the "dead babe" she and Friday encounter on their journey to Bristol (104–5). It is for this reason that the motif of the lost child features so prominently in *Foe*. In her quest to find the child she has lost, Barton must reject, and so abandon and betray, those possible impostors (such as the girl who claims to be her daughter) she encounters along the way. She must trust that which she cannot but doubt: namely, that when, or if, her actual daughter is eventually found, she will recognize her. Coetzee's point, here, is that Barton's quest is without term, that her responsibility is infinite.

It is exactly such a tyranny and persecution that await the reader who reads with eyes shut. As the fetal image in the ending of *Foe* implies, to read like this is to assume the burden of responsibility for Friday. It is to be taken hostage by an otherness that is otherwise than being and yet insists on coming into being. Implicit in both *Foe* and *Age of Iron* is thus a rather lugubrious irony. For the *Augenblick* to occur in reading, the reader must read with a "cold eye": he must betray the text in order to reduce its reductions, that is, the very reductions to which it itself, in its restless dissatisfaction with itself, has self-consciously drawn his attention. Should he succeed in doing this, the reader will have exposed himself to the otherness the text has inevitably reduced and, in the process, its restless dissatisfaction with itself will have become his own.

Levinas is, of course, famously suspicious of artistic representation, maintaining that the artwork, in its inability to approach the Other, is inherently irresponsible (*RS* in *CCP* 1–14). By contrast, my argument has been that Ondaatje and Coetzee's fiction demonstrates that literary art may traumatize the reader and thereby induce an effect that is uncannily similar (yet not identical) to the kind of traumatic temporal interruption of which Levinas repeatedly writes. I must emphasize that, in conducting this argument, I have sought not to counter Levinas's denunciation of the artwork by demonstrating the aesthetic's inherent ethicality. On the contrary, one of my principal contentions has been that the novels in hand draw attention to their referential inadequacy, their distance from the face, and therefore in fact concur with Levinas's assessment of the artwork's representational reduction of the Other. My point, though, is that the literary artwork, while not inherently ethical, may yet become so in its relationship with the reader. What is at stake then is not simply what the reader reads, but also how texts call the reader to read. With this in mind, I have shown that it is precisely through exposing their referential inadequacy that Coetzee's novels call on the reader to reduce their reductions. In so doing, they require their reader to share, rather than simply judge, their responsibility for the Other.

If the reader responds to the literary artwork's call, she will nevertheless have done so despite herself. As I have demonstrated, each of the novels discussed self-reflexively entertains the possibility of a pre-reflective encounter in which it unexpectedly visits itself upon the reader or, as Levinas might put it, slips into her like a thief in the night. In this *Augenblick*, the enraptured reader loses all control over what she reads. Should this happen, the work will have interrupted her ontological solitude, invaded her being, and so prevented her from returning to herself. In other words, it will have initiated the kind of irreversible movement of infinitization from Same to Other that distinguishes Levinas's ethical relationship.

NOTES

1. J. M. Coetzee, *Foe* (Johannesburg: Ravan, 1986), 30.

2. Jacques Derrida, *Of Hospitality: Anne Dufourmantelle Invites Jacques Derrida to Respond*, trans. Rachel Bowlby (Stanford: Stanford University Press, 2000), 77.

3. Maurice Blanchot, *The Unavowable Community*, trans. Pierre Joris (Barrytown, New York: Station Hill, 1988), 18–19.

4. Maurice Blanchot, "Literature and the Right to Death," in *The Work of Fire*, trans. Charlotte Mandell (Stanford: Stanford University Press, 1995), 327.

5. Michael Ondaatje, *The English Patient* (London: Bloomsbury, 2004), 147. Subsequent page references are to this edition of the novel.

6. David Roxborough, "The Gospel of Almásy: Christian Mythology in Michael Ondaatje's *The English Patient*," *Essays on Canadian Writing* 67 (Spring 1999): 239.

7. Quoted in Roxborough, 239.

8. Derrida, *Of Hospitality*, 61.

9. J. M. Coetzee, *Age of Iron* (London: Secker and Warburg, 1990), 13. Subsequent page references are to this edition of the novel.

10. In an e-mail letter to me, Don Wehrs points out that the description of Mrs. Curren's house is fairly close to the extended opening description of the Maison Vauquer, the rundown boardinghouse in Balzac's *Père Goriot*. He also notes that the figurative equation of house and isolated ego has many correlates—for instance, Edgar Allan Poe's House of Usher—and that the invasion or penetration of the self/house resonates interestingly with Julio Cortazar's "House Taken Over" ("Casa Tomada").

11. J. M. Coetzee, *In the Heart of the Country* (Johannesburg: Ravan, 1978). Subsequent page references are to this edition of the novel.

12. See Kristina Kyser, "Seeing Everything in a Different Light: Vision and Revelation in Michael Ondaatje's *The English Patient*," *University of Toronto Quarterly* 70, no. 4 (2001): 895.

13. Edward W. Said, "The World, the Text, and the Critic," in *The World, the Text, and the Critic* (Cambridge, MA: Harvard University Press, 1983), 35.

14. Jacques Derrida, "following theory: Jacques Derrida," in *life.after.theory*, ed. Michael Payne and John Schad (London: Continuum, 2003), 7.

15. Here my argument intersects with that of Johan Geertsema, "Irony and Otherness: A Study of Some Recent South African Narrative Fiction" (Doctoral thesis, University of Cape Town, 1999), 72–86. After commenting on Levinas's argument on the Other's ability to interrupt the Same, and the fact that such interruption becomes part of that which it interrupts, Geertsema considers the necessity of reducing "the degree of betrayal of the other" by incessantly interrupting interruption. He maintains that such an "interruption of the interruption of the conceptualisation of the other" may be explained in terms of irony.

16. J. M. Coetzee, *Foe* (Johannesburg: Ravan, 1986), 157. Subsequent page references are to this edition of the novel.

17. For an insightful discussion of Coetzee's staging of the paradox of expecting the unexpected in *The Master of Petersburg*, see Derek Attridge, *J. M. Coetzee and the Ethics of Reading: Literature in the Event* (Scottsville: University of KwaZulu-Natal Press/Chicago: University of Chicago Press, 2005), 121–24.

18. Attridge, 12.

VI

Levinas and Temporal Fracturing in New European and Postcolonial Fiction

Chapter Eleven

The Art of Time

Levinasian Alterity and the Contemporary Spanish Novel

Nina L. Molinaro

For Florence Belle Tuininga, *in memoriam*

For readers unfamiliar with any of the terms of my title, it may not be immediately obvious that the "time" of Emmanuel Levinas's revolutionary notion of ethical alterity can and perhaps even must be turned towards the "art" of the contemporary Spanish novel.[1] As a preliminary and partial starting point, Levinas offers to students and scholars of all literature, as well as to those who attempt to account for perception and subjectivity, a philosophical model of ethics as anticipating and exceeding metaphysics and epistemology. And temporality occupies a crucial place in his conception of otherness as a means to adduce the relationship between Being and Otherness that transcends the imposition of ontological symmetry.[2] Because for Levinas the structure of time animates the structure of ethics, I intend to track alterity, together with the interdependent stories of synchrony and diachrony, in Marta Sanz's *El frío* (*Cold*) (1995), Belén Gopegui's *Tocarnos la cara* (*To Touch Our Faces*) (1995) and Luisa Castro's *La fiebre amarilla* (*Yellow Fever*) (1994). These three contemporary Spanish novels suggest some of the ways in which narrative fiction shadows the temporal movement of ethicality.[3] What is exchanged in the narration of time and otherness and how is such an exchange realized? How can the intentional conscious perception of time surpass duration in order to broach otherness, without reducing it to so many chronologies of the Same?[4] Among the numerous (and ever increasing) manifestations of the contemporary Spanish novel, I am particularly interested in the texts of a recently emerged cohort of novelists in Spain, provisionally grouped under the derivative moniker of "Generación X."[5] Their fictional works have thus far defied easy classification, in part because they strive to communicate the urgency and timeliness of an ethics of alterity and in part because they strenuously contest the notion that knowledge is power. Spain's Gen X writers are not philosophers and they are not, for the most part, philosophically self-conscious. They generally do not articulate their primary concerns as either ontological or ethical, but they do maintain that, in varying ways and by various routes, human subjectivity is fragmented and contentious, and that it eschews both rationality and the so-called unity attributed to consciousness. Moreover, these writers uniformly explore subjectivity in relation to sociality and, I would propose, to time.

Any study of Levinas and fiction must acknowledge his difficult position on art, and more specifically on literature.[6] As Alain Paul Toumayan concisely summarizes, art for Levinas "is not the founding but the foundering of the world."[7] Although he ultimately dismantles many of the precepts of Platonism, Levinas shares with Plato a questioning of art, partly on the basis of its inherent illusion and capacity for mimicry (i.e., the image), and partly because art supposedly congeals time into some sort of timeless valuation. The first encourages disengagement, and discourages responsibility, in the perceiver, whereas the second consolidates subjectivity and reason. As Levinas states in the opening lines to one of his earliest commentaries on aesthetics, "the function of art is expression, and . . . artistic expression rests on cognition. An artist—even a painter, even a musician—tells. He tells of the ineffable. An artwork prolongs, and goes beyond, common perception" (*RS* 130). Telling unavoidably comprises and displays time as sequence and extension. And for Levinas the time of art dislodges alterity by universalizing, and therefore homogenizing, human subjects and human awareness.

Given Levinas's fluctuating antipathy towards aesthetic objects, whereby "the Infinity of the idea is idolized in the finite, but sufficient, image" (*TI* 140), one might well be tempted to discard narrative fiction, surely the quintessential expression of telling, as all too emblematic of the perilous distractions of literature. To make matters worse, the genre of narrative and the scholarly apparatus that accompanies it have long been pulled towards the pleasures of mimeticism, resolution, and the consolidation of identity, to name only some of the totalizing impulses gathered together under the broadly conceived label of realism. Nevertheless, and in spite of his protestations to the contrary, the majority of Levinas's philosophical expositions are rife with literary examples, many of them narrative, even to the point that he has astonishingly proposed that "it sometimes seems to me that the whole of philosophy is only a meditation of Shakespeare" (*TO* 72). In the specific milieu of narrative fiction, one might well counter that all narratives, fictional and otherwise, are always more or less about selves and others in relation and, as Levinas himself postulates, "every social relation leads back to the presentation of the other to the same without the intermediary of any image or sign, solely by the expression of the face" (*TI* 213).[8]

Perhaps the lingering ethicality of narrative fiction can be approached exegetically by means of temporality;[9] one might in fact assert that the story of ethical alterity is the story of time (and vice versa). To that end, Levinas opposes to the seductive rhythms of poetic activity "the language that at each instant dispels the charm of rhythm and prevents the initiative from becoming a role," and he further proposes that language "is *rupture and commencement*, breaking of rhythm which enraptures and transports the interlocutors—*prose*" (*TI* 203, emphasis mine). The discourse of prose, he appears to imply, pushes against the idolatry of the (poetic) image precisely by pursuing ethicality into time, by interrupting the duration of human perception, and by imagining the break of alterity as fundamentally temporal.

In its most simplistic formulation, for Levinas the entrance of alterity into being, our always already present ethical answerability to and for the Other and others, reveals diachrony, or what Sam B. Girgus has referred to as "a time of disruption,"[10] because of the impossibility of temporal coincidence between Self and Other; the perceiving self can never share the same time as the Other. Although Levinas develops and refines his theory of the temporalization of ontological asymmetry throughout the six decades of his scholarly career, he explicitly hinges time to alterity almost from the beginning, and in particular in *Time and the Other,* published originally in French as *Le temps et l'autre* in 1947. There he critiques Martin Heidegger's conception of the encounter between Being and itself, which is confirmed and prolonged through "ecstatic temporality": "in Heidegger there is a distinction [between *Sein* and *Seindes*, between *existing* and *existent*], not a separation. Existing is always grasped in the existent, and for the existent that is a human being . . . existing is always possessed by someone" (*TO* 45). Levinas posits that time is instead the necessary pre-condition for the encounter between Being and Other, an encounter that forestalls the autonomy of the transcendental Ego which has underwritten, in one form or another, all of Western philosophy. He assigns the term diachrony to his understanding of time as "this *always* of noncoincidence, but also the *always* of the *relationship*, an aspiration and an awaiting" (*TO* 32), and he devotes a considerable part of his life's work to the elaboration of diachrony as the temporal dimension of alterity.[11]

In order to contest the self-sufficiency of Heidegger's *Dasein*, by which Being comprehends itself through mortality, Levinas theorizes death as beyond "my" experience because it is incomprehensible:

> This approach of death indicates that we are in relation with something that is absolutely other, something bearing alterity not as a provisional determination we can assimilate through enjoyment, but as something whose very existence

is made of alterity. My solitude is thus not confirmed by death [as Heidegger
would have it] but broken by it. (*TO* 74)

He will later elaborate other metaphors such as fecundity, paternity and eros
to depict the encounter between the subject and others, but Levinas's initial
conceptualization of death as the defining futural event in human experience
remains critical to his successive efforts to conceptualize the time of alterity.

In order to better understand the time of diachrony, Levinas proceeds, in
Time and the Other, to unpack the reified temporal notion of synchrony. He
contends that Western philosophy has, at least since the exposition of Kant's
I think, privileged time as synchrony, whereby the Ego confirms coherence
and continuity through its unproblematic and unmediated consciousness.
This willed illusion of temporal omniscience, what Levinas calls "the egology of presence affirmed from Descartes to Husserl" (*TO* 99), celebrates the
dominion of individual self-awareness and the metaphysical ideal of rational
autonomy in which "'I think' comes down to 'I can'—to an appropriation of
what is, to an exploitation of reality" (*TI* 46). As part and parcel of such an
ideal, all temporal separation, rupture, discontinuity, unknowability and, to
use Levinas's preferred term, mystery is reduced to "the egology of synthesis, the gathering of all alterity into presence, and the synchrony of representation" (*TO* 100). As the next logical step in the so-called presentism of
Western metaphysics, the single and solitary subject successfully claims time
for itself: "The subject is alone because it is one. . . . Solitude is thus not only
a despair and an abandonment, but also a virility, a pride and a sovereignty"
(*TO* 54-55). In synchrony, so Heidegger's story goes, solitude is affirmed
through temporal duration, in which the perceiving self remembers the past
and anticipates the future as harmonious and supremely legible extensions of
the present; one present signifies all presents and "my now" flows unchecked
into "our now." The systematic reductiveness of synchrony forecloses all
(other) temporal possibilities, and with them the very notion of otherness.

In the third section of *Totality and Infinity* (1961), Levinas revisits the
detachment of synchrony as "the power that beings placed in relation have of
absolving themselves from the relation" and the pluralism of diachrony as
"the *surplus* of the social relation, where the subjectivity remains in face
of . . . and is not measured by truth" (220, 221). Ever careful to eschew
negative claims, he explains the independence beyond causality implied by
diachrony in the following way: "A being independent of and yet at the same
time exposed to the other is a temporal being: to the inevitable violence of
death it opposes its time, which is postponement itself" (*TI* 224). Here and
elsewhere Levinas contests the Heideggerian supposition that being is essentially temporal by arguing that, prior to temporal essence or synchrony, there
stretches "the other who, as infinity, opens time, transcends and dominates
the subjectivity (the I not being transcendent with regard to the other in the

same sense that the other is transcendent with regard to me)" (*TI* 225). He theorizes ontology as asymmetrically relational and therefore unavoidably temporal: because my indebtedness to the Other, who owes nothing to me, precedes my being, there can be no origin, no first cause, and neither can there "be" a future. Rather, as Levinas had already indicated in his previous work, "the future is what is not grasped, what befalls us and lays hold of us. The other is the future. The very relationship with the other is the relationship with the future" (*TO* 77). If ethical responsibility anticipates ontology, and if the self can only approach the Other in the futural face-to-face, the horizon of which is death, then alterity can only be conceived, perceived, and received temporally; the present and presence of the self is graspable only through the future of the other and the Other as future.

If time permeates the scene and story of ethics, of "telling being to the Other," then time, in the Levinasian paradigm, also stretches beyond discursive essence, or the Said, through Saying.[12] At the outset of *Otherwise than Being,* Levinas enunciates time as essence and then articulates "the temporal flow [as] the differing of the identical" (*OB* 9). Against temporal recuperation or synchrony, he juxtaposes "a lapse of time that does not return, a diachrony refractory to all synchronization, a transcending diachrony" (*OB* 9). Diachrony, or the temporalization of ontological ambiguity, expresses as equivocation and enigma by referencing an irrecoverable and unrepresentable past. We cannot experience or know the immemorial past through either memory or history. Levinas describes the immemorial past thus:

> This past is without reference to an identity naively—or naturally—assured of its right to presence, where everything must have begun. In this [ethical anteriority of] responsibility I am thrown back toward what has never been my fault or my deed, toward what has never been in my power or in my freedom, toward what has never been my presence, and has never come into memory. (*TO* 111)

The immemorial past is perforce beyond knowledge and chronology. Once again, however, the relational base of Levinasian ethics offers a measure of coherence: "the relationship with a past that is on the hither side of every present and every re-presentable . . . is included in the extraordinary and everyday event of my responsibility for the faults or the misfortune of others, in my responsibility that answers for the freedom of another" (*OB* 10). The freedom of another can never begin in the same present, occupy the same instant and/or make itself known to the perceiving subject. Ethical responsibility insures that an individual consciousness can never subsume the Other by means of duration because the knower is always already located in a chronology that it can never comprehend via the Said. In sum, synchrony constitutes the name that Levinas assigns to our illusion of temporal mastery and diachrony the name by which our experiences of the present become graspable through otherness.

How, then, does temporal alterity intercede in Spain's Gen X novels, especially given the fact that the novelists, in their literary texts, have all but effaced any reference to their recent traumatic national past?[13] While academics, journalists and publishers do not necessarily fix upon the same set of characteristics when they discuss this collection of writers, they do concur that the authors and texts in question diverge from their literary predecessors, that the novels project recurring elements and that the writers are noticeably affected by the discrete historical circumstances of post-Franco Spain.[14] Given that the definitive interpretation of Francoism is, to my knowledge, yet to be written, it is exorbitantly hasty to formulate a conclusive metaphysics concerning what has succeeded it. Nonetheless, as a prospective epigraph to any such elaboration, commentators agree that the writers of this generation, born between 1960 and 1971, have matured in a country dissimilar from but related to the Spain of their parents and grandparents; they have experienced neither the Spanish Civil War (1936–1939) nor the austerity measures and reactionary political regime that followed; they possess a technological savvy and accessibility that confirms their participation in a globalized (and globalizing) economy; they and their peers work, think, and play in the most liberal and heterogeneous political environment in Spanish history; this generation of writers has more publishing venues available to them; and more writers in Spain than ever before are vying for readership, literary prizes and book contracts.[15]

Within the generation, scholars have noted several additional phenomena. First, the Gen X writers, most of whom began publishing during the 1990s, were originally marketed by the national editorial complex as trendy, innovative, and young. Second, the writers themselves have generally ignored or rejected all claims of orthodoxy or shared identity, itself indicative of a commonality. And third, the critical and commercial fortunes of the generation as a whole were originally woven into the public recognition and circulation of a much smaller subgroup of writers whose novels explicitly imitate the style and ideology of "dirty realism," a North American literary phenomenon canonized in Douglas Coupland's popular novel *Generation X: Tales for an Accelerated Culture* (1991).[16] Bill Buford describes dirty realism thus: "it is realism so stylized and particularized—so insistently informed by a discomforting and sometimes elusive irony. . . . [I]t's what's not being said— the silences, the elisions, the omissions—that seem to speak the most."[17] In the arena of Hispanism, Coupland's term was appropriated to at least two ends: either critics conflated all of Spain's Gen X writers with the subgroup of "dirty realists" or they ignored (and, in the main, continue to ignore) any authors who did not pertain to the subgroup.

Moreover, most of these writers publish in multiple literary genres, are literary critics or journalists, and/or have taught or currently teach in Spain's educational system. As an indication of larger demographic and social changes in Spain and elsewhere, scholars have unanimously claimed gender as a predominant factor in both the publication and the reception of the generation. More women than ever before are writing and reading narrative fiction in Spain, and many of the most prominent women writers now publishing in Spain are affiliated with the Generation X.[18] Ironically, other markers of cultural heterogeneity within Spain vis-à-vis this generation, such as race and ethnicity, sexuality, and linguistic and regional specificity, have, by and large, been ignored by critics, a move that, in and of itself, corroborates the centripetal energies of homogenization inevitably at work in any generational criteria.

Although all of the aforementioned parameters have undoubtedly contributed to the acknowledgment and dissemination of Spain's Gen X writers, their novels far exceed such socio-historical considerations. While the novelists do not uniformly embrace a single approach to alterity, they, like Levinas, consistently attend to the insoluble quality of humanness and the inescapable violence that occurs when a subject attempts to incorporate into itself all that is other, external, unknowable, in a word *infinite*. Gen X novelists explicitly arrange their narrative texts around human relationships, around the perceptions of others and otherness, and around the ways in which alterity approaches, interrupts and inhabits being, language, perception, and responsibility. As three related yet distinct manifestations of these concerns, I now turn to the temporalization of ethical alterity in Sanz's *El frío*, Gopegui's *Tocarnos la cara* and Castro's *La fiebre amarilla*.[19] In electing a trio of novels I do not mean to suggest any kind of progression, temporal or otherwise, among them. Rather, in each novel I extract one exposition of temporal alterity from among the several that thread through all three novels. Although in each fictional text, time moves towards others and otherness to different ends and by different means, in all three novels at least one woman remembers herself and others (and remembers herself to others), with the apparent goals of restoration and return.[20] Each novel frames the responsibility of alterity from multiple perceptual thresholds. And each connects time to relationship and to ethical responsibility: *El frío* sifts the present violence of sameness through a failed amorous triangle; *Tocarnos la cara* stages the encounter between spectacle and fraternity against the backdrop of competing pasts; and *La fiebre amarilla* weaves a ghost story into paternity and death at the cusp of futurity. In conjunction, the three novels provocatively, albeit inconclusively, gesture towards the temporalization of Levinasian alterity.

Composed of thirty-five sequentially numbered chapters, Marta Sanz's *El frío* conjoins three shifting viewpoints: an unnamed woman recounts a bus trip to call on her lover Miguel, who is interned in a sanitarium for an undisclosed psychiatric disorder; Blanca Egar, a nurse at the sanitarium, sadistically infantilizes her patient, Miguel, until he conclusively rebels; and a man named Miguel rejects his visiting lover and punishes his perverse nurse. In the odd-numbered chapters, the woman recollects, mostly in the first-person and in the present tense, her journey to and from the sanitarium and her emotional history with Miguel. The even-numbered chapters seesaw between the conflicting visions of Blanca and Miguel as each invades and retreats from the other. Braided together, the chapters calculate the ways in which human subjects encounter and attempt to recover from the temporal trauma of otherness.

El frío novelizes the exhibition of failed proximity, the inside-out of eros, and the pathologization of selves who try to reclaim consciousness by dictating (to) the other. In order to lay claim to themselves, the three characters attempt to re-member each other, such that the novel elucidates synchrony as salvation. The first lines of the text, which are not, to be certain, the originary lines, read as follows: "Tú lo sabes ya de sobra, pero yo voy a repetírtelo. No me has dejado decir ni una palabra. Me has apartado suavemente; te has dado la vuelta" [You already know it only too well, but I'll tell you again. You haven't let me say a single word. You have gently removed me; you have turned your back on me].[21] The unidentified addressee to whom the narrating woman speaks already knows her story disproportionately, prior to the time of their shared story, and she, in turn, has already fitted the I to itself. She discursively predicts and remarks her lover's dismissal and distance, thus reinforcing the desirable solitude that she hopes to experience as an antidote to her current suffering. Synchrony names this aloneness as deeply temporal; as Levinas has declared, "Existing is mastered by the existent that is identical to itself—that is to say, alone. But identity is not only a departure from self; it is also a return to self. The present consists of an inevitable return to itself" (*TO* 55). It is this synchronous "return to self" that spreads into and throughout the temporal aspects of *El frío*.

In the early installments of her narrative, and as she metaphorically and literally travels towards Miguel, the woman simultaneously recalls and recoils from the illusion of their common time, which is completed and therefore past. She accomplishes this by lacing the times of before, during, and after into a causality; at the same time she dons and then discards, like so many ill-fitting coats, the identities of those around her. Whether it be the homeless woman, the disapproving businessman or the loquacious bus driver, all of those external to her immediate perceptual boundaries jeopardize her renewed control, based in the distinction between inside and outside. Insofar as she insists on lucidity by impressing her uncontested self-awareness into the events before and after her present, she affirms and sustains sequence and agency. Insofar as past and future disrupt and destabilize her presence, and insofar as others aggressively (re)insert themselves into her consciousness, alterity constrains any possible knowledge of self and other in the fictional world(s) created in and by Sanz's novel. But coherence and continuity, as expressions of Levinas's Said, win out as they must, according to the logic of affliction that girds *El frío*.

The opposite perceptual play molds the alternating plotline, filtered through an omniscient narrative voice, which teeters between the perspectives of Blanca and Miguel. As befits the rising tension that suffuses these intervals, specific details about their communal physical environment are grounded in the present moment and encroach upon any ethical interaction. Tellingly, Miguel appears, prior to Blanca, on the scene in the second chapter and, after finalizing a series of mundane activities, he contemplates his inverted reflection in the floor tiles beneath him. Blanca intrudes into the moment and initiates the chain of occurrences that will typify their relationship: "Blanca llega y le coge por el codo; cada día, en ese preciso instante, Miguel levanta la cabeza y sonríe" [Blanca arrives and takes him by the elbow; each day, at that precise instant, Miguel raises his head and smiles] (11). With painstaking precision, the all-seeing narrator describes the spatial arrangement of the rooms, doors, and walls in the same present tense that she or he uses to locate the unfolding subjugation between patient and nurse. The past, which can only be a perfect duplication of the current moment, does not interrupt and the only sign of a future incident consists of Blanca's announcement to Miguel that a visitor will arrive at three o'clock, effectively positioning the "other" woman's story inside of their joint futures, where it will languish as the narrative advances.

El frío concerns the ethics of relationality, but turned upside down. The proximity of the other person, which, for Levinas, commands ethical responsibility, has always already distressed the perceiving subject, who attempts to transform memory into causality and expectations into inevitability. The three characters drag themselves through time; that is, they justify their anguish by establishing and inserting themselves and each other into a chronology. As the original and final voice, the first-person woman upholds her victimization at the hands of Miguel, a role that she has repeated prior to her narration and is repeating in the process of telling her story. She transposes her now-terminated entanglement with Miguel onto the bus passengers around her and rehearses the phases of the pair's history by constantly reading herself against and into the actions that surround her. As only one among copious instances, after silently promising that she will ignore the kissing couple behind her on the bus, she mentally spews forth a litany of insults, only to recall that those very same insults were, at some other point in time, directed towards her and her lover.

The structure of the novel also twists time towards the additional characters who, to a certain extent, imitate the relational dynamics that emanate from the first-person narrator's recovery of her lover and their shared past. In the sections involving Miguel and Blanca, one perception pervades the omniscient voice, one character speaks and thinks, and one will clearly dominate. Their mutual story, which never ventures beyond the physical space of the psychiatric institution, could be described as the tale of Miguel's revenge and yet another chronicle of causality. The chapters devoted to the sadomasochistic duo are replete with horrific imagery and graphic language. In contrast to the intensely interiorized tone and direction of the unnamed woman's narrative, the omniscient narrator externalizes the incidents in the sanitarium by concentrating on the sensorial presentation of bodies, food, textures, surfaces, landscapes.

The pivotal moment in their history of reciprocal bondage transpires when Miguel grabs Blanca by the neck and threatens her with a stolen crochet hook, at which point he speaks for the first and only time: "'Voy a sacarte la yugular y cuando esté fuera de la piel voy a pincharla y te desangrarás de esa sangre rosa chicle que te hincha los pies y las varices de los muslos y la carne de la lengua'" [I'm going to rip out your jugular and when it's outside of the skin, I'm going to puncture it and you'll bleed to death with that bubblegum-pink blood that swells your feet and the varicose veins in your thighs and the flesh of your tongue] (101). The antithetical "thrust" of the quoted passage attests to a bloody circularity insofar as the present concentrates on the blood that literally flows through and bloats Blanca's body and the future merely intensifies or "bloats" that time. It is difficult to imagine a more challenging vision of sameness or a more chillingly violent fusion of Same and Other.

The return to the present extends through Blanca's shocked retreat and Miguel's understated bedtime ritual. In the first instance, the nurse dissimulates to her coworker and the two women agree to actively ignore Miguel and all other patients from that moment onward. In the second instance, the victorious Miguel carefully discards his used pajamas in favor of a brand-new pair, after which "Se acuesta, se arropa, lee un rato. Cierra los ojos" [He lies down, tucks himself in, reads awhile. He closes his eyes] (118). There is no interiority here. Each person has relegated the other to the past, and each moves forward seamlessly into continuity and reflection by sealing off both temporality and otherness.

Meanwhile, in the closing episode of her story the self-made singular woman arrives "home," both alone and in the company of strangers with whom she has refused to interact, preferring instead to cast them as foreign visitors (119). No one waits for her at the bus terminal and she has no luggage to claim, no baggage handlers to tip "porque mi vuelta es a destiempo. Estoy fuera de hora" [because my return is untimely. I'm outside of time] (121). She is "outside of time" in that she can conceive of no future, no time other than the present moment, no place other than the bus terminal. Levinas has commented in "Reality and Its Shadow" that "The characters of a novel are beings that are shut up, prisoners. Their history is never finished, it still goes on, but makes no headway" (138). For Levinas history stalls when being resembles and doubles itself, which is precisely the case with the fictional characters of *El frío*.

The last scene of the novel encodes directional blankness; "Camino hacia la salida con la mente en blanco" [I walk towards the exit with my mind blank] (121). In contrast to an affirmative ending, the concluding words of *El frío* underscore a loss of consciousness. After all of her memories, all of her self-motivated and self-directed coherence, the woman can think of nothing and no one. She has attempted (and failed) to make sense of her past, framed exclusively within the limits and substitutions of her relationship with Miguel. *El frío* temporalizes the unethicality of synchrony as one expression of the art of time. If, as Levinas theorizes, "identity is not only a departure from self; it is also a return to self" (*TO* 55), then the triple presents of and in the novel interrogate this illusory "freedom of beginning." In the three timelines the characters come back to themselves by abandoning the time(s) of others, mastering the possible and firmly grasping the present. In the absence of cultural, political, and even sociological histories that might reference contemporary Spain, Sanz's text exaggerates the solipsistic temporality of trauma in subjectivity.[22] Accordingly, the novel interlaces not one but three versions of solitude and calls each out of time and to a nonexistent future.

Belén Gopegui's *Tocarnos la cara* exposes a second approach to the art of time, one that exhorts, but does not arrive at, Levinasian alterity. Like *El frío*, Gopegui's text is quintessentially connective and, like the novel previously analyzed, the relations in *Tocarnos la cara* are directed towards discovering ethical responsibility for and to the Other. Moreover, in both novels the questing selves succumb to sameness because they commit to a chronology; each narration accentuates the causality of the past, the present as a problem, and the foreclosure of the future. But whereas *El frío* distends alternating narrative perspectives that acquire coherence through separation, *Tocarnos la cara* foregrounds a single narrator who attempts to summon the voices of others into her narration. Gopegui's text also concentrates more decisively on the past and winds more perspectives through more time. And instead of positioning erotic desire as the motor for all relationships, *Tocarnos la cara* surveys the possibilities and pitfalls of fraternity.

Briefly, the narrative weaves together, in a tripartite arrangement of consecutive chapters, the activities of an emergent experimental theater group known as El Probador (literally the Fitting Room) and composed of Óscar Azores, Ana Hojeda, Íñigo Martínez and Sandra, whose last name is never disclosed. El Probador is located in Madrid and directed by Simón Cátero, who brings together the four actors of varying abilities. Sandra, the most itinerant of the quartet, records and recalls the creation and dissolution of the collective, transcribes the words and thoughts of the other performers, inter-calates some of the documents that influenced Simón's original vision, and takes notes on the training sessions. In a strange melding of temporalities, she claims as her muses both fidelity and invention. Insofar as she re-reads the series of events leading towards and away from the foundation and disso-lution of El Probador, she organizes time and makes the past and the future contingent on a fixed set of texts. Insofar as she purposefully creates the history of those events, she incorporates herself and her contemporaries into that time and verifies that her history is their history. While the other actors do have a past, which periodically interrupts the story of El Probador, Sandra repeatedly characterizes herself as a vacant woman, alluding to her lack of employment as well as to her existential isolation. In theory she will be effortlessly shaped and filled. With her peripatetic participation in, and narra-tive responsibility for, El Probador, she willingly accepts the role of media-tor, but to what end? Sandra would seem to be perfectly positioned to perpet-ually await the other, but such is not to be the case.

The stated goal of the theater troupe consists of enabling a client's deep-est desire, such that the client will come away transformed. According to the official program, the selected patron discloses her or his innermost wish to one of the actors, who then projects a human mirror through which the customer may become the optimal image of her- or himself. In contrast to the reduced company of *El frío*, Gopegui's novel ushers forward an extended community of characters. In addition to the four principal actors, their teach-er and the numerous clients, three secondary figures, all whom are linked to Simón, intervene in the mission and the performances of El Probador. First, Pedro Alexéi works with the actors and arbitrates between them and Simón until he divulges, towards the close of the novel, that he is dying. Second, the journals of José Ángel Espinar lay out the conceptual map for El Probador and Sandra reads, in the course of the novel, from his written correspondence with Simón. And third, Fátima Uribe, Simón's former wife, forms a compet-ing theater group and convinces some of the actors to join her, thus hastening the demise of her ex-husband's theatrical experiment.

The members of El Probador believe, at different times, that they will literally touch the face of the Other in the course of their dramatic encoun-ters. By temporarily effacing their own identities in order to extend to the desiring others an alternative version of themselves, they consider their ef-forts to be highly ethical. In practice, however, the ideal runs aground from the start. As an early indication, during a preliminary session between Íñigo and a potential client named Pedro, the former charges "'[y]o sufro, tú sufres, él sufre. ¿No ves que eso es lo único que pasa? ¿No ves que nadie sabe lo que debe hacer?'" [I suffer, you suffer, he suffers. Don't you see that's all that happens? Don't you see that no one knows what they should do?].[23] Pedro responds by facing Íñigo and substituting for suffering the act of lying. He presumes that otherness is the result of, rather than the pre-condition for, change. In the exchange cited above, Pedro offers up to Íñigo an uncommon response, one that defines otherness as infinite acceptance and generosity, but he cannot accomplish alterity because he is not obligated to others in the present. Similarly, the other clients of El Probador avoid presence and the present. In keeping with Levinas's own concerns about art, the actors and their public experience the performances as images, as at least one step removed from the reality of their temporal dissonance from one another.

If *El frío* settles on the power of synchrony, then the art of time in and of *Tocarnos la cara* temporarily points towards the ethical potential of diachrony, the differing of the identical and the lapse of time that does not return. And it paradoxically accomplishes such a movement through the narrative dominance of Sandra. At the beginning of Gopegui's novel, Sandra narrates in the present tense about a historical (but not immemorial) past figure, and her narration immediately alludes to the difference and the lapse of time: "Ésta es la historia de un esfuerzo y una desbandada, pero hay algo que no consigo entender. Es como ver un avión parado en el cielo. O como aquel Palacio de los Deportes cuya cubierta de hierro se desplomó" [This is the story of an effort and a disbanding, but there is something that I don't understand. It's like seeing an airplane stuck in the sky. Or like that sports pavilion with the iron roof that collapsed] (11). When she undertakes to transcribe the story of El Probador, she can only summon up the outline, the temporal shape of the pertinent events rather than the sequence, and she can only secure that shape by means of analogous images; she cannot recall, much less recount, the sound or sight of the destruction that necessarily trails her memory.

Sandra attributes to the ensuing chronology the heavy promise of forward motion. But instead of knowing or seeing or relaying continuity, and thereby equating "I think" with "I can" (Levinas, *TI* 46), she situates time in the discontinuities of stories and of human comprehension. As a transcriber of texts and, therefore, as a producer of knowledge, she is assigned the task of converting the current and previous "records" of El Probador into a material discourse and a tangible past. As one of the actors, she is also ethically responsible to her colleagues, to her mentor and, to a greater or lesser degree, to all of the clients who approach the theater group. In an arguably purposeful move from epistemology to ethics, she promotes temporal discontinuity by taking on the responsibility of the past as unknowable and ungraspable.

As only one illustration of her repeated efforts to unhinge time from being, early in the overlapping histories of El Probador and Sandra's authorship, she follows Simón to a strip club. He introduces her to a sex worker whom he has named Fátima, after his ex-wife, and then proceeds to highlight the potential similarities, known only to him, between the young woman and the original Fátima.[24] In his role as teacher, he instructs Sandra on the facts of his failed marriage and on his inability to effect change in spite of the surrogate Fátima, who can never return Simón to the site of his definitive happiness. Simon wraps up the scene by reiterating his impotence and by decrying the corporeal return of his ex-wife to Madrid. They will not reunite but Simón will substitute a series of lovers, including Sandra herself, for Fátima, and Fátima will replace El Probador with her own theater company, staffed by most of Simón's actors. What looks like repetition, however, is in fact temporal noncoincidence, underscored by Sandra's representation of time as discontinuous.

Although Sandra's voice and vision permeate most of the novel, the conclusion is surprising for its irregularity. She revisits her initial image of the temporally frozen sports pavilion and sees it anew once gravity and time have resumed: "Ahora sí: los cables de acero que la sujetaban se han soltado, la cubierta está sola en el aire" [Now it's true: the iron cables that held the roof in place have released and the roof is hanging freely] (210). It is but a short step to equate the spectacular disappearance of the supporting roof and the more mundane failure of El Probador. Nature is multiple, she contends, thus confirming a translation of pluralism whereby all of the individual elements are equal, whereby responsibility is assumed after individuality, whereby alterity is an effect and not a cause. The actors of El Probador have echoed the fantasies of their peers, which are subsequently their own fantasies and, at the end of the novel, they have all retired to their own stories, and to futures that bear a striking resemblance to their desires.

Simón interrupts this homogeneity only after seducing Sandra, and he finalizes the narration with his authoritative account of the past, which confirms his starring role. He compares Sandra's story to his own and determines that she is a reliable witness; he writes that he recognizes himself in her words even though he facetiously maintains that he has become *her* reflection. Unfortunately, he comprehends the relationship between self and other, a relationship that he has been performing, staging and directing throughout the text, as one of incessant conflict: "Siempre hay violencia en el hecho de admitir a otro" (There's always violence in the fact of admitting another) (213). The key word here is "admitir." Agency and resolve saturate his description. As the teacher and prime mover of the theater group, as well as a self-proclaimed seducer, Simón is anything but receptive, anyone but the Other, despite, or perhaps because of, his pronouncements to the contrary.

If *El frío* and *Tocarnos la cara* ultimately cling to synchrony, then Luisa Castro's *La fiebre amarilla* purposefully turns towards diachrony. Instead of withdrawing into the temporal synthesis imposed by self-present consciousness (*El frío*) or paradoxically facing towards others *after* consolidating subjectivity (*Tocarnos la cara*), Castro's text faces towards the immemorial time of alterity. The previous two novels cultivate scenarios whereby the subjects recede into time, first by gathering all remembered pasts into a coterminous present and then by converting the future into a reflection of what has already been. *La fiebre amarilla* accomplishes something else altogether by invoking a responsibility for the other that precedes all genealogical beginning, exceeds the coherence of the present, and undoes the expectation of the future. Following Levinas's argument, the novel assembles temporal alterity in the mystery of death.

The plot unfolds in sixteen numbered chapters by means of at least three enmeshed temporal planes, each with its corresponding, yet divergent, perspective. In the first time zone Virginia Legazpi, a seventy-year-old woman who has always lived in a small village in Spain, tumbles down the stairs in her home just before joining a widow's excursion to the Shrine of Fátima, in Portugal.[25] In spite of the fact that she is not really a widow, she had intended to make the pilgrimage in order to finally fulfill a decades-old promise to her dying mother Amadora. When she goes to the hospital to have her broken arm set (again), the doctor informs Virginia that she has inoperable cancer and he sends her home. She floats in and out of delirium for two weeks and then apparently dies.

In the second time zone, generally paralleling Virginia's childhood, her father Jesús Legazpi abandons his daughter and his wife Amadora, when Virginia is ten years old, to emigrate to Cuba with an unidentified woman, presumably his lover. One year later, mother and daughter receive the astonishing news that Legazpi has expired from yellow fever,[26] but Virginia ignores the telegram to spend the next six decades awaiting both her father's explanation and his bodily return. Legazpi's arrival at his daughter's bedside coincides, in the first time zone, with her delirium during which she believes that, like her father, she suffers from yellow fever. He repeatedly begs Virginia to recognize him, approve of his impending marriage and meet his future wife, who has accompanied him. When she finally agrees to his pleas, "death," in the guise of a woman, enters Virginia's room and asks her to accompany them to Cuba. And in the third time zone, Ladislao Atare, the taxi driver who transported Legazpi and his lover to Ferrol in the first time, collects the couple in the second time at the dock, prior to their departure for Cuba, and drives them back to Virginia's village.

The three temporal strands carry equal narrative authority and interweave the supplementary stories of Virginia, her husband Francisco Pena, her adult daughter Juana, Amadora, Jesús Legazpi, the village priest don Sergio, the village doctor don Pablo, Ladislao Atare, and a peripatetic countess. All of these characters convene across competing times in order to inflect how one might recognize otherness anew. Virginia, as the connecting thread, presents the self who is summoned by the Other to account for its death. To glimpse that mystery, which escapes resolution, Virginia must be on the verge of—but not in--the future. On the cusp of the futural moment throughout the novel, it gradually dawns on her that in dying (and thus surviving yellow fever) she must return to the moment of trauma in which she was called to responsibility for her father's death.

La fiebre amarilla is paradoxically the most conventional of the three novels analyzed insofar as it features an omniscient narrator and displays the plot principally organized according to objectively verifiable details and dialogue. Castro also offers up a facile explanation, by way of Virginia's illness, for the temporal confusion that governs the plot. The novel is unusual, nonetheless, in that past, present, and future meet at mortality and death inhabits the novel as a person, as a kind of vision, as a place, as paternity, and as a metaphor for that which cannot be known or narrated.

The text commences in the present moment, recounted in the completed past of the preterit tense, when Virginia believes that she has contracted yellow fever and, several days later, "conoció por primera vez a su padre" [she met her father for the first time].[27] Her memories of Jesús Legazpi are based entirely on her mother's stories and the single photograph of her parents' wedding, which adorns the wall of her bedroom next to a bizarre painting in which a devil consumes the feet of a Christ figure. Significantly, when they meet, Legazpi calls his daughter by her first name and, instead of acknowledging him, she "sees" the village physician. The two temporal planes, embodied by Legazpi and don Pablo, will coexist throughout both Virginia's present and the remainder of the novel.

Although Virginia's perception predominates in the first chapter, the narrator-as-gatherer merges her self-directed memories of the past and her other-directed attentiveness to the present. Disease, old age and imminent death afford a reasonable motivation for her delusion but no narrative authority ever confirms this explanation. However, Virginia's pull to recover her father's imaginary past, and thus to hold him accountable for her current distress, is really about her own impending expression of Levinasian diachrony. Whereas the other two novels represent what might be termed "memorial encounters," the effect of which is to remind the subjects of themselves, *La fiebre amarilla* works through an immemorial encounter to rehearse the impossible meeting of self and other in the future of death.

In response to the "where" of such a future, the movement of "othering" displays in Castro's text as departing to and returning from the unknowable future destinations of Coimbra and Cuba. The Shrine of Fátima signals a site of maternal longing so fierce that Virginia's own mother has guaranteed her daughter's pilgrimage in several ways: Amadora bequeaths to her daughter a sum of money to make the journey that Amadora could never realize; Virginia recollects the reported appearance of the Virgin of Fátima (and thus the reason for the shrine) as a direct effect of her father's exodus to Cuba; and before her proposed trip, she imagines that she need never to return from Coimbra to her family, her village and her present life. The potential resonances among Virginia's own name, the requisite virginal status of Fátima,

Amadora's (remembered) eschewal of sexual relations with her husband, and the seemingly miraculous birth of their daughter all suggest that Virginia may be the literal manifestation of her mother's own temporal drive towards ethical alterity. Because most textual references to Amadora are filtered through someone else's consciousness, it is difficult to confirm such a move. Likewise, throughout the novel Virginia is fixated on her father's departure and return, with all that both of these actions imply, and she habitually summons the memory of her mother in support of what might be considered the primary paternal mystery. As a partial response to this mystery, she associates Cuba with refuge, yearning and foreignness, and she assumes that her father can and will rescue her from her present circumstances precisely because he has already traveled so far that, in Virginia's mind, his only recourse is to turn around, return "home" and reclaim his daughter.

In a peculiarly affirmative interrogation of the art of time in a Levinasian approximation, *La fiebre amarilla* links the narrative to the microhistory of the painting that faces Virginia's bed, which was her mother's bed before her's. The painting, periodically described by Virginia and the other characters, reveals a supposedly ethical confrontation between good and evil, the devil and Christ.[28] It also connects daughter and father. In one temporal strand, Ladislao delivers Legazpi and the unknown woman to the dock in time to board the ship that will take them to Cuba, only to then be directed to drive them back to Amadora's house (which is now Virginia's house) because Legazpi cannot depart without saying good-bye to his daughter. When the taxi arrives, Legazpi gives the painting to Amadora as a final gift for Virginia, with instructions to hang it in their bedroom.

When she returns from the hospital to see that in the painting Good consumes Evil, she deduces that she cannot possibly have cancer. Rather, she claims for herself the disease of yellow fever that she has always, in her imagination, associated with her father. Given that he could have contracted yellow fever, so the story goes, only by leaving the brisk rainy climate of Northern Spain for a tropical country such as Cuba, Virginia's self-diagnosis anticipates her definitive departure for Cuba (instead of the original destination of the Shrine of Fátima) in the company of her father and his mistress. The altered painting, in Virginia's mind, corroborates her father's mission of salvation, and it inspires her to reconsider the terms of her initial abandonment. As the only artistic object in the novel, given that the wedding photograph is presented as nothing more than a record, the religious iconography is the only visual stimulus in Virginia's ordinary domestic environment, and it moves her to reevaluate and re-inhabit her own time and the conflicting times of her parents. In sum, she sees in the painting a possible cipher for another time and the time of the Other, a time in which she embraces death, in a variety of literal and metaphorical manifestations, and recognizes ethicality.

At the end of the novel, the fate of the painting corroborates the temporal movement that has "undetermined" the future of death: "Así, como la voltereta del cuadro, tan enigmática en apariencia, el mundo podía revolverse de la noche a la mañana, y las casas, y las cabezas de los hombres, y hasta las palabras dentro de las cabezas de los hombres. Pues sí que podían. Podían eso y mucho más" [Thus, like the somersault of the painting, with its enigmatic appearance, the world could have turned upside down from night to morning, and the houses and the minds of men and even the words inside the minds of men. Of course they could have. They could have done that and much more] (165). The turnaround of the world and the words refers to the about-face of time, or the art of time, whereby the future and the past, across the present, trade places. In the time(s) of the novel, Amadora grows ever younger and death is not an occurrence but a human subject who accompanies Virginia into the immemorial past and unknowable future. But before she can meet Death, Virginia must perceive her father and become willing to assume responsibility, through the time of narration, for his death. Once she finally recognizes Jesús Legazpi, and once he removes the telegram from the painting and insistently names himself to and for her, she is prepared to meet his companion, who, not coincidentally, is referred to as death only once and only in the final paragraphs of the novel. On the brink of their long-awaited trip to Cuba, as the place of no-time, the personification of death lingers but don Pablo stands in for her father. His parting words of advice extend protection and comfort and sustain the mystery of alterity: "'Llevad ropa de verano—le oyó--, no creo que paséis frío" [Take your summer clothes—she heard him say—I don't think you'll get cold] (171). Under the guise of parental care, Virginia hears the unknowable, and yet familiar, tomorrow.

Because the futurity of death is unnarratable and beyond the chronology of time, as Levinas has theorized, *La fiebre amarilla* does not follow Virginia into death, although it does suggest that she follows her father into *his* death. She finally accepts responsibility for the Other by discarding "her" past, present and future and by giving up her claims to grievance. In so doing, she marks her future identity as fundamentally other-wise and in direct opposition to the self-obsessed (albeit blank) futures displayed in *El frío* and the reiterated failures of *Tocarnos la cara*. When Virginia finally hears and responds to the call of the other, outside of all rationality, all memory and all discourse, she refigures her paternal history; she becomes the parent and her father becomes the child, and death links them to one another. In Levinas's words, "the very relationship with the other is the relationship with the future" (*TO* 77) and that relationship is exposed, in Castro's novel, through the future of death and, more particularly, through Virginia's transcendent devotion to another, which is the time of alterity. This other is not only her father or his female companion, but also includes everything about her father that has always escaped her comprehension and her present and everything that makes the stranger unknowable and temporally immeasurable. Time traps the experiencing subjects in the previous two novels, but in *La fiebre amarilla* time liberates the self to encounter the Other in death.

In these three novelistic expressions of the art of time, then, we glimpse three very different relationships to alterity. In *El frío* the selves embark upon the tragedy of solitude as an antidote to present trauma. The time of the other must be subsumed again and again through the fiction of synchrony. Suffering forges coherence and forswears futurity. The internal causality of the individual displaces and fractures all possible futures and, therefore, any notion of alterity. By the same token, the novel ultimately critiques egology in terms of the collective frustration and frigidity of human desire. *Tocarnos la cara* approaches and then postpones alterity indefinitely. Others escape Sandra's present and she cannot sustain their histories; in the end even she is subsumed into Simón's story, which represents the communal drive of history. If, as Levinas postulates, time is the work of the face-to-face relationship, then time in Gopegui's novel eventually turns away from the Other. The difference of diachrony in *La fiebre amarilla* is that it contests sameness, consciousness and knowledge by pointing towards death as the origin of and the answer to anachrony. When Virginia remembers her father into his future death, she is released from the inevitable solitude and lament of her present as the only present and propelled towards sociality and the face-to-face encounter with the Other. The three novels explore Levinas's notion of ethical time based upon the immemorial past, the confrontational present and the unknowable future. If we read the texts allegorically, we can see the inevitable traces of Spain's painful exclusionary history in the nuanced conflicts between the individual and the collective, past and present, universalism and pluralism, Same and Other. Taken together, the three novels exhort us to consider again and always the price of temporal mastery and the promise of ethical responsibility.

NOTES

The present chapter has been immeasurably improved by the intellectual acumen and efforts of the editor. I thank him for his always engaging and pertinent comments, suggestions, and queries regarding Levinas, Spain, and the three novels here discussed.

1. Levinas's conception of ethics paradoxically seems more relevant to philosophical traditions anchored in either rationalism or mysticism. The formal history of Spanish philosophy has, by contrast, been irrevocably driven by the tenets and conundrums of Catholicism. In his succinct review of Spanish philosophy, Manuel Garrido notes both the spiritual stagnation of Spanish philosophy prior to 1870 and Spain's philosophical isolation from the rest of Europe, and he singles out Miguel de Unamuno (1864–1936) and José Ortega y Gasset (1883–1955) as the key Spanish philosophers of the twentieth century. See Manuel Garrido, "Spanish Philosophy," in *The Cambridge History of Philosophy 1870-1945*, ed. Thomas Baldwin (Cambridge: Cambridge University Press, 2003), 469–76.

2. It is an understatement to categorize Levinas's thought as methodologically dense. Two introductory sources have consistently proven helpful to me: Colin Davis, *Levinas: An Introduction* (Notre Dame: University of Notre Dame Press, 1996) and B. C. Hutchens, *A Guide for the Perplexed* (London: Continuum, 2004). The essays included in *The Cambridge Companion to Levinas*, edited by Simon Critchley and Robert Bernasconi (Cambridge: Cambrige University Press, 2002), are also accessible, insightful and wide-ranging.

3. Elsewhere I have addressed Levinas's ideas in the context of the contemporary Spanish novel but I have previously explored neither temporality nor aesthetics. See Nina L. Molinaro, "Facing Towards Alterity and Spain's 'Other' New Novelists," *Anales de la literatura española contemporánea* 30 (2005): 301–24; Nina L. Molinaro, "Looking for the Other: Peninsular Women's Fiction after Levinas," in *Women in the Spanish Novel Today: Essays on the Reflection of Self in the Work of Three Generations*, ed. Kyra A. Kietrys and Montserrat Linares (Jefferson: McFarland Press, 2009), 133–51.

4. Those familiar with Levinas's philosophy will no doubt recall his abiding interest in the work of Henri Bergson (1859–1941) and particularly in Bergson's notion of duration or *la durée*. Bergson attacked the Kantian idea that freedom pertains to a realm located outside of space and time and he instead theorized that the immediate data of consciousness are temporal. He understood duration as qualitative multiplicity, or a juxtaposition of events with no mechanistic causality. Levinas often references Bergson in his own texts. In "Martin Buber and the Theory of Knowledge," for example, Levinas writes, "For contemporary thought, the history of the theory of knowledge is synonymous with the history of the vanishing of the subject-object problem. . . . The consistency of the self is resolved into intentional relations as for Husserl, or into the being-in-the-world or *Miteinandersein* of Heidegger, or else it is identified with a continuous process of renovation, typified by Bergson's duration" (62). Levinas will use Bergson's duration as one of the primary points of departure for his own concept of diachrony.

5. A partial list of these writers, all of whom published at least one novel in the 1990s, includes (but is not limited to) the following names: Mercedes Abad, Antonio Álamo, Enriqueta Antolín, Javier Azpeitia, Nuria Barrios, Lola Becarria, Felipe Benítez Reyes, Juan Bonilla, Gabriela Bustelo, Martín Casariego, Francisco Casavello, Luisa Castro, Javier Cercas, Lucía Etxebarria, Susana Fortes, Espido Freire, Marcos Giralt Torrente, Belén Gopegui, Almudena Grandes, Ismael Grasa, Begoña Huertas, Andrés Ibáñez, Ángela Labordeta, Ray Loriga, José Machado, Pedro Maestre, Luis Magrinyá, José Ángel Mañas, Fernando Marías, Daniel Mújica, Antonio Orejudo Utrilla, Sergi Pàmies, Tino Pertierra, Juan Manuel Prada, Benjamín Prado, Blanca Riestra, Juana Salabert, Care Santos, Lorenzo Silva, Eloy Tizón, David Trueba, Clara Usón , Ángela Vallvey, Roger Wolfe and Pilar Zapata Bosch.

6. Numerous scholars have lucidly engaged Levinas's position vis-à-vis literature. See especially Steven Shankman, *Other Others: Levinas, Literature, Transcultural Studies* (Albany: State University of New York Press, 2010); *Levinas and Medieval Literature: The "Difficult Reading" of English and Rabbinic Texts*, ed. Ann W. Astell and J. A. Jackson (Pittsburgh: Duquesne University Press, 2009); *Levinas and Nineteenth-Century Literature: Ethics and Otherness from Romanticism through Realism*, ed. Donald R. Wehrs and David P. Haney (Newark: University of Delaware Press, 2009); Gabriel Riera, *Intrigues: From Being to the Other* (New York: Fordham University Press, 2006), 85–105; Gerald L. Bruns, "The Concepts of Art and Poetry in Emmanuel Levinas's Writings," in *The Cambridge Companion to Levinas,* ed. Simon Critchley and Robert Bernasconi (Cambridge: Cambridge University Press, 2002), 206–33; *In Proximity: Emmanuel Levinas and the Eighteenth Century*, ed. Melvyn New (Lubbock: Texas Tech University Press, 2001); Steve McCaffrey, "The Scandal of Sincerity: Towards a Levinasian Poetics," in *Prior to Meaning: Protosemantics and Poetics* (Evanston: Northwestern University Press, 2001*)*, 204–29; and Jill Robbins, *Altered Reading: Levinas and Literature* (Chicago: Chicago University Press, 1999).

7. Alain Paul Toumayan, "Levinas and French Literature," in *Levinas and Nineteenth-Century Literature: Ethics and Otherness from Romanticism through Realism*, ed. Donald R. Wehrs and David P. Haney (Newark: University of Delaware Press, 2009), 129. Toumayan follows the cited statement with a series of explanatory claims organized around the *tohubohu* and the fundamental foreignness of the uncreated.

8. In delineating between other and Other, I attempt to adhere to the distinction proposed by Alphonso Lingis in his note regarding Levinas's Preface to *Totality and Infinity*: "With the author's permission, we are translating '*autrui*' (the personal Other, the you) by 'Other,' and '*autre*' by 'other.' In doing so, we regrettably sacrifice the possibility of reproducing the author's use of capital or small letters with both these terms in the French text" (24–25).

9. Lorna Wood has recently argued in favor of the "said of exegesis" in Levinas's thought in order to postulate a positive interpretation of art in Levinas's philosophy See her article on "Emmanuel Levinas and the American Renaissance Canon" in *Levinas and Nineteenth-Century Literature: Ethics and Otherness from Romanticism through Realism*, ed. Donald R. Wehrs and David P. Haney (Newark: University of Delaware Press, 2009), 166–206.

10. Sam B. Girgus, *Levinas and the Cinema of Redemption: Time, Ethics, and the Feminine* (New York: Columbia University Press, 2010), 4.

11. In relation to *Time and the Other*, Levinas discusses dia-chrony in his "Preface," written and published in 1979 on the occasion of the French-language re-issue of the volume, and he utilizes both dia-chrony and diachrony in "Diachrony and Representation," written in 1982 and included, together with "The Old and the New," in the English-language translation of *Time and the Other*, published in 1987. In his 1982 essay, he suggests that dia-chrony corresponds to "the 'difference' of diachrony'" (118). He seems to employ dia-chrony and diachrony interchangeably in the four essays originally included in *Time and the Other*. I include these details because they seem to confirm that Levinas's thought was continually both evolving and returning to its sources. I have chosen, perhaps misguidedly, to use diachrony throughout my own essay, except when Levinas refers, in the relevant quotations, to dia-chrony.

12. Because I focus on Levinas's presentation of time in *Time and the Other*, and in a few of the complementary sections of *Totality and Infinity,* I have only preliminarily alluded to time as it relates to Levinas's highly complex, and much analyzed, distinction between Saying and Said in *Otherwise than Being or Beyond Essence*. As is his habit, Levinas both reiterates and substantially expands his earlier work in *Otherwise than Being*. For the relevant section on time in this volume, see especially 28–43.

13. I share Kathryn Everly's assessment that Spain's Gen X movement is characterized by detachment and evasion concerning historical themes. See her *History, Violence, and the Hyperreal: Representing Culture in the Contemporary Spanish Novel* (West Lafayette: Purdue University Press, 2010), x.

14. Although a parallel argument might be made for many, if not most, national cultures, Spain has historically been the site of repeated expulsions and erasures of its citizenry. One of the most noteworthy remains the forced exodus of the Jewish and Moorish communities from "Catholic" Spain in 1492. In his biography of Levinas, Salomon Malka has written that, while incarcerated in Stalag XIB during World War II, Levinas associated 1492, the number that marked the entrance of the prison camp, with Spain's expulsion of the Jews. See Malka's *Emmanuel Levinas: His Life and Legacy*, trans. Michael Kigel and Sonja M. Embree (Pittsburgh: Duquesne University Press, 2006), 67.

During its imperialistic heyday, which reached a zenith during the sixteenth century, the Spanish government sponsored a series of international campaigns designed to increase and enforce religious, political and linguistic homogeneity. Some four centuries later, Spaniards have only recently "transitioned" to a functional democracy, solidified in 1975 after a thirty-six-year military dictatorship that formally concluded with the death of the country's charismatic leader General Francisco Franco y Bahamonde. In addition to recording the highest level of unemployment in the European Union (19.79 percent as of October 2010), Spain's current social woes are manifold. Among the most pressing, and most publicized, of these, racism, domestic violence and clashes between the seventeen autonomous regions (las Comunidades Autónomas) of Spain and the centripetal Spanish government testify to a longstanding and profoundly rooted distrust of pluralism.

15. Early evaluations of Spain's Gen X included articles published during 1995 and 1996 in Spanish literary journals such as *Ínsula, Leer, Quimera, República de las Letras, Reseña*, and *El Urogallo*. During 1997 Toni Dorca and Carmen de Urioste published the first scholarly assessments of the new generation in the United States in *Revista de Estudios Hispánicos* and *Letras Peninsulares*, respectively. For recent treatments of the generation, see especially Car-

men de Urioste Azcorra, *Novela y sociedad en la España contemporánea (1994-2009)* (Madrid: Fundamentos, 2009); Dorothy Odartey-Wellington, *Contemporary Spanish Fiction: Generation X* (Newark, DE: University of Delaware Press, 2008); H. Rosi Song, "Anti-Conformist Fiction: The Spanish 'Generation X,'" in *A Companion to the Twentieth-Century Spanish Novel*, ed. Marta E. Altisent (Woodbridge: Tamesis, 2008), 197–207; and the essays contained in *Generation X Rocks: Contemporary Peninsular Fiction, Film, and Rock Culture*, ed. Christine Henseler and Randolph D. Pope (Nashville, TN: Vanderbilt University Press, 2007). For a critical argument against the Generation X writers as a discrete generation see especially *La pluralidad narrativa: Escritores españoles contemporáneos (1984-2004)*, ed. Ángeles Encinar and Kathleen M. Glenn (Madrid: Biblioteca Nueva 2005) and the essays included in the 2004 issue of *Ínsula* dedicated to "La novela española actual: ¿Un producto mercantil o un lugar de encuentro?"

    In an obvious parody of Pedro Almodóvar's classic film *¿Qué he hecho yo para merecer esto?* (1984), a collection of interviews with some of the Gen X writers was published by Noemí Montetes Mairal under the title *¿Qué he hecho yo para publicar esto?* (Barcelona: DVD Ediciones, 1999). Finally, many of the Gen X writers participated in a 2003 conference, the proceedings from which were published under the title of *En cuarentena: Nuevos narradores y críticos a principios del siglo XXI* and edited by Antonio Orejudo (Murcia: Universidad de Murcia, 2004).

    16. The Spanish novelists most often associated with the "dirty realism" subgroup include Bonilla, Bustelo, Casariego, Casavella, Etxebarria, Grasa, Loriga, Maestre, Mañas, Mújica, Prado and Wolfe.

    17. Bill Buford, "Editorial." *Granta* 8 (1983): 4-5.

    18. For an astute and far-reaching discussion of the women writers of the generation, see especially Carmen de Urioste, "Narrative of Spanish Women Writers of the Nineties: An Overview," *Tulsa Studies in Women's Literature* 20 (2001): 279–95, as well as my essay cited in note 3. I have purposefully chosen texts by women novelists as exemplary of the nexus between Levinasian alterity and Spain's Gen X because the vast majority of the existing criticism on Gen X focuses on male novelists. I do not mean to imply, however, that only novels by the women writers of the generation are germane to my larger argument.

    19. Other than the essays on *El frío* and *La fiebre amarilla* cited in note 3, no criticism exists, as of the writing of the present essay, on either novel. Gopegui's *Tocarnos la cara* has, by contrast, generated several scholarly articles. See especially Nuria Cruz-Cámara, "Notas sobre un 'Bildungsroman' posmoderno: *Tocarnos la cara* de Belén Gopegui," *Crítica Hispánica* 26 (2004): 41–48; Janet Pérez, "Tradition, Renovation, Innovation: The Novels of Belén Gopegui," *Anales de la literatura española contemporánea* 28 (2003): 115–38; and Eva Legido-Quigley, "La superación de una 'episteme' posmoderna saturada: El caso de Belén Gopegui en *Tocarnos la cara*," *Monographic Review/Revista Monográfica* 17 (2001): 146–64.

    20. For reasons of cohesiveness I do not take up, in the present essay, the problems and possibilities of gender in Levinas's theory or in the selected novels. For a superlative introduction to the issues associated with Levinas's ambiguous stance on gender, see the essays included in *Feminist Interpretations of Emmanuel Levinas*, ed. Tina Chanter (University Park: The Pennsylvania State University Press, 2001).

    21. Marta Sanz, *El frío* (Madrid: Debate, 1995), 7. Henceforth cited parenthetically. All English-language translations are mine.

    22. It could certainly be argued that *El frío* follows in the footsteps of such well-known novels of pathology as Günter Grass's *Die Blechtrommel (The Tin Drum)* (1959) and Ken Kesey's *One Flew Over the Cuckoo's Nest* (1962). Twentieth-century Spanish fiction includes among its ranks a number of noteworthy examples of the sub-genre that include *La familia de Pascual Duarte (The Family of Pascual Duarte)* (1942), by Nobel Laureate Camilo José Cela, Miguel Delibes's *Parábola del náufrago (Parable of the Shipwrecked Man)* (1969) and even *Veo Veo (I Spy)* (1996), by Gen X novelist Gabriela Bustelo.

    23. Belén Gopegui, *Tocarnos la cara* (Barcelona: Anagrama, 1995), 54. Henceforth cited parenthetically. All English-language translations are mine.

    24. Although a rehearsal of the aggressive history between Spain and the Middle East is far beyond the scope of the present essay, I would be remiss not to note that the name of Fátima

appears to anchor Gopegui's novel and the subsequent novel by Luisa Castro. Fátima is both the name of Mohammed's daughter and a common Islamic female name. Whereas the two Fátimas in *Tocarnos la cara* appear to embody Simón's recurring sexual fantasy of the unattainable female object, Castro emphasizes the spiritual and religious associations of the name by referencing the "real" Shrine of Fátima. However, the more abstract version of Fátima featured in Castro's novel is just as illusory (if not more so) than the two carnal women in Gopegui's novel.

25. The Shrine of Our Lady of Fátima (Nossa Senhora do Rosário da Fátima), located 75 kilometers to the south of Coimbra, Portugal, is a highly celebrated Marian shrine visited by some four million people each year. The shrine commemorates the apparition of the Virgin Mary to three local shepherd children in 1917. It is significant that in *La fiebre amarilla* neither the protagonist nor her mother has ever travelled outside of their village. The two characters erroneously place the Shrine in the city of Coimbra when it is in fact housed in the city of Fátima. Geographical reality has little currency in Castro's novel. Rather, the importance of the Shrine of Our Lady of Fátima rests on its metaphorical and temporal suggestiveness.

26. The disease of yellow fever suggests a number of associations relevant to Castro's novel. As an acute viral hemorrhagic illness, it is highly contagious and transmitted primarily through the bite of the female mosquito. Yellow fever occurs almost exclusively in tropical or sub-tropical climates and has played a crucial role in Cuban history.

27. Luisa Castro, *La fiebre amarilla* (Barcelona: Anagrama, 1994), 9. Henceforth cited parenthetically. All English-language translations are mine.

28. Other than a vague account of the exaggerated features of the two religious figures, the details of the painting remain oblique. There is no information in the novel concerning its origins, its artistic quality or the size of the canvas. Virginia recalls the artwork as the only keepsake from her father and hides his death notice behind the frame. The untitled image is thus initially assigned a synecdochical position vis-à-vis Legazpi.

Chapter Twelve

Answering the Summons of the "Other"

Reading the Literature of Migrant and Postcolonial Italy with Emmanuel Levinas

Norma Bouchard

With this chapter I follow the path of inquiry provided by Emmanuel Levinas's post-rationalist articulation of the humanism of the Other to focus on the recent, unprecedented emergence of the voices of migrant and postcolonial authors in Italian literature from the 1990s onwards. Drawing upon Levinas's conceptualization of ethics as a pre-rational, pre-cultural relation of responsibility, obligation, and submission to the call of a vulnerable, destitute Other, I argue that these voices constitute a moment of signification or, in Levinas's words, an "epiphany." Their testimonies and memories of the experience of migration and colonization provide a face-to-face encounter with an Other whose moral transcendence summons, disturbs, implicates, and ultimately unsettles modern definitions of Italian identity cultivated since the unification of the peninsula in 1860. I conclude by discussing how these voices, uttered in a political context marked by a rigid system of juridical borders and frontiers regulating the boundaries between the inside and the outside, the native and the foreign body, the Self and the Other, foreground the urgency of extending Levinas's ethical imperative towards forms of human sociality other than those sanctioned by the state.

OTHERNESS AND THE MODERN ITALIAN SELF

In the mid-1970s, Italy, like Greece and Spain, one of southern Europe's traditional out-migration countries, became a transit region for vast transnational migratory movements. By the end of the Cold War bipolar divide, Italy had fully evolved from a transit zone into a destination country. However, the arrival of immigrants from the "Souths" of the world—Eastern Europe, Africa, the Middle East, Asia, and Latin America—prompted Italians to perceive migration as a foreign invasion, a threat to a presumed Italian "authenticity," culture, and way of life.[1] A reactive mythology of Italian national identity based upon imaginary notions of shared civic values, territorial belonging and, at times, even a common ethnicity, quickly unfolded into a series of state legislations to control borders and reduplicate frontiers. From its first program to regularize immigration in 1986—a program that, up to that time, was still based on the Fascist laws of the 1930s—Italy put into place a number of legislations (Martelli Law of 1990 first and the Law of 1998 after) culminating in the Bossi-Fini immigration Law of July 30, 2002. Understanding migration only as a temporary condition affecting single individuals and framing it to be advantageous to the Italian national economy, the Bossi-Fini immigration Law is a repressive bio-political apparatus. It mandates fingerprinting by the police for all non-EU citizens (even those entitled to stay legally on Italian soil) and justifies confining immigrants to so-called Centers of Temporary Permanence as bodies to be controlled, detained, and punished. In short, this law subsumes human life to a juridical and institutional model, or a "politically qualified life," thus transforming the immigrant into the *homo sacer* and the *non habet personam*: the "non-person," the "bare life" of the *bios* of the *state of exception.*[2]

Italy's responses to migration are especially surprising. This is a country not only characterized by a high degree of cultural, linguistic, and ethnic hybridity but one whose founding moments as a modern nation-state in 1860 cannot be dissociated from the migratory movements resulting from colonialism and migration. As Antonio Gramsci reminds us almost at the outset of *The Southern Question*, Italy's founding moments—and, by implication, the concept of "Italianità," or Italian-ness—cannot be separated from processes of colonization and the global migratory flows that ensued."[3] With the territorial unification of the Italian peninsula in 1860, the independent Kingdom of the Two Sicilies was annexed to the Northern monarchy of the Savoy—a monarchy that had colonial ambitions even before unification when it had embarked in a naval display in front of Tunisia. But while Tunisia was out of reach, southern Italy was not. Within a few decades, the Savoy turned the South into a supplying base of natural resources and cheap human labor by way of a liberalized agenda that severely weakened the southern economy through trade blocks and tariff structures while impoverishing the peasantry in the erosion of rights to collective land use. Such colonial practices went in tandem with a discourse that represented the South as an exotic and bizarre land, very often compared to Africa and Turkey, and more generally, described in a relationship that reproduced the rhetoric of the European colonization of Africa, Asia, and the Americas.[4] At the end of the nineteenth century, a body of pseudo-scientific research further reified southern diversity in a very resilient discourse of racial inferiority established from the framework of biology, phrenology, anthropology, and criminology.[5] As the plight of Southern peasants continued to worsen, two related phenomena of social unrest took place that would lead to yet another fold in Italy's internal colonial history: rebellion and emigration. While some destitute masses fought against the Italian army in a class-based conflict that would claim more lives than all the battles of unification combined, the so-called "brigantaggio," or "brigand's war," the vast majority of them chose the path of mass migration in a postcolonial exodus that, from 1876 to 1976, saw the departure of 25 million people, two-thirds of them from the South. The Americas were their top destinations, but a significant number also left for French colonial holdings in Africa, such as Algeria and Morocco, but especially Tunisia. Here they settled in ports, rural areas, and mining regions from Goletta, Biserta, Monastir, and Sfax to Gafsa, Kelibia, and Cape Bon.[6]

The mass migration that followed the creation of the Italian nation-state would soon evolve into one more chapter of colonialism, a colonialism that now looked outside the Italian peninsula, particularly towards Northern and Eastern African territories.[7] These regions were seen not just as an opportunity for the acquisition of the so-called "place in the sun," a territorial expansion to solve the problems caused by an oversupply of labor and a large landless peasantry, but also as a means to affirm the legitimacy of the newly formed nation, a southern European state whose people had long been subject to negative stereotypes: the Italians as indolent, effeminate, morally and sexually lax.[8] In 1889 Italy occupied Somalia, after which followed the invasion of Eritrea in 1890.[9] Despite a number of catastrophic defeats, Italy pursued its colonial ambition and by 1912, proclaimed sovereignty over Tripolitania and Cyrenaica, lands that were under the control of the Ottoman Empire and inhabited by nomadic Berber populations that fiercely resisted the Italian occupation. With the fall of the Liberal State[10] and advent of Fascism, African colonialism entered its most violent phase. Mussolini gave free reign to his military leaders, empowering men such as the infamous General Rodolfo Graziani to pursue a most repressive military campaign that led to the proclamation of the *Colonia di Libia* in 1935 and the declaration, in 1936, of *Africa Orientale Italiana,* a territory that encompassed Eritrea, Ethiopia, and Somalia. However, the second chapter of Italian colonialism was also brief since the Paris Peace Treaty of 1947 forced Italy to abandon all claims to its colonies. Italian migration, however, did not cease in 1947. In the post-World War II era, the destinations shifted from the South of Italy to the North. In what would become the largest European interregional migration of the post-Word War II era, between 1951 and 1972, 2 million Southerners relocated to work in the factories of Genoa, Turin, and Milan. This was to be the last chapter of a long history of mass migration that would last till the first arrival of immigrants on Italian soil in the 1970s.

As this historical parenthesis illustrates, contexts of national and transnational colonialism and migration are undoubtedly part and parcel of modern definitions of Italian-ness in post-unification Italy. They constitute what Mark Choate has recently described as the global Italian nation, a transnational Greater Italy, originating from the subaltern classes, primarily from the southern regions of Italy but also from impoverished areas of the North, such as the Veneto region, for example,[11] and existing outside territorial jurisdiction, with frames of references encompassing Central and Northern Europe but also Africa, the Middle East, and the Americas. Yet, these transnational contexts have been repressed by the modern Italian consciousness.[12] In Italy, despite much evidence to the contrary, unification has been endlessly narrated, celebrated, and commemorated as a project of collective emancipation and resurgence (hence the word: *Risorgimento*) of Northern *and* Southern people alike. The migratory experience of the subaltern has been removed and repressed, as evidenced by the lack of attention in Italy to the literary culture that has emerged from the global Italian diaspora.[13] The colonial expansion into Africa was literally bracketed until very recently. Since Italy's loss of its African empire was an injury to national pride as well as an implicit failure of the newly born nation-state, modern Italian identity was built on a willed repression of its colonial Other. Archival collections were tightly controlled and, with very few exceptions,[14] it has been only since the 1980s and 1990s that the chapter of colonialism was reopened,[15] but without ever becoming the topic of a public debate necessary for a true decolonization to take place. Meanwhile, mainstream culture has continued to cultivate the idea of Italian colonizers as "brava gente," or good people, building roads and improving the urban planning and architecture of the cities of Tripoli, Bengasi, Addis Ababa, and Asmara, and of their colonialism as "straccione," that is to say, on the cheap with respect to other European empires and, for this reason, somehow more benign.[16] In sum, modern definition of Italian identity has been founded upon willed acts of historical amnesia and on the expulsion of its own Otherness. As a result, the full responsibilities and obligations towards the subject of migration and colonization have yet to take place.

ITALY'S MIGRANT AND POSTCOLONIAL VOICES AND LEVINAS'S ETHICAL IMPERATIVE

However, in this epochal moment of global migratory movements through and within Italy, the founding—if repressed—moments of Italian-ness, can no longer be forgotten and expelled. Notwithstanding the rigidity of Italy's legislative measures, the country continues to be a destination for those who are escaping poverty, destitution, political violence or are seeking to fulfill their aspirations for a better, more fulfilling life. More than 4 million immigrants are now residing on Italian soil where they are permanently reconfiguring the labor markets of the agricultural fields and domestic households while their bodies are transforming the ethnoscapes of squares and train stations in Italian cities and suburbs, the "non-places" of late Western modernity.[17] Yet, from the early 1990s, something unprecedented has also taken place. As Armando Gnisci[18] recognized before other scholars took notice, immigrants ceased to be just "hands," laboring silently in the tomato fields for a few euro a day or in the private homes of an aging Italian population in need of caretakers, and began to inscribe their presence through written words. Emerging as the newest voices in the panorama of late twentieth-century Italian literature, Pap Khouma, Salah Methnani, Mohamed Bouchane, Saidou Moussa Ba, and Nassera Chohra, among others, published what would become the first generation of migrant writing in Italy.[19] Having arrived on Italian soil primarily from countries colonized by other European nations,[20] they authored or, in many cases, co-authored testimonial, mimetic accounts of their lived experience as immigrants in Italy. Other voices soon followed and migrant writing now encompasses an ever-growing cohort of authors.[21] Their origins are varied and range from countries that escaped colonization to others that were colonized by Italy.[22] Together, they constitute a polyphony of voices that calls for a revisiting of archived episodes of Italian history and normative definition of Italian identity from the point of view of the excluded Other—the migrant and the colonized who have now irrupted onto the social and cultural scene of modern Italy.

The philosophy of Emmanuel Levinas, to which I will now turn, provides significant theoretical possibilities to assess the significance of these voices' emergence in an Italian context. In its description of a face-to-face encounter with a vulnerable, destitute Other whose summoning disturbs and unsettles the identity of the Self through a relation of proximity, it outlines a path for an ethics of obligation and responsibility. Situated before culture, Levinas's ethics indicates the necessity of moving beyond the exclusionary forces of a liberal tradition of European thought, of transcending the paradoxes and contradictions of a European consciousness that understands humanness only within forms of identities sanctioned and legitimized by the institutional and juridical models of the sovereign state.

Among the many bold moves made by Levinas in his 1961 *Totality and Infinity* is the claim that the relation with the human person must be freed from the ontological assumptions of modernity that require distance to thematize, objectify, and reduce the Other through a system of difference and oppositions so that rational comprehension and understanding can ultimately emerge. To the ontology of modernity and the epistemological orders of meaning upon which it is founded, Levinas opposes what he calls ethics "as first philosophy."[23] By this, Levinas means that the ethical moment is no longer derived from a rational system of morality and judgment located in the culture of a state or a nation. In the pages of *Totality and Infinity,*[24] he reverses the modern rationalist episteme and describes ethics as a primordial experience of proximity or, in the words of Derrida, "an Ethics of Ethics."[25] This ethical moment does not take place at the level of rational consciousness, but in the sphere of a primordial sensibility—"vulnerability, exposure to outrage, to wounding" (*OB* 14–15, also see *OB* 61–72 and *TI* 187–93)— originating from a relation of proximity with "the Other [a]s the signifier, he who gives a sign" (*TI* 181). Hence, ethics is no longer the product of a process of objectification of the Other by a distant, separate Ego, but depends upon a complete obligation to the Other despite the Other's irreducible and ultimately infinite alterity. This alterity is what Levinas calls the "face" of a being escaping the economy of sameness and identity of rationalism and its totalizing order of Being (*TI* 50–51). But the articulation of the ethical encounter as a primordial relation of proximity whereby the Self recognizes the face of another human being pre-culturally, that is, outside any pre-existing orders of meaning, has profound epistemological, cognitive, legal, and political implications. On the one hand, in his description of the ethical moment as an encounter that precedes, as well as exceeds, any rational understanding, Levinas no longer allows for a synthesis of phenomena by a subjectivity constituted *a priori*, that is to say, for the representational ability of the intentionality of the Ego situated outside of a relation and capable of forming totalizing interpretations. On the other hand, since the relation with the Other described by Levinas is the ethical relation, the failure to acknowledge the pre-cultural obligation to the Other's "face" leads to the loss of recognition of the humanity of the other person who remains a "face-less" being, a "bare life" whose life and death are inconsequential to me. As Levinas further describes in the essay "Peace and Proximity" (1984), the lack of recognition of the ethical order of human proximity not only bears witness to the epistemological and cognitive limits of European liberal thought, where "peace, freedom, and well-being" (*BPW* 163) find a justification in the unity of the state and the nation, rather than in the "the *fraternal* mode of proximity to the other (*autrui*)" (165), but explains the contradiction and paradoxes of European consciousness: "its millennia of fratricidal, political, and bloody struggles, of imperialism, of human hatred and exploitation, up to our century of world wars, genocides, the Holocaust, and terrorism; of unemployment, the continuing poverty of the Third World" (163). In his second major work, *Otherwise than Being, or Beyond Essence*, Levinas further develops his meditation on the subject. He does not conceive of it as an *a priori* state, but as an entity that acquires meaning and significance in its relation to the Other, a subjectivity-as-subjection completely hostage to the Other's demands, needs, and wants. And precisely because, as Alphonso Lingis has acutely commented, "[T]o acknowledge the imperative force of another is to put oneself in his place, not in order to appropriate one's own objectivity, but in order to answer to his need, to supply for his want with one's own substance" (*OB* "Translator's Introduction," xxviii), the ethical exposure to the alterity of the Other is a responsibility that requires a complete process of substitution. Nonetheless, substitution remains fundamental to the ontology of the Self. It is only by putting oneself in the place of another one, and assuming a total responsibility for the Other, that subjectivity finds its authentic constitution in an ethical relation between human beings.

In addition to further refining the notions of Self and Other, in *Otherwise than Being, or Beyond Essence* Levinas also departs from the ontological terminology that he had employed in *Totality and Infinity* to describe the ethical encounter with the "face." As a result of both self-critique[26] and following Derrida's essay "Violence and Metaphysics,"[27] Levinas submits his previous philosophical speech to a deconstructive process. The result of this operation is "amphibiology," a language described by Levinas as the product of the braiding of the "saying" with the "said" and that, for clarity's sake, can be usefully reformulated in terms of Derrida's articulation of the interweaving of writing and speech.[28] Like Derrida's logocentric speech, the "said" is the language of metaphysics. Its aim is that of making present, of re-presenting, of com-prehending, of turning diachrony into synchrony. Hence, the "said" designates and thematizes, assigns identity and establishes essence, states and asserts, totalizes and assimilates (*OB* 40). By contrast, the "saying," for which, in *Otherwise than Being*, Levinas can obviously not give a definition without the danger of falling into the realm of the "said,"[29] is the space where the ethical moment acquires signification. As such, it is the site where the identity of the one breaks down when summoned by the "face" of the Other. It is also the site of substitution and infinite responsibility for the Other.

It could be argued that, since any appearance of the "saying" would result in its betrayal, or better yet, in a thematized, re-presented Being belonging to the order of the "said," the ethical moment is fated to remain outside representation, forever confined to silence and oblivion by the totalizing system with which it is interwoven.[30] However, Levinas indicates that this is not the case. Through an often-employed metaphor of a thread whose continuity is interrupted by knots (*OB* 25, 105, 167–71), he repeatedly suggests that "amphibiology" implies two orders of meaning. These orders are the order of the "saying," which becomes readable as the non-thematizable, as the ethical supplement that prevents the order of the "said" from achieving the totalizing closure of ontological language: his *ex-ception* to being, as though being's other were an event of being (*OB* 6).[31]

Because of the emphasis placed by Levinas on the discursive structures that are constitutive of the "amphibiology" of language, it becomes clear, at this point, how his mediation between a humanist concern with the ethical imperative and a post-rationalist episteme extends far beyond the field of philosophical inquiry to encompass the practice of listening, that is to say, the activity of reading, interpreting, and critiquing. More precisely, Levinas's non-ontological ethical philosophy provides a model for conceptualizing the *ethos* of the narratives of migrant and postcolonial authors that have emerged in the contemporary Italian literary landscape. In pragmatic terms, this *ethos* equates with a labor of reading and scholarly inquiry that answers the summons of the textual voice by articulating those moments where the "saying" interrupts the totalizing truth of the "said".

These interruptions are well elucidated in the narrative model proposed by Adam Zachary Newton in his *Narrative Ethics*.[32] From the premise that narrative establishes a system of relations with readers dependent upon the uniqueness of the ethical situation, Newton proposes a Levinas-inspired model based upon "an interactive rather than a legislative order."[33] This model comprises a narrational, a representational, and a hermeneutic ethics. "Narrational ethics" articulates, for Newton, a moment of "saying" by activating "the dialogic system of exchanges at work among tellers, listeners, and witnesses, and the intersubjective responsibilities and claims which follow from acts of storytelling."[34] "Representational ethics" is associated to the otherness of Levinas's "face" and therefore is concerned with the issue of recognition, with "an anagnorisis that extends beyond the dynamics of plot to the exigent and collaborative unfolding of character, the sea change wrought when selves become either narrating or narrated."[35] The last category, "hermeneutic ethics," encompasses both "narrational" and "representational" ethics but relocates them from the literary space of the aesthetic to the political space of social reality.

Turning now to two works that exemplify the first and second generation of migrant and postcolonial writings in Italy, namely Salah Methnani's *Immigrato* (Immigrant) and Gabriella Ghermandi's *Regina di fiori e di perle* (Queen of Flowers and Pearls), I will illustrate how the framework provided by Levinas's philosophy and Newton's narratological model enables a practice of reading as a listening to ethical moments of signification. Expressed by the "face" of the migrant and postcolonial Others, these moments of signification call into question the themes and images of the modern Italian Self and, occasionally, even the African reading subject, while facilitating the imagining of forms of human sociality founded on the irreducible presence of the Other as a human being *simpliciter,* that is, a being before culture and representation.

SALAH METHNANI'S *IMMIGRATO* (1990)

Methnani's *Immigrato* has been rightly hailed as a milestone in the contemporary landscape of Italian literature. As one of the first examples of a migrant author speaking in the first person about his lived experience as an undocumented Tunisian in Italy, it undoubtedly exemplifies an act of "talking back," an illustration of how "Literature initiates a discourse in which the migrant is not only the 'foreigner'. . . but also a speaking subject."[36] However, Methnani's *Immigrato* represents much more than a gesture aimed at recovering the migrant from a condition of silence. When read from the path of inquiry opened by the philosophy of Levinas, Methnani's voice emerges as the "face" of the Other, a "visitation" that asserts the "Humanism of the Other," that is, the sacredness of "the human independent of culture and history" (*HOM* 38).

Contrary to the reading expectations encoded in its title, the first chapter of *Immigrato,* "In Tunis," opens with a description of Salah, a twenty-seven year-old Tunisian from a solid middle-class upbringing who holds a university degree in Russian and English.[37] As the chapter progresses, the reader learns of Salah's decision to migrate to Italy. Yet, his decision is variously associated with Italy as land of opportunities originating among Tunisian youth during the last years of the presidency of Habib Bourghiba as well as with sentiments of curiosity and desire for the unknown culture of a "foreign" country. In addition, Italy is also seen as providing a temporary resolution to a distant father-son relationship. In short, the motivations that lead Salah to Italy are many. Bound up with an alterity that is the result of historical and personal circumstances as well as a human desire and curiosity for the unknown, the motivations ultimately elude the full understanding of the reader. What is certain, however, is that from these initial pages, the image of the migrant as a "homogeneous, 'inferior' cultural mass"[38] is challenged by the voice of a multifaceted, complex person.

Upon his arrival in Sicily, however, the humanity of Methnani is put in question. His university degree does not provide him access to legal work and therefore to an employment contract necessary to obtain a stay-permit. Finding himself as "a North African immigrant, without work, without home, undocumented" (26) and in a state that defines the humanity of being in legal-political terms—a European, a native, a legal citizen of Italy—Salah comes to the realization that to Italian eyes he has becomes the *non habet personam,* the person in the biological sense only. Excluded from what

Agamben calls "the cities of men,"[39] Salah is increasingly transformed by the host society into a living body, struggling for the bare necessities to ensure his biological survival as countless other Tunisian, Moroccan, Senegalese, and Nigerians migrants do. In an excruciating quest for food and shelter, Salah decides to embark in a journey northward, from the Sicilian city of Mazara del Vallo to Milan. This journey, narrated in a series of chapters that bear the names of Italian cities noted for their high migrant population, "Palermo," "Naples, "Rome, "Florence," "Padua," "Turin," and "Milan," documents the many experiences of pain, exclusion, violence and abuse that Salah endures. The record of Salah's travels ends in the city of Milan where he finds a temporary shelter in the "Cascina Rosa," one of the many buildings condemned by Italian municipal authorities that are now occupied by undocumented migrants: from "Cascina Rosa," Salah departs for Rome. The book closes with the recollection of Salah's return to Tunisia described in the chapter "In Kairouan." Here, a casual reference discloses to the reader the passing of a law that allows undocumented migrants to remain in Italy with a stay-permit. Yet, Salah does not provide any information of how and when he received this permit and *Immigrato* concludes by announcing the beginning of other journeys towards unknown destinations.

Such overt omission of references to the juridical context surrounding migration is crucial and merits further reflection. As a work published in 1990, *Immigrato* is written against a political background that, after lengthy legislative debates over the undocumented presence of people, led Italian lawmakers to grant a series of amnesties, or "sanatorie," between 1979 and 1982. These temporary measures to control an ever-increasing flow of people, would eventually lead to the first program to regularize immigration in 1986, followed by the Martelli Law in 1990, or Law 39/90. Even though the final version of the law, vigorously opposed by the right, was much less liberal than it was originally proposed, it still represented a significant improvement over an existing legislation whose core principles were based on the Fascist Laws of 1931. While Law 39/40 included larger fines and harsher deportation regulations for undocumented migrants, it also allowed entry for family reunification, introduced the right of asylum and of self-employment, and continued to grant periodic amnesties while facilitating the issuing of stay-permits. Yet, Salah's voice is remarkably silent over this legislative debate and does not relate his testimony to the Italian juridical context against which it is obviously situated. Salah limits his reference to the brief line mentioned above, while in another passage of *Immigrato* he even voices his indifference towards the Italian juridical debate (121). This lack of engagement over a major legislative debate is significant and deserves more consideration, particularly when compared to the testimony of another writer belonging to the first-generation of migrant writers in Italy, Pap Khouma, the author of *I Was an Elephant Salesman*. In it, Khouma expresses his happiness following the issuing of stay-permits by the Italian legislative system [40] and voices sentiments of relief over the qualification of humanity that the law promises. [41] Yet, by trusting that the new legislation will guarantee migrants access to the fellowship of human beings, Khouma implicitly lends legitimacy to the juridical order of the state, validating its premises that human life is politically qualified life, that humanity is not a universal, invariable attribute but a socially and culturally defined role. By contrast, in the omission of any sustained references to Italy's legislative measures, Methnani's *Immigrato* questions juridical definitions of the human being sanctioned by the nation-state, forcing readers into taking responsibility for the suffering of those lives that, ungoverned and unprotected by the state sovereignty of the destination country, have become inconsequential. Otherwise stated, the silence of *Immigrato* over major Italian legislation indicates that the force of his testimony resides in an ethical relation "'before' history and 'before' culture" (*HOM* 38), in the signs that affirm the humanity of being in the "face" of a vulnerable, destitute Other who remains above and beyond the horizons of existing and emerging polities, including the relatively liberal Martelli Law. As Levinas comments in "The Rights of Man and the Rights of the Other,"

> The defense of the rights of man corresponds to a vocation *outside* the state, disposing, in a political society, of a kind of extra-territoriality, like that of the prophecy in the face of the political powers of the Old Testament, a vigilance totally different from political intelligence, a lucidity not limited to yielding before the formalism of universality, but upholding justice itself in its limitations. (*DF* 123)

An early example of the signs that affirm the humanity of being "extra-territorially," "the rights of man . . . *outside* the state," to reprise Levinas's words, occurs in the opening pages of Salah's testimony. Salah reacts to his newly found circumstances in Italy by refusing a form of existence limited to that of a physical body to be fed but also controlled, incarcerated, and punished. He thus assumes the role of a curious tourist, visiting the Sistine Chapel, the Vatican Museums, and the Roman Forum (52) while planning trips to other sites, such as the Egyptian museum of Turin (102). But besides describing acts that consciously seek to affirm the humanity of his being outside juridical categories, Salah also does so by questioning the distinction between Self and Other, native and foreign body, person and non-person sanctioned by modern state sovereignty. As early as the chapter "In Mazara," for example, his voice complicates boundaries by foregrounding a pre-modern Italian history of contaminations and crossovers, such as that recorded in the area of the city known as the Kasbah, where the memory of the Arab origins of Mazara, colonized by the Arabs in the ninth century, is revealed in its urban and anthropological landscape (21). Likewise, in the chapter "In Palermo," a shabby apartment in the neighborhood of Vucciria in Palermo, another city transformed by the Arabs, is described as a Tunisian *minaret* while the streets of Naples evoke a Middle Eastern "bazaar" (40).

As the testimony progresses, the casual evocation of a history of contaminations, hybridization, and crossings constitutive of Italian-ness across the centuries deepens into the conversion, or reconversion of the modern Italian Self into the vulnerable Other of *La storia*,[42] the Other of the Italian global diaspora who, from the unification of the peninsula in 1860 well into the post-World War II era, was expelled by modern definitions of Italian identity. In this challenge to consciousness, "[*mise en question*] by the face" (*HOM* 32), the significance of the short reference to the meeting between Salah and Tonino Cusumano, the author of a work entitled *Il ritorno infelice*, should not be lost. In this book, Cusumano had examined the post-World War II migration of Tunisians to the province of Trapani but his work placed the recent arrival of Tunisians within a much larger history of trans-Mediterranean migration binding the people of Sicily with those of Tunisia. This history[43] took place uninterruptedly throughout the centuries, becoming especially significant after the unification in 1860. By 1880, the Italian Consulate of Tunisia registered close to twelve thousand individuals but these figures were most likely higher since they were based on a census that excluded illegal migrants and those who had left Italy to avoid the lengthy military conscription that was introduced when the Italian state was formed in 1860. The ever-growing Sicilian presence became a concern for France, leading to the Treaty of Bardo in 1881 and the Convention of Marsa that established the French protectorate over Tunisia. Sicilian migration, however, continued and, by the first decade of the twentieth century, the French government resorted to repatriation. Nevertheless, the presence of Sicilians would diminish only with the Tunisian proclamation of independence from France in 1956 and the nationalization of private property that forced many to return to their island of origin. From there, they would once again leave, taking the path of other migrations, often towards the Italian cities of Northern Italy where industrialization had led to a demand of unskilled workers. However, as Cusumano's book illustrates, the patterns of emigration and immigration between Tunisia and Sicily have continued even after the 1950s, when the province of the Sicilian city of Trapani became the destination of Tunisians who returned to the same villages from where Sicilians had departed.

In addition to the reference to the meeting with Cusumano, other episodes analogously lead to the recovery of the expelled Other and concomitant loss of the Self 's "coincidence with self" (33) of modern definitions of Italian identity. Thus, for example, Salah recalls a conversation with Carmen, a Sicilian woman who speaks of the destitution of Southern Italy and the history of the Italian diaspora, or the portion of a journey by train that he shared with a Calabrese family en route to Rome to visit relatives separated by internal migration. An additional passage provides even a more powerful evocation of the Italian history of migration. Like another first-generation migrant writer, Moshen Melliti, the author of *Pantanella,* [44] Methnani explicitly stresses the specular function of the phenomenon of migration by citing the words of an Italian migrant, in this case an old Sicilian boatman, who describes the alienation that he felt as an immigrant in the North as being similar to that endured by the North Africans in Italy (21).

In his *The Suffering of the Immigrant,* Abdelmalek Sayad reflects on the specular function of migration that is expressed in the exchange between Salah and the old Sicilian boatman. Sayad argues that since immigrants are, at their origins, emigrants, that is, human beings with a history, a country, a memory, and a culture, emigration and immigration cannot and should not be separated by a system of difference and opposition: "One's country's immigration is another country's emigration. The two are indissociable aspects of a single reality." [45] Therefore, migrants reveal what is latent in our social order, bring to light who we are, forcing us to acknowledge that the Other, regardless of its legal and juridical status, is before all else a vulnerable "face," the same "face" that was once one's uncle or one's father. In this sense, the specularity of migration engenders dispositions necessary for an ethical relation of the one-for-the-Other. This is a relation that not only summons us to recognize the humanity of the one that is outside the legal systems sanctioned by the nation-state, lost in the anonymity of the crowds of today just as we were lost in those of yesterday, but enables the authentic constitution of our subjectivity in an ethical relation between human beings. In the words of Levinas's "Judaism," "The traumatic experience of my slavery in Egypt constitutes my very humanity, a fact that immediately allies me to the workers, the wretched, and the persecuted people of the world. My uniqueness lies in the responsibility I display for the Other" (*DF* 26).

Much more than an inscription of a literary voice in the landscape of contemporary Italian literature, then, *Immigrato* presents the reader with an ethical mandate. Through the voice of Salah, it allows the vulnerability and dispossession of the "face" to emerge in the nudity of a pre-cultural meaning, in a "visitation" where "mundane signification is disturbed and upset by another presence . . . non-integrated in the world" (*HOM* 31). And it is precisely in this upheaval of a mundane signification that would deny the visibility to the humanity of being, that the ethical dimension is disclosed. The Self, summoned by the one who has a "face," despite the legal and juridical institutions that would deny it, can no longer return to the certainty of the Same, to "the original form of identification" (*HOM* 29). Having been hailed by the Other's "trace," the imprint of an indelible human being that has irreparably disturbed the world's order of the modern Italian subject, the Self is now summoned to answer the call of responsibility in the realization of a more just polity. In the words of Levinas's *Humanism of the Other:*

"There, in the relation with the face—the ethical relation—the rectitude of an orientation or sense is traced" (34).

But in the contemporary Italian literary landscape, other presences, other "faces" compromise the Self's relationship with itself, challenging the forms of our consciousness and demanding that we assume responsibility not just for the migrant Other of yesterday and today but also for the indignities and atrocities suffered by all the subjects impacted by the horrors of colonialism.

GABRIELLA GHERMANDI, *REGINA DI FIORI E DI PERLE* (2007)

One of these voices is that of Gabriella Ghermandi. Born in Addis Ababa from an Italian father and an Italo-Eritrean mother, Ghermandi migrated from Ethiopia to Italy in 1979. Her first major work, *Regina di fiori e di perle* (Queen of Flowers and Pearl) is one of the very few examples of accounts of Italian colonization and its aftermath from the perspective of the colonized themselves. Ghermandi's historical novel is a collection of carefully researched testimonies of men and women who had a firsthand experience of the Fascist empire. In their defenseless "faces," the image of the modern Italian Self as the benevolent colonizer, bringing civilization to the "backward" people of the Horn of Africa, is not only shattered but demands are raised that this Self assume responsibility for events that span from the Fascist invasion to the present era.

Organized according to the principles of oral African storytelling, the novel opens in Debre Zeit, a town located about fifty kilometers from Addis Ababa. The elder of the house, Abba Yacob, extracts from the young character of Mahlet the promise to become one day the *azmari*[46] of the Ethiopian community, a figure similar to that of the *griot* in Western African tradition: "collect as many stories as you can. One day you will be our voice that tells. You will traverse the sea that Peter and Paul traversed and you will bring our stories in the land of the Italians. You will be the voice of our history that does not want to be forgotten" (6). Subsequent sections of the novel narrate the upbringing of Mahlet, born during the difficult years of the *Derg*, that is, the military junta that ruled the country from 1974 to 1987, her brief permanence in Italy to study at the University of Bologna, and her return to Ethiopia in the early 2000s where she fulfills her promise to Yacob and becomes the *azmari*. The stories that Mahlet collects, the "flowers and the pearls" of the title of the novel, come to configure a vast historical period that begins on October 3, 1935, when Ethiopia, one of the few countries that had escaped European colonization, was invaded by the Fascist imperial forces in a large scale war enterprise. Despite the condemnation of the Italian assault on a sovereign state on the part of the League of Nations, of which Ethiopia was a member, the advance continued till May 1936, when the Italian troops reached Addis Ababa, forcing the Negus, Hailè Selassié, to flee. After the military campaign, Italy requested from the League of Nations the recognition of the annexation of Ethiopia and all the members, with the exception of the Soviet Union, agreed to it. In the same year, Eritrea, Ethiopia and Somalia were brought together under the single unified colony of *Africa Orientale Italiana.* Italy's Savoy king, Victor Emmanuel III, was crowned Emperor of the African holdings. In 1941, after the defeat of Italy by British and Allied forces, Britain regained control of East Africa and Selassié returned to the throne. Six years later Italy lost claims to its colonies following the settlements agreed upon in the Paris Peace Treaty.

The testimony of this vast historical fresco comes to life in the oral, first person narratives of Abba Yacob, Abbaba Igirsà Salò, Farisa Alula, Dinke, the Lady with the Turtle, Kebedech Seyoum, Woizero Bekelech, and many others. Collected by Mahlet, these voices hail and summon us in a relation of ethical proximity, calling us to witness the suffering of the Other, the nakedness of the "face" that dispossesses the Italian Self from within.

Among the first stories to emerge is that of Abba Yacob who narrates the arrival of the frightful machinery of Italian tanks and airplanes and the strong counteroffensive that ensued. The counteroffensive brought together the army of Hailè Selassié with that of the resistance led by the *Arbegnà*, a group of male and female warriors that bear a number of similarities with the so-called "brigands" of southern Italy who fought against the army of the Savoy after 1860.[47] After the successful battle of Tekezza in 1935 under the command of Ras Imiru, the Italian forces reacted by strengthening their attacks on the Northern front. More battles ensued, including the one of Amba Alagi where, as the voice of another witness, Dinke, recalls, thousands of people were burned to death (163). But as the Ethiopian resistance continued to counter the Fascist advance, other weapons were used. Following the loss of the battle of Demberguina, the Italian General Badoglio ordered the use of gas, in full contravention of the Geneva Convention of 1925. Abba Yacob recalls the suffering of the Ethiopians and the killing of his parents, "two days before the *Timket,* killed by the gas" (29), as does Abbaba Igirsà Salò. The "effectiveness" of these military operations led to the Italian advance into the city of Addis Ababa, the site of a horrifying massacre told by the Lady of the Turtle. It is she who brings the testimony of the butchering of civilians on day 12 of *Yekatit.* One of the many episodes willfully buried in archives by modern Italian culture, this massacre originated in the reprisal that ensued after two boys attempted to assassinate General Rodolfo Graziani on February 19, 1937, at a public ceremony in Addis Ababa. In a state-sanctioned violence that lasted till February 21, a pogrom was unleashed against the defenseless population. Women and children were killed, houses and Copt churches were burned while thousands were rounded up to be deported to concentration camps:

> Addis Ababa was an inferno. There wasn't a single moment of silence. No truce, neither during the day nor at night. Always shootings and the rounds of machine-gun fire. And the excruciating screams of women, men, children. Screams like animals for slaughter. . . . Two days after the beginning of the inferno, vultures had appeared and falcons had multiplied in the sky. During the night the spectral screams of hyenas mixed with the growls of stray dogs fighting for pieces of the cadavers. . . . Cadavers of men, women, children and elderly . . . genital mutilations and the organs scattered on the ground . . . the sight of a pregnant woman, her belly cut open to reveal her fetus. (183–84)

In all of these testimonies the references to killings on the eve of *Timket,* a Christian celebration to commemorate the christening of Jesus, or the burning of Copt churches on day 12 of Yekatit, are not only striking reminders of the brutality of the Fascist state, but also foreground the moral ambiguity of Roman Catholicism during Fascism, an example of what Levinas calls Europe's "guilty conscience."[48] Seeking to solve the tensions that arose following the loss of territories incurred by the Papacy during the years of unification, Mussolini and Pope Pius IX signed the Lateran Pacts in 1929, a concordat that remained in place till 1984 and that gave the Pope sovereignty over the Vatican, provided him with a hefty financial settlement, and promoted Catholicism to religion of state, thus securing the legitimacy of Mussolini, "'the man sent by providence,' as the pope called him."[49] Yet, when the Lateran Pacts are set against testimonies such as the one provided by Abba Yacob or Abbaba Igirsà Salò, the moral ambiguities of Roman Catholicism during the interwar years become apparent. As the novel often reminds us through names such as Abba Yacob and Abba Chereka, references to the Madonna and the Apostles Peters and Paul, and frequent descriptions of Christian celebrations and liturgical rites, Ethiopia was then (as is now) one of the oldest Christian states, having converted to Orthodox Christianity at least as early as the fourth century. Yet, since neither Ethiopia's long Christian tradition nor the official recognition of the modern Italian state as a Catholic nation after the Lateran Pacts of 1929 provided Italy with the moral grounding to recognize in the Other a fellow human being, the novel summons readers to acknowledge the importance of a pre-cultural ethical relation, reminding us that "signification is situated before Culture . . . ; it is situated in Ethics, presupposition of all Culture and all signification. Morality does not belong to Culture; it allows us to judge culture, to evaluate the dimension of its elevation. Elevation ordains being" (*HOM* 36).

But besides summoning readers to answer to the horrors inflicted by the Fascist military forces onto a Christian population excluded from the right-bearing Catholic community of the Italian nation-state, other "faces" come forward to narrate the violence of Italian colonialism. These voices bear witness to the role of race in the definition of human beings that was introduced by the Fascist racial laws in the late 1930s to further perpetuate horrific acts against both the natives and Italians alike. Abba Yacob narrates how his younger sister Amarech had become pregnant with the child of an Italian soldier named Daniel. Whereas up to 1936 unions between Italian men and indigenous women were tolerated, even if regulated by laws of "madamismo", or concubinage, in 1937 a new racial legislation prohibited mixed familial arrangements, de-legitimated biracial children, criminalized mixed race unions, and punished the perpetrators with five years of imprisonment.[50] To escape the racial laws, the couple ran away to the mountains but shortly after the birth of their child, Daniel and Amarech were killed by Fascist militia. Since before her execution Amarech had expressed the wish that Yacob raise her child, an inter-racial baby girl named Rosa, Yacob abandoned the resistance movement. In his care, Rosa, a thinly veiled portrait of Gabriella Ghermandi's own mother,[51] was able to escape the fate of the vast majority of mixed race offspring, over ten thousand of them born in Ethiopia between 1936 and 1941. Unrecognized by the Italian government and subject to the prejudice of both Italians and Africans alike, these children were secluded in missionary centers where they worked to expiate the "sin" of being racially mixed.

The ethical force of Yacob's story clearly summons the Italian reader into taking responsibility for the racial policies of the Fascist regime and their impact on Italians and Ethiopians alike. However, this story is also significant because it broadens its ethical summons to include the African readership. Through the character of Yacob, it describes how totalizing frames of references initially prevented him from accepting Daniel. Thus, for example, upon discovering that Daniel was a *"tallian sollato"* (26), Yacob had fallen prey to a mad rage. Fuelled by his culture's designation of the Other as the malevolent Italian colonizer, Yakob's rage did not subside even when he learned that Daniel was the son of poor farmers from the Veneto region, conscripted in the Fascist army against his will. Yacob was eventually able to accept his sister's union with Daniel but only after the couple's death, when fellow resistance fighter Alemtsehay placed Rosa in Yacob's arms (55).

Testimonies such as the ones provided by Ghermandi's novel, then, call the Self—primarily the modern Italian Self but, as is the case of Yacob's story, also the African readership—into a submission to the call of the Other, to the "face" that, in an act of "traumatics,"[52] enters our field of consciousness to demand our responsibility for the unspeakable horror and suffering perpetrated by the order of a state which, to date, has yet to acknowledge the horrifying cost of imperialism and racism on human lives.[53] In post-World War II Italy, those who committed colonial crimes were briefly imprisoned or just acquitted. While the racial laws were abolished in the Paris Peace Treaty of 1947, Italo-Africans were not recognized as legitimate children of Italian fathers till 1975. Condemned to live a life of stigmatization, many Italo-Africans committed suicide.[54] Given the lack of responsibility over the violence inflicted on countless human lives, it comes as no surprise that reparation for war damages on public and private property was only partially honored and continues to be the subject of much debate in present-day Italy. These efforts at mystifying the horror of colonization coalesced around the publication of the multivolume *L'Italia in Africa* between 1953 and 1963. Promoted by the Ministry of Foreign Affair and managed by a committee of twenty members, fifteen of whom were former governors of the colonies or high officials, this publication presented Italian colonialism as fundamentally more humane than that of other European powers, perpetrating the myth of Italians as benign colonizers that continues to be widely believed by public opinion.

While Ghermandi's novel focuses primarily on bearing witness to the horrors of the Fascist colonizing efforts and racial policies, it should be noted that her work also summons a more global readership into taking responsibility for the ordeals of the Horn of Africa following World War II—a readership that encompasses Britain, America, the former Soviet Union, Eritrea and Ethiopia. More precisely, by extending past the 1940s to the year 2000, the novel's reach and scope spans a troubled postcolonial period that saw the restoration to the throne of Selassié in 1941 by Allied forces, the annexation of Eritrea by Ethiopia in 1962, the advent of the *Derg* in 1974, and the thirty year war between Eritrea and Ethiopia that ended in 1991 but ushered in a mass migration from the Horn of Africa towards Italy and other European nations.

In 1952, more than ten years after Selassié's restoration to the throne by British and Allied forces, the United Nations gave Eritrea in trusteeship to Ethiopia, which federated it as its fourteenth province. While initiating a broad program of Westernization of Ethiopia supported by renewed diplomatic ties with the United States, Selassié also pursued his imperial ambitions over Eritrea, a country strategically located on the Red Sea and rich in mineral deposits. Selassié's early efforts at the culturation of Eritrea, such as the compulsory teaching of Amharic in all Eritrean schools, gave way to a more overt political expansion. In 1962, he dismissed Eritrea's Parliament and annexed Eritrea to Ethiopia, causing a war of independence that ended only in 1991. By the early 1970s, criticism over Selassié's increasingly imperialistic monarchy, coupled with a lack of effective economic and political reforms, fuelled an Ethiopian Marxist movement that in 1974 staged a coup with the support of the Soviet Union and the Eastern Bloc. Selassié was removed from power, members of his government, including ministers, councilors, and court officials, were summarily executed, and Menghistu Hailè was named chairman of a socialist and military council, the Coordinating Committee of the Armed Forces, Police, and Territorial Army, or "Derg." Mahlet, who was born during the time of the *Derg*, narrates her upbringing during the seventeen years of Menghistu's totalitarian regime in pages that summon the African readership to bear witness and answer to the violence of postcolonial Ethiopia. Thus, for example, she recalls how her family's ancestral home in Addis Ababa was confiscated by a Soviet-style regime (98). Mahlet's father and uncles vainly sought to convince the authorities that their home in Addis Ababa belonged to a family that had fought the Fascists and that their ownership of a second property in Debre Zeit hardly qualified them as bourgeois landlords. Yet, the authorities answered their pleas with threats of imprisonment (98). Mahlet's memories also encompass descriptions of the massive militarization of the country financed by the Soviet Union and the Eastern Bloc, the period of purges of suspected enemies of the *Derg* known as the "Red Scare," the patrols led by terrifying bands of young soldiers armed with Soviet Kalashnikovs, and the evolution of political unrest into a civil war, a genocide that forced hundreds of thousands to leave the country in what is known as the first Ethiopian diaspora (91–2). By the late 1980s, discontent with the regime had mounted and opposition groups took over the capital of Addis Ababa in 1991. Menghistu was forced to flee Ethiopia for Zimbabwe and Eritrea finally separated from Ethiopia after decades of wars. The departure of Menghistu, however, did not bring peace. In a description of a state of violence that is reminiscent of the memories of the Fascist colonial advance, Mahlet narrates how Addis Ababa had become, one again, a theatre of war. Horror and abuse had returned, but victims and perpetrators were now fratricidal Africans: "Shootings, rounds of machine-guns fire, smoke, fire and explosion. . . . The elderly of our family had the gate closed and established guard duties among the men of the house. We, the women, barricaded ourselves between the house, the backyard, and the service rooms" (103).

While Mahlet's family was spared, the liberation of Addis Ababa further plunged the city in a state of chaos, as those who had lost property under Menghistu sought to regain it while the fighters who had opposed him could no longer adapt to a life of peace: "the disease had remained in the body of the fighters. . . . They had been accustomed to violence, to extreme sensations, to actions dictated by the instinct of survival. The poison of that war in the bodies of our fighters would take a long time before letting them free to return to us" (110).

Passages such as these, then, extend the ethical force of the novel beyond the Italian readership. In revisiting the upbringing of Mahlet during the years of the *Derg*, Ghermandi's *Regina di fiori e di perle* reveals a summoning that also complicates the themes and images of the postcolonial Selves, demanding from a global readership, which includes Ethiopians and Eritreans, a response to the Ethiopian civil war, the Eritrean war of independence, and the diaspora from the Horn of Africa that followed years of violence and abuse.

The last story of Ghermandi's *Regina di fiori e di perle*, "The Story of Woizero Bekelech and of Mister Antonio," well captures the broadening of the text's ethical force suggested by Abba Yacob's story and the narrative of Mahlet's upbringing in post-World War II Ethiopia through a nuanced representation that fractures the "said" of colonial and postcolonial discourse alike while pointing towards an order of "peace" to be found in "the *fraternal* mode of proximity to the other," in "the *surplus* of sociality and of love" (*OB* 165).

Bekelech's story is told to Mahlet after she has decided to fulfill the promise made to Yacob and therefore takes place around the year 2000. Bekelech recounts how she had left Addis Ababa for Italy to work, as many African migrant women do, as a domestic caretaker. One day, she met one of her neighbors who, as a young man, had enlisted in the Fascist militia in the hope of working in Ethiopia as a translator of Amharic. Most impressed by Antonio's fluency in oral and written Amharic, the illiterate Bekelech asks him to write letters to her family in Ethiopia. Yet, the cultural meaning that frames her understanding of Antonio, the "said" of a totalizing anti-colonial discourse, leads her to need repeatedly to verify that the words that she dictates to him have indeed been accurately transcribed. As Antonio continues to prove his trustworthiness, a relationship of proximity develops between them. Antonio not only listens to the stories of abuse that Bekelech endured but restores her sentiments of pride for her own heritage. In a powerful evocation of the ethical relation of the one-for-the-Other, Antonio, the officer of the Fascist militia in colonial time, answers Bekelech's needs by teaching her that Ethiopians come from the same land as the Queen of Sheba; that they are the rightful descendants of King Solomon; that their language is beautiful and rich in metaphors, with words that fill the mouth with poetry (222). As Bekelech draws closer to Antonio, she invites him to travel home with her. Yet, Antonio declines her invitation and, in a call for mercy, reveals to Bekelech how his shame for the horrors of colonization will forever prevent him from returning to Ethiopia: "I will not come because I would not be able to look at anyone in the face. In all these years, I reflected over many things, over many events that happened while I was there and I began to feel a great shame. Bekelech: I am ashamed, ashamed of what my country has done to yours" (231). In this powerful image of a human fellowship between the colonizer and the colonized, the novel allows us to imagine an order of sociality and love, a "peace" founded in the fraternal proximity between two inassimilable, irreducible, and unique others that is also affirmed in the final address to the reader of Ghermandi's choral novel: "today I am telling you his [Yacob's] story that is my story but also your story" (251).

TOWARDS COMING COMMUNITIES

Yet, despite the presence of more and more voices like those of Methnani and Ghermandi, it is important to recall that the ethical moments between self and Other, tellers and listeners, writers and readers emerge in a context where the nation and its totalizing orders of meaning continue to exert a great deal of hegemony. Despite Italy's endorsement of the supra-, if not post-national models of political, economic, and cultural integrations of the EU, as well as of various International Human Rights regimes (e.g., Geneva Conventions, Universal Declaration of Human Rights, etc.), the country has held fast to normative cartographies of state sovereignty that not only derive from an obsolete Westphalian model of territoriality but which, in recent years, have also been inflected by a frightful reaffirmation of racial policies. Thus, it is legitimate to ask how the ethical, face-to-face encounter with the self and the Other exemplified by the intersubjective relation that bind these voices with readers and listeners can find a translation into the political sphere.[55] Such relation, to which Levinas dedicates important pages in both *Totality and Infinity* (212–14) as well as *Otherwise than Being* (156–62), is named the third party, or *le tiers*.[56] As the collective site of all other human beings, this is the space where the ethical relation of interiority and proximity of the-one-for-the-Other can be opened to encompass the plurality of beings of a community. This community not only provides the ethical alternative to the political rationality of state and nation, but is also the location from where our institutional formations can be put under scrutiny for an on-going democratic project. This is the reason why, as Critchley acutely notes, "Levinas's thinking does not result in an apoliticism or ethical quietism. . . . Rather, ethics leads back to politics, to the demand for a just polity. . . . Ethics is ethical for the sake of politics, that is, for the sake of a more just society."[57]

Thus, in answering the call of migrant and postcolonial works, there lies the possibility of widening the ethical relation of proximity that binds self and Other, tellers and readers in the creation of new communities. To reprise Adam Zachary Newton, these communities will be founded on the responsibilities that follow from listening and reading but also from discussing and teaching works of fiction that are exemplified by the modest but ever growing number of grassroots initiatives, intercultural projects, civil associations and NGOs that are beginning to take hold on Italian soil. In the social performativity of this "hermeneutic ethics" the self-enclosed space of the aesthetic unfolds into that of social reality and communities founded on the ethical relation of sensibility arising from the narratives and testimonies of migrant and postcolonial experiences become agent of political change. Similar to what Giorgio Agamben, in *The Coming Community*, describes as the "singularities" of new forms of sociality born in a zone of indistinction between self and Other and based on models of non-essential solidarity, rather than on state-sanctioned bonds, these communities are also a "coming politics." As such they carry the promise of the advent of an ethical human sociality and, with it, a more just and democratic polity. In the words of *Humanism of the Other*, "Our era . . . is action for the world to come, surpassing one's era. . . . Léon Blum wrote . . . : 'We work *in* the present, *not* for the present. . . . May the future and the most distant things be the rule of all the present days'" (28).

NOTES

1. See Alessandro Dal Lago, *Non-Persons: The Exclusion of Migrants in a Global Society*, trans. Marie Orton (Vimodrone, MI: IPOC, 2009); Livia Turco, *I nuovi Italiani. L'immigrazione, I pregiudizi, la convivenza* (Milano: Mondadori, 2005); Corrado Bonifazi, *L'immigrazione straniera in Italia* (Bologna: Il Mulino, 1998); and Enrico Pugliese, *L'Italia tra migrazioni internazionali e migrazioni interne* (Bologna: Il mulino, 2006).

2. Giorgio Agamben, *Homo Sacer: Sovereign Power and Bare Life* (Stanford: Stanford University Press, 1998), 7. But see also his *State of Exception* (Chicago: University of Chicago Press, 2005).

3. Antonio Gramsci, *The Southern Question*, trans. Pasquale Verdicchio (West Lafayette, IN: Bordighera, 1995), 16. See also Pasquale Verdicchio, "The Preclusion of Postcolonial Discourse in Southern Italy," in *Revisioning Italy. National Identity and Global Culture*, ed. Beverly Allen and Mary Russo (Minneapolis: University of Minnesota Press, 1997), 191–212.

4. For an in-depth discussion, see Aliza Wong, *Race and Nation in Liberal Italy, 1861-1911: Meridionalism, Empire, and Diaspora* (New York: Palgrave Macmillan, 2006).

5. See John Dickie, *Darkest Italy: The Nation and Stereotypes of the Mezzogiorno* (New York: St. Martin's, 1999); Nelson Moe, *The View from Vesuvius: Italian Culture and the Southern Question* (Berkeley: University of California Press, 2002); and Vito Teti, *La razza maledetta: Origini del pregiudizio antimeridionale* (Rome: Manifestolibri, 1993).

6. See Ezio Giannotti, Giulia Miccichè, and Roberta Ribero, eds. *Migrazioni nel Mediterraneo. Scambi, convivenze e contaminazioni tra Italia e NordAfrica* (Torino: L'Harmattan Italia, 2002); Marcella Delle Donne and Umberto Melotti, *Mediterraneo. Di qua di là dal mare. Tunisia Italia* (Roma: Ediesse, 2002).

7. It should be noted that Italian imperialism would also extend to the islands of the Dodecanese archipelago and Albania.

8. In the eighteenth century, the superiority of Northern versus Southern Europeans was codified and explained through influential theories of climates, of which Montesquieu's *L'esprit des Lois* (1748) is probably the best-known representative. In it, Montesquieu argued for the negative impact of temperate climate on human behavior while attributing feminine traits to "Orientals" and southern Europeans. Montesquieu's work shaped an extremely vast library, coming to influence a host of other eighteenth and nineteenth century writings by northern travelers in the European Mediterranean, including, among others, von Riedesel, Marquis de Sade, Vivant Denon, Swinburne, Gibbon, Dryden, Lalande, Lenormant, Madame de Staël, Goethe, Renan, de Lesser, Stendhal. As products of the Enlightenment, the more benign writers of the *Grand Tour* often commented on the corruption of the government and the misery of the people while trusting in the teleological march of history towards progress that would be brought about through enlightened reforms. More frequently, however, travelers lamented the indolence, effeminacy, and lack of industriousness of Southern people. For additional discussion, see Silvana Patriarca, "Indolence and Regeneration: Tropes and Tensions of Risorgimento Patriotism," *American Historical Review* 110, no. 3 (2005): 380–408, and Moe.

9. It is also worth recalling that, while the Liberal Italian state was preparing for the invasion of Eritrea, it was starting the repression against the uprising of the Sicilian Fasci between 1890 and 1894. As Verdicchio comments, "Placed in such close proximity, the dates . . . suggest an imperialist program of Piedmontese origins that worked its way down the

peninsula before setting sail for the African continent" (*Bound by Distance. Rethinking Nationalism through the Italian Diaspora* [Madison and Teaneck, NJ: Farleigh Dickinson University Press, 1997], 27).

10. The term Liberal State refers to the post-unifications governments that lasted from 1861 till the dismissal of Parliament by Fascism in 1923.

11. See Mark Choate, *Emigrant Nation: The Making of Italy Abroad* (Cambridge: Cambridge University Press, 2008). For an excellent account of transnationalism from below, see Donna Gabaccia, *Italian Workers of the World* (Urbana and Chicago: University of Illinois Press, 2001) as well as her *Militants and Migrants* (New Brunswick: Rutgers University Press, 1988).

12. "The migratory experience of Italians has not yet been elaborated by the collective culture. It neither has a prominent position in the historical works nor has it produced memory, images, or symbols. One remembers only the grind; the private adventure has not been integrated into our national history, it does not make up part of our collective ethos, it does not feed the public feeling and *ethos*" (Turco, *I nuovi italiani*, 11; my translation).

13. While there is a long tradition in Italy of studies of Italian emigration authored by political scientists, historians, and anthropologists, including the major repository of data contained in *Bollettino dell'Emigrazione* (1902 to 1927), the literary voices of the diaspora struggle to acquire recognition since the study and teaching of the culture that originated from migration is mostly confined to works by autoctonous Italian authors. As Verdicchio writes, "A literature of emigration cannot include only *L'altro figlio* (The other son), by Pirandello; *Italy*, by Pascoli; *Sull'oceano* (On the ocean), by De Amicis, *Emigranti* (Emigrants), by Perri; *La patria lontana* (The distant homeland) by Corradini; and *Il canto degli emigranti* (The song of the emigrants), by Costabile," it must include the works of Pietro di Donato, John Fante, Dodici Azpadu, Mary Bucci Bush, and others . . . (*Bound by Distance*, 97). To Verdicchio's North Atlantic canon should also be added voices from the Italian diaspora in Latin America, Australia, Northern Europe and Africa.

14. Among the very few works that were published before 1980s are Angelo Del Boca's *La Guerra d'Abissinia 1935-1941* (Milano: Feltrinelli, 1965) and Giorgio Rochat, *Il colonialismo italiano* (Torino: Loescher, 1973).

15. For a discussion of Italian colonialism, see Jacqueline Andall and Duncan Derek, eds., *Italian Colonialism: Legacy and Memory* (Oxford: Peter Lang, 2005); Nicola Labanca, *Oltremare. Storia dell'espanzione coloniale italiana* (Bologna: Il mulino, 2002); Miguel Mellino, "Italy and Postcolonial Studies. A Difficult Encounter," *Interventions* 8, no. 3 (2006): 461–71; Patrizia Palumbo, *A Place in the Sun: Africa in Italian Colonial Culture from Post-Unification to the Present* (Berkeley: University of California Press, 2003); Alessandro Triulzi, "Displacing the Colonial Event," *Interventions* 8, no. 3 (2006): 430–43; Ruth Ben-Ghiat and Mia Fuller, eds., *Italian Colonialism* (New York: Palgrave Macmillan, 2005).

16. For a discussion of the myth of Italians as "brava gente" and of their colonialism on the cheap, see Angelo Del Boca, *Italiani, brava gente?* (Milano: Neri Pozza, 2005).

17. My reference is to Marc Augé, *Non Places: Introduction to an Anthropology of Supermodernity* (London and New York: Verso, 1995).

18. See Armando Gnisci, Armando, *Il rovescio del gioco* (Roma: Sovera, 1993) and *La letteratura italiana della migrazione* (Roma: Lilith, 1998).

19. Pap Khouma and Oreste Pivetta, *Io venditore di elefanti* (Milano: Garzanti, 1990), recently translated as *I Was an Elephant Salesman: Adventures between Dakar, Paris, and Milan*, trans. Rebecca Hopkins (Bloomington: Indiana University Press, 2010); Salah Methnani and Mario Fortunato, *Immigrato* (Roma: Theoria, 1990); Saidou Moussa Ba and Alessandro Micheletti, *La promessa di Hamadi* (Novara: De Agostini, 1991); Mohamed Bouchane, *Chiamatemi Alì*, ed. Carla de Girolamo and Daniele Miccione (Milano: Leonardo, 1990); Nassera Chora, *Volevo diventare bianca*, ed. Alessandra Atti di Sarro (Rome: E/O, 1993). But see also Shirin Ramzanali Fazel, *Lontano da Mogadisciu, Nuvole sull'equatore. Gli italiani dimenticati. Una storia* (Roma: Nerosubianco, 2010): Salwa Salem and Laura Mauritanc. *Con il vento nei capelli. Vita di una donna palestinese* (Firenze: Giunti, 1993); Thea Laitef, *Lontano da Baghdad* (Roma: Sensibili alle foglie, 1994); Maria de Lourdes Jesus, *Vengo da un'isola di Capo*

Verde (Roma: Sinnos, 1996); and Fernanda Farias De Albuquerque, *Princesa* (Roma: Sensibili alle foglie, 1994).

20. For many of these early writers, the countries of origin are former French colonies. Bouchane is from Morocco, Khouma and Moussa Ba are from Senegal, Methnani is from Tunisia, Nassera Chohra is the daughter of Algerian immigrants but was born in Marseilles. For a discussion of these writers, see Graziella Parati, "Foreigners and Shadows in Italian Literature," in *Revisioning Italy: National Identity and Global Culture,* ed. Beverly Allen and Mary Jo Russo (Minneapolis: University of Minnesota Press, 1997), 169–90, and Igiaba Scego, "Scrittori migranti di seconda generazione,"Eks & Tra. (2004) or http://www.eksetra.net/forummigra/relScego.shtml. English anthologies of these writers' works are Parati's *Mediterranean Crossroads: Migration Literature in Italy* (Madison & Teaneck, NJ: Farleigh Dickinson University Press, 1999), and Marie Orton and Graziella Parati, eds., *Multicultural Literature in Contemporary Italy.* Madison and Teaneck, NJ: Farleigh Dickinson University Press, 2007).

21. For a more complete bibliography, see the online journal *Kúmá Creolizzare L'Europa* as well as *El-Ghibli.*

22. These writers come from Albania, Serbia, Croatia, Slovakia, India, Cameron, Egypt, Ethiopia, Somalia, Eritrea, Zaire, Congo, Argentina, Venezuela, Brazil, Iran, Palestine, Poland, and Russia, among others. For more information on these writers' countries of origin, see the Banca dati di Basili, http://www.disp.let.uniroma1.it/basili2001.

23. For additional discussion of Levinas's reversal of the privilege of ontology for a pre-rational ethical obligation, see Fabio Ciaramelli, "Levinas's Ethical Discourse: Between Individuation and Universality," in *Re-Reading Levinas,* ed. Robert Bernasconi and Simon Critchley (Bloomington: Indiana University Press, 1991), 83–105.

24. See also Levinas, "Ethics as First Philosophy" (*LR* 75–87).

25. Jacques Derrida, *Writing and Difference,* trans. Alan Bass (Chicago: University of Chicago Press, 1982), 111.

26. Levinas once observed, *"Totality and Infinity* was my first book. I find it very difficult to tell you, in a few words, in what way it is different from what I've said afterwards. There is the ontological terminology. I spoke of being. I have since tried to get away from that language" (*The Provocation of Levinas: Rethinking the Other,* ed. Robert Bernasconi and David Wood (New York: Routledge, 1988), 171; quoted in Simon Critchley, *The Ethics of Deconstruction: Derrida and Levinas* (West Lafayette, IN: Purdue University Press, 2002), 51.

27. Derrida, *Writing and Difference* 79–153.

28. See especially the chapter "The End of the Book and the Beginning of Writing," from Jacques Derrida's *Of Grammatology,* trans. Gayatri C. Spivak (Baltimore and London: Johns Hopkins University Press, 1976), 6–18.

29. Robert Eaglestone proposes the following description of the "saying": "1. the break-up of identity and the approach to the other. 2. substitution, passivity beyond passivity, the state of being a hostage, exposure, proximity. 3. the relation to the other and the responsibility imposed by the other" (*Ethical Criticism: Reading After Levinas* [Edinburgh: Edinburgh University Press, 1997], 143). For further discussion, see also Adriaan Peperzak, "Presentation," in *To the Other: An Introduction to the Philosophy of Emmanuel Levinas,* ed. Robert Bernasconi and Simon Critchley (West Lafayette, IN: Purdue University Press, 1993), 51–66.

30. See for example, "The saying appears only as a betrayal of itself, a 'saying teleologically turned to the kerygma of the said' . . . . The saying is transformed into *doxa,* to such an extent that it is forgotten . . . in the said. It is impossible to say the saying because at the moment of saying it becomes the said, betrayed by the concrete language which is the language of ontology. The saying, which is unthematizable, impossible to delimit, becomes limited, thematized, said" (Eaglestone, 147).

31. Critchley observes, "[O]ntological thematization is the necessary condition for any consideration of the non-thematizable. One can see nothing without thematization, and all talks of an ethic without ontology is blind. Once again, the relation of the Saying to the Said is not one of absolute independence, but rather the interdependence of irreconciliable orders of discourse" (*The Ethics of Deconstruction,* 169).

32. Adam Zachary Newton, *Narrative Ethics* (Cambridge, MA: Harvard University Press, 1995). For additional treatment of the impact of Levinas's thought for the theory and practice

of reading, see also Eaglestone, *Ethical Criticism*, particularly the section "Conclusion Interpretation Continual Interruption," 175–79, and Critchley's "*Clôtural* Reading II: Wholly Otherwise: Levinas's Reading of Derrida," *The Ethics of Deconstruction*, 145–87.

33. Newton, 13.

34. Ibid., 18.

35. Ibid., 25.

36. Parati, *Migration Italy*, 174.

37. "For a year, I remained in boarding school. I was more or less nine years old. My father and my mother had been separated for a long time. He was still living in Tunis, just outside the city limits: he had a villa . . . . The boarding school was in Mateur . . . . With me, there was also my sister. My father came to pick us up every Saturday to take us in the city for the week-end. He had a blue Simca Ariane" (Salah Methnani and Mario Fortunato, *Immigrato* [Rome: Theoria, 1990], 9; my translation). Further references are to this edition and will be cited parenthetically in the text. Subsequent passages indicate that Methnani completed his education at a university in Tunis and, like every Tunisian of his social status, was expected to spend his leisure time and play money strolling on the avenue Burghiba dressed in the latest Western attire.

38. Parati, *Migration Italy*, 176.

39. Agamben, *Homo Sacer*, 7.

40. Pap Khouma and Oreste Pivetta, *Io venditore di elefanti* (Milano: Garzanti, 1990), 122.

41. Ibid., 123; emphasis added.

42. I am referring to Jerre Mangione and Ben Morreale's classic English-language account of Italian emigration, *La storia: Five Centuries of the Italian American Experience* (New York: HarperCollins, 1992).

43. See also Vincenzo Consolo, "The Bridge over the Channel of Sicily," in *Reading and Writing the Mediterranean*, ed. Norma Bouchard and Massimo Lollini (Toronto: University of Toronto Press, 2006), 241–45.

44. "Rosario, one of the bartenders, had a big belly and weighed more than eighty kilos. One time he told us: 'I worked abroad myself, in Germany. Life was difficult because of the hard work and the cold. The Germans treated us badly, but we had no choice and had to put up with the insults. We worked ten hours a day and even more, but the pay was lower than that of the Germans and we were the ones doing the worst jobs. I, too, have lived like you. I suffered from nostalgia, but I was able to save a little money, I bought a house, I got married, and decided to go back to my country. You will have to learn how to save money, you need to find fulfillment back home, not here. Work even ten hours a day, so that you can return to your families sooner. Here you will always be considered foreigners. I am Italian and I am your friend, but the truth is this: there are many who do not want you here, with us" (Moshen Melliti, *Pantanella. Canto lungo la strada* [Rome: Edizioni Lavoro, 1992], 71–72).

45. Abdelmalek Sayad, *The Suffering of the Immigrant* (Cambridge: Polity Press, 2004), 1.

46. Gabriella Ghermandi, *Regina di fiori e di perle* (Milano: Donzelli, 2007), 18. All further references are to this edition and will be cited parenthetically in the text. All translations are mine.

47. "[L]ike the brigands of Southern Italy, they are figures who straddle reality and myth, protected by Saint George and the peasants, young heroes and heroines ready to face anything" (Cristina Lombardi-Diop, "Postfazione," in Gabriella Ghermandi, *Regina di fiori e di perle*. Roma: Donzelli, 2007), 257–64, 262 cited.

48. See "Peace and Proximity" (*BPW* 164.). See also, "But the conscience of the European is henceforth guilty, because of the contradiction that rends it at the very hour of its modernity, which is probably that of the balance sheets drawn up in lucidity, that of full consciousness" (*BPW* 163).

49. Christopher Duggan, *A Concise History of Modern Italy*. (Cambridge: Cambridge University Press, 1994), 227.

50. For additional discussion, see Giulia Barrera, "Patrilinearity, Race, and Identity: The Upbringing of Italo-Eritreans during Italian Colonialism," in *Italian Colonialism*, ed. Ruth Ben-Ghiat and Mia Fuller (New York: Palgrave Macmillan, 2005), 97–108.

51. "I dedicate this book to my grandmother Berechtì, my grandmother Hagosà and my mother Rosina who were subjected to the racial laws of the Italian occupation" (254).

52. See Alexander Kozin, "The Sign of the Other: On the Semiotics of Emmanuel Lévinas," *Semiotica* 152-1/4 (2004): 235–49: "traumatics occurs when the personified meaning is ousted, pushed out by the primordial (first) signification that disrupts the normative order for the ethical call" (247).

53. "100,000 Libyans killed between 1911 and 1932 [. . .] 3,000 to 4,000 Ethiopians who died between 1935 and 1941" (Angelo Del Boca, "The Myths, Suppressions, Denials, and Defaults of Italian Colonialism," in *A Place in the Sun: Africa in Italian Colonial Culture*, ed. Patrizia Palumbo. Berkeley: University of California Press, 2003), 17–36, 20 cited.

54. See the interview with Erminia dell'Oro in Daniele Comberiati, *La quarta sponda. Scrittrici in viaggio dall'Africa coloniale all'Italia di oggi* (Roma: Caravan edizioni, 2009), 96.

55. Simon Critchley, "Introduction," in *The Cambridge Companion to Levinas*, ed. Simon Critchley and Robert Bernasconi (Cambridge: Cambridge University Press, 2002), 23.

56. For a discussion of Levinas's *tiers* and the democratic project that it foregrounds, see Critchley, "Conclusion: Philosophy, Politics, and Democracy," *The Ethics of Deconstruction*, 236–41.

57. Critchley, "Introduction," 24–25.

VII

Levinas, Apocalypse, and the Non-Imperializing Self

Chapter Thirteen

The Prophetic Thought of Emmanuel Levinas

Reading Two Contemporary Novels of the Shoah

Merle Williams

THE JEW AND THE GREEK

In the penultimate paragraph of "Violence and Metaphysics" (1964), Jacques Derrida attempts to tease out the complicated interwoven swathes of Levinas's earlier work:

> Are we Jews? Are we Greeks? We live in the difference between the Jew and the Greek, which is perhaps the unity of what is called history. We live in and of difference, that is, in *hypocrisy*, about which Levinas so profoundly says that it is "not only a base contingent defect of man, but the underlying rending of a world attached to both the philosophers and the prophets." (*TI* 24)[1]

This question about the inherent ambivalence of Levinas's enquiry has close bearing on the proposed reading of two contemporary novels of the Shoah,[2] both written by Jews and both addressing an event of irreducible trauma in the history of Jewish experience: *Fugitive Pieces* (1996) by Anne Michaels and *Everything Is Illuminated* (2002) by Jonathan Safran Foer. These texts are also inhabited by difference, as a taxing exploration of Jewish values becomes intertwined with the crafted, self-reflexive fragments of Michaels's fiction and the provocative postmodern experimentation of Foer's *debut* novel.

If, as Robert Bernasconi suggests, "Violence and Metaphysics" is to be understood as an examination of Levinas's relation to the Greek tradition and practice of philosophy,[3] this would encompass not only the putative death of philosophy as understood with reference to Marx, Nietzsche, or Heidegger, but also the well established opposition between philosophy and non-philosophy. Can the challenge to the Greek foundations of philosophy, for example, appropriately be called non-Greek?[4] In fact, Levinas himself remarks in one of his Talmudic readings, "Toward the Other," that "it is doubtful that a philosophical thought has ever come into the world independent of all [pre-established] attitudes or that there ever was a category in the world which came before an attitude" (*NiTR* 15). More specifically, one would need to investigate how a unique metaphysics of "radical separation and exteriority" could be conceived in the language of a *logos* which is governed by a complex of "spatial dualisms."[5]

As both Bernasconi and Seán Hand have argued,[6] Levinas's response to the conundrums posed by "Violence and Metaphysics" may be found in his 1975 essay, "God and Philosophy." Here he sharply takes up Derrida's view, attributed to an anonymous "Greek," that "if one has to philosophize, one has to philosophize; if one does not have to philosophize, one still has to philosophize (to say it and think it)."[7] Shortly before the end of "God and Philosophy," Levinas passionately retorts, *"Not to philosophize would not be 'to philosophize still'"* (*LR* 186). It is well known that this discussion adopts as its starting point the notion of an "insomnia" or "wakefulness" which cannot be thematized, so that it confounds the phenomenological construct of intentionality, opening the way instead for signification through the notion of infinity (see Hand's note *LR* 166; *LR* 169–73). This approach is reinforced by Levinas's interpretation of Descartes' Third Meditation, in which the idea of the infinite, implanted by a transcendent God in each individual consciousness, exceeds and breaks up every possible *cogitatum* attainable by the *cogito* (*LR* 173–75; *TI* 197). Such a mode of thinking deliberately undermines the universalizing and homogenizing tendencies of philosophical rationality, marking off the separateness of the self in its unique relation to the infinite. The infinite is shown to embrace "the Infinite in me," a negation of the finitude of totalizing intellectual and social systems, since the "in" of "infinite signals both the '*non*-finite' and the 'infinite' *within* the self" (*LR* 174).

On this basis, Levinas arrives at the notion of a transcendence beyond self-interestedness and erotic love, which prompts a desire for the paradoxically undesirable—the Other. This transcendence *is* ethics, nurtured by the subjectivity of an I that is "under the accusation of the other, even though it be faultless. It is a hostage for the other, obeying a command before having heard it, faithful to . . . a past that has never been present" (*LR* 178). This ineluctable, *anarchic* responsibility of the self to and for the Other soon comes to be co-ordinated with Levinas's view of prophesying as "pure testimony" in "subjection to an order before understanding the order. . . in prophesying . . . the Infinite passes—and awakens" (184).[8] While Levinas has retained elements of familiar philosophical diction and follows the sequential development of a reasoned argument, his essay strains against this confinement, exceeding itself into the language of prophecy. He underscores the predicament of an ethical self under commandment and deprived of freedom—"unless this would be the trauma of a fission of the self that occurs in an adventure undergone with and through God" (186).

"Revelation and the Jewish Tradition" (1977) describes just such an adventure, evincing striking affinities with its seemingly more philosophical counterpart. In fact, the content of the Revelation is predominantly ethical in a Levinasian sense. The foundational narrative of enslavement in Egypt gives the Jew a perception of closeness to "the wretched of the earth, to all persecuted people. 'My very uniqueness lies in my responsibility for the other; nobody can relieve me of this. . . . To obey the Most High is to be free'" (*LR* 202). Levinas points out that rabbinic tradition confers an openness to inspiration and prophetic capacity on all human beings by extrapolating from the presence of the Israelites when God spoke out of the fire at Mount Horeb. Understanding is thus shaped as language in the face-to-face encounter, although this is not construed as literal vision of the divine countenance, even for the supreme prophet Moses. The concerns of "God and Philosophy" therefore come to permeate the explanation of Jewish texts, beliefs and hermeneutic trajectories. Similarly, the conclusion of "Revelation in the Jewish Tradition" crystallizes certain key patterns in Levinas's thought, since it summarizes the relationship between same and other, or to use the terms of an earlier work, totality and infinity. Rather than launching the play of a dialectic, the notion of alterity inaugurates "an incessant questioning" without an ultimate solution, "like an inextinguishable flame which burns yet consumes nothing" (thus suggesting the unconsumed burning bush of Exodus 3:3). Levinas imagines that the "form" of this flame "is the prescription of the Jewish Revelation, with its unfulfillable obligation. . . . The 'less' is forever bursting open, unable to contain the 'more' that it contains, in the form of 'the one for the other'" (*LR* 209).

Simon Critchley shrewdly proposes that "Levinas's thinking is quite inconceivable without its Jewish inspiration," although he adds the qualification that Levinas should not be categorized merely as a "Jewish philosopher."[9] It is the Jewish flame of an "unfulfillable obligation" that burns within all of Levinas's writing, so that the "less" of strictly circumscribed philosophical discourse forever bursts open in its aspiration to encompass the "more" of a prophetic thought exceeding it. This is not to deny the philosophical dimension of Levinas's work, especially his repeated engagement with the seminal ideas of Parmenides, Plato, Descartes, Kant, Hegel, Husserl and Heidegger in such substantial texts as *Totality and Infinity* or *Otherwise than Being*. Nonetheless, Catherine Chalier points usefully to a hybrid dimension of Levinas's *oeuvre*. She cites the pertinence of Jewish material to his interrogation of philosophy and the influence of Greek concepts on his investigation of Jewish scholarship, noting that Levinas himself is sceptical of any rigid demarcation between "philosophy and simply thinking."[10] Again, one might include a thinking that stretches and reconfigures the putative domain of philosophy. These relationships are scrutinized from a different perspective in Bernasconi's essay on "Levinas: Philosophy and Beyond." He speculates that the field of philosophy might be interrupted by an "ethical cry which comes from outside it," hence constituting "the opening up within philosophy of a saying with another signification from that which belongs to philosophy and whose source is beyond it."[11] Not unlike Derrida, Bernasconi subtly grants priority to the theoretical enterprise, yet his "ethical cry" is not necessarily at odds with the "unfulfillable obligation" of the Jewish Revelation. If the prophetic human being is commanded, "man is also the irruption of God within Being, or the bursting of Being towards God; man is the fracture in Being which produces the act of giving, with hands which are full, in place of fighting and pillaging" (*LR* 202).

The antithesis of man with full hands is to be found in the experience of the Shoah. Robert Eaglestone, who thoroughly explores Levinas's response to these events in *The Holocaust and the Postmodern*, also regards his work as developing from both philosophy (especially the phenomenological praxis of Husserl) and a prophecy which bears witness to the Infinite. However, rather than considering the prophetic as the impulse of a thought striving beyond philosophy, Eaglestone pursues the argument in terms of an "ambivalence" or yoked separateness which becomes most compelling, for instance, in the discussion of murder.[12] He astutely tracks the imprint of the Shoah on Levinas's writing, noting the revealing imagery of "'good soup' and bread" in *Totality and Infinity*, as well as this text's openness to the effects of rhetoric on the practices of persecution.[13] Turning to *Otherwise than Being*, it would be remiss not to add the traditional dedication in Hebrew to Levinas's family members killed in the Shoah, as well as the universal memorialization of "the millions on millions of all confessions and all nations, victims of the same hatred of the other man, the same anti-semitism." The epigraphs from Ezekiel, the Talmudic commentator, *Rashi*, and Pascal obliquely gloss the preceding dedications by starkly demonstrating the horror of a violence driven by hunger for "a place in the sun," while locating the imperative to make an ethical beginning with those who sanctify the Infinite (*OB* v, vii). By the end of his chapter, Eaglestone has implicitly amended his reading of the interplay between philosophy and prophecy in Levinas's writing, connecting the effects of the Shoah with the failure of a philosophy whose totalizing (and often politicized) project excludes sceptical renewal and the intervention of external inspiration. Quoting Levinas's definition of philosophy in *Otherwise than Being* as "the wisdom of love at the service of love," he proposes that this wise loving should be included in the philosophical as a catalyst for reflection.[14] Ironically, though, Levinas's vivid formulation slyly turns inside out the literal Greek meaning of "philosophy" as "the love of wisdom." The "betrayal" and "reduction" of the ineffable that nonetheless remains subject to the transcendent signification of the "one for the other, as non-indifference to the other" shakes conventional disciplinary constructs, reversing them into a thinking that remakes the philosophical (*OB* 162).

The prophetic impulse of Levinas's thought, together with his strategic reframing of the philosophical project, frequently finds concrete realization in his Talmudic readings, especially in his account of the responsibilities of being "Israel." "Toward the Other" shows an austere alertness to the practical consequences of ethical commandment in its commentary on the "savage greatness" of 2 Samuel 21. In typical Talmudic style, the compelling heuristic potential of the story is laid bare. Because Saul is deemed to have wronged the Gibeonite people, justice is demanded from David according to the principle of talion required by the shedding of blood. Seven of Saul's descendants are given up to be nailed to a rock in satisfaction of the Gibeonites' insistence on retribution. Rizpah, the daughter of Aiah, is the mother of two of these young princes. She remains with the victims for six months, covering their tortured bodies each evening with bags to protect them from molestation by predatory birds and wild animals (*NiTR* 26). Levinas sharply draws attention to the Talmud's treatment of the historical fact that the Gibeonites belonged not to the children of Israel, but to the "rest of the Amoreans." This statement is reinterpreted as an ethical appraisal: "To belong to Israel one must be humble (place something or someone above oneself), one must know pity and be capable of disinterested acts" (*NiTR* 28). Although Levinas deduces from the Talmud a recognition of the absolute right of an appeal for justice—"it is better that a letter of the Torah be damaged than that the name of the Eternal be profaned"—he insists that to be Israel is neither to ask such justice for oneself nor to claim it. Moreover, he modifies the criteria for membership of Israel (by descent and as an ethical metaphor) so that "strict justice" is supplemented by "the impulse of disinterested goodness," thus giving rise to pity or *Rahamim*: "that special form of pity which goes out to the one who is experiencing the harshness of the Law."[15] Rising above the entire exposition, however, is the image of Rizpah bat Aiah whose "individual sacrifice . . . amidst the dialectical rebounds of justice and all its contradictory about-faces, without any hesitation, finds a straight and sure way" (27–29). Here the "wisdom of love" culminates in the consummate compassion of a mother for the child which she carries selflessly within her own body; this becomes the fulfilment of Israel's mission.

Yet again, although in the register of Talmudic interpretation, Levinas returns to the I as hostage, "the one for the other," the unfulfillable obligation, the "less" bursting open unable to contain the "more" paradoxically implanted within it. Without imposing a temporal priority on the relationship between Levinas's academic (or technically philosophical) production and his engagement with Judaism, it seems apt to confirm Critchley's intuition of the central importance of his Jewishness, albeit a Jewishness of a very particular order: rational, critical, hermeneutically inclined and deeply imbued with an outspoken prophetic sensibility.[16]

FUGITIVE PIECES: "THE FIRST WORD OF THE FACE—THOU SHALT NOT KILL"

Levinas's sense (*LR* 209) that an engagement with alterity leads to an "incessant questioning," which prefigures an "unfulfillable obligation," provides a helpful starting point for interpreting Anne Michaels's debut novel, *Fugitive Pieces*. The work is impelled by a search, not for narrowly intellectual insight, but for a "wisdom of love" which will rip the seams of normative moral systems by testing the limits of the self's commitment to the Other. To some degree this poetic enquiry proceeds through an almost Jamesian operative irony.[17] It projects the consequences of unrestrained persecution and murder in order to evoke and investigate the workings of their absolute inverse as the transcendent feminine compassion of *rachamim*. In a complex double gesture, Michaels manages to write horror "otherwise," never losing sight of the possibilities of a prophetic thought that eschews dialectical progressions in its commitment to the absolute command of the face of the Other. The aspiration towards justice and disinterested goodness slowly attenuates—even heals—the effects of trauma; in the rejection of mundane totalizing initiatives, the Infinite within the self claims restoration.

Fugitive Pieces is an unusually poised and accomplished novel. It won the Orange Prize, the Books in Canada First Novel Award and the Trillium Book Award, in addition to receiving almost dazzlingly favourable reviews in the British press.[18] Michaels honed her skills for this linguistically subtle and allusive fictional work by publishing two acclaimed volumes of poetry dealing with her characteristic themes of identity, alienation, memory and loss, *The Weight of Oranges* (1986) and *Miner's Pond* (1991).[19]

Fugitive Pieces is divided into two asymmetrical sections. The first describes the traumatic experience of Jakob Beer, a Jewish boy whose family is murdered by the Nazis during their invasion of Poland. He is rescued by a Greek archaeologist, Athos, who happens to be excavating the ancient waterlogged city of Biskupin.[20] Athos assumes the role of Jakob's *koumbaros* or godfather, taking him back to the island of Zakynthos during the Nazi occupation of Greece and later moving to Toronto. Jakob becomes a writer who is haunted by the losses of his childhood and unable to sustain intimate relationships, so that his first marriage fails. In his second marriage he finds a receptive partner who can at once accept his suffering by sharing her strongly contrasted memories and release him from his entanglement with the dead.

Both he and his wife are killed in an accident before the birth of a child. The second section of the novel (which is treated only briefly in this chapter) in many respects recapitulates, but also reshapes, Jakob's story through the experience of Ben, the son of survivors of the Shoah. Ben (which is the Hebrew word for "son") is a writer, too; he also has a predominantly erotic relationship with one woman, while seeking a mature reciprocity in his marriage to another. It is he who discovers Jakob's hidden notebooks during a visit to his house in the Greek islands. In effect, this detail of plot places Ben as the first-person narrator of Part II of the novel, with Jacob, by implication, as the narrator of Part I. The title *Fugitive Pieces* arouses multiple associations. "Fugitive" suggests an exile or refugee, as well as fearful flight and the fugue as a set of musical variations on a theme.[21] "Pieces" captures the sense of broken lives and the unstable, fragmentary, digressive composition of the novel, while hinting at the Nazi objectification of the Jews as *Stücke*. This poetic concentration foreshadows Michaels's plangent lament for, yet qualified recuperation of, personal histories maimed by the Shoah.

Fugitive Pieces presents a sequence of Levinasian aspects to the reader, although the text cannot sustain the pressure of an exclusively Levinasian interpretation.[22] The opening pages, however, powerfully encapsulate the kind of unconstrained violence that excludes the perpetrator from the community of Israel. The invasion of Jakob's home by nameless and faceless Nazi soldiers erupts in seemingly agentless actions: "The burst door. Wood ripped from hinges, cracking like ice under the shouts. Noises never heard before, torn from my father's mouth" (7)—the mouth also faceless and no longer capable of attesting to coherent selfhood as speech (*TI* 201). Jakob's recollection reaches its climax with "The soul leaves the body instantly . . . my mother's face was not her own. My father was twisted with falling. Two shapes in the flesh-heap, his hands" (7). This entropic degradation of a human being to a heap of flesh is incisively interrogated in Levinas's account of murder as a "claim to total negation" or "annihilation." It figures as an attempt to destroy the perceptible face, but disintegrates into impotence because "the face rends the sensible. . . . The Other is the sole being I can wish to kill" (*TI* 198). Although Michaels adopts the conventional diction of body and soul, the passage revolves around the distinction between the living and the dead. Jakob's mother has humbly been sewing a button on his shirt in familiar commitment to the claims of his childish vulnerability. The "spray of buttons" from her chipped saucer pathetically mimics the spray of bullets that kills her, just as the comparison with "little white teeth" collapses animate and inanimate in the instant of absolute incomprehension, reducing to the sensible a selfhood infused with Infinity.

As a young adult, Jakob interrogates the accumulating documentary and photographic evidence of the atrocities of the Shoah, finding confirmation of the formative traumatic moments of his childhood. He reflects first on the

Nazi policy of "anti-matter," whose linguistic vagaries deprived Jews of their humanity by classifying them as "figuren," "stücke," "dolls," "wood," "merchandise," "rags." Yet he begins to realize that this explanation is too reductive. He probes the "harrowing contradiction" that the expressions of torturers "contorted with laughter" betray the aporetic condition of regarding one's victims as simultaneously human and non-human; humiliation must depend on a knowledge of degradation. Jakob concludes that the rage to kill is unleashed as a means of finally taking revenge on the victim for "suddenly turning human" (165–66). This interpretation of the self-deceptions of Nazi reasoning has surprising affinities with Levinas's account of "hatred" in *Totality and Infinity.* Levinas is alive to the broken-backed logic of at once reifying the subject and willing to "maintain him superbly in his subjectivity." "Hatred," he contends, "wills both things. . . it is satisfied precisely when it is not satisfied, since the other satisfies it only by becoming an object, but can never become object enough" since "his lucidity and witness are [perversely] demanded" (*TI* 239). It is not only the agony inflicted on the innocent that convulsively deforms the lyrical prose of *Fugitive Pieces*, but also an amazed resistance to such distortion of the very processes of humane thinking.

Set against this disintegration of rational and moral values is the ethical roundedness of the instant in which Athos rescues Jakob, inverting and controverting the circumstances of his parents' murder through sheer goodness and fertile compassion. Since his family home has been burnt down, Jakob preserves himself by digging out hiding places in the damp soil of a nearby forest. When the loneliness, fear, and hunger become intolerable, he despairingly gives himself up to Athos, who is calmly absorbed in his excavations. Jakob limps "toward him, stiff as a golem, clay tight behind [his] knees." Athos vividly recalls that "your mud mask cracked with tears and I knew you were human, just a child. Crying with the abandonment of your age." Characteristically, the text foregrounds the tension between the human and the non-human, the golem or legendary clay figure sculpted as a last resort by a seventeenth-century rabbi to protect the Prague ghetto from devastating persecution, and a defenceless child (the Other who commands by his destitution). The dynamic movement of Jakob's disclosure is heightened by his frantically laying claim to his childish weakness, while plummeting from the folkloric monstrosity of a golem to the crude materiality of a *Figur* or *Stück*. Drawing on the only phrase he knows in "more than one language," and oblivious of the inherent dissonance between literal and metaphorical meaning, he screams "in Polish and German and Yiddish, thumping [his] fists on [his] own chest: dirty Jew, dirty Jew, dirty Jew" (12–13). Athos responds immediately not to Jakob's self-identification, but to the "first word of the face . . . 'Thou shalt not kill.' It is an order." Acting as a "first person" whose task is unique and inalienable, he "finds the resources" to obey this call (*EI*

88). So Michaels founds the relationship between Athos and Jakob, in which the *koumbaros* at his peril conceals his adopted son from the Nazis, coaxes him back to trust, and repeatedly demonstrates his willingness to sacrifice himself to his love for another.

Jakob's capacity to relate to others is severely complicated by his sense of failed responsibility towards his older sister, Bella. He bears witness to the death of his parents, but Bella simply vanishes without a sign, presumably killed or abducted by the local Nazi troops. From this point onwards, Jakob becomes haunted by elusive images of his sister, which trace themselves unbidden on his consciousness. After the brutal drowning in the Aegean Sea of the Jews from the millennium old ghetto on Crete, he "choke[s] against Bella's round face, a doll's face, immobile, inanimate, her hair floating behind her." She ghosts into his safe haven from the Nazi occupation of Zakynthos, just as barely decipherable intimations obscure his mental processes in Toronto, distracting him from the everyday (44–45). Consistently he recalls Bella's beauty (especially her long, dark, supple hair), her playfulness, and her passionate dedication to piano music. In his desire to remain close to her, he "blaspheme[s] by imagining," living vicariously her courage and the suffering through which a free being "ceases to be free," yet remains free by distanciating itself from its own pain (*TI* 238). So the nightmarish scene in a concentration camp dormitory unfolds, as the frail girl in an overcrowded bunk plays the piano on the diseased skin of her arms: "*Not too much pedal, you can spoil Brahms with too much pedal, the opening must be played clear—as water*" (167). Having internalized Bella so pervasively, Jakob inhabits the space of a delusory fantasy-memory and succumbs to social alienation. He figures himself as a touch-typist who cannot match his fingers to the keys; "the words [come] out meaningless, garbled" in parody of his sister's virtuoso piano performances, so that he and Bella frustratingly remain "a breath apart" (111).

The preceding aspects of *Fugitive Pieces* show close affinities with Levinas's prophetic concerns, both through the play of operative irony and in suggesting that Athos's saving of Jakob constitutes a form of "giving with full hands" that bursts the constraints of Being towards the Divine. Yet the novel's steady movement in the direction of the erotic as a remedy for introspective mourning and traumatic stress is at once at odds with Levinasian ethics and in keeping with certain tensions that characterize his earlier writing. If *Totality and Infinity* explicitly diminishes the role of the feminine Other, whose predominant function is to provide the virile self with a home which can later be hospitably offered to the stranger,[23] then Michaels, too, accords subordinate status to women. Susan Gubar argues that they are treated as instrumental to male needs in the novel, and that Jakob's two marriages counterpoint his experience with an "audaciously adventurous" partner to his subsequent fulfilment with a "more nurturing conventional one."[24] Meredith

Criglington reinforces this view by referring to the "auxiliary function of women within the overarching masculine quest for self-knowledge," juxtaposing the "'allegorical type' of the beguiler" to that of the "guide, sage or mediator."[25] Jakob's attraction to his first wife, Alex, is clearly at once sexual and an intellectual seduction; she is "a sword-swallower, a fire-eater. In her mouth English [is] dangerous and alive, edgy and hot." She is also "stunning," a "political debauchée" and "too proud to reveal her innocence," flirting to keep men at bay (132–33). When Ben has an intense affair with Petra during his visit to Idhra, he is in search of "the disruptive physical sexuality that unhinges ego boundaries,"[26] after the shock of discovering that his Holocaust survivor mother could lovingly confide in his wife while he remained permanently excluded. These interactions serve the physical and emotional needs of the male partner, without summoning him to the maturity of ethical responsibility.

Such relationships are, in fact, congruent with Levinas's oddly dismissive "Phenomenology of Eros" in *Totality and Infinity*. If Alex and Petra scarcely prompt the tender "epiphany of the Beloved" in terms of fragility and vulnerability, their behaviour often comes close to connoting a Levinasian "ultramateriality" or the "nudity of an exorbitant presence . . . already profaning and wholly profaned, as if it had forced the interdiction of a secret" (*TI* 256). Both Jakob and Ben long for satisfaction through "exorbitant" physical presence, but both discover in due course the telling absence of a transformative face-to-face encounter. Jakob feels that he has betrayed his quest for Bella in his passionate involvement with Alex, who envisages his salvation in persuading him to forget the past. As Ben returns home to Toronto, he conjures up images of reunion with his wife, Naomi, responding to her half hidden face (both as sensible phenomenon and transcendent existent) by calling her name and, in the spirit of the "one for the other," acknowledging that "I see I must give what I need most" (293–94).

The complex nurturing and mediating qualities identified by Gubar and Criglington are to a large degree evinced in Jakob's second marriage to Michaela and in Ben's relationship with Naomi. Michaela's mind is "a palace;" she is able to weep for Bella's suffering and Jakob's loss, opening herself without restraint to the destitution of the Other. So the traits of disinterested goodness and compassion make their appearance. Yet there are aspects of Michaels's narrative that seem distinctly un-Levinasian. Musing on his intimacy with Michaela, Jakob wonders, "What does the body make us believe? That we're never ourselves until we contain two souls" (189). This collapsing of the separation between self and Other might be construed as enmiring lovers in a voluptuosity of touch; because such an intentionality is "*without vision*, discovery does not shed light" (*TI* 260), producing instead an access of ultramateriality. In this way, Michaels's exploration of supportive relationships with women seems to fall disappointingly short of an awakening to ethical obligation, because the erotic impulse fails to break the deathly grasp of narcissistic identity.

Luce Irigaray's critical feminist reading of Levinas, however, carries the potential for escaping this *impasse* of disabling eroticism. Instead, her comprehensive recasting of the premises of *Totality and Infinity* promises to liberate the rich possibilities of prophetic thought (although with no pretension to uniting two souls in a single body). Irigaray argues that lovers' caresses carry inevitable traces of the immemorial intimacy of the maternal womb (the *rechem* of *rachamim*), since we cannot give birth to ourselves; thus a creative and discontinuous, cross-generational time is fostered, fecundating the erotic relationship. The male partner "searching for what has not yet come into being, for himself . . . invites [the woman] to become what [she] has not yet become."[27] Moreover, the pervasive trace of the mother's consummate gift of the Other in birth inspires ethical recognition in the lovers, for whom this sacrifice of the self, even to the extent of a reconfiguration of the contours of the body, becomes paradigmatic. As Levinas notes in *Otherwise than Being*, "The one-for-another has the form of sensibility . . . pure passivity . . . alterity in the same, the trope of the body animated by the soul, psyche in the form of a hand that gives even the bread from its own mouth. Here the psyche is the maternal body" (*OB* 67, translation slightly amended).[28] This shift in emphasis redresses the preoccupation of *Totality and Infinity* with paternity, now linking the responsibility of the "one-for-another" to the maternal body and the trans-generational trace of feminine fecundity.

In light of these liberating exchanges, Jakob's love for Michaela (whose name clearly associates her metafictionally with the novelist, Anne Michaels) may be seen to revivify his sense of resilient selfhood through a process similar to the search for "what has not yet come into being" described by Irigaray. Moreover, Michaela's capacity for nurturing subtly stirs his longings for lost maternal intimacy, which have been heightened by the sacrifice of his parents' lives for his sake. His relation to Bella similarly undergoes a radical transformation. Jakob realizes that "all the years I had felt Bella entreating me, filled with her loneliness, I was mistaken . . . *to remain with the dead is to abandon them*" (170).

This recasting of the processes of a painfully repeated, traumatized mourning is aptly elucidated by the Levinasian resonance of Derrida's *Memoires for Paul de Man*. Derrida argues that if it were feasible to interiorize the Other faithfully, as Jakob has attempted to incorporate Bella imaginatively, then the Other would be appropriated in terms of sameness, ceasing to be quite other. The self would have failed fundamentally to recognize the principles of metaphysical plurality and separateness between human beings that define Levinas's crystallization of the Other's right to command, even to the extent of snatching the bread from my mouth. Thus "an aborted interiorization [of a dead loved one] is at the same time a respect for the other as other, a sort of tender rejection, a movement of renunciation which leaves the other alone . . . in his death, outside of us."[29] The activity of mourning is at once ethically charged and irresolvable, because it demands the scrupulous cherishing of the deceased other, unassimilated and distinct, both within and from the self. Naomi tries gently to convey the necessity of this aporetic exteriority-in-interiority to Ben, who remains bitterly alienated by his parents' incapacity for emotional engagement. Her response is also extended to the dead of the Shoah, in the belief that "the only thing you can do for the dead is to sing to them." She explains that when a child died in the ghettos, the mother would compose a lullaby, mentioning its favourite toys to comfort it, "because there was nothing else she could offer of her self, of her body" (241). Once again, the latent psychism of the maternal body generatively traverses the space between husband and wife, mother and child, the living and the dead, confirming the gift of the Other that lies at the heart of Levinasian prophecy.

Although Irigaray emphasizes the fecundating possibility of erotic relationships that exceed the enervating regime of tenderness sketched by Levinas, the characters in *Fugitive Pieces* ultimately retain their awareness of loss and are left yearning for new life. Naomi grieves for her childlessness, as her eagerly chosen collection of lullabies seems to reproach her. Despite his happiness with Michaela, Jakob longs for a child, too; "my son, my daughter: may you never be deaf to love" (195). Just before Ben seeks sexual oblivion with Petra, they find a note tucked into the bedclothes in Jakob's bedroom on Idhra: "If she's a girl: Bella/ If he's a boy: Bela" (278). Michaela was clearly pregnant when she was run over and killed by a car in Athens. The novel ultimately refuses any redemption of the past by future generations, especially through a child bearing Bella's name. There is to be no restitution either for Hannah and Paul, Ben's young brother and sister, whose death in the Shoah is assiduously concealed until he belatedly discovers a photograph showing them with his parents. As Gubar puts it, "rebirth remains textual and subjective" in Michaels's novel.[30] Criglington echoes this view, proposing that the past can be restored only through the imaginative "re-presentation," while the "reunification of self/other—of Bela/Bella—remains an impossible dream."[31] Instead, the fugal structure of the text performs, varies, and re-enacts that suffering which is tyrannically inflicted by another or others. Nonetheless, as Levinas suggests, "violence does not stop Discourse; all is not inexorable" (TI 239). *Fugitive Pieces* is ambivalent as to whether such violence can or should be endured "in patience," yet the narrative accepts that in this world I may die *"as a result of someone"* and, more significantly, *"for someone."* The finely tuned lyricism of Michaels's novel eschews sentimental consolation; its major events are shadowed by a sensitivity to Desire for the Other and Goodness limited by nothing (*TI* 239). In its receptivity to the reverberations of prophetic thought, "the Infinite passes—and awakens" (*LR* 184).

EVERYTHING IS ILLUMINATED: FROM POSTMODERN EXPERIMENTATION TO "HERE I AM"

In *Everything Is Illuminated*, the passing and awakening of the Infinite is most productively construed as the Saying that establishes all human communication, together with signification, as a necessary precursor to constative discourse. The text is striking in its gymnastic manipulation of the said, radically remolding fictional form. Yet it equally captures the "trauma of a fission of the self that occurs in an adventure undergone," if not explicitly with God, then certainly with the command of the Other to assume responsibility (*LR* 186). Here the resources of the paternal are revisited; male fecundity is shown partially to redeem time by breaking the hold of fate and giving creative literary access to an infinite future. In this way, a staged rewriting of the tragic destruction of the Shoah can be enacted by reversing the flow of time and paradoxically allowing the figure of Jonathan to become the compassionate progenitor of his own ancestors. Most powerfully, however, the Saying of *hineni*, "Here I am—take me," comes to permeate the novel in an expression of unqualified integrity or uprightness that sweeps aside postmodern relativism and tears open complacent Western intellectual assurance in its comprehensive embrace of goodness.

At the age of only twenty-five, Jonathan Safran Foer earned remarkable acclaim for the publication of his first full-length fictional work, *Everything Is Illuminated* (2002), which examines Ukranian-Jewish relations in the aftermath of the Shoah. This novel received a Guardian First Book Award and the National Jewish Book Award; it was also voted "Book of the Year" by such critics as Joyce Carol Oates, Susan Sontag, and the Irish poet, Tom Paulin.[32] Foer's second novel, *Extremely Loud and Incredibly Close* (2005) continues his investigation of the traumatic. Focalized by a nine-year-old boy whose father was killed in the 9/11 World Trade Center disaster, the text is once again woven from different narratives which are not chronologically synchronized. In addition, this project marks Foer's concerted move into the field of visual writing, which is taken up in *Tree of Codes* (2010), making it as much a work of paper sculpture as fictional innovation shaped by challenging spatio-temporal disruptions.

In keeping with this brief sketch of Foer's exploratory writing, *Everything Is Illuminated* proves exuberantly postmodern in its formal experimentation. Realist narrative is juxtaposed to fantasy, magical realism and modern mythmaking, while epistolary revelations subtly wrap striking deductions around expressive silences.[33] The record of events produced by the young Ukrainian student of English, Alex, self-consciously exploits humor in a display of fluent virtuosity that is steadily modified under the pressure of the unspeakable. From the outset, he pushes language to and beyond its limits in a comically bizarre Russian version of English that "fatigue[s] the thesaurus . . . when [his] words [appear] too petite or not befitting" (23). The first chapter opens with:

> My legal name is Alexander Perchov. But all of my friends dub me Alex, because that is a more flaccid-to-utter version of my legal name. Mother dubs me Alexi-stop-spleening-me!, because I am always spleening her. If you want to know why I am always spleening her, it is because I am always elsewhere with friends, and disseminating so much currency . . . I have many girls, believe me. (1)

More than this wilfully innovative linguistic transgression, it is the structure of the novel that infuses postmodern iconoclasm with a searching ethical urgency. As Eaglestone has noted,[34] three obvious strands comprise the fictional narrative. Alex invests considerable effort in recording his involvement as translator in Jonathan's journey to find both his late grandfather's village of Trachimbrod on the Polish-Ukrainian border and a woman called Augustine, who saved his grandfather's life during the Nazi occupation. Jonathan, an American student, is writing a fanciful-mythopoeic novel which frames an imagined history of his family in the now-vanished Trachimbrod. Finally, Alex's letters to Jonathan facilitate a long-distance, delayed exchange that links the two stories in progress by including critical comments and promoting personal engagement. Yet this synopsis focuses on the evident discursive design of the novel, leaving out of count Jonathan's absent letters to Alex as they ghost through the printed pages, altering patterns of relationship. Similarly spectral is the implicit influence of the comprehensive authorial function associated with the inscription of "Jonathan Safran Foer" on the title page.

The postmodern fictional innovation of *Everything Is Illuminated* becomes inseparable from a postmodern ethical impulse that seeks to disentangle an *anarchical* Saying from the propositions in which it is at once formulated and assimilated to the pragmatic context of daily existence. Levinas thus argues that "the *otherwise than being* is stated in a saying that must also be unsaid" in order to pre-empt a mere reversion to "signify[ing] but a *being otherwise*" (*OB* 7). To qualify as genuinely *otherwise than being*, the Saying must be embraced as "antecedent to the linguistic signs it conjugates . . . a foreword preceding languages, [for] it is the proximity of one to the other . . . the very signifyingness of signification" (5). This explanation evokes a radical transmutation and remaking of philosophy as "the wisdom of love, at the service of love," "still synchroniz[ing] in the said the diachrony of the difference between the one and the other" (162). Foer's endeavour offers an arresting variation on this reading of prophetic thought. Preoccupied as the novel seems to be with its versatile linguistic cleverness, the unsaid repeatedly shadows the text with its incipient Saying. As the constitutive narratives progress, the trajectory of the enquiry aims beyond what can and will be stated to a silence that is redolent with surrender to Otherness. If Bernasconi regards Levinas as challenging the Western philosophical tradition by inter-rupting—or disrupting—it with a radically unique (and perhaps non-philo-sophical) innovation, so the Saying that founds communication with the Oth-er might be figured as the interruption of Foer's narrative by transformative ethical forces.

While these claims associate Foer's project explicitly with Levinas's pro-phetic embrace of the *otherwise than being*, the vibrant textuality of his fiction is equally important in its imbrication with the force of *différance* as the continuing displacement of linguistic signs together with sustained tem-poral deferral.[35] As Derrida explains in "Living On—Border Lines," such a text has no definitive edge, shoreline or boundary.[36] Rather than representing a "finished corpus of writing, some content enclosed in a book or its mar-gins," it becomes "a differential network, a fabric of traces referring endless-ly to something other than itself." By contrast with the poised poetic allusive-ness of *Fugitive Pieces*, Jonathan's novel bleeds into Alex's story, while both overflow into the monthly letters. At the same time, Foer's fiction plays into a vivid intertext that spans the postmodernism of Joyce and Pynchon, the magical realism of Borges and Gabriel García Márquez, and Isaac Bashevis Singer's magically fantastic fictions of Jewish life.[37] This fluid expansive-ness generates a variety of possible worlds, where the Levinasian tropes of violence and sacrifice, or the assertion of power rather than the acceptance of an irreducible responsibility to an (O)ther, find their enactment as readily in Alex's immediate family circle as in the colorfully invented *shtetl* politics of Trachimbrod.

The ethical dimension of *Everything Is Illuminated* is further entwined with its temporal structure. The relatively recent past of Alex's letters to Jonathan highlights the more distant past of the search for Augustine, and this narrative trajectory is cross-cut by the annals of Trachimbrod from the late eighteenth century until World War II. Yet each of these versions of the past is treated as carrying the seeds of corresponding future events; the inter-play-in-distinctness of different narrative strands opens the possibility of aesthetically reconstructing such fictional histories and the very acts of mem-ory from which they have been derived. For example, two irreconcilable accounts of the destruction of Trachimbrod are given; according to Augus-tine, the village is razed by a Nazi tank corps, while Jonathan's record of the *shtetl* describes a devastating air raid that drives many of the inhabitants to seek safety in the river, where they drown. Such deliberately cultivated in-consistencies are paralleled by excursions into a never-to be-realized future-yet-to-come: the reader is teased with what might have happened if Yankel had told Brod the truth about her birth or if Safran had married the Gypsy girl. The interwoven stories hover in the interstices of past and future, resisting the restrictions of a directly lived present, perhaps for the same reason that Derrida refuses simply to *present* his tribute to Emmanuel Levinas in "At this very moment in this work here I am." Derrida's use of the future anterior tense—*il aura obligé*—circumvents any straightforward economy of exchange and expected gratitude for his searching engagement with Levinas's writing,[38] much as Foer makes his readers the gift of a kaleidoscopically changing fiction that resists all attempts at totalizing interpretation.

Within the subtly unstable context of the narrative, however, the predominant affinities seem initially to lie with a self-conscious display of the permutations of the said, which partially occludes the Saying. When Jonathan begins to compose his fictitious record of life in Trachimbrod, he is clearly influenced by his own insecurities about loving. His parents remain shadowy figures, while his bond with his grandmother is at once ambiguous and disturbing, haunted by an awareness of her suffering during the Shoah. His childhood recollection of her picking him up, not to hug him but to determine whether he had gained weight during his visit, has the ring of veracity; on the other hand, the more salacious confession about hiding under her dress and running his hands along her varicose veins seems dubious, even calculatedly false (157–59). About women he is evasive, reluctantly confessing that he has never had a girlfriend (71). His attitude comes close to Levinas's analysis not of erotic voluptuosity, but of the gentler and more melancholy "pathos of love" in *Time and the Other*. Here the "insurmountable duality of beings"—the sheer impossibility of two persons ever becoming one, betrayed even by Jakob's image of *two* souls in *one* body—means that love must feed on its ever retreating future, on the alluring evanescence of a caress that relies on the immediacy of blind touch.[39] This sense of provocative attraction is portrayed (with wry qualification) in the interaction between Jonathan's maternal ancestor, Brod, and her foster father, Yankel: "Each was the closest thing to a deserving recipient of love that the other would find. So they gave each other all of it. He scraped his knee and said, *I too have fallen*" (83). Yet the effort of sustaining this uncertainty becomes too draining, so that Brod resorts to what Zygmunt Bauman terms "fixation"[40] in an attempt to congeal love into a safely malleable medium. She takes refuge in abstraction or "the *idea* of love," with love itself becoming "the object of her love." The refrain of "*I am not in love*" (80) runs throughout Jonathan's family history. Even his grandfather Safran's startling sexual exploits, which are invited by the fascinating unknowability of his dead arm, generally occur beyond the ambit of loving. The Gypsy girl, whom he meets in the strictest secrecy, appears to be the confounding exception to this rule, but she knows that "even if he thought he loved her, he did not love her" (232). Repelled by this expedient failure of commitment as the absence of meaningful relation, Alex writes angrily of Jonathan and his relatives: "*You are all cowards because you live in a world that is 'once-removed'*" (240).

Jonathan is not unaware of his sublimation of experience into writing as an avoidance of personal contact and responsibility. His mythical genealogy buttresses his mode of existence, enabling him to reconstitute himself as the patriarch of his lost ancestors in a kind of reversed paternity. This reading is endorsed by the repeated recastings of the Dial, a bronzed statue of his ancestor, the Kolker. When its surface becomes eroded by the kissing and fondling of subsequent generations of the community in search of folk reassurance, it is remodeled according to the features of the most recent representatives of the family (140). Jonathan feels bereft because the *shtetl* has been utterly destroyed, yet he senses an imperative to remember and cherish it faithfully. Deeply shocked by visiting the site, which is no more than an empty field, Alex writes, "I implore myself to paint Trachimbrod, so you will know why we were so overawed. There was nothing" (184). The narrative of the *shtetl* is thus transacted in the register of deeply desired fecundity, for, as Levinas (*TI* 267) suggests, a father is quite literally trans-substantiated by the birth of his son who recreates him as a "stranger" to himself. This is one of the effects of Jonathan's writing, for it facilitates multiple refashionings of himself as more attractive, more adventurous, tragic. At the same time, Levinas proposes that fecundity revivifies time by converting staid succession into access to "the absolute future, or infinite time" (*TI* 268). The child draws the parent into the stranger-self's new activities and desires, promising renewal and liberation from the fruitless repetitions of a fixed fate. In this regard, Menachem Feuer contends that Jonathan's novel about Trachimbrod delivers fresh opportunities for the molding of his complex identity as a Jew; effectively, the superseded past has mutated into a generative future-yet-to-come.[41] Most significantly, though, "the discontinuous time of fecundity" inaugurates a fresh orientation towards the past "in free interpretation and free choice, in an existence as entirely pardoned." As a moral phenomenon, "pardon" paradoxically operates retroactively, reversing the direction of temporality, virtually annulling commitments and "purifying" events (*TI* 282–83). So Jonathan as the literary patriarch of his murdered ancestors aporetically grasps at ethical redemption—or an impossible pardon—for his status as a privileged survivor. Substituting the past for the future described by Levinas, he can select and reconfigure, forgiving himself through the process of conceiving his ancestors in the intimately strange concreteness of their aspirations, faults, and foibles.

Jonathan's exercise of literary fecundity is not unlike his grandfather Safran's first experience of love in response to the conception of a daughter who is to die at the moment of her birth in the German bombing of Trachimbrod. Safran feels himself pulled forward towards the hope of transformative new life, yet tugged backwards into the flood of reminiscence that overwhelms other citizens of the *shtetl* as they helplessly prefigure the obliteration of their culture and history (263–64). With a similar double focus, Jonathan dramatizes the love between Brod and the Kolker that is to prove not to be love, both by verbal denial and by the violence of the husband's deranged actions after the blade of a circular saw has lodged itself in his cranium through a preposterous accident. To prevent further vicious assaults on Brod, their intimacy is conducted through a hole in the wall that keeps them apart. "The Kolker kissed the wall, and Brod kissed the wall, but the selfish wall never kissed either back." The "insurmountable duality" of the frustrated lovers is thus resolved by triangulation into a defense of plenitude withheld: "the absence that defined [the hole] became a presence that defined them" (135).

However, just as Jonathan seems to have squared the circle of his own disturbing disconnection, his proof is undercut. The Kolker, now preserved as the Dial, reveals to grandfather Safran that the hole in the wall was fictitious and that Brod used willingly to join him in bed at the cost of savage beatings, also caring for him gently and generously. *"She did all those things and so many more, things I would never tell anyone, and she never even loved me. Now that's love"* (264). This wryly ironic acknowledgment could scarcely serve as a sharper illustration of "the one for the other," giving with "full hands" regardless of the risk. Jonathan's narrative both brings him an imagined forgiveness through the creation of his literary (rather than biological) progeny and tentatively suspends the temporal pardon promised by fecundity, while projecting alternative possibilities that approach serious ethical awareness in a deceptively flippant or melodramatic tone.

Simultaneously in counterpoint to, and differential play with, Jonathan's family history is Alex's story, which commences confidently with a comic tendency to convenient intellectual manipulation. His account strives for dramatic tones that will allay his self-doubts and confirm his superiority. In wishful mode, he describes himself as roaring at a fastidiously dissatisfied Jonathan during their stay in a Lutsk hotel: "YOU WILL DRINK THE COFFEE UNTIL I CAN SEE MY FACE IN THE BOTTOM OF THE CUP"—only to be met with the riposte, "But it's a clay cup" (117). Yet Alex's latent ethical susceptibility is consistently unmasked and engaged on the journey to Trachimbrod. Up to this point, his sense of far from "unfulfillable" obligations has usually been awakened by financial reward or enforced by his father's fists. When he encounters the woman who at first appears to be Augustine, his whole manner of understanding alters. Puzzled by the oddity and defensive withdrawal of this figure from another era, he keeps pressing the question "Have you ever witnessed anyone in [this] photograph?" Despite his seemingly callous insistence, he has divined a half-veiled hunger for communion that contradicts the woman's reiterated denials of any appropriate knowledge. As his insight into her isolation deepens, irritable harshness becomes compassion for a wounded being who is utterly alienated from the contemporary world. The woman's tears of anguished welcome and her mysterious confession of a long delayed, yet consuming, expectation endorse his intuition: "I have been waiting for you for so long," Only this fragile individual is left to preserve and transmit the memories of a systematically annihilated community. So Alex commits himself to the Other in his determination both to ease Jonathan's disappointment at their apparently fruitless search for Trachimbrod and to comfort the ghostly stranger who controverts this assumption by releasing a "river of tears" while saying, "You are here [in Trachimbrod]. I am it" (117–18). Alex has been called to responsibility for the embodiment of a ruined *shtetl* in an intensely lived moment of recognition that vitiates his father's expedient rationalization of the self-serving infliction of pain, "It does not hurt."

Alex's palpable understanding of an ineluctable obligation to the Other is crystallized by the stark revelation of his grandfather's complicity in the death of his best friend during a Nazi selection. In the guise of the recently married Eli in the village of Kolki, Grandfather identifies Herschel as a Jew in order to save his wife and baby son from execution, even as Herschel despairingly grasps his hand, frantically repeating "Iamsoafraidofdying" (250). The dilemma seems irresolvable, for the narrative pushes Levinasian thought to and beyond its limits. In the event, Grandfather betrays the "first word of the face"; he turns away from the human being, created in the image of God, because he has failed to find "the resources to respond to the call" of the Other (*EI* 88–89). Yet Grandfather *has* met the demand of his wife's face in a situation where no just choice is possible. As Herschel is led away to the synagogue to be immolated with the other Jews, Grandfather kisses his wife, who in turn kisses him. He then takes his son from Grandmother, pouring out, "I loveyou I loveyou," struggling to expiate his proxy murder through the promise of fecundity. His baby son is his stranger-self, the earnest of an absolute future which can purify and renew the past. Yet Alex's rendering of this scene of exposure in the hotel bar closes in the modality of accumulating complication. He, Grandfather, and Jonathan point at one another, miming the gesture of singling out Herschel and reiterating "heisaJew." The "Jew" now stands as the archetypal victim, like the Biblical stranger, widow, and orphan who appear so frequently in Levinas's writing. The accusation spreads, implicating the young men in a past they could not have experienced, tying in the rest of Alex's family, whether living or dead (252). Feuer plausibly suggests that Grandfather may have been a Jew who conspired in the extermination of his own people, given the photographic evidence of his integration into the *shtetl* and his special association with Herschel.[42] But this is only one aspect of an urgent and universal ethical problem. Alex's narrative involves every individual in the victimhood of every Other, each of us as both perpetrator and victim, alternating roles and responsibilities under the authority of the unrelenting commandment, "Thou shalt not kill."

Grandfather's suicide at the end of the novel may be read as self-sacrifice for the murder of Herschel. This retrospective recognition would not be out of keeping with Levinas's disturbing argument that "I am responsible [even] for the persecutions that I undergo," answerable for ensuring that justice is done to my community. Under the influence of Aristotelian virtue ethics, Hilary Putnam admits to being shocked by this offering of oneself as a hostage,[43] despite Levinas's insistence that willing substitution alone can guarantee the meaningful humanity of being human. Yet Grandfather's avowed reasoning is different. He cannot but recognize the bitter irony that his son, the precious baby saved at such cost, has developed into a crassly abusive father given to manipulating and intimidating his own children. The consequences of this bullying are clearly discernible in Alex's nagging sense of inferiority and his nervous crafting of an often ludicrous image of asser-tive virility. Once he has gathered the courage to expel his father from the household, though, duly assuming the role of paternal protector, Grandfather acts decisively. He longs to set Alex and his brother free for the future—the potential of fecundity has skipped a generation. So Grandfather writes in a letter that Alex translates for Jonathan: "I would give everything for [the two grandsons] to live without violence. Peace. . . . They must begin again" (275).

In *Totality and Infinity* Levinas argues that peace must begin from the self and reach the Other "in desire and goodness, where the I both maintains itself and exists without egoism" (*TI* 306). The irony of Grandfather's communica-tion is that Jonathan and Alex have actually agreed to terminate their corre-spondence, foreclosing any desiring exchange. Feuer seems mistaken in at-tributing the break to Jonathan's refusal of forgiveness for the Ukrainian massacre of the Jews, in practice rejecting Alex's sincere wish for friendship and deeming him guilty of latent anti-Semitism.[44] The flow of letters dries up because Alex and perhaps Jonathan have reached a new stage of maturity beyond reductive egoism. Alex has certainly progressed beyond cheap sexual innuendo and cultivated comic extravagance. He has abandoned the illusion of leaving the Ukraine to start a charmed life of wealth and comfort in the United States. More revealingly, he has embraced responsibility in dedicat-ing himself to his mother and brother. This movement of the novel produces a significant tension with its wilfully aestheticizing, postmodern generation of alternative worlds, not to mention its slick remaking of the stark history of the Shoah through ingenious fabrication. As Levinas insists, it is the crucial moment of accepting the absolute right of the Other that transforms the selfish I, absorbed in satisfying enjoyment of the world, into a mature subjec-tivity. Through this prophetic inspiration, the intellectual versatility of philosophizing is transcended in a thought crossed by Godliness that brings the Divine into interpersonal experience.

In *Otherwise than Being*, Levinas explains the import of subordinating the self to the metaphysical height, or inherent dignity and rights, of the Other. The self becomes irreplaceable in its acceptance of uniquely imposed responsibility.

> To this command continually put forth only a "here I am" (*[hineni,] me voici*) can answer, where the pronoun "I" is in the accusative, declined before any declension, possessed by the other, sick [with love], identical. Here I am—is saying with inspiration. . . . There is a constraint to give with full hands [as in "Revelation in the Jewish Tradition"], and thus a constraint to corporeality. . . . [This] is a being torn up from oneself for another in giving to the other the bread out of one's own mouth [as in the case of maternal sacrifice]. (*OB* 141–42)

In *Everything Is Illuminated*, Alex's "here I am" resonates throughout the unfolding of the three parallel narratives, permeating the literary Said of the text with Saying. Simon Critchley aptly explains this ethical dynamic by working through Levinas's figure of the text as a fabric that is repeatedly torn and mended, or a thread that is successively broken and retied. The concept of *sériature* captures the relations between binding and unbinding, between being bound to the discourse of ontology and released from it. Thus a tension is maintained between "the thread (the ontological Said), the knot (the ethical Saying or interruption), and the hiatus (the interruption of interruption)."[45] In this context, Alex's *hineni* seems to occupy the special place of the "interruption of interruption." One of Derrida's speakers in "At this very moment in this work here I am" contends that Levinas himself never says *hineni*. He relies on a quotation, which in its grammatical particularity appears to submit the aphilosophical to ontological thematization or conceptual constraint. Nonetheless, the self in "here I am" slips out of the shackles of any theoretical interrogation of self-presence, finding itself a hostage who is "possessed with the other" in the spirit of the consuming love-sickness of the Biblical "Song of Songs."[46]

Hineni draws performativity to the transcendent limits of its performance. It calls to mind Moses facing the bush burning with "an inextinguishable flame" that "consumes nothing" (*LR* 109, p. 309, 20-21 above). His answer to the stern voice of God, "Here I am" (Genesis 3: 4), is repeated three times, emblematically, in the story of the binding of Isaac (Genesis, 22: 1–14). This terrifyingly majestic account moves from the apparent demand for the sacrifice of a son to an ethical transformation that underwrites the sanctity of human life, while still requiring that the self be ready "to be torn up" from itself. *Hineni* reverberates in *Otherwise than Being*, recurring repeatedly in the section on "The Glory of the Infinite" (*OB* 142–52). It becomes the pulse and watchword of Levinas's prophetic thought, inviting the Infinite to pass. In this movement—and to a lesser extent in the sustained ethical struggle of Foer's novel—the difference between the Greek and the Jew is all but absorbed into a more stringent, yet capacious, mode of thinking.

What is at stake in the *hineni* is mapped out in Levinas's Talmudic reading entitled "The Temptation of Temptation." This doubled temptation becomes an alternative name for the unreformed legacy of Greece, philosophy as the inclination towards detached intellectual investigation without bounds, as distinct from actually succumbing to the experiential allure of something forbidden. In sharp contrast stands the response of the children of Israel when offered the Torah. They construe the messenger as simultaneously "the very message," and request no "trial-knowledge" or "hypothesis-knowledge." They say immediately *na'aseh v'nishma*—in superficial illogic, "We will do and we will hear" (Exodus 24:7). In complete lucidity the Israelites embrace the Saying, meeting God as the absolute Other and becoming midwives to the birth of meaning (*NiTR* 48–50). In his funeral oration, "Adieu," Jacques Derrida cites this Talmudic reading, because he sees it as "set[ting] to work . . . all the great themes to which the thought of Emmanuel Levinas has awakened us." Thus he emphasizes in *na'aseh v'nishma* Levinas's response to "an innocence without naiveté, an uprightness without stupidity, an absolute uprightness, which is also absolute self-criticism." This upright movement toward the Other in defiance of death "is called *Temimut*, the essence of Jacob."[47]

In the closing sentences of *Everything Is Illuminated*, Grandfather writes in his suicide note that he is *"complete with happiness, and it is what I must do, and I will do it. . . . I will walk without noise, and I will open the door in darkness, and I will"* (276). This is how the text reaches beyond Greek aesthetic accomplishment to the *temimut* of *hineni*. As language with all its virtuoso ingenuity trails into silence, the Saying assumes its signification and darkness substitutes for the sought "illumination" the unshakeable lucidity of performed prophetic responsibility.

NOTES

1. Jacques Derrida, "Violence and Metaphysics: An Essay on the Thought of Emmanuel Levinas," in *Writing and Difference*, trans. Alan Bass (London and Henley: Routledge and Kegan Paul, 1978), 151.

2. In this essay, the Hebrew term "Shoah," meaning "destruction, ruin, catastrophe, cataclysm, or disaster" (Reuben Alcalay, *The Complete Hebrew-English Dictionary*, vol. 4 [Hebrew-English] [Tel Aviv and Jeusalem: Massadah Publishing Company, 1965], 2554) is consistently used in preference to the notion of a "Holocaust." The latter word is derived from ancient Greek via Old French, suggesting a "whole burnt offering." It thus places particular emphasis on the extermination of the Jews in the death camps at the expense of a broader context of violence, inflicted suffering, and various kinds of ethical resistance (see *The Concise Oxford Dictionary of Current English* [Oxford: Oxford University Press, 1964], 581, and

Liddell and Scott, *An Intermediate Greek-English Lexicon* [Oxford: Clarendon Press, 1968], 552).

3. Robert Bernasconi, "Levinas: Philosophy and Beyond," in *Philosophy and Non-Philosophy since Merleau-Ponty*, ed. Hugh J. Silverman (New York and London: Routledge, 1988), 237.

4. Ibid., 237.

5. Ibid., 237.

6. Bernasconi, 240; *LR* 166.

7. Derrida, "Violence," 152.

8. In *OB* 149, prophecy is defined with the same cogency, but modified emphasis, as "the reverting in which the perception of an order coincides with the signification of this order given to him that obeys it."

9. Simon Critchley, *The Ethics of Deconstruction: Derrida and Levinas* (Delhi: Motilal Banarsidass Publishers, 2007), 282.

10. Catherine Chalier, "Levinas and the Talmud," in *The Cambridge Companion to Levinas*, ed. Simon Critchley and Robert Bernasconi (Cambridge: Cambridge University Press, 2002), 100, 110.

11. Bernasconi, 258.

12. Robert Eaglestone, *The Holocaust and the Postmodern* (Oxford: Oxford University Press, 2008), 266–69, 259. Levinas's ethical understanding of murder is considered below (pp. 313-14).

13. Ibid., 256–63.

14. *OB* 162; Eaglestone, 276–78.

15. Levinas's translation seems strangely impoverished, diluting the force of his commentary. *Rachamim* has as its root the Hebrew word *rechem* (or "womb"), thus carrying connotations of the unqualified love of a mother for the child she carries and inviting translation as "compassion."

16. Hilary Putnam differentiates between Levinas's univeralization of Jewish values and his consciousness of Jewish particularism (see his "Levinas and Judaism," in *The Cambridge Companion to Levinas*, ed. Simon Critchley and Robert Bernasconi [Cambridge: Cambridge University Press, 2002], 48–53); however, this does not seem to me to undermine the fundamentally Jewish orientation towards ethical responsibility that infuses all his writing.

17. Henry James, *The Art of the Novel*, introduced by R. P. Blackmur (New York and London: Charles Scribner's Sons), 222.

18. Anne Michaels, *Fugitive Pieces* (London and New York: Bloomsbury, 1998 [1996]), i–ii. All further references are to this edition and will be cited parenthetically in the text.

19. See Eaglestone, 117–20.

20. Susan Gubar, "Empathic Identification in Anne Michaels's *Fugitive Pieces*: Masculinity and Poetry after Auschwitz," *Signs: Journal of Women in Culture and Society* 28, no. 1 (2002): 355, and Dalia Kandiyoti, "'Our Foothold in Buried Worlds': Place in Holocaust Consciousness and Anne Michaels's *Fugitive Pieces*," *Contemporary Literature* 45, no. 2 (2004): 310.

21. Donna Coffey, "Blood and Soil in Anne Michaels's *Fugitive Pieces*: The Pastoral in Holocaust Literature," *Modern Fiction Studies* 53, no. 1 (2007): 29, and Neal Bruss, "Anne Michaels's *Fugitive Pieces*, Object Relations, Internalization, and the Development of Discourse," *Reader: Essays in Reader-Oriented Theory, Criticism and Pedagogy* 48 (2003): 23.

22. The novel is frequently read within the context of Holocaust and trauma theory, with varying emphases on literary form, history and memory, or gender orientation (see, for example Kandiyoti, 300–30; Coffey, 27–49; Merle Williams and Stefan Ploatinsky, "Writing at its Limits: Trauma Theory in relation to Anne Michaels's *Fugitive Pieces*," *English Studies in Africa* 52, no. 1 (2009): 1–14; Meira Cook, "At the Membrane of Language and Silence: Metaphor and Memory in *Fugitive Pieces*," *Canadian Literature* 164 (2000): 12–33; Meredith Criglington, "Walter Benjamin's 'Thinking in Images' and Anne Michaels' Erotic Archaeology of Memory," *Canadian Literature* 188 (2006): 86–102; Elrud Ibsch, "Comfort and Scandal of Memory: Anne Michaels and Amir Gutfreund: Two Authors of the Second-and-a-Half Generation," *Journal of Modern Jewish Studies* 5, no. 2 (2006): 203–12; and Gubar, 249–76.

23. Lisa Guenther, *The Gift of the Other: Levinas and the Politics of Reproduction* (Albany: State University of New York Press, 2006), 57–58.

24. Gubar, 265.

25. Criglington, 95.

26. Gubar, 269.

27. Luce Irigaray, "The Fecundity of the Caress: A Reading of Levinas, *Totality and Infinity*, Section IV, B," in *Face to Face with Levinas*, ed. Richard A. Cohen (Albany: State University of New York Press, 1986), 233; Guenther, 86. For a lucidly innovative reinterpretation of Levinas's account of the erotic and fecundity, see Guenther's "Otherwise than Paternity: Irigaray Reading Levinas," in *The Gift of the Other*, 84–94.

28. See also Guenther, 104.

29. Jacques Derrida, *Memoires for Paul de Man*, trans. Cecile Lindsay *et al.* (New York: Columbia University Press, 1989), 35.

30. Gubar, 272.

31. Criglington, 97.

32. Jonathan Safran Foer, *Everything Is Illuminated* (London: Penguin, 2003), iv. All further references are to this edition, and will be cited parenthetically in the text.

33. See Robert E. Kohn, "Foer's *Everything Is Illuminated*," *Explicator* 65, no. 4 (2007): 245–47; Francisco Collado-Rodriguez, "Ethics in the Second Degree: Trauma and Dual Narratives in Jonathan Safran Foer's *Everything Is Illuminated*," *Journal of Modern Literature* 32, no. 1 (2009): 55; and Menachem Feuer, "Almost Friends: Post-Holocaust Comedy, Tragedy, and Friendship in Jonathan Safran Foer's *Everything Is Illuminated*," *Shofar: An Interdisciplinary Journal of Jewish Studies* 25, no. 2 (2007): 25, 36.

34. Eaglestone, 128–31.

35. Derrida elaborates the now familiar notion of *différance* in a deliberately provocative, sometimes humorous and philosophically wide-ranging essay bearing the same title. See his "Differance," in *"Speech and Phenomena"and Other Essays on Husserl's Theory of Signs*, trans. David B. Allison (Evanston, IL: Northwestern University Press, 1973), 129–60.

36. Jacques Derrida, "Living On—Border Lines," in *Deconstruction and Criticism*, ed. Harold Bloom *et al.* (London and Henley: Routledge and Kegan Paul, 1979), 81–84.

37. See Eaglestone, 129; Kohn, 245; Collado-Rodriguez, 55.

38. Jacques Derrida, "At this very moment in this work here I am," trans. Ruben Berezdivin, in *Re-Reading Levinas*, ed. Robert Bernasconi and Simon Critchley (Bloomington and Indianapolis: Indiana University Press, 1991), 11–15.

39. Zygmunt Bauman, *Postmodern Ethics* (Oxford and Cambridge, MA: Basil Blackwell, 1993), 92–93.

40. Ibid., 98.

41. Feuer, 36.

42. Ibid., 45–46.

43. Putnam, 55–56.

44. Feuer, 43–44.

45. Critchley, 128.

46. Derrida, "At this very moment,"18–19.

47. Jacques Derrida, *Adieu*, in *Adieu: To Emmanuel Levinas*, trans. Pascale-Anne Brault and Michael Naas (Stanford: Stanford University Press, 1999), 3. (Derrida slightly adjusts the text in *NiTR* 48.)

Chapter Fourteen

Against the *Akedah*

Levinasian Paternity in Cormac McCarthy's The Road

Daniel T. Kline

In "Cormac McCarthy's Venomous Fiction," one of the novelist's rare published interviews, *The New York Times*'s Richard B. Woodward writes that if "*Suttree* strives to be *Ulysses, Blood Meridian* has distinct echoes of *Moby-Dick*."[1] Extending the analogy, I argue in this chapter that *The Road* (2006) is McCarthy's *akedah*. In *The Road*, a worldwide disaster has reduced the earth to ashes, civilization to ruins, and society to cannibalism. We are never told why. Like the *akedah*, in which Abraham is commanded to take his son to Mount Moriah and offer him there as a sacrifice, *The Road* depicts a man and a boy on a journey to a moment of ultimate consequence, and like the story from Genesis 22, the man must continually weigh a sacrificial demand placed upon him by another. In both texts, a third party compels a man to kill his son to meet the exigencies of the moment. Both the *akedah* and *The Road* present the starkest ethical dilemma: should a father kill his son in response to a metaphysical demand? Søren Kierkegaard's *Fear and Trembling* provides one answer in the voice of Johannes de Silentio, who explains that in following God's command that he sacrifice Isaac, Abraham teleologically suspends all ethical demands in a "leap of faith." Emmanuel Levinas, whose "ethics as first philosophy" celebrates the preeminence of the Other, counters that Abraham's attention to God's second command, that he stay the knife and spare his son, reveals the *akedah*'s ethical heart. Through Emmanuel Levinas's dialogue with Kierkegaard concerning Abraham, Isaac, and Genesis 22, in this chapter I read McCarthy's *The Road* as an ethical and anti-sacrificial critique of the *akedah* in light of Levinas's meditations on paternity, subjectivity, and temporality.[2]

Although McCarthy's pervasive depiction of often perverse violence leads some to conclude his work nihilistic,[3] *The Road* reveals a severe, even moving, ethical vision in the paternal relationship between the man and the boy. While the commonplace interpretation of the *akedah* justifies Abraham's threatened sacrifice of Isaac as the height of faith, *The Road* opposes the rationalization of sacrifice and denigration of the child at the father's hands and for the father's needs. A Levinasian reading likewise accounts for the novel's emotional impact and counters the accusation that McCarthy's apocalyptic tale is hopeless, an allegory of the last days, or a triumph of language alone.[4] *The Road* is a harrowing and ultimately beautiful account of the triumph of ethics beyond love in the face of a world burned by fire, a holocaust. My analysis follows several trajectories. First, I examine the man and the boy's shared traumatic subjectivity in the midst of what Levinas terms the *il y a*. Second, I turn to *Fear and Trembling* and Levinas's reading of Kierkegaard. Next, I move to the ethical dimensions of *The Road* through Levinas's meditations upon fecundity and paternity. Finally, I conclude by examining *The Road* and Levinas's shared post-secular orientation. Seen through this Levinasian lens, *The Road* is a profound depiction of paternity, an ethical subjectivity that goes beyond love to the hither side of God, and it defies the sacred but embraces the holy in the face of a boy.

To begin I want to outline five suggestive relationships between the *akedah* and *The Road* to highlight their common concerns. First, both stories feature the same constellation of characters: a man, a son, and a mother. Although many question the possibility of God in McCarthy's world, a worldwide trauma presses upon the man with metaphysical certainty. Indelibly and spectrally present, both women are conspicuous by their textual absence, and though God puts Abraham to the ultimate test in Genesis 22, the woman in *The Road* demands the man kill the boy. Second, the boundaries of the two narratives provocatively complement one another. Like the *akedah*, *The Road* begins *in medias res*, and each text provides only a destination— south, to the sea—in *The Road* like "the land of Moriah" in Genesis 22. Third, the point of each journey seems diametrically opposed. In *The Road*, the man and the boy head south for survival. In the *akedah*, Abraham takes Isaac to Moriah to offer him as a holocaust or burnt offering. Fourth, the tales' configurations, the relationship of the structural elements of each narrative, differ in emphasis and proportion. The *akedah* depicts only the opening and the conclusion of the story, the motivating action and narrative resolution. God calls Abraham and gives the sacrificial command; Abraham and Isaac travel for three days; Isaac is delivered and the ram substituted; and Abraham returns, seemingly alone. The novel is, in a sense, "all middle." *The Road* depicts the man and boy in their quotidian activities, a continual fight for survival and demonstration of love as they encounter blood cultists, search for food, freeze in the snow, huddle in the night, stumble upon unexpected plenty, and meet horrific scenes of cannibalism and despair. In constant movement, the man and the boy are always strangers, homeless, in need, and neighbors to none. *The Road* presents the clearest articulation of Levinasian ethical subjectivity in contemporary literature.

THE MAN AND BOY: TRAUMATIC SUBJECTIVITY AND THE NAKED *IL Y A*

McCarthy's *The Road* immediately opens into a harrowing narrative whose origin is unclear and whose *telos* is unknown. McCarthy's two main characters are never named—the man and the boy—but they are set in a world, our world, in the aftermath of a catastrophe that is never explained but only suggested later, in a flashback that introduces a third character, the woman, who cradles "her belly in one hand"[5] (53). Three details emerge in this flashback. The first concerns the motivating event. Many readers reckon they know the nature of the incident, but McCarthy leaves the details ambiguous so as not to allow easy moralizing about ecological disaster or nuclear proliferation. The second concerns the relationship of the man and boy to the woman: she is the boy's mother and the man's partner. The third concerns the novel's fractured temporal co-ordinates, the multiple timelines that overlap but never coincide.[6] The man and the woman, like the reader, retain the memory of the world of the past, but the boy knows only the world after its undoing. It is the burnt-out ruin of a world, firestormed and ashblown. It is a world beyond the hither side of God, "Barren, silent, godless" (4).

The Road's oppressive environment suggests Levinas's *il y a*, the "there is" of brute reality, which he characterizes as "the total exclusion of light" (*EE* 52). As far back as 1935's *On Escape* (*De l'évasion*), the *il y a* formed the basis of Levinas's rethinking of the philosophical tradition: "Temporal existence takes on the inexpressible flavor of the absolute. The elementary truth that *there is being*—being that has value and weight—is revealed at a depth that measures its brutality and its seriousness" (*E* 52, emphasis Levinas's). For Levinas, "the ground of suffering consists of the impossibility of interrupting it [being], and of an acute feeling of being held fast [*rivé*]" (52). The man and the boy are riveted to the blasted world of *The Road*, and their trauma is that there is no escape from it or even interruption. This unmediated reality, "the horrible eternity at the bottom of essence" (176), describes the man's and the boy's physical as well as existential situation, a desolation without boundary or measure, in what McCarthy calls "the nameless dark come to enshroud them" (9). The relentless, creative beauty of McCarthy's prose, his ever fecund vocabulary of ash and blistered remains, gives the deadened world an insistent, oppressive vitality even as it afflicts the man and the boy on their journey. The man's and boy's traumatic "passivity beyond passivity," their hunger, nausea, fatigue, and insomnia yield the anarchic self as persecuted, vulnerable, destitute, and exposed to all Others.

The Road's oppressive environment, its irreducible *il y a*, highlights the man's and the boy's relationship, and the full range of Levinas's vision of subjectivity breaks forth in the novel's first few lines as the man and boy lay in their fetid cocoon of blankets: "When he woke in the woods in the dark and the cold of night he'd reach out to touch the child sleeping beside him. . . . His hand rose and fell softly with each precious breath"(3). The novel opens with a suffering, dying man beset by insomnia who reaches out to touch a sleeping child, both of them enveloped in a filthy cocoon, their only barrier against the merciless elements. The boy's breathing and the father's hand are synonymous and the only hint of life, an existence univocal and "each the other's world entire" (7). For the father, feeling his son's chest rise and fall bespeaks transcendence as face-to-face proximity; their uncontrolled shivering on a bitter cold night marks their unicity. For the son, his absolute trust in the father who remains hostage for his sake, persecuted on all sides, hungry and destitute, means that he, too, must remain vigilant for the one who stands responsible for him. The boy reprimands the man for denying himself the last bit of hot cocoa, rather than sharing it evenly (34). The ethical relation is revealed in its starkest terms, as Levinas writes, "To give, to-be-for-another, despite oneself, but in interrupting the for-oneself, is to take the bread out of one's own mouth, to nourish the hunger of another with one's own fasting" (*OB* 56). The novel's stark, relentless desolation amplifies each sensation, and as in so many moments of simple pleasure in the novel, a swig of hot chocolate takes on its full thermal, visual, gustatory, and gestural weight.

All their goods are packed in a knapsack and into a dilapidated grocery cart, and their lives are reduced to the barest immediate needs of the present—food, shelter, survival—except for one thing: their relationship to each other, in Levinasian terms a plural existence. They are at once rootless, displaced, and constantly strangers to everyone they encounter, others who are more likely to be predatory than benign. Even so, they are bound together in a living filiation so powerful that it looks beyond even death:

> What would you do if I died?
> If you died I would want to die too.
> So you could be with me?
> Yes. So I could be with you.
> Okay. (10–11)

In what other work of literature does the simple phrase "okay," its quotidian banality thrown into sharp relief by McCarthy's harrowing story, rise to liturgical heights? The boy's "okay," picked up at times by the man as well, signifies acknowledgment and awareness, a willingness to respond prior to volition as well as a readiness to accede prior to understanding the request. "Okay" is before passivity and proximity, both an acquiescence and a recognition. In Genesis 22, God calls Abraham's name, and the patriarch responds, "Here I am" (or, in Hebrew, *hineini*). Abraham could have just as easily said, "Okay." For Levinas, "Here I am," or "okay," signifies transparency and witness "of a subjectivity responsible for the other" (152).

SILENTIO READS THE *AKEDAH,* LEVINAS READS KIERKEGAARD

As is well known, in Genesis 22 God "tempted" (or tested) Abraham and commanded him to journey to Moriah to offer his son Isaac as a burnt offering.[7] Johannes de Silentio's explication of Genesis 22 in Kierkegaard's *Fear and Trembling* has attained canonical status since its publication in 1843, introducing influential concepts like "the knight of faith," the "leap of faith," and "the teleological suspension of the ethical." Reacting specifically to Hegel's understanding of the "universal" as conformity to public morality (the "ethical") necessary to state coherence, Silentio argues that Abraham rises above the ethical (and universal) by establishing an "absolute relation to the absolute" (God) that, from the perspective of the "universal" (because it ethically applies to everyone), is absurd. Abraham is therefore ethically and socially unintelligible to others because he ascends as a specific individual above the universal by a "teleological suspension of the ethical."[8] His willingness to sacrifice Isaac is itself absurd, incapable of mediation. Unlike tragic heroes Agamemnon, Jephthah, and Brutus, Abraham "overstepped the ethical altogether, and had a higher *telos* outside it, in relation to which he suspended it" because his actions neither conformed to public morality nor served the interests of state.[9] In other words, Silentio justifies Abraham's threat against Isaac because it reaches a higher good, a singular relation to God. The substance of Abraham's faith is that he will receive Isaac back "by virtue of the absurd" and the proof of Abraham's faith is his silent torment, his singular anguish before God, because to speak of his faith or give evidence of his suffering would place him back within the universal (or ethical) domain. Faith is therefore a "monstrous paradox . . . capable of making a murder into a holy act well pleasing to God, a paradox which gives Isaac back to Abraham, which no thought can grasp because faith begins precisely where thinking leaves off."[10] Thus, Abraham's righteousness consists precisely in the unutterable extremity of his personal torment, and Silentio finds Abraham baffling from any normative perspective. Of course, Silentio already knows the outcome of the story, and as a Christian Kierkegaard sees in the *akedah* the prefiguration of Christ's crucifixion. Christianity traditionally calls Genesis 22:1–19 "the sacrifice of Isaac" because of its prophetic fore-shadowing of Christ's crucifixion. Significantly, neither Kierkegaard nor Silentio imagine that Isaac suffers beneath his father's blade. [11] Isaac exists for Abraham's exaltation. In contrast, Judaism calls the *akedah* "the binding of Isaac," which is a faithful understanding of the literal Hebrew text, since, as Rashi, the important medieval rabbi, notes, God asked only that Abraham "offer" Isaac, not kill him. [12] Levinas likewise reads Genesis 22 according to the rabbinic tradition, although he does not provide a straightforward commentary. [13] Instead, Levinas's understanding of the *akedah* emerges in his broader assessment of Abraham and in his colloquy with Kierkegaard, particularly in two brief essays: "Kierkegaard: Existence and Ethics" and "A propos of *Kierkegaard Vivant*." [14]

Levinas critiques Kierkegaard's definition of the ethical stage and his account of subjectivity. For Levinas, the Kierkegaardian subject tensed upon itself in "egotism" requires a truth found only interiorly, in subjective suffering, and this subjective infolding turns the self away from any Other to attain Kierkegaard's religious realm. "Violence emerges in Kierkegaard," Levinas writes, "at the precise moment when, moving beyond the esthetic stage, existence can no longer limit itself to what it takes to be the ethical stage and enters the religious one, the domain of belief" (*PN* 72). Turned ever inward and separated from social attachment, Kierkegaard's autonomous self provides the only basis for relationship to God, the absolute, who stands beyond all ethics and sociality. The problem, according to Levinas, is that Kierkegaard's version of the self opens itself only to God and not to others, making Kierkegaard "the first philosopher who thinks God without thinking Him in terms of the world" (*EN* 74). In contrast, Levinas summons the face of the Other as the call to ethical responsibility as an antidote to reflexive inwardness: "The putting in question of the *I* in the face of the Other is a new tension in the *I*, a tension that is not a tensing on oneself. Instead of destroying the *I*, the putting in question binds it to the other in an incomparable, unique manner" (*PN* 73). Levinas's key thematic, the face of the Other, indicates the individual's vulnerability to violence and inveighs against murder, "Thou shalt not kill." Thus, rather than finding itself in solitary suffering before God, the "uniqueness of the *I* consists in the fact that no one can answer in his or her place" for the Other (*PN* 73). Being placed thus in the accusative rather than the nominative, the Kierkegaardian I is "elected" and "promoted to a privileged place on which all that is not me depends," rather than being separated from the ethical in an absolute relation to the absolute (73). Levinas fears that Kierkegaardian subjectivity, without regard for the Other and turned ever inward away from reason toward affect alone, "leads us to other forms of violence" (68).

The Road's apocalyptic "blood cults" vividly depict the violent consequences of substantiating belief through suffering and isolating religion from an ethical commitment to any Other.[15] In the aftermath of worldwide apocalypse, *The Road* imagines bands of crazed, half-starved survivors joined together not as communities but as collective predators. Self-mutilating and tattooed by arcane symbols, totems, and "creeds misspelled" (90), they march four abreast with red scarves, chanting and on the lookout for their next meal. They leave only a trail of death. Elementary social forms have disappeared, replaced by a cannibalistic hierarchy of predation and sexual violence. Even those who have settled into vaguely recognizable domestic arrangements have fallen into routine horror, preying on the weak and infirm and treating other humans as foodstuffs, their abjection embodied in a beheaded, eviscerated baby roasting on a spit. After going without food and sleep for five days, the man and boy fall into a scene of unrelieved terror. In the horrid stench of a basement, amidst a huddle of naked men and women who hide their faces with their hands, a man lays on a mattress, the stumps of his legs "blackened and burnt" (110). By a hair's breadth the man and boy avoid capture by the house's inhabitants, four bearded men who live with two women. Any remaining rudimentary society in *The Road*'s post-cataclysmic world is built upon the flesh of others.

The logic of survival, of all against all, undoubtedly animates the habitual horrors of *The Road*. The subject tensed upon itself to the absolute disregard of any social obligation or ethical commitment is capable of any violence because there are no restraints upon its self-serving desires and no brakes upon its self-justifying logic. The Kierkegaardian movement from the ethical sphere to the religious is exactly the opposite of Levinas's insistence that the self is asymmetrically responsible to (and for) the Other. In contrast to Silentio, Levinas argues that the Other to whom we are indebted ultimately calls the self into subjectivity, for "only irreducible subjectivity can assume a responsibility. That is what constitutes the ethical" (*PN* 73).Whereas Kierkegaard's account of subjectivity, like the Enlightenment valorization of the rational mind, simultaneously isolates and elevates the individual self, Levinas maintains that Kierkegaard's sovereign *I* must be challenged in its ipseity or selfhood. This challenge comes through the face of the Other. The asymmetry of self and Other, my responsibility to and for the Other, is altered only by the appearance of a third party.

In the crucial final paragraph of "Kierkegaard: Existence and Ethics," Levinas notes that Kierkegaard reads the *akedah* selectively, concentrating only upon God's demand that Abraham sacrifice Isaac and Abraham's acquiescence while ignoring Abraham's willingness to spare his son and offer the ram. Incredulous, Levinas describes Kierkegaard's "encounter with God as a subjectivity rising to the religious level: God above the ethical order!" (*PN* 74). Kierkegaard's selectivity likewise concerns this single moment in Abraham's life and disregards those moments when Abraham acknowledges the Other and intervenes on behalf of the third party as in Genesis 18. Levinas notes that when God condemns Sodom and Gomorrah (Genesis 18:16–33), Abraham audaciously confronts God "in the name of the just who may be present there." Levinas shows that in the Talmudic tradition Abraham is "above all the one who knew how to receive and feed men: the one whose tent was side open on all sides" as he welcomes the visitors under the oaks of Mamre in Genesis 18 (*NiTR* 99).[16] Abraham's boundaryless shelter signifies that he is continually oriented toward, and responsible for, Others, accepting "the form of obligation toward the body, the obligation of feeding and sheltering" (99). In fact, Levinas accounts for the entirety of Genesis 22:1–19, rather than focusing exclusively upon the sacrificial threat. Levinas famously reads the *akedah* against Kierkegaard by noting the crucial moment is not when Abraham raises the knife to his son but when he heeds the angel's command *not* to harm Isaac. Even if God's test severs Abraham from the social realm, the angel's second call returns Abraham to the ethical order (*PN* 74).

THE LEVINASIAN FATHER AND CHILD: PATERNITY, FILIATION, AND TEMPORALITY

Levinas's reading of the *akedah*, and his account of subjectivity generally, differs from Silentio's not only in his understanding of Abraham but also in the central position he grants Isaac specifically and, throughout his work, to children categorically.[17] For Kierkegaard via Silentio the child must always remain subordinated to the adult, and Abraham must remain unassailably isolated from all Others, particularly his son, in his religious ascent. Rather than seeing Isaac's face as uniquely Other yet linked to him, in *Fear and Trembling* Abraham sees Isaac as an instrument to fulfill God's demand. In contrast, Levinas's *Totality and Infinity* finds in the child the paradigmatic other who prevents the Kierkegaardian closure of the self in agonizing, secreted isolation. In language that could be directed toward the ascent of Kierkegaard's Knight of Faith, Levinas writes, "The profanation that violates a secret does not 'discover,' beyond the face, another more profound I which this face would express; it discovers the child" (*TI* 267).[18] The relationship with the child through filiality, fecundity, and paternity, expressed in voluptuousity and tenderness, reorients subjectivity as consociality, and the return of the I in paternity continually alters the self. The self in paternity becomes simultaneously multiple without division, for the "fecundity of the I is its very transcendence" (277). In *The Road*, this transcendence finds the self responsible to and for the Other in the Other's infinite immediacy: "He held the boy close to him. So thin. My heart, he said. My heart" (29). For Levinas, paternity reconfigures epistemology, for what one knows is irrevocably extended into multiple unknowns. Paternity reshapes ontology, for the self issues beyond the self to another who is both stranger and self-same. Paternity shakes the foundational categories of subjectivity and sociality because, for Levinas, "I do not have my child; I am my child. Paternity is a relation with a stranger who while being Other . . . *is* me, a relation of the I with a self which yet is not me" (277). Levinas refuses to construct the child as an instrument or object, for such a regard for the Other is the essence of the sacrificial—that is, to regard the Other as mine to use for my own purposes, as Abraham regards Isaac as an object to elevate his relationship to God in Silentio's account.

Paternity likewise reconfigures temporality. For Levinas, the child is not a means to an end but opens the range of possible futures, nor is the child an end for she or he calls the parent to continuing responsibility that goes beyond any theodicy. In the Kierkegaardian "tensing of being," the self is foreclosed in interiority, a teleology without dimension but ever present, yet the "relation with the child—that is, the relation with the other that is not a power, but fecundity—establishes relationship with the absolute future, or infinite time," according to Levinas (*TI* 268). This absolute future is smeared spatially in *The Road* so that the conventional coordinates of space and time are nearly meaningless. A service-station roadmap, the ones that are so hard to fold again in the correct sequence, has shredded at each seam with its continued usage. The man and the boy number and stack each rectangular shard, laying out the sequence anew at each moment they consult it as if the coordinates of the world have no relation each to the other any longer. The boy memorizes the names of the towns in a world long dead as he follows their progress on the map from the road to the sea (214–15). Despite their intimacy, the man knows that his past is not the boy's; nor are their futures co-terminal. That another future is possible for the boy keeps the man alive.

"The converse of paternity," the father–son relationship or "filiality," designates "a relation of rupture and a recourse at the same time," according to Levinas. As the son opens the father to new forms of futurity and subjectivity, so too "in the form of the son being *is* infinitely and discontinuously, historical without fate. The past is recaptured at each moment from a new point" that disrupts continuity with persistent resumption (*TI* 278). McCarthy's achievement here is the utter lack of nostalgia for the past or sentimental attachment to an unrealistic future. The man and boy live in an unfettered present, a diachrony that recognizes their differences yet nurtures their consociality. What becomes clear in *The Road* is that their goodness consists not in a set of beliefs nor in their avoidance of anything bad but in their continued openness toward one another, their non-indifference to Others, and their refusal—particularly the father's refusal—to embrace theodicy or teleology, to foreclose the son's future because of his own circumstances. There is no "teleological suspension of the ethical" in *The Road* because there is no future, no higher good than their presence one to another, no reality beyond the present moment of sensation and unicity. The difference between the man and the woman in *The Road* is that the son allows the father to imagine a future different for the boy than for him, but the mother can see only her son's fate determined in her own.

A simple formalist reading of *The Road*'s historical sensibility might say that the woman symbolizes the past, the man represents the present, and the boy symbolizes the future. However, McCarthy also gestures toward a particularly Levinasian sense of temporality, a deformalization of time that emerges in the encounter with the Other (person) as otherness (alterity) itself.[19] Levinas's early reflections upon temporality and otherness insist upon the interruption the Other brings to the self, for "time is not the achievement of an isolated and lone subject, but . . . is the very relationship of the subject with the Other" (*TO* 39). Reacting to a Bergsonian conception of time as duration, Levinas eschews synchrony for multiple noncoincident *dia-chro-nies* (in Levinas's locution). The self is never temporally concurrent with an Other; they cannot meet in/at the same time. The Other's temporality interrupts the self, and this interjection joins the structure of time with the possibility of ethical relation. In *The Road*, the father *knows* nothing of time as *chronos*, for he has lost track of the days, months, and years. Even the seasons seem indistinct in a world that knows only twilight and darkness. His *experience* of time is in the rise and fall of his son's chest and the changes in the boy's face as he grows hungry, fearful, anxious. There is no knowledge of time apart from the man's relationship to the boy. For the man, the boy's concrete, embodied existence keeps alive the promise of a future, the possibility of futurity itself or what Levinas terms the "hither side," while at the same time it maintains the absolute alterity of the past as lived with another Other, a third party, the woman. The boy is also the woman's child, but the cataclysm forecloses all futures for her. Unlike the man, she cannot separate her own temporality, her *telos*, from the boy's. Their temporal, and thus experiential, horizons are coincident and co-terminal, and the man must continually contend with her inconsolable demand from the past that continually colors their future. In flashback the man and woman argue over whether or not they should fight to remain alive or kill themselves to avoid the horror of becoming someone else's meal. The woman states: "I'd take him with me if it weren't for you. You know I would. It's the right thing to do" (56). Unlike the *akedah*, where God commands Abraham to offer his son, and Sarah mysteriously disappears from the narrative, the sacrificial demand in *The Road* comes from the mother. We find that the mother, blinded, takes her own life to escape the horrors of that world, while the father remains faithful to his dying breath. She is convinced she knows what time will bring as it unveils its horrors to her and her son, while the man has little conception of time apart from the quotidian efforts to preserve and extend his son's life. The boy's gestation enseams these two temporalities of the man and woman, joining while sundering them eternally. In contrast to the woman, the man's existence is accomplished in his temporal experience of the boy, which approaches Levinas's understanding of temporality, as taken from Rosenzweig: the past as creation, the present as revelation, and the future as redemption, not as abstract concepts but as the lived experience of fatigue, horror, anxiety, insomnia, sickness, hunger, and (in fleeting moments) as something approaching pleasure in the bite of an apple, a swig of cola, a withered morel, water from an old cistern, or shivering beneath a winter waterfall. The Rabbis considered Abraham's three day journey, otherwise undeveloped in the Genesis account, and Rashi asks, "Why did He delay from showing it to him immediately [that is, the place of sacrifice]? So that people should not say that He suddenly perplexed and confused him and confounded him suddenly and deranged and, had he had time to contemplate it, he would not have done it."[20] In McCarthy's novel, in contrast, the man is confronted at every moment by the choice to end his and his boy's suffering or to continue on in the face of horror and finding, in Levinasian terms, transcendence in proximity to his son, whose heartbreaking refrain of "okay," of total faith in his father, flies in the face of their shared trauma. It is crucial to remember that Isaac never explicitly agrees to be sacrificed in the *akedah*. He simply calls to his father and is met with knife and fire.

ON THE ROAD WITH LEVINAS

Critical analysis of the *akedah* too often and too quickly either ignores Isaac or claims in the absence of any evidence that Isaac simply acquiesces to Abraham's violence or, even more tellingly, actively supports his father's actions. In an otherwise nuanced Levinasian reading of Genesis 22 in terms of community versus collectivity, James E. Faulconer writes that "we see not only Abraham's ethical stance, but Isaac's, for Isaac continues, though he must at least suspect what is to come. He continues willingly."[21] Rashi, the medieval rabbi and Talmudic exegete, elegantly solves the problem by closely attending to the Hebrew and noting that God commanded Abraham to offer or "to bring him [Isaac] up," not to slaughter him.[22] In *The Road*'s ash-strewn world, the man continually faces a Levinasian dilemma so stark that I would call it a form of *triage*, and that is, how does one remain continually open to the demand of the other, his child, while continuously facing the needs of the third party—those in their death throes whom they encounter on the road. For the man, the choice is always clear. He must protect, feed, and nurture his son within the narrowed range of possibilities in this fire-blasted world. Hardened by the horrors of survival, the man begins in what Levinas would term an "egological" mode, the subject tensed back upon itself in doubt and trauma. As such, the man, though not indifferent to the suffering of others, resists intervening because life to him is a zero-sum proposition. What he gives is what he loses, and what he loses he cannot give to his son. In contrast, perhaps because in his naiveté he is not as hardened against the world as his father, the boy wishes to help those in need. One of the beauties of McCarthy's novel, as well as one of its heartbreaks, is how the man and boy affect each other across the novel's characterological arc. From his boy's example—the boy's "suffering the suffering of the other," in Levinasian terms—the man regains a sense of compassion for the suffering of others, even when all he can do is witness their anguish. Out of his experience on the road with his father, the boy learns that he has the ability to choose to intervene or not. As his sensibility is toughened by horror, he discovers that he must choose to make ethical decisions, and he no longer responds simply, reflexively out of overwhelming pity.

McCarthy makes these developments clear by depicting parallel encounters across the novel. Early on, the man and the boy encounter a lightning-struck man. The boy wants to help the man, but the father insists that he's beyond hope. As a result, the boy falls silent and distant even when the man tries to explain again why they cannot intervene: "He's going to die. We can't share what we have or we'll die too" (52). Later they meet another old man tottering in the middle of the road. Perhaps a reference to the mythical "Wandering Jew," the man's name is Ely, or perhaps not, and in a fascinating sequence they discuss the nature of God and humanity. Ely says he has "always been on the road" (160) and "knew this was coming" (168). This time they stop at the boy's insistence, and seeing the old man's face they feed him a can of fruit cocktail from their meager stores because he is still alive and, like them, moving down the road (163–64). When the man questions him as to why he is still alive, the old man replies, "People give you things" (170). In McCarthy's novel, it is the child, the boy, who because of what he has experienced is anything but innocent, yet he continually returns his father's attention to those third parties whose faces demand an ethical response and whose suffering commands their witness.

Rather than being the excluded third party, the sacrifice in the *akedah*, that enables Abraham's relationship to God, the boy here is the one who, in his relationship with the other, his father, remains compassionately receptive, hostage even, to the third party. To attract such attention in this world is to court death and become someone else's meal. In a particularly harrowing moment in the novel, the boy and the man come upon a group of people chained in a basement, as food. The boy asks the man if they would ever eat anyone—a human sacrifice—and he replies that they would not because "we're carrying the fire" (129). "Carrying the fire" becomes a refrain in *The Road*, an image of home, hearth, and goodness in a world lacking all three. In the same way that paternity and filiality exceed biological relationship, so too McCarthy's "fire" need not be material to invoke the power of ethical relationship that surpasses the boundaries of physical life.[23] But its materiality gives the man and the boy life.

THE HITHER SIDE OF GOD

Jacques Rolland makes the provocative claim that "Levinas should be understood as a thinker of 'the death of God,'" in the sense that God for Levinas is "not contaminated by Being."[24] Levinas himself writes, "We propose to call religion the bond that is established between the same and the other without constituting a totality" (*TI* 40).The "infinity" of the other traverses ontotheology to reach an "otherwise than being." McCarthy's novel also looks beyond the death of God in a narrative that, like Levinas, spurns onto-theology or a God synonymous with the totality of being. *The Road* is therefore less postmodern than post-secular, characterized by the ethically informed rethinking the relationship of politics, theology, and philosophy and, in particular, as in Levinas, rethinking God apart from metaphysical categories.[25] Like Levinas, *The Road* disavows theodicy and teleology to find eschatological fulfillment in the bond between the man and the boy. McCarthy's tactic is, like Levinas's, to use theological language to reach beyond being and even beyond atheism to a thoroughly embodied, ethical sociality. The boy looks back at the man from "[s]ome unimaginable future, glowing in that waste like a tabernacle" (273), and as his father lay down to die, he watches the boy: "'Look around you,' he said. 'There is no prophet in the earth's long chronicle who's not honored here today'" (277). In the same way that Levinas defines transcendence in the face of the other and so moves to an awareness of "the hither side" of God, so too *The Road*'s theology is relationally and ethically defined apart from metaphysics. In a passage so Levinasian and so beautiful I can hardly bear to read it, the man finds transcendence in his son: "He only knew the child was his warrant. He said: If he is not the word of God God never spoke" (5). The boy reaches toward the hither side of God through others, for he prays twice in what might be called a Levinasian mode—first, when he thanks those who left behind the bounty of an abandoned fallout shelter, hoping they're safe in heaven (145–46) and finally after his father's death: "He tried to talk to God but the best thing was to talk to his father and he did talk to him and he didn't forget" (286). The space between these two prayers marks the boy's disenchantment with the sacred, a metaphysical space set apart from social existence, and his embrace of the holy, "the holiness of the other" and "the holiness of the holy."[26]

In the same way that Levinas rethinks "God," he challenges conventional notions of love, and the relationship between the man and the boy is loving but is also so much more. Western culture is accustomed to regarding love as the highest good, but in Levinas's elegant, challenging formulation, "To love is to exist as if the lover and the loved one were alone in the world. The intersubjective relation of love is not the beginning of society but its nega-tion" (*EN* 20). Love ignores the third party, the other of the other, for an exclusive focus upon the lover and the beloved, and "Thus, the love that contemporary religious thought, cleared of magical notions, has promoted to the rank of the essential situation of religious existence, does not contain social reality" (21). Even love, since it is limited to the two, can justify horror, because love ignores the third party to whom we are also responsible. Abraham indeed loved Isaac, but it did not prevent him from raising the blade. Thus, Abraham places the divine command above Isaac because of his love for God, but in *The Road*, the man nurtures, protects, and suffers (with) the boy, and all the while he struggles against the memory of his wife's despair and the demands of those third parties they encounter on their jour-ney.

Even so, the *akedah* and *The Road* pose a similar set of questions: Given the naked *il y a* of God's command to offer Isaac as a sacrifice and its postsecular equivalent of a father and son caught in a traumatized world devoid of life, hope, and any form of community or hospitality, what then is one's ethical responsibility to the other, specifically a father to his son and son to father, and the two of them to any third party? What ethical choice is available when one has already taken the food out of one's mouth for the other, but the third party still is hungry or suffering? At the same time, the fire-blasted, denuded world of *The Road* fundamentally challenges the Levi-nasian account of subjectivity in *Totality and Infinity*, which begins in enjoy-ment, nourishment, and fecundity. Can ethics survive a world in which food will not grow nor animals reproduce? Levinas resists creating an ethical system that might be applied programmatically, but the shift from *Totality and Infinity* to *Otherwise than Being* outlines a response that McCarthy dra-matizes through the man suffering the boy's suffering: the self remains non-indifferent to that suffering—in hunger, insomnia, nausea, and anxiety—to be witness and to bear the memory of it, and most importantly, to remain *respons-ible* to the other. By one's resisting the temptation to foreclose the future in a fatalistic teleology, the infinite holiness of the other remains in the self's asymmetrical responsibility to, and for, the other, as a hostage. The unique, asymmetrical relation "signifies an inequality in the oneself due to substitution, an effort to escape concepts without any future, but attempted anew the next day." In an-archical passivity, the oneself-for-another, has "a meaning despite death. Contrary to the ontology of death, this self opens an order in which death can be not recognized" (*OB* 115).

The Road depicts a final, moving example of the primacy of the ethical, returning, as it were, to the beginning. After the man has died, the boy mourns over his body for three days, not knowing what to do. He carries the revolver with its single bullet, knowing what it can be used for, but he sees on the road a figure in the distance. A man and a woman, with a boy and girl of their own, approach the boy. The man tells the boy simply that he can stay with his father's body "and die or you can come with me" (283). McCarthy suggests that *others* had been watching the man and the boy without their knowledge, before knowing who they were, what they wanted, or what they could offer, and the solitary boy calls them into response and responsibility. In a world where nothing could be "made right again" (287), the boy leaves his father behind and tells the man, "Okay."

NOTES

1. Originally published on April 19, 1992, in The *New York Times*, the interview is accessible online. See Richard B. Woodward, "Cormac McCarthy's Venomous Fiction" at http://www.nytimes.com/1992/04/19/magazine/cormac-mccarthy-s-venomous-fiction.html?pagewanted=all.

2. In "Secular Scripture and Cormac McCarthy's *The Road*, (*Renascence* 61, no. 3 [Spring 2009], 153–67), Thomas Schaub writes that the novel's central problem concerns "the status of the ethical, as well as the reason for being, in the absence of the social" (158), and he notes that "The Father's foundation, from the beginning of the novel, is the son, and there is perhaps in this coupling of his own existence to that of his son's a degree of selfishness, an unnatural reliance of the father upon the son" (158). I agree completely that the novel concerns "the ethical," but a Levinasian understanding of paternity sees the very heart of the "the social" in the father-son relation. What is unnatural is their artificial separation through an appeal to a sovereign subjectivity inherited from the Enlightenment.

3. McCarthy's supposed nihilism stretches back to John Ditsky's early article, "Further into Darkness: The Novels of Cormac McCarthy," *Hollins Critic* 18, no. 2 (1981): 1–11.

4. Ashley Kunsa argues that "[t]he novel is best understood as a linguistic journey toward redemption, a search for meaning and pattern in a seemingly meaningless world—a search that, astonishingly, succeeds" (57) ("'Maps of the World in Its Becoming': Post-Apocalyptic Naming in Cormac McCarthy's *The Road*," *Journal of Modern Literature* 33, no. 1 [2009]: 57–74).

5. Cormac McCarthy, *The Road* (New York: Random House, 2006), 52–53. All subsequent references are to this edition and will be indicated by page number parenthetically in the text.

6. For this suggestion, I am indebted to Richard Middleton-Kaplan's comments following my presentation of an earlier version of this essay at the 2008 North American Levinas Society meeting, held at Seattle University.

7. All biblical citations are from the King James Version.

8. "Faith is just this paradox, that the single individual as the particular is higher than the universal, is justified before the latter, not as subordinate but superior, though in such a way, be it noted, that it is the single individual who, having been subordinated to the universal as the particular, now by means of the universal becomes that individual who, as the particular, stands in an absolute relation to the absolute. This position cannot be mediated, for all mediation occurs precisely by virtue of the universal; it is and remains in all eternity a paradox inaccessible to thought. And yet faith *is* this paradox" (Søren Kierkegaard, *Fear and Trembling*, trans. Alastair Hannay [New York: Penguin, 2003], 84–85, emphasis is Kierkegaard's).

9. Kierkegaard, 88.

10. Ibid., 82.

11. In his reading of Rembrandt's "The Sacrifice of Isaac," Steve Shankman notes that Abraham is depicted placing his hand over Isaac's face both to hide his horror and shame, and to prevent Isaac from seeing the drawn blade, indicating that Abraham could not fulfill the command if he saw Isaac's face. See his *Other Others: Levinas, Literature, Transcultural Studies* (Albany: State University of New York Press, 2010), 7–8. Claire Katz has written, that "Abraham was changed when he looked into Isaac's face" ("The Voice of God and the Face of the Other: Levinas, Kierkegaard, and Abraham," *The Journal of Textual Reasoning* 10 (2001), available online at http://etext.virginia.edu/ journals/tr/archive/volume10/Katz.html.

12. Shankman notes the same point in *Other Others*, 10.

13. The literature interpreting the *akedah* is vast and varied, but the best single volume concerning rabbinic commentary is Shalom Spiegel, *The Last Trial: On the Legends and Lore of the Command to Abraham to Offer Isaac As a Sacrifice* (Woodstock, VT: Jewish Lights Publishing, 1967; rpt. 1993).

14. Both essays appear in Levinas's collection, *Proper Names*: "Kierkegaard: Existence and Ethics" *PN* 66–74 and "A propos of *Kierkegaard Vivant*" *PN* 75–79.

15. I am indebted to Don Wehrs for suggesting this line of analysis.

16. See Levinas's entire argument in "Judaism and Revolution" (*NiTR* 94–119).

17. I detail a similar set of concerns in Daniel T. Kline, "Doing Justice to Isaac: Levinas, the *Akedah*, and the Brome Play of Abraham and Isaac," *Levinas and Medieval Literature: The "Difficult Reading" of English and Rabbinic Texts*, ed. Ann W. Astell and J. A. Jackson (Pittsburgh: Duquesne University Press, 2009), 107–36.

18. Many of these observations appeared in earlier form in *TO*.

19. Richard Cohen gives a lucid account of these relationships in his Translator's Introduction to *TO*, 1–27.

20. Rashi's commentary on Genesis 22 is from *Metsudah Chumash*, 2nd ed., ed. Nachum Y. Kornfeld and Abraham B. Waltzer, trans. Avrohom Davis (Jersey City, NJ: KTAV Publishing, 1009), available online at http://www.tachash.org/metsudah/b04r.html.

21. "The Past and Future Community: Abraham and Isaac, Sarah and Rebekah," *Levinas Studies* 3 (2008), 94.

22. Genesis 22 (ParshahVayeira), http://www.chabad.org/library/ bible_cdo/aid/8217/show-rashi/true.

23. I think it no accident that the motif of "carrying the fire" in *The Road* looks back to the closing moments of McCarthy's *No Country for Old Men*, so memorably delivered by Tommy Lee Jones in the Coen brothers' movie, when the sheriff recounts two dreams about his father: "*I don't remember the first one all that well but it was about meetin him in town somewheres and he give me some money and I think I lost it. But the second one it was like we was both back in the older times and I was on horseback goin through the mountains of a night. Goin through this pass in the mountains. It was cold and there was snow on the ground and he rode past me and kept on goin. Never said nothing. He just rode on past and he had this blanket wrapped around him and he had his head down when he rode past I seen he was carryin fire in a horn the way people used to do and I could see the horn from the light inside of it. About the color of the moon. And in the dream I knew that he was goin on ahead and that he was fixin to make a fire somewhere out there in all that dark and all that cold and I knew that whenever I got there he would be there. And then I woke up.*" (*No Country for Old Men* [New York: Random House-Vintage, 2005], 309, italics McCarthy's). I think it would be possible to read *The Road* together with *No Country for Old Men* in light of this passage.

24. Jacques Rolland, Annotation 10 in Levinas, *OE*, 89.

25. A key early anthology is *Post-Secular Philosophy: Between Philosophy and Theology*, ed. Phillip Blond (New York: Routledge, 1998). Martin Beck Matustik's *Radical Evil and the Scarcity of Hope: Postsecular Meditations* (Bloomington: Indiana University Press, 2008) is the most recent profound approach to these questions.

26. Jacques Derrida, "Adieu," in *The Work of Mourning*, trans. Pasquale-Anne Brault and Michael Naas (Chicago: University of Chicago Press, 2001), 202. In his eulogy for Levinas, Derrida recalled, "he said to me: 'You know, one often speaks of ethics to describe what I do, but what really interests me in the end is not ethics, not ethics alone, but the holy, the holiness

of the holy'" (202). Shankman likewise addresses Levinas's distinction between the sacred and the holy in *Other Others*, 12–13.

Contributors

Todd Avery is an associate professor of English at the University of Massachusetts, Lowell, where he teaches nineteenth- and twentieth-century British literature. His publications include *Radio Modernism: Literature, Ethics, and the BBC, 1922-1938* (2006*); Desmond and Molly MacCarthy: Bloomsberries* (2010); the edited collection *Unpublished Works of Lytton Strachey: Early Papers* (2011); and essays on the Bloomsbury Group, ethics, and early radio.

N. S. Boone (Ph.D., Auburn University) is Assistant Professor of English at Harding University. He has published a number of essays, including "Ontological Blending and the Absence of Agency in Mark Strand's *Reasons for Moving*"; "Escaping Emersonian Egocentrism: Poe's Moral Tales of the Haunting Other" (2009); "The Minister's Black Veil and Hawthorne's Ethical Refusal of Reciprocity: A Levanasian Parable" (2005); and "Openness to Contingency: *Huckleberry Finn* and Phronesis" (2004).

Norma Bouchard is Associate Professor of Italian Studies and Comparative Literary and Cultural Studies at the University of Connecticut, Storrs. She teaches courses in nineteenth- and twentieth-century Italian Culture and Literature, including Migrant and Postcolonial Writers, Italian American Studies, Film, and Critical Theory. Among her publications are *Southern Thought and Other Essays on the Mediterranean* (2011); *Reading and Writing the Mediterranean: Essays by Consolo* (2006); *Italian Cultural Studies: Negotiating Regional, National and Global Identities* (2006); *Risorgimento in Modern Italian Culture: Revisiting the 19th century Past in History, Narrative, and Cinema* (2005); *Céline, Gadda, Beckett: Experimental Writers of the 1930s* (2000); *The Politics of Culture and the Ambiguities of Interpreta-*

tion: Umberto Eco's Alternative (1998), as well as critical essays and translations. She has edited a journal issue on the 150th anniversary of Italian Unification (1861–2011) and is completing two monographs, *Writing, Screening, and Sounding Beyond the Nation: Italy and the Mediterranean from the Cold War into the Twenty-first Century*, with Valerio Ferme; and *Umberto Eco's Historic Imaginary*. She is Vice President elect of the American Association of Italian Studies, Associate Editor of *Annali d'Italianistica* and Book Review Editor of *Italian Culture*.

Benjamin J. Doty is a Ph.D. student in the Department of English and Comparative Literature at the University of North Carolina at Chapel Hill. He studies American literature, cognitive neuroscience, and philosophy.

Mike Marais is Professor of English at Rhodes University in Grahamstown, South Africa, where he teaches twentieth-century and postcolonial literature. His recent publications include *Secretary of the Invisible: The Idea of Hospitality in the Fiction of J. M. Coetzee* (2009); "Violence, Postcolonial Fiction, and the Limits of Sympathy" (2011); "Coming into Being: J. M. Coetzee's *Slow Man* and the Aesthetic of Hospitality" (2009); "From the Standpoint of Redemption: Aesthetic Engagement and Social Engagement in J. M. Coetzee's Fiction of the Late Apartheid Period" (2008); "J. M. Coetzee's *Disgrace* and the Task of the Imagination" (2006); "Bastards and Bodies in Zoë Wicomb's *David ' s Story*" (2005); "'After the death of a certain god': A Case for Levinasian Ethics" (2002); "'The Rest Should Be Silence': Blanchot, Conrad, and the Impossibility of Silence" (2001).

Richard Middleton-Kaplan is Professor of English and Humanities at Harper College where he teaches American and Russian nineteenth- and twentieth-century literature, Holocaust literature, and the literature of peace and nonviolence. His publications include "Using Literature to Teach Peace," with Patrick Henry (2010); "'Play It Again, Herman': Melville at the Movies" (2009); "Facing the Face of the Enemy: Levinasian Moments in *All Quiet on the Western Front* and the Literature of War" (2008); "Romantic and Realist Rubble: The Foundation for a New National Literature in Dostoyevsky's *Poor Folk* and Melville's *Pierre*" (1998).

Daniel T. Kline (Ph.D., Indiana University) specializes in Middle English literature and culture, literary and cultural theory, and digital medievalism, and his research concerns children, violence, sacrifice, and ethics in late-medieval England. He has published in *Chaucer Review*; *College Literature*; *Comparative Drama*; *The Journal of English and Germanic Philology*; *Philological Quarterly*, among others, and has chapters in *The Cambridge Companion to Medieval Women's Writing*; *Translating Desire in Medieval and*

Early Modern Literature; *Mass Market Medievalism*; and *Levinas and Medieval Literature*. He edited *Medieval Literature for Children* and the *Continuum Handbook of Medieval British Literature*. The author/webmaster of *The Electronic Canterbury Tales*, www.kankedort.net, Kline is Professor of English at the University of Alaska, Anchorage.

Nina L. Molinaro is Associate Professor of Spanish and Associate Director of the Honors Program at the University of Colorado at Boulder. She is author of "Looking for the Other: Peninsular Women's Fiction after Levinas" (2009); "Facing Toward Alterity and Spain's 'Other' New Novelists" (2005); and *Foucault, Feminism, and Power: Reading Esther Tusquets* (1991).

Rebecca Nicholson-Weir (Ph.D., Purdue University) is an assistant professor of English at East Central University in Ada, Oklahoma. A founding board member and treasurer of the North American Levinas Society, she co-guest edited a special issue of *Shofar* on Levinas and Jewish Thought (Summer 2008). Her current book project examines the interstices of phenomenology and life writing in women's modernism.

Donald R. Wehrs is Professor of English at Auburn University where he teaches comparative and postcolonial literatures, critical theory, and eighteenth-century British literature. He is co-editor with David P. Haney of *Levinas and Nineteenth-Century Literature: From Romanticism Through Realism* (2009), author of three books on twentieth-century African fiction—*Pre-Colonial Africa in Colonial African Narrative* (2008); *Islam, Ethics, Revolt* (2008); and *African Feminist Fiction and Indigenous Values* (2001)—and has published essays on Shakespeare in *Poetics Today*, *Modern Philology*, and *College Literature*; on postcolonial fiction and theory in *MLN*, *New Literary History*, *Ariel*, *Modern Language Studies*, and *The Comparatist*; and on eighteenth-century British literature in *SEL*, *ELH*, *The Eighteenth Century: Theory and Interpretation*, *Comparative Literature Studies*; as well as book chapters in *Theology and Literature in the Age of Johnson* (2012), *Swiftly Sterneward* (2011), *Divine Rhetoric* (2010); and *In Proximity: Emmanuel Levinas and the Eighteenth Century* (2001), among others.

Merle A. Williams is a Personal Professor of English and former Assistant Dean for Graduate Studies in the Faculty of Humanities at the University of the Witwatersrand in Johannesburg, South Africa. She is the author of *Henry James and the Philosophical Novel: Being and Seeing* (1993, reprinted 2009), and is currently editing *The Awkward Age* for Cambridge University Press's forthcoming *Complete Fiction of Henry James*. A monograph on Percy Bysshe Shelley's poetry and thought, with particular emphasis on the creative endeavor of the last year of his life, is close to completion. Williams has edited several special issues of journals. Her articles and book chapters lie principally in the fields of Romantic Poetry, Modernist Fiction, American Studies and Trauma Studies, reflecting a sustained interest in the relations between literature and philosophy.

Lorna Wood is an independent scholar and instructor at the Schwob School of Music Preparatory Program at Columbus State University, Georgia. She holds a B.M. in Violin Performance from Oberlin College's Conservatory and a Ph.D. in English from Yale University, has taught English at Auburn University and Southern Union Community College, serves as concertmaster of the Auburn Community and LaGrange orchestras, plays in the Columbus Orchestra and teaches violin privately. She is author of "Emmanuel Levinas and the American Renaissance Canon" (2009).

Zahi Zalloua is Associate Professor of French and Interdisciplinary Studies at Whitman College and editor of *The Comparatist*. He has published *Montaigne and the Ethics of Skepticism* (2005), and has a forthcoming book titled *Reading Unruly: Interpretation and Its Ethical Demands* with the University of Nebraska Press. He has edited two volumes on Montaigne: *Montaigne and the Question of Ethics* (2006) and *Montaigne After Theory, Theory After Montaigne* (2009), and has also published articles, edited volumes and special journal issues on globalization, literary theory, ethical criticism, and trauma studies.

Index

www.ingramcontent.com/pod-product-compliance
Lightning Source LLC
Chambersburg PA
CBHW071147100726
47908CB00002B/284

* 9 7 8 1 6 1 1 4 9 6 5 0 5 *